Ottoman Law of War and Peace

# Ottoman Law of War and Peace

*The Ottoman Empire and Its Tribute-Payers from the North of the Danube*

SECOND REVISED EDITION

*By*

Viorel Panaite

BRILL

LEIDEN | BOSTON

Cover illustration: Turcici Imperii Descriptio – Map of Abraham Ortelius, Flemish cartographer (1528-1598) (BAR, Bucharest).

Library of Congress Cataloging-in-Publication Data

Names: Panaite, Viorel, 1958- author.
Title: Ottoman law of war and peace : the Ottoman Empire and its tribute-payers from the north of the Danube / Viorel Panaite.
Other titles: Ottoman Empire and its tribute-payers from the north of the Danub
Description: Second revised edition | Leiden ; Boston : Brill, 2019. | Includes bibliographical references and index.
Identifiers: LCCN 2019023140 (print) | LCCN 2019023141 (ebook) | ISBN 9789004406377 (hardback) | ISBN 9789004411104 (ebook)
Subjects: LCSH: Turkey--Foreign relations--Law and legislation--History. | Turkey--History--Ottoman Empire, 1288-1918. | International law (Islamic law) | Romania--International status--History. | Romania--Relations--Turkey--History. | Turkey--Relations--Romania--History.
Classification: LCC KKX2400 .P36 2019 (print) | LCC KKX2400 (ebook) | DDC 342.56/0412--dc23
LC record available at https://lccn.loc.gov/2019023140
LC ebook record available at https://lccn.loc.gov/2019023141

Typeface for the Latin, Greek, and Cyrillic scripts: "Brill". See and download: brill.com/brill-typeface.

ISBN 978-90-04-40637-7 (hardback)
ISBN 978-90-04-41110-4 (e-book)



This book is printed on acid-free paper and produced in a sustainable manner.

# Contents

# Preface and Acknowledgments

Historians and jurists have paid scant attention to the Ottoman law of war and peace, and those specialists who have dealt with Islamic Ottoman law ignored as a rule the status of tributary princes. In turn, Romanian scholarship developed a veritable tradition of addressing the issue of "Ottoman–Romanian relations," focusing particularly on the autonomous status of the principalities of Wallachia, Moldavia and Transylvania towards the Porte.

The purpose of this book is to improve and partially revise these assertions, focusing not on the elements that set the provinces north of the Danube apart from the rest of the Ottoman Empire, but rather on the legal and political methods applied to extend the *pax ottomanica* system in the area.

Accordingly, two central questions underlie the present study. First, what was the Ottoman legal and political standpoint on the empire's relationship with non-Muslim individuals, communities and states? Second, what position did the tributary states and provinces of Southeastern Europe occupy vis-à-vis the Ottoman Empire? From the outside, I have to stress the difficulty of providing unambiguous answers to either of these questions, first and foremost due to the dearth of information and the vagueness of available sources. To address these issues, I have firstly tried to decipher and define concepts and rules that underpinned Ottoman notions of war, peace, treaty, custom and protection. Finally, to elucidate the issue, perspectives other than the Ottomans– those of local voivodes, nobles, Christian neighbors and Western Europeans – must be taken into account.

Subsequently, I turned my attention towards the political and legal status of the principalities of Wallachia, Moldavia and Transylvania, which provide us with case studies of tributary status within the Ottoman context. This second stage is by no means an afterthought; on the contrary, it constitutes the crux of the study.

These imperatives shaped the structure of this five-part book. In Part One, I discuss legal and diplomatic sources, focusing on the Islamic tradition as a cornerstone of the Ottoman law of nations. Part Two deals with the impact of Ottoman holy war (*cihad* and *gazavat*) on the territories north of the Danube, paying special attention to the period spanning from the end of the fourteenth to the mid-sixteenth century. In Part Three, I shift my attention towards the Islamic–Ottoman law of peace and the ways submission and conquest in Southeastern Europe were acknowledged and recognized. In doing so, I emphasize peculiarities and commonplaces, with regard to both their historical circumstances and legal–political consequences. Part Four focuses on legal sources of Wallachia, Moldavia and Transylvania's tributary status, investigating Ottoman peace agreements and the procedure of *aman – ʿahd – ʿahdname*. This topic includes the role of the temporary covenants of the fifteenth and early sixteenth centuries, the impact of imperial diplomas and customary norms in outlining the rights and duties of the voivodes, as well as the Porte's attitude towards the *pacta sunt servanda* principle when dealing with its tributaries. Part Five, entitled 'Tribute-payers and Protected Peoples,' investigates power relations between sultans and voivodes, the latter's duties towards the Porte and the legal status of Wallachian, Moldavian and Transylvanian subjects as protected-peoples (*zimmi*s). As I argue, a comprehensive examination of these relations between the sultan and his tributaries allows us to depict the place of the three tributary-protected principalities within the system of *pax ottomanica,* from both a legal and political point of view.

Terminology lies at the heart of my investigation. Developing a coherent terminological grid necessary to define the status of Moldavia, Wallachia and Transylvania required me to adopt a critical attitude towards both the vocabulary employed in official documents and chronicles of the period (be they Ottoman, European or Moldo-Wallachian), as well as the terms utilized by modern historians and jurists. Moreover, a clear distinction had to be made between the conceptual framework of twentieth-century international law and that of fifteenth–eighteenth century law of nations; between European legal terminology and Islamic; finally, between legal terms and political vocabulary. As an example of this, Dimitrie Cantemir, who realized and criticized the sultans' tendency to call "tribute" any sum of money received from Christians,[1] a purpose of my research has been to determine terminological abuses, which can be constantly found in historical sources, and to correlate the legal and political theory and terminology with the actual power relations.

Although the terms of "tribute-payer" (*haracgüzar*) and "protection" (*himayet*) had been employed in fifteenth-century sources, and some legal elements of these concepts were applied in relations with the Wallachian voivodes from 1417[2] and the Moldavian ones from 1456, it was only during the reign of Süleyman Kanunî (1520–1566) that a coherent Ottoman interpretation of the legal and political position of the princes, inhabitants and territories north of the Danube crystallized. In these circumstances, I believe it would be wrong to

1 Demetrius Cantemir, *The History of the Growth and Decay of the Othman Empire.* Translated by N. Tindal, London, 1734, 276, n. 2.

2 The dates throughout the book are given in the Gregorian calendar. In footnotes, I have also indicated the dates in the Hijrah calendar in certain cases, such as extensively quoted Ottoman documents, collections of documents in archives and libraries, and publishing years of Ottoman books.

adopt the legal vocabulary of early modern sources and to retroactively apply this to the period when power relations between the sultans and Moldavian-Wallachian princes were at their inception, as some chroniclers did – such as Idris Bitlisi and Kemalpaşazade. Only in the third and fourth decades of the sixteenth century did the process of integrating Moldavia, Wallachia and Transylvania into the *pax ottomanica* reach its conclusion, defining their status as tributary principalities and buffer protectorates.

To remedy the relative dearth of information regarding Moldavia and Wallachia, particularly prominent until the mid-sixteenth century, I have opted for a comparative approach. The comparison involved a variety of cases, ranging from Ottoman provinces (particularly *salyaneli* regions), Christian neighbors, as well as other examples of tributary status. The latter included both the blueprints developed in the early Islamic period (like Nadjran) and other Southeastern European polities that temporarily or permanently enjoyed similar status (such as Ragusa and the Crimean Khanate). Adopting this more encompassing perspective is particularly important, since Moldavia and Wallachia were frequently invoked as blueprints, utilized as legal and political frameworks for new additions to the *pax ottomanica* system.

At the same time, when speaking about vassal or tributary principalities of the Ottoman Empire, many historians tend to lump these together into a single, undifferentiated group. However, despite similarities between them, we should keep in mind the peculiarities and idiosyncrasies of each individual case, produced by specific historical circumstances surrounding their entry into Ottoman orbit, such as their geopolitical position, economic features, as well as religious and dynastic identity. Obviously, ignoring these divergences would produce a distorted image of the polities' relationship to the Porte. Thus, I consider it necessary to take into account the legal and political trajectory between the fifteenth and the eighteenth centuries, and the distinct political status of Transylvania in comparison to the Danubian principalities. Yet, my main objective throughout the study remains the legal status of tributary states or provinces in the Ottoman Empire; from this point of view, commonalities outweighed differences. Probably this is why French geographer Nicolas Sanson d'Abbeville opted to depict the borders of Wallachia, Moldavia, Transylvania and Ragusa with the same red line on a map he produced in 1655.[3]

•••

3 *Estats de l'Empire des Tvrqs en Evrope; et Pays circomvoisins; entre lesquels sont Hongrie, Transilvanie, Valaqvie, Moldavie, Petite Tatarie. Sujets, ou tributaires des Turqs. Par N. Sanson d'Abbeville, Geographe ordinaire du Roy*, Paris, Chez Pierre Mariette, 1655 (BAR, Bucharest, Maps Division).

It would be impossible to mention here all those who through their help or advice have contributed to this book.

Financial support for various stages of the research and writing was generously made available to me by a number of institutions, including the Institute for South-East European Studies of the Romanian Academy, the Faculty of History of University of Bucharest, the Soros Foundation, Institut Français d'Études Anatoliennes in Istanbul, the Europa Institute in Budapest, Maison des Science de l'Homme in Paris, the Council for International Exchange of Scholars in Washington, the Fulbright Commission in Washington and Bucharest, American Research Institute in Turkey and Mellon Foundation. They each allowed me to enrich my documentation in Bulgarian, Hungarian, Turkish, Polish, French, British, Italian and American archives and libraries, besides my usual research in the Romanian libraries and archives. My warmest thanks go to these organizations and institutions.

At the same time, I would like to express my gratitude to all who helped me in the archives and libraries in Sofia, Istanbul, Budapest, Warsaw, Krakow, Paris, London, Venice, Florence, Princeton and Washington. The list is too long to permit individual mentions. I wish to thank all those who generously placed their time and knowledge at my disposal and to acknowledge the facilities provided by the National Archives and the Romanian Academy Library in Bucharest; the "Cyril and Methodius" Library in Sofia; the Library of the Hungarian Academy of Sciences and Hungarian National Archives in Budapest; the Archives of Old Documents in Warsaw and Czartoryski Library in Krakow; Bibliothèque Nationale de France and Archives du Ministere des Affaires Étrangers in Paris; the State Archives of Venice; Princeton University Library and the Library of Congress in Washington; The Prime Minister's Archives, Süleymaniye Library, Topkapı Palace Library and Archives, Libraries of the American Research Institute in Turkey, Institut Français d'Études Anatoliennes, Centre for Islamic Studies and Research Centre for Islamic History, Art and Culture, all in Istanbul.

While writing this book, I have tried not to assume an exclusively critical tone. I feel indebted to all the scholars whose findings and ideas – even if I disagreed with them – opened my eyes to many pleasant vistas. In the course of researching and writing my earlier books and articles, as was also the case with this book, I had the good sense to consult with colleagues specializing in areas outside my primary research field. I am grateful to all colleagues and friends from whom I received comments, guidance, encouragement, or admonition. Each of them offered valuable criticism that helped me refine the argument and stay on course where I might otherwise have gone astray. For the defects that remain, I alone am responsible.

It has been nearly twenty years since the first edition of the *Ottoman Law of War and Peace. The Ottoman Empire and Tribute Payers* (Boulder, 2000). Ever since its publication, it has been noticed that this book was in need of a good and careful editor. Meanwhile, my documentation of this issue has become enriched, and with it the interpretations have gained a clearer outline, and some dilemmas have become certainties. During this period of time several studies dedicated to the political and legal status of Wallachia, Moldavia and Transylvania towards the Porte appeared in specialized journals or were included in volumes of Islamic and Ottoman history.[4] It was therefore necessary to publish a new edition of the 2000 book, but a deeply revised and augmented one.

I do not want to end this foreword without expressing my gratitude to Michał Wasiucionek, who significantly improved the English text and made valuable historical comments, to David-Linus Neagu and Radu Dipratu, who helped me with bibliographical list and index, and to George MacBeth, who copy-edited the manuscript. I also owe my warmest thanks to Maurits van den Boogert, who found a way to publish this book at Brill.

*Viorel Panaite,*
December 2018

4 I note here the most recent papers: Viorel Panaite, "The Legal and Political Status of Wallachia and Moldavia in Relation to the Ottoman Porte," in G. Kárman and L. Kunčević, eds. *The European Tributary States of the Ottoman Empire in the Sixteenth and Seventeenth Centuries*. Leiden–Boston: Brill, 2013, 9–43; idem, "The Danubian Principalities," in K. Fleet, G. Krämer, D. Matringe, J. Nawas, and E. Rowson, eds. *The Encyclopaedia of Islam. Three*, Leiden: Brill, 2014, 85–89.

# Facsimiles, Illustrations and Maps

# Transliteration and Pronunciation of Turkish and Romanian

Transliteration is the perennial problem of historical scholarship in different branches of Islamic studies. Materials in pre-modern Turkish rendered in the Arab script, as in almost all the sources used in this study, are particularly difficult to standardize, and any transliteration system is bound to be aesthetically displeasing. In this book the Ottoman Turkish technical vocabulary is transliterated in conformity with modern Turkish spelling, and is italicized on each isolated occurrence in the text (e.g. *zimmi, cihad, cizye* etc.). The Arab and Ottoman names of persons, places, states and dynasties are printed in their modern forms, without diacritical marks. It should be noted that I have not modified the titles of books and articles according to the above-mentioned rules. As concerns the pronunciation of those Turkish and Romanian letters which either do not appear in the English alphabet, or which differ markedly from their English pronunciation, here are the correspondences for more difficult pronunciation cases:

Turkish consonants and vowels:

| | |
|---|---|
| c | j as in jam |
| ç | ch as in church |
| ğ | a fricative sound |
| ş | sh as in shop |
| â | long a as in father |
| ı | i as in cousin |
| ö | eu as in French jeu |
| ü | u as in French tu |

Romanian consonants, vowels, diphthongs and triphthongs:

| | |
|---|---|
| ş | sh as in shop |
| ţ | ts as in nuts |
| ă | a as in awake |
| â, î | i as in cousin |
| ce | che as in check |
| ci | chi as in cheese |
| ge | ge as in gesture |
| gi | gi as in genius |
| chi | ki as in kilo |
| ghi | ghi as in gift. |

# Abbreviations

## Usual Abbreviations

| | |
|---|---|
| AD | Anno Domini |
| AH | Anno Hegira |
| Ar. | Arabic |
| Bulg. | Bulgarian |
| c. | century |
| cf. | conform to |
| Ch. | Chapter |
| d. | dead |
| ed. | edition, editor |
| eds. | editors |
| fr. | frame |
| f. | folio |
| Fr. | French |
| Gk. | Greek |
| K | Karton (in Polish Archives) |
| Lat. | Latin |
| mf., MC | microfilm, Microfilm Collection |
| n. | note |
| n.d. | no date |
| o.n. | our note |
| P. | Persian |
| pl. | plural |
| r. | reel |
| Rom. | Romanian |
| sing. | singular |
| Supl. | Supplement |
| Sl. | Slavic |
| t | *teczka* (small file in Polish archives) |
| Tk | Turkish |
| vol. | volume |

## Archives, Libraries, Collections

AGAD — Archiwum Glowne Akt Dawnych (The Archives of Old Documents). Warsaw.
*AKW-Tureckie* — *Archiwum Korone Warszawskie, Tureckie.*
AMAE — Archives du Ministere des Affaires Étrangers du France. Paris.
ANIC — Arhivele Naționale Istorice Centrale (National Historical Central Archives). Bucharest.
BAR — Biblioteca Academiei Române (Romanian Academy Library). Bucharest
BnF — Bibliothèque Nationale de France. Paris.
BOA — Başbakanlık Osmanlı Arşivi (Prime Minister's Archives). Istanbul.
*DED* — *Düvel-i Ecnebiye Defterleri* (*Ecnebi Devletler Defterleri*)
EEN — Early English Newspapers
GYC — Garrett Yahuda Collection
IUK — Istanbul Üniversitesi Kütüphanesi
*LED* — *Lehistan 'Ahdnamesi Defteri*
*MD* — *Mühimme Defterleri*
MeD — *Mémoires et documents*
MOL — Magyar Országos Levéltár (Hungarian National Archives). Budapest.
*NAD* — *Nemçelü 'Ahd Defteri*
DO — Division orientale
PRUL — Princeton University Library
SK — Süleymaniye Kütüphanesi (Süleymaniye Library). Istanbul.
TKSMA — Topkapı Sarayi Müzesi Arşivi (Topkapı Palace Archives). Istanbul.
TKSMK — Topkapı Sarayi Müzesi Kütüphanesi (Topkapı Palace Library). Istanbul.

## Periodicals, Collective Volumes

*AARMSI* — *Analele Academiei Române. Memoriile Secțiunii Istorice* (Bucharest)
*AAS* — *Asian and African Studies. Journal of the Israel Oriental Society* (Haifa)
*AAWG* — *Abhandlungen der Akademie Wissenschaften in Gottingen. Philologish-Historische Klasse* (Göttingen)
*AFDI* — *Annales de la Faculté de Droit d'Istanbul*
*AHDO* — *Archives d'Histoire du Droit Oriental* (Brussels)
*AHROS* — *Arab Historical Review for Ottoman Studies* (Zaghouan, Tunisia)

| | |
|---|---|
| *AHY* | *Austrian History Yearbook* (Rice University) |
| *AI* | *Anale de Istorie* (Bucharest) |
| *AIESEE-B* | *Association Internationale d'Études du Sud-Est Européen. Bulletin* (Bucharest) |
| *AIIAI* | *Anuarul Institutului de Istorie și Arheologie «A.D.Xenopol»* (Iași) |
| *AIIC* | *Anuarul Institutului de Istorie* (Cluj) |
| *AION* | *Annali dell'Istituto Orientale di Napoli* (Naples) |
| *AIPHOS* | *Annuaire de l'Institut de Philologie et d'Histoire Orientales et Slaves* (Brussels) |
| *AJIL* | *The American Journal of International Law* (Washington) |
| *AJSMLL* | *American Journal of Semitic Languages and Literatures* (Chicago) |
| *AKOG* | *Archiv für die Kunde Österreichischer Geschichtsquellen* (Vienna) |
| *Annales* | *Annales. Economies. Sociétés. Civilisations* (Paris) |
| *AO* | *Archiv Orientálni* (Prague) |
| *AOtt* | *Archiwum Ottomanicum* (The Hague–Leiden) |
| *AOH* | *Acta Orientalia Academiae Scientiarum Hungaricae* (Budapest) |
| *Arabica* | *Arabica. Revue d'études arabes* (Paris) |
| *AUBI* | *Analele Universității din București. Istorie* (*Filozofie. Drept*) |
| *AÜSBFD* | *Ankara Üniversitesi Siyasal Bilgiler Fakültesi Dergisi* |
| *Belgeler* | *Belgeler. Türk Tarih Belgeleri Dergisi* (Ankara) |
| *Belleten* | *Belleten. Türk Tarih Kurumu* (Ankara) |
| *BEO* | *Bulletin d'Etudes Orientales* (Damascus) |
| *BOA.Rehberi* | *Başbakanlık Osmanlı Arşivi Rehberi,* Ankara, 1992. |
| *BS* | *Balkan Studies* (Thessaloniki) |
| *BSOAS* | *Bulletin of the School of Oriental and African Studies* (London) |
| *Bul. Com. Ist.* | *Buletinul Comisiei Istorice a României* (Bucharest) |
| *Byzantion* | *Byzantion. Revue internationale des études byzantines* (Paris, Liège, Brussels) |
| *BZ* | *Byzantinische Zeitschrift* (Leipzig, Munich) |
| *CCM* | *Cahiers de Civilisation Médievale* (Poitiers) |
| *CI* | *Cercetări istoric* (Iași) |
| *CICSEE* | *Cercetări de istorie și civilizație sud-est europeană* (Bucharest) |
| *CL* | *Convorbiri Literare* (Iași) |
| *CLSO* | *Caietele Laboratorului de Studii Otomane* (Bucharest) |
| *CMRS* | *Cahiers du monde russe et soviétique* (Paris, Mouton, La Haye) |
| *CSISD* | *Crestomație pentru studiul istoriei statului si dreptului RPR. II. Feudalismul I*, eds. Șt. Pascu and V. Hanga, Bucharest, 1958. |
| Decei, *RRO* | Aurel Decei, *Relații româno-orientale. Culegere de studii*, Bucharest: Editura Științifică și Enciclopedică, 1978. |
| *DO* | *Dissertationes Orientales* (Prague) |

| | |
|---|---|
| *DOP* | *Dumbarton Oaks Papers* (Washington) |
| *EB* | *Études Balkanique* (Sofia) |
| *EI-1* | *The Encyclopaedia of Islam*, I-IV. First Edition. Edited by H.Th. Houtsma, R. Basset, T.W. Arnold, R. Hartmann, Leiden: Brill, 1913-1936. |
| *EI-2* | *The Encyclopaedia of Islam.* I-XIII, Second Edition (French edition, *Encyclopédie de l'Islam*). Edited by P. Bearman, Th. Bianquis, C.E. Bosworth, E. van Donzel and W.P. Heinrichs Paris, Leyden: Brill, 1986–2004. |
| *ETR* | *Études Théologiques et Religieuses* (Montpellier) |
| *FHDR* | *Fontes Historiae Daco-Romanae*, vol. IV: *Scriitori și acte bizantine. Secolele IV-XV*, H. Mihăescu, R. Lazarescu, N. Ș. Tanașoca, T. Teoteoi, eds., Bucharest, 1982. |
| *GOTR* | *The Greek Orthodox Theological Review* (Brookline, Massachusetts). |
| Hurmuzaki, *Documente* | *Documente privitoare la istoria românilor culese de Eudoxiu de Hurmuzaki*, eds. E. de Hurmuzaki – I. Bogdan; N. Densușeanu; N. Iorga; Gr. G. Tocilescu, Bucharest, 1880–1900. |
| *IDR* | *Istoria dreptului românesc*, ed. Ioan Ceterchi, *Istoria dreptului românesc*, vol. I, Buharest, 1980; Vol. II/1, București, 1984. |
| *IJMES* | *International Journal of Middle East Studies* (London–New York) |
| *IJTS* | *International Journal of Turkish Studies* (University of Wisconsin–Madison). |
| *IQ* | *The Islamic Quarterly* (London) |
| *ITED* | *Islâm Tetkikleri Enstitüsü Dergisi* (*Review of the Institute of Islamic Studies*) (Istanbul) |
| *JA* | *Journal Asiatique* (Paris) |
| *JAH* | *Journal of Asian History* (Wiesbaden) |
| *JAOS* | *Journal of the American Oriental Society* (Michigan) |
| *JESHO* | *Journal of the Economic and Social History of the Orient* (Leiden) |
| *JMH* | *The Journal of Modern History* (Chicago) |
| *JNES* | *Journal of Near-East Studies* (Chicago) |
| *JPHS* | *Journal of the Pakistan Historical Society* (Karachi) |
| *JRAS* | *Journal of the Royal Asiatic Society* (London) |
| *JTS.TBA* | *Journal of Turkish Studies. Türklük Bilgisi Araştırmaları* (Harvard University) |
| *MHR* | *Mediterranean Historical Review* (London) |
| *Mircea* | *Marele Mircea Voievod.* Ed. I. Pătroiu, Bucharest, 1987. |
| *MOG* | *Mitteilungen zur Osmanischen Geschichte* (Vienna) |
| *MOS* | *Mitteilungen des Österreichischen Staatsarchivs* (Vienna) |
| *NÉH* | *Nouvelles Études d'Histoire* (Bucharest) |

| | |
|---|---|
| *OA.JOS* | *Osmanlı Araştırmaları. The Journal of Ottoman Studies* (Istanbul) |
| *OCP* | *Orientalia Christiana Periodica* (Rome) |
| *OLP* | *Orientalia Lovaniensia Periodica* (Leuven) |
| *RA* | *Revista Arhivelor* (Bucharest) |
| *RdC* | *Recueil des cours de l'Académie de Droit International de la Haye* |
| *RdI* | *Revista de Istorie* (Bucharest) |
| *REI* | *Revue des Études Islamiques* (Paris) |
| *RER* | *Revue des Études Roumaines* (Paris) |
| *RESEE* | *Revue des Études Sud-Est Européennes* (Bucharest) |
| *RFR* | *Revista Fundaţiile Regale* (Bucharest) |
| *RGDIP* | *Revue générale de droit international public*, Paris |
| *RHD* | *Revue d'histoire diplomatique* (Paris) |
| *RHDFE* | *Revue Historique de Droit Français et Étranger* (Paris) |
| *RHMC* | *Revue d'Histoire Moderne et Contemporaine* (Nanterre) |
| *RHSEE* | *Revue Historique des Études Sud-Est Européennes* (Bucharest) |
| *RI* | *Revista Istorică* (Bucharest) |
| *RIDC* | *Revue Internationale de Droit Comparé* (Paris) |
| *RIU* | *Românii în Istoria Universală* (Iași) |
| *RIR* | *Revista Istorică Română* (Bucharest) |
| *RMM* | *Revue du monde musulman* (Paris) |
| *RMMM* | *Revue des mondes musulmans et de la Mediterranée* (Aix-en-Provence) |
| *RO* | *Rocznik Orientalstyczny* (Warsaw) |
| *ROMM* | *Revue de l'Occident musulman et de la Mediterranée* (Aix-en-Provence) |
| *RRH* | *Revue Roumaine d'Histoire* (Bucharest) |
| *SA* | *Studia Asiatica* (Bucharest) |
| *SAI* | *Studii și Articole de Istorie* (Bucharest) |
| *SAO* | *Studia et Acta Orientalia* (Bucharest) |
| *SEER* | *The Slavonic and East European Review* (London) |
| Sertoğlu, *ROTA* | Sertoğlu, Midhat. *Resimli Osmanlı Tarihi Ansiklopedisi*, Istanbul, 1958 |
| *SF* | *Südost Forschungen* (Munich) |
| *SI* | *Studia Islamica* (Paris) |
| *SMIM* | *Studii și materiale de istorie medie* (Bucharest) |
| *St.RdI* | *Studii. Revistă de Istorie* (Bucharest) |
| *TAD* | *Türk Araştırmaları Dergisi* (Ankara) |
| *TD* | *Istanbul Üniversitesi Edebiyat Fakültesi. Tarih Enstitüsü Dergisi* (Istanbul) |
| *TM* | *Türkiyat Mecmuası* (Istanbul) |

| | |
|---|---|
| *TOEM* | *Tarih-i Osmanı Encümeni Mecmuası* (*Türk Tarih Encümeni Mecmuası*) (Istanbul) |
| *TRHS* | *Transaction of the Royal Historical Society* (London) |
| *Turcica* | *Turcica. Revue des études turques* (Paris, Louvain, Strasbourg) |
| *TV* | *Tarih Vesikaları* (Istanbul, Ankara) |
| *WZKM* | *Wiener Zeitschrift für die Kunde des Morgenlandes* (Vienna) |
| *ZDMG* | *Zeitschrift der Morgenlandischen Gesellschaft* (Wiesbaden) |

# PART 1

## *Ottoman Law of War and Peace*

CHAPTER 1

# Islamic Tradition and the Ottoman Law of War and Peace

Students of Romanian history often decry the dearth of sources at their disposal, although these are in fact extraordinarily abundant and varied. This apparent discrepancy stems from the fact that, within the corpus, sources of Ottoman origin vastly outnumber those produced in Moldavia, Wallachia, Transylvania, or Western Europe. However, many scholarly studies ignore Ottoman documents and chronicles in discussing the topic. Thus, the issue is not the number of sources available, but rather engaging the extant ones in a meaningful manner, even if the sheer amount of evidence forces one to rely on published editions.

Thus, approaching tributary states necessitates, first and foremost, grasping the character of the extant sources and asking the correct questions. In this respect, Islamic juridical and religious sources provide us with a theoretical model concerning warfare, peace-making and defining the juridical status of non-Muslim subjects and foreigners.

However, examining the Ottoman stance on the ideology of holy war, "international" law and the political status of tributary states, provinces, rulers and subjects, forces us to go beyond juridical theory and address the administrative and diplomatic documents produced by the sultanic chancellery. By casting our net wider, we are able to construct a more comprehensive picture of the political, military and diplomatic practice in "Ottoman–Romanian relations" in the early modern period. These documents, which involve a variety of different genres, such as imperial charters, orders, diplomas and petitions, bridge the gap between theory and practice. However, the information contained within official documents is insufficient for the topic at hand and must be complemented by Ottoman chronicles, which form the backbone of our knowledge regarding Ottoman policy in Southeastern Europe in the fourteenth and fifteenth centuries.

Thus, the scope of this chapter is to map out the sources that are most relevant for investigating Ottoman "international" law, the place of tributary provinces within this framework and to distinguish between questions they may answer, and those that they cannot.

 | DOI:10.1163/9789004411104_002

## 1 Juridical and Diplomatic Sources

To talk about juridical sources of Ottoman "international" law, one must identify and define juridical "instruments" that established, confirmed and fine-tuned rules and notions concerning war, peace, tributary status and the legal status of foreigners.

Ottoman law of war and peace derived from a variety of sources, including sacred Islamic traditions (*şeriʿat*), secular law (*kanun*), peace agreements (*ʿahdname*) and international customs. As a result, the development of a systematic approach towards provincial governance and its rules developed only gradually and over time.

Islamic juridical and religious sources provided the basic theoretical grid for matters of war-making, peace-making and defining the legal status of non-Muslim subjects and foreigners. This tradition originated primarily in the *Kur'an*, Traditions (*hadis*), treatises on Islamic law (*kitab al-siyar, kitab al-cihad*) and juridical opinions (*fetva*).

Ottomans, who adopted a pragmatic approach in their relations with non-Muslims, made few original and notable contributions to the development of Islamic law.[1] Since the prohibition of religious "innovations" in the ninth century,[2] treatises on Islamic law written by Ottomans were mostly summaries, compilations, annotations, commentaries or Turkish–Ottoman translations of earlier juridical works.[3] Nonetheless, Ottoman scholars sought to reassert the juridical tradition and harness it for political purposes, even if this legitimacy was deployed post-factum and in a derivative form.

Islamic tradition was thus one of the cornerstones of Ottoman law of war and peace. The imperial authorities, in their relations with non-Muslims, had to obey the stipulations of *şeriʿat*, the "path" dictated by Allah, and proclaimed by Prophet Muhammad, in his capacity as God's envoy– a "code of behavior" binding all Muslims.[4] This divine will was mediated through religious law

1 There is a recent attempt to revisit this traditional claim by Guy Burak, *The Second Foundation of Islamic Law. The Hanafi School in the Early Modern Ottoman Empire*, Cambridge: Cambridge University Press, 2015, which argues that the Ottomans did make contributions of note.

2 E. Tyan, "Méthodologie et sources de droit en Islam," *SI*, X, 1959, 79–111.

3 Ya'kov Meron, "The Development of Legal Thought in Hanefi Texts," *SI*, XXX, 1969, 73–119; Halil Inalcık, *The Ottoman Empire. The Classical Age. 1300–1600*, translated by Norman Itzkowitz and Colin Imber, New York, Washington, 1973, 173.

4 S.G. Vesey-Fitzgerald, "Nature and Sources of the Shari'a," in *Law in the Middle East*, ed. Majid Khadduri and Herbert J. Liebesny, vol. I. *Origin and Development of Islamic Law*, Washington D.C.: The Middle East Institute, 1955, 85–112; Ebül'ula Mardin, "Development of the Shari'a under the Ottoman Empire," in *Law in the Middle East*, I, 279–291; Savvas-Pacha, *Étude sur la théorie du droit musulman*, Paris: Marchal et Billard, 1892, 96–291; J.

(*fikh*), constructed by jurists from the exegesis of the *Kur'an* and *sünnet*, two basic sources of Islamic jurisprudence (*usul al-fikh*).[5] In doing so, the jurisconsults' utilized consensus (*icmaʿ*)[6] and reasoning by analogy (*kıyas*)[7] – the juridical interpretation and explanation of the *şeriʿat* – so that every member of the Muslim community (*ʿUmma*) would know what had been allowed or forbidden.[8] Social and customary divergences in these legal developments led to the emergence of four Sunni juridical schools (Ar. *madhhab*) during the eighth and ninth centuries. Their names originated from their founders: Hanafi (Abu Hanifa, d. 767), Maliki (Ibn Malik, d. 795), Shafiʾi (al-Shafiʾi, d. 820) and Hanbali schools (Ibn Hanbal, d. 855).[9]

Of the four schools, the Ottomans adopted the Hanafi tradition, a choice that marked a departure from the Seljukids, who had been preferred Hanbali and Shafiʾi doctrines. Moreover, the Hanafi approach was more malleable and flexible, providing the *ulema* with more leeway in using analogy (*kıyas*) and individual opinion (*raʿy*) in their rulings, which made it particularly fitting to Ottoman internal and external policy.[10] Abu Hanifa became the object of veneration by the Ottomans and, in official documents, he came to be described as

---

Schacht, "Usul," *EI-1*, IV, 1112–1116; Tyan, "Méthodologie," 79–111; Chaygan, *Essai*, 25–35; S. M. Yusuf, "The Supremacy of Shari'at Law in Islamic Society," *IQ*, 1–2, 1978, 20–21; N. Çagatay, "Laiklik nedir. Şeriat nedir? (Qu'est-ce que le laicisme, qu'est-ce que le Şeriat?)," *Belleten*, XLII, 167, 1978, 427–436.

5 The four sources of Islamic law established in the nineth century were *al-Kur'an, sünnet, icma'* and *kıyas* (Savvas-Pacha, *Droit musulman*, 96–291; J. Schacht, "Usul," *EI-1*, IV, 1112–1116; Tyan, "Méthodologie," 79–111; Chaygan, *Essai*, 25–35; David, *Droit*, 457–496.

6 On *icma'* see M. Bernard, "Idjma," *EI-2*, III, 1046–1052; Laoust, *Ibn Taimiya*, 80, 83, 103, 111–112, 170; Milliot, *Droit*, 125–133; Yusuf, "Shar'ia," 20–21; Bravmann, *Arab Concepts*, 194–198; G.F. Hourani, "The Basis of Authority of Consensus in Sunni Islam," *SI*, XXI, 1964, 13–61; Bernard Weiss, "Al-Amidi on the Basis of Authority of Consensus," in *Essays on Islamic Civilization. Presented to Niyazi Berkeş*, Edited by D. P. Little, Leiden: Brill, 1976, 342–356.

7 On *kıyas* see M. Bernard, "Kıyas," *EI-2*, V, 238–242; Laoust, *Ibn Taimiya*, 114; Tyan, "Méthodologie," 82–83; Milliot, *Droit*, 134–144; Yusuf, "Shar'ia," 19–20. In Turkish, *kıyas etmek* means "to compare" (*Redhouse*, 660).

8 For details see I. Goldziher, J. Schacht, "Fıkh," *EI-2*, II, 906–912; Alfred Morabia, *La notion de ğihad dans l'Islam médiéval (des origines à al-Gazali)*, thèse presenté devant l'Université de Paris IV, 1 er Juillet 1974, Université de Lille III, 1975, 277–282; Kramers, "Droit islamique," 401, 404, 411–412; Milliot, *Droit*, 182–183; Hamidullah, *Conduct of State*, 4; M. el-Shakankiri, "Loi divine, loi humaine et droit dans l'histoire juridique de l'Islam," *RHDFE*, 59, 2, 1981, 161–182.

9 On Muslim schools of jurisprudence see I. M. d'Ohsson, *Tableau général de l'Empire Othoman*, Paris: De l'Imprimerie de Monsieur, 1787, I, 45; Bianchi, "Fetvas," 173; Chaygan, *Essai*, 36–41; Miquel, *Géografie humaine*, 26; Caurroy, "Législation," I, 5, n. 1; Sourdel, *Islamul clasic*, I, 153, 180, 219 and III, 233; Morabia, *Ğihad*, 178–179.

10 Several reasons were considered by historians. See Inalcık, *Ottoman Empire*, 181; Cardahi, *Droit*, 513–514, n. 1; Miquel, *Islam*, 184 (the Seljukids were Shafi'is and Hanbalis). Paul Coles considered that, by adopting the Hanafi school, the Ottomans became more tolerant towards Christians (Coles, *Ottoman Impact*, 18).

> the grand imam (*imam al-aʿzam*) [...] the leader of knowledge and wisdom, *kıbla*[11] of modesty and kindness, the leader of the law, the head of the greatest *ulema*.[12]

The Ottoman conquest of Baghdad in November 1534 was thus considered a major event, which liberated the grand imam's tomb from Shiʾite domination of the Safavids. A decade later, Süleyman Kanunî built a mausoleum, which would gain considerable significance for the dynasty and was visited by several sultans, including Murad IV, who visited the tomb in 1638, following his reconquest of Baghdad.[13]

## 1.1 Kur'an *and* Sünnet

*Kurʾan*[14] and *sünnet*[15] – the latter preserved in the form of "traditions" (*hadis*),[16] constitute the primary sources of Islamic law.[17] They also sketch the guiding principles regarding the relationship between the Muslim community and non-Muslims. It is important to remember that political and military circumstances had a profound impact on the verses of *Kurʾan*[18] that touch on the

11 *Kıbla is* the direction of Mecca towards which a Muslim turns during worship; generally it is a place or person towards which or whom everyone turns (*Redhouse*, 648).

12 In a letter of Grand Vizier Mustafa paşa to the *padişah*'s son of Hindustan, from the first part of the seventeenth century (Hammer, "Memoir," 486).

13 Decei, *Imp. otoman*, 181, 364, n. 2, 366.

14 For researching and quoting, I have used the following editons: *The Glorious Kurʾan*, ed. Abdullah Yusuf Ali, Lahore, 1973; *Le Saint Coran*, translation and commentary by Muhmmad Hamidullah, Nouvelle Edition, Publiée par Amana Corporation, 1989; *Kurʾan-ι Kerim ve Türkçe Açıklamalı Meali*, Hazırlayanlar: Prof. Dr. Ali Özek (and collaborators), Medine-i Münevere, 1412 AH/1992; *Coranul*, translated from Arabic by Dr. Silvestru Octavian Isopescul, Chernivtsi, 1912 (reedited Cluj-Napoca, 1992).

15 On *sünnet*, see A. J. Wensinck, "Sunna," *EI-1*, III, 581–3; D. W. Brown, "Sunna," *EI-2*, IX, 878–881; Morabia, *Ğihad*, 224–275; Bravmann, *Arab Concepts*, 159–160.

16 On *hadis*, see J. Robson, "Hadith," *EI-2*, III, 24–30; J. Schacht, "A Reevaluation of Islamic Tradition," *JRAS*, 3–4, 1949, 143–154; Morabia, *Ğihad*, 246–248, 269–275; Tyan, "Méthodologie," 81; A. J. Wensinck, *Concordance et indices de la tradition musulmane*, 8 vols., Leiden: Brill, 1936–1988.

17 Many historians and jurists affirmed that Islamic law is based on the *Kurʾan* and *sünnet* only. 'Traditionalists,' such as Ibn Taimiya (d. 1328), stated that any reading contrary to the unchanging principles stated in the *Kurʾan* should be considered a harmful novelty (*bidʿa*) or even heresy (Laoust, *Ibn Taimiya*, 61, 80; Milliot, *Droit*, 105; Shaltut, *Koran*, 26–27, 52; Bianchi, "Fetvas," 172).

18 On the *Kuʾran*, see Cantemir, *Sistemul*, 85–106; Fr. Buhl, "al-Kur'an," *EI-1*, II, 1124–1139; J. D. Pearson, "al-Kur'an," *EI-2*, V, 400–432; M. A. Draz, *Initiation au Koran*, Paris, 1951; Milliot, *Droit*, 105; Laoust, *Ibn Taimiya*, 61, 72; Schacht, *Law and Justice*, 565; Peters, "Djihad," 284; Tyan, "Djihad," *EI-2*, II, 551; Watt, "Jihad," 290–291; Watt, *Mahomet. Mecca*, 48; Watt, *Mahomet. Medine*, 377, 389; Morabia, *Ğihad*, 178–223.

issue. The verses IX, 29–32 regarding hostility towards Christians – and their analysis by W. Montgomery Watt – is particularly relevant here, since they were frequently invoked by Muslim rulers to justify their actions against non-Muslims. The warlike attitude contained in this fragment originated from the conflict between Muhammad and the Christians of northern Arabia, who had been under Byzantine rule and refused to accept poll-tax. In contrast, Christian communities of central and southern Arabia had concluded pacts (*ʿahd*) with the Prophet.[19] Analyzing Ottoman petitions of the early modern period, Suraiya Faroqhi pointed out that, in the case of Muslims,

> both petitioners and officials placed a special religious value upon all practice rightly or wrongly believed to go back to the times of the Prophet Muhammad.[20]

Moreover, the Prophet provided a ready model for Muslim rulers to aspire to in their conduct of military, political, diplomatic and theological affairs. The fact that Muhammad's actions, gestures and utterances had been a product of his time was ignored.

*Kur'an* and *hadis* were frequently invoked by Ottoman sultans, grand viziers and *şeyh ül-Islam*s to start wars, conclude, observe or break peace agreements, or to regulate the juridical position of non-Muslim subjects.[21] It is worth illustrating this practice with several examples. In a review of peace agreements concluded with Uzun Hasan, in 1474, Mehmed II justified his peaceful attitude through *Kur'an* VIII, 61: "but if the enemy incline towards peace, do thou also incline towards peace, and trust in Allah."[22] Just a couple years later, though, the same sultan reminded the Moldavian voivode, Stephen the Great, to observe his oath, which he had taken on the conclusion of the 1480–1481 *ʿahdname*, invoking another passage, *Kur'an* XVII, 34: "fulfill (every) commitment, for (every) commitment will be enquired into (on the Day of Reckoning)."[23] The *Kur'an* IX, 29 was most frequently cited by Muslims, including Ottomans, to justify actions against enemy infidels[24] and the conclusion of covenants with tributaries. One of the various renditions of this famous verse says:

19 Watt, *Mahomet. Medine*, 389; Watt, "Christianity," 651–656.

20 Faroqhi, "Ottoman Taxpayers," 5.

21 In a Crimean official's letter, Mehmed II was also entitled as "he who maintains the Prophet's *sünnet*" (Mehmet, *Documente turcești*, I, doc. 4).

22 Mokri, "Farman," 75–76.

23 Decei, "Sulhname," 122–124.

24 For exemple, it can be found at the end of the summon to the Byzantine emperor Heraclius (M. Hamidullah, *Documents sur la diplomatie musulmane à l'époque du Prophète et des Khalifes Orthodoxes*, Paris: G. P. Maisonneuve, 1935, doc. 15).

> Fight those who believe not in Allah nor the Last Day, nor hold that forbidden which hath forbidden by Allah and His Messenger, nor acknowledge the religion of Truth, (even if they are) of the People of the Book, until they pay the *cizye* with willing submission, and feel themselves subdued.[25]

After 1395, this verse was quoted by Idris Bitlisi to define and justify an alleged peace agreement between Bayezid I and Wallachian Voivode Mircea the Elder. This instance demonstrates the role of the *Kur'an* as juridical source for the Ottoman law of peace, though it did not fit well with the Ottoman–Wallachian realities of the late fourteenth century.[26]

What is more, Muhammad's covenants with non-Muslim communities, such as the *ʿahd* with Nadjran in 632, became a blueprint for peace arrangements between the Ottomans and their tributaries from the fourteenth until the sixteenth centuries, including those with Wallachia and Moldavia.[27] In turn, a ten-year treaty of Hudaibiya, which the Prophet concluded with the Meccans in 628 and broke two years later, served to legitimize conclusion of temporary peace arrangements with European states and the sultan's right to break them. A juridical opinion (*fetva*), issued in 1570 by *şeyh ül-Islam* Ebussuud Efendi to justify Selim II's decision to break a treaty with Venice and attack Cyprus, is illustrative in this respect:

> His Excellency the Caliph of the Lord of the Worlds [Selim II] [...] has, in his imperial actions, been guided by the noble acts of His Excellency the Bearer of Prophecy.[28]

## 1.2 Kitab al-siyar

Islamic law treatises, written in the pre-Ottoman period or by Ottoman scholars (*ulema*), provided the sultans with another source for defining their relations with non-Muslims. Virtually all juridical works produced between the eighth and eleventh century contained a set of rules and practices regarding the conduct of a Muslim polity in conducting war or making peace with non-Muslims; other chapters addressed the matters of holy war (*cihad*), tribute

---

25 I am quoting the translation from *The Glorious Kur'an*, ed. Abdullah Yusuf Ali, Lahore: Sh. Muhammad Ashraf Publishers, 1973.

26 Idris Bitlisi, *Heşt Behişt*, ms. Nurosmaniye Kütüphanesi, no. 3209, f. 181a (cf. Decei, "Mircea," 143).

27 A. Abel, "La convention de Najran et le developement du "droit des gens" dans l'Islam Classique." *RIDA* 2, (1949): 1–17; Maxim, *ŢRÎP*, 146–151.

28 Düzdağ, *Fetvalar*, no. 478; D'Ohsson, *Tableau*, V, 73–74; *Journal-Lepante*, 52. Here I am quoting the English version in Imber, *Ebu's-suʿud*, 85.

(*harac*), poll-tax (*cizye*), sovereignty (*hükümet*), foreigners (*müste'min*), intended as a systematic compilation of existing practices.[29] These issues were usually covered within a single chapter, entitled *kitab al-siyar*.

*Siyar* denoted the branch of *şeriʿat* dealing with Muslims' dealings with infidels (*kafir*s): enemies (*harbi*s) and signatories of treaties (*muʿahid*s), either foreigners (*müste'min*s) or tributaries (*zimmi*s). The term also encompassed the treatment of rebels (*bagy*) and apostates (*mürteddin*). It is in *siyar* that we may find the classical definition of what modern jurists tend to call Islamic "international" law; in fact, it was born from the transformation of the doctrine of *cihad* into a fully-fledged juridical system operating on two levels of inter-state relations: external relations with non-Muslim world, and internal relations among Muslim states.[30] In addition to the treatises covering Islamic law as a whole, some Muslim scholars also produced more specialized works dealing with the conduct of Muslims towards infidels.

Given that the Ottoman Empire followed the Hanafi school, the writings from within this *mezheb* (Ar. *madhhab*) are particularly relevant for the topic at hand. Although none of the works by the school's eponymous founder, Abu Hanifa al-Nu'man b. Thabit have been preserved,[31] his teachings on "international" law were inherited and developed by his disciples, particularly Abu Yusuf Ya'kub (d. 798)[32] and Muhammad al-Shaybani (d. 805). The former wrote an essential book on the Islamic law of nations, entitled *Book of the Land Tax* (*Kitab al-harac*),[33] which Ottoman *müfti*s employed – in its Arabic version – as the source for juridical opinions. The book was also translated in 1683 into Turkish, by Rodosizade Mehmed Ayasluği (d. 1702). The translation was commissioned by Grand Vizier Kara Mustafa paşa, who was interested in the issue

29 Morabia, *Ğihad*, 286; Rechid, "Islam," 384; Najib Armanazi, *L'Islam et le droit international*, Paris : Picart, 1929, 42, n. 1.

30 H. Kruse, "Notion of Siyar," *JPHS*, II, 1954, 16–25; *Shaybani's Siyar*, 3; Morabia, *Ğihad*, 301-306; Shai Har-El, *Ottoman-Mamluk*, 8. On the historical and juridical background of the şeriʿat and *kanun* in the Ottoman period, see Imber, *Ebu's-suʿud*, 3–64.

31 On his life see J. Schacht, "Abu Hanifa," *EI-2*, I, 126–128; Özel, *Hanefi*, 11–13.

32 He was a juristconsult in Kufa and Baghdad. On his life see Abu Yusuf, *Kitab*, IX–XVI (Avertissment); Morabia, *Ğihad*, 289.

33 Abou Yousuf Ya'koub, *Le livre de l' impôt foncier* (*Kitab al-kharadj*), translated and annotated by E. Fagnan, Paris: Paul Geuthner, 1921. For comparison, I have used also "Book of the Land Tax" of Yahya bin Adam (d. 818) (*Taxation in Islam. Volume I: Yahya bin Adam's Kitab al-kharaj*, edited, translated, annotated and introduced by A. Ben Shemesh, Revised Second Edition, Leiden: Brill, 1967, 23–109).

of tribute from non-Muslims. Abu Yusuf Yakub's work was in fact also compiled at the behest of Abbasid Caliph Harun al-Rashid.[34]

However, the most complete synthesis of Hanafi "international" law was *The Grand Book of Conduct of Government* (*Kitab al-siyar al-kabir*) by Muhammad al-Shaybani, dubbed the "Hugo Grotius of Islam" by European scholars.[35] This crucial text has not been preserved in its original form, but reached us in the form of commentaries by another medieval scholar, al-Sarakhsi (d. 1090).[36] Ottoman *ulemas* used the Arabic version of the text until the nineteenth century, when the text was translated into Ottoman Turkish by Mehmed Munib ʿAyntabi (d. 1822) between 1796–1798 and published on Sultan Mahmud II's orders.[37]

The original Hanafi precepts of *siyar* ("ancient law") underwent a process of revision, annotation and codification between the tenth and twelfth centuries by several scholars originating from Central Asia, Syria and Egypt. Their

34 Manuscripts in: TKSMK, R. 615 (ms. of 127 folios, written during the expedition of 1683); SK, Lala Ismail 85. On the first page is written: *sadr'azam sabık Kara Mustafa paşa'nın tevsiyesi üzere tercüme eyledüği Kitab-ı harac-ı Abu Yusuf.*

35 Reviewing the Turkish translation published in 1825, J. von Hammer called al-Shaybani for the first time a "Hugo Grotius of Islam" ("Jahrbücher der Literatur," Vienna, vol. 40 1827, 40, cf. Kruse, "Treaties," 153; *Shaybani's Siyar*, 56). Latter, H. Kruse used this appellation in a famous article (H. Kruse, "Die Begrundung der islamischen Volkerrechtslehre – Muhammad al-Shaybani – «Hugo Grotius der Moslimen»," *Saeculum* (Munich), 5, 1954, 221–241; English version, Hans Kruse, "The Foundation of International Islamic Jurisprudence (Muhammad al-Shaybani – Hugo Grotius of the Muslims)." *JPHS*, III, IV, 1955, 231–267). On his life, see Morabia, *Ğihad*, 289–290; Özel, *Hanefi*, 22–24; *Shaybani's Siyar*, 26–38.

36 See T. Osman *The Jurisprudence of Sarakhsi with particular Reference to War and Peace: A Comparative Study in Islamic Law*, PhD thesis, University of Exeter, 1993.

37 The translation was presented by the grand vizier and *şeyh ül-Islam* to Selim III, who refused its publication. Only in 1825 was ʿAyntabi's translation published. See al-Sarakhsi, *Şerh al-Siyar al-Kabir*, türkçeye tercüme: Mehmed Münib ʿAyntabi, Vols. I–II, Istanbul, 1241 AH/1825. Many copies are housed in the Süleymaniye Kütüphanesi in Istanbul. A copy can also be found in the "Cyrill and Methodius" Library in Sofia. A translation into modern Turkish is available, *Siyer-i Kebir. İslam Devletler Hukuku*, translated by M. Said Şimşek and I. Sarmuş, Istanbul, 1980. Excerpts from this work were also translated into French by A. J. du Caurroy and included in his capacious article on Sunni law (M. du Caurroy, "Législation musulmane Sunni: rite hanéfi," *JA*, IV, 12 (1848) – V, 2 (1853). The most recent translation into a Western language was made by M. Hamidullah (Muhammad ibn al-Hasan ach-Chaibânî, *Le Grand Livre de la Conduite de l'Etat* (*Kitâb al-Siyar al-Kabîr*). *Commenté par... al-Sarakhsî.* Translated by M. Hamidullah, vols. I–IV, Ankara: Editions Türkiye Diyanet Vakfı, 1989–1991. An abbreviated version of al-Shaybani's *siyar* was translated and published by M. Khadduri (*The Islamic Law of Nations. Shaybani's Siyar*, translated with an introduction, notes and appendices by M. Khadduri, Baltimore, Maryland: The Johns Hopkins Press, 1966).

writings were subsequently adopted and compiled by Ottomans during the early modern period, becoming the backbone of Ottoman legal doctrine.[38]

The first steps of the recovery process of Islamic law by the Ottomans took place in the first part of the fifteenth century and continued until the end of the century. This enterprise was led by Muslim scholars, some originating from older centers of Muslim learning, whose writings furnished the imperial authorities with legal precedents and expertise.[39] Among the first wave of Ottoman scholars, the most important figure was undoubtedly Molla Hüsrev (d. 1480), who Mehmed II appointed as *şeyh ül-Islam* in 1469, following his tenures as the *kadı* of Edirne and *kadıasker* of Rumeli. His prestige and knowledge led many contemporaries, including the sultan himself, to praise the scholar as the "Abu Hanifa of our time."[40]

Molla Hüsrev's most important work in the field of Islamic law was composed between 1473 and 1479 in Arabic and set out to compile and explain the legal opinions of his predecessors. The treatise was subsequently translated into Ottoman Turkish in 1632 by Ahmed b. Ali al-Ankaravi (*Terceme-i Dürer al-hükkam ve gurar al-ahkam*) and was repeatedly republished in print during the nineteenth century.[41] Hüsrev dealt briefly with questions concerning relations with non-Muslims in short chapters entitled "Book of the Holy War" (*Kitab al-cihad*), "Chapter of the Poll-Tax" (*Fasl fi al-cizye*) and "Chapter of the Foreigners" (*Bab al-müste'min*).[42]

In the sixteenth century, particularly following the Ottoman conquest of Arab lands, the assertion of the Islamic tradition by the ascendant dynasty intensified, and the corpus of *siyar* expanded and improved considerably. A major figure in this process was Ibrahim al-Halebi (d. 1549), who came to Istanbul from Egypt following Selim I's conquest of the province in 1517.[43] His oeuvre

38 See Meron, "Hanefi Texts," 73–119. Thirteenth- and fourteenth-century Anatolian writings on holy war are also worth mentioning here (Şinasi Tekin, "XIV. Yüzyılda yazılmış Gazilik Tarikası "Gaziliğin Yolları" adlı bir eski Anadolu Türkçesi metni ve gaza/cihad kavramları hakkında," *JTS-TBA*, 13, 1989, 139–204).

39 Inalcık, *Ottoman Empire*, 174–175; Tekin, "Gaziliğin Yolları," 139–204; Coles, *Ottoman Impact*, 30.

40 Or Khosrew, Hosrov, Hosrou, Hosrowa. He remained in office until his death. On his life and work, see F. Babinger, "Molla Khosrew," *EI-2*, V, 33; Özel, *Hanefi*, 102–103; Meron, "Hanefi Texts," 115–116; R. C. Repp, *The Müfti of Istanbul. A Study in the Development of the Ottoman Learned Hiera rchy*, Oxford: Oxford University Press, 1986, 154–166; Shaw, *Ottoman Empire*, I, 144; A. Abel, "La djizya: tribut ou rançon?" *SI*, xxxii, 1970, 7.

41 Many manuscripts and published copies can be found in the Süleymaniye Library in Istanbul and "Cyrill and Methodius" Library in Sofia. I have used Molla Hüsrev, *Dürer al-hukkam fi şerh gürer al-ahkam*, I–II, Istanbul, 1258 AH/1842–1843.

42 Hüsrev, *Dürer*, I, 205–210.

43 J. Schacht, "al-Halebi," *EI-2*, III, 90; Özel, *Hanefi*, 114–115. Beldiceanu-Steinherr, "Le règne de Selim I," 35–48.

was a crucial contribution to the growth of Islamic law in the empire, and his treatise "The Confluence of Seas" (*Mülteka el-Ebhür*), came to be regarded as "one of the most important books on the fully developed doctrine of Hanafi Law."[44] Judging by its title, al-Halebi's goal was to synthesize the opinions of six Arab jurists active between the eleventh and fourtheenth centuries.[45] *Mülteka el-Ebhür* saw several translations into Ottoman Turkish, the first undertaken by Mehmed Tahir b. Mehmed Rahimi (d. 1655) in the first half of the seventeenth century.[46] However, by far the most well-known of these translation was that by Mehmed b. Mehmed Efendi Mevkufati (d. 1761),[47] frequently republished throughout the nineteenth century under the title "Commentary upon The Confluence of Seas" (*Şerh-i Mülteka el-Ebhür*).[48] Observing the tradition of *şeriʿat* scholarship, Ibrahim al-Halebi penned distinct chapters regarding relations with non-Muslims (*Kitab al-siyar, Bab al-ʿuşr ve al-harac, Bab-ı ahkam al-müsteʾmin*).[49] In Western Europe, al-Halebi's work became known by way of eighteenth-century French translation by Ignace Mouradgea d'Ohsson, entitled *Tableau général de l'Empire Othoman*, which constituted a major watershed for European knowledge of Islamic law.[50]

44 F. le Blanc Hackluya, *Histoire de l'Islamisme*, Paris, 1892, 29–30; Schacht, *Islamic Law*, 112.

45 It is about al-Kuduri (d. 1037), al-Marghinani (d. 1197), Tadj al-Shari'a (d. 1263), Madj ed-Din (d. 1284), Muzafer al-Din ibn Sa'di (d. 1293) and al-Nasafi (d. 1310) (Milliot, *Droit*, 24).

46 Mehmed Tahir b. Mehmed Rahimi, *Tercüme-i Mülteka el-Ebhür* (TKSMK, E.H. 788; ms. of 637 folios, copied in 1221 AH/1806–1807).

47 Mehmed b. Mehmed Efendi Mevkufati, *Tercüme-i Mülteka el-Ebhür* (TKSMK, A 892, ms. of 360 folios; also, TKSMK, A. 892). There are many manuscripts of *Mülteka el-Ebhür* in the Süleymaniye Library, Istanbul (for example, SK, Nazif Ef. 8).

48 M. Mevkufati, *Şerh-i Mülteka el-Ebhür*, Vols. I–II, Istanbul, 1254 AH/1838–1839) is one of almost eighteen editions from "Cyrill and Methodius" Library in Sofia. The last edition is Ibrahim Halebi, *Şerh-i Mülteka el-Ebhür* (*Mevkufat*), Tercüme ve Açıklamalar Nedim Yılmaz, vols. 1–4, Istanbul, 1993. The ninth chapter deals with *siyar* (*Ibidem*, Vol. 2, 550–628).

49 Halebi, *Mülteka*, I, 336–338 (in edition of 1254 AH/1838– 1839).

50 I. M. d'Ohsson, *Tableau général de l'Empire Othoman*, vol. I–VII, Paris: De l'Imprimerie de Monsieur, 1787–1824. Louis Milliot accused d'Ohsson of distorting the original by restructuring his translation and suggesting that *Mülteka el-Ebhür* was a collection of religious, civil, criminal, political and military law-codes (Milliot, *Droit*, 24). Later, F. A. Belin and and M. Du Caurroy made ample use of al-Halebi's juridical text for writing their own studies of Islamic law (F. A. Belin, *Étude sur la proprieté foncière en pays musulman et spécialement en Turquie*, Paris: Impr. Impériale, 1862; M. Du Caurroy, "Législation musulmane Sunni: rite hanéfi," *JA*, IV, 12 (1848) – V, 2 (1853).

## 1.3 Fetva

Juridical opinions (*fetva*),[51] issued by a *müfti* were, according to Halil Inalcık, the Ottoman's most important contribution to the *şeri'at*.[52] For our topic, the most important ones were those issued at the behest of Muslims and discussing the matters of the holy war. The origins and functions of *müftis* in Ottoman history produced a variety of sometimes contradictory opinions.[53] According to Haim Gerber, the *müfti* was a religious–juridical expert particularly qualified to provide juridically authoritative answers; he stood in the Ottoman juridical hierarchy between jurists (authors of juridical manuals who occupied the highest rank) and judges (the *kadıs*, situated on the lowest level), but closer to the latter.[54] The chief *müfti* of Istanbul and the highest-ranking religious official in the empire, called *şeyh ül-Islam*, was also called "the chief (*reis*) of the ulemas" in Mehmed II's code of law.[55] Most *fetvas* were issued for the purposes of private cases heard in the *kadı* courts. Yet, *şeyh ül-Islams* were deeply embedded in political, diplomatic and administrative affairs, providing legal opinions and advice for the sultan, a phenomenon that had begun in the fifteenth century, but which became a standard in the seventeenth and eighteenth centuries. The *fetvas* provided religious–juridical legitimization of imperial orders, providing them with legal justification. The best illustration of this political–legal nexus are *fetvas* calling up Ottomans to fight European infidels (the so-called *cihad fetvaları*, i.e. juridical opinions on holy war), or justifying attacks on Muslim heretics.[56]

51 For the general aspects concerning *fetvas*, I have used: Sertoğlu, ROTA, 106 (*Fetva*); U. Heyd, "Some Aspects of the Ottoman *Fetva*," BSOAS, XXXII, 1, 1969, 35–56; Hilmar Krüger, *Fetwa und Siyar*, Wiesbaden: Otto Harrassowitz, 1978; Gerber, *Ottoman Law*, 79–112 (Chapter 3: "The *Fetva* in the Juridical System"); E. Tyan, J. R. Walsh, "Fatwa," *EI-2*, II, 866–867 (II. Ottoman Empire, by J. H. Walsh); Imber, *Ebu's-su'ud*, 24–64 (Chapter "The Law: *shari'a* and *qanun*").

52 Colin Imber defined *fetva* "as one of the three major categories of Ottoman juridical documents," the other two being Sultanic decrees and certificates issued by judges (Imber, *Ebu's-su'ud*, 51–55); Inalcık, *Ottoman Empire*, 173–174.

53 Most recently, between J. H. Walsh and R. C. Repp. On the institution of the *müfti* and *şeyh ül-Islam*, see R. W. Bulliet, "The Shaykh al-Islam and the Evolution of Islamic Society." SI xxxv, 1, (1972): 53–69; J. H. Kramers, R. W. Bulliet, R .C. Repp, "Shaykh al-Islam," *EI-2*, IX, 399–402.

54 Gerber, *Ottoman Law*, 79–88.

55 On *müftilik* in the later fifteenth century, see Repp, *Müfti*, 125–196; Paul Rycaut, *The Present State of the Ottoman Empire. Containing the Maxims of the Turkish Politie, the Most Material Points of the Mahometan Religion, Their Sects and Heresies, Their Convents and Religious Votaries. Their Military Discipline with an exact Computation of Their Forces both by Land and Sea*, London: Printed for John Starkey and Henry Brome, 1668, 105–109: Ch. IV. "The power and office of the Mufti's, and of their Government in Religious Matters").

56 Repp, "Shaykh al-Islam," 402; Gerber, *Ottoman Law*, 79–112. J. L. Bacqué-Grammont, *Les Ottomans, les Safavides et leurs voisins…*, Istanbul, 1987. On the Christian states' rationale

The generic format of a *fetva* is a document issued as a reply to a legal question, worded in a way that eliminated any personal and contextual details, thus preventing any influence on the *kadi*'s decision. It consisted of two sections: a question (*mesele*) and an answer (*el-cevab*). The first part provided a concise query, asking "is it possible?" The answer section provided a laconic reply of the *müfti*, either "yes" (*olur*) ot "no" (*olmaz*); sometimes, the opinion was accompanied by an explanation citing relevant religious-juridical texts.[57] Usually, the names used in the *fetva* were conventional ones, both with regard to individuals (Zeyd, ʿAmr, Bishr for males, Hind, Zeynab and Khadija for women) and territories (*dar al-harb* and *dar al-Islam*).

Fortunately for us, divergences from this rule exist. For instance, in a collection of *fetvas* by Ali Efendi Akkermani, several opinions refer directly to Moldavian–Wallachian and Polish territories and their inhabitants. Most *fetvas* have not been preserved in their original, standalone form, but rather by way of *kadı* court records (*şeriʿat sicilleri*), sultanal orders (*hüküm*) and particularly *fetva* collections.[58] Usually, the latter brought together juridical opinions issued by a single *şeyh ül-Islam*; however, from the seventeenth century we find a growing number of thematic collections, which gradually became scholars' manuals for Islamic law. Such collections also contained separate chapters, focusing on relations with non-Muslims: *siyar*, *cihad*, *zimmi*, *müsteʾmin*, *harac* and *cizye*.[59]

One of the questions relevant to this study is the degree of influence *fetvas* could have on the juridical status of the tributary principalities of Wallachia, Moldavia and Transylvania? Although we lack clear evidence that they were used for juridical purposes, some conclusion can be drawn, nonetheless. I believe that the *fetvas* can provide us with the most detailed picture of the status of tribute paying rulers, inhabitants and territories under their rule in their relations with the Sublime Porte. In this respect, three types of *fetvas* are particularly relevant.

First among these are *fetvas* dealing with general matters of sovereignty (*hükümet*), conduct of state (*siyar*), holy war (*cihad*), protected peoples (*zimmi*), tribute (*harac*), poll-tax (*cizye*) and foreigners (*müsteʾmin*). In the

regarding war, the same Papal bulls served a similar purpose to the declarations of holy war (Brummett, *Ottoman Seapower*, 7). The European observers underlined also this role of *fetvas* (D'Ohsson, *Tableau*, V, 71; Castellan, *Moeurs*, I, 9–10).

57 Sertoğlu, *ROTA*, 106; Heyd, "Fetva," 35–56. J. R. Walsh was wrong to state that the answer was "never supported by reasons of citations from authority" (Walsh, "Fatwa," 867).

58 I have found some original *fetvas* among the pages of *fetva* collections in the Topkapı Saray Müzesi Library and Süleymaniye Library in Istanbul. For details on the structure of these collections, see Krüger, *Fetwa*, 136–139.

59 For instance: *Defter-i sukuk* (TKSMK K. 778); *Siyasete müteʿallik fetvalar* (*Fetvas* concerning politics) (TKSMK, H. 1650); *Fetava fi hakk-i müsadere* (*Fetvas* concerning the right of capture) (TKSMK, B 107).

sixteenth century the most famous juridical opinions on these matters were issued by great *şeyh ül-Islam*s Zenbilli Ali Efendi[60] and Ebussuud Efendi,[61] which emerged as the basic sources addressing the Ottomans' relations with non-Muslims. In the latter centuries, other well-known *fetva* collections were those of *şeyh ül-Islam*s Minkarizade Yahya Efendi (in office between 1662–1674),[62] Çatalcalı Ali Efendi (*1674*–1686, 1692),[63] Ankaravi Mehmet Emin Efendi (1686–1687),[64] Ebu-Saʿidzade Feyzullah Feyzi Efendi (1690–1694, with a short interruption),[65] Menteşizade Abdurrahim Efendi (1715–1716)[66] and Yenişehirli Abdullah Efendi, who enjoyed a long tenure between 1718–1730.[67]

60 Zenbilli-Ali Efendi served as şeyh ül-Islam between 1503–1526, until his death. I have consulted the manuscript *Fetava-yi 'Ali Ef.* (SK, Fatih 2390), but there are three other manuscripts in the Süleymaniye Library in Istanbul.

61 Ebussuud Efendi (d. 1574) served as *şeyh ül-Islam* for thirty years between 1545 and 1574, being considered one of the greatest Ottoman *şeyh ül-Islam*. His *fetvas* were taken as pattern during the seventeenth–eighteenth centuries (Repp, *Müfti*, 272–304; Hasan Basri Erk, *Meşhur Türk Hukukçuları* (*Célébres juristes turcs*), Istanbul, 117–139; Shaw, *Ottoman Empire*, I, 139; Özel, *Hanefi*, 120). Certain *fetvas* were published by M. E. Duzdağ, F. Selle and A. Akgündüz (M. E. Düzdağ, *Şeyhülslam Ebussuud Efendi fetvalar ışıgında 16. asır türk hayatı*, Istanbul, 1983; Friedrich Selle, *Prozessrecht des 16. Jahrhunderts im Osmanischen Reich. Auf Grund von Fetwas des Scheichülislame Ebüssuud und anderer unter des Regierung des Sultans Süleiman des Prächtingen*, Wiesbaden: Otto Harrassowitz, 1962; Akgündüz, *Osmanlı Kanunnameleri*, IV, 40–100).

62 I have consulted three manuscripts: *Fetava-yi Yahya Efendi* (SK, Hamidiye 601: *Bab al-üşr ve al-harac*, f. 12a-16b; *Kitab al-siyar*, f. 17a–21b; on *zimmis*, f. 21b–25b); *Fetava-yi Yahya Efendi* (TKSMK, A 788); *Fetava-yı Minkarızade Yahya Efendi* (PRUL, GYC, 2389 Y, ms. of 1798).

63 Many manuscripts of his *fetvas* collections are preserved in the Princeton University Library: *Fetava-yi Ali Efendi* (PRUL, GYC, 2509Y, ms. of 1183 AH/1769, 286 folios; 2456Y; 3027Y; NSC, 1014. Also, *Fetava-yi Ali Efendi* (TKSMK, M. 378, ms. of 223 folio). At the same time, his juridical opinions were frequently published in the nineteenth century (*Fetava-yi Ali Efendi*, Ali Çatalcalı Şeyh ül-islamdan toplayıp tertip eden Salih ibn-i Ahmed El-Kefevi, Istanbul, 1245 AH/1829 (6th ed. 1311 AH/1893; Ali Efendi, *Fetava*, Istanbul, 1324–1325 AH/1906–1907).

64 *Fetava-yi Ankaravi*, Istanbul, 1281 AH/1864–1865.

65 His *fetvas* collection is better known as *Fetava-yi Feyziyye*. A manuscript is in PRUL, GYC, 3762 Y: *Kitab al-siyar*, f. 17a–18a. More published editions: Feyzullah Şeyh ül-islam, *Fetavayi Feyziyye Maan Nükul*, Istanbul, 1266 AH/1850; Feyzullah Efendi, *Fetava-yi Feyziyye*, Istanbul, 1324–1325 AH/1906–1907.

66 Published *fetvas*: Abdurrahim Efendi, *Fetava*, Istanbul, 1243 AH/1827; Abdürrahim Menteşizade, *Fetava-yi Abdürrahim*, Dar üt-Tabaat ül-Mamuret üs-Sültaniye, Vols. I-II, 1243 AH/1847.

67 Manuscripts: *Fetava-yi Abdullah Efendi* (TKSMK H. 173); *Behcet ül-fetava* or *Fetava-yi Abdullah Efendi el-Yenişehir* (MOL, Budapest, Török Qu. 18). Published *fetvas*: *Behcet ül-fetava Maan-Nükul*, Istanbul: Matbaa-i Amire, 1266 AH/1849.

Second, several *fetvas* from the western shore of the Black Sea were issued for private trials and employed a juridical terminology with explicit connection to Moldavia and Wallachia. Most were penned by *müfti* Ali Efendi Akkermani (d. 1621). Unfortunately, we know little about his life and activity. According to Mehmed Süreyya, he was professor (*müderris*) and *müfti* in various regions of the empire for over three decades, although I suspect his main area of activity was the port of Akkerman on the mouth of Dniester, where he had likely been born.[68] A large number of manuscripts containing his *fetvas* – seven I am acquainted with – suggest his fervent and vigorous activity among the *ulema*.[69]

The third group are opinions directly addressing military and administrative measures taken by the Porte towards voivodes, territories and inhabitants of Wallachia, Moldavia and Transylvania. Launching a punitive campaign against rebels, their imprisonment and execution had to be legitimated by a *fetva*. Unfortunately, the *fetvas* regarding the Ottoman response to a great revolt in Moldavia, Wallachia and Transylvania in 1594–1595 have not yet been discovered. However, as Mustafa Selaniki's account clearly shows, the decisions taken by the Porte relied on the legal opinions of *şeyh ül-Islam* Bostanzade Mehmed Efendi.[70] Similarly, Moldavian chronicler Miron Costin also referred to a *fetva* by the chief *müfti*, requested by Murad IV to justify the execution of the Moldavian voivode Miron Barnovschi. The incumbent *şeyh ül-Islam*, Ahi-zade Hüseyin Efendi (also known as Şehid-Hüseyin Efendi), condemned Barnovschi as the "head" of the rebellion.[71] However, the most famous example in this respect was the dethronement of Wallachian voivode Constantin Brâncoveanu. The order issued in 1714 by Ahmed III to *mübaşir* Mustafa, which commanded the latter to bring the voivode to Istanbul, included a *fetva* by *şeyh ül-Islam* Imam Mahmud Efendi, which ruled Brâncoveanu's execution to be lawful.[72] A mere three years later, during the Ottoman–Habsburg war of 1716–1718, *şeyh*

68 Süreyya, *Sicill-i 'Osmani*, III, 509; Süreyya, *Sicill-i 'Osmani* (ed. 1996), vol. 1, 251.

69 *Fetava-yi 'Ali Akkermani* (TKSMK, A 842, ms. of 458 folio, 203 x 124, nesih). It is a collection (*mecmu'a*) which contains the *fetvas* issued by Akkermani Ali Efendi, gathered by Derviş Mehmed b. Hasan Istanbuli in 1040 AH/1630–1631. The most important chapter for our research is *Kitab al-siyar*, f. 94b–108b. Other manuscripts: *Fetava-yi Akkermani Maa Üskubi* (SK, Hkm. 405; ms. of 397 folio, nesih, *Kitab al-siyar*, f. 87a-98b; *Fetava-yi Akkermani* (SK, M. Hafid Ef. 98, ms. of 206 folio, talik; Millet Kütuphanesi, Istanbul, Murad Moll, 1118; Beyazit Devlet, Veliyüddin, 1470, 1471). There is also a manuscript in Konya.

70 In the şeyh ül-Islam office between 1589–1592 and 1593–1598 (Selaniki, *Tarih*, in *Cronici turcești* I, 367).

71 Miron Costin, *Letopiseţ*, 102; Danişmend, *OTKronolojisi*, III, 530.

72 Veliman, *Documente turcești*, doc. 11. Imam Mahmud Efendi was in office between 1713–1714 (Danişmend, *OTKronolojisi*, IV, 533).

فهرست الجلد الاول من ترجمة شرح السير الكبير المشتمل على ما فيه من الابواب والفصول وما يحويه من غرائب المسائل ورغائب الفصول

| | | | |
|---|---|---|---|
| ٦ | ترجمة احوال مؤلف الكتاب الامام الهمام محمد بن الحسن الشيبانى | ٥٣ | باب من قاتل فاصاب نفسه وفيه حكم من قتل نفسه عمدا |
| ٩ | ترجمة اوصاف شارح الكتاب شمس الائمة محمد ابن ابى سهل السرخسى | ٥٥ | باب قتل ذى الرحم المحرم وفيه حبس الاب لنفقة ولده لا لدينه |
| ١١ | سبب وقوع المنافرة بين الامامين محمد وابى يوسف رحمة الله تعالى عليهما | ٥٥ | باب البكاء على القتلى وفيه استماع بكاء النساء على الميت |
| ١٢ | بيان سبب تأليف السير الكبير بعد تصنيف السير الصغير | ٥٦ | باب حمل الرؤس الى الولاة |
| ١٣ | افتخار امير المؤمنين هارون الرشيد على اجداده بكتاب السير الكبير | ٥٧ | باب السلاح والفروسية وفيه ذكر فضائل القوس وتوفير الاظفار والشوارب فى الحرب |
| ١٣ | سلسلة استاد شمس الائمة السرخسى الى الامام محمد بن الحسن الشيبانى رحمه الله تعالى | ٥٨ | باب الحرب كيف يعبى له وفيه الخدعة فى الحرب وحكم الكذب |
| ١٤ | تفسير المرابطة وفضلها وعذاب القبر حق | ٦١ | باب الفرار من الزحف وفيه عد بعض الكبائر |
| ٢٩ | باب وصايا الامراء فى الحرب وفيه بيان معنى الذمة | ٦٢ | باب من اسلم فى دار الحرب ولم يهاجر الينا |
| | | ٦٣ | باب دواء الجراحة وفيه المداواة بالعظم البالى |
| ٣٩ | باب الامارة وفيه ينبغى للمسافرين ان يؤمروا عليهم اميرا | ٦٤ | باب اتخاذ الانف من الذهب والفضة وفيه اتخاذ السن منهما |
| ٤١ | باب مبعث السرايا وفيه فضل الابتكار فى طلب الحاجات وطلب العلم | ٦٤ | باب اموال المعاهدين وفيه حكم دخول المشرك فى المسجد الحرام وغيره |
| ٤٣ | باب الرايات والالوية وفيه الفرق بين الراية واللواء | ٦٥ | باب الجعائل وفيه حكم فضل النفقة اذا حج غيره |
| ٤٥ | باب الدعاء عند القتال وفيه دعوة المشركين الى الاسلام | ٦٨ | باب آنية المشركين وذبائحهم وطعامهم وفيه حكم اكل طعام الكافر |
| ٤٧ | باب البركة فى الخيل وما يصلح وفيه ما يتبرك من اوصاف الخيل ويتشأم به | ٦٩ | باب الاسلام وفيه حكم نصرانى او يهودى قال انا مسلم |
| ٤٩ | باب كراهة الجرس وفيه اباحة الحدى | ٧١ | باب الجهاد مع الامراء وفيه الوعيد على من كتم علما وحكم مرتكب الكبيرة |
| ٥٠ | باب رفع الصوت وفيه كراهية رفع الصوت عند الذكر والسماع والجنائز | ٧٤ | باب من يحل له الخمس والصدقة وفيه اخذ العامل عمالته من الصدقة |
| ٥٠ | باب العمايم فى دار الحرب وفيه ارخاء الذنب العمامة ونقضها | ٧٥ | باب ما يجب من طاعة الوالى وما لا يجب وفيه لا طاعة لمخلوق فى معصية الخالق |
| ٥١ | باب القتال فى الاشهر الحرم وفيه انه عليه السلام غزا الطايف فى المحرم | ٨١ | باب قتال النساء مع الرجال وشهودهن الحرب |
| ٥١ | باب هجرة الاعرابى | ٨٢ | باب الجهاد ما يسع منه وما لا يسع وفيه ان القتال فرض على التدريج |
| ٥٢ | باب صلة المشرك وفيه جواز التصدق على المشركين | ٩١ | باب صاحب الساقة اذا وجد فى اخريات الناس رجلا مع دابته |
| ٥٣ | باب المبارزة وفيه جواز التغنى حال وحدته لدفع وحشته | ٩٣ | باب سجدة الشكر وفيه تفسير المترجم لفظ النجاشى |

باب صلوة

FIGURE 1 Muhammad al-Shaybani (d. 189 AH/805), *Kitab al-Siyar al-Kabir*, page from Table of content (from the Turkish translation made by Mehmed Ayntabi, *Şerh al-Siyar al-Kabir*, Istanbul, 1241 AH /1825, cild I, p. 2)

FIGURE 2 Ibrahim al-Halebi (d. 956 AH/1549), *Mülteka el-Ebhür / Confluence of Seas,* page from the chapter *Kitab al-siyar* (from the Turkish commented translation of Mehmed Mevkufati, *Şerh-i Mülteka el-Ebhür / Comments to the Confluence of Seas,* I, Istanbul, 1254 AH/1838–1839, p. 329)

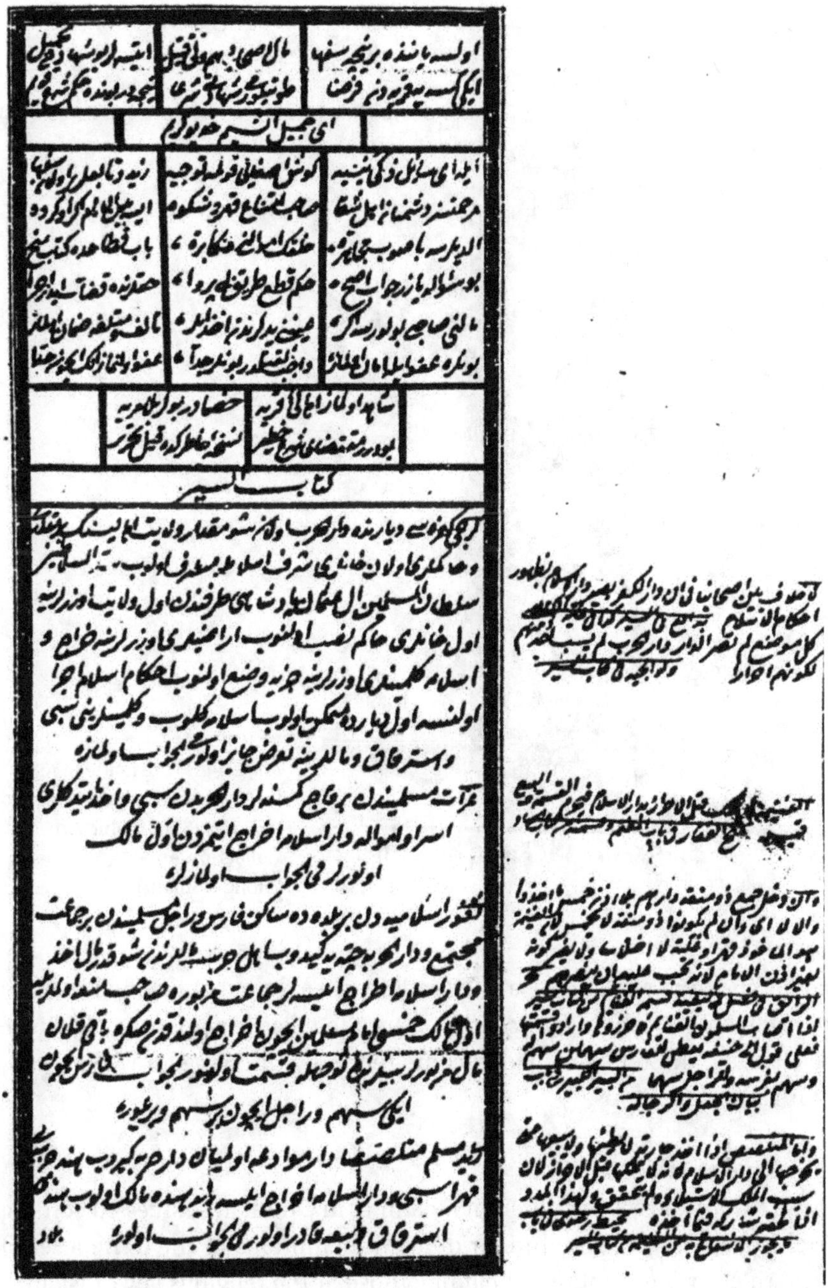

FIGURE 3 *Fetvas* issued by *şeyh ül-Islam* Abdallah Efendi al-Yenişehir (d. 1156 AH/1743), gathered in the chapter *Kitab al-Siyar* of *Behcet ül-fetava* (from the manuscript *Fetava-yi Abdullah Efendi al-Yenişehir*, Library of the Hungarian Academy of Sciences, Oriental Collection, Török Qu.18, f. 56)

FIGURE 4
*Müfti* – gravure made in 1687 by Andreas Matthaüs Wofgand (1660–1736) (Graphic Art Collection Abbey – Wikipedia. Public Domain)

*ül-Islam* Ebu-Işak Kara Ismail Na'im Efendi issued a *fetva* that justified military action against Wallachian *haracgüzar*s from the villages across the Olt River. As he claimed, these people had become rebels by throwing away their support for Habsburg troops.[73]

## 1.4 *Sultan's Will*

The term *kanun* had several different meanings in Ottoman sources. According to Uriel Heyd, one can discern four different definitions of the term: a set of juridical rules or prescriptions, including those of the religious law of Islam; a single regulation or statute of secular law enacted by the sultan (in this case synonymous with *'adet*); a collection of such regulations relating to one or

73 Veliman, *Documente turceşti*, doc. 24.

more matters; finally, the whole body or institution of secular state laws (having as a synonym the term *ʿörf*), juxtaposed to the *şeriʿat*.[74] Generally, historians and jurists have emphasized the radical difference between *şeriʿat* ("sacred Islamic law") and *kanun* ("civil and secular law").[75]

The *kanunnames* or the *ʿörf* laws were the written materializations of the sultans' will (*ʿörf-i padişahi* or *ʿörf-i sultani*) to enact laws, cancel or strengthen habits and confirm covenants with non-Muslim communties within the empire.[76] Halil Inalcık has divided the *ʿörf* laws into three categories:[77] general law-codes, applicable for the empire as a whole (such as those enacted by Mehmed II,[78] Bayezid II,[79] Selim I,[80] Süleyman Kanunî,[81] Selim II,[82] Murad III

74 Heyd, *Ottoman Law*, 167–168.

75 Heyd, *Ottoman Law*, 167–176; Halil Inalcık, "Osmanlı Hukukuna Giriş. 'Örf-i Sultanı Hukuk ve Fatih'in Kanunları," *AÜSBFD*, XIII, 2, 1958, 102–126; H. Inalcık, "Kanun," *EI-2*, IV, 580–584; H. Inalcık, "Kanunname," *EI-2*, IV, 584–588. See also Imber, *Ebu's-suʿud*, 65–97 (Chapter 3: The Sultan and Juridical Sovereignty).

76 R. Anhegger, H. Inalcık, *Kanunname-i Sultanı ber muceb-i örf-i Osmanı. II.Mehmed ve II. Bayezid devirlerine ait yasakname ve kanunnameler*, Ankara: TTK Basımevi, 1956, X; Inalcık, "Örf-i Sultanı," 102–126; Heyd, *Ottoman Law*, 167–176.

77 Inalcık, "Süleyman," 115–116; Inalcık, "Kanunname," 584–588. See also Mario Grignaschi, "Le problème du droit coutumier dans l'Empire Ottoman," in *La coutume. Custom, Troisième partie. Third Part. Europe Orientale, Asie et Islam. Eastern Europe, Asia and Islam*, Transactions of the Jean Bodin Society for Comparative Institutional History, Brussels: De Boeck Université, 1992, 281–298; Yunus Koç, "Early Ottoman Customary Law: The Genesis and Development of Ottoman Codification," in *Shattering Tradition: Custom, Law and the Individual in the Muslim Mediterranean*. Ed. Walter Dostal and Wolfgang Kraus (The Islamic Mediterranean, 8). London: IB Tauris, 2005, 75–121.

78 Mehmed Arif Bey, "Kanunname-i ʿal-i Osman," *TOEM*, I, 13, 1330 AH/1912, 1–16 and 14, 1330 AH/1912, 17–32; Fr. Kraelitz, "Kanunnamé des Sultans Mehmeds des Eroberers," *MOG*, Vienne, I, 1921, 13–48; R. Anhegger, H. Inalcık, *Kanunname-i Sultanı ber muceb-i örf-i Osmani. II.Mehmed ve II. Bayezid devirlerine ait yasakname ve kanunnameler*, Ankara: TTK Basımevi, 1956; N. Beldiceanu, *Code de lois coutumières de Mehmed II*, Wiesbaden, 1967; A. Akgündüz, *Osmanlı Kanunnameleri ve Hukukı Tahlilleri. 1 Kitab. Osmanlı Hukukunda Giriş ve Fatih Devri Kanunnameleri*, Istanbul: Fey Vakfı, 1990.

79 A. Akgündüz, *Osmanlı Kanunnameleri. II. Kitab: II. Bayezid Devri Kanunnameleri*, Istanbul: Fey Vakfı, 1990.

80 Selami Pulaha, Yaşar Yücel, *Le code (Kanunname) de Selim Ier (1512–1520) et certaines autres lois de deuxième moitie du XVIe siécle. I Selim Kanunamesi (1512–1520) ve XVI yüzyılın ikinci yarısının kimi kanunları*, Ankara: TTK Basımevi, 1988; A. Akgündüz, *Osmanlı Kanunnameleri, III. Kitab: Yavuz Sultan Selim Devri Kanunnameleri*, Istanbul: Fey Vakfı, 1991.

81 A. Akgündüz, *Osmanlı Kanunnameleri. IV. Kitab: Kanunî Sultan Süleyman Devri Kanunnameleri. I. Kasım. Mekezi ve Umumi Kanunnameler*, Istanbul: Fey Vakfı, 1992.

82 A. Akgündüz, *Osmanlı Kanunnameleri. VII. Kitab/II*, Istanbul: Fey Vakfı, 1994, 218–820.

THE

HISTORY

OF THE

GROWTH *and* DECAY

OF THE

*OTHMAN EMPIRE.*

---

PART I.

---

CONTAINING THE

Growth of the *OTHMAN EMPIRE*,

FROM THE

Reign of *OTHMAN* the Founder,

TO THE

Reign of *MAHOMET* IV.

THAT IS,

From the Year 1300, to the Siege of *Vienna*, in 1683.

---

Written Originally in LATIN,

By DEMETRIUS CANTEMIR, late Prince of *Moldavia.*

---

Tranflated into ENGLISH, from the Author's own Manufcript,

By N. TINDAL, M. A. Vicar of *Great Waltham* in *Effex.*

---

Adorn'd with the HEADS

Of the TURKISH EMPERORS, Ingraven from Copies taken from ORIGINALS in the Grand SEIGNOR's Palace, by the late SULTAN's Painter.

---

*LONDON:*

Printed for JAMES, JOHN, and PAUL KNAPTON, at the *Crown* in *Ludgate Street.* MDCCXXXIV.

FIGURE 5 Demetrius Cantemir, *The History of the Growth and Decay of the Othman Empire.* Written Originally in Latin. Translated into English by N. Tindal, London, 1734 – title page

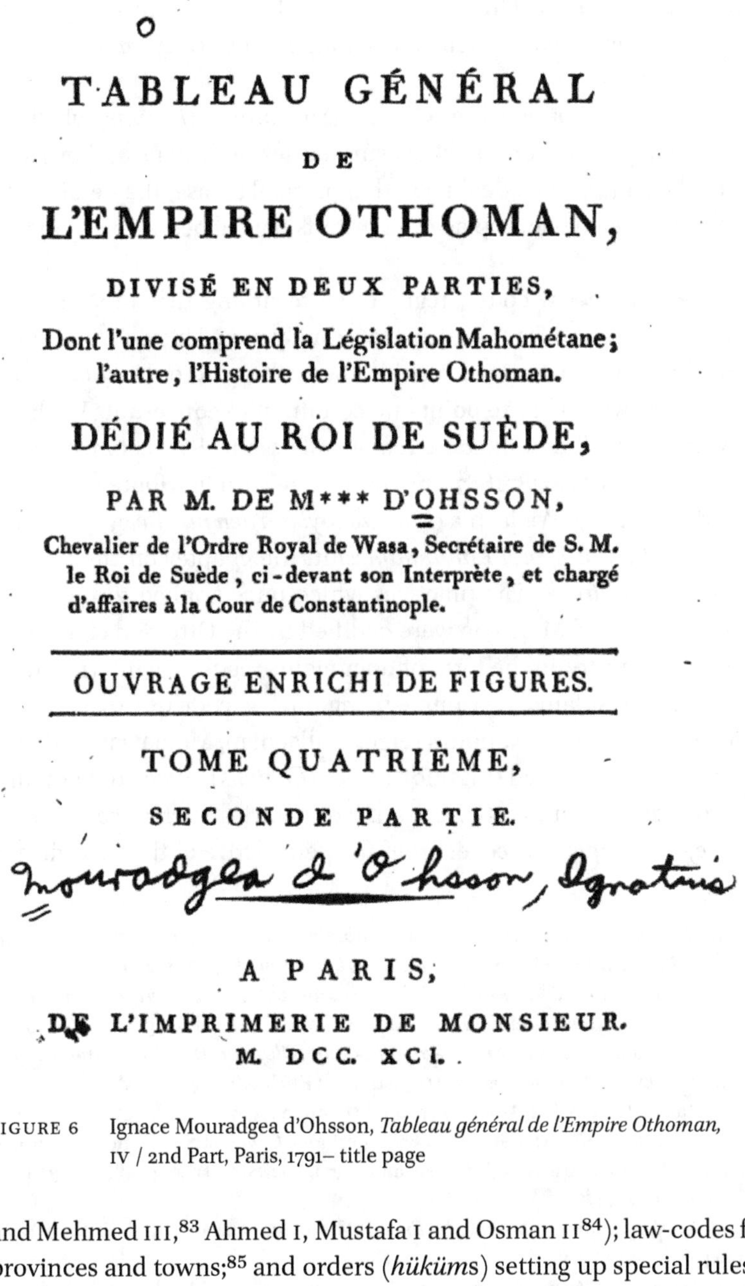

TABLEAU GÉNÉRAL

DE

L'EMPIRE OTHOMAN,

DIVISÉ EN DEUX PARTIES,

Dont l'une comprend la Législation Mahométane; l'autre, l'Histoire de l'Empire Othoman.

DÉDIÉ AU ROI DE SUÈDE,

PAR M. DE M*** D'OHSSON,

Chevalier de l'Ordre Royal de Wasa, Secrétaire de S. M. le Roi de Suède, ci-devant son Interprète, et chargé d'affaires à la Cour de Constantinople.

OUVRAGE ENRICHI DE FIGURES.

TOME QUATRIÈME,

SECONDE PARTIE.

Mouradgea d'Ohsson, Ignatius

A PARIS,

DE L'IMPRIMERIE DE MONSIEUR.

M. DCC. XCI.

FIGURE 6 Ignace Mouradgea d'Ohsson, *Tableau général de l'Empire Othoman*, IV / 2nd Part, Paris, 1791– title page

and Mehmed III,[83] Ahmed I, Mustafa I and Osman II[84]); law-codes for specific provinces and towns;[85] and orders (*hüküms*) setting up special rules. Defining

83 A. Akgündüz, *Osmanlı Kanunnameleri. VIII. Kitab*, Istanbul: Fey Vakfı, 1994.

84 A. Akgündüz, *Osmanlı Kanunnameleri. IX. Kitab: I. Ahmed, I. Mustafa ve II. Osman devirleri kanunnameleri*, Istanbul: Fey Vakfı, 1995.

85 See Ö. L. Barkan, *XV ve XVI-inci asırlarda Osmanlı Imparatorluğunda zirai ekonominin hukuki ve mali esasları. Birinci Cilt: Kanunlar*, Istanbul: Bürhaneddin matbaası, 1943;.

the juridical character of the Ottoman law-codes, Uriel Heyd has emphasized the strong connection between them and sultanal orders (*hüküms*):

> The Ottoman *kanunname*s are collections of statutes (*kanuns*) which [...] were originally in most cases short summaries of firmans and other decrees of the sultan, each dealing with a particular case, the details referring to individual persons, place, and events having been eliminated.[86]

In the aforementioned law-codes, regulations regarding the three tributary principalities north of the Danube are exceedingly rare. This does not mean, though, that their rulers remained outside the realm where the sultan could impose his will; as I would like to point out, certain rules concerning Wallachia and Moldavia were included in *kanunname* collections. For instance, during the reign of Mehmed IV (1648–1687), regulations regarding tribute paid by the voivodes of Moldavia and Wallachia (*Mukataʿa-yi maʿden maʿa-cizye-yi Boğdan ve Eflak*) entered *Eyyubi Efendi Kanunnamesi* in the chapter on the Imperial Treasury (*Hazine-i amire*).[87] The practices which once applied to the principalities of Wallachia and Moldavia were codified by the Ottoman chancellery in the eighteenth century, in the form of documents regulating internal affairs of the empire, the most famous example being the law-code of 1793.[88]

Beginning with Süleyman Kanunî's reign, Wallachian, Moldavian and Transylvanian princes also received sultanic decrees (*hüküms*), which did not differ in any way from those sent to other Ottoman dignitaries, such as *beys*, *sancakbeyis*, *beylerbeyis*, or *kadıs*. Moreover, from the perspective of the classification

---

A. Akgündüz, *Osmanlı Kanunnameleri... V. Kitab: Kanunî Sultan Süleyman Devri Kanunnameleri. II. Kasım. Kanunı Eyalet Kanunnameleri*, Istanbul: Fey Vakfı, 1992; A. Akgündüz, *Osmanlı Kanunnameleri...VI. Kitab: Kanunî Sultan Süleyman Devri Kanunnameleri. II. Kasım. Kanunı Eyalet Kanunnameleri (II)*, Istanbul: Fey Vakfı, 1993; A. Akgündüz, *Osmanlı Kanunnameleri... VII. Kitab: Kanunî Sultan Süleyman Devri Kanunnameleri. II. Kasım. Kanunı Eyalet Kanunnameleri (III)*, Istanbul: Fey Vakfı, 1994. See also M. Berindei, M. Kalus-Martin, G. Veinstein, "Actes de Murad III sur la région de Vidin et remarques sur les qânun ottomans," *SF*, XXXV, 1976, 11–68; M. Berindei, G. Veinstein, "Règlements fiscaux et fiscalité de la province de Bender-Aqkerman. 1570," *CMRS*, XXII, 2–3, 1981, 251–328.

86 Heyd, *Ottoman Law*, 171.

87 *Eyyubi Efendi Kanunnamesi. Tahlil ve Metin.* ed. Abdülkadir Özcan, Istanbul: EREN Yayıncılık, 1994, 31.

88 Veliman, *Documente turcești*, doc. 210 (*kanunname* of 28 March 1793). See, also, M. A. Mehmet, "O nouă reglementare a raporturilor Moldovei şi Țării Româneşti faţă de Poartă la 1792. O carte de lege – Kanunname – în limba turcă," *St.RdI*, XX, 6, 1976, 691–707.

mentioned above, the documents also entered the realm of *kanun*. Everyday issues arising between the Porte and its tributary rulers were managed through simple orders that could be invoked when either side failed to uphold them. These orders could confirm to established customs, impose Ottoman practices or establish new obligations. As a rule, the scope of *hüküm*s was limited to the matter at hand and bound only the sultan who issued it and the voivode to whom it was dispatched; nevertheless, their contents could be confirmed by the next sultan.[89]

The summaries of most 'decrees,' which, apart from *hüküm*s, were also called *emr*s or *ferman*s, starting from the mid-sixteenth century were registered in over 260 volumes of *Mühimme Defterleri*; covering the period between 1553 and 1906,[90] they are preserved to this day in the Prime Minister's Archives in Istanbul, and their publication has recently begun.[91] I found copies of *hüküm*s in other registers like *Hüküm-name-yi mecmuʿası* or *Ahkam-ı Defterleri*, which organize the documents regarding Ottoman provincial administration according to a thematic key. For instance, two collections of imperial orders (*Hüküm-name-yi mecmuʿası*) of 1544–1546[92] and 1551–1553,[93] preserved in the Archives of the Topkapı Palace, contain *hüküm*s issued to the rulers of Wallachia, Moldavia and Transylvania and the 1552 conquest of Temeşvar. In the eighteenth and nineteenth centuries, the orders regarding Moldavia and

89 H. Busse, U. Heyd, P. Hardy, "Farman," *EI-2*, II, 822–825; A. M. Goichon, H. Fleisch, "Hukm," *EI-2*, III, 568–570; Uriel Heyd, *Documents*, 7–31.

90 Series of *Mühimme defterleri* have numerous gaps. Lists of *Mühimme defterleri* are given in Gliša Elezović, *Iz carigadskih turskih arhiva. Mühimme Defteri*, Belgrade, 1950–1951 (who dealt especially with *Mühimme Defterleri* no. 5–6, for years 1564–1566) and *Başbakanlık Osmanlı Arşivi Rehberi*, Ankara, 1992, passim. See also U. Heyd, "The *mühimme defteri* (registers of decrees): A Major Source for the Study of Ottoman Administration." In *Actes du XXIVe Congrès international des orientalistes*, ed. H. Franke, Wiesbaden, 1959, 389–391; U. Heyd, *Ottoman Documents on Palestine. 1552–1615. A Study of the Firman according to the Muhimme Defteri*, Oxford: Clarendon Press, 1960, 3–6.

91 *3 Numaralı Mühimme Defteri (966–968/1558–1560) <Özet ve Transkripsiyon>*, Ankara, 1993; *5 Numaralı Mühimme Defteri (973/1565–1566). <Özet ve Indeks>* and *<Tıpkıbasım>*, Ankara, 1994; *6 Numaralı Mühimme Defteri (972/1564–1565). <Özet – Transkripsyon ve Indeks>*, I–II, Ankara, 1995; *7 Numaralı Mühimme Defteri (975–976/1567–1569). <Özet – Transkripsyon – Indeks>*, I–II, Ankara, 1998; *12 Numaralı Mühimme Defteri (978–979/1570–1572). <Özet – Transkripsyon ve Indeks>*, I–II, Ankara: T.C. Başbakanlık Devlet Arşivleri Genel Müdürlüğü, 1996.

92 951–952 AH. Gilles Veinstein and Mihnea Berindei have translated and published most documents from the volume TKSMA, E. 12321 in their work entitled *L'Empire Ottoman et les Pays Roumaines, 1544–1545. Étude et documents*, Paris: Éditions de l'ÉHÉSS, Cambridge : Harvard Ukrainian Research Institute, 1987.

93 959–960 AH.

Wallachia entered a separate collection, *Romanya Nam-ı Diğer Boğdanlu'nun Ahkam Defteri*. Part of them have already been published in Romanian translation by Mustafa Ali Mehmet, Tahsin Gemil and Valeriu Veliman.[94] This implies that my frequent quotations from these volumes of documents are as a matter of fact arguments which expressed the sultans' will.

## 1.4 *Peace Agreements*

The peace agreements concluded between the Ottoman Empire and Christian states by their juridical and diplomatic nature could institute new bases for bilateral relations, as well as renew or abrogate established ones. In this way, they gave rise to a prolonged series of customary practices.

The treaties were among the most frequently published sources of Ottoman origin, entering eighteenth- and nineteenth-century antologies published in Western Europe.[95] This interest was intimately connected to the prominence of the "Oriental Question" and the capitulatory regime in this period, which saw a proliferation of treaties' collection focusing solely on the Ottoman Empire.[96] Such editions varied in their quality and completeness,[97] but it is important to note that most Ottoman and Turkish editions – somewhat

94 Mehmet, *Documente turcești*, I–III, passim; Gemil, *Documente turcești*, passim; Veliman, *Documente turcești*, passim.

95 Some instances: J. du Mont, *Corps universel diplomatique du droit des gens...*, vol. I–VIII, À Amsterdam: Chez P. Brunel..., À La Haye: Chez P. Husson et Charles Levier, 1726–1732, and *Suppliment*, vol. I–II, À Amsterdam: Chez P. Brunel..., À La Haye: Chez P. Husson et Charles Levier, 1739; Comte d'Hauterive et Baron F. de Cussy, *Recueil des traités de commerce...*, vol. I–II, Paris: Rey et Gravier, 1834–1844; *Hertslet's Commercial Treaties*, 31 vols., London: Butterworth, 1820–1925.

96 *Treaties between Turkey and Foreign Powers. 1535–1855*, Foreign Office, London, 1855; Grégoire Aristarchi Bey, *Législation ottomane ou recueil des lois, règlements, ordonnances, traités, capitulations et autre documents officiels de l'Empire Ottoman*, Vol. I–VII, Publiée par Demétrius Nicolaides, Constantinople, 1873–1888; *Mu'ahedat Mecmu'ası*, Cilt I–V, Istanbul, 1294–1298 AH/1877–1881; Gabriel Noradounghian, *Recueil d'actes internationaux de l'Empire Ottoman*, vol. I–IV, Paris: F. Pichon, 1897–1900; I. de Testa, *Recueil des traités de la Porte Ottomane avec les puissances étrangères*, vols. I–VIII, Paris: Amyot, Leroux, 1864–1896; vols. IX–X, ed. A. de Testa and L. de Testa, Paris: E. Leroux, 1898–1901; *Kapitulasyonlar. Tarihi, menşei, asılları*, eds. Macar Iskender ve Ali Reşad, Istanbul: Der-Sa'adet, 1330 AH/1911–1912.

97 Reşat Ekrem, *Osmanlı Muahedeleri ve Kapitülasyonlar (1300–1920) ve Lozan Muahedesi (24 Temmuz 1923)*, Istanbul: Muallim Ahmet Halit Kitaphanesi, 1934; Nihat Erim, *Devletlerarası Hukuk ve Siyası Tarih Metinleri. Cilt I: Osmanlı Imparatorlugu Andlaşmaları*, Ankara: Ankara Üniversitesi, Hukuk Facültesi, 1953; Necdet Kurdakul, *Osmanlı Devletin'de Ticaret Andlaşmaları ve Kapitülasyonlar*, Istanbul: Döler Neşriyat, 1981.

paradoxically – did not use Ottoman originals of *ʿahdname*s, relying instead on English and French translations.

Locating Ottoman originals of *ʿahdname*s today is no easy task, since most exist solely as copies or translations. However, we have at our disposal the longest continuous sequences of such original documents in Ottoman–Polish *ʿahdname*s preserved in the Central Archives of Old Documents in Warsaw, spanning the period of 1489–1699.[98] Additionaly, original texts of sixteenth- and seventeenth-century Ottoman–Habsburg *ʿahdname*s are also preserved in the Austrian Archives in Vienna, three of them (1559, 1562, 1565) published by A. C. Schaendlinger.[99]

Considering their role in the evolution of the Ottoman law of nations, seventeenth- and eighteenth-century manuscripts containing only peace agreements deserve our special attention. These registers contain *ʿahdname*s granted to either one or more Christian states.[100] To the first category belong the "Registers of the Foreign States" (*Düvel-i Ecnebiye Defterleri* or *Ecnebi Devletler Defterleri*) from the Prime Minister's Archives in Istanbul, where *ʿahdname*s are organized by states to whom they had been granted. These registers were compiled in *Divan-i Hümayun Amedi Kalemi*, one of the chanceries of the Imperial Council handling foreign relations, including the incoming correspondence from abroad.[101]

98 Archivum Glówne Akt Dawnych in Warsaw, Collection Archiwum Korone Warszawskie, dz. Tureckie. Most of these texts are microfilms in ANIC, Bucharest, mf. Poland, r. 1. In this day, the originals are published by Dariusz Kołodziejczyk, *Ottoman-Polish Diplomatic Relations (15th – 18th Century). An Annotated Edition of ʿAhdnames and Other Documents*, Leiden–Boston–Cologne: Brill, 2000. See my review of this book: Viorel Panaite, "On Ottoman-Polish Diplomatic Relations," *SA*, III, 2002, no. 1–2, 179–187.

99 Schaendlinger, *Süleyman*, doc. 23, 25, 32.

100 For example: *1567–1796 Osmanlı devleti ile Nemçe ve sa'ir devletler arasında ʿakd olunan bazi muahedeler*, Belediye Kütüphanesi, Muallim Cevdet, K. 4, and ANIC, mf. Turkey, r. 53, fr. 894–1004. An interesting manuscript containing texts of *ʿahdnames* from the second half of the seventeenth century, granted (sing. *mukaleme*; pl. *mukalemat*) to eight European states: France (*Franca*), Britain (*Ingiltere*), Holland (*Nederlanda*), Habsburg Empire (*Roma Imparotoru*), Russia (*Mosku, Moskof*), Venice (*Venedik*), Raguza (*Dubrovnik*), Poland (*Leh kıralı*) (TKSMA, Defter 7018 and MOL, mf. Turkey, r. 10131).

101 The Persian word *amed* meant "received," and an *amedçi* was that official who received the letters addressed to the grand vizier (*BOA Rehberi*, 142). For a complete list in *BOA. Rehberi*, 142–147. For example, *Lehistan ʿAhdnamesi Defteri* of 1016–1173 AH/1607–1759; *Nemçelü ʿAhd Defteri* of 975–1210 AH/1567–1795); *Venedik ʿAhdname Defteri* of 1081–1211 AH/1670–1796 etc. Copies of seventeenth–eighteenth century *ʿahdnames* can be found also in "Registers of Imperial Letters" (*Name-yi Hümayun Defterleri*). A catalogue of these registers, which include documents from 1111–1336 AH/1699–1918, is in *BOA. Rehberi*, 95–96.

Many *ʿahdnames* also found their way into Ottoman official epistolographic anthologies, called *münşeʾat*, designed "to provide chancery officials with formularies to guide them in the composition of elegant and formally correct state documents."[102] The most famous *münşeʾat* was penned by Ahmed Feridun bey (d. 1583) and dedicated to Sultan Murad III in 1575. Entitled *Mecmuʿa-yı Münşeʾat al-Selatin* ("Collection of Sultans' Correspondence"), it included various types of documents issued in the sultans' name, including *ʿahdnames*, *fetihnames*, *berats* and *fermans*. Two nineteenth-century editions of this oeuvre are complemented with documents produced after the original date of composition. Most likely, both relied on an eighteenth-century manuscript copy, which would explain the inclusion of *ʿahdnames* concluded with Poland (1577–1667), England (1601), France (1604), and the Habsburgs (1606).[103] Although the context of these nineteenth-century editions and the original do not differ significantly, some shifts in terminology can be detected, for instance the use of "Christian" (*Hıristiyan*) rather than "infidel" (*kafir*). The *münşeʾats* are invaluable for addressing the issue of the Porte's relation with its tributaries, since the 1480–1481 charter, as well as imperial diplomas of 1577 and 1586 have been preserved only in such collections.

The importance of the peace agreements concluded between the Ottoman Empire and its Christian neighbors lies in the fact that such treaties habitually refer to Moldavia, Wallachia and Transylvania. Essential in this respect is the series of Ottoman–Hungarian treaties between 1428 and 1519,[104] the sequence of sixteenth- and seventeenth-century Ottoman–Polish *ʿahdnames* granted

102 Humphreys, *Islamic History*, 41. *Münşi* was the official who wrote drafts of documents for Ottoman chanceries.

103 Ahmed Feridun bey, *Mecmuʿa-ı Münşeʾat al-Selatin*, I–II, Istanbul: Takvimhane-yi Amire, 1264–1265 AH/1848–1849 (2nd edition, in 1274–1275 AH/1858. Ahmed Feridun was *divan katibi*, *reʾis ül-küttab*, and finally *nişanci* in 981 AH/1573). (Danişmend, *OTKronolojisi*, vol. 2, 455–456). Details in: J. H. Mordtmann – V. L. Ménage, "Feridun Beg," *EI-2*, II, 901–902; A. Antalffy, "*Münşeʾat al-Salatin* al lui Rukhsanzade Ahmed Feridun, Et-Tevkii (pomenit şi sub numele de Ahmed Feridun Bei Nişangi), ca izvor pentru istoria românilor," *Bul. Com. Ist.*, XIII, 1, 1934, 4–23.

104 The treaties of 1451, 1483, 1488 and 1503 have survived until today (*DRH*, D, I, doc. 305; Iorga, "Privilegiul," 20–23; Iorga, *Acte şi fragmente*, III, 23–27; TKSMA, E. 5861; ANIC, mf. Turkey, r. 4, fr. 312; G. Hazai, "Urkunde des Friedensvertrages zwishen König Matthias, und dem türkischen Sultan 1488," in *Beiträge zur Sprachwissenschaft Volkskunde und Literaturforschung* (*Steinitz-Festschrift*), Berlin, 1965, 141–145; TKSMA, E. 7675; ANIC, mf. Turkey, r. 1, fr. 1–9; Gökbilgin, "1503," 369–390; Hammer, *Empire Ottoman*, IV, 393–400; Hurmuzaki, *Documente*, II/1, doc. XXIV).

after 1533;[105] sixteenth-to-eighteenth-century Ottoman–Habsburg *'ahdnames* between 1547 and 1791;[106] and instruments of peace between the Porte and the Russian Empire, complemented with conventions specifically devoted to Romanian affairs.[107]

105 For originals of almost all treaties, see AGAD, AKW-Tureckie; ANIC, mf. Poland, r. 1. For copies, see BOA, *DED* 55/1, *Lehistan 'ahdnamesi Defteri*, 1016–1173 AH/1607–1759. Also: for 1553–1554 (Gökbilgin, "Belgeler I," 128–132; Hurmuzaki–Bogdan, *Documente*, Supl. II/1, doc. XCIX; Mehmet, *Documente turceşti*, I, doc. 45; Corfus, *Documente. XVI*, 86–87). For 1565 (Hurmuzaki–Bogdan, *Documente*, Supl. II/1, doc. CXXX). For 1577 (Mehmet, *Documente turceşti*, I, 127–128). For 1591 (Hurmuzaki, *Documente*, III, doc. CXLIX; Mehmet, *Documente turceşti*, I, 136–137). For 1598 (Mehmet, *Documente turceşti*, I, 142–143). For 1605 (Feridun, *Münşe'at*, II, 414–417; Corfus, *Documente. XVII*, 50–51; Hammer, *Empire Ottoman*, VIII, 407–415). For the February 1623 *'ahdname* issued by Mustafa I (AGAD, Akw-Tureckie, k. 71, t. 304, no. 557; ANIC, mf. Polonia, r. 1, fr. 22160). For the 10 October 1623 *'ahdname* issued by Murad IV (AGAD, AKW-Tureckie, k. 71, t. 307, no. 564). For the 1634 *'ahdname* issued by Murad IV to Vladislav IV (AGAD, AKW-Tureckie, k. 75, t. 362, no. 643; ANIC, mf. Polonia, r. 1, fr. 74–78). For the 1640 *'ahdname* issued by Ibrahim to Vladislav IV (AGAD, AKW-Tureckie, k. 75, t. 376, no. 663; ANIC, mf. Polonia, r. 1, fr. 87–91; BOA, DED 55/1, doc. 4; Feridun, *Münşe'at*, II, 435–438). For the 1667 *'ahdname* issued by Mehmed IV to John Casimir (AGAD, AKW-Tureckie, k. 77, t. 453, no. 772; BOA, *DED* 55/1, doc. 5; Feridun, *Münşe'at*, II, 4205). For 1678 (Czartoryski, IV, 859, 412). For 1699 (Czartoryski, IV, 859, 43–44).

106 Copies in: BOA, *DED* 57/1, *Nemçelü 'Ahd Defteri* 975–1210 AH/1567–1795; Belediye Kütüphanesi, Muallim Cevdet, K. 4; ANIC, mf. Turkey, r. 53, fr. 894–1004 (*1567–1796 Osmanlı devleti ile Nemçe ve sa'ir devletler arasında 'akd olunan ba'zı mu'ahedeler*). In details, see for 1547 (Feridun, *Münşe'at*, II, 341–342: *Roma imparatoru tarafına ısdar buyurulan 'ahdname-yi hümayun sureti*; Petritsch, "1547," 49–80). For 1559 (Schaendlinger, Süleyman, doc. 23; Hurmuzaki, *Documente*, II/1, doc. CCCXLII; Hammer, *Empire Ottoman*, VI, 114–117. For 1562 (Schaendlinger, *Süleyman*, doc. 25; Hurmuzaki, *Documente*, II/5, doc. CCXXXI). For 1565 (Schaendlinger, *Süleyman*, doc. 32; Hurmuzaki, *Documente*, VIII, doc. CXXXIII). For 1568 (BOA, *DED* 57/1, 1–3; ANIC, mf. Turkey, r. 53, fr. 896–897: *dokuz yüz yetmiş beş semesinde merhum sultan Selim Han zamanında Nemçe çesarina virilen 'ahdname-yi hümayun*; Feridun, *Münşe'at*, II, 324–328). For 1576 (BOA, *DED* 57/1, 2–5; ANIC, mf. Turkey, r. 53, fr. 897–898; Hurmuzaki, *Documente*, III/1, doc. 1). For 1606 (BOA, *DED* 57/1, 5–7; ANIC, mf. Turkey, r. 53, fr. 898–899; Feridun, *Münşe'at*, II, 346–350; Fekete, *Esterházy*, 3–14). For 1615 (BOA, *DED* 57/1, 7–10; ANIC, mf. Turkey, r. 53, fr. 899–904: *merhum sultan Ahmed Han zamanında bin yirğmi dört senesinde*; Feridun, *Münşe'at*, II, 321–324; Fekete, Esterházy, doc. 2; Noradounghian, *Actes*, I, 113–118). For 1627 (BOA, *DED* 57/1, 10–14; Feridun, *Münşe'at*, II, 330–334). For 1664 (BOA, DED 57/1, 17–19; ANIC, mf. Turkey, r. 53, fr. 905–909: *bin yetmiş beş senesinde tecdid 'ahd olunduğda taraf-ı hümayunun Nemçe çasarına verilen 'ahdnamedir*). For 1699 (*BOA*, *DED* 57/1, 21–27; *BOA*, *Amedi Kalemi Odası* (*Kamil Kepeci tasnifi*), 53, 2–16: *Amedi odası defterlerinden Nemçe çasarına verilen 'ahdname-yi hümayun kayıtı. Tarihi 1110;* IUK, ms. 3514, ANIC, mf. Turkey, r. 1, fr. 301–429: *1110 tarihindeki sulhnamesi*). See also Sturdza, Petrescu, *Acte şi documente*, I, 32–40 (1718 treaty of Passarowitz), 48–58 (1739 treaty of Belgrad), 79–81 (1791 treaty of Şiştov).

107 Ottoman copies in BOA, *DED* 83/1, *Rusya 'Ahdname Defteri* 1113–1249 AH/1701–1833. For 1711 (Czartoryski Library, ms. no. 1685/35, 491–492; Hurmuzaki, *Documente*, VI, doc. XLV). See

In addition, solemn documents issued by the sultans to the voivodes, both imperial charters (*ʿahdname-yi hümayun*) and diplomas (*berat-ı hümayun*)[108] are crucial for the topic at hand. Unfortunately, only a handful of such documents remain from the fifteenth century. The only original fifteenth-century document is one issued to Moldavian Voivode Stephen the Great at the end of Mehmed II's reign (in 1479, according to A. Decei; in 1480–1481, according to M. Guboglu and M. A. Mehmet). The only document directly available to modern historians, it was discovered in 1945 by Aurel Decei, who found it in a late fifteenth-century *münşe'at* collection in the Süleymaniye Library in Istanbul.[109] The situation is only slightly better for the Moldavia and Wallachia in the later centuries: only the *berat*s granted to Wallachian Voivode Mihnea II in 1577 and 1585.[110] Fortunately, virtually all diplomas granted to Transylvanian princes exist today, most part of them finding their way into print.[111] Since the publica-

---

Sturdza, Petrescu, *Acte și documente*, I, 131 (1774 treaty of Küçük Kaynarca); 219–225 (1791/1792 treay of Jassy); 298 (1812 treaty of Bucharest); 311–314 (1826 agreement of Akkerman); 321–329 (1829 treaty of Adrianople); 338 (1834 treaty of St. Petersburg); 357–360 (1849 agreement of Balta Liman).

108 Jan Reychman and Ananiasz Zajaczkowski, *Handbook of Ottoman-Turkish Diplomatics*, Mouton, The Hague, Paris: Mouton, 1968, 136–137.

109 A. Decei, "Tratatul de pace – *sulhname* – încheiat între sultanul Mehmed al II-lea și Ștefan cel Mare la 1479," *RIR*, XV, fasc. IV (1945) 465–494 (reprinted in Aurel Decei, *Relații româno-orientale. Culegere de studii*, Bucharest, Ed. Științifică și Enciclopedică, 1978, 118–129. Other editions: Guboglu, *Paleografia*, 132, 165; Mehmet, *Documente turcești*, I, doc. 5.

110 For the first reign, the diploma of *evahir-i Cemazi ül-evvel* 985/ 6–15 August 1577 (Bayazid Kütüphanesi, Istanbul, fd. Veliyüddin Efendi, no. 1970, f. 9–10; ANIC, mf. Turkey, r. 74, fr. 8–9, cf. Tahsin Gemil, "Documente turcești inedite. Sfârșitul sec. XVI și sec. XVII." *RA* 3, (1981), 353–356.). For the second reign, the *berat* of 22 *Ramazan* 993/ 17 September 1585 (BOA, *Maliyeden Müdevver Defteri*, no. 17932, 11–12; ANIC, mf. Turcia, r. 155, fr. 618–620, cf. Maxim, *CTO*, doc. 14).

111 Among these are certain addressees of *berat-ı hümayuns:* John Sigismund Zápolya by Süleyman Kanunî in 1566 (Sándor Szilágyi, *Erdélyország törtenete tekintettel müvelö désére*, I, Pesta, 1866, 385–388; *CSISD*, II, 421–422; O. Spies, "Ein Ferman Sultan Sülejmans des Prächtigen an König Johann Sigismund von Siebenbürgen," in *Jean Deny Armağanı*, Istanbul: Türk Dili Kurumu, 1958, 221–229); Stephen Báthory by Selim II in 1571 and Murad III in 1577 (Uzunçarşılı, *Osmanlı Tarihi*, III, 2, 46–47, n. 2); Paul Márkházy by Murad III on 20 *Receb* 989/ 20 August 1581 (Veliman, "Carte de legământ," 27–44); Sigismund Báthory by Murad III in 1581 (Uzunçarşılı, *Osmanlı Tarihi*, III/2, 47, n. 3); Stephen Bocskai by Ahmed I in 1605 (Feridun, *Münşe'at*, II, 356–358); Sigismund Rákóczy by Ahmed I *evahir-i Ramazan* 1015/ 20–29 January 1607 (Guboglu, "Arhive. Brașov," doc. 1); Gabriel Báthory by Ahmed I in January 1608 (A. Behrnauer, "Sultan Ahmad's I. Bestallungs-und Vertrags-Urkunde für Gabriel Báthory von Somlyó, Fürsten von Siebenbürgen, vom Jahre 1608 der Christlichen Zeitrechnung," *AKOG*, XVIII, 1857, 299–330); Gabriel Bethlen and Transylvanian nobles by Ahmed I in June–July 1614 (Gemil, *Documente turcești*, doc. 61); George Rákóczy I by Murad IV on *evaʾil-i Ramazan* 1040 / 3–12 April 1631 (A. Handzić, "Diploma sultana Murada IV erdeljskom knezu Đorđu Rakociju," *Prilozi*, VI–VII, 1956–1957, Sarajevo, 1958, 182–186; Guboglu, *Catalog*, II, doc. 220); Ákos Barcsay by Mehmed IV in 1658 (I. H. Uzunçarşılı,

tion of the first edition of this book, Sándor Papp collected and published a critical edition of the inauguration documents (*'ahdnames* and *berats*) granted to Transylvanian rulers up to 1605.[112]

It is necessary to compare the imperial chapters and diplomas with those issued to other tribute-payers throughout Southeastern Europe. Particularly important in this respect is the Ragusan Republic (Dubrovnik), whose juridical status was similar to that of the principalities under discussion. Three fifteenth-century charters (1430, 1442, 1458) written in Slavic languages and housed in the State Archives in Dubrovnik have been published in French translation by Boško Bojović.[113] For the later period, two transcripts of Ottoman *'ahdname* of 1512–1513,[114] and the original acts of 1575, 1595 and 1649 provide useful comparison.[115] Copies of seventeenth-century *'ahdnames* were included in the "Registers of the Orders to Dubrovnik" (*Dubrovnik Ahkam Defteri*), have been compiled in one of the chanceries of the Imperial Council since 1604.[116]

The Aegean islands were tribute-payers to the Porte during the fifteenth and sixteenth centuries, their status regulated by imperial charters and diplomas similar to those of the principalities of Wallachia, Moldavia and Transylvania.[117] Thus, one can compare the Andros *'ahdname* of 1539,[118] part of a wider set of imperial charters issued by Sultan Süleyman, intended to define the political status of the Cyclades in the first part of the sixteenth century. Also, two

---

"Akos Barçay'ın Erdel Kırallığına ait tayını hakkında birkaç vesika," *Belleten*, VIII, 1943, 361–377).

112 Sándor Papp, *Die Verleihungs-, Bekräftigungs- und Vertragsurkunden der Osmanen für Ungarn und Siebenbürgen. Eine quellenkritische Untersuchung*, Vienna: Verlag der Österreichischen Akademie der Wissenschaften, 2003. See also Gábor Kármán, "The *'ahdname* of Sultan Mehmed III to András Báthori, Prince of Transylvania," in Stoica Lascu, Melek Fetisleam, eds. *Contemporary Research in Turkology and Eurasian Studies*, Cluj–Napoca, 2013, 435–445.

113 Bojović, "Dubrovnik I," doc. 2 (1430), doc. 4 (1442), doc. 6 (1458).

114 918 AH. It is recorded in *Şeri'ye Sicilleri* of Brusa (*Bursa Şer'iye Sicilleri*, A, 20, f. 387/b; Dalsar, "Dubrovnik muahede," 410–414; Akgündüz, *Osmanlı Kanunnameleri*, 3, 385–387).

115 These *'ahdnames* have been preserved at The State Archives in Dubrovnik. On the *'ahdname* of 1575, see Biegman, *Ragusa*, 48–59.

116 BOA, *DED* 13, 1013–1028 AH/1604–1618. A draft of the *'ahdname* granted by Mehmed IV in the second part of the seventeenth century can also be found in a manuscript from the Topkapı Palace Archives (TKSMA, Defter 7018; MOL, mf. Turcia, r. 10131, fr. 31–33: *Dubrovnik namesi*).

117 Matei, "Domination," 87.

118 946 AH. They are called "*lettres de privilège du sultan*," in the French translation of 1686 presented by the priest Saulger to the French ambassador in Constantinople (R. Saulger, *Histoire nouvelle des anciens ducs et autres souverains de l'Archipel*, Paris, 1698, 349–351, cf. Slot, *Archipaelagus Turbatus*, II, 76–77).

ʿ*ahdname*s of 1564 and 1565, granted by the same sultan to the Duke of Naxos, can be used for comparison.[119]

## 1.5 *International Custom*

Historians and jurists have long emphasized the co-existence and parallel operation of two distinct systems of "international" law – European and Islamic – until the nineteenth century. Whereas Christian powers adhered to the former, the latter informed the standpoint of the Muslim world. One might assume that this parallelism and religious difference inevitably led to mutually exclusive interpretations, but centuries of religious coexistence in the Eastern Mediterranean and Southeastern Europe led to the emergence of pragmatic customary rules mediating this gap. Thus, it is crucial to underline that Ottoman laws of war and peace cannot be boiled down to their purely Islamic component, forcing us to elucidate customary norms adhered to in the practice of governance.

As I have mentioned, Ottoman rules on foreign relations were rooted in traditional Near Eastern Islamic law. However, by the time the dynasty emerged, "international" law had already been transformed through contact with the Mongol's traditions (following the conquest of Baghdad in 1258) and those of Latin Christendom during the time of Crusades.[120] Later, when dealing with non-Muslim individuals, communities and states, Ottoman authorities invoked rules and practices that had been employed throughout the Middle Ages. Moreover, according to Hans Kruse, since the seventeenth century

> the decline of the Turkish empire [...] compelled the Muslims to submit more and more in their dealings with the occidental states to the usages practiced by them, but without, however, actually adopting inner-European international law.

Finally, through the Treaty of Paris in 1856, the Ottoman Empire was admitted into the European community of states, which meant "the official renunciation to practice the rules of its own canonical law."[121] For a long time, custom has been one of the essential sources for the practice of internal, as well as

119 On 16 *Cemazi ül-evvel* 972/20 December 1564 (Uzunçarşılı, *Osmanlı Tarihi*, III, 2, 102–103); and on 28 *Ramazan* 972/29 April 1565 (Safvet, "Nakşe (Naksos) Dukalığı, Kiklad Adaları," *TOEM*, IV, 1329, 1446–1448).

120 Khadduri, *War and Peace*, 268–296; Khadduri, "Impact," 47–49.

121 Kruse, "Shaybani," 231–232. See also Thomas Naff, "Ottoman Diplomatic Relations with Europe in the Eighteenth Century: Patterns and Trends," in *Studies in Eighteenth Century Islamic History*, Carbondale and Edwardsville: Southern Illinois University Press; London

"international" law. It was employed as a juridical basis for creating new rules and for validating the old ones. In the internal law, custom referred to the unwritten law, as opposed to the written law.[122] In a similar manner, the law of nations, juxtaposed custom and treaty.[123] According to the jurists' opinion, international custom can exist only on the basis of two elements:

a. a historical element ("repetition of facts" or "past practices"), implying a continuous practice in time and multiplication of precedents in space;
b. a mental element (the *opinio juris sive necessitatis*), which means that the subject of the law believes in the necessity of that practice.[124]

In international law, a customary rule holds true either for the international community as a whole, or for a part of it. Thus, Paul Guggenheim has classified the international custom into three categories: general custom as accepted by the totality of states; regional custom, observed by a particular group of states; and, bilateral custom, which derives only from prolonged relations between two states.[125] Consequently, one can say that, besides Islamic, Byzantine, Turkish and European characteristics, the precepts, concepts and regulations of the law of nations also arose through the mechanism of custom. That is why studying the Ottoman law of war and peace involves investigating not only theoretical structures but also political, military and diplomatic practices. In this regard, it is enough to engage only in a brief search through sources of the relations between Ottomans and non-Muslims to find many common methods and techniques of establishing interstate relations that belong neither to Islamic nor to European laws of international relations. The most conspicuous instances include: tribute payments in exchange for protection; the vassal's military support of the suzerain; establishment of the same foreign policy for vassal and suzerain; the use of oaths and hostages as guarantees for peace agreements; the custom of protocol gifts; the paying of homage to the suzerain; renewals of covenants when one of the contractors died or was substituted; the principle of observing treaties (*pacta sunt servanda*); and the inviolability of envoys.[126]

---

and Amsterdam: Feffer and Simons, 1977, 88–107; Th. Naff, "Reform and the Conduct of Ottoman Diplomacy," *JAOS*, 83, 1963, 295–315.

122 V. Al. Georgescu, "La place de la coutume dans le droit des états feodaux roumains de Valachie et de Moldavie jusqu'au milieu de XVIIe siècle," *RRH*, VI, 4 (1967) 553–586; V. Al. Georgescu, "Structura şi izvoarele dreptului," in *IDR*, II/1, Bucharest, 1984, 65–85.

123 Guggenheim, *Droit*, I, 94. See also Charles de Visscher, "Coutume et traité en droit international public," *RGDIP*, 3, 1955, 353–369; R. R. Baxter, "Treaties and Custom," *RdC*, 129, I (1970) 27–105.

124 Gianni, *Coutume*, 120–135; Rousseau, *Droit*, I, 834–844.

125 Guggenheim, *Droit*, I, 107–109.

126 François L. Ganshof, *Histoire des relations internationales*, ed. Pierre Renouvin. Vol. I. *Le Moyen Age*, Paris: Hachette, 1953, 36–54, 119–156, 263–302.

Let us emphasize that these customary observances were also applied by the Ottomans in their relations with their tribute-payers, including the principalities of Wallachia, Moldavia and Transylvania. As a matter of fact, tributary status in Southeastern Europe was born from a customary practice rather than from an *ad litteram* application of Islamic law, even though when Muslims applied the conditions of tribute-payers, they respected the Prophet's *sünnet*, such as the pattern of the *ʿahd* granted to Nadjran in 632.

# PART 2

## *The Danube as a* Gazi *River*

CHAPTER 2

# The Ottoman Ideology of Holy War

The Islamic concept of holy war has been given special attention not only by historians, jurists, and sociologists, but also by political scientists and theologians.[1] As a consequence, there have been differing opinions among these scholars. Some of them have studied the holy war (*cihad*) as the main ideology in the Arab Caliphate;[2] others have compared *cihad* with the Crusades.[3] Most frequently, Muslim scholars, both Arabs and Turks, have treated the doctrine of *cihad* as part of Islamic law,[4] comparing it with Western "international" law.[5]

1 Here are certain cases: Cl. Huart, "Le Khalifat et la Guerre Sainte," *RHR*, LXXII, 1915, 288–302; O. Houdas, "La Guerre Sainte islamique," *RSP*, XXXIII, 1915, 87–95; J. E. Jurji, "The Islamic Theory of War," *The Moslem World*, 30, 1940, 332–442; L. Massignon, "La guerre sainte supreme de l'Islam arabe," in *Opera Minora*, II, Paris, 1969, 305–320; A. K. S. Lambton, "A Nineteenth Century View on *Jihad*," *SI*, XXXII, 1970, 181–193; W. M. Watt, "The Significance of the Theory of *Jihad*," *AAWG*, 98, 1976, 390–394; B. Lewis, "Politics and War," in *The Legacy of Islam*, ed. J. Schacht and C. E. Bosworth, 2nd edition, London, 1974, 156–210; E. Kohlberg, "The Development of the Imami Shii Doctrine of *Jihad*," *ZDMG*, 126, 1, 1976, 64–88; R. Peters, *Islam and Colonialism. The Doctrine of Jihad in Modern History*, Uitgeverij Mouton's Gravenhage, 1979, 9–37; R. Peters, "Djihad: War of Aggression or Defense?" *AAWG*, 98, 1976, 282–289; M. Bonner, *Aristocratic Violence and Holy War. Studies in Jihad and the Arab-Byzantine Frontier*, New Haven: American Oriental Society, 1996; R. Firestone, *Jihad. The Origin of Holy War in Islam*, Oxford: Oxford University Press, 1999.

2 An example is Khalid Yahya Blankinship, *The End of the Jihad State: The Reign of Hisham Ibn 'Abd al-Malik and the Collapse of the Umayyads*, SUNY Series of Medieval Middle East History, Albany, NY: State University of New York Press, 1994 (reviewed by Nina J. Safran, in *IJMES*, 28, 1996, 591–592).

3 M. Canard, "La guerre sainte dans le monde islamique et dans le monde chrétien," *Revue Africaine* (Alger), 1936, 605–623; A. Noth, *Heiliger Krieg und heiliger Kampf in Islam und Christentum: Beitrage zur Vorgeschichte und Geschichte der Kreuzzuge*, Bonn: Ludwig Röhrscheid Verlag, 1966; E. Sivan, *L'Islam et la Croisade: Idéologie et propagande dans les réactions musulmanes aux Croisades*, Paris: Maisonneuve, 1968; *Just War and Jihad: Historical and Theoretical Perspectives on War and Peace in Western and Islamic Traditions*, edited by John Kelsey and James Turner Johnson, New York: Greenwood Press, 1991.

4 M. Hamidullah, *Muslim Conduct of State*, 4th Edition, Revised and Enlarged, Lahore, 1953; Majid Khadduri, *War and Peace in the Law of Islam*, Baltimore: The Johns Hopkins Press, 1955 (2nd ed. 1969); A. Morabia, *La notion de ǧihad dans l'Islam médiéval (des origines à al-Gazali)*, Université de Lille III, 1975.

5 Some of them accused Western scholars of flawed interpretations of the Islamic law of peace and war. See: N. Armanazi, *L'Islam et le droit international*, Paris, 1929; M. Chaygan, *Essai sur l'histoire de droit public musulman aux premiers siècles de sa formation*. Paris: Thèse pour le doctorat, 1934; A. Rechid, "L'Islam et le droit des gens," *RdC*, 60, II, 1937,

 | DOI:10.1163/9789004411104_003

The role of holy war in Ottoman history has provoked discussions among historians from Fuat Köprülü[6] and Paul Wittek,[7] up to Halil Inalcık,[8] Colin Imber,[9] Cemal Kafadar[10] and Heath Lowry.[11] Irrespective of their conclusions,[12] the works devoted to the foundation and expansion of the Ottoman state include unchanging expressions like "the spirit of *gaza*" ("l'esprit *gazi*" or "la

---

375–504 S. Mahmassani, "The Principles of International Law in the Light of Islamic Doctrine," *RdC*, I, 1966, 205–328; M.T. al-Ghunaimi, *The Muslim Conception of International Law and the Western Approch*, The Hague, 1968; Ahmed Özel, *Islam Hukukunda Ülke Kavramı. Darülİslam. Darülharb*, Istanbul, 1988.

6 M. F. Köprülü, *Les origines de l'Empire Ottoman*, Paris: E de Boocard, 1935 (see also the expanded Turkish version, M. F. Köprülü, *Osmanlı Devleti'nin Kurulusu*, Ankara: TTK Basımevi, 1959, and the English translation, *The Origins of the Ottoman Empire*, tr. and ed. Gary Leiser, Albany: State University of New York Press, 1992). See also H. A. Gibbons, *The Foundation of the Ottoman Empire. A History of the Osmanlis up to the Death of Bayezid I (1300–1403)*, New York: The Century Co., 1916.

7 Paul Wittek, "Deux chapitres de l'histoire des Turcs de Roum," *Byzantion*, XI, 1, 1936, 285–319; P. Wittek, "Le Sultan de Rum," *AIPHOS*, VI, 1938, 361–390; P. Wittek, "De la défaite d'Ankara à la prise de Constantinople," *REI*, 12/1, 1938, 1–34; P. Wittek, *The Rise of the Ottoman Empire*, London: The Royal Asiatic Society of Great Britain and Ireland, 1938. Wittek's *gazi* theory, which envisaged holy war and its requirements as the principal *raison d'être* behind the early Ottoman *beylik*, and later as the fatal flaw of the succeeding empire, and which concluded that the life-force for the empire came from religious zeal, the *gazi* spirit of holy war, influenced particularly Ottoman historiography (Kunt, "State," 3–29).

8 H. Inalcık, *The Ottoman Empire. The Classical Age. 1300–1600*, New York, Washington: Praeger Publishers 1973, 5–22; H. Inalcık, "The Emergence of the Ottomans," in *The Cambridge History of Islam*, ed. P. M. Holt, A. K. S. Lambton and B. Lewis, vol. I, Cambridge: Cambridge University Press, 1970, 263–291; P. Coles, *The Ottoman Impact on Europe*, London: Thames & Hudson, 1968. See also I. Mélikoff, "Ghazi," *EI-2*, II, 1068–9; Gy. Káldy-Nagy, "The Holy War (*jihad*) in the First Centuries of the Ottoman History," *HUS*, III–IV, 1, 1979–1980, 467–473; Pál Fodor, "Ahmedi's Dasitan as a Source of Early Ottoman History," *AOH*, XXXVIII, 1–2, 1984, 41–54; R. C. Jennings, "Some Thoughts on the Gazi-Thesis," in *Festschrift Andreas Tietze zum 70. Geburtstag* (*WZKM*, vol. 76, Vienna, 1986), 151–161; J. F. Guilmartin, "Ideology and Conflict: The Wars of the Ottoman Empire, 1453–1606," *Journal of Interdisciplinary History*, XVIII, 4, 1988, 721–747; Viorel Panaite, *Război, pace şi comerţ în Islam. Ţările române şi dreptul otoman al popoarelor*, Iași: Editura Polirom, 2013.

9 Colin Imber, "Paul Wittek's "De la défaite d'Ankara à la prise de Constantinople," *OA-JOS*, V, 1986, 65–79; C. Imber, *The Ottoman Empire. 1300–1481*, Istanbul: Isis Press, 1990, 65–81. See also Rudi Paul Linder, "Stimulus and Justification in Early Ottoman History," *GOTR*, 27, 2, 1987, 207–224.

10 Cemal Kafadar, *Between Two Worlds: The Construction of the Ottoman State*, Berkley, Los Angeles, London: University of California Press, 1995.

11 Heath Lowry, *The Nature of the Early Ottoman State*, Albany, NY: Suny Press, 2003.

12 Wittek's conclusions has been plausibly challenged by Colin Imber, Cemal Kafadar and Heath Lowry's accurate studies, mentioned in above quotes.

mystique *gazi*"), "l'état de *gazis*," "principauté de *gazis*," "frontier *gazi* state" or "Empire of the *gazis*."[13] The main argument has been to establish the importance of the "*gaza* ideal" for the expansionist thrust of the Ottoman state in the fourteenth and fifteenth centuries. Thus, Ottomanists have sought to answer the following questions: can the Ottoman Empire be described as a *gaza* state, committed to the advancement of the realm of Islam as directed by the precepts of the faith? Can it be argued that the first sultans, beginning with Osman I, hoped to establish their legitimacy by continuing the *cihad* policy of medieval Muslim caliphs? Can it be said that the *cihad* policy became the "fundamental pillar of state ideology," the basis of Ottoman legitimacy and the source of Ottoman prestige? No matter what the answers to these questions have been, in my opinion excessive interpretations must be rejected.

It is obvious that the "*cihad* with sword," i.e. the *gazi* ideal, was the political expression of an ideology built and used by the Ottomans to justify the rule of the dynasty. Generally, then, students of the empire have posited the importance of *cihad* to Ottoman legitimacy largely due to continuous warfare characterizing the first three centuries of Ottoman history. As Colin Imber has emphasized,

> the most celebrated of these legitimizing ideals was the notion that the sultans and their armies were *gazis*, warriors of the faith, whose war against Christians represented an Islamic holy war against infidelity. The ultimate source of this idea was the *şeri'at*, the holy law of Islam, which, to simplify greatly, makes the prosecution of holy war an obligation on the Islamic community. By invoking the *şeri'at*, Ottoman rulers were able to project their wars against Christian neighbors and their subjects' raids on Christian territories as the necessary fulfilment of a divinely imposed obligation, a claim which gave them legitimacy in the eyes both of their own subjects and of other Muslim sovereigns.[14]

At the same time, offensive *cihad* had an important impact on Ottoman individual and collective religious conscience from as early as the fourteenth

13 Lemerle, *L'Emirat d'Aydın*, 12 (he quoted P. Wittek); Wittek, "Turcs de Roum," 311; Sugar, *Southestern Europe*, 10. Even in the title of Stanford J. Shaw's work: S. Shaw, *History of the Ottoman Empire and Modern Turkey. Vol. I: Empire of the Gazis: The Rise and Decline of the Ottoman Empire. 1280–1808*, Cambridge, London, New York, Melbourne: Cambridge University Press, 1976.

14 Imber, "Ideals," 138–139. An accurate analysis of the holy war as basis of the Hanafi theory of rulership, and its connection with the sultan's juridical sovereignty, in Imber, *Ebu's-su'ud*, 65–73.

century. And so, the religious element embodied in the *gazi* spirit has been considered by most historians as the main impulse for Ottoman expansion.[15]

From the eighth and ninth centuries onwards, the doctrine of holy war (*cihad*) was based upon warlike activities throughout the Islamic world.[16] This interpretation of the doctrine was therefore adopted by the Ottomans as part of their political ideology, and used to justify both military conflicts and peaceful relations with the non-Muslim individuals, communities and states in Southeastern and Central Europe, even though these were motivated in fact by purely military and political considerations. In forging an efficient political interpretation, Muslim scholars endowed the holy war with the exclusive, offensive, compulsory and *bellum justum* qualities. Despite being diminished somewhat in military and political practice, these attributes remained the most important juridical aspects of the doctrine of *cihad* during the Ottoman period. It is important to emphasize that *cihad* gradually came to be interpreted more as a defensive than as an offensive principle. Two stages of this evolution can be distinguished in Ottoman history.

The ideology of an offensive holy war prevailed during the fifteenth and sixteenth centuries,[17] but the ideology of a defensive *cihad* was expressed clearly only after the failed second siege of Vienna (1683). According to the Ottoman official position in the late seventeenth and eighteenth centuries, the "holy campaign and holy war" (*gaza ve cihad*) were launched only to repulse the attacks against the Islamic territories and remove the damages made by the infidels, especially by the Habsburg Empire and Russia.[18] In this period of military decline, the transition from the idea of a holy war to a "holy peace" took place, in part because in the Ottoman chancery the attribute "sacred" (*mübarek*) now came to regularly accompany the term "peace." For example, the Ottoman–

15 The attributes assigned by historians are significant for this problem. In this respect, Halil Inalcık considered the holy war as the ideal of the Turkoman tribes in Anatolia which then became "the main factor of the Ottoman expansion" (Inalcık, *Ottoman Empire*, 6; Inalcık, "Emergence," 291). On this point I agree with Metin Kunt's observation that "the old masters' analysis (i.e. that belonging to Fuad Köprülü and Paul Wittek – o.n.), is still valid that Ottoman origins can be understood only in a wider context, with reference both to Byzantium and to the Islamic world of West Asia" (Kunt, "State," 3–29).

16 *Cihad* did not mean only "war with the sword," but also moral, spiritual or intellectual efforts for building an ideal community. On the general doctrine of *cihad*, see: Khadduri, *War and Peace*, 51–140; Morabia, *Ğihad*, 480–554; Özel, *Islam Hukuku*, 49–76; Panaite, *Război, pace și comerț în Islam*, 95–101).

17 E. A. Zachariadou, "Holy War in the Aegean during the Fourteenth Century." *MHR* 4, (1989): 212–225. Kortepeter spoke on the decline of *gazas* since the sixteenth century (Kortepeter, "Arabs," 333).

18 Expression excerpted from the order of *evahir-i Cemazi ül-ahir* 1101/ 22–31 March 1690 (Gemil, *Documente turcești*, doc. 184). See also Hurmuzaki, *Documente*, XVI, doc. DCXII.

Habsburg treaty of Vasvár (1664) was called the treaty of "holy peace" (*mübarek sulh*), even though it was concluded for a twenty-year period.[19] Even later, the idea of holy war continued to be a guiding principle of Ottoman juridical and political thought, even though its application was intermittent and pragmatic.[20] Further, it is clear that the ideology of a defensive *cihad* appeared in certain circumstances during the expansive period of the Ottoman history, as well as in the eighteenth century. However, this more peaceful ideology was actually full of nostalgia for the offensive definition of the holy war.[21]

## 1 Enemy Infidels in Southeastern Europe

Considering that the Ottoman Empire was an Islamic state, it is necessary to emphasize the Muslim factor in defining the Ottoman juridical standpoint regarding non-Muslims. Thus, the question arises as to the terminology used for non-Muslims in Islamic law:

> Among Muslims as among other peoples there was a tendency to see others as a reflection of themselves. While Islam was conceived as a single entity, it was natural to think of the Abode of war in the same terms. The subdivisions among the infidels, particularly those of them who lived beyond the Islamic frontier, were of no interest or significance.[22]

One can say that Muslim jurisprudence ignored, as a rule, the notion of ethnic groups. Consequently, major juridical disjunctions were made between "believers" (sg. *mümin*, pl. *mümінin*), seen also as "subjects to Allah" (sg. *müslim*, pl. *müslimin*), and "infidels" (sg. *kafir*, pl. *küffar*, *kefere*, *kafirler*) considered also as "potential enemies" (sg. *harbi*, pl. *harbiler*). The Ottomans took from the

19 BOA, *DED* 57/1,19; Silahdar, *Tarih*, in *Cronici turcești II*, 329. Also, the treaty of Karlowitz (1699) was defined as a "holy peace," even though it took twenty-five years to conclude, and the *re'is ül-küttab* Rami Mehmed Efendi and the official chronicler Mustafa Na'ima characterized it as a "temporary peace" (BOA, *Amedi Kalemi Odası, Kamil Kepeci tasnifi*, 53, 2–16; R. A. Abou-el-Haj,. "Ottoman Attitudes toward Peace Making: The Karlowitz Case." *Der Islam* 51, 1, (1974): 130–137.

20 The last Ottoman juridical opinions concerning holy war (*cihad fetvaları*) were enacted in the First World War (Pakalin, *Sözlük*, I, 291; Uzunçarşılı, *Ilmiye*, 203; Maxim, *CTO*, doc. 34; Lewis, "Jihad," 157–163).

21 Some examples may be seen in the Ottoman–Austrian–Russian war of 1787–1791, and the conduct of the Phanariot princes of Wallachia and Moldavia, in M. A. Mehmet, "O condică domnească din a doua jumătate a veacului al XVIII-lea, scrisă în limba turcă, privind Țara Românească." *RA*, 2, 1958, doc. 44.

22 Lewis, *Muslim Discovery*, 171, 202.

*Kur'an* the differentiation between "believers" and "infidels," and this differentiation was later amplified by jurists in treatises on Islamic law.[23]

### 1.1 *Infidels*

Terms for infidels (*küffar*, sing. *kafir*, *gavur*) were abundantly used in juridical texts, as well as in Ottoman chronicles and documentary sources, encompassing all people of faith other than Islam.[24] These "infidels" were then divided into two categories: "polytheists" (*müşrik*; pl. *müşrikin*)[25] and "people of the Book" or "Scripturaries" (*ehl-i kitab*). The latter name was given specifically to Christians and Jews as followers of religions which Islam considered revealed. It was also used (although less consistently) for Zoroastrians and Sabians.[26]

Even though the Ottomans considered that "all unbelievers form a community" (*cümle kefere millet vahide*),[27] their juridical outlook distinguished between two kind of infidels:

a. infidels of the Abode of War (*harbi küffar* or *harbi*), and
b. infidels of the Abode of Islam (non-Muslim Ottoman subjects, called in Turkish *re'aya*, *zimmi* or *kefere ki dar al-harbdan olmıya*).

Considering the fact that in the Ottoman period the juridical categories *kafir*s and *zimmi*s were not applied widely to Jews, the "infidels" par excellence were the Christians. Likewise, those countries outside the Abode of Islam were

---

23 In his "Introduction" to the *Tableau général de l'Empire Othoman*, Ignace Mouradgea d'Ohsson pointed out that: *De la distiction que fait la loi dans ses prononcés, entre les différentes Religions de la Terre, les Nations elles-mêmes et les diverses Conditions de l'Homme.* He performed four major "general disjunctions." Two of them are relevant to our topic, i.e. the first, according to the religious criterion between "believers" and "infidels" and the third, according to the juridical criterion between *muslims*, *zimmis*, *müste'mins* and *harbis* (D'Ohsson, *Tableau*, I, 12–3). According to the Muslim faith, "les hommes, tout comme les territoires, sont de deux categories, bien tranchées: Croyants et Incroyants" (Morabia, *Ğihad*, 313, 431).

24 "The opprobrious name *Gaur*, Infidel, is bestowed on all Christians; and *Kiafir* or Blasphemer; and *Kiefere*, a blasphemous Nation; as likewise in the plural, *Kiuffar* blasphemous Men" (Cantemir, *Othman History*, 50, n. 7). See also W. Björkman, "Kafir," *EI-2*, IV, 425–427.

25 Abu Yusuf, *Kitab*, 100; Shaybani, *Kitab al-siyar*, cf. Williams, *Islamic Civilization*, 277.

26 During the Prophet's life, peoples from outside of Arabia were considered "peoples of the Book" (G. Vajda, "Ahl al-Kitab," *EI-2*, I, 272–274; Watt, *Islam*, 33; Watt, *Jihad*, 291; Decei, "Sulhname," 138, n. 1; Panaite, "Djihad," I, 714; Panaite, "Pacea," 573).

27 In the *'ahdname*s issued to Venice by Bayezid II and Selim I in 1503 and 1513 (Şakiroğlu, "1503," 1559–1569; Gökbilgin, "Belgeler I," 47–50; Ménage, "Capitulation," 378).

perceived by Muslims as "lands of the infidels," or Christendom.[28] Nevertheless, it is necessary to distinguish between the different states or nations of Christendom in both official documents and historical writings. In some cases, the Ottomans referred to English infidels, French infidels, Hungarian infidels, Polish infidels etc., or simply, Englishmen, Frenchmen, Venetians etc. For instance, a 1750 *hüküm*, listed as infidels of the Abode of War (*dar al-harb tüccarından* [...] *ba'zi kefere*) Venetians (*Venediklü*), Bosnians (*Bosna'lu*),[29] Armenians and Jews of Poland (*Leh ermeniler* ve *yahudiler*). They were denounced as infidels because they had bought certain merchandise from the principalities of Wallachia and Moldavia and sold them in all places that had been defined as territories of the Abode of War (*dar al-harb*).[30]

### 1.2 *Harbi küffar*

Theoretically, there was a permanent state of holy war between the Ottoman Empire and Christian states; hence, the latter were described as "the enemy" (*harbi*) even if only a potential one. *Harbi* (pl. *harbiler*) generally designated the "infidel" who did not pay tribute or poll-tax (*harac* or *cizye*) and lived in the Abode of War. On the other hand, certain jurists defined *harbi* as only those infidels who had not concluded peace agreements with Muslims, or had not received a safe-conduct from them. It must be emphasized that this identification was applied not only to the inhabitants of Abode of War but also to countries they inhabited (*harbi vilayetler*), their ships (*harbi gemiler*) and their merchandise (*meta'-yi harbi*), as well as the foreign merchants who entered Ottoman territories (*harbi tüccar*).[31]

The Wallachians and Moldavians themselves were deemed *harbi* in their early relations with the Ottomans, that is from the end of the fourteenth century, during the fifteenth century, and even during the sixteenth-century

28 In the fiscal documents a customary formula was "*kafir* and Jews" (Lewis, *Muslim Discovery*, 172–173).

29 This is interesting given that Bosnia was part of the Ottoman Empire. It is possible the document did refer to Dalmatians or Montenegrins under the guise of the term 'Bosnian.'

30 Veliman, *Documente turcești*, doc. 122: *hüküm* of *eva'il-i Safer* 1164/ 30 December-8 January 1750. See also Mehmet, *Documente turcești*, I, doc. 265 (*hüküm* of *evahir-i Zilhicce* 1177/ 21–30 June 1764)..

31 *Redhouse*, 519; Caurroy, "Législation," IV/12 (1848), 13, n. 6 and IV/17 (1851), 219; Morabia, *Ğihad*, 331; D'Ohsson, *Tableau*, V, 70; Biegman, *Ragusa*, 124–125 (*ferman* of 1582); Panaite, "Străinii," 31; Groot, *OEDR*, 239–245 (the *'ahdname* of 1612, issued by Ahmed I to Dutch Republic).

episodes of open conflict with the Porte, when the thrust of the holy campaigns (*gazavat*) was directed against them.

### 1.3 *Christian View*

Given the relationship between Islam and Christendom under the Ottoman Empire, one can say that the notion of the "infidel" was one of mutual exclusion.[32] The Islamic world, represented by the Ottoman Empire, was the eternal enemy of Christianity against which Christianity had to fight in unity.[33] This formula was routinely repeated in the majority of the political literature addressing the contacts between Christianity and Islam during the medieval and early modern history of both until to the end of the eighteenth century.

Generally, according to the late fourteenth- to mid-sixteenth century Christian view, the "infidel" was identified with the Muslim, whose prevailing image was that of the Turk. German traveller Johann Schiltberger called the Turks "infidels," and their territory "the land of the infidels."[34] Yet, European observers who actually lived in Islamic territories, like the Serbian Konstantin Mihajlović, who stayed many years as a captive in the Ottoman world, presented a less homogenous depiction of Muslims, differentiating between ethnic groups and speaking of "The Persians, the Turks, the Tatars, the Berbers, and the Arabs; and diverse Moors…"[35] In fourteenth- and fifteenth-century Southeastern European sources, the Ottomans were called Turks and were

32 About the Christian view on Turks, see: Clarence Dana Rouillard, *The Turk in French History, Thought and Literature (1520–1660)*, Paris: Boivin, 1938; Carl Göllner, *Turcica.* I–II Vol. *Die europäischen Türkendrucke des XVI. Jahrhunderts*, Bucharest: Editura Academiei, Berlin: Akademie-Verlag, 1961; Bucharest: Editura Academiei, Baden-Baden: Verlag Librarie Hertz, 1968; III. Vol. *Die Türkenfrage in der öffentlichen Meinung Europas im 16. Jahrhundert*, Bucharest: Editura Academiei, Baden-Baden: Verlag Librarie Hertz, 1978; Andrei Pippidi, *Visions of the Ottoman World in Renaissance Europe*, London: Hurst&Company, 2012.

33 Éva Bóka, "In search of a Stereotype: «the Turkish Question»," *SF*, Vol. 55, 1996, 1–24. Alexandru Duțu has spoken about two levels of perception of the Turks by Christians. The first, a consequence of frequent military conflicts, was characterized as the popular one, and according to it the Turk was seen as a cat, with the habit of cheating Christians. The second tried an "academic" exclusion, defining Turks as barbarians, as the exclusive communities of earlier times did. He emphasized that due to "military contact" the negative features prevailed in both cases, and "cultural contact" gave rise to a few positive features which could be attributed to the Turks (Duțu, *Călătorii*, 118–159).

34 "I was also in Wallachy and in its two chief cities…; also in a city called Übereil <o. n. Brăila>, situated on the Tunow. There were the kocken < n. ed. koggen or coggo was a vessel with rounded bow and stern> and galleys, in which merchants bring their goods from the land of the Infidels" (Schiltberger, *Travels*, passim).

35 Mihajlović, *Memoires*, 3.

seen primarily as "native enemies" of the whole of Christendom and the Christian faith. Only after they were so identified could they be characterized as enemies of Christian states like Hungary and Wallachia at end of the fourteenth and first half of the fifteenth century.[36] For instance, the treaty of alliance of 7 March 1395 between Sigismund I, the king of Hungary, and Mircea the Elder, the prince of Wallachia, mentioned Hungarian support against "Turks, those enemies of Christ's name and our fierce enemies…"[37] As a rule, then, Turks were identified as "infidels," "pagans," and described as "barbarous," "brutal" and "knavish" (*perfidissimis infidelibus*).[38] Certain formulas were often used in fifteenth-century Hungarian, Wallachian and Moldavian documents, written in Latin, for example, "the savage Turks, persecutors of Christ's cross, hated by God and his peoples" (1426),[39] "the very wretched Turks and inborn enemies" (1427),[40] "Turks, the cruel oppressors of Christ's cross and of the whole Orthodox faith" (1427).[41] In sixteenth and seventeenth-century Moldavian and Wallachian documents, Tartars, like the Turks, were also defined as "infidels," "pagans" and "enemies of Christians."[42] The Moldavian and Wallachian chroniclers reinforced the traditional image of Turk and Tartar, particularly the vision of a perpetual enmity between them and Christians. This adversarial relationship came to be considered a defining feature of the Muslims' relationship with Christian Europe; as Nicolae Costin remarked "the pagan was never loved by Christians."[43]

36 DRH, D, I, doc. 99, 108, 114, 132, 149, 153, 162, 196 etc.

37 DRH, D, I, doc. 87.

38 DRH, D, I, doc. 85, 140 (*contra saevissimorum Turcorum*), 159. See also letters of Christian rulers of the second part of the fifteenth century (*Războieni. 1476*, 125–127; C. Esarcu, *Documente descoperite în arhivele Veneției*, Bucharest, 1874, 23–24; Hurmuzaki, *Documente*, VIII, doc. XII; Bogdan, *Documente. Ştefan*, II, 318–319).

39 DRH, D, vol. I, doc. 149 (of 8 May 1426: *hostiliter invadentibus*).

40 DRH, D, vol. I, doc.153 (27 January 1427: *nefandissimis Turcis et ini<mi>corum natis*).

41 DRH, D, vol. I, doc. 157 (6 April 1427 from Câmpulung: *contra perfidiae alumnos, puta Turcas, crucis Christi et totius orthodoxae fidei dirissimos persequitores*).

42 In the letters of Moldavian voivodes and boyars (Hurmuzaki, *Documente*, Supl. II/1, doc. CLXVII (letter of 5 March 1594), CLXXIII (letter of 29 July 1594); Hurmuzaki, *Documente*, Supl. II/2, doc. CCXXXVIII (letter of 13 September 1624).

43 Nicolae Costin, *Letopiseț*, 164 (*ce niciodată creştinilor drag păgânul n-au fost*).

## 2 The Abode of Islam vs. the Abode of War in Southeastern Europe

As the expansion of the Caliphate came to a halt after the mid-eighth century and it gradually became clear that the establishment of universal Islamic rule was impossible, Muslim jurists (especially the Hanafi ones), started to view the world as consisting of two adversarial blocs: the Abode of Islam and the Abode of War. Therefore, they imposed, as the underlying principle and basic polarity of Islamic "international" law, the binary opposition between the Muslim and non-Muslim worlds, i.e. *dar al-Islam* vs. *dar al-harb*.[44]

Adopting the Hanafi view, Ottoman juridical texts also clearly emphasized the rivalry between *dar al-Islam* and *dar al-harb*.[45] Let us note that the Arab word *dar* (translated as abode, house, realm, territory, dominion, country etc.) was used as an abstract notion, being strongly associated with sovereignty, rulers and laws.[46]

### 2.1 *Abode of War*

The formulas "the Abode of Infidels" (*dar al-kefere*) and "the Abode of War" (*dar al-harb*) designated any part of the world which had not yet accepted Islam, including the territories where *şeri'at* was not applied and where Muslims were in danger. According to Ibrahim al-Halebi's definition, all countries outside the Abode of Islam might be considered as belonging to the Abode of War. In the Islamic juridical view, the Abode of War and everything related to it was open to conquest and violence.[47]

---

44 On this disjunction in early Islam, see: Abu Yusuf, *Kitab*, passim; Caurroy, "Législation," IV/17, 218 (*pays de l'islamisme* and *pays de la guerre*); Khadduri, *War and Peace*, 51; Özel, *Islam Hukuku*, 78, 121–152 (*Dar ül-Islam – Dar ül-harb Taksimi*); Shai Har-El, *Ottoman-Mamluk*, 8. W. M. Watt underlined the Kuranic origins of these concepts (IX/29, 33; XLVIII/28; LXI/9) and the notion of *dar al-takiyya* ("the sphere of prudent concealment"), used by Kharijites before 700 AD., which could be considered as the Abode of Islam (W. M. Watt, *The Formative Period of Islamic Thought*, Edinburgh: Edinburgh University Press, 1973, 29–31; Watt, "Jihad," 393–394). The Hanafi jurist Debusi (d. 1039), stated simply: "According to our opinion, the basic principle is the existence of two domains: the Abode of Islam and the Abode of War" (cf. Özel, *Islam Hukuku*, 151).

45 Bianchi, *Fetvas*, 180–181: *dar-ı harbdan... dar-ı Islam'a çıkub*. A recent work offers an original perspective on sovereignty and territory in the Ottoman Mediterranean (Palmira Brummett, *Mapping the Ottomans. Sovereignty, Territory and Identity in the Early Modern Mediterranean*, New York: Cambridge University Press, 2015).

46 *Redhouse*, 272; Shaybani, *Kitab al-siyar*, cf. Caurroy, "Législation," IV/17, 224; A. Abel, "Dar al-Islam," *EI-2*, II, 127–128 (for its meanings in pre-Islamic period); Özel, *Islam Hukuku*, 77.

47 D'Ohsson, *Tableau*, V, 41. See also Shaybani, *Kitab al-siyar*, cf. Caurroy, "Législation," IV/17, 218; A. Abel, "Dar al-harb," *EI-2*, I, 126.

In order to define foreign territories and states, the Ottomans used the concept *dar al-harb*, but also its synonyms: *diyar-ı harb* (enemy lands), *kefere vilayetleri* (infidel's countries), *kafirlerin illeri* (unbelievers' possessions), *diyar-ı küfr* (non-Muslim lands), *kafiristan* (country of the infidels, Europe especially). From the sixteenth century onwards, the attribute *harbi* came to be used in official documents, such *kanunname*s, *ʿahdname*s and *hüküm*s, as well as in chronicles. For instance, in seventeenth-century *ʿahdnames* granted to Western states we can find the formula *harbi vilayet* (pl. *harbi vilayetler*) for designating those Christian countries that had not concluded peace treaties with the Porte and, therefore, did not enjoy commercial rights.[48] In the Ottoman chronicles this terminology was employed, more or less, depending on the authors' training in Islamic law.

According to the Ottoman view in the fifteenth century, the territories to the north of the Danube, including the principalities of Wallachia and Moldavia, were considered part of the Abode of Infidels or "the countries inhabited by infidels."[49] As a result, the Ottoman chroniclers of this period always referred to Moldavia ruled by Stephen the Great as a "territory of infidels" (*dar al-kefere*), in spite of the fact that the ruler paid tribute in exchange for peace. Moreover, when the princes rebelled, – an act epitomized by their refusal to pay the established *harac* – the Porte responded by launching *gazavat* (a term used for instance in Mehmed II's Moldavian campaign of 1476),[50] Wallachia and Moldavia were labelled as "territories of war"[51] rather than by the generic name of infidel countries. For instance, in 1484, Kıvami considered the territory north of the Danube, Moldavia particularly, as part of the Abode of War (*dar al-harb*). This Ottoman chronicler estimated that, by crossing the great river, the army led by Bayezid II could only reach the Abode of War: "they crossed the waters to the other bank of the Danube to the Abode of War."[52] With respect to the 1538 campaign, Nasuh Matrakçi defined Moldavia as a "*harbi* country," and Süleyman Kanunî's campaign against his prince, Petru Rareș, had as its objective "the conquest of an enemy [country]."[53]

48 Veliman, *Documente turcești*, doc. 54 (*hüküm* of 1138 AH/1726), doc. 122 (*hüküm* of 1164 AH/1750–1751). In the 1612 *ʿahdname* granted to Holland (Groot, *OEDR*, 239–245).

49 Several formulas: *dar al-kefere, diyar-ı küffar, diyar-ı küfr, kefere vilayetleri, kafiristan* (*Şükrullah, Tevarih*, cf. Veliman, "Mircea," 426; Ibn Kemal, *Tevarih*, cf. Decei, "Mircea," 144). *Küfr* means "infidelity" (*Redhouse Lexicon*, 305, 694).

50 Neşri, *Tarih*, in *Cronici turcești I*, 128. See also Tursun bey, *Tarih*, in *Cronici turcești I*, 74.

51 Several formulas: *dar al-harb, dar-ı harb, diyar-ı harb, harbi vilayetler.*

52 *sulere Tunanın öte kenarına dar al-harb'e geçdiler* (Kıvami, *Fetihname*, 304, 306).

53 Nasuh Matrakçi, *Fetihname*, in *Cronici turcești I*, 228.

### 2.2 *Abode of Islam*

To define the concept of the Abode of Islam (*dar al-Islam*), the juridical texts of classical Islam insisted on the free practice of Islamic religion, safety guarantees for Muslims and the application of *şeri'at*.[54] According to the Hanafi jurists, one might speak of a transformation of the Abode of War into the Abode of Islam only when the Islamic faith had become established:

> *Dar al-harb* becomes *dar al-Islam* by public exertion of the Islamic cult in practices like Friday prayer, the two *bayramlar and* other feasts, even though [the territory] continues to be inhabited by indigenous infidels. Furthermore, the identity would be given even though the territory might not be adjacent to *dar al-Islam*, that is, even though another country belonging to the *harbis*, might lie between the old territory of Islam and the new Abode of Islam.[55]

In the Ottoman period, the Abode of Islam (in Turkish, *dar al-Islam, dar-ı Islam* or *diyar-ı Islam*)[56] was identified with the territories whose sovereign was the sultan, although they might be called *Memalik-i mahrusa* (Well-Protected Domains) in narrative and official sources. Moreover, the Abode of Islam included all the territories ruled by the sultan, even if a Muslim community was absent in particular regions.

## 3 The Danube as Border between Abode of War and Abode of Islam

In the fifteenth and sixteenth centuries and even later, the Danube was one of the most disputed areas at the frontier between Islam and Christianity.[57] Some

---

54 Shaybani, *Kitab al-siyar*, cf. Caurroy, "Législation," IV/17, 218; A. Abel, "Dar al-Islam," *EI-2*, II, 127–128; Parvin, Sommer, "Dar al-Islam," 4. According to M. Boisard, its synonym would be *dar al-a'dl*, a territory which ruled the law, order and harmony by observing Allah's and Muhammad's precepts (Boisard, *Islam*, 208).

55 Apud Caurroy, "Législation," IV/17, 219.

56 "Our territory" (*bizim darımız*) in the Turkish translation of al-Halebi's work (M. Mevkufati, *Şerh-i Mülteka el-Ebhür*, II, Istanbul, 1254 AH/1838–1839, 336); Bianchi, "Fetvas," 180–181; Şükrullah, *Tevarih*, in Veliman, "Mircea," 426; Ibn Kemal, *Tevarih*, in Decei, "Mircea," 144.

57 On the frontiers in the Ottoman world, see Mark L. Stein, *Guarding the Frontier. Ottoman Border Forts and Garrisons in Europe*, London, New York: I.B. Tauris, 2007; Andrew Peacock, ed. *The Frontiers of the Ottoman World*, Oxford, New York: Oxford University Press, 2009; Gábor Ágoston, "Defending and Administering the Hungarian frontier," in Christine Woodhead, ed., *The Ottoman World*, London, New York: Routledge, 2012, 220–236;

fifteenth-century chroniclers shared this Islamic view of the Danube, even though it was not so obvious in the language current at the time. Thus, Şükrüllah spoke of *dar al-Islam*, led by Sultan Bayezid I (1389–1402), against whom the infidel king of Hungary (*kafir*) had waged war. Obviously, in accordance with this view, the fortress of Niğbolu could only be situated "at the frontier of Islam" (*serhadd-ı Islamda*).[58] Similarly, according to Idris Bitlisi (d. 1520), Bayezid I's holy campaign (*gaza*) to Wallachia in 1394 was altogether tantamount to the strengthening of the "Islamic frontier."[59]

The theoretical disjunction between the two areas was retroactively emphasized and reinforced in sixteenth-century Ottoman sources, after the conquest of Arab provinces by Selim I and Süleyman Kanunî brought about the ascendancy of Islamic law at the sultanic court. A persuasive example of such usage can be found in the chronicle of Ibn Kemal (d. 1535), who was *şeyh ül-Islam* for almost a decade under Süleyman Kanunî, precisely at the juncture of Islamic law's ascendancy. Recounting the conflict between Bayezid I and Mircea the Elder (1386–1418), the Ottoman historian distinguished between the territory of Islam (*dar-ı Islam* or *diyar-ı Islam*), situated on the east and southern side of the Danube, and the territories of infidels (*dar al-kefere* or *diyar-ı küffar*), including Wallachia. In this context, the Wallachian prince "was – according to Kemalpaşazade – the most famous prince of the infidels' countries of his time."[60] From the late-sixteenth-century perspective, Mustafa Ali (d. 1599), while describing the ethnic, geographic and political realities in the Balkans during the fourteenth and fifteenth centuries, classified Wallachia (*Eflak*) as part of the "infidel territories" that were situated "on the borders of this river" (the Danube).[61]

---

M. P. Pedani, *The Ottoman-Venetian Border (15th -18th Centuries)*, translated by Mariateresa Sala, Venice: Edizioni Ca' Foscari – Digital Publishing, 2017.

58 Şükrullah, *Tevarih*, in Veliman, "Mircea," 426.

59 In this respect, the chronicler invoked a "famous commandment of *şeri'at* and [...] a juridical opinion (*fetva*)" (Idris Bitlisi, *Heşt Behişt*, in *Cronici turcești I*, 156–157). For details, see A. Decei, "Expediția lui Mircea cel Bătrân împotriva acîngiilor de la Karinovasi (1393)," *RER*, I, 1953, 130–151 (Decei, *RRO*, 140–155); A. Decei, "Două documente turcești privitoare la expedițiile sultanilor Baiazid I și Murad al II-lea în Țările Române," *RRH*, XIII, 3, 1974, 395–413 (Decei, *RRO*, 209–222); Gemil, *Românii și otomanii*, 69–85.

60 *Rüzgarında olan diyar-ı küffar şehryarlarının şehiriydi* (Ibn Kemal, *Tevarih*, in Decei, "Mircea," 144 and n. 1).

61 Mustafa Ali, *Künh al-ahbar*, in *Cronici turcești I*, 336. Also, referring to Süleyman Kanunî's expedition in 1538, Mustafa Celalzade (d. 1568) affirmed that the South of Moldavia runs the river of Danube and towards this part lay the borderline with the Ottoman Empire (Mustafa Celalzade, *Tabakat*, in *Cronici turcești I*, 263).

One of the important attributes that defined territories of the Abode of Islam was the protection and defence of the Muslims' life and assets, a point emphasized by Hanafi jurists such as al-Shaybani.[62] Hence, one may consider that this perspective – one going beyond military and strategic considerations – is discernible when Ottoman chroniclers insist on the retreat of the Ottoman army, for reasons of safety, to the east of the Danube. Even following the conquest of Moldavia in 1538, Süleyman Kanunî, eager to reach the Abode of Islam which was the safest place for any Muslim, hurried to the south of the Danube.

> Then, the sultan of Islam left Suceava without delay and, marching without stopping and covering great distances – Lütfi paşa wrote – went back to the Danube.[63]

In the sixteenth and seventeenth centuries the Danube continued to represent the boundary that separated the territories of infidels from the Abode of Islam both for Ottomans and Christians. In this regard, Katip Çelebi claimed that: "As there are few Muslim countries north of it [the Danube], most of them are infidel countries."[64]

How do we define the late-fourteenth- to mid-sixteenth-century juridical status of the Danube in terms of the Islamic law of war? We can do so on the basis of information from historical sources, some of which has been mentioned above. Despite the gradual assertion of Ottoman control over the great river as a frontier between the Abode of War and the Abode of Islam, I have been tempted to adopt one of the Hanafi opinions, according to which the frontier areas (mountains, rivers, seas etc.) were not part of either *dar al-Islam* or *dar al-harb*. Starting again from the criterion of guaranteed protection for Muslims – perhaps the best definition of the Abode of Islam status – and from the jurists' recommendation in this respect,[65] Ottomans considered the Danube, at least in the period referred to herein and in times of open conflicts, as still belonging to the Abode of War. Furthermore, the areas characterized by intense and recurring conflicts between Muslims and non-Muslims also belonged – according to historical sources – to the Abode of War (*dar al-cihad*).[66]

62 Shaybani, *Kitab al-siyar*, cf. Caurroy, *Législation*, IV/12, 218.

63 Lütfi paşa, *Tevarih*, in *Cronici turcești I*, 248.

64 Katib Çelebi, *Cihannüma*, in *Cronici turcești II*, 110. Evliya Celebi expresses the same sentiment, when giving the description of his stay in Silistre (*Călători străini*, VI, 368–376).

65 Caurroy, "Législation," IV/12, 224–225.

66 During the tenth century, due to the yearly campaign against Christians, Spain was known

Thus, the city of Belgrade and its surroundings got this name in the context of fifteenth–seventeenth century military conflicts between the Ottomans and Hungary, specifically between the Ottomans and the Habsburg Empire.[67]

In their turn, the Christians saw the Danube as the natural barrier that could stop the Ottoman advance towards the Christian territories, and as a possible launching pad for the expansion of Christendom. In effect, Wallachian princes of the fifteenth and early sixteenth century emphasized the difference between the territories to the south of the Danube, considering them to be part of the "Turkish country," while dubbing those on the other side as "our country."[68] Likewise, foreign travellers noticed this difference even in the seventeenth century. In 1608, travelling from Lvov to Constantinople, the Armenian Simeon Dbir Lehaţi wrote: "I reached Galaţi, the last Moldavian town and the gate to the Turkish country."[69] In one of the diaries from Miaskowski's embassy of 1640, the author remarks upon crossing to Hotin from Poland that they are entering Turkey; however, upon crossing the Danube, he says that they crossed at this point into a "wholly Turkish country."[70]

When their relations with the Porte escalated into an open conflict, Wallachian rulers in their correspondence with Christian princes did not describe the exact route of the Ottoman campaign but focused on their crossing of the Danube. Thus, Mircea the Elder perceived the Danube as a frontier; the arrival of the Ottoman army on the banks of the river would have seriously threatened

---

in Arab world as *dar al-cihad* (Watt, *Islamic Spain*, 34–35). During the Ottoman period, Tunis was also characterized in early seventeenth-century *'ahdname*s as *dar al-cihad*.

67 Mehmed Raşid (d. 1735), relating the Ottoman–Habsburg war of 1683–1699, more precisely to the year 1695, defined Belgrade by a formula appeared during early Ottoman expansion to Central Europe, i.e. *dar al-cihad* (Mehmed Raşid, *Tarih*, in *Cronici turceşti III*, 180).

68 Documents issued during the reign of Laiotă Basarab (in 1476) and Neagoe Basarab (1512–1521) (Tocilescu, *534 documente*, doc. 99).

69 *Călători străini*, IV, 347.

70 Here is the main paragraph: "We left Kam'janec' to easier cross the Dnester. As the night fell, we arrived to Hotin, three miles from Kam'janec', which lies in the Turkish monarchy beyond the Dnester, which we crossed over a glass bridge [i.e. ice]." (Adam Przyboś (ed.), *Wielka legacja Wojciecha Miaskowskiego do Turcji w 1640 r.*, Krakow 1985, 107). Michał Wasiucionek, who gave me this information, has also discussed the related topic of the Danube's role as a boundary and the strategies of crossing in the article: Michał Wasiucionek, "Danube-hopping. Conversion, jurisdiction and spatiality between the Ottoman Empire and the Danubian principalities in the seventeenth century," in *Conversion and Islam in the Early Modern Mediterranean: The Lure of the Other*, ed. Claire Norton, London: Routledge, 2017, 77–99.

Wallachia's safety. In 1399, he wrote to Sigismund of Luxemburg, the king of Hungary,

> that Bayezid himself, the lord of the Turks, lies with a great army in the town of Adrinople, on this side of the sea, at a five days' distance, easy to cover to the Danube.[71]

An almost identical wording can be found almost two hundred years later, in the petition of 17 January in 1601 that Wallachian Prince Michael the Brave presented to Emperor Rudolph II: "My province, Wallachia, lies not farther than five days' distance from the tyrant's residence."[72] Thus, in every conflict in Southeastern and Central Europe which involved the Ottoman Empire and Christian states –Hungary, Poland, the Habsburg Empire but particularly the principalities of Wallachia and Moldavia – the borderline of the Danube was of utmost strategic importance. In this vein, Petru Rareș considered the conquest of Buda – the key to the control of the Middle and Lower Danube – by the Ottomans, as a tragedy for Christendom. This is why in 1541 the Moldavian prince asked the king of Poland, Sigismund I, to rally Christian forces with the goal to recover the town and buttress Christendom beyond the Danube:

> Besides, we bring to the knowledge of Your Highness that you should advise King Ferdinand to strike in the name of Christians and retake Buda from the Turks, and if he conquers it to destroy it and let the Danube sweep its ruins, so that the Turks should not strike roots there, for this could not help the Christians in any way, but only harm them.[73]

Over half a century later, during the 'Long War' of 1593–1606 between the Ottomans and the Christian coalition (which included among its members Wallachia, Moldavia and Transylvania), the strategic importance of the Danube again came to the fore. In his efforts to involve Poland in this war, Michael the Brave invoked the danger, hovering over Moldavia and Wallachia, of their transformation into *sancak*s under direct Ottoman administration. During his discussions with a Polish envoy, Lubieniecki, the voivode stated in July 1595:

71 In the Hungarian king's letter of before 23 March 1399 (*DRH*, D, I, doc. 105).

72 *Mihai. Documente*, I, doc. 226.

73 Corfus, *Documente. XVI*, doc. 35. This idea was also affirmed in a 1542 letter: Corfus, *Documente. XVI*, doc. 47.

> And if that fire should cross the Danube into my country and then into the country of Moldavia, then the same fire will be in store for the countries of His Royal Highness the king. Therefore, it would be better for their lordships (*hetmans*) not to wait for the Turks by the Dnestr but by the Danube.[74]

Moreover, even after the battle of Călugăreni (1595), sources registered the Danube as the main axis in the ongoing conflict between Christendom and the Ottoman Empire. In April 1599, Polish dignitaries stressed that "meanwhile the imperial armies will leave in the Danube."[75] The next year, on 4 October 1600, Piotr Tylicki, the bishop of Culm and the Vice-Chancellor of the Polish Crown, acknowledged the threat hovering over Michael the Brave by drawing the attention to the Ottoman troops gathering south of the Danube: "Likewise the Turkish army lies in a fairly great number by the Danube."[76]

74 *Mihai. Documente*, I, doc. 16.

75 Corfus, *Documente. XVI*, doc. 205.

76 Corfus, *Documente. XVI*, doc. 227.

CHAPTER 3

# Ottoman Holy War to the North of the Danube

## 1 Efforts to the Way of Allah

Initially, as vassals of the Seljukid sultans, the Anatolian *beys*, including the fledging Ottoman dynasty, accompanied their suzerains in holy campaigns (*gaza*) against Byzantine territories.[1] Adopting the ideology of *cihad*, the Ottoman sultans assumed for themselves the task of leaders of the holy war against infidels of Southeastern Europe. This idea was directly and most categorically declared in "letters of conquest" (*fetihnames*), accounts of victorious campaigns against unbelievers, distributed both domestically and abroad by the sultans. The most relevant examples of this genre are to be found in Mehmed II's statements in letters sent to Muslim rulers.[2] Furthermore, both Byzantine and Ottoman sources indicate that sultans were conscious of their obligation to conduct *cihad*. For instance, in 1421, after Mehmed I's death, as Nişancı Mehmed paşa informs us, his son,

> Gazi Sultan Murad Han, came to the imperial throne. Murad Han did not abandon but rather followed the right way, hoisted the banners of the holy campaign and the holy war (*gaza ü-cihad bayraklarını yücelten*) and confided in the glorious Allah.[3]

Step by step, but especially after the conquest of Arab territories, the image of sultans as leaders of holy wars was recognized across the Muslim world.[4] In the sixteenth century, stereotypes dominated the image of the sultan as a holy warrior. As Christine Woodhead pointed out in her analysis of campaign

1 According to the chronicler Nişanci Mehmed paşa, Ertoğrul had accompanied his suzerain Alaaddin Kay-Kubad III in sacred campaigns (*gaza ü cihadda sultanla birlikte bulunmak istedi*) (Mehmed paşa, *Tarih*, in *Osmanlı Tarihleri*, I, 344).

2 To the Mamluk sultan after the conquest of Constantinople in 1453 (Critobul, *Mehmed II*, 56–74; Inalcık, *Ottoman Empire*, 56). To Uzun Hasan, in 1476, after the campaign against the Moldavian prince (Guboglu, "Izvoare turco-persane," 139).

3 Mehmed paşa, *Tarih*, in *Osmanlı Tarihleri*, I, 348. On Bayezid I (Ducas, *Istoria*, III/4; Chalcocondil, *Expuneri*, 77). On Mehmed I, Mustafa Çelebi and Güneyt (Ducas, *Istoria*, XXIV/5, XXIV/12, XXI/10).

4 Inalcık, *Ottoman Empire*, 57; Carl Max Kortepeter, "How the Ottomans governed the Arabs: The Observations recorded by Evliya Çelebi in 1672." In *Studia Turcologica Memoriae Alexii Bombaci Dicta*, Naples: Istituto universitario orientale, 1982, 318–333.

 | DOI:10.1163/9789004411104_004

accounts (*gazavatnames*) produced during the reign of Süleyman Kanunî (1520–1566):

> Here Süleyman's role as warrior king, the sultan of the *gazis*, dominates: he surpasses the achievements of his predecessors in extending the territorial bounds of empire and of Islam; he marches with a magnificently arrayed, invincible force, reduces the strongest fortresses, slays the irredeemable infidel, and puts rebels to flight.[5]

According to Ottoman juridical theory, there was a permanent state of war between the Abode of Islam (*dar al-Islam*) and the Abode of War (*dar al-harb*) that would last until infidels' territories were brought under the sultan's authority. To accomplish this goal, the ideology of offensive *cihad* was built and promoted as the main element of fifteenth- and sixteenth-century Ottoman political thought. This meant the only just war was *cihad*, i.e. that war which had as final aim the achievement of a *pax ottomanica* or *imperium mundi* for the Ottoman Empire.[6] From this perspective, the Moldavian scholar Dimitrie Cantemir insisted that the rationales for war were purely theological:

> they [the Ottomans] call those Wars just, (and only those) which are undertaken for the Propagation of the *Mahometan* Religion: On the contrary, unjust Wars with them are such as are entered into for the enlarging the Bounds of their Empire, or the Royal Revenue…[7]

Contemporary analysts also attempted to prove that Ottoman wars were waged for just causes by insisting that all victories and defeats were ultimately decided by "divine Providence."[8] Actually, this mentality originated in the standard reaction of the Ottoman dignitaries: "it was so the Allah's will," chroniclers

---

5 She quoted especially *Tabakat ül-memalik* of Mustafa Celalzade (Christine Woodhead, "Perspectives on Süleyman," in *Süleyman the Magnificent and His Age. The Ottoman Empire in the Early Modern World*, Edited by Metin Kunt and Christine Woodhead, London and New York: Longman Publishing, 1995, 172–173).

6 E. Tyan, "Djihad," *EI-2*, II, 1991, 538–540; Morabia, *Ǧihad*, 416; Cl. Cahen, "Harb. II. Sous le califat," *EI-2*, III, 185. On the just war in Western Europe, see R. Regnant, *La doctrine de la guerre juste de s. Augustin à nos jours, d'après les théologiens et canonistes catholiques*, Paris, 1934; F. M. Russel, *The Just War in the Middle Ages*, 2nd ed., Cambridge, 1977.

7 Cantemir, *Othman History*, 79, n. 4.

8 Chalcocondil, *Expuneri*, 279; Kara-Çelebi-Zade, *Ravdat ül-Ebrar*, in *Cronici turcești I*, 544; Cantemir, *Othman History*, 79, n. 4.

recorded.[9] In any case, once a war was defined as an "effort in the way of Allah" (*cihad fi sebil-i Allah*), its results – such as title of *gazi*, the quality of the martyr and the right of sword – would become lawful.[10]

The sources prove that Wallachia and Moldavia, and then Transylvania were between the late fourteenth to middle sixteenth century objectives of the Ottoman policy of conquest. All the campaigns during that period – from the incessant predatory raids (*akın*) launched by frontier *bey*s in order to back loyal princes or punish defiant ones[11] to full-scale military expeditions organized and led by sultans, grand viziers or *beylerbeyi*s of Rumelia – were considered holy campaigns (*gazavat*). With regard to the frontier raids, Ottoman chronicles and documents provided sufficient evidence to conclude that the terms *akın* and *akıncı* (raider) were considered synonymous and interchangeable with *gaza* (holy campaign) and *gazi* (holy war warrior).[12] For instance, in the second half of the fifteenth century, Mihaloğlu Ali bey was one of the most famous leaders of the *gazavat*s against Moldavia, Hungary and Poland.[13] Describing the 1485 campaign against Stephen the Great, led by another famous frontier *bey*, Malkoçoğlu Bali bey, chronicler Koca Hüseyin wrote:

> This [*bey*] in his turn according to the great ferman, having gathered the *gazi*s, launched [this campaign] with holy war (*cihad*) on his mind.[14]

Ottoman narrative sources particularly emphasized the *gaza* aspect of campaigns led personally by sultans, such as Bayezid I's expedition in 1394 or 1395;[15]

9 Mehmed II would say after the defeat of the Belgrade's siege, in 1456 (Oruc bin Adil, *Tarih*, in *Cronici turcești I*, 59).

10 D'Ohsson, *Tableau*, V, 71; Cantemir, *Othman History*, 210, n. 94; Cantemir, *Sistemul*, 425.

11 A. S. Levend, *Gazavatnameler ve Mihaloğlu Ali Bey'in Gazavatnamesi*, Ankara: Harbiye Kitabevi&Sahaf ve Ecrin Kitabevi, 1965, 1–178.

12 Colin Imber offered more examples in this respect. "Those servants of religion made raids against the infidels. For that reason, they called holy war (*gaza*) *akın*" (Ahmedi, cf. Imber, "Ideals," 140). See also: Chalcocondil, *Expuneri*, passim; Ducas, *Istoria*, passim; Tocilescu, *534 documente*, passim; Mehmet, *Documente turcești*, I, passim; Neșri, *Tarih*, passim; B. Cvetkova, A. Razboynikov (eds.), *Fontes Turcici Historiae Bulgaricae*, Sofia, 1972, 30–41; Sertoğlu, ROTA, art. *Akıncı*; Pakalın, *Sözlük*, I, 36; A. Decei, "Akındji," *EI-2*, I, 350–351; Decei, "Mircea," 140–155; Decei, *Imp. otoman*, 114–115; Berindei, Veinstein, *Documents*, 308–309; Beldiceanu-Steinherr, "Pengyek," 28–32.

13 *Mihaloğlu Ali Bey'in Gazavatnamesi*, in Levend, *Gazavatname*, 179–358.

14 Koca Hüseyin, *Beda'i ül-Veka'i*, in *Cronici turcești I*, 464. See also Suzi Çelebi, *Gazavatname-yi Mihaloğlu Ali Bey*, in *Cronici turcești I*, 141–148.

15 *Cronici turcești I*, 38–39 (Enveri); 48–49 (Oruc bin Adil); 13 (Mehmed Neșri); 157–159 (Idris Bitlisi); 290 (Mehmed pașa); 304 (Sa'adeddin); 339 (Mustafa Ali); 441–442 (Koca Hüseyin); 543 (Kara-Çelebi-Zade).

Mehmed I's in 1417;[16] Mehmed II's in 1462,[17] which targeted the rulers of Wallachia; the campaigns launched against Moldavia by Mehmed II in 1476;[18] Bayezid II's in 1484[19] and Süleyman Kanunî's in 1538 were portrayed in a similar manner.[20] For instance, Mehmed Neşri's account of the dynasty's history, also contained a set of "stories" (*hikayets*) on the *padişah*-led campaigns against the Danubian principalities, such as "The Story of the Holy Campaign in Wallachia" in 1462 (*Hikayet-i gaza-yı Eflak*),[21] or "The Story of the Second Holy Campaign in Moldavia" of 1476.[22] However, the author applied the same term to the raids organized by frontier campaigns, led either by grand viziers or provincial governors. Recounting the defeat Süleyman paşa had suffered in Moldavia in 1475, Neşri described it as "taking place during the holy campaign in Moldavia" (*Hikayet-i Inhizam-ı Süleyman bey der gaza-yı Kara Boğdan*).[23]

In the light of the doctrine of *cihad*, these military campaigns (*gazavat*) were part of the effort every Muslim made on the path of Allah (*fi sebil-i Allah*). Thus, in Ottoman sources, military campaigns, whether led by the sultan or by a frontier warlord, appear as manifestations of *cihad*, and embody the unceasing obligation of the faithful to expand the boundaries of the Abode of Islam.[24]

---

16 *Cronici turcești I*, 32 (Şükrüllah); 51(Oruc bin Adil); 85 (Asıkpaşazade); 116 (Mehmed Neşri); 160–164 (Idris Bitlisi); 181 (*Tevarih*); 238 (Lütfi paşa); 291 (Mehmed paşa); 307–8 (Sa'adeddin); 402–3 (Mehmed bin Mehmed); 445 (Koca Hüseyin).

17 *Cronici turcești I*, 42–44 (Enveri); 59–60 (Oruc bin Adil); 67–72 (Tursun bey); 93–4 (Aşıkpaşazade); 126–127 (Mehmed Neşri); 186 (*Tevarih*); 201–206 (Ibn Kemal); 244 (Lütfi paşa); 294 (Mehmed paşa); 317–320 (Sa'adeddin); 405–406 (Mehmed bin Mehmed); 455–456 (Koca Hüseyin). For Mehmed II's reign, see F. Babinger, *Mohamet II le Conquérant et son temps (1432–1481)…*, Paris: Payot, 1954.

18 *Cronici turcești I*, 62 (Oruc bin Adil); 74–75 (Tursun bey); 95–97 (Aşıkpaşazade); 127–128 (Mehmed Neşri); 211–214 (Ibn Kemal); 294 (Mehmed paşa); 322–324 (Sa'adeddin); 407 (Mehmed bin Mehmed); 458–460 (Koca Hüseyin).

19 *Cronici turcești I*, 63 (Oruc bin Adil); 75–78 (Tursun bey); 98–100 (Aşıkpaşazade); 130–2 (Mehmed Neşri); 245 (Lütfi paşa); 253 (Rustem paşa); 326–327 (Sa'adeddin); 408 (Mehmed bin Mehmed); 461–462 (Koca Hüseyin); 545 (Kara-Çelebi-Zade).

20 *Cronici turcești*, I, 189 (Mühieddin el-Cemalı); 221–232 (Nasuh Matrakçi); 248 (Lütfi paşa); 254–255 (Rustem paşa); 261–272 (Mustafa Celalzade); 351–352 (Mustafa Ali); 412 (Mehmed bin Mehmed); 480–482 (Ibrahim Peçevi); 532–547 (Kara-Çelebi -Zade).

21 Neşri, *Tarih*, ed. Unat-Köymen, II, 755–758.

22 Neşri, *Tarih*, ed. Unat-Köymen, II, 829–833.

23 Neşri, *Tarih*, ed. Unat-Köymen, II, 829.

24 John F. Guilmartin made a distinction between two kinds of war in the Ottoman expansion: the war of imperial campaigns, formally legitimized by the Ottoman state's chief religious authority, and the perpetual war of raid and counter-raid along the borders of the Ottoman Empire and its Christian neighbours (called *gazi* warfare, from the term *gaza*, a raid) (Guilmartin, "Ideology," 726).

This understanding is made clear in a document from 1476, summoning Crimean Tatars to attack Stephen the Great of Moldavia:

> His Highness the Emperor has decided to wage holy war (*gaza*) against the damned Kara-Boğdan. That is why it is also brought to your knowledge that you should support the Islamic faith and rise and head from those parts, by joining the imperial army with all your forces.[25]

Actually, *niyyet-i gaza fi sebil-i Allah*, i.e. to "intend to wage a holy war on the path of Allah" or to "plan of holy war on the path of Allah," became a standard expression in the Ottoman chronicles for defining campaigns against enemy countries. As a rule, Ottoman chroniclers shied away from elucidating more mundane causes for imperial war-making. In the case of the 1476 Moldavian campaign, both Aşıkpaşazade and Tursun bey dwelt extensively on the sultan's desire to broaden the scope of the holy war and bring new territories into the Abode of Islam. At the same time, they de-emphasized the immediate *casus belli*, namely the assistance the Moldavian ruler had provided to his relatives in Kefe against the Ottoman siege. Such punitive raids were in many respects a routine task for any frontier *bey*.[26] For Kıvami, who accompanied Sultan Bayezid II during his conquest against Kili and Akkerman in 1484, considered it a holy campaign under the circumstances of *niyyet-i gaza fi sebil-i Allah* imposed by the sultan. Recounting the events, he expressed his admiration of the sultan who had fought the infidels north of the Danube:

> But, with very few of the Islam's *padişah*s it happened that, crossing the Danube, they fought the infidel in holy war [...] Sultan Bayezid han the Gazi, with fortune on his side, was confident to cross – ahead of his army – on the other side of the Danube, the waters of which were stained with blood.[27]

---

25 This order is mentioned in a Tatar dignitary's letter of *evahir-i Cemazi ül-ahir* 881/10–19 October 1476 (Mehmet, *Documente turcești*, I, doc. 4).

26 Tursun bey, *Tarih*, ed. Inalcık, Murphey, 147a–152b; Tursun bey, *Tarih*, in *Cronici turcești I*, 74. "Mehmed Han the *Gazi*, the heroic sultan of Islam, having in mind to wage a holy campaign, left Istanbul and marched forward with his victorious army" (Aşıkpaşazade, *Tevarih*, in *Cronici turcești I*, 96).

27 *Amma Islam-i padişahlarından azına vaki' olmuşdur ki Tuna suya geçüb kafirle gaza eylemek... la-cerem sultan Bayezid han Gazi devlet ile gelüb Islam asker ile kanlu Tunanın öte yakasına geçdi* (Kıvami, *Fetihname*, 304–307). See also Guboglu, *Crestomație turcă*, 178–179.

To mobilize and encourage his troops, the sultan issued an "order for the holy campaign" (*gaza fermanı*), one of the few such documents from the fifteenth century that exist to this day.[28] In it, he proclaimed the campaign – undertaken to conquer two fortresses on the Black Sea shore – a holy war. Obviously, this pragmatic scope was left out from the *hüküm*:

> When the sublime sign arrives, it shall be known: in these moments, invoking help from Allah's Court – may His glory increase – and support from the Prophet's generosity – may blessing and peace be with Him – to increase and multiply the conquests, I have in my mind to wage great holy war (*ulu gazaya niyyet etdim*).[29]

Even in the first half of the seventeenth century, the clash between the Ottoman troops from Lipova and the Habsburg detachment led by the Captain of Ineu, Bornemissza Pál, were described as *gaza*. Similarly, the sum of six thousand *guruş*, paid by the Transylvanian Prince George Rákoczy I to reconcile with the *beylerbeyi* of Buda, Nasuhpaşazade Hüseyin paşa came to be regarded as proceeds from war booty:

> My enduring sultan – the *beylerbeyi* of Buda reported to the grand vizier, Tabanıyası Mehmed paşa –, the infidel race will not give money to the Muslims till they see the wonders of the sword. With help from the almighty Allah, the above-mentioned money shall be a *gaza* asset.[30]

According to the same juridical logic, Ottoman documents and chronicles alike described the 1659–1660 campaign to oust Rákoczy's son – George Rákoczy II (1648–1660) – from the throne as a holy war. Thus, cavalry commander (*serdar*) Seydi Ahmed paşa reported of their "obeying the order which asked

28 Called also *ʿasker ihracı fermanı*, these documents were enacted for calling up soldiers from certain *sancak*s. Gilles Veinstein wrote a case study on the call-up for a sacred expedition by sea in 1552. Identical orders had been sent by Süleyman Kanunî to certain *sancakbeyi*s, including that of *Midillü*, announcing to them his plan to wage a *gaza*. Consequently, each *sancakbeyi* had to advertize the *sipahi*s from his *sancak* to come to *Midillü* and join to other soldiers (Veinstein, "Les préparatifs," 47–48). Other example can be found during the 1683–1699 war, in a *hüküm* of 1690 (Gemil, *Documente turceşti*, doc. 184).

29 *Bursa Şer'iyye Sicilleri*, A/4, 87, cf. Akgündüz, *Osmanlı Kanunnameleri*, II, 135–136.

30 *Kefere taʿifesi kılıç kerametin görmeyince müslümana akçe virmez; in-şa'-Allahu teʿala meblağ-ı mezbur gaza malı olur* (Gemil, *Documente turceşti*, doc. 102: Report of 1636).

him to fight for Allah in the holy war and obeying the sublime order [...] launched against Rákoczy-oğlu."[31]

## 2 From Communal to Individual Obligation

Even though the effort to follow the path of Allah was not one of the five basic pillars of Islam (*arkan*, sing. *rukn*), most jurists considered it a religious obligation for all Muslims.[32] Whenever Muslims enjoyed superiority over their enemies and sufficient number of soldiers partook in regular campaigns against infidels, offensive *cihad* remained only a communal obligation (*farz-ı kifaya*) of the Islamic community.[33] Thus, primary sources of Islamic law required the community to battle against its enemies, and – as al-Sulami stated – "the *Kur'an, hadis* and *icma'* are in agreement, proving to us that holy war is a communal duty when it is an offensive one."[34]

In theory, waging war against infidels should be a permanent, individual duty for the sultans, due to their status as leaders of the state and the Muslim community.[35] However, when an Islamic polity found itself in dire straits and its troops were unable to defeat the enemy or to repulse their attacks, *cihad*

31 Mehmed Halifa, *Tarih-i Gilmanı*, in *Cronici turcești II*, 195. Also, Hasan Vecihi, writing on the battle of 29 May 1660 in the vicinity of Cluj, called it *cihad* (Hasan Vecihi, *Tarih*, in *Cronici turcești II*, 184).

32 Profession of faith, prayers, donations, fasting, pilgrimage to Mecca. For details and nuances on the place of *cihad* among the religious obligations according to various denominations, see Shaybani, *Kitab al-siyar*, IV, 145–149; Laoust, *Ibn Taimiya*, 74; Sulami, "Kitab al-djihad," 214; E. Tyan, "Djihad," *EI-2*, II, 1991, 538–540; I. Goldziher, *Le dogme et le loi de l'Islam*, Paris: Librarie Paul Geuthner, 1920, 117; Morabia, *Ğihad*, 405–408; Kohlberg, "Jihad," 65; Hitti, *Arabes*, 49; Mahmassani, *Islamic Doctrine*, 17; Carra de Vaux, *Penseurs*, IV, 137; Panaite, "Djihad," I, 409–413.

33 The opinions of Ibn Hazm (d. 1064), Ibn Kudama (d. 1223), Ibrahim al-Halebi (d. 1549), in: Banna,' *Five Tracts*, 147–149; Sulami, "Kitab al-djihad," 216; Caurroy, "Législation," IV/17, 236–237; Morabia, *Ğihad*, 337; E. Tyan, "Djihad," *EI-2*, II, 1991, 538–540; L. Gardet, *Dieu et la destinée de l'homme*, Paris: Vrin, 1967, 446–447; Williams, *Islamic Civilization*, 268.

34 He invoked *Kur'an*, IX/123, IV/95 (Sulami, "Kitab al-djihad," 217). Children, women, cripples, demented people, old men, slaves, and even debtors, poors and best jurists [meaning of this phrase is unclear] were generally excepted from attending the sacred expeditions (al-Hilli, cf. Williams, *Islamic Civilization*, 268; Peters, *Islam*, 17).

35 Mawerdi, *Le droit de califat*, 145–146; E. Tyan, "Djihad," *EI-2*, II, 1991, 538–540; Hitti, *Arabes*, 49; Ducas, *Istoria*, III/4, XXIV/5; Chalcocondil, *Expuneri*, 77; Mehmed pașa, *Tarih*, in *Osmanlı Tarihleri*, I, 348; Guboglu, "Izvoare turco-persane," 139.

became an individual obligation (*farz-ı 'ayn*), like prayer, for any Muslim.[36] This idea was strongly emphasized in a propagandistic manner during the Crusades.[37]

Between the fourteenth and sixteenth centuries there was no apparent need to legitimize the holy war in the eyes of the Muslim community by means of juridical opinions (*fetvas*).[38] However, the situation changed significantly in the second half of the sixteenth century, when rampant absenteeism from imperial campaigns (*sefer-i hümayun*)[39] caused Ottoman sultans to employ both their administrative power and their prerogative to declare *cihad* an individual obligation to reinforce discipline and punish deserters. Facing a lukewarm response to their calls for *cihad*, the authorities began to emphasize juridical and religious arguments in support of wars against infidels. *Şeyh ül-Islams* were called upon to provide *fetvas* against those who eluded the call-up, and their opinions were often included in imperial orders. For instance, a register of *sipahis* of Rumeli from 1571–1573, opens with a *fetva* by Ebussuud Efendi regarding those who avoided *gaza* and martyrdom.[40] The Porte employed similar tactics during its conflicts with Russia in the eighteenth century, "the campaigns against infidels" being legitimized by "illustrious *fetvas*" inserted in orders of mobilization.[41]

---

36 Moreover, in these circumstances, to attend to defensive war became a duty for slaves, women, children, cripples or, even, non-Muslim subjects (Halebi, *Mülteka*, cf. Banna,' *Five Tracts*, 147–148; Sulami, "Kitab al-djihad," 216 (who quoted more precedent jurists, such as al-Shafi'i, al-Ghazali etc.); Averroes, *Jihad*, 10–11; Loust, *Ibn Batta*, LXXXIII; Caurroy, "Législation," IV/17, 240–241; E. Tyan, "Djihad," *EI-2*, II, 1991, 538–540; Morabia, *Ǧihad*, 338).

37 For instance Ali b. Tahir al-Sulami (d. 1106), who wrote *Kitab al-djihad* during the first Crusade, 1096–1099 (E. Sivan, "La genèse de la contre-croisade: un traité damasquin du début du XII-e siècle," *JA*, CCLIV, 2, 1966, 214–222; al-Sulami's text was recently published in a critical edition: Niall Christies, *The Book of the Jihad of 'Ali ibn Tahir al-Sulami (d. 1106)*, Text, translation and commentary, Aldershot: Ashgate, 2015).

38 For Káldy-Nagy, one piece of evidence is the absence of any declaration of *cihad* from the orders of mobilization for the war against the Habsburgs of autumn 1565 (Káldy-Nagy, "Holy War," 471–472).

39 Initially, the participants on expeditions were registered in so-called "registers of inspections and stipends" (*yoklama ve mevacib defterleri*) (Káldy-Nagy, "Holy War," 472). The negative attitude of certain *sipahis* (with *timars*) during the war with Iran (1603–1612) was presented by the grand vizier Bosnalı Lala Mehmed paşa (1604–1606) to Ahmed I in a *telhis* (Orhonlu, *Telhisler*, doc. 109; Maxim, CTO, doc. 22). The situation during the war of 1683–1699 was described by the French ambassador Castagnères, in a letter of 31 January 1692 (Hurmuzaki, *Documente*, XVI, doc. DCXII).

40 979–980 AH (BOA, *Bab-ı Asafi, Nişanci (Tahvil) Kalemi*, Defter 1066).

41 "The illustrious *fetva* or consultation issued by the *müfti*" was included in the order of 20 November 1712 to viziers, paşas and beys, where the sultan shew the causes of the war with Russia and ordered the mobilization of troops in the encampment of Edirne

At particularly dire moments, an extreme solution was to declare participation in the holy campaign an individual duty of all Muslims. This was the case during the 1683–1699 war, when – after the failure of the Second Siege of Vienna – the conflict with the Christian coalition was proclaimed a defensive holy war waged "to guard the Law of Muhammad."[42] Thus, in 1690, a *hüküm* of Süleyman II, intended to rally the troops from the *sancak*s of Ochakov (*Özü*) and Dobruja (Dobruca), emphasized that the coming of the holy war was an individual obligation (*farz-ı 'ayn*):

> It is the holy individual duty (*farz-ı 'ayn olub*) of each Muslim to plentifully support the holy campaign and holy war (*gaza ü-cihad*) which will be launched soon for removing the damages made by the damned Hungarian who intends to attack the Islamic territories.[43]

The understanding of the defensive *cihad* as an individual obligation of all capable Muslims remained until the very end of the empire's existence. Arguably the most famous *fetva*s on the topic, issued in November 1914 by then-incumbent *şeyh ül-Islam* Esad Efendi, declared the Ottomans' entry into the war a defensive *cihad*, in which every Muslim should take part.[44]

## 3 Booty as Stimulus

Since pillage and plunder constituted the main rationale of pre-Islamic *razzia*s, the Prophet Muhammad could not ignore them and, consequently, justified

(Hurmuzaki, *Documente*, VI, doc. LXVIII). Also, *fetva*s can be found in two *hüküm*s sent to the Moldavian voivode, Alexandru Ipsilanti, on 3 *Zilkade* 1201/17 August 1787 (Mehmet, *Documente turcești*, II, doc. 134, 135). Before the Ottoman–Russian war of 1828–1829, a *hatt-ı şerif*, called a "proclamation" by the French consul in Bucharest, was read in the mosques from the provinces south of the Danube river (Hurmuzaki, *Documente*, XVII, doc. LIV: Hugot's letter to Laferronnays of 6 February 1828, in which was underlined actually the missing of any ardor for war).

42 Hurmuzaki, *Documente*, XVI, doc. DCXII.

43 In the order of *evahir-i Cemazi ül-ahir* 1101/22–31 March 1690, sent to the *beylerbeyi* of Ochakov (Özü)) and local officials (*kadı, kethüdayeri, yeniçeri, serdarı* etc.) from Silistre, Babadağı, Karasu, Isakçı, Tulçi etc., which is a part of a general call-up (*asker ihracı fermanı*) to imperial expedition (*sefer-i hümayun*) (Gemil, *Documente turcești*, doc. 184). A copy was also sent to Morea. According to the French ambassador, considering "*l'expérience du mauvais ordre*," in 1692 the imperial orders for calling-up were not observed (Hurmuzaki, *Documente*, XVI, doc. DCXII).

44 Pakalin, *Sözlük*, I, 291; Uzunçarşılı, *Ilmiye*, 203; Maxim, *CTO*, doc. 34.

and regulated their status in both *Kur'an* and *sünnet*.[45] Accordingly, booty became a major topic of numerous juridical treatises, the most important work being al-Shaybani's *Kitab al-siyar al-kabir*.[46] Thus, any attempt to sketch the doctrine of *cihad* makes it necessary to address rules regulating the status and division of its material proceeds.[47]

Plundering enemy territory and taking captives was an essential part of the approach to war shared by the Ottomans and their Islamic predecessors.[48] It is, therefore, unsurprising that depictions of Ottoman *gaza*s in the Balkans, found in fifteenth-century Byzantine and Ottoman chronicles, are invariably associated with pillage and capture of infidels.[49]

The right to plunder and seize enemies' property was a constant feature of medieval wars and rebellions. The Prophet himself, the first four Caliphs, and – subsequently – Muslim jurists, discussed the legitimacy of plunder and enslavement, often expressing conflicting opinions.[50] According to the Hanafi tradition, a commander had the right to plunder enemy territory if it fit his military and political interests and allowed him to the defeat the enemy and force infidels to seek peace.[51]

In the fourteenth and fifteenth centuries, Wallachia and Moldavia were both considered territories of the House of Infidels or the House of War, and as such could be plundered under Islamic law, and their inhabitants enslaved.

---

45 *Kur'an* VIII, al-Anfal (Spoils of War), appeared after the battle of Badr in 2 AH/624: "But now enjoy what ye took in war, lawful and good: but fear Allah: for Allah is All-forgiving, Most Merciful" (*Kur'an* VIII, 69). See also Turpin, *Histoire de l'Alcoran*, I, 241; Morabia, *Ğihad*, 108.

46 Of 218 chapters, about 100 were dedicated to booty and prisoners (Shaybani, *Kitab al-siyar*, I, 418–471; II, 7–531; III, 5–233, 334–361, 398–401. Also see Yahya bin Adam, *Kitab*, 23–26 (18 "traditions" on booty); Halebi, *Mülteka*, II, 571–585.

47 Chaygan, *Essai*, 127–142; Khadduri, *War and Peace*, 118–132.

48 In Umayyad Spain summer expeditions were organized (*sa'ifa*) for taking captives (Levi-Provençal, *L'Espagne musulmane*, III, 104–105; Wenner, "Arab/Muslim," 62). Sums of money from the caliphal treasury were also paid to warriors (P. M. Holt, A. K. S. Lambton and B. Lewis, eds. *The Cambridge History of Islam. Vol. 2: Further Lands. Islamic Society and Civilisation*, Cambridge: Cambridge University Press, 1970, II, 825).

49 Chalcocondil, *Expuneri*, 29, 30, 38, 54; Ducas, *Istoria*, 34; Tursun bey, *Tarih*, passim; Aşıkpaşazade, *Tevarih*, in *Cronici turcești I*, 87, 97; Inalcık, "Emergence," 75; Káldy-Nagy, "Holy War," 472. For the seventeenth century, see Pál Fodor, "Ungarn und Wien in der osmanischen Eroberungsideologie (im Spiegel der Târîh-i Beç krâlı – 17. Jahrhundert)." *JTS* 13, (1989): 81–98.

50 According to the Prophet, Abu Bakr, al-Awzai and Ibn Hazm's sayings, such seizure was generally forbidden (Morabia, *Ğihad*, 364–365, 466–467; Lewis, *Islam*, I, 212).

51 Muslim warriors might destroy goods which could not be carried in the Abode of Islam and would enforce the enemy (Abu Yusuf, *Kitab*, 301, 308; Morabia, *Ğihad*, 366).

Fierce struggles between multiple claimants to the Wallachian throne exposed the principality to continuous raids by *akıncı* troops stationed on the southern bank of the Danube; such incursions took place every time an Ottoman-leaning ruler was ousted by a rival with Hungarian support. Sultans frequently ordered such raids north of the river, using them as a check on Wallachian princes. One of them, Alexandru I Aldea (1431–1436) wrote to the city of Brașov:

> And you shall thus know that the Turks have invaded all the fords of the Danube and are heading for our country to plunder and destroy everything.[52]

In 1435, to punish Vlad the Evil who had previously attacked Silistre, Murad II gave orders to his subject Firuzbeyoğlu Mehmed bey, that

> any time he on any occasion would have to cross [the Danube] with the *gazi*s and attack, destroy and set fire to his country, and enslave all the men, as well as women, he found on his way.[53]

In the late fifteenth century, Mihaloğlu Ali bey led numerous holy campaigns (*gazavat*) with his *gazi*s to fight on the path of Allah against the infidels in campaigns that involved pillaging the territories to the east of the Danube.[54]

On the other hand, in the course of Ottoman–Wallachian conflicts during the late fourteenth and fifteenth century, the Wallachian rulers frequently crossed the Danube to lay waste to the territories under Ottoman rule. In 1427, Prince Dan II, after ousting his rival, Radu II Praznaglava, prepared to launch – with Hungarian support – a predatory raid against Ottoman lands, "if the Danube freezes and they will be able to [cross]." Once these conditions were satisfied, the Sigismund of Luxembourg advised the Christian warriors

> not to stop destroying the Turkish country, burning it to the ground and laying waste to it; advancing towards the seashore, they will have to do all the damage they can to those wicked Turks…[55]

Taking booty provided a universal stimulus for war. In Arab and Ottoman sources, commanders of campaigns against the lands of infidels always

---

52 Tocilescu, *534 documente*, doc. 25 (no date).

53 Aşıkpaşazade, *Tevarih*, in *Cronici turcești* I, 86.

54 Suzi Çelebi, *Gazavatname-yi Mihaloğlu Ali bey*, in *Cronici turcești* I, 145.

55 Stephen Rozgony defined Turks as *inimicorum natis* in his letter (DRH, D, I, doc. 153).

invoked booty and fiefs (*timar, dirlik*)[56] as crucial incentives for their troops. The promise of rich rewards attracted fighters and boosted their morale. In this respect, Dimitrie Cantemir wrote:

> It is customary with the *Turkish* Emperors to promise their Soldiers all the Goods of the Enemy unless the City is taken by surrender, the Walls only and the Government of it reserved to Themselves. It is not to be expressed what fire this gives to Men naturally greedy for Plunder and Rapine.[57]

In the *hüküm* of 1484, occasioned by the campaign waged to conquer the fortresses of Kili and Akkerman, Bayezid II promised the participants the pleasures of robbery and of fiefs (*timar*):

> Therefore, each of you is due to call and announce to everyone in the territories under your jurisdiction, so that those who have participated in the *gaza* and *cihad* from generation to generation, as well as the plunderers and those who live on the sword [participating in campaigns] and those who wish to get a *timar* as a result of their [participation] in the campaign shall come fully armed and equipped for war.[And] joining me in this blessed campaign (*mübarek gaza*), they shall be pleased and satisfied with the advantages of this *gaza* and *cihad* and they shall obtain booty.[58]

Later, in 1598, Mehmed III promised that he would repay by fiefs all who were attending the next campaign against the Wallachian rebel prince, Michael the Brave, in a *hüküm* issued to mobilize troops from the *sancak* of Silistre.[59]

56 For details on the Byzantine *pronoia*, Arab *ikta* and Ottoman *timar*, see: Cl. Cahen, "Contribution à l'histoire de *l'iqta*," *Annales*, VIII, 1953, 25–52; Brezeanu, *Imp. bizantin*, 228–229; Belin, "Étude," 113–152: Ch. IX. *Concessions souveraines. Bénéfices. Constitutions des anciens bénéfices militaires en Turquie*; M. Belin, "Du régime des fiefs militaires dans l'islamisme et principalement en Turquie," *JA*, 6e série, 15, 1870, 187–301; H. Inalcık, "Timariotes chrétiens en Albanie au XVe siècle d'aprés un régistre de *timar* ottoman," *MOS*, 4, 1951, 118–138; V. P. Mutafcieva, A. Dimitrov, *Sur l'état du système des timar des XVI-XVIII siècle*, Sofia, 1968; N. Beldiceanu, *Le Timar dans l'Etat Ottoman* (*début du XIVe – XVIe siècles*), Wiesbaden: Otto Harrossowitz, 1980; M. M. Alexandrescu-Dersca Bulgaru, "Date noi despre transmiterea timarului în Imperiul otoman," *CLSO*, 1, 1990, 37–68.

57 Cantemir, *Othman History*, 73, n. 6.

58 In 889 AH (*Bursa Şer'iyye Sicilleri*, A/4, 87, cf. Akgündüz, *Osmanlı Kanunameleri*, II, 135–136: *suret-i hükm-ü padişah*); Beldiceanu "La campagne ottomane de 1484," 66–77.

59 *Mihai. Documente*, I, doc. 75: *hizmetlerine göre dirlik ile ber-murad kılınurlar.*

According to Islamic law, only those goods taken from the enemy during a holy war – the unique *bellum justum* in Islam – were considered lawful booty. Consequently, the belongings plundered, and persons enslaved without the sultan's authorization, could not be considered lawful spoils of war. Relying on Ebussuud's juridical opinions, Colin Imber emphasized that in Hanafi theory the sultan exercises exclusive authority with regard to the spoils of war.[60]

In juridical texts, booty appears under two names, *ganimet* and *fey'*. The former refers to all spoils of war taken by force during battles, thus constituting the "personal booty," divided among soldiers partaking in the campaign. In contrast, *fey'* refers to those goods given willingly by the enemy infidels as ransom for peace; these included lands and taxes (*harac* and *cizye*).[61]

Where and how was the booty of war divided? According to Ibrahim al-Halebi, the spoils of war became lawful property of the Muslims warriors only after their conveyance to the Abode of Islam.[62] The first step in this process was the partition of booty into five parts. One fifth was originally earmarked for the Prophet and his family, and, in the later period, assigned to the Muslim sovereign; the remaining spoils were divided between warriors as a reward for their victory.[63]

In Ottoman practice one can find more rules of *şeriʿat*, but the sultans and other commanders had the right to provide soldiers with larger or smaller shares, depending on their merit. Sources prove that the sultan customarily claimed "the fifth" or "the usual part" of the booty (called *pencik*, *mal-ı hums* or *hums-i şerʿi*)[64] to which he was entitled. In practice, its collection was executed

60 Imber, *Ebu's-su'ud*, 84–89.

61 Halebi, *Mülteka*, Vol. 2, 571–585; D'Ohsson, *Tableau*, V, 76–85; Shaybani, *Kitab al-siyar*, I, 418–428; Belin, "Étude," 13–14; Yahya bin Adam, *Kitab*, 23; Mawerdi, *Ahkam*, ed. Fagnan, 267; Laoust, *Ibn Batta*, 66, n. 1, 2; Morabia, *Ğihad*, 329; *Redhouse*, 384, 370; F. Lokkegaard, "Ghanima," *EI-2*, II, 1028–1030. Al-Hilli (d. 1278) named gold, silver, military equipment as examples of *fey'* (Williams, *Islamic Civilization*, 271).

62 Halebi, *Mülteka*, Vol. 2, 571–585 (*Ganimetler ve ganimetlerin taksimi; Ganimetler nasıl bölüşülür*); D'Ohsson, *Tableau*, V, 77. See also Abu Yusuf, *Kitab*, 303; *Shaybani's Siyar*, 52. The Shafi'is and other jurists affirmed that it was lawful to divide booty in Abode of War, too (Braymann, *Arab Concepts*, 164; *Shaybani's Siyar*, 52; Williams, *Islamic Civilization*, 267).

63 For details on the criteria and methods of allocation, see: Shaybani, *Kitab al-siyar*, II, 164–203, 307–414; Abu Yusuf, *Kitab*, 27–33, 302–306; D'Ohsson, *Tableau*, V, 79–85; Savary, *Lois morales*, 238–241; Sourdel, *Islamul clasic*, I, 261; Williams, *Islamic Civilisation*, 267. For peculiarities in Umayyad Spain: Lévi-Provençal, *L'Espagne musulmane*, III, 105.

64 *Pencik* came from the Persian *pence* (*pençe*). It referred to the tax collected on captives and, also, the document issued by custom authorities to the slave's owner after its paying. In Arabic, *hums* means "the fifth" (*Redhouse*, 493, 925; I. Beldiceanu-Steinherr, "En marge d'un acte concernant le *pengyek* et les *aqıngı*," *REI*, XXXVII, 1, 1969, 21–47; Naima, *Tarih*, in *Cronici turcești III*, 17; Critobul, *Mehmed II*, 158 (I, 73/1).

by special officials following the orders of military commanders.[65] Following his campaign against Wallachia in 1391, Firuz bey assumed the task of choosing "the fifth part (*hums*) for sultan" from the spoils of war, taken from "the enemies of the Islamic faith."[66] As Kritobulos of Imbros recorded, one of the first measures undertaken by Mehmed II following the conquest of Constantinople was "taking for himself the usual part of [the booty]."[67]

To collect the fifth on crossing the Danube also became a customary practice. After the Moldavian campaign in 1485, Malkoçoğlu Bali bey took the *pencik* "on the side of Danube."[68] Later, in 1497, coming back from the campaign against Poland, he gathered and kept the fifth part of spoils for Bayezid II in Kili, the fortress on the Danube at the border of the Islamic territories.[69]

A significant example can be seen during the retreat of the Ottoman army in October 1595, following the campaign intended to punish the Wallachian voivode Michael the Brave. According to an established tradition, upon crossing the Danube in Giurgiu, the fifth part of the booty and captives (*mal-ı hums*) of each soldier was to be collected in *akçes*. According to Mustafa Naima's rendition of the story this operation was called off only due to the fear of Wallachian and Hungarian armies approaching the positions of retreating Ottoman troops.[70] In difficult circumstances, the sultans could promise – even before the campaign began – to renounce their part of the spoils in order to encourage more soldiers to join. In 1598, Mehmed III ordered Ahmed paşa, the commander of Silistre, to launch a new attack against Michael the Brave, specifying that "the spoils taken by Islamic warriors should not be confiscated in any way; each of them is to take his own booty."[71]

65 In 1595, in Giurgiu, "emins and scribes" (Naima, *Tarih*, in *Cronici turcești III*, 17); Koca Hüseyin, *Beda'i ul-veka'i*, in *Cronici turcești I*, 464.

66 Idris Bitlisi, *Heșt Behișt*, in *Cronici turcești I*, 156.

67 Critobul, *Mehmed II*, 158 (I, 73/1).

68 Koca Hüseyin, *Beda'i ül-veka'i*, in *Cronici turcești I*, 464.

69 Sa'adeddin, *Tevarih*, in *Cronici turcești I*, 332.

70 Naima, *Tarih*, in *Cronici turcești III*, 17.

71 *Mihai.I.Documente*, doc. 75 (*ve asker-i islamın garet edüb ellerine giren doyumluklaruna bir vechile ta'arruz olunmayub herkesin ele getürduği doyumluğu alub*). In October 1595, the commander renounced "the fifth," but this decision was taken during the retreat of the Ottoman army to the South of the Danube river (Naima, *Tarih*, in *Cronici turcești III*, 17).

## 4 "Hero or Martyr"

The participants in holy war had only two alternatives, victory or death.[72] This attitude can be found in a sixteenth-century *fetva* on the topic, subsequently reproduced by Dimitrie Cantemir in his *The System of Muhammedan Religion*:

> If any Muslim – Turk, Arab or of any other kind – belonging to those called *sunni*, which means right-believers, in a just war, that is a war meant to spread the [Muslim] faith, ever kills an infidel, i.e. a Christian, a Jew or an idol worshipper, that Muslim shall be *gazi*, who is a hero whose place is in paradise. If he is killed by the enemy, he shall be *şahid*, that is a martyr also inheriting heaven.

This belief was the reason why Muslims would utter, when engaging in holy war, *Ya Şehid, ya Gazi* ("Either martyr or victor"), which meant if they die, "they become Martyrs in God's sight, and if they conquer, *Gazi*."[73]

### 4.1 *Gazi*

In Islamic juridical texts, the term employed for participants in holy wars was that of *mücahid*.[74] In the Arab world, the name initially referred to all those partaking in campaigns against infidels (*gaza*); however, in the later period, *mücahid* and *gazi* became honorary titles granted only to those who had distinguished themselves in holy wars.[75]

As later chronicles indicate, with the Ottoman advancement in Europe in the fourteenth and fifteenth centuries, *gazi* warriors became a daily presence at the frontier with Christian states in the Balkans.[76] Under these circumstances,

---

72 A *hadis* says: "If you die you will become a martyr; if you kill you will become a hero of faith" (Guer, *Meurs*, II, 263; Canard, "Une lettre," 721).

73 Cantemir, *Sistemul*, 315–316, 425; Cantemir, *Othman History*, 210, n. 94. An interesting reflection regarding this particular phrase in fifteenth- and sixteenth-century Islamic Asia is provided by Ali Anooshahr, *The Ghazi Sultans and the Frontiers of Islam*, London and New York: Routledge, 2009, as it circulated both among Ottoman sources and even as far as Babur's India.

74 On the participants of holy wars, see: Khadduri, *War and Peace*, 83–93; Morabia, *Ğihad*, 342–351.

75 *Gazis* were called especially those who fought on the borders between Abode of Islam and Abode of War. On *gazi* see: Shaybani, *Kitab al-siyar*, I, 5–28; Wittek, "Turcs de Roum," 285–319; I. Mélikoff, "Ghazi," *EI-2*, II, 1043–1045; T. M. Johnstone, "Ghazw," *EI-2*, II, 1055–1056; Pakalin, *Sözlük*, I, 654.

76 Initially, holy war warriors were often led by dervishes, who played a double role, that of spiritual guides and of military commanders, often escaping the control of the sultan (Beldiceanu-Steinherr, "Selim I," 36).

reciprocal pillage and predatory raids coalesced into a mode of life, even if the causes invoked to justify them focused on spreading Islam or – on the other side of the pale – defending the Christian faith.[77] A thorough analysis of the legitimizing myths and ideals in the early history of the Ottomans was provided by Colin Imber's research into chronicles from the fourteenth to the sixteenth centuries.[78] For instance, Ahmedi (d. 1412), the first poet and moralist to give a literary formulation of Ottoman claims, ignored any reference to the tribal origin tradition of Turks[79] and constructed a genuine Ottoman ideology of holy war. As a result, in Ahmedi's rendition, the fledging Ottoman polity was cast as a *gazi* kingdom *par excellence*. Ahmedi's evocative definition of *gazi* survived throughout the centuries:

> A *gazi* is one who is God's carpet-sweeper, who cleanses the earth of the filth of polytheism. Do not imagine that one who is martyred in the path of God is dead. No, that blessed martyr is alive.[80]

Ahmedi's view, who wrote the first comprehensive Ottoman chronicle, was taken over by the chroniclers of the second half of the fifteenth century. For instance, in Oruc bin Adil's view, it was natural for these "frontier beys" (*uc beyleri*), as leaders of the robbing and enslaving *razzia*s against *dar al-harb*, to wash "their hands in the infidels' blood."[81]

The Ottoman chronicles abound in the idea that *gazi*s were primarily those destined to fight against infidels. From the fifteenth through the seventeenth

77 Between the eleventh and thirteenth centuries, the Turks coming from the Central Asia were pushed to the borders (in Turkish *uc*) of the Byzantine Empire to fight with Christians. On the other side, the Byzantine border troops were called *akritai* and played the same role. On life from within the Muslim–Byzantine borders, see A. Pertusi, "Tra storia e leggenda: *akrítai* e *ghazi* sulla frontiera orientale de Bisanzio," in *XIVe Congrés International des Etudes Byzantines. 6–12 setembre 1971, Rapports II*, 27–70; I. Mélikoff, "Ghazi," *EI*-2, II, 1043–1045.

78 Colin Imber, "Paul Wittek's "De la défaite d'Ankara à la prise de Constantinople." *OA-JOS*, V, 1986, 65–79; C. Imber, "The Ottoman Dynastic Myth," *Turcica*, XIX, 1987, 7–28; Imber, *Ottoman Empire*, 65–81; C. Imber, "Ideals and legitimation in early Ottoman history," in Kunt, Metin and Christine Woodhead (eds). *Süleyman the Magnificent and His Age. The Ottoman Empire in the Early Modern World*, London, New York: Routledge, 1995, 138–153.

79 This tradition was established later, during Murad II's reign (1421–1451) (Wittek, "Turcs de Roum," 304; Pitcher, *Ottoman Empire*, 36).

80 There are more translations of that excerpt. I used the last one, from Imber's "Ideals," 139. See also Wittek, "Turcs de Roum," 304; N. S. Banarlı, "Ahmedi ve Dasitan-i tevarih-i müluk-i Al-'Osman," *TM*, 6, 1936–9, 111–135; Ahmedi, *Iskender-name*, ed. Ismail Ünver, Ankara: TTK Basımevi 1983; Pál Fodor, "Ahmedî's Dâsitân as a Source of Early Ottoman History." *AOH* XXXVIII, (1–2), (1984): 41–54.

81 Oruc bin Adil, *Tevarih*, in *Cronici turcești I*, 53.

centuries, the name *gazi* was given to all the participants in "holy campaigns" (*gazavat*) because the conflicts between the Ottoman Empire and European states constituted, from both a juridical and religious point of view, an integral part of the former's holy war (*cihad*).[82] Usually, the term "*gazi*" applied to warriors active in the frontier zone with Christian polities, such as garrison troops on the border. Even at a later stage, during the prolonged Ottoman–Habsburg wars of 1593–1606 and 1683–1699, the soldiers were considered "boundary *gazis*" by the chroniclers Katib Çelebi[83] and Silahdar Fındıklılı Mehmed Ağa.[84]

Although the title of *gazi* had been used in the Muslim–Turkish world in earlier periods,[85] it was the Ottomans that established and solidified the image of sultans as leaders of Islam in *cihad*, ubiquitous in both documentary and narrative sources.[86] By analyzing several fifteenth- and sixteenth-century

---

82 The Ottoman and Tartar warriors in the 1593–1606 war with Habsburgs were called the "*gazis* of Islam" by Katib Çelebi (Katip Çelebi, *Fezleke-i Tarih*, in *Cronici turcești II*, 52–55).

83 Katib Çelebi wrote about the *gazis* of Solnoc in 1598 (Katib Çelebi, *Fezleke-i Tarih*, in *Cronici turcești II*, 55; also, Naima, *Tarih*, in *Cronici turcești I*, 29). Also, Katip Çelebi wrote of the *gazis* of the Bender province called by the *bey* of Bender, Ahmed paşa, to fight in 1595 with the Moldavian voivode, Ștefan Răzvan (Katib Çelebi, *Fezleke-i Tarih*, in *Cronici turcești II*, 35). In a 1572 document it is about the *gazis* from the *sancak* of Pancota, the *beylerbeyilik* of Temeşvar (Mehmet, *Documente turcești*, I, doc. 108). In a 1635 document it is about the *gazis* of Lipova (*Lipova gazileri*) (Gemil, *Documente turcești*, doc. 100).

84 Their activity was encouraged by the sultan's visit to Temeşvar in September 1695 (Silahdar, *Nusretname*, in *Cronici turcești II*, 431). Silahdar also recorded that in 1683, Kör Hüseyin paşa had six thousand *gazis* to conquer the Pojon fortress (Silahdar, *Tarih*, in *Cronici turcești II*, 360; see, also, 299). In 1690, Süleyman II called his soldiers who were fighting against Habsburgs "my slaves dedicated to sacred campaigns" (*gazavat kullarım*) (Gemil, *Documente turcești*, doc. 186).

85 Herbelot de Malainville, *Bibliotèque Orientale ou Dictionnaire Universel, contenant généralment tout ce qui regarde la connaissance des peuples de l'Orient*, Maastricht, DCCLXXVI (1776), 338. For pre-Ottoman cases, e.g. Ghaznavids, Danișmend princes, Seljukid sultans, see *The Cambridge History of Iran*, edited by J. A. Boyle, Cambridge: Cambridge University Press, 1968, IV, 170 and V, 13; Wittek, "Turcs de Roum," 306–308; Turan, "Les souverains seldjoukides," 85). In Arabic, Islam used several titles for Muslim rulers who led holy wars: "defenders of the faith" (*nasır al-din*), "fighter for the faith on Allah's way" (*al-mujahid fi sebil-i Rabb al-'alamin*) (H. Basset et E. Lévi-Provençal, "Chella: une nécropole mérinide," *Hesperis*, 1–2, 1922, 1–93). Other cases are recorded in Lewis, *Islam*, II, 16.

86 For details concerning the sultans' titles, and the place of the title *gazi*, see Suha Umur (Suha Umur, *Osmanlı Padişahı Tuğraları*, Istanbul: Cem Yayınevi, 1980, passim). He also published the *fetvas* by which this title was granted to Abdülhamid II in 1877 and Mehmed V in 1915 (Umur, *Tuğraları*, 48–51). Here, I also address Anooshahr's argument, which traces the initial model of *gazi* rulers to a tradition originating from the Ghaznavids and Utbis *Yamani*. He also argues that the model of a *gazi* ruler in the Ottoman context crystallized in the context of Bayezid I–Timur confrontation. While the argument is open to criticism, I think it also has the potential to address why Bayezid was not always called a *gazi* by the

chronicles, one comes to realize that the most annalists ascribed the title *gazi* to all Ottoman rulers, from Osman I to Bayezid II.[87]

In the second part of the seventeenth century, this title was also granted to those grand viziers from the Köprülü family, who practically became commanders of the Ottoman army against Christian states.[88]

A reflection of *gaza* as a source of legitimacy was the active promotion of the ruler's image as primarily that of a military leader preoccupied with campaigning and conquest. A literary expression of this trend was the proliferation of the *gazavatname* genre,[89] with 350 manuscripts of this type composed between 1444 and 1853.[90] Some of them were devoted to a single campaign led by sultans, grand viziers or governors-general,[91] while others addressed broader topics.[92]

---

chroniclers Ahmedi and Nişanci Mehmed paşa (Ali Anooshahr, *The Ghazi Sultans and the Frontiers of Islam*, London and New York: Routledge, 2009).

87 Here are various combination of imperial titles: *Osman Gazi* (*Sultan Osman Gazi*); *Gazi Orhan Beg, Orhan Beg Gazi, Orhan Gazi, Sultan Orhan Gazi; Murad Beg Gazinin Padişahlığı, Gazi Murad, Sultan Murad Hünkar Gazi, Hudavendigar Gazi, Hünkar Gazi, Murad Han Gazi, Gazi Sultan, Sultan Murad Gazi, Sultan Murad Han Gazi; Bayezid Beg, Gaziler Sultan Yıldırım Bayezid Beg, Bayezid Hünkar, Gazi Sultan, Gazi Şah, Bayezid Han Gazi, Sultan Bayezid, Sultan Yıldırım Bayezid Han Gazi, Sultan Bayezid Han Gazi; Mehmed Gazi, Sultan Mehmed Han, Çelebi Sultan Mehmed Han Gazi; Sultan Murad Han Gazi, Sultan Murad, Gazi Sultan Murad Han, Sultan Mehmed Han, Ikinci Sultan Murad Han Gazi; Sultan Mehmed Han, Sultan Mehmed Han Gazi, Bayezid Han Gazi, Sultan Bayezid Han, Sultan Bayezid Han Gazi* (Ahmedi, Nişanci Mehmed paşa, Şükrullah, Aşıkpaşazade, Bayatlı Mahmud Oğlu Hasan and Mehmed Neşri, in *Osmanlı Tarihleri*, I, passim). Even Mehmed Neşri wrote on *Ertoğrul Gazi* (Neşri, *Tarih*, ed. Unat, Köymen, I, 24–26).

88 Mehmed IV's travel to Hungary in 1683 had as its object the granting of a *kaftan* and the Prophet's banner to the grand vizier Kara Mustafa paşa. According to P. Coles, this was an official investiture with the quality of "official leader of Islam in the holy war against Christianity" (Coles, *Ottoman Impact*, 36).

89 Woodhead, "Perspectives on Süleyman," 173.

90 Levend, *Gazavatnameler*, 15–177.

91 Tacizade Ca'fer Çelebi (d. 1514), "Mahruse-i Istanbul Fetih-namesi." *TOEM*, 20–21, Istanbul, 1331 AH/1913; Nasuh Matrakçi, *Fetihname-yi Kara-Boğdan*, in *Cronici turceşti I*, 221–232; A. Decei, "Un Fetih-name-i Kara-Boğdan (1538) de Nasuh Matrakçi," in *Fuad Köprülü Armağanı*, Istanbul: Osman Yalçin Matbaası, 1953, 113–124; *II. Osman adına yazılmış Zafername*, ed. Yaşar Yücel, Ankara: Ankara Üniversitesi Dil ve Tarih-Coğrafya Fakültesi Yayınları, 1983.

92 H. Inalcık, *Fatih Devri üzerinde tetkikler ve vesikalar*, I, Ankara: TTK Basımevi, 1954 (2. Baskı 1987), 185–225; *Gazavat-i Sultan Murad bin Mehmed Han. Izladi ve Varna savaşları (1443–1444) üzerine Anonim Gazavatname*, ed. H. Inalcık, M. Oguz, Ankara: TTK Basımevi 1978; Kıvamı, *Fetihname-i Sultan Mehmed*, ed. F. Babinger, Istanbul: Maarif Basımevi, 1955. See also *Mihaloğlu Ali Bey'in Gazavatnamesi*, in Levend, *Gazavatnameler*, 179–358.

### 4.2 *Martyrdom*

Apart from taking booty, martyrdom (*şehadet*) was essential to the whole doctrine of *cihad* and occupied a special place in treatises of Islamic law.[93] The term of "martyrs" (*şehids*) generally pertained to those Muslim warriors killed on the path of Allah.[94] However, its meaning was wider than just that of warriors who perished while waging war. According to Dimitrie Cantemir, there were seven steps of martyrdom in Islam, broadly divided between military martyrs (Muslim who killed on battlefields, either on sea or on land) and civil martyrs (victims of rebels, brigands, and natural calamities).[95] We encounter the same classification system in Ignace Mouradgea d'Ohsson, who extrapolated from al-Halebi's work.[96]

According to juridical texts, martyrdom constituted one of the reasons for Ottomans to engage in holy war.[97] Its appeal becomes intelligible when we take into account the idea of predestination in the Muslim world.[98] While booty constituted material compensation for the martial effort, the prospect of martyrdom was presented as a spiritual reward for holy war combatants, a point frequently reinforced in sultanic orders. In a *hükum* from mid-February 1770, in the midst of the conflict with the Russian Empire, Mustafa III promised that

> Those who make [an] effort to and attend [to] holy war for the true faith are honoured in both this world and the afterlife.[99]

---

93 Shaybani, *Kitab al-siyar*, I, 158–166. On martyrdom in Islam, see J. Wensinck, *The Oriental Doctrine of the Martyrs*, Amsterdam: Koninklijke Akademie van Wetenschappen, 1921; Abdul-Sattar al-Sayyid, "The Martyr in Islam," in *The Sixth Conference of the Academy of Islamic Research*, Cairo: General Organisation for Government Printing Offices, 1391 AH/1971, 231–251; Qasim Ghalib, "The Martyr in Islam," in *The Sixth Conference*, 251–301.

94 "And say not of those who are slain in the way of Allah: «They are dead». Nay, they are living, though ye perceive (it) not" (*Kur'an* II, 154); "And if ye are slain, or die, in the way of Allah, forgiveness and mercy from Allah are far better than all they could amass." (*Kur'an* III, 157). Ibrahim al-Halebi defined martyrs as those Muslims who had unnaturally received their death (cf. D'Ohsson, *Tableau*, II, 319).

95 Cantemir, *Sistemul*, 314–317.

96 D'Ohsson, *Tableau*, II, 319–324. For some "traditions" and juridical opinions on martyrs, see Lewis, *Islam*, I, 210–211; Williams, *Islamic Civilisation*, 32 (Ibn Hanbal's opinion).

97 Sulami, "Kitab al-djihad," 216; Cantemir, *Sistemul*, 314–317.

98 An eighteenth-century European scholar considered that this mentality influenced Ottoman conquests (Guer, *Moeurs*, II, 263).

99 *Din-i mübin içün gayret ve gaza idenlerin iki cihanda yüzleri akdır* (Veliman, *Documente turcești*, doc. 168).

The Ottoman chroniclers constantly insisted on the tight connection between *cihad/gaza* and martyrdom. Thus, when war against the infidels broke out, one of the purposes declared by the combatants was: "to sacrifice ourselves in celebration of the holy campaign."[100] Therefore, in the moment of death, Muslim warriors should utter on the battlefield the following words: "our aim is the holy war" (*niyyet-i gaza*).[101] As for the champions of the Islamic faith during the holy campaigns, their wounds testified to the *gazis*' heroic accomplishments and their triumph of Islam, as their radiance and musk perfume would embellish the Resurrection Day.[102] Referring to János Hunyadi's 1443 campaign to the southern bank of the Danube, Idris Bitlisi marked – while describing the Ottoman defeat at *Izladi* – the role of the wounds as a "testimony" of obtaining martyrdom:

> most of heroes died like martyrs of the holy law and, according to the custom of the ruthless war, they endured the pains of their wounds.[103]

Given that all Ottoman campaigns north of the Danube – either led by the sultan or one of the officials – were considered "holy campaigns" (*gazavat*), the sources universally considered dead soldiers martyrs. As Solakzade Mehmed wrote with the reference to the battle of Valea Albă (1476):

> But, as many *gazis* died on that heroic battlefield their blood was running just like the river Ceihun (Amu-Daria).[104]

A common thread in Ottoman chronicles was to emphasize the role and place of martyrdom in the holy war, in particular to minimize the consequences of an Ottoman defeat. This was the case of Idris Bitlisi; narrating the defeats suffered by imperial troops in Wallachia in 1442–1443, he insisted on the essential difference between the Muslims who fled the battlefield ("avoided a martyr's death") and those slain by the infidels ("finding their salvation in a martyr's death"). The former "erased their names from the list of the braves," while the

100 Suzi Çelebi, *Gazavatname-yi Mihaloğlu Ali Bey*, in *Cronici turcești I*, 146.

101 During the military campaign led by Evrenosoğlu Isa bey against the fortress of Kocacuk in Albania (846 AH/1442–1443), most warriors "perished as martyrs crying «our aim is the holy war»" (*niyyet-i gaza deyü şehid oldılar*) (Aşıkpaşazade, *Tevarih*, in *Osmanlı Tarihleri*, I, 178, and also in *Crestomație turcă*, 101).

102 *Şehid* also means "evidence" (*Redhouse*, 1053–1054; D'Ohsson, *Tableau*, II, 319; Kohlberg, "Jihad," 66–67).

103 Idris Bitlisi, *Heşt Behişt*, in *Cronici turcești I*, 173.

104 Solakzade, *Tarih*, in *Cronici turcești II*, 142.

latter "mostly joined the martyrs and under the banner of the Kerbala martyrs, passed away among the eternally forgiven [peoples]."[105]

## 5 The Danube as a Gazi River

During the late fourteenth and through the sixteenth century, the Danube had its own victims that the Ottomans considered martyrs. When Kıvami reached the southern bank of the river in 1484 while accompanying Sultan Bayezid II on the campaign against Moldavia, he expressed mixed feelings of fear and admiration while crossing the river.[106] Without any doubt, many a *gazi* shared Kıvami's impressions. The author then relates a discussion about the Danube between the late Sultan Murad II (characterized as a "martyr hero") and the poet Yusuf Sinan, nicknamed Şeyhi (d. 1429):

> Şeyhi said: "The Danube river, which lies in our neighborhood, is to be preferred to the Spring of Paradise (*kevser*)."[107] In doing so, he exaggerated the Danube's beauty. The sultan Murad Han Gazi objected and asked Şeyhi: "How can the Danube river be more miraculous than the spring of Paradise?" In his answer the Şeyhi shows that the spring of heaven was meant for the *gazi*s, being conceived as compensation. But the Danube itself, in its essence, is a *gazi* river (*amma Tuna kendü... mahza gazi sudur*). Every year it beheads the thousand Turks (*on bin türkün başı*) with no swords and knifes and no bloodshed.[108]

In this way, Kıvami expanded upon the meaning of the metaphor uttered by poet Yusuf Sinan over fifty years prior. For Kıvami, who by that point had participated in three Wallachian campaigns,[109] the majestic river was "the bloody Danube" (*kanlu Tuna*), as it witnessed the death of numerous Ottoman soldiers who died either by drowning in its waters or in violent battles along its banks.[110] The association of the Danube with the martyrs' blood had become a

105 Idris Bitlisi, *Heşt Behişt*, in *Cronici turceşti I*, 171.

106 Kıvami, *Fetihname*, ed. Babinger, 306, and in *Crestomaţie turcă*, 178.

107 In Muslim tradition, *Kevser* is a river of Paradise from where believers drink. *Kevser* is the title of the *Kur'an* CVIII (*Redhouse*, 647).

108 Kıvami, *Fetihname*, ed. Babinger, 306–307.

109 *Crestomaţie turcă*, 159.

110 Muhammad's tradition claimed that a maritime warrior should receive a double compensation if he drowned (Lewis, *Islam*, I, 211).

literary topos in Ottoman chronicles. Describing the failed siege of Belgrade in 1456, Kemalpaşazade depicted it as one during which

> the Islamic warriors, struggling on the river with the infidel combatants worthy of hell, the Danube river reddened with blood at the surface.[111]

Thus, we may conclude that between the fourteenth and sixteenth centuries, the Ottomans employed the ideology of an offensive *cihad* as a way to legitimize their military push against Christian polities of Southeastern and Central Europe. As all these territories were included in the Abode of War (*dar al-harb*), the ultimate aim of the Ottoman leaders was to bring them under their authority by incorporating them into Abode of Islam (*dar al-Islam*). As the sultans' domains in Europe expanded, the *gazi*s made their presence felt along the frontier with Christendom. Thus, from the fourteenth to the late sixteenth century, the histories of Ottoman *gazi*s and that of the Danube became intimately entangled one with another, the latter becoming the "river of *gazi*s," its name evoking the images of holy war, the prospect of the spoils of war, and the promise of martyrdom.

111 Ibn Kemal, *Tevarih*, VII, ed. Turan, 126; *Cronici turcești I*, 195.

# PART 3

## *Submission and Conquest*

CHAPTER 4

# The Islamic Ottoman Law of Peace

*Pax ottomanica* is a notion that elicits strong rejection or, at best, guarded acceptance among non-Ottomanists,[1] and even students of the empire's history rarely utilize it in their works. Sometimes it was defined by comparison with other cases,[2] such as *pax romana*,[3] *pax byzantina*,[4] *pax christiana*,[5] *pax mongolica*,[6] or *pax islamica*.[7] Among the first to emphasize similarities between *pax romana, pax byzantina* and *pax ottomanica* was Nicolae Iorga, who wrote: "Romans, Byzantines, Turks mean the same thing: the same peace, the same freedom concerning small groups, the same routes established for the great trade."[8] His opinion was adopted and occasionally expanded upon by other scholars,

1 In 1981, a debate on peace in Southeastern Europe took place at Institute for South-East European Studies of the Romanian Academy (Andrei Pippidi, Tudor Teoteoi, Alex. Duţu, V. A. Georgescu, M. A. Mehmet, Sergiu Iosipescu, E. Stănescu, "Forme ale păcii în sud-estul european în secolele XIV-XVII. Dezbatere la Institutul de Studii Sud-Est Europene. 10 iunie 1981." *RdI*, 35, 1, 1982, 139–160). Certain historians exaggerated the sixteenth to seventeenth-century European view and affirmed that the concepts of peace and empire were incongruous for the Ottomans. Periods of peace would cause the demolition of empire. N. Djuvara has used the formula *pax turcica* but denies its content (Neagu M. Djuvara, *Civilisation et lois historiques. Essai d'étude comparée des civilisations*, Paris, La Haye: Mouton, 1975, 158).

2 See G. I. Brătianu, "Formules d'organisation de la paix dans l'histoire universelle. Première partie," *RHSEE*, XXII, 1945, 67–104 and "Deuxième partie," *RHSEE*, XXIII, 1946, 31–56; Raoul Manselli, R. I. Burns, Philippe Contamine, Y. Amino, "Formes et problèmes de la paix dans l'histoire. 1. Moyen Age." *In Actes XVe Congrès international des sciences historiques, Bucarest, 10–17 août 1980. Grandes thèmes et méthodologie*, Bucharest : Editura Academiei, 1980, vol I. 149–90; IV/1, 123–196; A. Pippidi, "Formules d'organisation de la paix dans l'histoire universelle par G. I. Brătianu," *AIIAI*, XXIV, 1987/2, 45–61.

3 Coleman Phillipson, *The International Law and Custom of Ancient Greece and Rome*, I–II, London: Macmillan, 1911; Maxime Lemosse, *Le régime des relations internationales dans le Haut-Empire Romain*, Paris: Librairie Sirey, 1967.

4 For Pax Byzantina, see D. Obolensky, *The Byzantine Commonwealth. Eastern Europe. 500–1453*, London: Weidenfeld and Nicolson 1971.

5 Roger Bonnaud-Delamare, "Fondement des institutions de paix au XI-e siècle," in *Mélanges d'histoire du Moyen Age dédiés à la mémoire de Louis Halphen*, Paris: Presses universitaires de France, 1951, 19–26; C. Seroux d'Agincourt, *Exposé des projets de paix perpetuelle de l'Abbé de Saint-Pierre, de Benthen et de Kent*, Paris: H. Jouve, 1905.

6 W. Kotwicz, "Les mongols, promoteurs de l'idée de paix universelle au début du XIIIe siècle," in *VII-e Congres International des Sciences Historiques*, I, Varsovie, 1933, 199–204; Ch. Lemercier-Quelquejay, *La pace mongola*, Milan: Ugo Mursia Editore, 1971.

7 Khadduri, *War and Peace*, 55–73; Morabia, *Ğihad*, 135, 314; Panaite, "Djihad," I, 713–718.

8 N. Iorga, *Ce este sud-estul european?* Bucharest: Datina Românească, 1940, 11.

 | DOI:10.1163/9789004411104_005

most of them Ottomanists, who promoted the concept of the *pax ottomanica* system.[9]

Considering the permanent state of war between Christendom and Islam that dominated the premodern period, scholars were looking for a solution by which a long-term peace between the two civilizations could be achieved. Religious peace was habitually considered an efficient method but statesmen and theologians perceived it most frequently in a confessionally exclusive manner, as either a *pax christiana* or a *pax islamica*, with few of them promoting a community of faith.[10] The Ottoman religious attitude and behavior towards non-Muslims has long been subject to historians' assessment, producing a variety of opinions ranging from an overstatement of open-mindedness to indictments of intolerance. Given that religious toleration – though not as it is understood today – applied to Christians and Jews (either as subjects or foreigners) in the Ottoman Empire in the fifteenth and sixteenth centuries corresponded to intolerance and repression throughout Western Europe, many historians agreed to characterize the concept *pax ottomanica* primarily as a "religious peace."[11]

*Pax ottomanica* can be also seen as an "imperial peace." The concept of *imperium unicum*, or *imperium mundi*, preceded the modern notion of statehood in medieval Europe and Asia, both in Islam and in Christendom. The early Islamic period saw the development of the theory of a monistic caliphate as a universal polity, bound by one law and governed by one ruler. In fact, the classical doctrine of Islam leaned heavily on this concept that would later be adopted by the Ottomans. There were no territorial limits on the sultan's sovereignty, and no other ruler could aspire to hierarchical parity with the caliph. Within the internal realm, the concept implied order and unity, peace and justice. From this perspective, the ultimate goal of Islam was to subordinate the

9 Gorovei, "Însemnări," 40–41 ("Ottoman family," "Ottoman Commonwealth"); Decei, *Imp. otoman*, 107; Gemil, *Românii și otomanii*, 23.

10 For the Christian view on religious peace, see Nicolaus of Cusa's conception (1401–1464), in Mgr. Cristiani, "La tolérance et l'intolérance de l'Eglise en matière doctrinale, depuis les premiers siècles jusqu'à nos jours," *Cahiers d'Histoire Médievale*, v, 1, 1959, 81. For the Islamic–Ottoman view, see the *sufi* movement of Bedr ed-din of Simavna, until his death by a *fetva* in 1421 (Decei, *Imp. otoman*, 83, 168; Ducas, *Istoria*, XXI/11); M. Boisard, *L'Islam et la morale internationale*, Paris: Albin Michel, 1979, 208.

11 See Rechid, "Islam," 382; Miquel, *Islam*, 245; K. Binswanger, *Untersuchungen zum Status der Nichtmuslime im Osmanischen Reich des 16 Jahrhunderts. Mit einer Neudefinition des Begriffes Dimma*, Munich: R. Trofenik, 1977; Géza Dávid, "Administration," 75; Gemil, *Românii și otomanii*, 23.

whole world to one system of law and religion, thus bringing harmony to the world of chaos and conflicts situated outside the Abode of Islam.[12]

## 1 Summons

In Islamic juridical theory,[13] as a first step to cancelling the state of war and regulating peaceful relations with enemy, the summon (*daʿvet*) was frequently considered the most deserving *cihad* by Muslim scholars.[14] Drawing from the *Kurʾan* and Muhammad's *sünnet*, jurists almost unanimously stated that Muslims were not allowed to begin hostilities without enjoining the enemy.[15] However, opinions differed on how to proceed towards infidels who had never received the "invitation to Islam."[16] According to Hanafi scholars enjoining the enemy before every attack was preferable, although by no means obligatory.[17] "The *Turks* are forbid by their law, to wage war without acquainting the enemy of their coming," Dimitrie Cantemir stated.[18] In fact, Ottomans considered this requirement not only a stipulation of the *şeriʿat* but also an international custom that had to be followed even when dealing with Christian polities. "The emperors have this custom, of announcing to each other when they make war one against other," said the Moldavian chronicler Miron Costin when he described Osman II's expedition to Poland in 1621. Fulfilling this practice, the sultan first dispatched his envoys to the king, "announcing that he is coming with all force against his kingdom."[19] Political or military emergencies

12 Khadduri, "International Law," 350–351; Dimitri Kitsikis, "Le concept ottoman de relations internationales et le service diplomatique ottoman au XIXe siècle," in *CIÉPO, 9th Symposium*, 23–26 July 1990, Jerusalem, 50; Shai Har-El, *Ottoman-Mamluk*, 8.

13 For details, see Abu Yusuf, *Kitab*, 295–334; Shaybani, *Kitab al-siyar*, I, 53–58 ("Summon before fighting"); IV, 136–145 ("The invitation to Islam").

14 Ibn Hazm's opinion (d. 1064), cf. Morabia, *Ǧihad*, 519.

15 "When we decide to destroy a population, We (first) send a definite order to those among them who are given the good things of this life and yet transgress; so that the word is proved true against them: then (it is) We destroy them utterly" (*Kurʾan* XVII, 16). See also Abu Yusuf, *Kitab*, 295; D'Ohsson, *Tableau*, V, 55; Morabia, *Ǧihad*, 358.

16 Averroes analyzed several opinions on this subject (Averroes, *Jihad*, 19–21). See also Rechid, *Islam*, 464–465; M. Khadduri, "Harb," *EI-2*, III, 184–185; Malik ibn Anas, cf. Morabia, *Ǧihad*, 358–359; al-Shafiʿi, cf. Williams, *Islamic Civilization*, 278.

17 Abu Yusuf, *Kitab*, 296; Morabia, *Ǧihad*, 358; Shaybani, *Kitab al-siyar*, cf. Williams, *Islamic Civilization*, 278; D'Ohsson, *Tableau*, V, 64.

18 Cantemir, *Othman History*, 210, n. 94.

19 Miron Costin, *Letopiseţ*, 76: *Au acestu obicei împăraţii, de dau ştire unul altuia, cându voru să facă războaie unul asupra altuia.*

could justify departures from strict adherence to the practice.[20] Although historical sources claim that the Ottomans scrupulously observed the rule of enjoining the enemies before starting a war, they also mention frequent departures from this practice:[21]

> However, [the Turks] do not always so strictly observe this custom, but often interpret the law according to urgent emergencies, nor proclaim war before they have sheathed the sword in the Bowels of the enemies [...] But it is wrong to blame the *Turks* for what is the common practice of all Mortals.[22]

In 1808, the Turkish ambassador to Paris blamed Russia for attacking the "territories of the Sublime State," that is the fortresses of Hotin and Bender (Tighina), and invading Moldavia and Wallachia without enjoining the Porte, which he considered "against the law" (*gayr-ı hakk*).[23]

According to the international practice, a summon had to include two elements: the statement of claims and the declaration of war.[24] The first summon to the "People of the Book" and idolaters, as stipulated by Islamic law, should enjoin them to embrace Islam (also called a "religious summon" by Ignace Mouradgea d'Ohsson), whereby the infidels were called to adopt and observe individual duties of all Muslims.[25] Should the "People of the Book" reject the invitation to convert, a Muslim ruler was allowed to encourage them to recognize the supremacy of Islam by paying a legal poll-tax (*cizye*).[26] The summon

20 Abu Yusuf, *Kitab*, 296; Morabia, *Ğihad*, 358; Shaybani, *Kitab al-siyar*, cf. Williams, *Islamic Civilization*, 278; D'Ohsson, *Tableau*, V, 64.

21 According to Ion Neculce, before the expedition against Kameniçe, in 1672, the Poles knew nothing and were unprepared for fighting (Neculce, *Letopiseț*, 40: *Leșii neștiindu nemic, nice avându veste, nu se gătise nemic de oaste*).

22 Cantemir, *Othman History*, 210, n. 94.

23 Veliman, *Documente turcești*, doc. 237.

24 For the Western European practice, see Hugo Grotius (Grotius, *Drept*, 638–639).

25 Shaybani, *Kitab al-siyar*, IV, 136–145; Shaybani, *Kitab al-siyar*, cf. Williams, *Islamic Civilization*, 277; Abu Yusuf, *Kitab*, 100; Ibrahim al-Halebi, *Mülteka*, cf. D'Ohsson, *Tableau*, V, 53–54,67–68; Morabia, *Ğihad*, 357–358; Mills, *Histoire de mahométisme*, 59. Examples from early Islam are collected in Abu Yusuf, *Kitab*, 296–300 (to idolaters of Fars); Hamidullah, *Documents*, doc. 15 (to the Byzantine emperor Heraclius, 610–641), 28, 29, 37, 41 (Muhammad to Kisrá, the Persian emperor), 66 (to the tribe Banu al-Harith), 67, 68, 69, 77 (to the tribes Banu ad-Dibah, Yazid b. at-Tufail and Banu Kanan); Lewis, *Islam*, I, 228.

26 Examples from early Islam are collected in Hamidullah, *Documents*, doc. 15 (to Heraclius of Byzantium); Abu Yusuf, *Kitab*, 296; Lewis, *Islam*, I, 228 (Fars). See also D'Ohsson, *Tableau*, V, 53–54, 70–71.

uttered by Muhammad to Nadjran in 631 became, along with the *ʿahd* he granted the following year, a diplomatic blueprint included in Arabic chronicles and Islamic legal treatises, as well as diplomatic handbooks, such as that of al-Kalkashandi:

> So, I invite you to abandon the idols worship in favor of the God adoration [...]; if you refuse, [I summon you to pay] *cizye;* if you reject *cizye* too, I shall declare war to you.[27]

Ignace Mouradgea d'Ohsson defined this kind of invitation as a "political summon."[28] From the fifteenth until the seventeenth century, the Ottomans did not employ a standardized enjoining formula in practice,[29] but the calls sent to Southeastern European princes comprised, either explicitly or implicitly, the demand to submit to the sultan and pay demanded tribute; the alternative was war.[30]

The oldest known official document in Ottoman–Moldavian relations, issued by Mehmed II on 5 October 1455 and addressed to Voivode Petru Aron, can be considered one such "political summons" from the perspective of Ottoman law of war and peace. Its importance for the topic at hands merits quoting the source in its entirety:

> You have sent this envoy and your boyar, Mihul the Logothete, and by him your words which were transmitted to us. Therefore, if you will annually send me two thousand golden ducats as tribute, then peace will be concluded. And, for this purpose, we have established three months as term. If it will arrive by then, in that case the peace will be concluded with me. But if it will not arrive you know this [consequence]![31]

---

27 9 AH (Hamidullah, *Documents*, doc. 79).

28 D'Ohsson, *Tableau*, V, 53–54, 70–71.

29 In fifteenth-century Byzantine chronicles, the military summons, e.g. "to send word to surrender the town," was frequently used in front of the besieged cities and fortresses (Chalcocondil, *Expuneri*, 258; Ducas, *Istoria*, 406; Critobul, *Mehmed II*, 184, 220). Seventeenth century chroniclers wrote on military written summons, called "mercy letters" (*amanname*), like those sent to the soldiers of Sotvin (Schottwien) and Benfurt (Ebenfort) (Kazazzade Ahmed Ağa, *Vakayi'name*, in *Crestomație turcă*, 873).

30 To the envoys of Rhodos after 1453: "If you do not accept giving tribute, you will not have the sultan's friendship [...]" (Ducas, *Istoria*, 402). The Bosnians were frequently called to conclude a peace agreement by paying of tribute (Critobul, *Mehmed II*, IV/15, 2).

31 22 *Şevval* 859 AH. The original was written in Slavic (Mehmet, *Documente turcești*, I, doc. 1). Historical comments in: Gorovei, "Casa păcii," 629–639; L. Şimanschi, "Închinarea de la Vaslui (5 iunie 1456)," *AIIAI*, XVIII, 1981, 613–617.

The document proves that, following Mehmed II's show of his military might on the southern bank of the Danube, the Moldavian ruler decided to initiate peace negotiations, sending his dignitary to the Ottoman court. Although fifteenth-century sources regarding Wallachia are no longer extant, we can safely assume from narrative accounts that similar political summons were also addressed to them.

## 2 The Islamic Ottoman Law of Peace

Taking into consideration that historians and jurists encountered considerable difficulties in trying to define Islamic notions of peace, the Ottoman understanding of peace remains a largely uncharted territory. Did the Ottomans have the right to conclude peace with non-Muslims? This question is a necessary and crucial one, since the legal theory divided the world into two irreducibly antagonistic realms, with a theoretically permanent state of war between them.[32]

In Islamic legal treatises, even if most space was devoted to the rules of war, it was the concept of peace that proved most controversial.[33] Already by the eighth and ninth centuries, Muslim jurists tried to address the conditions justifying definitive conclusion or interruption of the holy war, which eventually formed the core of the Islamic law of peace. Drawing on the Hanafi jurist al-Kashani's statements on *aman* in his *Kitab al-siyar*, Hans Kruse has concluded that

> the *cihad* ends when its purpose is reached, i.e. when its opponents have been subjected to the commands of Islam either by their embracing of Islam or by their submission to the Muslim rule.[34]

The Moldavian prince and scholar Dimitrie Cantemir excellently grasped the meaning of the Ottoman law of peace, affirming that although the *Ku'ran* exhorted Muslims to fight Christians, to spread Islam, the jurists also addressed the circumstances under which Muslims were allowed and had to conclude peace ("the manner in which peace may and ought to be made.") A passage

32 Armanazi, *Islam*, 98, 100; Peters, *Islam*, 149.

33 H. Kruse, "The Foundation of Islamic International Jurisprudence," *JPHS*, III, 1955, 264.

34 Al-Kashani (d. 1191) counted the following three conditions as causes which cancel the holy war: "embracing Islam (*iman*), grant of safety (*aman*), and sheltering in the holy sites (*iltija' ila'l haram*)" (Kruse, "Treaties," 155).

from Dimitrie Cantemir's *The History of the Growth and Decay of the Othman Empire* stipulates these conditions:

> But though they are commanded by the precepts of the *Koran* to make war upon the *Christians*, even when there is no other cause for it but the propagation of *Mahometism*, yet that law determines the manner in which peace may and ought to be made. For first it permits to make a truce, if the enemy be stronger than the Musulmans, that these may have time to augment their forces, and to heal their wounds, if they have received any. And it commands, that a firm and lasting peace be made, when the enemy embraces *Mahometism*, the enlargement whereof is the sole end of a just war, or promises to pay an annual tribute. For in such a case, he cannot be compelled further to *Mahometism*, nor be hurt any way unless he revolts. And if any one commits hostilities upon such a tributary, he shall be punished as severely as if he had attacked a Musulman's house or lands. For the *Fetvah* answers upon that point: *Anlerun mali bizum malimuz gibi cane can, gözi göz, &c.* Such a man's substance and riches, are as our substance, his soul as our soul, his eye as our eye, &c.[35]

By distinguishing between the standard situations, Dimitrie Cantemir suggests the conditions which allowed Muslims to conclude peace with non-Muslims:

a. If the infidels accepted embracing Islam or paying a poll-tax (*cizye, harac*), the Ottomans were obliged to halt the holy war and conclude a 'permanent peace' with non-Muslims, who thus became subjects of Ottoman sultans;
b. If the infidels rejected entering the *pax ottomanica*, the Ottomans had the right to temporarily halt the holy war and merely conclude truces with Christian polities.

These conditions allow us to conclude that the state of war between the Abode of Islam and the Abode of War could be permanently ended only following the infidels' conversion to Islam[36] or their recognition of the supremacy of the Muslim sovereign. Taking into consideration that the acceptance of *pax ottomanica* by non-Muslims was the sole envisioned outcome, we can describe the

35 Cantemir, *Othman History*, 276, n. 1. See also Watt, "Jihad," 390–394.

36 On conversion to Islam as a "permanent peace," see Panaite, *Război, pace și comerț în Islam*, 159–162. On the connection between conquest and conversion in the Ottoman Empire, see Marc David Baer, *Honoured by the Glory of Islam. Conversion and Conquest in the Ottoman Empire*, Oxford, New York: Oxford University Press, 2006.

Ottoman law of peace as a "law of force," justifying the policy of conquest. At the same time, it furnished juridical and religious legitimacy for establishing peaceful relations between the Ottomans and non-Muslim polities.

Political and military practice had a profound impact on the Islamic law of war and peace, and the principle of "public utility" (*maslaha*) became not only a means to develop juridical rules, but also informed Muslim jurists' use of formal sources of Islamic law: *Kur'an, sünnet, icma'* and *kıyas*.[37] Throughout the Ottoman period, war-making and peace-making, especially the agreements concluded under inauspicious circumstances, followed an overriding principle to serve the interests of "faith and state" (*din ü -devlet*).[38] Dimitrie Cantemir noted:

> If a peace is to be made with some *Christian* Prince, the same Canons are consulted, least any thing be done contrary to the Law of the *Koran* or the *Othman* Empire.[39]

In effect, the central idea guiding both temporary and permanent peace with the infidels was one of a "profitable peace" that, according to Ibrahim al-Halebi, meant that "there is no peace, if it is not an useful one."[40]

---

37 Laoust, *Ibn Taimiya*, 245–250; Tyan, "Méthodologie," 100–101; Bishai, "Peace Agreements," 53–54. In Islam, the Roman principle of *salus populi suprema lex esto* also worked (Morabia, *Ğihad*, 317).

38 In 1595, Mehmed III ordered the grand vizier Sinan paşa to act to punish the rebels from Wallachia and Moldavia "according to what would be most profitable to the faith and state" (*din ü devlete enfa' olan her ne ise ana göre*) (*Mihai. Documente*, I, doc. 29). In 1598, punishing Mihai the Brave was still "an important question of the faith and state" (*mühimmat-i din ü devletden olmağin*) (*Mihai. Documente*, I, doc. 75). Peace had to serve the interests of the Ottoman state (Veliman, *Documente turcești*, doc. 240: on the peace with Russia of 1812).

39 Cantemir, *Othman History*, 174, n. 1.

40 D'Ohsson, *Tableau*, V, 61. The sultan had the right to establish which peace was profitable and which was not (Armanazi, *Islam*, 98). Nuances, details and cases in Shaybani, *Kitab al-siyar*, III, 237; Abu Yusuf, *Kitab*, 320. According to Idris Bitlisi, the payment of tribute by Mircea the Elder before 1395 was "a useful and profitable submission" for the Ottomans (Idris Bitlisi, *Heşt Behişt*, cf. Decei, "Mircea," 143). The same attribute was applied by Kritobulos to the peace concluded by Mehmed II before the conquest of Constantinople (Critobul, *Mehmed II*, I, 5, 3). The treaty of Zsitvatörök (1606) with the Habsburgs was characterized as a "useful peace and friendship" (*bu hayirli sulh ü salah*) (BOA, *DED*, 57/1, doc. 3). The peace of Vasvár of 1664 was also seen as a useful peace by Silahdar Findiklili Mehmed Ağa (Silahdar, *Tarih*, in *Cronici turcești II*, 329).

### 2.1 *Temporary Peace*

Once one of the aforementioned conditions – conversion to Islam or the payment of *cizye* – was met by the infidels, the Ottomans were obliged to terminate the state of war. However, what if the goal of the holy war was not achieved? It was permissible to halt it, if, as jurists themselves briefly sketched, "the manner in which the peace – of course, a temporary one, a truce – may and ought to be made."[41]

The Ottoman approach to conducting peace negotiations, as was the case for the Arabic caliphate, was influenced by the balance of power. Jurists theorized three procedures that a Muslim sovereign could follow in concluding a temporary truce with non-Muslims, depending on whether the Muslims were in a position of supremacy, an equilibrium of power, or inferiority vis-à-vis their adversaries.[42] These three scenarios included, respectively: Muslims receiving a fixed sum of money in exchange for temporarily ceasing hostilities; no tribute payment by the contractual parties; Muslims' payment of an annual established tribute to the enemy. All these solutions revolved around the concepts of emergency[43] and tribute. Invoking several verses from the *Kur'an*, Abu Yusuf Ya'kub and al-Shaybani stated that generally an *imam* was prohibited from concluding a truce (*muvada'a*) with infidels if he had sufficient troops to vanquish the infidel adversary.

There were exceptions, though; for instance, it was permissible to the Muslim ruler to adopt peaceful methods, if he hoped to sway the infidels to embrace Islam or submit themselves to him.[44] Another influence underpinning these theoretical constructs came from precedents and truces, including the Arab–Byzantine peace agreements concluded in the eighth and ninth century;[45] consequently, a Muslim sovereign could strike a peace agreement and promise

41 Cantemir, *Othman History*, 276, n. 1.

42 Bishai, "Peace Agreements," 51. In this respect, let us quote Vlad the Impaler's words from the letter of 10th September 1456: "when a humble individual or ruler is strong and powerful he can make peace how he wants; but, when he is unpowerful, somebody stronger will come against him and do what he wants." (*DRH*, *D*, I, doc. 339).

43 "According to *Kur'an* – wrote Cantemir – the Muslims were allowed to grant peace when the emergency urges it" (Cantemir, *Sistemul*, 322–323; Cantemir, *Othman History*, 276, n. 1).

44 Abu Yusuf, *Kitab*, 319–320; Shaybani, *Kitab al-siyar*, III, 236. In this respect they invoked for instance *Kur'an* III, 139 and XLVII, 35 ("Be not weary and faint-hearted, crying for peace, when ye should be uppermost: for Allah is with you, and will never put you in loss for your [good] deeds").

45 To avoid Arab raids, the Byzantine emperors, e.g. Irina (780–790, 797–802) and Nikephoros I Logothete (802–811), paid 70,000 annually (90,000 dinars respectively) to Harun al-Rashid, according to the truces of 782, 798, or 806 (Canard, "Héraclée," 345).

not to attack infidel territory, if non-Muslims agreed to pay a fixed annual tribute.[46] By paying this "protection money," that – according to al-Mawerdi – did not constitute *cizye* or *harac* from a legal point of view,[47] the infidels could temporarily ransom their peace (*sulh*) and remove the threat of attack. For these reasons, such infidels were called the "people of ransom" (*ehl-i fidye*). It is worth emphasizing that, for the jurists, peace agreements including the tribute clause constituted an extreme solution and could be concluded "for a certain number of years," thus constituting temporary truces rather than permanent peace agreements.[48]

Throughout their history, Ottomans collected such sums of money (called *vergü, kesim, pişkeş, hedaya, armağan*, but also *harac* and *cizye*) from a number of foreign princes across Europe and Asia. Certain Christian neighbors of the empire, such as Venice, the Habsburg Empire, or Safavid Iran, paid tribute in return for keeping certain territories;[49] others, like Poland and Russia, remitted a yearly 'tax' to the Crimean Khanate – an Ottoman vassal – to prevent

46 "608. I asked: If some of the inhabitants of the territory of war wished the Muslims to enter into a peace agreement with them for a specified number of years on condition that they would pay a fixed annual tribute to the Muslims, provided that the Muslims abstain from entering their territory or enforce their jurisdiction on them, do you think that the Muslims should make a peace agreement with them on such terms? 609. He replied: No, unless it were better for the Muslims to do so. 610. I asked: And if it were better for the Muslims to do so? 611. [He replied: It would be permissible.]" (*Shaybani's Siyar*, 155). See also Shaybani, *Kitab al-siyar*, III, 262–281 ("On the ransom paid by the enemy infidels for a truce").

47 Terminological abuses can be frequently found in historical sources. The sum of money paid by Byzantium was sometimes defined as *cizye*, and the emperors as *zimmi* (Canard, "Héraclée," 345, 354). Dimitrie Cantemir realized and criticized the sultans' tendency to call "tribute" any sum of money received from Christians: "For the Turks aim at nothing more, than to have an enemy bound to pay them a small sum of money, which they may easily call a tribute. That once obtained, they do not want contrivances to increase that sum daily, and reduce it to a real tribute." (Cantemir, *Othman History*, 276, n. 2). As a rule the sums of money paid by Poles and Russians were called *vergü* (pl. *vergüler*) and *'adet* (pl. *'adetler*), which can be translated as "tax," but in 1520 Mehmed Giray termed *cizye* and *harac* the sum of money promised by the Polish king (Gemil, *Documente turcești*, doc. 117; Gemil, "Relațiile moldo-otomane," 137, n. 24; Mehmet, *Documente turcești*, I, doc. 161).

48 Shaybani, *Kitab al-siyar*, III, 262–281; *Shaybani's Siyar*, 155; Mawerdi, *Ahkam*, 101, 325; Morabia, *Ǧihad*, 323; Canard, "Héraclée," 352, n. 5.

49 Venice paid for their possessions in Albania, for Cyprus between 1517–1571 and for Zante until 1699. The Habsburg Empire paid for the Hungarian territories between 1547–1606. Thus, 30,000 gold pieces was to be paid for the Hungarian lands which were left in the hands of Habsburgs. Starting with 1612, Iran paid a sum of money for certain territories in Armenia and the Caucasus (Schaendlinger, *Süleyman*, doc. 23; Inalcik, "Power Relationships," 209; Pitcher, *Ottoman Empire*, 132).

predatory raids undertaken by Crimean Tatars. Even if these lump sums did not entail actual submission and dependence, both the Ottomans and Crimean Tatars equated them with Islamic legal taxes, *cizye* and *harac*.[50]

The state of the parity of power with the infidels was considered infrequent and exceptional by jurists, hence scant information on this scenario can be found in juridical works. Yet, al-Shaybani stated that if the inhabitants of the Abode of War were too strong for the Muslims to prevail, it was preferable for the latter to make peace for a specified period, even without the payment of *cizye*.[51] Muslim jurists could not totally ignore the critical circumstances between the eighth and tenth centuries, when the caliphs were forced to temporarily ransom their peace and pay tribute to non-Muslim adversaries. Consequently, without offering details, al-Shaybani and Abu Yusuf Yakub legitimized a peace agreement concluded for a period of years, whereby Muslims would pay their enemies a fixed annual tribute "if they were afraid of destruction and realized that an agreement would be better for them."[52]

The juridical theory remained unchanged during the Ottoman period, and – as Ibrahim al-Halebi (d. 1549) noted – Muslims rulers were allowed to ransom peace if they had no means to mount an armed opposition.[53] Moreover, starting from the end of the sixteenth century, when the empire found itself in dire straits, some Ottoman scholars began to promote peace while repudiating war. Illustrative of this current are several passages written by Hasan al-Kafi el-Bosnevi Akhisari (d. 1616) during the Long War of 1593–1606:

50 Poland paid "tribute" of up to 1699 to the Khan of Crimea, and for a short period, between 1672–1678, directly to the sultan. In 1520, Mehmed Giray spoke about 15,000 filoris. In 1634, Murad IV (1623–1640) reminded Vladislav IV Vasa (1632–1648) to pay "your taxes (*'adetleriniz*) which you had given from ancient times to the Khan" (Pitcher, *Ottoman Empire*, 132; Gemil, "Relațiile moldo-otomane," 137, n. 24; Mehmet, *Documente turcești*, I, doc. 161). Russia paid the Tartar Khan constantly until 1592 and irregularly from then until 1700. "Considering that we pay our taxes (*vergülerimiz verüb*) and send our envoys (*elçilerimiz gönderüb*) to His Majesty, the glorious Khan," Aleksei Mihailović (1645–1676) was right to object against the Tartar razzias (Pitcher, *Ottoman Empire*, 132; Gemil, *Documente turcești*, doc. 117: from a letter to the Moldavian voivode. Details in Inalcık, "Power Relationships," 208–211: "Notes on tribute paid to the Tatars").

51 *Shaybani's Siyar*, 154.

52 It was even possible to give back the captives converted to Islam. Being so humiliating, both Abu Hanifa's disciples were agreed that the *imam* had the right to violate these truces whenever he become stronger than their enemies (*Shaybani's Siyar*, 155; Shaybani, *Kitab al-siyar*, III, 236; Abu Yusuf, *Kitab*, 319–320; Averroes, *Jihad*, 21–23). For instance, according to the chroniclers al-Mas'udi and al-Tabari, the Caliph 'Abd al-Malik (685–705) concluded a peace with Justinian II by paying a monthly tribute of 1,000 dinars (cf. Bishai, "Peace Agreements," 59).

53 Ibrahim al-Halebi, *Mülteka*, cf. D'Ohsson, *Tableau*, V, 62.

> During conflicts nothing is more preferable than peace; The greatest guilt [...] is to launch war against somebody who is asking peace; A treaty is a sacred thing; to violate it is a crime.[54]

In practice, from the fifteenth until seventeenth centuries, the Porte concluded a series of peace agreements with Hungary, Poland and the Habsburg Empire, which reflected the parity of power between the adversaries. Between the Treaty of Karlowitz in 1699 and until the Treaty of Paris in 1856, the weakness and military inferiority of the Ottomans changed the parameters of war and peace with European powers. Consequently, they concluded peace treaties which brought constant territorial losses. As Hans Kruse pointed out:

> The rules and provisions of Muslim law, which were built up to the principle of perpetual enmity with, and of coercive advance against the unbelievers, were hardly fit for a situation like this.[55]

Yet, until the mid-eighteenth century the agreements with European powers continued to be considered temporary truces from the Ottoman juridical point of view.

### 2.2 *Firm and Lasting Peace*

Conversion to Islam was initially formulated as a "religious summon" and was the most desired solution for concluding the holy war, which aimed to spread the Muslim faith around the globe.[56] Forced conversion was prohibited in Islamic law, a point vehemently emphasized in Ottoman sources. For instance, an *'ahdname* issued by Mehmed II for the Genoese of Galata in June 1453 stated "that no infidel be converted to Islam against his will."[57] This was confirmed by a number of Christian sources from the Ottoman period.[58] Informative in

54 In 1595–1596, Akhisari wrote *Usul el-hikam fi nizam el-alem*, dedicating it to Mehmed III ("Principes de Sagesse, touchant l'art de gouverner, par Ac-hissari. Petit Traité traduit du turc par M. Garcin de Tassy," *JA*, IV, 1824, 289). See also M. A. Mehmet, "La crise ottomane dans la vision du Hasan Kiafi Akhisari (1544–1616)," *RESEE*, 13, 3, 1975, 385–402.

55 Kruse, "Shaybani," 232.

56 Cl. Huart, "Le droit de la guerre," *RMM*, II, 1907, 344. Al-Gazali's opinion (d. 1111), in Lazarus-Yafeh, *al-Gazzali*, 448–449.

57 Inlacik, "Galata," 19, 77; Iorga, "Privilegiul," 153–154. L. Mitler. "The Genoese in Galata: 1453–1682." *IJMES*, 10, 1, (1979): 71–91.

58 Chalcocondil, *Expuneri*, 86; Georgius of Hungaria, *Tractatus de moribus, condicionibus et nequicia turcorum*, Rome, 1480, cf. Káldy-Nagy, "Holy War," 473. For early Islam, see

this respect is a case from the reign of the Wallachian Voivode Radu the Great (1495–1508). A household servant, who had been brought from Brașov by a Wallachian merchant, fled to the Ottoman town of Hârșova "without his [master's] consent and knowledge, and turned Turk." According to the letters dispatched from Wallachia, the fugitive willingly remained under Ottoman protection, even though his master continued to affirm that "the Turks keep him under compulsion."[59]

Conversion to Islam put an end to any hostilities against the infidels who embraced the Islamic faith and exempted those who had been tributaries from their obligation to pay poll-tax (*cizye*). Moreover, their life, liberty and property entered under Allah's protection, providing them with the same rights and duties as other members of the *'Umma*.[60] According to *Kur'an* IX, 11:

> But (even so), if they repent, establish regular prayers, and practice regular charity, they are your brethren in Faith.

Historical circumstances in the Ottoman Empire favored conversion to Islam, but from the perspective of Islamic law of peace[61] it was important that they promised "peace to the people who accepted Islamic faith and law."[62] Thus, spreading Islam was the ideal path towards the establishment of *pax islamica*, which could be threatened solely by apostasy.[63]

The "political summon" addressed to non-Muslim individuals, communities or states was a dilemma of either choosing to pay tribute or confronting an

---

G. E. von Grunebaum, "La première expansion de l'Islam: élan et arrêt," *Diogene* (Paris), LIII, 1966, 71.

59 Tocilescu, *534 documente*, doc. 196, 412. There are individual cases of conversion to Islam, like certain voivodes of the Romanian principalities: Mihnea II the Renegate (1577–1583, 1585–1591); Paul Márkházi, pretender to the Transylvanian throne in 1581, converted to Islam in 1593, calling himself Ibrahim and being named *bey* of Lipova (Szamosközy, *Însemnări ungurești*, 95, 97; I. H. Uzunçarşili, "On altıncı yüzyıl ortalarında Islamiyeti kabul etmiş olan bir Boğdan voyvodası," *Belleten*, XVIII, 69, 1954, 83–87.

60 Abu Yusuf, *Kitab*, 94–95, 104; Shaybani, *Kitab al-siyar*, IV, 136–188. Examples from early Islam in Hamidullah, *Documents*, doc. 23, 37, 41, 42, 43, 56, 66, 67, 68, 69, 77; Abu Yusuf, *Kitab*, 296. See also W. M. Watt, "Conditions of Membership of the Islamic Community," *SI*, XXI, 1964, 5–13; Watt, *Mahomet-Medine*, 377; Rechid, "Islam," 395.

61 Miquel, *Islam*, 244–245. For instance, the case of the Islamization of Bosnian population in the fourteenth century (Todorov, *Ville balkanique*, 60–61).

62 Hamidullah, *Documents*, doc. 10; Morabia, *Ğihad*, 358.

63 Morabia, *Ğihad*, 322; Cantemir, *Othman History*, 276, n. 1. For the Islamic law on apostasy and renegades, Shaybani, *Kitab al-siyar*, III, 412–510. Cases from Ottoman history in Bartolomé Bennassar, Lucile Bennassar, *Les chrétiens d'Allah. L'histoire extraordinaire des renégats. XVIe et XVIIe siècles*, Paris, 1989.

Islamic army on the battlefield. The former option frequently appears in historical sources from the early Islamic period. The population of Hirah responded to Khalid b. al-Walid's demand:

> We do not need your war. Conclude rather an agreement like those you have already concluded with other people of the Book, and which consists in paying of *cizye*.[64]

The manner in which the Prophet Muhammad and the first four caliphs had established their relations with Christians and Jews as subjects of the new Islamic polity would be theorized by eighth and ninth-century jurists, including Abu Yusuf Ya'kub and al-Shaybani, who frequently quoted these solutions. Consequently, a Muslim ruler had to accept with as "protected subject" (*zimmis*) any non-Muslim *harbis* who submitted to him by agreeing to pay *cizye* or *harac*.[65]

The *Kur'anic* verse IX, 29, was often invoked to justify this type of peace, and its importance for the Islamic law of peace and war has been frequently emphasized by scholars:

> Fight those who believe not in Allah nor the Last Day, nor hold that forbidden which hath been forbidden by Allah and His Messenger, nor acknowledge the religion of Truth, (even if they are) of the People of the Book, until they pay the *cizye* with willing submission, and feel themselves subdued.[66]

---

64 Hamidullah, *Documents*, doc. 220. See, also, the case of the Christians and Jews from fortresses around Damascus in 634–635, narrated by al-Baladhuri (d. 892) (cf. Williams, *Islamic Civilization*, 265–266). For financial, administrative and religious advantages offered by the Arab Caliphate and then by Seljukids in comparison with the Byzantine Empire, see Iorga, *Istoria vieții bizantine*, 193–197; Sourdel, *Islamul clasic*, I, 55; O. Turan, "Les souverains seldjoukides et leur sujets nonmusulmans," *SI*, I, 1953, 65–101.

65 Abu Yusuf, *Kitab*, 213–230; Khadduri, *War and Peace*, 195–197; Laoust, *Ibn Taimiya*, 270; Özel, *Islam Hukuku*, 203.

66 *The Glorious Kur'an*, Translation and Commentary by Abdallah Yousuf Ali, Lahore, 1973, 447. Other translation: "Fight against such of those who have been given the Scripture as believe not in Allah nor the Last Day, and forbid not that which Allah hath forbidden by His messenger, and follow not the religion of truth, until they pay the tribute readily, being brought low." This verse suggested a procedure which intended to humiliate the non-Muslim ruler (Turki, "Tributaire," 42, n. 3; Cl. Cahen, "Documents et notules: C. IX-29 – Hatta…" *Arabica*, IX, 1, 1962, 76–79). Muslims, including the Ottomans, often invoked this verse in summons addressed to infidels or in the peace agreements concluded with tributary princes (Hamidullah, *Documents*, doc. 15; Idris Bitlisi, *Heşt Behişt*, ms. Nurosmaniye Kütüphanesi, nr. 3209, f. 181a, cf. Decei, "Mircea," 143). The Ottoman sultans

From the perspective of Islamic law of peace, one can conclude that the state of war between the Abode of Islam and Abode of War ceased and a firm peace was established not only by converting to Islam but also by accepting Islamic supremacy.[67]

In fifteenth-century Ottoman sources, non-Muslims who had accepted to pay tribute were called either "tribute-payers" (*haracgüzarlar*) or "infidels who are not from the Abode of War" (*kefere ki dar al-harbdan olmıya*); however, in the later period, the term *zimmi* became the main juridical concept applied to non-Muslim subjects of the empire. The recognition of Ottoman sovereignty by these individuals, communities and polities established a permanent peace, described by Dimitrie Cantemir as "firm and lasting." From the Ottoman point of view, it essentially hinged on granting these non-Muslims protection in exchange for the payment of tribute. By these means, the state of *pax ottomanica* proliferated throughout Southeastern and Central Europe.

considered the personal payment of the tribute by the fifteenth century Wallachian and Moldavian princes as a humiliation (practically, a verification of submission), frequently asking them to come to the Porte with tribute. Stephen the Great's case is accounted in Aşıkpaşazade, *Tarih*, in *Cronici turcești*, I, 95.

67 Watt, "Jihad," 390–394.

CHAPTER 5

# Obeying Ottoman Sultans in Southeastern Europe: a Chronological Survey

Sources mention frequent instances of non-Muslim communities and polities across Southeastern Europe accepting tribute payments and submitting to the Ottoman sultans. For instance, the cities of Thessaloniki and Christopolis became tribute-payers between 1387 and 1391, enjoying "a condition of privileged vassalage," according to A. E. Vacalopoulos. This meant that Murad I did not opt to incorporate the two cities into his empire but only demanded the payment of the customary poll-tax and the maintenance of a small Ottoman garrison. These "peaceful and privileged conditions" were abrogated after the towns' conquest following the death of John V (February 1391).[1] In 1453, after the inhabitants of Galata have submitted "willingly" to Mehmed II as subjects, the sultan "imposed upon them the Islamic poll-tax (*harac*) which they pay each year as other non-Muslims do."[2] As narrative and documentary sources indicate, the capitulations of Christian towns in Southeastern Europe and Anatolia generally implied, in terms of Islamic law, imposing *şeriʿat*-stipulated taxes, *cizye* and *harac*, and transforming obedient non-Muslims into *zimmi*s.

The decisions of Christian rulers to accept to pay tribute is particularly important for the topic at hand. The fourteenth and fifteenth centuries provides us with several clear-cut examples of tributary states (*haracgüzar*s): Byzantium between 1372–1453; Serbia between 1372–1459; the Bulgarian tsardoms in the 1380s and 1390s; Bosnia in the period 1389–1463; Albania from 1385–1478, with interruptions; the Morean Despotate in the fifteenth century; the North Aegean islands of Lesbos, Lemnos and Imbros in the fifteenth century. These cases can be adopted as a point of reference for the fifteenth-century legal and political position of Moldavia and Wallachia.

1 A. E. Vacalopoulos (Bakalopoulos), *History of Macedonia. 1354–1833*, Translated by Peter Megann, Thessaloniki: Institute for Balkan Studies, 1973, 64–67.

2 In the *ʿahdname* of June 1453 (Inalcık, "Galata," 18; Critobul, *Mehmed II*, 148). On the fortresses surrounding Kaffa (Tursun bey, *Tarih*, in *Crestomaţie turcă*, 198).

 | DOI:10.1163/9789004411104_006

## 1 The Byzantine Empire

In regard to Byzantium, historians have generally agreed that in summer 1372, following the Ottoman victory at Çirmen (26 September 1371), Emperor John V Paleologus, became a "tributary to Amurat, following him in any of his expeditions," as recorded by Chalcocondylas.[3] This event was but one episode from a prolonged history of war and peace spanning over a century. It began in 1348 when Anna of Savoy acquiesced to presenting to Orhan, among other things, "a great sum of money" as a single payment, whereas John VI Cantacuzino bestowed "plenty of gifts" upon the Ottomans who had assisted him during the civil war. Once on the Byzantine throne, John V Paleologos (in 1379) and John VII Paleologos (in 1390) institutionalized yearly payments of "many hundreds of gold and silver coins" to Murad I and Bayezid I, respectivly. However, in the span of merely three decades following 1424, Byzantine–Ottoman relations took a sharp turn to the detriment of Byzantine rulers, which eventually led to the fall of Constantinople in 1453 and of Trebizond in 1461.[4]

## 2 Albania

Ottoman–Venetian rivalry over Albania played an essential role in the region's historical evolution, in a manner similar to the parallel Ottoman–Hungarian competition for Wallachia. According to Ottoman chronicles, the first instance of submission by Albanian lords took place following the defeat and death of Balša II during the battle of Savra in 1385. One of Murad I's tribute-payers was Gjergj Stratsimirović, Balša's heir in Scutari and Dulcigno.

A curious development that merits attention is that, in order to keep their tributaries on their side, the Ottomans guaranteed the possession of their lands as *timar*s. Nonetheless, it was only after almost a century of conflict, truces and conquests – Skanderbeg's career being the most known episode during this time – that Mehmed II succeeded in bringing all of Albania under Ottoman direct administration.[5]

3 Chalcocondil, *Expuneri*, 42. See also Dölger, *Regesten*, no. 3136; Danişmend, *OT Kronolojisi*, I, 55–56; G. Ostrogorsky, "Byzance, État tributaire de l'Empire turc." *Zbornik Radova* (Novi Sad), vol. V, (1958): 49–58.

4 The Byzantines paid Murad I and Bayezid I 30,000 hiperpers (i.e. 15,000 Venetian ducats or 480,000 akçes), and after 1424 Murad II, 9,090 ducats or 300,000 akçes (Ducas, *Istoria*, VIII/1, IX/1–2; Chalcocondil, *Expuneri*, 35, 54–55; Melissenos, *Memorii*, I/13; Octavian Iliescu, "Le montant du tribut payé par Byzance à l'Empire Ottoman en 1379 et 1424)," *RESEE*, IX, 3, 1971, 427–432).

5 For details see H. Inalcık, "Arnawutluk," *EI-2*, I, 650–658; Critobul, *Mehmed II*, 246;

## 3 The Tsardoms of Tarnovo and Vidin

Bulgarian tsardoms of Tarnovo and Vidin became Ottoman tributaries in the 1380s, although a precise date is impossible to determine; we know that this took place either following the Ottoman victory at Çirmen in 1371 or during the military campaign of 1376–1377, and both polities continued as the sultans' tributaries for two decades. According to Sa'adeddin, Tsar Ivan Shishman of Tarnovo (1371–1393), "took the way to the court of heaven. And bringing proper greetings and pure gifts and preferring to be tributary (*haracgüzar olmağı ihtiyar idüb*), he hurried to be received in the presence of the shah." Ivan Stratsimir, who ruled in Vidin, followed suit.[6]

Few sources – mostly narrative ones – address the status of both polities; nonetheless, Ottoman historians, including Mehmed Neşri, called them tribute-payers (*haracgüzarlar*) of the sultan.[7] Apart from tributary obligations, the tsars were also to bring their troops for Ottoman campaigns. Ivan Shishman's failure to comply triggered a punitive campaign led by Grand Vizier Candarlı Ali paşa in the Winter of 1388–1389, which ended with the conquest of numerous Bulgarian towns. The chronicles also mention two acts of submission by Ivan Shishman to Murad I prior to the battle of Kosovo Polje. The first one took place in Varna in Spring 1389, at the heels of Ali paşa's campaign, whereby the tsar promised to surrender the town of Silistre. However, his refusal to give up the city led to a renewed threat of Ottoman attack, forcing Shishman to renew his act of submission on the outskirts of Tarnovo.

Bayezid I, following his conquest of Tarnovo (1393) and Niğbolu (Nikopol) in 1395, put Ivan Shishman to death and, following the victory in the battle of Niğbolu (28 September 1396), Bayezid I turned against the Tsardom of Vidin, ruled by Ivan Stratsimir. The conquered territories were transformed into *sancaks* and frontier troops (*uc beys*) were settled in the main urban centres of Bulgaria to serve as a springboard for repeated raids into Wallachia and Hungary.[8]

---

Chalcocondil, *Expuneri*, 206; Decei, *Imp. otoman*, 52, 95, 112–113; Danişmend, *OT Kronolojisi*, I, 300 ; J. O. Schmitt, *Skanderbeg (Der neue Alexander auf dem Balkan)*, Regensburg: Pustet, 2009.

6 Sa'adeddin, *Tac üt-tevarih*, I, Istanbul, 1280, 93–94, cf. Decei, "Sulhname," 134, n. 1; *Cronici turceşti I*, 300–301. Also, Mehmed Neşri, Idris Bitlisi, Mehmed bin Mehmed, Koca Hüseyin, in *Cronici turceşti I*, 110–111, 300–301, 400–401, 440.

7 TKSMA, E. 6374 (Inalcık, "Document," 220–222; Decei, "Două documente," 210–214).

8 In 1365, Tsar Ivan Alexander divided his realm between his two sons. Ivan Shishman received Tarnovo, while Ivan Stratsimir – Vidin (H. Inalcık, "Bulgaria," *EI-2*, I, 1302–1304).

## 4 Serbia

Serbia became the Porte's tributary following the battle of Maritsa (Çirmen) in 1371, when Lazar Hrebljanović agreed to pay *harac* to Sultan Murad I. According to Sa'adeddin, in 1375–1376, the Serbian *knez* made his "acknowledgment of submission" (*ʿarz-ı ʿubudiyet*) and "gathering a three-year tribute, prayed to be counted among other tributary princes."[9] Another lord who became an Ottoman tributary was Marko Kraljević of Prilep, whose father had perished on the banks of Maritsa.[10] However, in 1402, the defeat suffered by Bayezid I in the battle of Ankara meant the effective abolition of tributary relations throughout Southeastern Europe. Murad II eventually succeeded in reinstituting Ottoman control over Serbia, defeating a Christian coalition at Golubac fortress in 1428. George Branković (1427–1456) was forced, like other Southeastern Christian princes, to ransom the peace by resuming tribute. Even though he maintained their alliance with Hungary, the Serbian *knezi* were also Ottoman tribute payers until 1459, when Serbia was transformed into a province under direct Ottoman administration.[11]

## 5 Bosnia and Herzegovina

Bosnia and Herzegovina became targets of Ottoman attacks prior to the battle of Kosovo Polje in 1389, in the final years of King Tvrtko I's reign (1377–1391); some sources indicate that Bosnians began to pay tribute to Sultan Bayezid I (1389–1402). During the reign of Mehmed I (1413–1420), Ottoman raids intensified, while the sultans also increasingly interfered in the internal conflicts between local barons and pretenders. As a result, Tvrtko II (1420–1443) had to acknowledge his submission to Murad II and become tribute-payer in 1428–1429. According to the Greek chronicler Makarios Melissenos, it was Sultan Murad II who "transformed a large part of [Bosnia] in a tributary territory."[12]

Bosnia's last two rulers, Stjepan Tomaš (1444–1461) and Stjepan Tomašević (1461–1463), attempted but failed to escape from under Ottoman suzerainty. In this regard, Stejpan Tomašević refused to send the due tribute and formed an

9 *Üç yıllık harac ihraç edüb müluk-i haracgüzar adadından olmağı istidʿa eyledikde* (Sa'adeddin, *Tac üt-tevarih*, I, Istanbul, 1280, 93, cf. Decei, "Sulhname," 134, n. 5).

10 *Anonymous Greek Chronicle*, 126–127.

11 Chalcocondil, *Expuneri*, 150, 189, 193, 241–242, 263; Mihailović, *Memoirs*, 87, 97; Sphrantzes, *Memorii*, XXXVI/2, 7; XXXVII/15; Ducas, *Istoria*, XXX/4 and p. 38, 256, 260, 288, 396; Critobul, *Mehmed II*, 178–180, 184–186, 208, 216; *Cronici turceşti I*, 123 (Mehmed Neşri); 542, 544 (Kara-Çelebi-Zade); Moxa, *Cronica*, 190; Decei, *Imp. otoman*, 51, 56, 83–96, 91, 109–110; Danişmend, *OTKronolojisi*, I, 287; Vaughan, *Europe and the Turk*, 49.

12 Melissenos, *Cronica*, 231.

alliance with Hungary, the Pope and Venice. As a reprisal, Mehmed II launched a swift campaign that took control of Bosnian territories, including the capital of Jajce, and established the *sancak* of Bosnia (1463). The same year, a campaign led by Grand Vizier Mahmud paşa defeated the ruler of Herzegovina, Duke Stjepan Vukčić-Kosača, who submitted himself, paid tribute and sent hostages to the Porte, effectively signalling the submission of Herzegovina. A few years later, in 1470, part of Herzegovina was transformed into a *sancak*, but it was only in 1482, following Vukčić-Kosača's death, that the annexation of all territories took place.[13]

## 6 Despotate of Morea

Greek historian A. Savvides drew a direct connection between the destruction of Hexamilion by Murad II, only just refortified by Constantine XI Paleologus after the crusade of Varna in 1444, and the acknowledgment of submission by the Despot of Morea in 1446. According to Nicolae Iorga, in 1455 – on the heels of the fall of Constantinople – the Despot of Morea agreed to pay an increased tribute of 10,000 ducats, as did other rulers of Southeastern Europe. In the following years, Mehmed II thwarted any attempts by Morea to ally itself with the anti-Ottoman camp or to delay the payment of tribute, launching punitive raids in the case of non-compliance (those led by Turahan in 1452 and ʿÖmer Bey in 1456, which also led to the conquest the Florentine duchy of Athens). In 1458, a third of the Morean territory was annexed and transformed into a *sancak* under ʿÖmer Bey's governorship, while the tribute imposed on the Paleologi dynasty was increased. Finally, the campaigns of 1460–1461 brought a systematic conquest of Morean strongholds, and the whole polity was put under Ottoman administration, its lands distributed as *zeʿamet*s and *timar*s. Despot Demetrius, brother of Constantine XI, received the islands of Thasos, Samothrace and Lemnos, and continued for a brief period as Mehmed II's tribute-payer.[14]

---

13 Tursun bey, *Tarih*, in *Crestomaţie turcă*, 186–195; Melissenos, *Cronica*, I/23; Chalcocondil, *Expuneri*, 153; Mihailović, *Memoirs*, 137, 177; Decei, *Imp. otoman*, 110; Inalcık, *Ottoman Empire*, 27; Danişmend, *OTKronolojisi*, I, 302; Branislav Djurdjev, "Bosna," *EI-2*, I, 1261–1275.

14 On this topic, see: Chalcocondil, *Expuneri*, 189–190, 202, 205; Sphrantzes, *Memorii*, XLII/2, XLIV/2; A. Savvides. N. A. Bées, "Mora," *EI-2*, VII, 236–241; Iorga, *Istoria vieţii bizantine*, 550–599; Zakynthinos, *Morée*, I, 241–285 and II, 71–90; Decei, *Imp. otoman*, 94–95; Inalcık, *Ottoman Empire*, 27; Pitcher, *Ottoman Empire*, 85–86 (who speaks about three conquering campaigns of 1452–1454, 1458 and 1460).

## 7 North Aegean Islands

The northern Aegean islands of Lesbos-Mytilene, Tenedos, Imbros, Samothrace, Thasos, Lemnos, along with the towns of Phocaea and Enoz (Aenos) had a common history and their relations with the Ottoman Empire followed a similar path.[15] Lesbos-Mytilene (or *Midilli*, by its capital), Lemnos and Thasos constituted a fief granted to a Genoese Gattilusio family by the last three Byzantine emperors. After 1453, Duke Dorino Gattilusio (1426–1455)[16] recognized Ottoman suzerainty and began to pay a tribute of 3,000 ducats in exchange for the right to retain his holdings. Just two years later, the annual sum was more than doubled to 7,000 ducats, an increase imposed on Dorino's successor, Domenico (1455–1458). However, once Domenico was murdered by his brother, Niccolò, who took power with Catalan corsairs' support, the Ottoman Grand Vizier Mahmud paşa annexed Mytilene outright.

The Ottoman policy towards Morea and Lesbos reverberated in the islands of Lemnos (*Limni*), Imbros (*Imroz*), and Thasos (*Taşoz*). Even prior to 1453, Mehmed II granted Lemnos to Dorino Gattilusio as a fief. Once Constantinople fell, the tributary status of Lemnos and Thasos was upheld in exchange for the annual payment of 2,325 ducats, which continued when Domenico succeeded his father in 1455. An important role in the relations between the Porte and Imbros was played by Kritovoulos of Imbros, a judge and chronicler who originated from the island. Thanks to his intercession in 1453, Imbros was granted to Domenico Gattilusio of Aenos, who was to pay 1,200 ducats annualy. In 1456, when the Ottomans took Aenos, the three islands were transformed into maritime dependencies of the Gallipoli *sancak*,[17] directly administrated by Ottoman officials. Following a short interlude of Papal rule, in 1459–1460

15 On this topic, see: Ducas, *Istoria*, XI/3,67, XII/5,73; Critobul, *Mehmed II*, 13/1, 195/15; Sphrantzes, *Memorii*, XLII/2, XLIV/2; Chalcocondil, *Expuneri*, 267–268; Iorga, *Istoria vieții bizantine*, 573, 595; A. E. Bakalopoulos (Vacalopoulos), *The Greek Nation. 1453–1669: the cultural and economic background of modern Greek society*, New Brunswick, N.J.: Rutgers University Press , 1976; A. E. Bakalopoulos (Vacalopoulos), *Thasos, son histoire, son administration de 1453 à 1912*, Paris: De Boccard, 1953; W. Miller, "The Gattilusi of Lesbos (1355–1462)," in *Essays on the Latin Orient*, Cambridge: Cambridge University Press, 1921 (reprinted, Amsterdam, 1964), 313–353. A. H. de Groot, "Limni," *EI-2*, V, 1986, 763–764; V. L. Ménage, "Enos," *EI-2*, II, 698; Ed., "Imroz," *EI-2*, III, 1176; S. Soucek, "Midilli," EI-2, VI, 1035–1037; S. Soucek, "Tashoz," *EI-2*, X, 1999, 352–353; Decei, *Imp. otoman*, 109–111; Inalcık, *Ottoman Empire*, 27.

16 Francesco Gattilusio had received Lesbos from John V (1355–1362) for the help he gave to Byzantium: *Privilegium aurea bulla munitum: der Kaiser gibt an Francesco Gattilusi die hand seiner schwester Maria und die insel Lesbos* (Dölger, *Regesten 5*, no. 3043; Ducas, *Istoria*, XI/3,67, XII/5, 73; Iorga, *Istoria vieții bizantine*, 573; Vacalopoulos, *Greek Nation*, 63).

17 The Ottoman chroniclers Aşıkpaşazade and Tursun bey claim that, after the death of Domenico Gattilusio in 1455, family quarrels and complaints of neighboring Muslims ensued, giving Mehmed II the pretext to intervene.

Mehmed II retook Lemnos and restored it as a tributary territory along with Imbros, Thasos, Samothrace and the town of Aenos. As mentioned above, the territory was granted to the former Despot of Morea, Demetrius Paleologus, in return for a tribute of 3,000 ducats.

Following the Venetian–Ottoman war of 1464–1479, when Lemnos experienced a period of Venetian occupation, Ottoman rule was reestablished and a regular provincial administration set up in 1479. Thus, Chalcocondylas could conclude that under Mehmed II "Turks took over administration of islands" in the northern Aegean.[18]

## 8 South Aegean Cycladic Islands

The Duchy of Naxos, Paros, Andros and Chios[19] also paid tribute to the Porte from the fifteenth until the early nineteenth centuries. The turning point in their political status were the raids by Hayr al-Din paşa, which swept throughout the Cyclades,[20] Naxos capitulating on 11 November 1537 and the Kephalos fortress of Paros the following month. The first tribute payment was collected the following year. The conquest was followed by a set of imperial charters issued by Süleyman the Magnificent – such as the Andros *ʿahdname* of 1539[21] – that established the legal status vis-à-vis the Porte. Thus, Naxos and other Cycladic islands, in the words of Richard Knolles, "becometh tributary unto the Turks."[22] Ottoman suzerainty was subsequently recognized and ratified on the "international" stage with the conclusion of the 1540 Ottoman–Venetian treaty.

---

18 Chalcocondil, *Expuneri*, 268.

19 For details, see: Chalcocondil, *Expuneri*, 267–268; Melissenos, *Cronica*, 233; Ducas, *Istoria*, 410–411, 418–419; R. Saulger, *Histoire nouvelle des anciens ducs et autres souverains de l'Archipel*, Paris, 1698; Safvet Bey, "Nakşe (Naksos) Dukalığı. Kiklad Adaları," TOEM, IV, 1329, 1446–1448; Matei, "Domination," 87; B. J. Slot, *Archipelagus Turbatus. Les Cyclades entre colonisation latine et occupation ottomane. c. 1500–1718*, I–II, Nederlands Historish – Archaeologisch Institut Te Istanbul, 1982; A. Savvides, "Nakshe," *EI-2*, VII, 939–941 (with bibliography in Greek); A. Savvides, "Para," *EI-2*, VIII, 265–266.

20 The Duchy of Naxos (*Nakşe*) is the largest Cycladic island. Despite the Ottoman raids against the archipelago, which had begun in 1416, in the first part of the fifteenth century Ottoman–Venetian treaties granted control over the Duchy and other islands to Venice. Even after the Ottoman–Venetian wars of 1463–1479 and 1499–1503, the island of Naxos remained under Venetian control, the *status quo* between Venice and Ottoman Empire ratified by the 1479 and 1503 peace agreements.

21 Slot, *Archipaelagus Turbatus*, II, 76–77.

22 Knolles, *Turkish History*, 455. A. Savvides defined the legal status of Paros as "a semi-autonomy under a kapudan paşa," but Latins and local notables took an important role in governing the island (A. Savvides, "Para," *EI-2*, VIII, 265–266).

Step by step, Naxos and the other Cycladic islands were integrated into the Ottoman administrative system. In 1564–1565, the last member of the incumbent Crispo dynasty managed to secure favorable *ʿahdname*s from Süleyman Kanunî;[23] however, between 1566 and 1579, Naxos received an administrator on behalf of the Jewish merchant Joseph Nasi, installed as the duke by Piyale paşa after the conquest of Keos and Andros in 1566.[24] After Nasi passed away in 1579, the extensive privileges granted by the *ʿahdname* of 1580 meant "a new era for the Cyclades," according to A. Savvides. Naxos became the center of the *sancak* of Cyclades, which was ruled by a dignitary (*sancakbeyi*) named either among the Turks (*Soleiman bei de ducat di Naxia, signor di Andro* in 1580 or 1582; Otural bey up to 1606) or Greek–Italian notables, as "dukes" (Constantine Cantacuzino in 1582, John Choniates in 1598, Gasparo Graziani in 1617–1618 etc.). These privileges were subsequently renewed by Sultan Ibrahim, following the ravages a new war with Venice brought to Paros in 1645–1646. The *ʿahdname* of 1646 recognized a local government in Naxos, consisting of a voivode and six local notables, while Paros' ruling council consisted of a voivode, two *koca-başı*s and a *kadı*. Local notables could lobby at the Porte or buy the position of the voivode, although they could face dismissal and execution, much like the rulers of Wallachia and Moldavia. This was the fate suffered by Constantine Konddyles in 1716, who faced accusations of providing a safe haven for pirates. The privileged status of Cycladic islands as Ottoman provinces, continued until the early nineteenth century (1830–1832), when most Cycladic islands were incorporated into the newly established Kingdom of Greece.

Chios (*Sakız*) was autonomously ruled by a *podestà* from the Giustiniani family, sent by the government of Genoa. The Giustinianis had paid tribute to the Byzantine emperors, which the Anatolian Emirate of Aydın took over. Ottomans continued these practices and it was said that, following the conquest of Constantinople, the Giustinianis "fearing to lose the sovereignity of the island, sent ambassadors to Mahomet, who, in consideration of a yearly tribute of 6,000 ducats, consented to leave them in the enjoyment of their former privileges." This annual tribute gradually increased, reaching 14,000 ducats under Süleyman Kanunî. Finally, in 1566, following the islands' refusal to pay double the sum, Chios was conquered and transformed into a *sancak*.[25]

---

23 Precisely, they were granted on 16 *Cemazi ül-evvel* 972/20 December 1564 and 28 *Ramadan* 972/29 April 1565 (Safvet, "Nakşe," 1446–1448; Uzunçarşılı, *Osmanlı Tarihi*, III, 2, 102–103). Savvides indicated 29 August 1565 (A. Savvides, "Para," *EI-2*, VIII, 265–266).

24 A. Saviddes considered that date as a "definitive annexation" (A. Savvides, "Para," *EI-2*, VIII, 265–266).

25 Karl Hopf, *Les Giustiniani, dynastes de Chios*, translated by Etienne A. Vlasto, Paris: Leroux, 1888; P. P. Argenti, *Bibliography of Chios from Classical Times to 1936*, London, Oxford: Clarendon Press, 1940; *Diplomatic Archive of Chios. 1577–1841*, edited by Philip P. Argenti, vol.

## 9 Ragusa

Many controversies surround Ragusa[26] and the precise moment the republic began to pay tribute to the Porte.[27] As the Ottomans reached Dalmatia in the early fifteenth century and succeeded in subduing the Western Balkans, the Ragusan rector and patriciate accepted the new powerful ruler as protector of their international trade, even though they continued to recognize the Hungarian king as their suzerain. This practice was in many respects similar to other minor polities of the Balkans, such as Serbia and Wallachia. The conditions in which Dubrovnik initiated its contact with Ottoman authorites seem to be quite similar.

Given that the charter of 1365 is undoubtedly an invention,[28] it was only in the fifteenth century that the Porte granted Dubrovnik *ʿahdname*s (called in Italian *privilegio*), which included the documents from 1430, 1442, 1458, 1480 and 1481–1482; interestingly, all of them were composed in Serbian and written in Cyrillic letters.[29] The first document of this series, issued 1430, was the product of an attempt by Ragusan diplomats to secure Ottoman support against aggressive neighbors; Murad II guaranteed protection for Ragusan merchants, even though the arrangement did not include tribute payments. The issue of tribute first entered Ragusan–Ottoman relations in 1442, when the republic

---

I–II, Cambridge: Cambridge University Press, 1954; S. Turan, "Sakız'ın türk hakimiyeti altına alınması," *TAD*, IV (1966), 173–184; D. Goffman, *Izmir and the Levantine world, 1550–1650*, Seattle–London: University of Washington Press, 1990, 61–64; S. Soucek, "Sakız," *EI-2*, VIII, 1995, 889–892.

26 For details, see: N. H. Biegman, *The Turco-Ragusan Relationship according to the Firmans of Murad III (1575–1595) Extant in the State Archives of Dubrovnik*, The Hague–Paris, 1967; Zdenko Zlatar, *Between the Double Eagle and the Crescent. The Republic of Dubrovnik and the Origins of the Eastern Question*, Boulder, New York: East European Monographs, 1992; Sertoğlu, *ROTA*, 267; Orhonlu, "Kharadj," 1086; Matei, "Domination," I, 87; F. Babinger, "Raghusa," *EI-2*, VIII, 391–393; Boško I. Bojović, *Raguse (Dubrovnik) et l'Empire Ottoman (1430–1520). Les actes imperiaux ottomans en vieux-serbe de Murad II à Selim Ier*, Paris: Association Perre Belon, 1998; Vesna Miović, "Diplomatic Relations between the Ottoman Empire and The Republic of Dubrovnik," in *European Tributary States*, 187–208.

27 There are three main opinions concerning the early legal status of Ragusa: firstly, the protectorate of Hungarian kings from 1358 to 1526 (according to the nineteenth-century historians' view, the "old school"); secondly, that Dubrovnik became an Ottoman tributary of the Porte only in 1458 (the "new school" headed by J. Tadić); finally, that Dubrovnik was under dual protection *de jure* from 1458 to 1526 (Foretić's opinion) (Zlatar, *Dubrovnik*, 95, n. 1).

28 I. Božić, *Dubrovnik i Turska u XIV i XV veku*, Belgrade, 1952, cf. Biegman, *Ragusa*, 26, n. 22.

29 The charter of 1458 was discovered and published by Branislav M. Nedeljković (B. M. Nedeljković, "Dubrovačko-turski ugovor od 23. oktobra 1458 godine," *Zbornik filozofskog fakulteta*, XI (Belgrade, 1970), 363–392. French translations in B. Bojović, "Dubrovnik et les Ottomans (1430–1472). 20 actes de Murad II et de Mehmed II en médio-serbe," *Turcica*, XIX, 1987, doc. 2 (1430), doc. 4 (1442), doc. 6 (1458).

was to pay 1,000 ducats annually, but Zdenko Zlatar argues that "it was only after the Charter of 1458 had been granted that the Ragusan Republic decided to stake its survival as a political unit on the Ottoman protection," even though Dubrovnik had already accepted by then a tributary relationship to the Porte.[30]

Effectively until the end of eighteenth-century Ragusa enjoyed a status of tributary protection within the Ottoman Empire, very similar to that of Wallachia, Moldavia and Transylvania. These two basic elements – the tribute and Ottoman protection – were confirmed by the charters issued in the sixteenth and seventeenth century.[31]

## 10 The Khanate of Crimea

The Crimean Khanate[32] recognized Ottoman suzerainty in the context of the 1463–1479 Ottoman–Venetian war, which saw Mehmed II's troops conquer the towns of Kaffa, Mangop (*Menküp*) and the peninsula's southern shores in July 1475. Hadji Giray founded the khanate, but his son, Mengli Giray I, was frequently credited with establishing the Crimean Khanate as a power to be reckoned with. At the same time, he was also the one who accepted Ottoman protection. In this respect, some sources mention a charter (*ʿahdname*) by Mehmed II, which named Mengli Giray, who at that time was the prisoner of the sultan, to the Crimean throne.[33] In exchange, the khan assured Mehmed II of his commitment to serve "in our sultan's state" (*sultanımın devletinde*), according to a letter from 1475.[34] Most importantly, the khans retained their right to conduct the internal affairs of their domains, including minting their own

30 Biegman, *Ragusa*, 26; Zlatar, *Dubrovnik*, 69–70.

31 *Bursa Şer'iye Sicilleri*, A, 20, f. 387/b; Dalsar, "Dubrovnik muahede," 410–414; Akgündüz, *Osmanlı Kanunnameleri*, III, 385–387; Biegman, *Ragusa*, 48–59. See also "Registers of Orders to Dubrovnik" (*Dubrovnik Ahkam Defteri*), 1013–1028 AH/1604–1618 (BOA, *DED* 13) and TKSMA, Defter 7018; MOL, m. Turcia, r. 10131, f. 31–33 (*Dubrovnik namesi*).

32 On the Khanate of Crimea, see: Akdes Nimet Kurat, *Topkapı Sarayı Müzesi Arşivindeki Altınordu, Kırım ve Türkistan hanlarına ait yarlık ve bitikler*, Istanbul, 1940 (doc. IV-IX); Halil Inalcık, "Yeni vesikalara göre Kırım Hanlığının Osmanlı Tabiliğine girmesi ve ahidname meselesi," *Belleten*, VIII, 29 (1944), 185–229; *Tarih-i Sahib Giray Han* (*Histoire de Sahib Giray, Khan de Crimée de 1532 à 1551*), ed. Özalp Gökbilgin, Ankara: Atatürk Üniversitesi Edebiyat Fakültesi Yayınları, 1973; Özalp Gökbilgin, *1532–1577 yılları arasında Kırım Hanlığı'nın siyasi durumu*, Ankara: Atatürk Üniversitesi Edebiyat Fakültesi Yayınları, 1973; *Le Khanat de Crimée dans les Archives du Musée du Palais de Topkapı*, edited by Alexandre Bennigsen, Pertev Naili Boratov, Dilek Desaive, Chantal Lemercier–Quelquejay, Paris: ÉHÉSS, The Hague: Mouton Éditeur, 1978.

33 Called the "Treaty of Vassalage" in Noradounghian, *Actes*, I, 392. It was also proved by Mengli Giray I's letter of 5–15 July 1475 (Cazacu, Kévonian, "Caffa 1475," 511).

34 Gemil, "Două documente tătărăști," 191.

coins, offering sanctuary, or even being named in the *hutbe* after the sultan's name since Islam Giray II, 1584–1585.[35]

Most historians have characterized the Crimean Khanate as a "vassal" or client state of the Porte, which enjoyed large autonomy until the 1783 annexation of the khanate by the Russian Empire. Its status is frequently compared with that of Moldavia, Wallachia, Transylvania or Ragusa. Yet, as Alan Fisher and C. M. Kortepeter rightly point out, unlike Christian tributaries, the khans did not pay any tribute to the sultan. On the contrary, the voivodes of the two Danubian principalities were obliged to send annual payments (*vergü*) to the Crimean capital of Bahçesaray.[36]

## 11 Wallachia

One of the first references to Ottoman–Wallachian relations dates back to the reign of Vladislav I, who sought Ottoman help after he had turned against the Hungarians.[37] However, the contacts did not take off until the reign of Mircea the Elder (1386–1418),[38] whom sixteenth-century chronicler Kemalpaşazade regarded as "the most famous prince of the Abode of Infidels in his time."[39] Despite claims found in the Ottoman chronicles of Mehmed Neşri and Idris Bitlisi regarding Wallachians and Moldavians' participation in the famous battle of Kosovo Polje on 15 June 1389, most Romanian scholars reject this idea.[40]

35 On the Ottoman–Crimean legal arrangement, see Natalia Królikowska, "Sovereignty and Subordination in Crimean–Ottoman Relations (Sixteenth–Eighteenth Centuries)," in *European Tributary States*, 43–66.

36 C. M. Kortepeter, "Gazi Giray II, Khan of the Crimea, and Ottoman Policy in Eastern Europe and the Caucasus, 1588–1594," *The Slavonic and East European Review*, XLIV (102), 1966, 139–166; Alan W. Fischer, "Les rapports entre l'Empire ottoman et la Crimée. L'aspect financier," CMRS, XIII 3, (1972), 368–381. See also M. A. Mehmet, "La politique ottomane à l'égard de la Moldavie et du Khanat de Crimée vers la fin du règne du sultan Mehmed II «Le Conquérant»," *RRH*, 3, 1974, 509–533; Decei, *Imp. otoman*, 121–122; B. Spuler, "Kırım," *EI-2*, V, 136–143; Hurmuzaki, *Documente*, Supl. I/1, 55–56; Uzunçarşılı, *Osmanlı tarihi*, II, 434.

37 Inalcık, "Rise," 23. Then, Radu I (1377–1383) concluded an alliance with the Bulgarians and Ottomans to oppose Hungary and re-conquer the Banat of Severin but was defeated by Louis I, the king of Hungary, on 7 June 1377 (Brătianu, *Marea Neagră*, II, 216).

38 For early Ottoman–Wallachian relations, see: I. Minea, *Principatele române și politica orientală a împăratului Sigismund. Note istorice*, Bucharest: Convorbiri literare, 1919; P. P. Panaitescu, *Mircea cel Bătrân*, Bucharest, 1944; *Marele Mircea Voievod*, ed. I. Pătroiu, Bucharest: Editura Academiei, 1987; Gemil, *Românii și otomanii*, 69–85.

39 *Rüzgarında olan diyar-ı küffar şehryarlarının şehiriydi* (Ibn Kemal, *Tevarih*, in Veliman, "Mircea," 410–411).

40 On this famous battle, see: Şükrüllah, *Tevarih*, in *Cronici turcești I*, 31; Enveri, *Düsturname*, in *Cronici turcești I*, 38; Sa'adeddin, *Tevarih*, in *Cronici turcești I*, 301–303; Mehmed bin

Still, the principality had to grapple with the aftermath of the battle, most notably the Ottoman annexation of Dobruja.[41] The 1391 raid (*akın*) against Wallachia, led by Firuz bey marked the first time the Ottomans crossed the Danube, although its chronology is by no means certain.[42]

Several sources on both the Ottoman and Wallachian sides claim that one of the Wallachian princes became an Ottoman tribute-payer prior to the 1390s.[43] Other accounts, all produced at the later date, allude to Mircea the Elder accepting the status of *haracgüzar* before launching his campaign against Karınovası in 1393 and the battle of Argeş in 1395.[44] However, no document regarding these events is known at this moment. Finally, another local tradition in Wallachia included the 1772 petition by boyars to the congress of Focşani claiming that two rulers had accepted their status as Ottoman vassals. The first would have taken place before the battle of Argeş, although the year it was supposed to have happened is clearly wrong, as it falls beyond Mircea's reign.[45] Mircea the Elder's campaign against the *akıncıs* of Karınovası in 1393 is a cer-

---

Mehmed, *Tevarih*, in *Cronici turceşti I*, 401. The Christian alliance was initiated by the Serbian *knez*, Lazar (1371–1389), after the victory of Pločnik in 1387: "Laz had sent envoys to all infidels (*tamamiyet-i kefereye*) and asked for help. Helpers came from Wallachia (*Eflak*) and Hungary..., and from Serbians and from Albanians and from Bulgarians and from Franks, thus the infidels gathered (*küffar cemʿ oldılar*)" (Neşri, *Tarih*, in Veliman, "Mircea," 399–402). P. P. Panitescu definitely rejected it (Panaitescu, *Mircea*, 219–223).

41 Anca Ghiaţă, "Condiţiile instaurării dominaţiei otomane în Dobrogea," *Studii istorice sud-est europene*, I, Bucharest, 1974, 43–126.

42 *Tevarih*, in *Cronici turceşti I*, 180; Aşıkpaşazade, *Tevarih*, in Veliman, "Mircea," 405–406. Here is Richard Knolles's account on this event: "And Ferises-Beg, not content to have taken Vidin (as is aforesaid) passed over the great River of Danubius, and grievously spoiled Valachia; from whence he returned laden with a great Prey" (Knolles, *Turkish History*, 140).

43 Aşıkpaşazade quoted Bayezid I's appeal to the Wallachian prince, made after the battle of Alaca Hısar in 1391–1392: "Here Bayezid Han waged holy war [...] Bosna country and Laz gave tribute (*harac verdi*). He told to [the prince] of Wallachia: «Come immediately, and be my subject»" (Aşıkpaşazade, *Tevarih*, in Veliman, "Mircea," 406).

44 Yet, Idris Bitlisi will speak inaccurately about a "renewal of submission and obedience" and the doubling of the Wallachian prince's annual tribute (Idris Bitlisi, *Heşt Behişt*, in Veliman, "Mircea," 423, 424, and n. 202, 205). Rustem paşa said: "and in that part, the prince of Wallachia, despite he was the padişah's tribute-payer, cross the Danube on this side, plundering Karinovasi" (*Eflak voyvodası padişahın haracgüzarı iken*) (Rustem paşa, *Tevarih*, in Veliman, "Mircea," 407). Later, at the beginning of the nineteenth century, Joseph von Hammer-Purgstall quoted a record of 1391 which seems to be the first appearance of Wallachia on a register of tribute-payer princes (*haracgüzarlar*) to the Sublime Porte (Hammer, *Empire Ottoman*, I, 87; Seton–Watson, *Roumanians*, 33).

45 "The first capitulation (*proskynesis*) of Wallachia under Mircea Voivode. In the year 1383" (*Genealogia Cantacuzinilor*, 495–499). This idea was reaffirmed by the Tunusli brothers in the Greek translation of Mihai Cantacuzino's work, published in Vienna, in 1806, and later

tainty, accounted for by most fifteenth- and sixteenth-century Ottoman annalists.[46]

In Spring 1395, Bayezid I launched a campaign, intended to intimidate the Hungarians and subdue the Wallachians. His troops ravaged southern Hungary before entering Wallachia.[47] Details of the campaign found their way into the correspondence between the sultan and Timur Lenk, as well as most historical works of the fifteenth and sixteenth centuries.[48] According to Idris Bitlisi (d. 1520), a *fetva* was issued, declaring Bayezid I's expedition a holy campaign (*gaza*) meant to buttress the borders of Islam on the Danube in response to Wallachian aggression against the *akıncı* haven of Karınovası.[49]

All sources agree that Bayezid and Mircea fought at least one battle,[50] although its place and date remain unknown. According to Richard Knolles, Bayezid I led two campaigns against Wallachia, which would permit us to overcome difficulties with regard to their chronology.[51] Most accounts claim the

---

translated into Romanian by G. Sion (*Istoria Ţerei Romănesci de fraţii Tunusli*, Bucharest, 1863, 66).

46 Neşri, *Tarih*, in *Cronici turceşti I*, 113; Idris Bitlisi, *Heşt Behişt*, in *Cronici turceşti I*, 156–157; Sa'adeddin, *Tac üt-Tevarih*, in *Cronici turceşti I*, 303; Rustem paşa, *Tevarih*, in Veliman, "Mircea," 406–407. According to Richard Knolles' account, "the voivode of Wallachia, hearing of Bajazet's troubles in Asia, passed over Danubius to the South, where he spoiled the countries, slew great numbers of the Turks, retired back again into *Valachia*, carrying with him also many of the Turks Prisoners" (Knolles, *Turkish History*, 141). A comprehensive article on this topic was published by Decei, "Mircea," 140–155.

47 ANIC, mf. Turkey, r. 4, fr. 293; Decei, "Două documente," 209–210; Inalcık, "Rise," 25; Imber, *Ottoman Empire*, 44–45; Gemil, *Românii şi otomanii*, 25, 69–85.

48 *Cronici turceşti I*, 38–39 (Enveri); 48–49 (Oruc bin Adil); 13 (Mehmed Neşri); 157–159 (Idris Bitlisi); 290 (Mehmed paşa); 304 (Sa'adeddin); 339 (Mustafa Ali); 441–442 (Koca Hüseyin); 543 (Kara-Çelebi-Zade); Ibn Kemal, *Tevarih*, in Veliman, "Mircea," 410–411.

49 Idris Bitlisi, *Heşt Behişt*, in *Cronici turceşti I*, 156–157; Ibn Kemal, *Tevarih*, in Veliman, "Mircea," 410–411. The same details are in an anonymous chronicle from the end of the sixteenth century (Gemil, *Românii şi otomanii*, 25).

50 In trying to reconstruct Bayezid I's route during the Wallachian campaign, historians most often refer to a controversial mid-fifteenth-century Ottoman document (Imber, *Ottoman Empire*, 44–45). "Then [Bayezid I], came to the Wallachian country; Voivode Mircea, who is the *bey* of Wallachia, to confront him and prevent him from going any further, fought and battled together with the army of Wallachia for a week on the river called Argeş" (*andan Eflak ili diyarına gelüb, Eflak beği olan Mirce voyvoda askeriyle karşu gelüb geçid vermeyüb Arciş nam suyin üzerinde bir hafta mikdarı Eflak askeriyle muharebe ve mukatele olub*) (ANIC, mf. Turkey, r. 4, fr. 293; Inalcık, "Document," 220–222; Decei, "Două documente," 209–222).

51 The first battle is described as follows by Richard Knolles: "... thus at once invaded both in *Asia* and *Europe*; deferred his Wars purposed against the Prince of Pontus, until a more convenient time, converting his Forces against the *Valachians*. Wherefore passing over the Strait to Hadrianople, he sent his Army from thence to *Nicopolis*, and there passing

battle took place in the vicinity of the Argeș river (*Arciș nam suyin üzerinde*), although Idris Bitlisi described the battlefield as a "mountainous and dangerous place." Romanian historians have considered so far two possible dates of the clash, either 25 November 1394 or 17 May 1395.[52] It is also clear that prior to the battle in Spring 1395, an alliance was struck on 7 March 1395 between Mircea the Elder and the king of Hungary, Sigismund of Luxemburg; the voivode expressed his gratitude for the support the Hungarian ruler had granted him, and promised to join the king's army against the Ottomans and their allies. It seems that the conclusion of the alliance triggered the sultan's campaign, which was relatively swift, since soon "Bayazet had ended his Wars in Valachia, and was with Victory returned to Prusa."[53]

What happened after the battle became the subject of heated debates among historians, although it garnered less attention among students of Ottoman history. Halil Inalcık and Colin Imber dealt with Bayezid I's campaign against Wallachia as part of the wider conflict between the Ottomans and Hungary, Serbia, Bulgaria and Byzantium, unfolding from 1389 until 1402. Their treatment on the outcomes of Bayezid I's Wallachian campaign was largely limited to a brief mention of the sultan's having crossed the Danube at Nikopol and brought an end to the existence of Bulgarian tsardom, whose last ruler, Shishman, was detained and executed.[54]

---

the River of *Danubius*, entered into *Valachia*, burning and spoiling the Country before him as he went. Where the Vayvod to repress his Fury, met him in the Field and gave him Battle, but was therein overthrown, and many of his People slain" (Knolles, *Turkish History*, 144).

52 B. P. Hașdeu cited a source indicating 17 May 1395 as the date of Constantin Dragoš' death. It is known that this Serbian despot died on the battlefield (See A. V. Diță, "17 mai 1395, o dată importantă în istoria universală – victoria românească de la Rovine," in *Mircea*, 254–278). Moreover, Tahsin Gemil concluded that the battle took place in "Autumn 1395" (Gemil, "Mircea," 330–365).

53 "In the Wars against Sigismund, the Vayvod of Valachia had given aid to the Hungarian King; wherewith Bajazet being offended, determined now at length to be revenged; and therefore intending to make War upon the Valachian Prince, left Temurtases his great Lieutenant at Ancyra in Asia, and so passed over Hellespontus himself against the Valachians" (Knolles, *Turkish History*, 144). See also DRH, D, vol. I, doc. 87. Imber supposed that the aim of Bayezid I's campaign was to preempt the consequences of this agreement (Imber, *Ottoman Empire*, 44).

54 Inalcık, "Rise," 25; Imber, *Ottoman Empire*, 44–45. One can quote here both the Bulgarian chronicle ("put Bulgaria under his power") and the Ottoman text (*merhum Yıldırım Han dahi Arciș suyin geçüb, Nikeboli kalesinin karșusunda konub ol zamanda Nikeboli vilayetinin Șișman nam bir beği var imiș Eflak voyvodası gibi Hüdavendigarun haracgüzarımıș*) (ANIC, mf. Turkey, r. 4, fr. 293; Decei, "Două documente," 210–211).

There is no doubt that a peace agreement was concluded between Bayezid I and a Wallachian voivode, although the name of the incumbent (Mircea the Elder or Vlad I) and the conditions of peace remain unknown.[55]

A document produced in the period the events took place, a letter sent by King Sigismund I in December 1395, depicts Vlad I as hostile towards the Hungarians, since he had been installed by the Ottomans and continued to receive their support against the Crown of Saint Stephen. A similar image emerges from other Hungarian documents issued in this period.[56] Unfortunately, Ottoman historians offer no details concerning Vlad I's bid for the throne and his usurpation of the Wallachian throne. Another source, seen either as the document from the late fourteenth century or as an excerpt from a sixteenth-century chronicle, mentions "peace with the voivode of Wallachia" (*Eflak voyvodasıyla sulh edüb*) concluded after the battle of the Argeş.[57] Unfortunately, chronicles provide no details regarding the terms of the peace, with the exception of Idris Bitlisi who – writing about the "renewal of the submission and obedience pact" and the doubling of the Wallachian prince's annual tribute – anachronistically applied Islamic vocabulary, closer to the sixteenth-century juridical texts rather than fourteenth-century realities (for instance *ʿahd-ı zimmet,* and *cizye*).[58] Wallachian historical traditions of the eighteenth century opposed this Ottoman standpoint. Among them, Radu Popescu recorded the conclusion of a peace agreement after the battle of "Rovine" and noted that Mircea the Elder,

> realizing the Turks' arrogance, made peace with them and gave them a gift so that the country can rest unruffled.[59]

Historians have frequently cited this passage to characterize the first Ottoman–Wallachian agreement as a temporary truce and the first sum of money paid to the sultan as merely a "gift" (*plocon*). Worth mentioning in this respect is the opinion of Richard Knolles, who claimed that the voivode, defeated by Bayezid I

55 Gh. I. Constantin, "Le traité entre le sultan Baiazet I et la Valachie," *Der Islam*, vol. 59, no. 2, 1982, 254–284.

56 *DRH*, D, vol. I, doc. 101. In Romanian historiography Vlad I is considered as being the first Wallachian prince who took the throne with Ottoman support. See also the letter of 21 March 1396 or 10 April 1397, which speaks about envoys to Vlad I in order to obtain news on the Turks (*DRH*, D, vol. I, doc. 97).

57 ANIC, mf. Turkey, r. 4, fr. 293; Decei, "Două documente," 210–214.

58 Idris Bitlisi, *Heşt Behişt,* in Veliman, "Mircea," 423–424, n. 202, 205.

59 Popescu, *Istoriile*, 240 (*văzând obrăznicia turcilor, s-au împăcat cu ei şi le-au fost dat plocon pentru ca să se odihnească ţara cu pace*).

> at last he was glad to sue for Peace, which he obtained, by submitting himself to *Bajazet*, and yielding to pay him a yearly Tribute.[60]

When the Ottoman army returned to the southern bank of the Danube, Bayezid I seized Nikopol, thus establishing control over one of the most important crossings from Rumelia to Wallachia.[61] It was in the vicinity of this fortress, which Ottoman authors described as located on the "Islamic frontier" (*serhadd-ι islamda*), the sultan confronted on 25 September 1396 a crusader army led by King Sigismund.[62] Mircea's participation in the disastrous battle of Nikopol and his eagerness to strike against the Ottomans are referred to only in Christian sources, including Johann Schiltberger, but not the Ottoman ones.

After his decisive victory, Bayezid I invaded and annexed in Fall 1396 yet-unconquered vestiges of Bulgarian territories – the Tsardom of Vidin, ruled by Ivan Stratsimir, thus consolidating the Ottoman control over the southern bank of the Danube.[63] However, north of the river the Ottoman foothold was soon undone. In their correspondence from 1399, both Mircea and King Sigismund continued to refer to Wallachia as the lands that Bayezid I failed to conquer, with the Danube separating the Ottoman lands from Christian territories. Still, both expressed anxiety over the presence of Ottoman troops on the right bank of the great river, a mere five days of march from their domains, and carefully assessed the negative consequences of Mircea's submission to the Porte.[64]

It is important to remember that the position of Anatolian and Balkan rulers was strongly affected by the battle of Ankara, where Timur Lenk vanquished Bayezid I on 28 July 1402.[65] For the following decade, until 1413, Mircea repeatedly intervened in a succession struggle between Bayezid's successors,[66]

---

60 Knolles, *Turkish History*, 141.

61 Inalcık, "Rise," 25; Imber, *Ottoman Empire*, 44–45.

62 Şükrullah, *Tevarih*, in Veliman, "Mircea," 426; Idris Bitlisi, *Heşt Behişt*, in *Cronici turceşti I*, 156–157; Koca Hüseyin, *Beda'i ül-veka'i*, in *Cronici turc I*, 442; Imber, *Ottoman Empire*, 45–47.

63 Imber, *Ottoman Empire*, 47.

64 In King Sigismund's letter of 23 March 1399: *non est vorbis incognitum in quanto postea pericolo et discrimine existeret regnum nostrum* (DRH, D, vol. I, doc. 105).

65 The participation of the Wallachian troops was also addressed by historians (A. Decei, "A participat Mircea cel Bătrân la lupta de la Ankara?" RIR, VII, fasc. III–IV, 1937, 339–357 (reprinted in Decei, RRO, 5–14).

66 In King Sigismund's letter of 16 April 1404 addressed to the Duke of Burgundy, Wallachia and Moldavia were mentioned as being in an alliance against the Turks (Hurmuzaki, *Documente*, I/2, 429; DRH, D, vol, I, doc, 109). A good summary of these struggles is provided in Dimitris J. Kastritsis, *The Sons of Bayezid. Empire Building and Representation in the Ottoman Civil War of 1402–1413*, Leiden, Boston: Brill, 2007.

particularly in favour of Musa Çelebi, who even resided in Wallachia between 1409 and 1410.[67]

The Ottoman civil war was brought to an end in 1413, when Mehmed I Çelebi prevailed over his brothers and became the new Ottoman sultan.[68] According to Ducas, Wallachian emissaries attended his ceremony of accession together with other foreign envoys.[69] Christian and Ottoman sources alike mention a campaign launched by Mehmed I against Wallachia, which brought a renewal of hostilities after a period of relative calm, as well as a peace with the voivode between 1416 and 1420; unfortunately, it is impossible to provide precise dates nor to determine the name of the incumbent voivode.

The majority of Ottoman authors identify the sultanic campaign (which they call *gaza*) of 1417,[70] which resulted in the capture of the Giurgiu fortress, an important strategic foothold on the northern bank of the Danube, and the *akıncı* raid to the northern areas of the principality. A peace agreement is said to have been reached between the warring sides, stipulating an annual tribute (*harac*) and the requirement to send one or more "sons" (in this case, boyars) as hostages to the Porte.[71] Şükrullah, Aşıkpaşazade and Mehmed Neşri's narrations are essentially the same in this respect:

---

67 Neşri, *Tarih*, in *Cronici turcești I*, 114–116; Sa'adeddin, *Tevarih*, in *Cronici turcești I*, 302–307; Koca Hüseyin, *Beda'i ül-veka'i*, in *Cronici turcești I*, 443–444; M. Alexandrescu-Dersca Bulgaru, "Les relations du prince de Valachie Mircea l'Ancien avec les émirs seldjoukides d'Anatolie et leur candidat Musa au tróne Ottoman," *TAD*, VI, 1968, 10–11 (1972), 113–225; Ș. Papacostea, "La Valachie et la crise de structure de l'Empire Ottoman (1402–1413)," *RRH*, XXV, 1–2, 1986, 23–33.

68 The Ottoman policy for conquering the territories around the Delta of Danube, as well as Ottoman–Wallachian relations during Mehmed I's reign, have been deeply studied by: V. Ciocîltan, "Competiția pentru controlul Dunării inferioare. 1412–1420," *RdI*, 10, 1982, 1090–1100 and 11, 1982, 1191–1203; V. Ciocîltan, "Poarta Osmană și Gurile Dunării în secolul al XV-lea," *RdI*, 11, 1985, 1058–1074; N. Pienaru, "Relațiile lui Mircea cel Mare (1386–1418) cu Mehmed I Çelebi (1413–1421)," *RdI*, 8, 1986, 774–794; N. Pienaru, "Les Pays Roumains et le Proche Orient (1420–1429)," *RRH*, XXVIII, 3–4, 1989 (I) and XXIX, 1–2, 1990, 69–103 (II).

69 Ducas, *Istoria*, XX/2 (in *FHDR*, 419).

70 819 AH. See: Neșri, *Tarih*, II, 536–537; Aşıkpaşazade, *Tevarih*, in *Cronici turcești I*, 85 ("reaching the side of Danube"); *Tevarih*, in *Cronici turcești I*, 181 ("he stopped at Danube").

71 See: *Cronici turcești I*, 32 (Şükrüllah); 51 (Oruc bin Adil); 85 (Aşıkpaşazade); 116 (Mehmed Neşri); 160–164 (Idris Bitlisi); 181 (*Tevarih*); 238 (Lütfi paşa); 291 (Mehmed paşa); 307–308 (Sa'adeddin); 402–403 (Mehmed bin Mehmed); 445 (Koca Hüseyin). The same account can be found in a 16th century Ottoman chronicle written in Greek (*16. Asırda Yazılmış Grekçe Anonim Osmanlı Tarihi. Giriş ve Metin (1373–1512)*, Hazırlayan: Şerif Baştav, Ankara: Ankara Üniversitesi Basımevi, 1973, 113).

> The sultan, with fortune on his side, marched on to Rumeli. And he crossed the Danube, building Giurgiu [...] After that, the prince of Wallachia sent tribute through his envoy, acknowledged his submission (*Eflak'un beği dahı elçiyle haracın göndürdü ita'at-i külli etdi*) and dispatched his sons to serve the Porte.[72]

Chalcocondylas' account is basically the same, as he narrates the Wallachian campaign, the peace agreement and an annual tribute imposed by Mehmed I.[73] There are indications that this campaign took place after Mircea's death, during the reign of his son and successor, Mihail I (January 1418–August 1420) and was triggered by the violation of a covenant by the Wallachian ruler. Indeed, a much later chronicle by Koca Hüseyin sets its date on the year 1420,[74] while the eighteenth-century Wallachian boyar Ienache Văcărescu affirmed that Mihail I (*Mihai Voda sin Mircea Voda*) was the first Wallachian voivode to pay homage to an Ottoman sultan and become his tribute-payer, although he gives the year 1418 as the date of the events in question.[75]

---

72 Aşıkpaşazade's account is as follows: *Bu bab anı beyan eder kim Sultan Mehmed Gazi ibn-i Bayezid Han Bursaya gelüb Eflaka 'azm etdüğini bildirür... Devlet ilen vilayet-i Eflak'a yürüdü. Tuna kenarına vardı. Dahı akıncılar göndürdü. Kendü oturdu. Yergögüyi yapdı. Akıncılar mubalağa doyum geldiler. Eflakun beği dahı elçiyle haracın göndürdü. Ita'at-i külli etdi. Ve oğlanların Kapu'ya hizmete göndürdü* (Aşıkpaşazade, *Tevarih*, in *Osmanlı Tarihleri*, 151, and in *Cronici turceşti I*, 85). Şükrullah was the closest chronicler to that event. See, Şükrüllah, *Tevarih*, in *Osmanlı tarihleri*, 61, and in *Cronici turceşti*, I, 32 (*Dinsiz, kötü düşünceli Eflaka yöneldi. O yörede üç kale vardı ki karganmış kafirlerin yüzünden yıkılmıştı. Üçünü de yaptırdı. Birinin adı Sakçı, ikincinin adı Yeni Sala, üçünçünün Yörkövi idi. Oradan Üngürüse yönelip Savarin kalesini aldı. Tanrı onları aşağılatsın, karganmış kafirler Islamların ululuk ve yüceliğini görüb bilince barış dilediler. Harac vermeği boyunlarına aldılar. Kendilerini sultanın yüce eşiği kulları sırasında saydılar. Üç kafir beği oğlunu yarağı yasağı uşağı ile hizmete gönderdiler... ve onun üzerine and ettiler ki... Barış kıldılar...*). Mehmed Neşri's account is: *Hikayet-i Zihab-ı Sultan Mehmed ila Ungurus ve feth-i kal'a Severin ve ta'at ül-küffar lehü... andan hicretün sekiz yüz on dokuzunda sultan etrafun leşkerin cem' idüb Karaman oğlu dahi leşker gönderüb Isfendiyar oğlu Kasım Beği gönderdi. Andan devletle yürüyüb* (*Rumeli'ne geçti ve* – ed. U.K) *Tuna'yı geçti. Kenarında durub, Yerköyünü yapdurub* (*Isakçı* – ed. U.K.) *ve Yeni-Sale'yi ma'mur idüb, andan akıncılar salı virüb seğirdüb mübalağa* (*ile*) *doyumluklar oldı. Andan Eflak Beyi harac* (*ını*) *gönderüb elçiyle ita'at etdi. Ve dahi oğlanların*(*ı*) *hizmete Kapuya gönderdi ki, ayrık yağılık etmiye. Eğer edecek olursa oğlanlarını helak edeler. Eflak oğlu'yla bu vech üzere musalaha idüb, barışıklık etdiler* (Neşri, *Tarih*, ed. Taeschner, II, 214; Neşri, *Tarih*, ed. U.K., II, 536, 537, and in *Cronici turceşti I*, 115–116).

73 Chalcocondil, *Expuneri*, 120.

74 823 AH in Koca Hüseyin, *Beda'i ul-Veka'i*, in *Cronici turceşti I*, 446–447: "since that treacherous infidel broke the pact (*'ahd*) and agreement (*misak*)."

75 Văcărescu, *Istorie*, 204.

During the communist regime, some Romanian historians invoked this information in an attempt to dissociate Mircea, regarded as a great ruler and a national hero, from what was interpreted as a humiliating submission to the Ottomans. However, these debates seem unfounded given that Richard Knolles, whose *Turkish History* appeared for the first time in 1603, on the basis of Byzantine and Ottoman sources clearly stated that Mircea had become Mehmed I's tributary following the Ottoman campaign of 1417:

> 1417. Valachia Tributary to the Turk. The Caramanian War thus happily ended, he went into Europe, and passing over Danubius, foraged the Country of Valachia Transalpina, making there great spoil; for redress whereof, the Valachian Prince by his Embassadors sent him such Tribute as he demanded, and his Son also to serve him in his Court. About which time happened a great Earthquake in Prusa, and other places of Asia.[76]

Since 1417, also, all territory south of the Danube mouths (*Dobruja*) was annexed definitively by Ottomans.

For several decades following Mircea's death, until 1456, the situation in Wallachia degenerated into factional infighting between his sons and rival claimants to the throne, known in historiography as the fight between Danești (descendants of Dan I) and Draculești (Mircea's descendants).[77] The policy of

76 Knolles, *Turkish History*, 170. Later, Dimitrie Cantemir would analyse this issue in a similar manner: "VIII. Mahomet makes the *Walachians* tributary. H. 820/A.C. 1418. After weakening all his Enemies in *Asia*, *Mahomet* assembles his *European* and *Asiatic* forces, and departs from *Prusa* to *Adrianople*. From thence he marches against the Wallachians, routs their Army, lays waste [to] great part of the Province, takes *Severia*, where is a bridge said to be built by *Trajan*, and the Castles *Sakche* and *Cale*, situate on the other side the Danube, and fortifies *Girgiow* with new Works and a good Garrison, so that the *Walachians* could not any more pass the *Danube*. Pent up in this manner and pressed by the sword of the Enemy and the want of warlike Stores, desparing also to preserve their liberty, they purchase their safety with the promise of an annual tribute, for the performance whereof the Sons of Prince and theree Great Men are given to the Emperor in hostage. After which he returns to *Adrianople*" (Cantemir, *Othman History*, 73–74).

77 For instance, between 1420 and 1427, Dan II ruled four times, incessantly struggling against his rival, Radu II Praznaglava, who also reigned four times in this period, the longest period being from December 1424 to May 1426. In 1420, one of the Wallachian princes being kept hostage at the sultanic court, most likely Dan II, entered Wallachia with the *akıncıs*' support, and dethroned Mihail I; the latter perished in battle. Shortly thereafter, in autumn 1420, Dan II switched his allegiance and recognised the Hungarian king, Sigismund, as his overlord, with the assistance of Filippo of Scolari/Pippo Spano, Count of Timișoara and Ozora. In 1421 Radu II Praznaglava was installed on the throne by chieftans

Wallachian princes and their status were profoundly influenced by the geopolitical position of the principality, incessantly oscillating between Hungary and the Porte.[78] The reign of Vlad the Evil provides a telling depiction of this tumultuous period.[79] The voivode had been enthroned by the Hungarians in December 1436 to stand guard against the Ottomans but the absence of substantial support caused by the prompt death of Sigismund I in 1437 led him to pay to Murad II soon after "he got the throne." The Wallachian voivode's submission, recorded by most Ottoman and Byzantine chroniclers, obliged him to resume tribute payments (including arrears from the previous two years), send hostages to the Porte (his sons Vlad and Radu, accompanied by offspring of high-ranking boyars) and join his forces with the Ottoman troops in their military campaigns against Hungary.[80]

The conditions suggest that Vlad the Evil became tribute-payer (*haracgüzar*) and concluded a pact (*ʿahd*) with Murad II, according to Idris Bitlisi, who used an Islamic legal terminology.[81] In exchange, Vlad the Evil, like his

---

on the Danube, Turahan and Evrenosoğlu, and obliged to join them in their raids into Transylvania. He was subsequently ousted by Dan II, supported by Hungarian troops, with the back and forth continuing throughout the 1420s. By 1422–1423, Dan II was unquestionably hostile to the Porte, and crossed the Danube together with Pippo Spano, plundering Silistre and its vicinity. Probably on that occasion, Giurgiu and Turnu fortresses were conquered. Firuzbeyoğlu Ali bey responded through an expedition of January 1423 in an attempt to install Radu II, but the victory belonged to Dan II (Some information on this is offered by official Hungarian and Wallachian documents published in *DRH*, D, I, doc. 139, 141, 150, 151, 153, 157, 160, 161, 162, 209. For details on that period, see: A.D. Xenopol, "Lupta dintre Dănești și Drăculești," *AARMSI*, 2, XXX, 1907, 183–272; Decei, *Imp. otoman*, 85–86; Giurescu, *Istoria românilor*, II, 112–114).

78 C. C. Giurescu and Dinu Giurescu spoke about a permanent oscillation of the Wallachian voivodes between a "political solution" (tribute-payer status) and a "military solution" (alliance with Hungary against Ottomans) (Giurescu, *Istoria românilor*, II, 112).

79 He ruled twice: Dec. 1436–March 1442 and Autumn 1443–Nov./Dec. 1447. On Vlad the Evil, see: I. Minea, *Vlad Dracul și vremea sa*, Iași: Viața Românească, 1928 (off-print from *Cercetări istorice*, IV); C. I. Karadja, "Poema lui Michel Beheim despre cruciadele împotriva turcilor din anii 1443 și 1444," *Bul. Com. Ist.*, XV, 1936, 3–59; P. P. Panaitescu, N. Stoicescu, "La participation des Roumains à la bataille de Varna (1444)," *RRH*, IV, 1965, 2, 221–231; V. Ciocîltan, "Între sultan și împărat: Vlad Dracul în 1438," *RdI*, 29, 11, 1976, 1767–1790.

80 Ducas, *Istoria*, XXIX/10; Decei, *Imp. otoman*, 87–88. Vlad the Evil participated in Murad II's campaign, in Transylvania in 1438.

81 Idris Bitlisi, *Heşt Behişt*, in *Cronici turcești I*, 167. The same policy applied after Vlad the Evil's attack against Silistre. "At this time also, Dracula Prince of of Valachia, passing over Danubius, did the Turks much harm boust Silistra, but was afterwards enforced to submit himself to Amurath, and become his Tributary." (Knolles, *Turkish History*, 175).

predecessor Alexandru I Aldea, was able to ransom Wallachians enslaved before,[82] and ensured Wallachian territory would not be pillaged by Ottoman troops crossing the principality.[83]

Soon after Mehmed II's failure to conquer Belgrade in 1456, the Wallachian throne was taken by Vlad's son, known as Vlad the Impaler.[84] Kritobulos mentioned that the sultan "bound him by treaties and oaths" immediately after he took the reins of power, thus confirming the voivode's position as an Ottoman tribute-payer.[85] However, in 1460, when the sultan demanded Vlad personally travel to the Porte with the due *harac*, the voivode refused. By denying the tribute he had been paying for the past years the aim, from the prince of Wallachia's point of view, was to shake off "the *Turkish* yoke."[86] Consequently, in 1462, Mehmed II personally led a campaign against Vlad, recounted in most Ottoman narrative sources of the fifteenth and sixteenth century. Mehmet Neşri, in his history of the Ottoman dynasty, recounted "The story of the holy campaign of Wallachia" (*Hikayet-i Gaza-yı Eflak*).[87] According to Richard Knolles, Mehmed II aimed "to extrap Wladus Prince of Valachia," and consequently

82 *Genealogia Cantacuzinilor*, 64 (*Şi aşa Turcii i-a dat şi pe toţi Romanii, ce-i robise mai înainte*). They were probably the captives taken during the raids commanded by Firuzbeyoğlu Mehmed bey (Aşıkpaşazade, *Tarih* and Neşri, *Tarih*, in *Cronici turceşti I*, 86, 118).

83 Like in 841 AH/1437–1438, on the occasion of Murad II's expedition to Hungary (Idris Bitlisi, *Heşt Behişt*, in *Cronici turceşti I*, 167).

84 He had three reigns: Oct. 1448; 22 Aug. 1456–Nov. 1462 and 1476. On Vlad Tepeş, see: *DRH*, D, I, doc. 338, 339; Tocilescu, *534 documente*, doc. 73, 75; I. Bogdan, *Vlad Ţepeş şi naraţiunile germane şi ruseşti asupra lui*, Bucharest: Ed. Socecu, 1896; Radu Florescu, Raymond T. McNally, *Dracula: A Biography of Vlad the Impaler. 1431–1476*, New York: Hawthorn, 1973; N. Stoicescu, *Vlad Ţepeş*, Bucharest: Ed. Academiei, 1976; Şt. Andreescu, *Vlad Ţepeş (Dracula). Între legendă şi adevăr*, Bucharest: Ed. Minerva, 1976.

85 It is not clear if he was referring to the first reign, in 1448, or to the second one (Critobul, *Mehmed II*, IV/10, 3). There is a discussion on this topic in Stoicescu, *Vlad Ţepeş*, 15–25, 35–37. Narrating the campaign against Vlad Ţepeş (*Kazıklu Voyvoda*), Tursun bey began, like other chroniclers, by defining the previous legal condition of the Wallachian voivodes towards the Porte (Tursun bey, *Tarih*, 47, 93a–103a).

86 Ducas, *Istoria*, XXIX/20; Cantemir, *Othman History*, 108.

87 Neşri, *Tarih*, II, 755–758. See also *Cronici turceşti I*, 42–44 (Enveri); 59–60 (Oruc bin Adil); 67–72 (Tursun bey); 93–94 (Aşıkpaşazade); 126–127 (Mehmed Neşri); 201–206 (Ibn Kemal); 244 (Lütfi paşa); 294 (Mehmed paşa); 317–320 (Sa'adeddin); 405–406 (Mehmed bin Mehmed); 455–456 (Koca Hüseyin). William Wey, as well, on his pilgrimage to the Holy Land, heard and accounted for the Ottoman action against Vlad the Impaler in 1462 (F. Pall, "Notes du pélerin William Wey à propos des opérations militaires des Turcs en 1462," *RHSEE*, XXII, 1945, 246–266; Tappe, *Documents*, no. 2).

> the year following, which was the year 1462, Mahomet having Intelligence, that Wladus Dracula Prince of Valachia, his Tributary, was resolved to cast from him his Obedience, and to join himself unto the Hungarians, his mortal Enemies; thought it best to prove if he could by policy circumvent him, before he were altogether fallen from him.[88]

From the Ottoman perspective, following Mehmed II's campaign, Wallachian "infidels" came in droves and submitted to the sultan, who installed Radu the Fair after the latter took his "oath of fealty." In comparison with "homage paying" with a personal charge, a collective "homage paying" took place in 1462:

> The padişah of Islam [...], crossed the Danube, entering Wallachia; all Wallachian people came [and] paid homage to him.[89]

According to Dimitrie Cantemir, Mehmed II considered that in the face of Vlad the Impaler's imminent threat,

> instantly turns his arms against *Walachia*, and expelling the rebellious Prince, makes his younger brother Governor of the Province.[90]

Let us note that, for seventeenth- and eighteenth-century Wallachian authors, the first voivode to acknowledge his subordination to the Porte was Basarab Laiotă (who ruled intermittently between 1473 and 1477), engaged in a struggle for the throne with Mehmed's erstwhile appointee, Radu the Fair, and frequently confused with his rival.[91] In turn, modern Romanian historiography

88 Knolles, *Turkish History*, 246–248.

89 *Padişah-ı Islam* [...] *Tuna'yı geçüb Eflak vilayetine girüb cemi' Eflak'ın vilayeti halkı gelüb tapdılar* (Neşri, *Tarih*, II, 756–757); ANIC, mf. Turkey, r. 65, fr. 751–752, cf. Gemil, *Românii și otomanii*, 144, n. 375; Critobul, *Mehmed II*, IV, 10, 1–3 (*ta pista labon*). See also Chalcocondil, *Expuneri*, in *FHDR*, IV, 515, 517. Radu the Fair ruled four times between 1462 and 1475, the longest reign being between Nov. 1462 and Nov. 1473.

90 Cantemir, *Othman History*, 108. According to Mihai Cantacuzino's view, in 1460–1462, "the Hospodar himself (and he wrongly indicated Basarab Laiotă), willingly, submitted the country" (*Genealogia Cantacuzinilor*, 67, 495–499).

91 *Letopisețul Cantacuzinesc*, 4; Popescu, *Istoriile*, 252 (*care au închinat țara turcilor*); *Genealogia Cantacuzinilor*, 67 (*Laiot Basarab Voevod, la anul 1460. Acesta este carele cu totul s'a supus, închinând Țara-Românească la Turci*), 495–499; Filstich, *Istorie*, 104–105. An article regarding the tribute of Wallachia and Moldavia in this period was published by Mihail Guboglu, "Le tribut payé par les Principautés Roumaines à la Porte jusqu'au début du XVIe siècle d'après les sources turques," *REI*, 37, 1, (1969): 49–80.

overwhelmingly interpreted the year 1462 as a turning point in the political relations between Wallachia and the Porte.[92]

In the 1520s and 1530s, the reign of Süleyman Kanunî brought important changes in the power relations in Southeastern and Central Europe. The Ottomans captured Belgrade in 1521, vanquished the Hungarian army in the battle of Mohács (1526), and occupied the capital Buda in 1529, effectively destroying the Kingdom of Hungary.[93] Moreover, Polish claims and Habsburg encroachments in the course of the 1530s prompted Süleyman to definitively establish the issues of Ottoman control north of the Danube. A campaign launched in 1538 against the Moldavian Voivode Petru Rareş, the second conquest of Buda and the transformation of Transylvania into a tributary principality in 1541 had a profound impact on the political status of Wallachia as well.

Consequently, by the 1520s Wallachia faced an imminent threat of being put under direct Ottoman administration, headed by a Muslim governor. This danger led Wallachian boyars to suspend internal infighting and successfully resist the attempt by performing a collective act of homage, similar to that of 1462.[94] Recounting the events, Radu Popescu described an attempt to sooth the attitude of the Porte, undertaken by Voivode Radu of Afumaţi (1522–1529, intermittently) and Wallachian boyars, most likely in 1524:

> But putting heads together, they found this: that they could not fight [because] they were few in a small country, an emperor who conquered and overran so many countries and has many arms. They all decided that the voivode should go to the Porte and bow his head to the emperor's lap. And so he did. He went with many boyars.[95]

These conditions elucidate an unguarded joy of the voivode, expressed in a letter of 1 February 1525 to the inhabitants of Sibiu:

---

92 For details, see Stoicescu, *Vlad Ţepeş*, 85–136; Maxim, *ŢRÎP*, 230–240. Yet, Halil Inalcık ignored Mehmed II's expedition against Wallachia in 1462. In turn, V. J. Parry claimed that Wallachia had only been ravaged by the Ottomans, but the Ottoman hold on Wallachia was not yet assured (Parry, "Bayezid II-Selim I," 55).

93 For details see Gábor Basta, *La route qui mene à Istanbul 1526–1528*, Budapest: Akadémiai Kiadó, 1994.

94 This initiative belonged to Mehmed bey, *sancakbeyi* of Nikopol (*Cronica lui Macarie*, in *CSR*, 93; Popescu, *Istoriile*, 272–274; Michael Bocignoli, in *Călători straini*, I, 178; Tocilescu, *534 documente*, doc. 308, 426; Nicolae Stoicescu, *Radu de la Afumaţi*, Bucharest, 1983, 81–88).

95 Popescu, *Istoriile*, 274.

> I went to the Turkish Porte and I stayed in the presence of the Turkish emperor and all high officials of the Turkish country. The Wallachian reign was given to me by God, firstly, and then by the Turkish emperor, and I came back again alive and healthy [...] , and I took the Wallachian throne and reigned.[96]

Despite certain voivodes' attempts to regain their independence or secure protection of Christian powers, Wallachia, remained as an autonomous principality under the Ottoman system of government up to the Russian-Ottoman war in 1877–1878.[97] According to the treaty of Berlin signed in 13 July 1878,[98] the independence of Romania (since 1859 Wallachia unified with Moldavia) was recognized by the European powers.

## 12 Moldavia

Following the conquest of Constantinople, Mehmed II continued his policy of extending his mastery over the Black Sea by forcing Geneose colonies of the region to pay tribute to the Porte, and subsequently annexing them one by one into his expanding polity.[99] At this juncture, on 5 October 1455, while en route to besiege Belgrade, the sultan forced Moldavia to accept a 2,000-ducat annual tribute.[100] Following the sultan's ultimatum, the Moldavian Voivode Petru Aron (1451–1456, intermittently) sent Chancellor Mihul to deliver "those two thousand Hungarian *zloty* so that we may have peace and our country may not be robbed,"[101] unless the envoy was able to obtain better conditions from the sultan. In response, on 9 June 1456, Mehmed II issued an imperial order (*nişan-ı hümayun*) to local Ottoman officials (*sancakbeyi*s, *bey*s, *sübaşı*s, *kadı*s), in which he announced the establishment of peaceful relations with the Moldavian ruler, and guaranteed protection to the merchants from his countries and

96 Tocilescu, *534 documente*, doc. 308, 426.

97 On Russia's involvement in the Balkans, see Barbara Jelavich, *Russia's Balkan entanglements. 1806–1914*, Cambridge: Cambridge University Press, 1991.

98 *The Concert of Europe*, 272–273.

99 Inalcık, "Rise," 45.

100 22 *Şevval* 859 AH (Mehmet, *Documente turcești*, I, doc. 1). According to the Sbigniev Olesnicki's letter of 10 September 1453, Mehmed II would have already sent a challenge in June–August 1453, asking Alexandru II (1449; 1452–1454; 1455) to pay tribute: *gravia tributa requirit* (Papacostea, "1455–1456," 446, n. 2).

101 *DRH* , A, II, doc. 58.

especially those from Akkerman who would come to trade in Edirne, Brusa and Istanbul.[102]

In the Ottoman chronicles, at least those published so far, the events of 1455–1456 remain unmentioned, although two Ottoman documents I have discussed refer to this episode at length.[103] In turn, the Moldavian chronicles recount the events, although they frame it not as a decisive political juncture, but merely as the first instance a "tax" (in Romanian *bir* or *dajde*) was paid to the Porte. For instance, Grigore Ureche wrote that "this Petru voivode was the first who devised and began to pay tax to the Turks."[104]

In 1457, Stephen the Great took the throne of Moldavia and began paying an increased *harac* of 3,000 ducats. However, fifteen years later he refused further payments, and after the set date passed in 1474, Mehmed II dispatched an ultimatum, summoning Stephen personally to come to Istanbul along with the tribute, in order for the voivode to demonstrate his loyalty. The Moldavian voivode refused (*kafir gelmedi*),[105] and consequently a punitive campaign was launched against Moldavia, under the *beylerbeyi* of Rumelia Süleyman paşa. The Ottoman chronicles unanimously describe an ignominious defeat of the Ottoman Army on 10 January 1475 at the battlefield of Vaslui.[106] Next year, after issuing another ultimatum,[107] and meticulous preparations (including securing Crimean support),[108] Mehmed II routed Moldavians at Valea Albă on 26

102 5 *Receb* 860 AH. This document was published and commented several times (Mehmet, *Documente turcești*, I, doc. 2; Guboglu, *Paleografia*, doc. 3: *Boğdan ile beyi Pitri voyvoda ile barışıklık edüb aradan duşmanlığı götürdüm*).

103 For details, see: F. Babinger, *Cel dintîi bir al Moldovei către sultan* (off-print), Bucharest, 1936; A. H. Golimas, *Sensul închinării de la Vaslui a lui Petru Vodă Aron. Din legăturile de drept ale Moldovei cu Poarta Otomană*, (off-print), Iași, 1941; Papacostea, "1455–1456," 445–461; L. Șimanschi, "Închinarea de la Vaslui (5 <iunie>1456)," *AIIAI*, XVIII, 1981, 613–637; M.A. Mehmet, "Din raporturile Moldovei cu Imperiul Otoman în a doua jumătate a veacului al XV-lea," *St. RdI*, 5, 1960, 160–178; Gorovei, "Casa Păcii," 631–639.

104 Ureche, *Letopiseț*, 33.

105 Aşıkpaşazade, *Tevarih*, ed. Giese, 178 (*Padişah... Kara Boğdanın tekurunu Kapuya okudular. «Bu kez sen kendün getür haracını» dediler*).

106 See, for instance: Neşri, *Tarih*, ed. Unat, Köymen, II, 829 (*Hikayet-i Inhizam-ı Süleyman Bey der Gaza-yı Kara Boğdan*).

107 One can deduce this from Nicolae Costin's chronicle. The Moldavian historian claimed that Mehmed II would grant peace to the Moldavians if Stephen the Great sent his annual tribute, released the captives and surrendered the fortress of Kili (Nicolae Costin, *Letopiseț*, 119: *Ar fi dat pace moldovenilor, de nu ar fi oprit birul cel legat pre an și de ar fi slobozit robii și de ar fi întorsu cetatea Chiliei*).

108 Letter of *evahir-i Cemazi ül-ahir* 881/10–19 October 1476 of a Crimean official (Mehmet, *Documente turcești*, I, doc. 4).

July 1476.[109] Peace negotiations followed and, eventually, an imperial charter was granted in the last year of Mehmed II's reign (1480–1481).[110]

Many historians claim that, despite the *ʿahdname*, the Ottoman hold on the principality of Moldavia was not yet secure.[111] Moreover, from the perspective of the Ottoman doctrine of the holy war, this peace agreement was but a temporary one, since Moldavia continued to be regarded part of the Abode of War.

In 1484, Bayezid II organized a massive campaign intended to impose control over the northwestern shores of the Black Sea, which garnered considerable attention from Ottoman historians. Kıvami, who accompanied the sultan during his expedition, provided a description of the conquest of Kili in the Danubian estuary and Akkerman at the mouth of the Dniester in July and August.[112] These events convinced Stephen of the necessity of reaching peace with Bayezid II. In 1486, a Moldavian embassy arrived at Istanbul, bringing with them the tribute of Moldavia (called *cizye* or *harac* by Kara-Çelebi-Zade), and asking the sultan for peace in exchange. According to Kara-Çelebi-Zade (d. 1658), the resulting agreement granted Moldavian voivodes sultanic protection (*aman*) and, consequently, allowed them to retain their throne.[113]

---

109 Mehmet Neşri (d. 1520) narrated this second sacred expedition to Moldavia in a special chapter, *Hikayet-i Gaza-yı Kara Boğdan saniyen* (Neşri, *Tarih*, ed. Unat, Köymen, II, 829–833; Neşri, *Tarih*, in *Cronici turcești I*, 127–128; Aşıkpaşazade, *Tevarih*, in *Cronici turcești I*, 95–97; Tursun bey, *Tarih*, in *Cronici turcești I*, 74–75; Solakzade, *Tarih*, in *Cronici turcești II*, 142. See also *Cronici turcești I*, 62 (Oruc bin Adil); 211–214 (Ibn Kemal); 294 (Mehmed pașa); 322–324 (Sa'adeddin); 407 (Mehmed bin Mehmed); 458–460 (Koca Hüseyin); *Războieni. 500 de ani de la Campania din 1476*. Monografie și culegere de texte, ed. Manole Neagoe, Bucharest: Direcția Generală a Arhivelor Statului, 1977, passim; Parry, "Bayezid II-Selim I," 55.

110 The author of the *Münşeʿat*, which was discovered by the Romanian ottomanist A. Decei, called it *sulhname*. For details, see Decei, "Sulhname," 465–494. See also B. Murgescu, "O nouă reglementare de pace moldo-otomană in 1481?" *SAI*, II–III, (1985): 268–274; M. A. Mehmet, "La politique ottomane à l'égard de la Moldavie et du Khanat de Crimée vers la fin du règne du sultan Mehmed II "Le Conquérant," *RRH*, 3, 1974, 509–533.

111 But, also, of Wallachia, according to V. J. Parry (Parry, "Bayezid II-Selim I," 55).

112 Kıvami, *Fetihname*, 304–306. See also *Cronici turcești I*, 63 (Oruc bin Adil); 75–78 (Tursun bey); 98–100 (Aşıkpaşazade); 545 (Kara-Çelebi-Zade); N. Beldiceanu, "La conquete des cités marchandes de Kilia et Cetatea Albă par Bayezid II." SF xxiii, (1964): 36–90; Parry, "Bayezid II-Selim I," 58.

113 *Menakib*, in *Cronici turcești I*, 137; Kara-Çelebi-Zade, *Süleymanname*, in *Cronici turcești I*, 532; Neculce, *O samă de cuvinte*, II/1, 162. For comments, see: Ș. Papacostea, "Relațiile internaționale ale Moldovei în vremea lui Ștefan cel Mare," *RdI*, 5–6, 1982, 607–638; T. Gemil, "Observații referitoare la încheierea păcii și stabilirea hotarului dintre Moldova și Imperiul Otoman," *RA*, 2, 1983, 117–128; Gorovei, "1486," 807–821; Parry, "Bayezid II – Selim I," 58.

Until the end of his reign in 1504, Stephen remained the sultan's tribute-payer (*haracgüzar*), and it was in this capacity that he requested protection and committed his troops to the Ottoman war effort. When in 1497, Polish King John Albert invaded the principality, Stephen appealed for Ottoman assistance, which allowed the voivode to defeat the Poles on 26 October 1497 at Kozmin in the Bucovina. The following year, he reinforced Malkoçoğlu Bali bey's troops sent by Bayezid II to invade Poland as a reprisal for the king's attack on his vassal.[114]

Although later Moldavian tradition, including Dimitrie Cantemir, claimed that Stephen's successors, Bogdan III the Blind and Petru Rareș acknowledged their submission to the Porte in 1511–1513 and 1529, respectively,[115] it seems that essential changes in the legal and political status of Moldavia did not take place until the year 1538.[116]

Nasuh Matrakçi defined Moldavia in 1538, ruled by the hostile voivode Petru Rareș, as an "enemy country," and the voivode's attitude led Süleyman Kanunî's to conduct a campaign aimed at conquering and subjugating the principality.[117] The 1538 invasion was reported by Edmund Harvel, English resident in Venice in his dispatches to Thomas Cromwell. On 25 October 1538, the Ottoman troops were in Moldavia and "beseigid three townis of strenght wiche ben defeindid valiantly." Petru Rareș, called in this source *Caraboldan* (from the Turkish *Kara-Boğdan*) and the "Duke of Moldavia," had at his disposal about 30,000 horsemen, good warriors, and received further 40,000 horsemen from John of Hungary (i.e. John Zápolya).[118] However, the troops proved insufficient to resist the invading army. The surrender of the capital of Suceava sealed the success

114 Koca Hüseyin, *Beda' ül-veka'i*, in *Cronici turcești*, I, 465; Ureche, *Letopiseț*, 54; Nicolae Costin, *Letopiseț*, 129; Parry, "Bayezid II-Selim I," 60–61.

115 It should be emphasized that Richard Knolles, who provided an accurate interpretation of sources, did not mention the alleged documents of 1512 or 1529. In turn, see Cantemir, *Othman History*, 186–189, and n. 28–34. These traditions were taken over by eighteenth- and nineteenth-century Western scholars, as Thomas Thornton (Thornton, *Turkey*, II, 312).

116 For details on the preparations, unfolding and the outcome of the campaign, see: *Cronici turcești I*, 189 (Mühieddin el-Cemalı); 221–232 (Nasuh Matrakçi); 248 (Lütfi pașa); 254–255 (Rustem pașa); 261–272 (Mustafa Celalzade); 351–352 (Mustafa Ali); 412 (Mehmed bin Mehmed); 480–382 (Ibrahim Peçevi); 532–547 (Kara-Çelebi -Zade).

117 Süleyman Kanunî's letter of October 1538 to the Polish king (Hurmuzaki, *Documente*, Supl. II/1, doc. LX). See also Nasuh Matrakçi, *Fetihname*, in *Cronici turcești*, I, 228; Mustafa Celalzade, *Tabakat al-memalik*, in *Cronici turcești I*, 263.

118 Tappe, *Documents*, no. 20.

of Süleyman's campaign, after which he returned to the southern bank of the Danube with his troops.[119] Mehmed Paşa Küçük Nişanci wrote:

> Young princes and boyars (*boyarları*) of the Moldavian *vilayet*, kowtowing in all possible ways and taking large bows, begged for a new hospodar (*hakim*) to be appointed to rule over them. Then, on 21 *Rebi ül-ahir* of the year 945 [16 September 1538], one of the young princes of their descent was appointed, and they pledged themselves to send annually their *harac*.[120]

In fact, immediately after concluding the campaign in October 1538, Süleyman wrote to King Sigismund I of Poland that he had named Ștefan Lăcustă, a former hostage at the Porte and a devotee of the Ottoman ruler, as "voivode of the *vilayet* of Moldavia."[121] Nasuh Matrakçi and Ibrahim Peçevi relate how Ștefan Lăcustă was invested in Suceava, as any *bey* of an Ottoman province, granted – according to the old Ottoman custom – an imperial diploma (*berat-ı hümayun*), a banner (*ʿalem*), with a robe of honor (*hilʿat*) bestowed upon him, along with a knitted cap with a tassel (*üsküf*), worn usually by officers of the Janissary corps.[122]

Ottoman chronicles emphasized the political fallout of Süleyman's campaign of 1538, described as a watershed in the Porte's relationship with Moldavia. In 1538, just as had been the case for Wallachia in 1462, a collective act of homage took place, whose significance outmatched the previous peace agreements of 1456, 1480–1481 and 1486. In this regard, Muhieddin el-Cemalı wrote that the country of Moldavia and all its inhabitants "submitted to the *padişah*" in 1538, and Ibrahim Peçevi concluded that "on that day, the Moldavian country came under the domination of the Ottoman countries."[123] Moreover, henceforward, the Ottoman legal view gained a prominence it had not previously enjoyed. Accordingly, the Moldavia came to be regarded as an integral part of the Well-Protected Domains (*Memalik-i mahrusa*) and Moldavians were

119 Lütfi paşa, *Tevarih*, in *Cronici turcești I*, 248. See also *Petru Rareș*, 161–162 (Chapter: Șt. S. Gorovei, "Domnia lui Ștefan Lăcustă").

120 Mehmed paşa, *Tarih*, in *Cronici turcești I*, 295.

121 In a letter sent in 1540 by some local boyars to the Polish king, they spoke of the sultan's will to establish a Turkish *sancakbeyi* in Moldavia (Hurmuzaki, *Documente*, Supl. II/1, doc. LX).

122 Nasuh Matrakçi, *Fetihname-i Kara-Boğdan* (TKSMK, R. 1284); Nasuh Matrakçi, *Fetihname*, in *Cronici turcești I*, 230; Peçevi, *Tarih*, in *Cronici turcești I*, 481.

123 Muhieddin el-Cemalı, *Tevarih*, in *Cronici turcești I*, 188; Peçevi, *Tarih*, in *Cronici turcești I*, 480.

assimilated with non-Muslim Ottoman subjects (*zimmi*) in most Ottoman documents.

From the local point of view, Süleyman's campaign against Petru Rareș in 1538 was not regarded as a turning point in the legal status of Moldavia, like the non-existent homage performed by Bogdan III the Blind in 1512. In this regard, Dimitrie Cantemir provided a relatively neutral account:

> XXXVI. Whilst these things were performing by his Generals,[124] he himself with numerous forces, as a friend, enters *Moldavia*, but contrary to the expectation of the inhabitants, from the *Danube* to *Soczava*, then the Metropolis, destroys all with fire and sword. Moreover pitching his tents near the City, he demands the yearly tribute. The *Moldavians* seeing no way to withstand so great a storm, humbly sue to him for peace, and promise the payment of the annual tribute, only they petition that the choice of a prince may remain in the state, and that he may, as before, be invested with regal authority. *Soliman* grants their requests, confirms the Prince chosen by them, and restoring the captives, assembles the Nobles next day, and severely reprimands them, saying, that unmindful of the favours received from the Musulman Emperors, they had dared to draw the sword against so powerful an Empire, and not only burnt the Town of *Kili*, but slain many Musulmans. Though for this proceeding all by the *Mahometan* Law were guilty of death, he as a demonstration of his clemency, was ready to give them life and liberty, on condition they would deliver up the Treasurers of thier late Prince. As the wretched *Moldavians* could refuse nothing, the *Defterdar* with a company of Janizaries comes into the town, and plunders both the publick and the Prince's private Traesury, where are found scepters, crosses, and holy images adorned with precious jewels, which *Soliman* abusing as he pleased, leads back his forces to *Constantinople*.[125]

Moldavia's trajectory in the following centuries largely mirrors that of Wallachia, plotted in the previous section.[126]

---

124 Cantemir noted that "Soliman takes Yemen by his Generals. H. 945 / A.C. 1538" (Cantemir, *Othman History*, 201).

125 "On his return, he orders *Kili*, destroyed by the *Moldavians*, to be rebuilt, and because there was no woods in those parts, he gives them the timber of a bridge he had run over the *Danube*" (Cantemir, *Othman History*, 202–203).

126 For Moldavia in 1538, see E. Stănescu, "Le coup d'état nobiliaire de 1538 et son role dans l'asservissment de la Moldavie par l'Empire Ottoman," *NEH* (Bucarest), 1955, 241–264; M. Guboglu, "L'inscription turque de Bender relative à l'expedition de Soliman le Magnifique

FIGURE 7 Sultan Mehmed II the Conqueror and his army during the siege of Constantinople (1453) – outside fresco (c. 1532) attributed to Toma of Suceava, from Moldovița Monastery, Romania (personal photo)

FIGURE 8 Vlad III Țepeș (The Impaler), Voivode of Wallachia (1456–1462, 1476) – Portrait from Ambras Castle (c. 1560), a copy of an original made during his life time (Kunsthistorisches Museum Wien, Gemäldegalerie; Wikipedia. Public Domain)

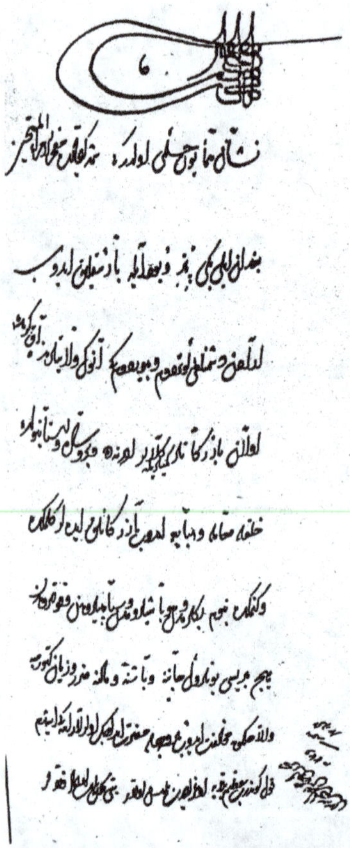

FIGURE 9
*Nişan-ı hümayun* enacted on 5 *Receb* 860 AH / 9 June 1456 by Mehmed II, confirming the peace concluded with voivode Petru Aron of Moldavia and guaranteeing safe commercial activities in Ottoman territories (AGAD, t. 2, no. 3; Guboglu, *Paleografia*, doc. 3 and facismile 3)

FIGURE 10
Stephen the Great (1457–1504), Bogdan III the Blind (1504–1517) and Petru Rareș (1527–1538; 1541–1546), voivodes of Moldavia – inside fresco from Dobrovăț Monastery, painted in 1527–1531, Romania (personal photo)

## 13 Transylvania

After the capture of Belgrade in 1521, Sultan Süleyman launched a new invasion of Hungary in 1526, which culminated in the destruction of the Hungarian army in the battle of Mohács and the death of King Louis II. The subsequent election of John Zápolya by the Hungarian nobility as the King of Hungary (1526–1540), plunged him into a twelve-year war with Archduke Ferdinand of Austria (the future Holy Roman Emperor Ferdinand I), who also claimed the throne.[127]

In response, in 1529 Süleyman Kanunî returned to Hungary, throwing his support behind Zápolya. After the capture of Buda on 8 September 1529, the Ottomans drove Ferdinand's army back to Vienna, and unsuccessfully besieged the Habsburg capital. Backed by the Ottoman army, John Zápolya secured control over much of Hungary. During that campaign, the "ban of Transylvania (*Erdel banı*) came and submitted himself. Bringing gifts, he kissed [the] sultans's hand." This passage was penned by Muhieddin el-Cemali, an Ottoman chronicler who managed to capture in a few words all the essential elements associated with the political "recognition of allegiance," except for the treaty concluded on 28 February 1528.[128] From that moment, Zápolya became a "tributary King" of the sultan, labelled as *haracgüzar* in the Ottoman sources, exacting sums of money "to pay the Turks his Tribute" from his own subjects.[129]

Ferdinand of Austria finally recognized John Zápolya's royal title in 1538, on the condition that he would decide his rival's succesor. However, the arrangement was cast aside in 1540 with the birth of Zápolya's son. Still an infant, John Sigismund Zápolya was elected as the new king shortly after his father's death, but his claim was contested by Ferdinand. As a result, under the pretense of protecting John's interests, Süleyman the Magnificent again invaded Hungary in 1541, occuping Buda and incorporating all of central Hungary into

en Moldavie (1538)," *SAO*, I, 1957, 175–187; Decei, *Imp. otoman*, 190; Gorovei, "Casa Păcii," 659–666; *Petru Rareș*, 151–175 (chapters of T. Gemil and Șt. S. Gorovei); Veinstein, "Oceakov," 128–136; Ștefana Simionescu, "Les relations de la Moldavie avec les Habsbourgs pendant le règne de Petru Rareș (1527–1538; 1541–1546)." *RRH*, XVI, 3, 1977, 463–475.

127 Pál Fodor, "Ottoman Policy towards Hungary, 1520–1541." *AOH* 55, 2–3, (1991): 271–345. Perjés, Géza. *The Fall of the Medieval Kingdom of Hungary: Mohács 1526 – Buda 1541*, Boulder, New York, East European Monographs, 1989; Géza Dávid, and Pál Fodor (eds.), *Hungarian-Ottoman Military and Diplomatic Relations in the Age of Süleyman the Magnificent*, Budapest: Loránd Eötvös University, Hungarian Academy of Sciences, 1994; Gábor Barta, *La route qui mene à Istanbul 1526–1528*, Budapest: Akadémiai Kiadó, 1994.

128 Muhieddin el-Cemalı, *Tevarih* (ed. Giese), 140; Guboglu, *Crestomație turcă*, 293; Gorovei, "Casa Păcii," 659–660. See also A. Decei and M. T. Gökbilgin, "Erdel," *EI-2*, II, 702–705.

129 Knolles, *Turkish History*, 468–469.

his empire.[130] Richard Knolles commented on this episode by saying that Süleyman the Magnificent entered into Buda on 30 August 1541 and immediately issued a decree stating that,

> Buda should from that day be kept with a Garrison of Turks, and the Kingdom converted into a Province of the Turkish Empire.[131]

Soon after, the sultan transformed Transylvania, which was the bastion of the Zápolya party, into a tributary principality, appointing as its ruler – as he had promised – the young king, John Sigismund Zápolya and his mother, Isabella. The Ottoman legal standpoint and the rationales guiding imperial policy towards Transylvania are most evident in Süleyman Kanunî's letter of conquest of 1541:

> By the grace of God and with the help of my victorious sword, I conquered Hungary and its capital Buda in the mentioned years; but since it was very far from the Muslim Empire and thus it would have been hard to govern it, and since King Janos (John Szapolyai) undertook the obligation of paying tribute, I bestowed the kingship of Hungary on him and after his death, I donated it to his son King Istefan (John Sigismund).[132]

Here is also Richard Knolles's opinion in this regard:

> almost all the Country of *Transylvania*, was by Solymans consent delivered to the young King, unto whom all the People most willingly submitted themselves, and took the Oath of Obedience, remembering that

130 Pál Fodor emphasized the aims and results of Süleyman Kanunî's Hungarian campaign, summed up in the *fetihname* the sultan sent in 1541 to the grand vizier Süleyman paşa: "My true aim was to make the capital Buda one of the abodes of Islam and take possession of the town of Buda with its inhabitants and the area belonging to it, I had the great churches converted into camis in which Friday service was held with the participation of all the warriors and the prayer included my princely name [...] Having attached Hungary with all her fortresses, provinces and inhabitnts to the rest of the provinces of the Ottoman Empire, I ordered kadıs, castle commanders and garisons, and I appointed my vizier Süleyman paşa, who possesses the wisdom of Asaf, to defend and guard the province and assigned him a valiant corps from the world-conquering army," (Feridun, *Münşe'at*, 553–554, cf. Fodor, "Ottoman policy," 273). Subsequently, "that women (Isabella) and her son (János Zsigmond) were granted by the sultan the country and the vilayet of Transylvania" (Muhieddin el-Cemalı, *Tevarih*, in *Cronici turcești I*, 189).

131 "The Queen with her young Son should presently depart the City, and live in *Lippa*, in a fertile an quiet Country Beyond the river *Tibiscus* [i.e. Transylvania]" (Knolles, *Turkish History*, 481).

132 Feridun, *Münşe'at*, I, 551, cf. Fodor, "Ottoman policy," 274.

> his Father had almost for thirty years space with great Justice and quietness governed that Province; and with many Presents honoured the young King lying in *Lippa*, with the Queen his Mother, and his two Tutors, the Bishop, and *Vicche*.[133]

These events came to be universally regarded as the cornerstone of the submission and conquest of Transylvania.[134]

The final act of Transylvania's transition into the status of the Ottoman tributary took place on 29 June 1566, when John Sigismund Zápolya arrived at Süleyman's military camp in Zemun to prostrate himself before the sultan.[135]

Despite certain attempts to escape from under Ottoman protection and either enter the Habsburg camp or to become an independent principality, Transylvania remained under the sultans' suzerainty until 1699. The Treaty of Karlowitz, concluded between the Habsburgs and the Porte, recognized its occupation by the Habsburg troops and effectively brought an end to the existence of Transylvania as a distinct entity.[136]

•••

The political and military context in the closing decades of the fourteenth until the mid-sixteenth century had a profound impact on all Southeastern European tributaries, shaping their individual arrangements with the Porte. Nonetheless, we can identify some common features. In the face of an

133 Richard Knolles indicated that this event took place after the town of *Fogaras* (Făgăraş) surrendered to the Ottomans (Knolles, *Turkish History*, 481). Discussing Süleyman's campaign against Hungary and its consequences for Transylvania, Dimitrie Cantemir followed a similar line: "The enemies being thus dispersed, *Soliman* enters *Buda*, send into *Transylvania Stephanus* the heir of the kingdom with his mother, because he believed them incapable (the one for his youth, and the other for her sex) of defending the kingdom, and assigns them a *Sanjak* for their subsistence" (Cantemir, *Othman History*, 205).

134 For details, see: Cristina Feneşan, *Constituirea principatului autonom al Transilvaniei*, Bucharest: Editura Enciclopedică, 1997; R. Constantinescu, *Moldova şi Transilvania în vremea lui Petru Rareş. Relaţii politice şi militare (1527–1546)*, Bucharest: Direcţia Generală a Arhivelor Statului, 1978.

135 Selaniki, *Tarih*, I, 21.

136 "I. The Reign of Transylvania, as it is at present in the Possession, and in the Power of his Caesarean Majesty, so it shall remain under his Dominion, Bounded by the Confines of Podolia, and with the Mountain of the side of Wallachia, which were its Ancient Limits before the present war, between Transylvania on one part, and Moldavia and Wallachia, on the other…" (Rycaut, *Turkish History. 1679–1700*, 575). For Ottoman texts of this treaty, see: BOA, *DED* 57/1, 21–27; BOA, *Amedi Kalemi Odası* (*Kamil Kepeci taşnifi*) 53, 2–16: *Amedi odası defterlerinden Nemçe çasarına verilen ʿahdname-yi hümayun kayıtı. Tarihi 1110*; Istanbul Üniversitesi Kütüphanesi, ms. 3514, ANIC, mf. Turkey, r. 1, fr. 301–429: *1110 tarihindeki sulhnamesi*).

Ottoman onslaught, the capacity of minor Balkan polities hinged on their ability to curb internal political infighting and establish anti-Ottoman alliances with major powers, which would be supported by the whole of Christendom.

Political and military practice provides us with many examples of how the Ottomans managed to exploit dynastic conflicts, such as those ravaging the Byzantine Empire, Wallachia following Mircea the Elder's death in 1418, or Moldavia in the fifteenth century. For instance, chroniclers recounted peace talks between the sultans and Byzantine emperors in the midst of conflicts of the throne (1322–1328, 1351–1354, 1390). Orhan, Murad I and Bayezid I offered to support pretenders and incumbent emperors, in exchange for promises and cessions of territory and even rights inalienable to any of the sovereign polity.

The Ottomans also reaped the benefits from the political isolation of the Southeastern European states facing these dire circumstances.[137] This lack of support constituted, from the Christian perspective, the main cause that prompted local rulers to enter unequal peace settlements with Ottoman rulers and accept their inferior status. For instance, Ducas claimed that John V agreed to pay a 30,000-ducat tribute in 1379, as did Manuel II in 1390–1391, and to provide 12,000 troops, due to the fact that they had "no help from any of the kings or state leaders."[138]

Wallachian, and later Moldavian, princes found themselves in a similarly helpless position that forced them to adopt available political and diplomatic solutions to navigate the geopolitical realities of their time. As a result, blaming Christian rulers and their hesitance to provide substantial help became a common thread in Moldavian and Wallachian sources. Such a cliché of extreme political isolation can be found in the document from 5 June 1456, which reflects on the attitude Petru Aron and the Moldavian boyars, gathered at Vaslui, adopted towards Mehmed II's ultimatum. The demand of a 2,000-ducat tribute was accepted because "we have no support and help from any part."[139]

Pondering about Petru Aron's rationale for accepting Ottoman suzerainty, the eighteenth-century historian Nicolae Costin would point out the Polish

---

137 There is enough evidence to demonstrate that, whenever a strong alliance system was established by first-line states, the success against the Ottomans was guaranteed. One can emphasize, for instance, John Hunyadi's activity in this respect (F. Pall, "La condizioni e gli achi internationali della lotta antiottoman del 1442–1443 condotta da Giovanni di Hunedoara," *RESEE*, III, 1965, 433–463; C. Mureşan, *Iancu de Hunedoara*, Bucharest: Editura Ştiinţifică, 1968).

138 Ducas, *Istoria*, XIII/1.

139 *DRH*, A, II, doc. 58. On the political and military difficulties of the Moldavian voivode, Nicolae Iorga remarked that he "was threatened by Tartars, hated by Hungarians and abandoned by Poles" (Iorga, *Istoria Românilor*, IV, 113–114).

refusal to provide assistance against the Porte: "the Poles answered that they could not be of help to the Moldavian voivodes."[140] Petru Rareș explicity placed the blame for his submission to Sultan Süleyman with the entirety of Christendom: "We have been abandoned to the pagans by Christians," the Moldavian voivode wrote to Sigismund I of Poland in 1541, justifying his participation in the Ottoman campaign.[141] Even neighbors, who should have provided military support, were keenly aware of the consequences of the Wallachian and Moldavian princes' polical isolation. In this respect, the Hungarian king Sigismund of Luxemburg (1387–1437), informed Count John of Paszto in his letter from 23 March 1399 that "lacking our support [...], the Wallachians will soon submit to the Turkish yoke."[142] Trying to justify the voivodes' submission to the Porte, some Romanian scholars also placed the blame with the policy of compromise and appeasement of major powers in the region, while glossing over multiple conflicts of political interests between them and the principalities.

During the period of Ottoman expansion into Southeastern Europe, the fear of reprisal and harsher conditions or the threat of war[143] often led Christian princes to recognize Ottoman suzerainty and,[144] as a consequence, their own status as tribute-payers. During 1375–1376, the Serbian knez Lazarus Hrebljanović (1371–1389) agreed to pay tribute and submit to Murad I only after the conquest of Niš had left him with few options. The following year, the Bulgarian tsar Ivan Shishman (1371–1393) was aware of "the impossibility to resisting" and opted to become the sultan's *haracgüzar*.[145] Wallachian voivodes were also aware of the Ottoman threat looming from across to the Danube. In his letter to the Hungarian king in 1399, Mircea the Elder remarked that Bayezid I "camps with a great army in the city of Adrianople [...] from where in five days'

140 Nicolae Costin, *Letopiseț*, 105. See also Papacostea, "1455–1456," 445–461.

141 Corfus, *Documente. XVI*, doc. 35, 52.

142 *DRH*, D, I, doc. 105.

143 Liviu Pilat and Ovidiu Cristea, *The Ottoman Threat and Crusading on the Eastern Border of Christendom during the 15th Century*, Leinden: Brill, 2017.

144 Ottomans themselves were also conscious of this fact, once we take into account the *beylerbeyi* of Buda, Nasuhpașazade Hüseyin pașa's remark made in 1636, regarding the "request of submission" (*ʿarz-ı ʿubudiyet*) of the Transylvanian prince, George Rákoczy I: "My most enduring sultan," the governor said to the grand vizier, "the infidels will not give money to the Muslims until they see the wonders of sword" (*kefere taifesi kılıç kerametin görmeyince*) (Gemil, *Documente turcești*, doc. 102).

145 Sa'adeddin, *Tac üt-tevarih*, I, Istanbul, 1280, 93–94, cf. Decei, "Sulhname," 134; *Cronici turcești I*, 300–301. See also Mehmed Neșri, Idris Bitlisi, Mehmed bin Mehmed, Koca Hüseyin, in *Cronici turcești I*, 110–111, 400–1, 440.

time he can easily reach the Danube."[146] Later, in 1417, Mehmed I Çelebi personally conducted a show of force on the banks of the Danube, and subsequently sent *akıncıs* across the river:

> The sultan, having luck on his side, marched on passing to Rumeli. And he crossed the Danube, building Giurgiu.[147]

Only under these circumstances, would the Wallachian voivode accept to ransom for peace by paying a sum of money, the *harac* or *cizye*.

Another stereotype frequently found in the sources also merits our attention. Other Christians, particularly the rulers of polities adjacent to Wallachia and Moldavia, considered these acts of submission as undertaken of the voivodes' own initiative and thus worthy of condemnation. In a letter from 5 December 1433, the Hungarian king Sigismund stated that Dan II of Wallachia "in defiance of our Majesty, donned willingly the colors of the aforementioned Turks."[148] In turn, Alexandru I Aldea was accused by the inhabitants of Sibiu of "having abjured the royal ruler," the Hungarian king, and "surrendered to the Turks."[149]

Similarities between the tributary status of the voivodes and that of other Balkan rulers sometimes found their explicit reflection in the sources. For instance, Ivan Shishman, the tsar of the Tarnovo tsardom (1371–1393) "was a tribute-payer to Murad I, just like the voivode of Wallachia."[150] However, it is important to keep in mind that for most of the aforementioned polities, the tributary status proved temporary, and they were eventually transformed into territories under direct Ottoman administration.

The cases of the Cycladic islands in the southern Aegean (the Duchy of Naxos together with its dependencies, Paros and Andros) and the Ragusan Republic, which enjoyed a long-term status of tributary-protection, deserve special mention, since their longevity as tributary polities was similar to that of

146 Sigismund of Luxemburg's letter to Ioan de Paszto of 23 March 1399 (*DRH*, D, I, doc. 105).

147 *Sultan devletle yürüyüb Rumeli'ne geçti ve Tuna'yi geçti kenarında durub Yerköy'ünü yaptırıb* (Neşri, *Tarih*, II, 536–537). See also Aşıkpaşazade, *Tevarih*, in *Cronici turcești I*, 85; *Tevarih-i Al-i Osman*, in *Cronici turcești I*, 181. About thirty years later, Alexandru I Aldea (1431–1436) invoked the support of the inhabitants of Brașov, as "the great emperor Amurat Beğ (Murad II – o.n.) is at three days' distance from me" (*DRH*, D, I, doc. 191).

148 *DRH*, D, I, doc. 209.

149 *DRH*, D, I, doc. 197.

150 *Eflak voyvodası gibi Hüdavendigarun haracgüzarımış* (TKSMA, E. 6374; Inalcık, "Document," 220–222; Decei, "Două documente," 210–214; Guboglu, "Le tribut," 58–59; Alexandrescu, "Khatt-ı şerifs," 253). *Hüdavendigar* was a title given to Murad I (*Redhouse*, 496).

Wallachia and Moldavia between the fifteenth and nineteenth centuries, as well as that of the Principality of Transylvania in the period 1541–1699. Their common feature was their ability to preserve the position of autonomous principalities or provinces although in an altered legal and political form. Finally, the Crimean Khanate, a client polity with extensive internal autonomy vis-à-vis the Porte, should be also included in the comparison, even though the Giray khans did not pay any tribute to the Ottoman sultans.

CHAPTER 6

# From Allegiance to Conquest: Terminology, Meanings, Myths

In the following pages I will focus on deciphering various meanings of the notions of "submission" and "conquest," often understood here in a narrow and restricted sense. This analysis relies on a great variety of information provided by Ottoman narratives and documentary sources, but also others, produced in the Byzantine Empire, the Danubian principalities, Transylvania and Western Europe.

## 1 Acknowledgement of Allegiance

### 1.1 *Terminology*

Simple or phrasal verbs from Ottoman chronicles and documents, such as *boyun eğmek, boyun vermek, tapmak, itaʿat ve inkıyad etmek, yüz sürümek,* or *yüz sürmek,* have both concrete and abstract meanings. They can be translated with a figurative meaning, such as "to obey," "to submit," "to pay homage," "to reverence," "to acknowledge allegiance," or, with a proper signification, as "to bend," "to hang one's head down," "to make a low bow." In this regard, one must take into account the use of nouns, both concrete – like "head," "neck" (*baş, boyun*), – and abstract terms, like "submission," "obeisance," "allegiance" (*itaʿat, inkıyad, muti, münkad*) in the structure of such phrasal expressions.

Worth mentioning here is the abundant, albeit diffuse, descriptive use of ceremonies at the sultan's court (including the reception of tributary princes, envoys, and Ottoman dignitaries), in Ottoman phrases such as "to rub one's face," "to pay one's humble respect or homages to a superior," "to prostrate oneself," "to bow," "to humbly kowtow," or to denote the acknowledgment of submission. For instance, the terminology employed in the 1480–1481 *ʿahdname* suggests that the conclusion of peace with Mehmed II demanded Stephen the Great to "rub his face against the land of servitude" (*zemin-i hizmete yüz sürüyüb*). Also, Saʾadeddin used the verb *yüz sürmek* to describe the ceremony when the sultan received Anatolian and Rumelian *beylerbeyi*s, as well as the envoy of the Hungarian king Matthias Corvinus: "the Hungarian envoy, coming as well, rubbed his face against the Court-shelter of the world."[1] Yet, Mehmed

1 *Ungurus kıralın dahi elçisi gelüb Dergah-ı Cihanpenaha yüz sürdü* (Sa'adedin, *Tevarih*, in Decei, "Sulhame," 125, n. 6).

 DOI:10.1163/9789004411104_007

Neşri, in his description of Mehmed II's Wallachian campaign in 1462 and the subsequent submission of the Wallachian boyards, opted for the verb *tapmak*, which means "to bend," "to hang one's head down," "to make low bows," but also "to meet someone."[2] Similarly, the Ottoman chancery developed its own vocabulary meant to define the relationship with tributary princes. This included: *sadakat ü-istikamet*, two synonyms that can be translated as "faithfulness and loyalty" or "fidelity and devotion"; *ʿubudiyet ü-itaʿat*, *ʿubudiyet ü-rıkkiyet*, *itaʿat ü-inkıyad*, meaning "obedience and submission," "obeisance and servitude," "homage paying," or "acknowledgment of allegiance."[3] Unfortunately, it is difficult to precisely define the legal meanings of these terms, as they were abundantly employed in both *ʿahdname*s granted to Western states like Venice, England, or Poland,[4] and documents regarding tribute-payer princes. Thus, before 1475, Stephen the Great, was – according to the 1476 *fetihname* – in:

> a state of obeisance and of tribute-payer condition and of real submission and servitude towards my Imperial Threshold.[5]

In a similar vein, in 1641 George Rákoczy I sent a "letter of submission" (translated in Turkish as *ʿubudiyetname*) to Sultan Ibrahim (1640–1648), promising to deliver the tribute due to the Porte in his quality of *haracgüzar*.[6]

The Greek word *proskynesis* was invariably translated by Byzantinists as "bowing," "prostrating," or "adoring" encountered in fifteenth-century Byzantine chronicles along with similar expressions, like "to bow one's head," "to bend."[7] From this vocabulary emerged the Romanian term *închinare* abundantly employed in the Wallachian and Moldavian sources.[8]

---

2 Neşri, *Tarih*, ed. Unat, Köymen, II, 757.

3 *Redhouse*, 540, 564, 804, 823, 1095, 1267; Decei, "Sulhame," 122; Gemil, *Documente turceşti*, 42, 209, 304; Veliman, *Documente turceşti*, doc. 1, 73, 164, 437.

4 In 1540 *ʿahdname* to Venice, "request of submission" (*ʿarz-ı ʿubudiyet*) (Gökbilgin, "Belgeler I," 121).

5 *Atebe-i ʿaliyeme şol ki resm-i itaʿat ve haracgüzari ve mahz-ı ʿubudiyet ü hidmetkari der-i müeddi kılurken* (Gemil, "Fetih-name," 254, 257).

6 Gemil, *Documente turceşti*, doc. 106. In October 1613, Radu Mihnea, Ştefan II Tomşa and Gabriel Bethlen were sworn in submission to the serdar Iskender paşa, as "tributaries" (*haracgüzarlar*) (Decei, *Imp. otoman*, 370).

7 *Proskyno* means "to prostrate" (M. A. Bailly, *Dictionnaire grec-français*, Paris: Hachette, 1894, 1670; Ducas, *Istoria*, 262–3, 429, 430, 435).

8 See *Letopiseţul cantacuzinesc*, passim; Miron Costin, *Letopiseţ*, passim; Nicolae Costin, *Letopiseţ*, passim; Berza, "Turcs, Empire Ottoman et relations roumano-turques," 595–627 .

### 1.2 *General Meanings*

An analysis of Moldavian–Wallachian sources proves that the term *închinare* encompassed a wild variety of meanings. Here I will focus on the most important ones, paying special attention to the way they were employed in the context of the principalities' relations with the Sublime Porte.

Prostration was a custom specific to the Christian rituals that expressed the recognition of God (and, implicitly, of God's church) as the supreme lord. *Închinare* was used with this sense frequently by Wallachian and Moldavian authors in all types of the sources.[9] At the same time, it constituted a ceremonial gesture, which was frequently performed in the sovereign's presence, and could be imbued with political undertones. At the etiquette-conscious Byzantine court, the reception of envoys and vassal princes was accompanied by their "prostration" (*proskynesis*) in front of the *basileus*. Ducas, narrating the siege of Constantinople by Murad II in 1422, mentions Dan (the future Dan II of Wallachia) who, after he had defected from the Ottoman camp to the Byzantine one "prostrated in front of the emperor (*proskynesas to basilei*) and asked for permission to return directly to his country." A custom of Middle Eastern origin, the humble act of prostration in the presence of a political superior was subsequently adopted by the Romans and Byzantines, eventually taking hold in the ceremonial court throughout Southeastern Europe and the Middle East. Envoys dispatched to the sultanic court for the purpose of negotiating problems or handling minor issues, invariably bowed in front of sultans. Here is a case, chosen at random. In 1484, "an envoy came from the Hungarian king too, bowing before the world-protecting Court."[10]

Prostration also marked the recognition of a new ruler by his subjects, dignitaries and noblemen. The word *închinare* was frequently employed in this sense in both the narrative and documentary sources. Upon his third ascension to the Wallachian throne in 1476, Vlad the Impaler wrote to the inhabitants of Brașov "the whole country of Wallachian and its boyars paid homage to me."[11] According to the *Cantacuzino Chronicle* and other narrative sources, the ceremony of the boyars' submission was a standard practice performed whenever a new voivode ascended to the throne, from the legendary founder of the principality, Voivode Radu, until Șerban Cantacuzino's reign, coterminous with the composition of the chronicle.[12]

9 *Letopisețul cantacuzinesc*, 25, 190; Nicolae Costin, *Letopiseț*, 164.

10 Ducas, *Istoria*, XXIX/7; Solakzade, *Tarih*, in *Cronici turcești I*, 145; Sa'adeddin, *Tevarih*, in *Cronici turcești I*, 327, 329.

11 Tocilescu, *534 documente*, doc. 102.

12 *Letopisețul cantacuzinesc*, 2, 19, 45–6, 50, 89, 103, 175.

This customary practice, which indicated the recognition of a new sovereign, proliferated during the Middle Ages and also found its way into the Ottoman court. Homage was performed by imperial dignitaries (*bey'at*), loosely translated as an acknowledgment of allegiance, accompanying and complementing the ceremony of enthronement (*cülüs*).

In the eighteenth century, when the thrones of Moldavia and Wallachia became the exclusive preserve of Phanariot rulers appointed directly by the Porte, the Ottomans interpreted the homage paid by local officials and boyards as a renewal of homage to the Sublime Porte. In a *hüküm* issued for the Moldavian elite in Summer 1711, Sultan Ahmed III ordered them to obey Ioan Mavrocordat as the voivode's *kaymakam*, for

> paying homage and submitting to my High State (*taraf-ı Devlet-i aliye'me ita'at ve inkıyad edüb*) [...] and obeying him, they shall be protected as before under my imperial shelter.[13]

*Proskynesis/închinare* could also be understood as a "surrender," either militarily or politically. In fifteenth-century Byzantine chronicles, the term *proskynesis* was used whenever fortresses or towns surrendered to victorious Ottoman troops. In a similar vein, the meaning of "surrender" was conveyed through *închinare* in the Romanian sources. After his attempts to resist the Ottoman army in 1574, Moldavian voivode John the Terrible was forced to surrender and "he started sending messages of capitulation to them."[14] However, this instance of capitulation was a purely military one, despite the fact that some boyars had encouraged him to pay homage to the sultan even before he initiated the revolt:

> either acknowledge allegiance towards the sultan or depart for foreign countries, but do not set out against the Turks.[15]

Acknowledgment of allegiance marked in the Medieval period a political juncture, whereby a prince accepted the trusteeship of a superior power center, thus recognizing a more powerful ruler as his suzerain. This understanding of the term is particularly widespread in narrative sources, although it also features prominently in documents issued by the Moldavian and Wallachian

13 Veliman, *Documente turcești*, doc. 1: *hüküm* of *evasıt-ı Cemazi ül-ahir* 1123/27 July-6 August 1711.

14 Ureche, *Letopiseț*, 147 (*Începu a trimite la dânșii că să va închina*).

15 *Cronica lui Azarie*, in CSR, 151; Berindei, "Le problème des Cosaques," 338–367.

chancelleries. It is commonly employed to express the relationship between the voivodes and their overlords, such as the kings of Hungary and Poland. Several examples are in order here. At the beginning of the sixteenth century, Vladislav III informed the inhabitants of Brașov:

> I paid homage with absolute fairness to the Holy Crown and to His [Royal] Highness the king and to the Transylvanian voivode, as well as to all Hungarian noblemen and to you.[16]

According to the *Cantacuzino Chronicle*, the Wallachian voivode Nicolae Alexandru (1352–1364), following his conflict with the Hungarian Crown:

> submitted and went to the king [to present him] with plenty of gifts, with a thousand golden *hrivne*, paying homage and promising an annual tribute.[17]

At Kolomyja in 1485, Stephen the Great performed the last personal act of homage to the Polish king, Casimir IV. According to the chronicle, he did it by:

> prostrating before the king in accordance with the Moldavian custom, and reclining the flag to the king's feet.[18]

Wallachian and Moldavian chroniclers also employed *închinare* to describe the political bonds established between Transylvania and the Habsburgs. Following the death of Michael the Brave, who had for several months held the authority in Transylvania, the Hungarian nobility offered the throne to the Habsburg general Giorgio Basta, promising "and we shall pay homage the emperor with all the country."[19] From this point of view, the homage paid to the Porte, which I discuss below, is a particular case belonging to a wider category

16 Tocilescu, *534 documente*, doc. 279 (letter of 2 July, without year, anyway between 1523–1525).

17 *Letopisețul Cantacuzinesc*, 80 (*plecă capul și mersă la craiul cu mari daruri, cu mie de hrivne de aur de s-au închinat și s-au făgăduit că-i va da dajdie pe an*).

18 Nicolae Costin, *Letopiseț*, 124 (*închinându-se craiului după obiceiul moldovenesc, plecând steagul țării la picioarele craiului*). Later, John Albert besieged the fortress Suceava "hoping that the country would obey <him>" (Ureche, *Letopiseț*, 54: *să va închina țara*). See also other examples in Nicolae Costin, *Letopiseț*, 129 (*Ștefan vodă să nu se închine la Turcu*); Ureche, *Letopiseț*, 83 (in 1509, *Vasco oarecarile de ai noștri… s-au închinat la leși*). See also Victor Eskenasy, "Omagiul lui Ștefan cel Mare de la Colomeea (1485). Note pe marginea unui ceremonial medieval." *AIIAI*, XX, 1983, 257–267.

19 *Letopisețul Cantacuzinesc*, 198 (*și noi să fim închinați împăratului cu toată țara*).

of medieval customs and practices. Thus, in Grigore Ureche's opinion, Selim II banished Bogdan Lăpușneanu (1568–1572) because of his close relationship to Poland, which could have turned into the voivode's "homage" to the Polish king. Therefore, the sultan,

> forewarned [the Moldavian voivode] not to break his oath and turn his thoughts to that country and to surrender his country, lest he should have many accounts to settle with the Poles.[20]

### 1.3 *The Myth of Original Submission*

Eighteenth-century Wallachian and Moldavian chroniclers depicted the term *închinare* as a series of crucial, military, political and diplomatic decisions that had taken place from the late fourteenth until the mid-sixteenth century, and had a profound impact on the legal status of the tributary principalities for the centuries to come.[21]

In Wallachia, both the author of the *Cantacuzino Chronicle* and Radu Popescu, associated this decision with Basarab Laiotă (ruling intermittently in the period 1473–1477), "who yielded the country to the Turks."[22] The late eighteenth-century boyar Ianache Văcărescu considered that the first act of submission took place during the reign of Mircea the Elder's successor, Mihail I (1418–1420):

> Wallachia yielded [...] They decided it and in a public assembly in the year 1418 and 820 the voivode and the boyars willingly yielded Wallachia to the emperor Mehmed the First and became tributaries.[23]

Still, differences of opinion persisted. In a petition submitted in August 1772 to the Russian representative at the peace congress of Focșani, Count Orloff, the boyars promoted the idea of two Wallachian acknowledgments of allegiance towards the Porte. The first allegedly took place on the initiative of Mircea the Elder, who, on an unspecified date before the 1395 battle of the Argeş, "yielded

20 Ureche, *Letopiseț*, 139 (*socoti să nu să lepede dispre dânsul și să să lipască spre aceia parte și să închine țara, mai apoi să nu aibă mai multă gâlceavă cu leșii*).

21 In Wallachian and Moldavian chronicles: *întîiași dată; mai întîi; au izvodit întăi și au început; de atuncea* etc.

22 *Letopisețul Cantacuzinesc*, 4; Popescu, *Istoriile*, 252 (*care au închinat țara turcilor*).

23 Văcărescu, *Istorie*, 204 (*Mihai Vodă sin Mircea Vodă* [...] *S-a închinat Valahia* [...] *Au hotărât și cu sfat de obște la leat 1418 și 820, domnul cu boierii au închinat Țara Românească fără război la înpăratul Mehmed cel dîntîiu și s-au făcut tributar*).

the country to the Turk" (*a închinat țara turcului*). A seventy-year interval followed, when the voivodes would be "released" from the dependence, with the second act of submission performed by Basarab Laiotă (although dated inappropriately on the year 1460!), when "the Voivode himself, of his own accord, yielded the country."[24] However, we can identify significant differences between the two episodes, regarding the circumstances in which they were performed (in contrast to Mircea, it was Basarab Laiotă himself who took the initiative), and the irreversibility of the later act ("Laiotă Basarab Voivode, in the year of 1460. The one who in absolute submission, yielded the country to the Turks").[25]

The idea that Wallachian rulers acknowledged their submission to the Porte twice can also be found in the Greek edition of *Ban* Mihai Cantacuzino's chronicle, published by the Tunusli brothers in 1806 in Vienna, and subsequently translated in Romanian. The text conflated the notions of homage, submission, *proskynesis* and capitulation, although it contained numerous chronological ambiguities and frequently confused individuals involved in the events. The chronicle discusses both "the first capitulation (*proskynesis*) of Wallachia towards the Ottoman Porte under Mircea Voievod. In the year of 1383" and "the second surrender" (*Devtera proskynesis. En etei 1460*) by Basarab Laiotă, dated for the year 1460.[26]

In the case of Moldavia, the local tradition of the seventeenth and eighteenth centuries, preserved by Dimitrie Cantemir and other historians of the period, was – as was the case with Wallachia – rife with confusions and ambiguities. The information they furnished was subsequently taken at face value by nineteenth-century Western scholarship that, like Thomas Thornton, accepted their spurious claims regarding homages performed by Bogdan III in 1512 and Petru Rareș in 1529. Hence, erroneous claims regarding the reign of Bogdan III as a turning point in Moldavian–Ottoman relations continue to be repeated in modern scholarship.[27]

According to this spurious tradition, Stephen the Great (1457–1504)

> alarmed by the conquests of the Turks over the Hungarians, the Tartars and the Wallachians, and fearing to rely either on the Poles and the

24 *Genealogia Cantacuzinilor*, 495–499.

25 *Genealogia Cantacuzinilor*, 67 (*Laiot Basarab Voevod, la anul 1460. Acesta este carele cu totul s'a supus, închinând Țara-Românească la Turci*).

26 *Istoria politică și geografică a Țerei Românesci de la cea mai veche a sa întemeere până la anul 1774, dată mai ântâiu în limba grecească la anul 1806 de Frații Tunusli*, translated by G. Sion, Bucharest, 1863, 66.

27 For instance, Sugar, *Southeastern Europe*, 121, 322 ("1512 Moldavia becomes vassal state").

> Germans, advised with the last breath the surrender of his country to the Ottoman power in the name of a fief, if the inhabitants could obtain peace on honorable terms, together with the preservation of their civil and ecclesiastical laws.[28]

Thus, Bogdan III would be the first one to follow his father's advice and submit Moldavia to the Turks in 1512, receiving in return a so-called "capitulation." Grigore Ureche wrote in this respect:

> Learning the lesson from his father, Stephen the Great, he sent Grand Chancellor Tăutu to the Turkish empire, with servants, infantry, foot soldiers [...] to deliver the tribute, ten burdens of money and acknowledged allegiance of the whole country to Sultan Süleyman, the Turkish emperor.[29]

Consequently, the sultan accepted the Moldavian prince's homage and his "small sum of money" which, once obtained, soon turned out to be interpreted as an actual tribute. In exchange, the sultan granted the boyars the privilege to elect their governors in case of vacancy on the throne, although the elect had to secure the sultan's confirmation.[30] Here is Dimitrie Cantemir's account from his history of the Ottoman Empire:

> XVII. *Moldavia* made a fief of the Empire. Whilst *Soliman* after the taking of the City, stayed in the neighborhood some days to refresh his army, *Teutuk Lagotheta* is sent in embassy by *Bogdan* Prince of *Moldavia* to the *Turkish* camp. Having obtained an audience, he declares his mission from the *Moldavian* Prince and People, to offer the Sultan both *Moldavia's* upon honorable terms, particularly that their Religion should be preserved entire, and the country be subject as a fief to the Empire. Nothing

28 Thornton, *Turkey*, II, 312.

29 Ureche, *Letopiseț*, 78 (*Pre învățătura tătîne-său, a lui Ștefan vodă, trimis-au la împărăția turcilor pre Tăutul logofătul cel mare, cu slujitori, pedestrime, dărăbani de au dus birul, zece povară de bani și s-au închinatu cu toată țara la sultan Suleimanu împăratul turcescu*). See also Nicolae Costin, *Letopiseț*, 154 (*i s-au închinat cu toată țara*); Cantemir, *Descrierea Moldovei*, 270 (*Bogdan cel Chior a închinat turcilor Moldova*); Neculce, *O samă de cuvinte*, X/12 (*când au închinat țara la turci*); *Tractaturile*, BAR, ms. 566, f. 126v–136. For discussions on this event, see N. Bălcescu, "Ioan Tăutul, marele logofăt al Moldovei," *Magazin istoric pentru Dacia"* (Bucharest) I, 1845, 135–137; Maxim, "Cantemir," 69–78; Gorovei, "Casa Păcii," 629–667 (with accurate interpretations of sources).

30 Thornton, *Turkey*, II, 312.

> could be more grateful to *Soliman*, whose more weighty affairs hindered him from turning his arms that way, and yet the defeats received from the *Moldavians*, obliged him to have always an eye to their motions. Wherefore readily accepting the offered terms, he confirms them with his own hand, and delivers him the instruments to be carried to his Prince at *Soczava*. Afterwards in his return from that year's expedition he is met near *Sophia* a City of *Servia* by *Bogdan* with some of his Barons, and presented by him with four thousand gold Crowns, forty bred Mares, and twenty four Falcons, with a promise to send yearly to *Constantinople* the like present in token of his feudal subjection. The Emperor admits the Prince to his presence, and again ratifies the conditions made with the Ambassador, gives him a larger *Cucca* adorned with jewels, with a *Chylaat fahire*, and a horse with all the imperial trappings. Moreover he orders four of his guard to attend him, which custom is still observed whenever the Prince of *Moldavia* comes to the *Othman* Court.[31]

According to the same tradition, following the fall of Buda to the Ottomans, Voivode Petru Rareș (1527–1538, 1541–1546), allegedly performed the act of homage towards Sultan Süleyman in 1529. It is important to note that the description of these episodes is marred by confusion regarding their participants and when they took place. This should raise our scepticism regarding the accuracy of such narratives and see them more as legends and rumours. English scholar Richard Knolles, whose information is more accurate, fails to mention any substantial changes in Moldavian affairs either in 1512 or 1529.

In comparison with Moldavia and Wallachia, Transylvanian homage in the first part of the sixteenth century presents itself much clearer. The crucial moment that defined subsequent evolution of the principality's relationship with the Porte took place under John Sigismund Zápolya in 1541. George Branković described the events in the following manner:

> 7049. Süleyman, after King Janos' death, took hold of Buda and the Hungarian Belgrade […], and gave Transylvania to the king's son. And it is ever since that Transylvania had remained under the infidels' domination.[32]

---

31 Cantemir, *Othman History*, 186–189.

32 Brancovici, *Cronica*, 73 (*7049. Suliiman, dupre moartea craiului Ianoș, au luat Buda și Belgradul cel unguresc* […] *iar fiului craiului au dat Ardealul. Și de atuncea au rămas Ardealul supt ascultarea păgânilor*).

Seventeenth- and eighteenth-century Ottoman sources also invoke – when decrying abuses – ancient acts of submission by Wallachian and Moldavian voivodes, although they offer no chronological details. For instance, a 1769 *hüküm* reiterated the Moldavians' obligation to obey the sultan's orders, but also confirmed their right to protection. In the document, Mustafa III referred to the fact that Moldavia (*Memleket-i Boğdan*) "has since the times of yore been yielded to and obeyed my Sublime *Devlet*."[33]

## 2 Constituent Elements of the Acknowledgment of Allegiance

Şükrüllah, describing the peace concluded between Mehmed I Çelebi and Mircea the Elder in 1417, provides an example regarding the way in which such acts of allegiance were performed. Like other depictions of fifteenth-century pacts with princes of the region, it is a summary record, allowing us to identify the main features of the process. The chronicler briefly narrates the run-up to the pact, including the threat of force, a petition for peace, subsequent negotiations and the act of submission proper. The first stage was the threat of an attack, as the sultan "went to the infidel from Wallachia." In response, the Wallachian prince sued for peace ("seeing the greatness of Muslims, the infidels asked peace"). Negotiations followed, which established a set of obligations imposed on the new tributary (tribute payment, sending of hostages and military support for sultan). To secure the enforcement of the agreement reached, both sides took oaths to uphold the conditions. The whole process, as Şükrüllah, amounted to establishing peace with the Wallachian ruler ("thus, they make peace"). He did not forget to specify that peace was valid only for "the sultan's life."[34] This pattern can be called the act of paying homage, as Mehmed Neşri did in no uncertain terms:

> After that, the prince of Wallachia, sending the tribute by his envoy, acknowledged his submission.[35]

Regardless of the exact year and voivode with whom it was concluded, most historians have considered this episode as the first time a Wallachian ruler

---

33 *Öteden berü Devlet-i aliye'me muti ve münkad olan* (Veliman, *Documente turcești*, doc. 164: *hüküm* of *evahir-i Receb* 1183/ 20–29 November 1769).

34 Şükrüllah, *Tevarih*, in *Cronici turcești*, I, 32.

35 *Andan Eflak Beyi elçiyle haracını gönderüb ita'at etdi* (Neşri, *Tarih*, II, ed. Unat, Köymen, 536–537).

submitted himself to the Porte, acknowledging Ottoman suzerainty and commencing tribute payments.

Fifteenth- and sixteenth-century sources associate the acts of submission performed by Wallachian, Moldavian and Transylvanian rulers towards the Porte with at least one of the following measures: personal attendance of the voivode at the Porte, or sending of an envoy or high-ranking officials; voluntary submission to the sultan rather than an open military confrontation concluded with Ottoman victory; the payment of a certain sum of money, invariably interpreted by the Ottomans as a tribute (*cizye* or *harac*); the sultan's grant of protection; and recognition of accession to the throne, usually accompanied by a bestowal of distinctive insignia to the voivode or his envoy.

### 2.1 *Acknowledgment of Allegiance and Voluntary Submissions*

It is important to note from the outset that the act of submission was frequently regarded as an outcome of military inferiority, whereby the weaker party surrendered to a stronger adversary, thus recognizing the latter's supremacy. From this point of view, an acknowledgment of allegiance presents itself as a direct consequence of the threat or use of force. A legend narrated by Ion Neculce, presents it in the following manner:

> And Stephen the Great asked the hermit what he should do, for he could no longer fight the Turks, should he yield the country to the Turks, or should he not?[36]

Sooner or later, all Balkan princes chose this path. Ducas recognized these circumstances when he described the hegemony Ottomans achieved following their conquest of Constantinople in 1453:

> Thus, involuntarily and under duress, they obeyed and brought gifts to [Mehmed II] for fear that they might share the same fate.[37]

In Byzantine and Ottoman chronicles, the act of homage was always equalled with submission. For instance, Vlad the Evil arrived to Murad II's court in Bursa, "paying his homage, submitted to [the sultan]."[38] According to an anonymous Ottoman chronicle, in the aftermath of Mehmed II's campaign of 1462,

---

36 Neculce, *O samă de cuvinte*, 166 (*Și au întrebat Ștefan-vodă pe sihastru ce va mai face, că nu poate să să mai bată cu turcii, închina-va țara la turci, au ba?*).

37 Ducas, *Istoria*, XLII/6; Melissenos, *Cronica*, IV/18, 2, 543–545.

38 Ducas, *Istoria*, XXIX/10. For another example, see Ducas, *Istoria*, XLV/17.

Wallachian "infidels [...] came in droves willing to pay homage and submitted to His Majesty the Emperor."[39] In 1538, Muhieddin al-Cemali remarked that Moldavia "submitted to the *padişah*."[40]

Later sources also associated the acknowledgment of allegiance with submission and considered both as a moment of transition under Ottoman domination. Transylvanian historian J. Filstich stated with regard to Basarab Laiotă:

> It is under his reign that the Turks first laid their hands on Wallachia, a country they had been unable to take hold of ever before.[41]

For Mihai Cantacuzino, Mircea the Elder "acknowledged allegiance of the country towards the Turks" by paying *harac* "under the oath of submission," and Laiotă Basarab "submitted completely, the acknowledging allegiance of Wallachia to the Turks."[42] Generally speaking, early modern authors saw the declaration of allegiance by the rulers as a critical juncture which put them in the state of submission to and dependence upon the Porte: "And ever since hath the country remained subject to the Turkish Porte."[43]

The same principle applied to Moldavia. Dimitrie Cantemir claimed that prior to the times of Bogdan and Süleyman the Magnificent, when the Moldavian prince "subjects to him Moldavia by the name of a fief," the country had not yielded to the Turks.[44]

A difference of interpretation must be emphasized here. If, from the Ottoman standpoint, an indissoluble link existed between the tribute (and other voivodal duties) and the state of submission to the Porte (*ʿubudiyet*), this connection was by no means obvious to Christian rulers, for whom the obligation to pay what the Ottomans called *cizye* or *harac* did not necessarily mean a political dependence. For instance, the Polish king Sigismund II Augustus expressed his opinion that prior to 1538 the Porte did not subdue Moldavia, even if the principality had been paying the tribute.[45]

Thus, acknowledging allegiance to the sultan did not imply political submission except a voluntary one, which took place without military confronta-

---

39 ANIC, mf. Turkey, r. 65, fr. 751–752, cf. Gemil, *Românii și otomanii*, 144, n. 375.

40 Muhieddin el-Cemalı, *Tevarih*, in *Cronici turcești I*, 188.

41 Filstich, *Istorie*, 104–105.

42 *Genealogia Cantacuzinilor*, 67–70.

43 *Genealogia Cantacuzinilor*, 67–70 (*Și de atunci până astăzi a rămas țara supusă la Poarta turcească*).

44 Cantemir, *Othman History*, 187, n. 29.

45 *Terra ejus Turco non est subjecta* (cf. Ciurea, "Relații," 6–7; Gemil, *Românii și otomanii*, 35, n. 83).

tion. According to Ianache Văcărescu, in 1418 "the voivode and the boyars yielded Wallachia without war to the emperor Mehmed the First."[46] For Mihai Cantacuzino, in 1460–1462, "the voivode himself [inappropriately identified by the author Basarab Laiotă] on his own accord, yielded the country."[47]

In the 1520s, Radu of Afumați and Wallachian boyars, aware of the overwhelming Ottoman military superiority, voluntarily engaged in the efforts to secure peace after they successfully repelled the challenge by Mehmed bey, the *sancakbeyi* of Nikopol:

> The wish of them all was for the voivode to go to the Porte and take a low bow before the emperor.[48]

Acknowledging allegiance as a means to avoid military conflict also found its expression in a letter of Mehmed bey, the *sancakbeyi* of Nikopol (former voivode Mihnea II the Renegate) from 14 December 1594. Earlier that year, the Wallachians had revolted against the Porte, forcing the Porte to undertake military action the following year. However, the punitive campaign was preceded by an attempt to replace the rebel voivodes. As Mihnea II wrote,

> they sent me ahead, so that I may sway the country to yield before the war is waged and harms the land.[49]

The tradition of accepting allegiance was also strong in the case of Moldavia, circulating among Moldavian historians and the local boyars who submitted their petition to the Focșani congress. Dimitrie Cantemir, discussing the alleged act of submission performed by Bogdan III the Blind claimed that it was distinguished by the fact that the "country [...] made a voluntary surrender to *Soliman* I"[50] rather than being forced to do so.

46 *Văcărescu, Istorie*, 204 (*domnul și boierii au închinat Țara Românească fără război la înpăratul Mehmed cel dintîiu*).

47 *Genealogia Cantacuzinilor*, 67–70 (*însuși Domnul, din a lui voință, a închinat țara*).

48 Popescu, *Istoriile*, 274 (*Au voit cu toții să meargă domnul la Poartă să plece capul la poala împăratului*).

49 Hurmuzaki, *Documente*, XIV/1, doc. CLXXXIII (*pe mine m-au trimis înainte, poate să fac țara să se închine și să nu mai fie războiu și să se strice locul*).

50 Cantemir, *Othman History*, 56, n. 24. See also Golimas, "Închinare," 14.

## 2.2 *Acknowledgments of Allegiance and Covenants*

Submission was also often associated with concluding peace agreements negotiated between both parties. This type of allegiance was specific to the tributary states, being also called "conditioned submission."[51]

At the state level, the conclusion of a pact did not necessarily imply the acknowledgment of allegiance of one party to the other. Still, whenever sources discuss the performance of such acts, it appears very likely that they were reinforced by official regulations of the relations between the parties. After all, this was a customary practice present in suzerain–vassal relations throughout Southeastern and Central Europe. A treaty could stipulate acknowledgment of allegiance in the future while the latter could, in turn, be reinforced by a bilateral agreement.[52]

Sources frequently linked acknowledgment of allegiance with issuing or renewal of oaths (in Ottoman *ʿahd*, in Romanian *jurămant*) between sultans and voivodes. However, eighteenth-century Moldavian and Wallachian authors overstated the connection between homage and the grants of ancient privileges (so-called "capitulations"). Thus, according to Mihai Cantacuzino, the declarations of allegiance by Mircea the Elder and Basarab Laiotă were accompanied by their covenants with the Ottoman rulers (in Romanian *învoială* or *tocmeală*), whose alleged "clauses" (*legături*) Wallachian boyars listed in their memorandum to Count Orloff.[53] Later, according to the tradition, Voivodes Bogdan III the Blind and Petru Rareș submitted Moldavia to the sultan, who granted them privileges in the form of "covenants" (*tractaturi*).[54]

## 2.3 *Acknowledgment of Allegiance and Tribute*

The practice of "gift giving" upon ascension to the throne, dispatch of envoys or avoiding military conflicts was widespread not only in the Christian–Ottoman relations but was a customary practice throughout the premodern world. Before John Albert's invasion of Moldavia in 1497, Stephen the Great sent Chancellor Tăutu and Treasurer Isaac,

51 This formula was applied by T. Gemil to Moldovia in and after 1538 (*Petru Rareș*, 158).

52 The case of the treaty concluded between Stephen the Great and Cazimir iv in 1462 is relevant (Bogdan, *Documente. Ștefan*, II, doc. CXXIX).

53 *Genealogia Cantacuzinilor*, 67–70.

54 *Tractaturile prin care s-au închinat țara, de către Bogdan voevod, domnu al Moldoviei, împărățind Baizet al 2-lea* (*The Covenants by which the country was submitted by Bogdan voivode, ruler of Moldavia, during the reign of Bayezid the Second*) (BAR, ms. 566, fol. 126v–136). Published by M. Kogălniceanu in *Arhiva Românească*, 1845, II, 347–364 and then in Kogălniceanu, *Letopisețe*, III, 450–459.

> with many gifts and greeted [the king] on the other side of the Dnestr and presented the gifts before him.[55]

Yet, acknowledgment of allegiance towards the Porte implied a distinct procedure. First, the homage was inextricably associated with the presentation of gifts. Particularly after the conquest of Constantinople, the Christian princes "acknowledged their allegiance to [Mehmed II] by offering gifts."[56] Moreover, for tributary princes, paying their homage to the sultan was always accompanied with the payment of tribute. As Ducas points out, it was Mehmed II who asked "all peoples around the Black Sea to come and acknowledge their allegiance every year," not only with gifts but also with tribute. Similarly, Vlad the Impaler was summoned to the Porte, to pay his homage and "bring by all means [...] the annual tribute."[57] This difference was observed by Stephen the Great in a letter which compared the advantages of his submission to the Polish king with paying the homage to the sultan, the latter involving tribute payments:

> I admit I had acknowledged allegiance to the king [of Poland], as a benefactor of mine [...] lest I should become tributary to the Turks. [58]

Later, when the peace with Bayezid II was concluded, most probably in 1486, the homage-paying – a phrase which is not explicitly used either in Moldavian and Ottoman sources – was accompanied by a tribute payment.[59]

### 2.4 *Acknowledgment of Allegiance and the Oath of Fealty*

Since the act of homage had an obvious political meaning, fifteenth-century sources frequently present it as a method to keep Ottoman tributaries in check and periodically ascertain their continued loyalty to the sultan. Following the conquest of Constantinople, Mehmed II demanded that the despots of Serbia and Morea, the rulers of Chios, Mytilene and the emperors of Trebizond, as well as all living,

---

55 Ureche, *Letopiseț*, 54.

56 Ducas, *Istoria*, XLII/6.

57 Ducas, *Istoria*, XLII/6 and XLV/20.

58 Papacostea, "Colomeea," 536.

59 For details, see: Ș. Papacostea, "Relațiile internaționale ale Moldovei în vremea lui Ștefan cel Mare," *RdI*, 5–6, 1982, 607–638; Tahsin Gemil, "Observații referitoare la încheierea păcii și stabilirea hotarului dintre Moldova și Imperiul Otoman." *RA*, 2, 1983, 117–128; Șt. S. Gorovei, "Pacea moldo-otomană din 1486," *RdI*, 7, 1982, 807–821 (French version in *RRH*, 3–4, 1982, 405–421).

> by the Black Sea, should come every year and acknowledge their allegiance by presenting gifts and paying their tribute.[60]

The demand that the Wallachian and Moldavian princes personally attend the sultan's court with due tribute were thus utilized to verify the loyalty of tributaries towards their suzerain. Few voivodes prior to the mid-sixteenth century personally attended the Ottoman court, and the few exceptions were caused by their prior revolts that understandably spiked distrust of the Porte. Acknowledgment of allegiance could take place at the special request of the Porte or at the voivode's initiative. To re-establish amicable relations with Murad II, Vlad the Evil "came to Bursa," was received by the sultan and "paid homage to him." In turn, Vlad the Impaler was summoned by Mehmed II in 1460 "to come hastily and perform homage" (*proskynesis*), an act which the Wallachian voivode would reject for understandable motives. According to Ducas, "as for [Vlad] coming in person to pay homage was even more inconceivable."[61] In the same manner and under similar circumstances, Stephen the Great received an ultimatum: he was expected come to Istanbul and deliver the tribute personally, which automatically meant an act of submission. According to Aşıkpaşazade's rendition of that episode:

> The *padişah* [...] summoned the Moldavian voivode to the Porte, telling him: «This time you shall bring the tribute yourself». [Obviously] the infidel did not come (*kafir gelmedi*).[62]

On the other hand, Stephen's son, Petru Rareş "went to Tsarigrad" in 1541 to regain his throne,[63] concluding this trip by "paying homage" to Sultan Süleyman.

A frequent practice was to acknowlede one's allegiance through personal envoys. In 1451, soon after Mehmed II's rise to the throne, numerous Christian princes dispatched their embassies with gifts to "pay homage" to the sultan.[64] However, in the seventeenth century, the Porte insisted on personal attendance of the voivodes whom it suspected of preparing a rebellion. In 1658–1659, Dimitros Ramadanis relates that the grand vizier tried:

60 Ducas, *Istoria*, XLII/6.

61 Ducas, *Istoria*, XXIX/10 and XXIX/20.

62 *Padişah* [...] *Kara Boğdanın tekurunu Kapuya okudular. «Bu kez sen kendün getür haracını» dediler* (Aşıkpaşazade, *Tevarih*, ed. Giese, 178).

63 Ureche, *Letopiseţ*, 104.

64 Or "paid their respect to him" (Ducas, *Istoria*, XXIX/20).

> to inquire about Wallachia and Moldavia, whether they would submit to the Ottoman Empire or not [...], summoned the voivodes, that is Constantin Șerban, the voivode of Wallachia, and Gheorghe Ștefan, the voivode of Moldavia, to come and kiss [the sultan's robes], for they had not done it when they had come to the throne.[65]

When the voivodes in question attempted to evade this demand by offering further gifts, this proposal was rejected by the grand vizier, who reiterated the order. When the summon was ignored for a second time, the voivodes were deposed and forced to flee their principalities.

### 2.5 *Prostration and Official Appointments*

From the second half of the sixteenth century, but on several occasions earlier as well, the appointment of voivodes was accompanied by the bestowal of insignia of investiture, the most important being the roble of honor (*hil'at*) and the banner (*sancak*).[66] This took place during the ceremony of "submission" to the Porte, either personally or through representatives. In this respect, power relations, voivode's political position, international circumstances and immediate interests of the Porte were of considerable importance. In 1605, Radu Șerban received the banner and an implicit confirmation as the voivode of Wallachia through "submission embassies."[67] An illustrative example in this respect is the "charter of submission" (*'ubudiyetname*) of 28 September 1641, with which the Transylvanian prince George Rákoczy I reaffirmed his loyalty to the sultan. By sending his "head ambassador" (*baş elçimiz*) Stephen Serédi with the tribute, the prince performed the act "paying homage (*yüz sürmek*) to the blessed Imperial Stirrup of His Majesty, my glorious and sublime *padişah*."[68] If Radu Șerban and George Rákoczy I paid homage through intermediaries, other princes, including Radu Leon (1664–1669) and Gheorghe Duca (as voivode of Moldavia, 1678–1683) attended the Porte in person:

---

65 *Cronicul lui Chesarie Daponte de la 1648–1704*, in C. Erbiceanu, *Cronicarii greci carii au scris despre Români în epoca fanariotă*, Greek text and Romanian translation, Bucharest: Tipografia cărților bisericesci, 1888, 7. Actually, this chronicle is not written by Chesarie Daponte, but instead by Dimitros Ramadanis (see Machi Paizi-Apostolopoulou,. "Dimitrios Ramadanis: Enas istoriographos tou 18ou aiona se aphaneia," *O Eranistis* 20, 1995, 20–35; Machi Paizi-Apostolopoulou, "To cheirographo tou "Chronographou tou Daponte kai i lysi enos ainigmatos: To chf 4 Kyriazi tis 4 tis Gennadeiou," *O Eranistis*, 24, 2003, 85–94).

66 Examples in *Letopisețul Cantacuzinesc*, 45, 47, 48, 53, 103, 176 etc. See also Selaniki, *Tarih*, in *Cronici turcești*, I, 361.

67 Decei, *Imp. otoman*, 292.

68 Gemil, *Documente turcești*, doc. 106.

> As Radu bey, the current Wallachian *bey*, came to pay homage (*yüz sürüb*) to the imperial Stirrup, was deemed worthy of the imperial favour, the reign he has in his care was further entrusted to him and confirmed for three years henceforward.[69]

In his turn, Gheorghe Duca left for the Porte in the summer of 1681 "to lay his face at the Emperor's feet, on the occasion of obtaining a new province, as is the custom at the Porte."[70]

In the mid-eighteenth century, the practice of homage demanded of newly-appointed voivodes included an audience with the sultan and "kissing the earth [before] His Imperial Highness, the all-joyous *şahinşah*." The new position of the principalities of Wallachia and Moldavia in the Phanariot period, as their legal standing came closer to that of other Ottoman provinces, diminished the political role of the homage, and their structure became a simple ceremony similar to other appointments within imperial administration. That is why by August 1758 Voivode Ioan Teodor Callimachi protested the fact that his homage took place at the same time as that of foreign ambassadors (*müste'min elçiler*).[71]

### 2.6 *Ceremony of Prostration*

Prostration (*inclinare* in Latin, *proskynesis* in Greek) generally denotes an act of "inclining one's head" or bowing. The gesture can also involve kneeling (in Latin *ingenuculare*, in Romanian *îngenunchere*). Since kneeling occupies a prominent spot in Christian liturgy, the act of tributaries kneeling before the sultan and its importance was not lost on Ottoman chroniclers; "he kneeled in accordance to their custom,"[72] wrote Mustafa Selaniki about the submission of Prince John Sigismund Zápolya of Transylvania in 1566.

Until Murad III's reign, the gesture most prominently expressing submission and loyalty towards the sultan was the kissing of *padişah*'s hand, also practiced during the ascension ceremonies.[73] This custom also features in the homagial ceremonies of voivodes at the sultan's court. Thus, Oruc bin Adil described the ceremony of homage by Basarab Laiotă (1473–1477, with intermissions) with the following passage: "coming to the Imperial Threshold, he kissed the

69 Gemil, *Documente turcești*, doc. 148

70 Hurmuzaki, *Documente*, Supl. II/3, doc. LXX (letter of 26 June 1681), LXXI, LXXII.

71 Veliman, *Documente turcești*, doc. 134.

72 Selaniki, *Tarih*, ed. Ipşirli, I, 26–27; *Cronici turcești I*, 360.

73 Decei, *Imp. otoman*, 241.

*padişah*'s hand and donning of the *hil'at*." This ceremony was repeated "a couple years later."[74]

During Süleyman the Magnificent's campaign in Hungary in 1529, King John Zápolya "kissed the sultan's hand."[75] His son, John Sigismund Zápolya, would also perform the gesture during the ceremony in Zemun, while also kneeling before the sultan three or four times. In fact, the event that took place on 29 June 1566 represented a distinct (and possibly unique) moment in the evolution of the homage ceremonial. Mustafa Selaniki, who was in attendance, recounted:

> When the abovementioned prince, Istepan, came with the viziers to the presence of the glorious *şahinşah*, taking off his sophisticated gem-adorned cap, he kneeled in accordance with their custom as a token of submission. Then his Highness the All-happy *padişah* ordered him to stand up. After doing so he made another two steps, then kneeled again. Then, after kneeling for a third time, he went and bowed at the sultan's feet.

Triple kneeling and a bow, accompanied by kissing the sultan's hand thrice, were an exception even in the sixteenth-century relations with Ottoman tributaries, in a somewhat paradoxical manner that the chronicler's own words seem to indicate. According to him, John Sigismund Zápolya said "His Majesty made me faint; I lost all strength to speak." But, if we are to believe Mustafa Selaniki, it would be wrong to attribute this lavish ceremony to mere confusion that supposedly overwhelmed the prince. One also has to take into account the uncertain situation of John Zápolya's son, who badly needed recognition and assistance from the most powerful ruler of his age.[76]

Still, by the mid-eighteenth century, the ceremony of "prostration" compelled the appointees to Moldavian and Wallachian throne to "kiss the earth [before] his Imperial Highness the all-happy *şahinşah*."[77]

74 Oruc bin Adil, *Tevarih*, ed. Babinger, 74.

75 Muhieddin el-Cemalı, *Tevarih*, ed. Giese, 140.

76 Selaniki, *Tarih*, ed. Ipşirli, I, 26–27 (*ve mezbur Istefan kıral, vüzera-i izam hazretleryle izz-i huzur-ı şehenşahiye girdüklerinde ayın ü ka'ideleri üzre cevahir ile müzeyyen takyesin çıkarup, Padişah-ı cihan-penah hazretleri nazar-ı şerifinde makam-ı 'ubudiyetde diz çöküp oturmuş, sa'adetlü Padişah hazretleri «kalksun» diyü buyurmışlar emre imitisal edüp, kalkup iki kademe gelüp yine oturmuş, üçinci mertebe varup damen-i saltanata yüz sürüp*). See also the account of Ibrahim Peçevi (Decei, *Imp. otoman*, 197).

77 Veliman, *Documente turcești*, doc. 134.

## 3 Submission in Long-Term Perspective

The acts of submission (*închinare*) by Wallachian and Moldavian rulers have caused many controversies in Romanian historiography, addressed whenever new sources and interpretations have been allowed. Historians and jurists studying the principalities' relationship with the Porte used the word *închinare* – a term specific to the medieval chronicles – giving it two different meanings. The first meaning was employed to describe the first instance when the voivodes agreed to pay tribute as a token of submission to the sultan.[78] In turn, the second referred to any new peaceful arrangement between the voivodes and the sultan from the end of the fourteenth to the middle of the sixteenth century.[79]

Refining our understanding of these early episodes in the Moldavian–Ottoman and Wallachian–Ottoman relations requires us to identify historical events that contain enough legal and diplomatic elements specific to "homage" (*închinare*) in the sources from the late fourteenth until mid-sixteenth century. It is important to note that the extant sources clearly show that acceptance of tribute and submission, as well as conclusion of relevant pacts, cannot be attributed to any single moment in time:

> Even when there was some reason why they came to fight each other, yet, through new agreement they came again to terms.[80]

This passage by Ducas referred to the renewal of Ottoman–Byzantine peace agreements. However, the same description can as easily be applied to the early contacts between the Porte and the principalities of Wallachia and Moldavia.

On the other hand, given that the term "homage" acquired multiple meanings in the sources of the period, it should not be treated in an exclusive and restrictive manner. The adoption of the later meaning, which conceived the act of submission as singular and decisive, would be unfortunate, as it did not reflect the meaning usually applied to the term in fifteenth and sixteenth-century sources. Instead, it is better to talk about temporary peace agreements

78 See, for instance: Gorovei, "Casa Păcii," 649, 654; Gorovei, "1486," 815, 820; L. Şimanschi, "«Închinarea» de la Vaslui (5 <iunie> 1456)," *AIIAI*, 1981, 613–638; A.H. Golimas, *Sensul închinării de la Vaslui a lui Petru Vodă Aron. Din legăturile de drept ale Moldovei cu Poarta Otomană*, Iaşi, 1941 (off-print from *Cuget moldovenesc*, Iaşi, 9–12, 1940).

79 For example: Xenopol, *Istoria Românilor*, vol. II, 80, 88–89, 144–145, 351, 426–428; Decei, *Imp. otoman*, 139.

80 Ducas, *Istoria*, XXXIV/6; Ştefănescu, *Ţara Românească*, 37–100.

– with their logical implications – that were usually broken by one or both parties. Moreover, speaking of a single moment of submission would assume political and juridical stagnation, which should alert historians. Historical reality itself militates against such "pinpointing," since – along with reinforcing some basic principles – it encompassed changes, either short- or long-term.

In this context, my concern is whether it is accurate to limit the notion of homage – as seventeenth- and eighteenth-century chroniclers did – to a single event and a single voivode. On the contrary, the development of the tradition of homage, with its welter of personalities involved and its ambiguous chronology, suggests a genuine evolution of relations between the Porte and its Moldavian–Wallachian tributaries. This trajectory was marked by a series of events which involved multiple temporary pacts between sultans and voivodes rather than a single defining moment.

As I have already shown in the previous chapter, the submission of Wallachia began in the last decade of the fourteenth century and had concluded by the reign of Süleyman Kanunî. Particularly important moments in this evolution were the reigns of Mircea the Elder, Mehmed II's Wallachian campaign of 1462 and the period between 1521 and 1529.

In the case of Moldavia, the process started in 1455–1456 and was brought to a conclusion in 1538, with Stephen the Great's peace agreements with Mehmed II in 1480–1481 and Bayezid II in 1486 constituting important milestones of this evolution.

As for Transylvania, the submission was performed for the first time in the first half of the sixteenth century, and stemmed from Süleyman the Magnificent's policy in Central Europe. This conjecture produced a treaty with John Zápolya in 1528, and subsequently led to the granting of Transylvania to John Sigismund Zápolya as a *sancak* in 1541 and, ultimately, to the prince's prostration in 1566.

Taking into consideration these three timetables, we may safely conclude that the 1520s and 1530s bookended the first period of Ottoman relations with tributary rulers and ushered in a new stage in their history, profoundly shaped by the political changes in Hungary and Transylvania.

## 4 Conquest North of the Danube

One of the most important topics on which the sources diverge and contradict each other is the modality by which the Porte imposed its hegemony over Wallachia, Moldavia and Transylvania.

A similar ambiguity characterized records of early Arab expansion. In this respect, it is worth citing D. R. Hill's effort to present the data regarding the cessation of hostilities and estimate its military and political effects in the immediate aftermath of the early conquests.[81] Nonetheless, it is clear that the ambiguity of sources cannot be ignored altogether. Iraq (al-Sawad), which jurists considered a test case for their theories, is significant for the ambiguity which characterized the status of land and early Islamic methods of conquest:

> I do not know anything I can say about the land of Sawad – invoked as example by the famous jurist al-Shafiʾi himself – except conjecture because the most accurate report by the school of Kufah in relation to Sawad is obscure conjecture. Furthermore, I have found some other reports to be conflicting with it. Some say that Sawad was a land which surrendered peacefully, without war; others that it was a conquered land: still others that part of it was of the first, but the other part was of the latter.[82]

Questions regarding methods of conquest arose in a series of *fetva*s issued in the closing decades of the tenth and beginning of the eleventh centuries, which raised the question of the status of land seized by Muslim soldiers from Christians in Sicily.[83] Similar controversies arose in the well-known Ottoman dilemma that followed the conquest of Constantinople in 1453. On this issue, Dimitrie Cantemir and other Christian authors, tried to prove that a full half the city was taken "by surrender" and only the other half "by force."[84]

The legal status of conquered lands, population, churches and synagogues under Muslim rule stemmed directly from whether they were conquered "by

81 D. R. Hill, *The Termination of Hostilities in the Early Arab Conquests.* AD *634 – 656*, London: Luzac and Co. Ltd., 1971.

82 Shafi'i, *Al-ʿumm*, cf. Ali Abd al-Kader, "Land Property and Land Tenure in Islam." *IQ*, v, 2 (1959), 8.

83 Abu Jaʿfar al-Daʿudi (d. 1012), *Kitab al-amwal*, ed. Ridha Shahada, Rabat, n.d., 70–81, cf. W. Granara, "*Jihâd* and Cross-Cultural Encounter in Muslim Sicily." *HMEIR*, 3, 1/2, 1996, 47–48: "He was asked: When Sicily was conquered by force, the inhabitants of some of the (fortified) towns resisted until they made peace treaties. Some of them later fled and their houses were left abandoned. [What is the status of them?]. He said: «If those who made peace treaties stipulated as a condition of the treaties that the land would remain their property for which in turn they would pay a poll-tax, then they may keep the land and do with it as they may. As for those who converted to Islam, the poll-tax is dropped, and they get to keep the land. Concerning those upon whom both a poll-tax and a land tax were imposed, they may not sell their land because the one cannot be separated from the other. Those who convert to Islam need not pay a poll-tax, are exempt from a land tax, and may keep their land and do with it as they may»").

84 Cantemir, *Othman History*, 367–368, n. 20.

force" or "by surrender." For instance, in al-Mawerdi's opinion, the lands conquered "by force" would become territories of Islam, and those acquired "willingly," with a peace agreement, could become a territory of covenant.[85]

### 4.1 *"By force" or "Willingly"*

According to D. R. Hill, the occurrence of the terms *ʿanveten* or *kasran* in early Islamic sources indicated that the conquest took place "by force" which naturally ruled out the use of the term *sulhen*.[86]

In Dimitrie Cantemir's view, "by right of arms" meant that one side was subdued or surrendered under the threat of force. His claims are laid out in an annotation entitled "annual tribute," while describing how Mehmed I "makes the *Walachians* tributary. H. 820 / A.C.1418." Recounting the sultan's Hungarian–Wallachian campaign, Cantemir singled out the conquest of Severin and Giurgiu situated on the Danube's left bank. Giurgiu was reinforced with new walls and a sizeable garrison to bar Wallachians from crossing the river. The fact that Wallachians agreed to ransom their peace by paying an annual tribute after the sultan started his campaign should mean in Cantemir's view a submission "by right of arms":

> Pent up in this manner, and pressed by the sword of the Enemy and the want of warlike Stores, despairing also to preserve their liberty, they purchase their safety with the promise of an annual tribute, for the performance whereof the Sons of Prince and three Great Men are given to the Emperor in hostage.[87]

The occurrence of the terms *sulh* or *sulhen* in early Islamic sources indicated that the conquest took place "by surrender" or "voluntarily." Also, even if the circumstances strongly indicate a settlement, for instance the lack of references to a battle, or if the existence of an *ʿahd* puts the conquest into the *sulhen* category, still the very term does not appear.[88] According to early fourteenth-century traveller al-Tijani, the continued existence of Christian churches in

---

85 Mawerdi, *Ahkam*, 301; Ibn Taimiya, cf. Laoust, *Ibn Taimiya*, 272 ("la question se pose de savoir si le pays a été enlevé de vive force (*ʿanwatan*), ou s'il s'est rendu par capitulation (*sulhan*)." See also Biegman's reflections on this subject (Biegman, *Ragusa*, 31–32).

86 Hill, *Hostilities*, 4. In Roman law, the legal concept of *debellatio* was applied to defining the process by which a state of war ended with a transfer of territorial sovereignty (Grotius, *Drept*, 666).

87 Cantemir, *Othman History*, 74 and n. 10.

88 Hill, *Hostilities*, 4.

Tunis served as a proof that it was conquered "by surrender," even though the churches themselves laid in ruins.[89]

Dimitrie Cantemir's interpretation of a "voluntary" surrender can be deduced from his account of Moldavia's submission to the Ottomans.[90] It seems to have consisted of the following elements: the Moldavian prince's recognition of vassalage (which Cantemir attributed to Petru Rareș in 1529), an embassy which offered both the people and the land to the sultan (tradition identified the emissary as Chancellor Tăutu/*Teutuk Lagotheta*), obtaining honorable terms of surrender and privileges granted by the sultan (safeguards for the Orthodox Church in Moldavia and the status of the principality as an imperial fief) and drafting the instruments of peace (the sultan ratified the conditions, with the documents brought by the envoy to the prince in Suceava/*Soczava*). Thus, according to Cantemir, the circumstances of the submission proved "that Moldavia voluntarily and without compulsion offered her obedience to the Turkish Empire."[91]

### 4.2 *Differences between Wallachia and Moldavia*

Moldavian sources did not draw parallels between the ways Wallachia and Moldavia submitted to the Porte.[92] On the contrary, eighteenth-century Moldavian authors, including Dimitrie Cantemir and Ion Neculce, emphasized divergences in favour of Moldavia. Thus, Cantemir recognized that "Wallachians were subject to the Turks by right of Arms," but he categorically rejected the same claim with regard to Moldavians, whom he saw as those who "voluntarily put themselves under the Protection of the Turks."[93]

It is instructive that, while trying to juxtapose "submission" to "conquest," with regard to Wallachia Cantemir applied different criteria than he did for Moldavia. Reading his account on the ravages of Süleyman's campaign in 1538, one could expect that Moldavia would be regarded as subdued "by right of arms." However, Cantemir claimed this was not the case. Instead,

---

89 *Voyage du Scheikh et-Tidjani dans la régence de Tunis, pendant les années 706, 707 et 708 de l'Hégira* (1306–1309 de J.C.) translated from Arabic by M. Alphonse Rousseau, Paris: Imprimerie Impériale, 1853, 147; Mas-Latrie, *Traités*, 4.

90 Cantemir, *Othman History*, 188–189 and n. 28–34.

91 Cantemir, *Othman History*, 189, n. 32.

92 C. Orhonlu, compared the political status of Wallachia and Moldavia, which were compelled to pay tribute as a result of Ottoman conquest, with that of Ragusa, emphasizing that the latter accepted paying tribute but by the conclusion of a peace treaty (C. Orhonlu, "Kharadj," *EI-2*, IV, 1086).

93 Cantemir, *Othman History*, 74, n. 10.

> The *Moldavians*, seeing no way to withstand so great a storm, humbly sue to him for peace, and promise the payment of the annual tribute, only they petition that the choice of a prince may remain in the state, and that he may, as before, be invested with regal authority. *Soliman* grants their requests, confirms the Prince chosen by them, and restoring the captives…[94]

At the beginning of the nineteenth century, Alexandru Beldiman adopted a similar approach, emphasizing the difference between Moldavia and its southern neighbour, claiming that Wallachia the sultan "had taken by military power" (*le luase cu puterea armelor*).[95]

Western scholars adopted this view without adopting a uniform chronology and vocabulary to describe the events. In 1809, Thomas Thornton wrote that "Wallachia submitted to the force of the Ottomans arms in 1418," but Moldavia "surrendered its liberties to Soliman the First in 1529."[96] Also, according to Bois-le-Comte's opinion from 1834, "Wallachia was defeated by Mehmed II's armies," but "Moldavia surrendered willingly to great Süleyman to avoid inevitable conquest."[97] Indeed, one cannot deny that certain differences existed between the obligations of Wallachia and those of Moldavia, the duties being far more onerous in the former case. Considering this, one should deduce that this divergence originated from two different methods of conquest.

However, two caveats have to be made in this regard. First, Ottoman control over Wallachia was imposed around fifty years earlier than in Moldavia. Secondly, the geographical position of Moldavia was more peripheral than Wallachia's, which was geographically closer to Ottoman power centers, Adrianople and Istanbul.

### 4.3 *Sultan's Right of Sword*

To affirm the right of the sword over a territory after a military victory was a widespread custom in the premodern period, since the conqueror could decide the legal status of a subdued territory.[98] No matter the method of con-

---

94 Cantemir, *Othman History*, 202–203.

95 *Tractaturile*, 451.

96 Thornton, *Turkey*, II, 307.

97 "Report on the Romanian principalities" of 10 May 1834, to the Count of Rigny (Hurmuzaki, *Documente*, XVII, doc. DXI: *la Valachie abattue par les armes de Mahomet II, en 1460; la Moldavie se soumettant volontairement au grand Soliman, pour se soustraire à une conquête devenue inévitable, 1536*). Of course, the dates are wrong.

98 For example, the prince of Moldavia, Petru Rareș (1527–1538, 1541–1546), affirmed his "right of sword" over the principality of Transylvania in a letter to the inhabitants of 14

quest, either "by force" or "voluntarily," according to the Hanafi view, the sultan had the right to unilaterally determine the legal condition of the conquered territories and their population.[99]

In regard to the territory, a Muslim sovereign could choose between multiple options, taking into consideration the geographical, military and political circumstances.[100] Firstly, he could distribute them among the warriors after setting apart his due fifth of the territory, thus transforming his conquests into *ʿöşr* lands (*arazi-yi ʿöşriye*).[101] Secondly, he could leave the lands in the hands of the local population in exchange for a land tax, thus transforming them into *harac* lands (*arazi-yi haraciye*); finally, he could declare them a property of the whole Muslim community.[102]

Abu Yusuf Ya'kub recounted the conflicts between Umar ibn al-Khattab (634–644) and the Arab warriors, caused by the caliph's decision not to share the territories conquered by force in Syria, Iraq and Egypt, but rather to organize them as "frontier provinces."[103] Even though the peace had been imposed by force, non-Muslims were to be treated as "protected peoples" (*zimmis*), paying either an individual poll-tax or a collective one.

An *ʿanveten* conquest provided a Muslim sovereign with a theoretical right to transform the churches and synagogues into mosques, and only within a territory conquered "by surrender" had non-Muslims the right to build new religious buildings. In practice, a Muslim sovereign could deny this right and decide the future of the churches and synagogues by historical and local circumstances. Thus, despite the fact that Thessalonika (Selanik) was conquered

---

January, without year: "…I have won the country of Transylvania with the sword…" (Tocilescu, *534 documente*, doc. 500). But the "conqueror's right" could be modified or even cancelled by concluding a peace treaty (Armanazi, *Islam*, 87–88).

99 D'Ohsson, *Tableau*, V, 57–58; Morabia, *Ğihad*, 454–455; Inalcık, "Policy," 231.

100 See: Max von Berchem, *La propriété territoriale el l'impôt foncier sous les premiers califes*, Geneva: H. Georg, 1886 (he analyzed the work of the Shafi'i jurist al-Mawerdi); A. N. Poliak, "Classification of Lands in the Islamic Law and its Technical Terms," *AJSMLL*, 1, 1940, 50–63; Decei, *Imp. otoman*, 213; Sertoğlu, *ROTA*, 15.

101 In the fourteenth and fifteenth centuries, the Ottomans applied an old Turkish and Mongol practice of dividing the conquered territories between the members of a frontier *bey*'s family (*uc beyi*), ruler of *gazis* troops, being charged to wage sacred expeditions to *dar al-harb* (Inalcik, "Emergence," 76).

102 According to a *hadis*, "The land taken by peace treaty belongs to Allah and His Prophet," i. e. to the sultan in the Ottoman Empire (Berchem, *Propriété*, 10; D'Ohsson, *Tableau*, V, 97; Sourdel, *Islamul clasic*, I, 261; Decei, "Sulhname," 138, 4).

103 Abu Yusuf, *Kitab*, 36, 43–65, 103–104, 302. He invoked the *Kur'an* LIX, 7–10.

"by force" and plundered in 1430, Murad II ordered the Saint Dimitri church "be kept by Christians," as Ducas claimed.[104]

The outbreak of war because of non-Muslim prince's refusal to pay tribute, diminished the infidel state's right to exist. Given that, according to a medieval custom, a victory over non-Muslims granted supplementary rights to the conqueror, Muslim sources emphasized or even fabricated conquests "by force." In this way subsequent claims of alteration of non-Muslims' legal and political position could be justified.

According to the Ottoman legal standpoint, the lands that entered under Muslim control were considered "conquered," regardless of whether they were taken "by force" or "voluntarily."[105] Despite the resistance mounted since the end of the fourteenth until the mid-sixteenth century resistance and the peace agreements reached with the voivodes, Moldavia, Wallachia and Transylvania were regarded by the Ottomans as lands conquered by the sultans. Narrating the 1538 expedition and the surrender of Suceava, Ibrahim Peçevi affirmed that

> in that day, the land of Moldavia came under the rule of the Ottoman state, [although] documents with conditions and obligations were drafted."[106]

In the same way, regardless of the methods used by the Ottomans, beginning with Süleyman the Magnificent (1520–1566), Wallachia and Moldavia "definitively entered under their domination."[107] In regard to Wallachia, Ottoman chroniclers used the notion of "conquest," particularly when discussing the 1462 expedition against Vlad the Impaler. The image of Wallachia as an Ottoman conquest increasingly spread in the 1540s and 1550s, however, featuring both in chronicles, but also in official documents. At the same time, the idea

104 Ibn Taimiya, cf. Laoust, *Ibn Taimiya*, 272; Ducas, *Istoria*, XXIX/5. Let us here note the opposite case, when the transformation of a mosque in Jerusalem to a Christian church was not allowed by Süleyman Kanunî as it was deemed contrary to Islamic law (Charrière, *Négociations*, I, 130–131).

105 Many historians used the term of Ottoman "conquest," while also emphasizing differences in the methods of conquest. Many Southeastern European states, such as Bulgaria, Serbia, Byzantium and Bosnia, were crushed and dismantled by the invading Ottomans during late fourteenth and fifteenth century, and were directly incorporated into the rising Ottoman state. In turn, Wallachia and Moldavia "were preserved as puppet states in name only" for almost half a millennium (Denis P. Hupchick, *Culture and History in Eastern Europe*, New York: St. Martin's Press, 1994, 59).

106 Peçevi, *Tarih*, in *Cronici turcești I*, 481.

107 Bois-le-Compte, cf. Hurmuzaki, *Documente*, XVII, doc. DXI: *passèrent définitivement sous leur domination.*

was fleshed out. According to this new narrative, Wallachia was actually subdued "by sword." Even the most solemn and important records regarding Wallachia, the *berat* granted to the voivodes, categorically asserted the "right of sword." An "imperial cipher" (*nişan-ı hümayun*) issued by Murad III on 17 September 1585, on the occasion of Mihnea II's appointment to the throne stated that "the above-mentioned country was conquered by the power of our swords."[108]

The expedition of 1538 was considered in Ottoman sources a turning point in the evolution of the status of Moldavia.[109] It was at this point that Ottoman authorities began to invoke the claim to justify increasing interference in the principality's internal affairs, since "the country of Moldavia is our country, conquered by our victorious and defeating sword." This statement featured most prominently in the Porte's correspondence with the Polish kings, who had their own claims to Moldavia.[110] However, it must be noted that Ottoman chronicles – even when authored by the same individual – often provide two contradictory opinions regarding the method by which Moldavia had been subdued.

In the seventeenth and eighteenth centuries, most works emphasized the sultan's "right of sword" over Moldavia. Nonetheless, some historians affirmed that Moldavians had surrendered "voluntarily" and were conquered "peacefully." Thus, in a chapter included in *Süleymanname* and devoted to the "sacred expeditions" of 1484 and 1538, Kara-Çelebi-Zade spoke of "the submission of Moldavia country by the power of sword." However, another work by the same author claimed that the "annexation" of Moldavia took place "without resistance."[111] In Nasuh Matrakçi, Mustafa Ali and Ibrahim Peçevi's opinion, the "surrender" of Suceava that represented a conspiracy of Moldavian boyars against the incumbent voivode, and the capture of the prince's fabulous treasure justified Süleyman Kanunî's right to decide unilaterally in 1538 on the

108 Maxim, *CTO*, doc. 14: 22 *Ramazan* 993.

109 The Romanian historians have advanced different interpretations on the consequences of the expedition of 1538. For details, see: E. Stănescu, "Le coup d'état nobiliaire de 1538 et son role dans l'asservissment de la Moldavie par l'Empire Ottoman." *NEH*, 1955, 241–264; *Petru Rareş*, red. coordonator Leon Şimanschi, Bucharest, 1978, 151–174 (T. Gemil, Şt. S. Gorovei); Maxim, "Statutul politico-juridic," 111; Gorovei, "Casa păcii," 656–666; Andreescu, "Dominaţia," 409–410.

110 Mehmet, *Documente turceşti*, I, doc. 87 (Selim II's letter of 26 *Ramazan* 1568/25 March 1568 to Sigismund II, king of Poland). See also Süleyman Kanunî's letter of 6 October 1564 to the same ruler (Hurmuzaki, *Documente*, Supl. II/1, doc. CXXVII).

111 Kara-Çelebi-Zade, *Süleymanname*, in *Cronici turceşti I*, 532; Kara-Çelebi-Zade, *Ravdat ül-Ebrar*, in *Cronici turceşti I*, 547.

future status of Moldavia.[112] Moreover, issuing the "conquest letter" (*fetihname*) in October 1538,[113] the sultan – who called himself "the conqueror of the country of Moldavia" in the inscription of Bender[114] – was willing to reject the privileges grand boyars had earned by the "conditional capitulation" of Moldavia.

As a result, the Ottoman sources describe Süleyman Kanunî as entitled, from the perspective of the Islamic law of peace, to grant "forgiveness (*aman*) to the whole Moldavian population." Nevertheless, due to serious political–military and financial concerns, it was deemed preferable to confirm or appoint only Christian voivodes rather than transform the principality into a province governed by a Muslim official. Towards the mid-sixteenth century, the image of Moldavia and Wallachia as provinces conquered "by sword" increasingly dominated the official Ottoman standpoint, as it was frequently cited in *hüküm*s. For instance, in 1559, Süleyman Kanunî affirmed that

> Wallachia and Moldavia are dominions and countries of mine that have been conquered and invaded with my own sword, the guide to victory.[115]

Transylvania was also given the label of a "conquered country," beginning with the Süleyman the Magnificent's reign. Later, in a 1613 letter addressed to Brașov, the grand vizier Nasuh pașa insisted that:

> Transylvania has been conquered with the own sword of our fortunate, honoured and glorious *padișah* [Süleyman].[116]

In fact, this notion originated from the Mohács victory in 1526, which allowed the Ottomans to consider Hungary as ruled by the "right of his sword" (*kendi kılıç hakkı*).[117] Let us note that to consolidate these "conquests," the Ottomans issued "letters of conquest" (*fetihname*) which announced sultanic victories "throughout the world and to all the peoples."

112 Nasuk Matrakçi, Mustafa Ali and İbrahim Peçevi, in *Cronici turcești I*, 229–302, 353–354, 480–481.

113 *Cemazi ül-ahir* 945 (Nasuk Matrakçi, *Fetihname-yi Kara-Boğdan*, in *Cronici turcești I*, 232).

114 Guboglu, *Paleografia*, doc. 7; M. Guboglu, "L'inscription turque de Bender relative à l'expedition de Soliman le Magnifique en Moldavie (1538)," *SAO*, I, 1957, 175–187.

115 *vilayet-i Eflak ve Boğdan benim șimșir-i zafer-rehberim ile feth ü-teshir olmuș memleket ü-vilayetimdir* (Veliman, "Carte de legământ," 29).

116 Guboglu, "Arhive. Brașov," doc. II.

117 Mehmet, *Documente turcești*, I, doc. 21; Decei, *Imp. otoman*, 175.

### 4.4 *"Since the Imperial Conquest..."*

In the Ottoman documents from the early modern period, the idea of conquest was usually associated with Süleyman the Magnificent's reign, seen as a watershed in the empire's relationship with its Wallachian, Moldavian and Transylvanian tributaries. Still, as a rule, neither the Ottoman authorities nor the locals invoked the conquest in a negative sense. In this regard, it is important to correctly interpret the phrase "being separated at chancery and spared the violations and free in all respects" (*mefruz ül-kalem ve maktuʿ ül-kadem min-küll-il-vücuh serbest olub*), invoked so frequently in Ottoman documents of the late seventeenth and eighteenth centuries.[118]

Romanian historians and jurists considered this phrase solely as an expression of Wallachia and Moldavia's autonomous status. In fact, this statement was quoted only in part, to avoid a rather embarrassing fact that this assumed autonomy was put in place "since the imperial conquest" (*feth-i hakaniden berü*).

Moreover, the idea that the Ottoman conquest took place was also invoked by Moldavian–Wallachian elites throughout the seventeenth and eighteenth century in order to retain or reassert ancient practices and governance. The petitions (*ʿarz*) they drafted interpreted the tribute of the principalities as a collective one (*miri maktuʿ*) that had been established "since the imperial conquest" (*feth-i hakaniden berü*) both in Wallachia and Moldavia.[119] For instance, a document from 1728 claimed that since the conquest of the principality by Sultan Süleyman, a poll-tax was imposed as a communal obligation. This constituted evidence for a Moldavian agent in Istanbul (*Boğdan kapu-kethudası*) against the abuses of the *cizye* collector of Burgas, who had asked for the poll-tax from Moldavian cavalrymen.[120] Also, "since the imperial conquest" the tribute (*cizye*) from Wallachian subjects was to be collected by the voivode alone, thus shielding his subjects from financial abuses by Ottoman authorities, we read in a document of 1759.[121] "Since the imperial conquest" the boundaries between Wallachia and adjacent *sancak*s, including Brăila (Ibrail) were also established, their governors and inhabitants forbidden from intruding in Wallachian territories.[122]

---

118 Veliman, *Documente turcești*, doc. 93, 104, 107, 112, 140, 117, 118, 121, 127, 130, 141, 210 etc.

119 In a petition of Voivode Ștefan Cantacuzino (1714–1715), one can read: *Eflak memeleketi feth-i hakaniden berü mirisi maktuʿ olub* (Gemil, *Documente turcești*, doc. 205).

120 *Feth-i hakaniden berü memleket-i Boğdanın cizyesi maktuʿ olub* (Veliman, *Documente turcești*, doc. 61).

121 Veliman, *Documente turcești*, doc. 140.

122 In a *hüküm* of *evahir-i Zilhicce* 1104/ 23 August-1 September 1693, added to Voivode Ștefan Cantacuzino' petition of 1715 (Gemil, *Documente turcești*, doc. 205).

The Shakespearean dilemma "to be or not to be" does not work for Romanian historians in respect to the Ottoman conquest. Following the nationalistic ideal of "neither conquerors, nor conquered," some scholars attempt to solve the problem by inverting the question: "Why did the Ottomans never conquer the Romanian countries?"[123] In my view, it is necessary to clearly affirm that – after a long period of paying homage – the Ottomans succeeded in conquering Wallachia and Moldavia during the reign of Süleyman the Magnificent.[124]

---

123 Most modern Romanian historians strongly reject the idea of the Romanian principalities' conquest (especially, see P. P. Panaitescu, "De ce n-au cucerit turcii Ţările Române," in P. P. Panaitescu, *Interpretări româneşti: Studii de istorie economică şi socială*, edited by Ştefan S. Gorovei and Maria M. Székely, Bucharest: Editura Enciclopedică, 1994, 111–119; Maxim, *ŢRÎP*, 111–142: Ch. "De ce n-au cucerit Otomanii Ţările Române").

124 Panaite, "Legal and Political Status," 9–17.

# PART 4

## *Covenants and Customs*

CHAPTER 7

# Ottoman Peace Agreements

Discussing official documents issued by Muslim chanceries up to the beginning of the fourteenth century, Ahmad al-Kalkashandi (d. 1418), the author of the most comprehensive manual of chancellery draftsmanship, classified the documents which could regulate the relationship between Muslims and non-Muslims into three categories: safe-conducts (*aman*), pacts of tributary protection (*ʿahd-ı zimmet*) and peace agreements (*muvadaʿa*).[1]

> Apart from the acceptance of Islam and a faint trace of a provision to grant asylum, the *siyar* – Hans Kruse wrote, basing on al-Shaybani's *Kitab al-siyar* – had three institutions which provided security for individual unbelievers of unbelieving communities against belligerent acts of the Muslims: the promise of security (*aman*), the subjects as semi-citizens with inferior rights (*zimmet*) and the international treaty (*muvadaʿa*).[2]

In concluding peace agreements, the Ottoman sources indicate the concepts of *aman*, *ʿahd* and *ʿahdname* as central legal and diplomatic steps for establishing peaceful relations with non-Muslim communities and states.

## 1 Aman

The legal debate over treaties with non-Muslim communities and states in the Abode of War has found its place in the law of *aman*. The sheer amount of space devoted to the concept in legal treatises, such as al-Shaybani's *Kitab al-siyar al-kabir*, allows one to say that the safe-conduct (*aman*) was one of the main concepts of the Islamic "international" law. By its nature, the concept of *aman*, which can be translated also as "mercy," "safety" or "protection," was

1 Ahmad al-Kalkashandi, *Kitab subh al-aʾsha*, 14 vols., Cairo, Dar al-Kutub al Misriyyah, 1922, cf. Wansborough, "Safe-Conduct," 25. A short al-Kalkashandi's biography in C. E. Bosworth, "al-Kalkashandi," *EI-2*, IV, 531–533. He finished his work in 1415, being used also in the Ottoman chancery (Wansborough, "Safe-Conduct," 26, 31, n. 49; Zachariadou, *Trade and Crusade*, 179–185).

2 Kruse, "Shaybani," 247.

 | DOI:10.1163/9789004411104_008

connected to both the law of war and that of peace. Similarly, the status of foreigners also relied on this notion.[3] According to Joseph Schacht, *aman* is,

> a safe conduct or pledge of security by which a harbi or "enemy alien," i.e. a non-Muslim belonging to the *dar al-harb*, becomes protected by the sanctions of the law in his life and property for a limited period.[4]

The main questions the treatises aimed to address were the following: who had the right to grant *aman*; when and how was *aman* to be granted; who could enjoy *aman*; what were the consequences of *aman* to the legal status of enemy infidels (*harbi küffar*); and finally, when did the validity of *aman* end and what ramifications did it have?

In the Ottoman sources, as well as in documents of the Early Islamic period, the concepts of *aman*, *zimmet* and *ʿahd* were considered synonymous, frequently leading to confusion. For instance, the formula *ʿahd ü-aman* ("pact and mercy") could attest a peace granted to Christian ruler, and *emn ü-aman* ("safety and mercy") could mean the protection granted to the enemy troops which had capitulated during the war.[5]

Al-Shaybani devoted a significant section to "the protection (*aman*) granted by a free Muslim, a minor boy, a woman, a slave or a non-Muslim subject (*zimmi*)," implying that the aforementioned categories had the right to grant *aman*. But only the Muslim sovereign or his delegate could grant a collective *aman* to a group of non-Muslims (e.g. besieged enemies, inhabitants of a country) or to a non-Muslim ruler.[6] To avoid misinterpretations, Christians were frequently anxious to surrender to the suitable authority, the best way being to "put all their families and goods on the ground of the *padişah*'s feet," because the sultan was the highest authority with the right to frame the relations between the conquerors and conquered peoples.[7]

3 Shaybani, *Kitab al-Siyar*, I, 176–414; III, 364–399. See also Abu Yusuf, *Kitab*, 313–318; Morabia, *Ǧihad*, 331; J. Schacht, "Aman," *EI-2*, I, 441; Wansborough, "Safe-Conduct," 30.

4 Schacht, "Aman," 441.

5 Mehmet, *Documente turcești*, I, doc. 26, 64; Maxim, *CTO*, doc. 14.

6 Shaybani, *Kitab al-Siyar*, I, 176–181; Caurroy, "Législation," IV/8, 304; Peters, *Islam*, 29.

7 In 1738–1739, the infidels of Mehadia wanted to capitulate to the "true commander" (Mehmed Subhi, *Tarih*, in *Cronici turcești III*, 263). For the case of John the Terrible (1572–1574), see Dinu C. Giurescu, *Ion vodă cel Viteaz*, Bucharest: Editura Științifică, 1966, 172. The cited formula features prominently with regard to the surrender of fortresses to the Ottomans (Kıvami, *Fetihname*, in *Crestomație turcă*, 180–183).

Adopting as the main criteria whether *aman* was granted during the time of peace or war, and the number of its beneficiaries (either an individual or a larger group), we can construct a typology of *aman*.

*Aman* granted during the time of hostilities bestowed protection to the inhabitants' life, freedom, property, or faith. Generally, *aman* could not be refused if an enemy had asked for it, with the exception made for rebels.[8] *Aman* granted during peacetime was, in practice, a temporary safe-conduct which provided guarantees of life, freedom and property of *harbi* merchants, travellers, or envoys in the Abode of Islam.[9]

With regard to the number of beneficiaries, legal texts distinguished between individual or special protection (*has aman*) and collective or general protection (*ʿamm aman*). The former constituted an Islamic equivalent of Western safe-conduct. The latter, in turn, was granted to the inhabitants of a conquered community or even the whole country, as well as to the merchant groups allowed to travel and trade in the territories of Islam.[10]

The Ottomans also employed *aman* as a basic legal concept to establish and legitimize peaceful relations with both non-Muslims and Muslims, during wartime and the time of peace. First, *aman* was granted upon the surrender of fortress and towns and was frequently mentioned by the chroniclers. For instance, in 1484 Bayezid II granted mercy and protection to the infidels of the Moldavian towns of Kili and Akkerman, who had requested an *aman*.[11] Second, some historians claimed that the non-Muslim communities' status within the empire, from the legal point of view, hinged on the notion of *aman*.[12] Third, the peace and trade agreements granted as *capitulations* to the Christian states implicitly conveyed a general *aman* for foreigners who travelled to the Ottoman territories, particularly merchants. Yet, in practice, the general *aman* was followed by an individual one by the imperial chancellery, which took the form of a written safe-conduct (in Turkish *izn-i hümayun*, *icazetname* or

8 *Kur'an*, IX, 6; Shaybani, *Kitab al-siyar*, I, 220–244; Peters, *Islam*, 32; Morabia, *Ğihad*, 332, n. 183); Decei, *Imp.otoman*, 365, n. 3; Schacht, "Aman," 442; D. Ayalon, "Harb. III. Le sultanat mamluk," *EI-2*, III, 192; Cantemir, *Othman History*, 72, n. 4.

9 Abu Yusuf, *Kitab*, 187–188, 290–295; Shaybani, *Kitab al-Siyar*, I, 170, 358–361; Armanazi, *Islam*, 103; Peters, *Islam*, 29–32; J. Schacht, "Aman," 441–442; Wansborough, "Safe-Conduct," 29.

10 Wansborough, "Safe-Conduct," 24–25, 30; Shaw, *Ottoman Empire*, I, 163; Schacht, "Aman," 442; Morabia, *Ğihad*, 333.

11 Kıvami, *Fetihname*, 304–306. See also *Cronici turcești I*, 63 (Oruc bin Adil); 75–8 (Tursun bey); 98–100 (Aşıkpaşazade); 130–132 (Mehmed Neşri); 245 (Lütfi paşa); 253 (Rustem paşa); 326–327 (Sa'adeddin); 408 (Mehmed bin Mehmed); 461–462 (Koca Hüseyin); 545 (Kara-Çelebi-Zade).

12 Hadrovics, *Peuple serbe*, 73.

*yol-tezkere*).[13] In *ʿahdname*s, the sultanic *aman* was constantly invoked as the cornerstone underpinning other stipulations of the treaty. For instance, the formularies of *şerayt-i ʿahd ü-peyman* ("conditions of pact and pledge"), *şerayt-i sulh ü-aman* ("conditions of peace and protection"), *şerayt-i ʿahd ü-aman* ("conditions of pact and protection"), *şerayt-i emn ü-aman* ("conditions of safety and protection") feature prominently in Ottoman documents.[14] Even though the concept of *aman* was explicitly and constantly invoked by *ʿahdname*s starting from the second half of the sixteenth century, this does not mean that it was not implicitly present before.

Drawing on the statements of Hanafi jurist al-Kashani's (d. 1191) discussion of *aman*, contained in his *Kitab al-siyar*, Hans Kruse concluded that the "grant of safety to infidels individually or collectively suspends the principle of *cihad* and prevents for a definite or indefinite time its realization by armed disputes." Therefore, it played a crucial role, constituting a prerequisite for peaceful arrangement of relations with non-Muslims.[15]

## 2 ʿAkd and ʿahd

Islamic law stipulated that peaceful relations between Muslims and non-Muslims could be established by means of *ʿahd* or *muʿahada* – translated as a covenant, pact, oath, or compact – that in fact consisted of two categories: a permanent covenant (*ʿahd-ı zimmet*, *ʿakd-ı zimmet*) and a temporary truce (*muvadaʿa*, *hüdne*, *sulh*).[16]

### 2.1 *Permanent Covenants*

*ʿAkd-ı zimmet* (or *ʿahd-ı zimmet*) is a complex concept, which is hard to cover concisely. Generally, we can say that this kind of a "covenant" implied a permanent peace, which concluded the theoretical state of war between the Abode of Islam and the Abode of War, whose main parameters were the submission of non-Muslims and the payment of tribute in exchange for protection granted to them by a Muslim sovereign. *ʿAhd*s issued during the early Islamic period

13 H. İnalcık, J. Wansborough, "Imtiyāzāt." *EI*-2, III, (1971), 1210–1211. In the sixteenth-century *ʿahdnames* granted to Venice contained a stipulation which obliged every merchant to have a permission from the *bailos* (*icazetname*) if he wanted to travel into the Ottoman Empire (Şakiroğlu, "1521," 398).

14 For instance, see the *ʿahdnames* granted to England in 1580 and 1601 (Skilliter, *Harborne*, 236; Feridun, *Münşeʾat*, II, 385).

15 Kruse, "Treaties," 157.

16 J. Schacht, "ʿAhd," *EI*-2, I, 263; M. Fayda, M.S. Kütükoğlu, "ʿAhdname," *IA*, I, 535–540; Özel, *Islam Hukuku*, 141–144.

state this arrangement in a concise manner: "For them protection (*zimmet*) and upon them a poll-tax (*cizye*)."[17] Such a contract gave non-Muslims the right to stay in the Abode of Islam, protections of their person and property, freedom to practice their own religion and defence against enemies.[18] According to al-Shaybani, the *zimmet* (the acceptance of the People of the Book as "semi-citizens of the Islamic commonwealth") was stronger than *aman* (the promise of security) and followed the latter, thus implying an indissoluble agreement between the Islamic community and *zimmis*.[19] The rules governing the *zimmi* status originated with the practices of Muhammad and the first caliphs, and were subsequently compiled as the famous Covenant of Umar. Jurists suggested that this elaborate text, which can be described as an *ʿahd-ı zimmet*, should be regarded as the archetypical agreement between Muslim rulers and the People of the Book, and provided the blueprint for later interactions, including the status of non-Muslims within the Ottoman domains.[20]

The official document issued by Mehmed II to the Genoese of Galata immediately after the conquest of Constantinople has been considered as a veritable *ʿahd-ı zimmet*. The formal treaty, written in Greek, was sworn by both parties, and Zaganos paşa guaranteed the community of Galata – in terms reminiscent of the Covenant of Umar – their life and property, and exempted their male offspring from the Janissary levy. The Ottoman authorities would not interfere with the religious institutions and practices, while Muslim soldiers and civilians were barred from entering Galata. Moreover, the Genoese were permitted to carry out their commercial activities undisturbed and tax-free.

---

17 Hamidullah, *Documents*, doc. 17; al-Tabari, cf. Lewis, *Islam*, I, 234–235. See also Özel, *Islam Hukuku*, 203–205, 216–218; Peters, *Islam*, 36.

18 From studies concerning the *zimmi* status in classical Islam, see: A. C. Tritton, *The Caliphs and their Non-Muslims Subjects*, London: Oxford University Press, 1930; Antoine Fattal, *Le statut légal des non-musulmans en pays d'Islam*, Beirut: Imprimerie Catholique, 1958; B. Ye'or, *Le dhimmi. Profil de l'oprimé en Orient et en Afrique du Nord depuis la conquête arabe*, Paris; Anthropos, 1980; B. Lewis, "L'Islam et les Non-Musulmans," *Annales*, 35, 3–4, 1980, 784–799.

19 The Pact of Umar, which was supposedly the peace accord that Caliph Umar offered to the Christians of Syria, opens with the invocation of *aman*, requested by Christians: "When you came against us, we asked you for safe-conduct (*aman*) for ourselves, our descendants, our property, and the people of our community, and we undertook the following obligations toward you [...]" It concludes with Umar's accord: "Sign what they ask" (Tritton, *Non-Muslims*, 5–16). In the words of Hans Kruse, "[t]he discussion of the limitations and restrictions to which the non-Muslim "semi-citizens" are subjected will lead us into the realm of the law of religious minorities and thus to the public law of Islam." (Kruse, "Shaybani," 249).

20 Texts and comments in: Tritton, *Non-Muslims*, 5–16; Laoust, *Taimiya*, 267; Khadduri, *War and Peace*, 194–195; Maxim, *ȚRÎP*, 169–173; Cohen, *Jews*, 52–76.

In return, they were subjected to the poll-tax and banned from constructing new church buildings and using church bells and wooden gongs (semantrons); they were also forced to surrender their weapons, cannon and ammunition, and to attend to razing the walls of Galata.[21] *ʿAhdname-yi hümayun* or *berat-ı hümayun*, as imperial diplomas were usually called by the Ottoman sources, which set the juridical status of non-Muslim communities, be they cities (Ioanina, Antivari)[22] or Christian monasteries (e.g. St. John Prodromos of Serres, Monasteries of the Athos Mountain, Saint Catherine of the Sinai Mountain), also fall into this category.[23]

### 2.2 *Temporary Agreements*

*ʿAkd-ı muvadaʿa*, *sulh* or *hüdne* were frequently used in Islamic legal texts,[24] conveying an idea of a temporary reconciliation which should offer the conditions for a permanent peace that was to follow. For instance, the concept *akd-ı muvadaʿa* can be found in a short *fetva* collection on the matters of governance (*Siyasete muteʿallik fetvalar*), preserved in the Topkapı Palace Library, grouped in a chapter devoted to the relations with the inhabitants of the Abode of War (*ehl-i harb*).[25]

Throughout the Middle Ages, and particularly in Muslim–Christian relations, striking long-term truces habitually substituted for permanent peace

21 The original text has been preserved in London. The most recent published edition and comments belong to Inalcık, "Galata," 117–118. See also M. H. Şakiroğlu, "Fatih Sultan Mehmed' in Galatalılara verdiği fermanın Türkçe metinleri," *TAD*, 1983, 211–216; Iorga, "Privilegiul," 2–3 (the Greek original); Akgündüz, *Osmanlı Kanunnameleri*, 1, 476–479; Beldiceanu, *Ville ottomane*, 153–154. On 29 May 1453, Angelo Lomellino, *podestà* of the Genoese of Galata, sent the keys of fortress to sultan (Babinger, *Mehmed II*, 101–102).

22 The 1430 *ʿahdname* of Ioannina (C. Amantos, "La reconnaisance par les Mahométans des droits politiques et religieux des Chrétiens et le décret de Sinan Pacha," *Epirotika Kronika*, 1930, 197–210; Pantazopoulos, *Church and Law*, 21). The 1571 *ʿahdname* of Antivari (Grignaschi, "Ahdname," 105–127).

23 Beldiceanu-Steinherr, "Serres," 15–24; Zachariadou, "Prodromos," 1–12; Wittek, Lemerle, "Monastères athonites," 411–472; Oikonomidès, "Monastères," 1–10; Veselá-Prenosilova, "Sinai," 326–338. Documents issued by sultans for this monastery were published by Klaus Schwarz, *Osmanische Sultansurkunden des Sinai-Klosters in türkisher Sprache*, Freiburg im Breisgau: Klaus Schwarz Verlag, 1970. For comparing with the precedent policy towards Saint Catherine monastery of Sinai, see S. M. Stern, "Two Ayyubid Decrees from Sinai," in *Documents from Islamic Chanceries*, ed. S. M. Stern, Columbia: University of South Carolina Press, 1965, 10–25.

24 Also, *mühadene, mutaraka* (*Redhouse*, 497, 784, 804, 978, 1035; Heffening, "Sulh," *EI-1*, IV, 566–567; Tornauw, *Droit*, 201–202; Özel, *Islam Hukuku*, 141; M. Khadduri, "Hudna," *EI-2*, III, 565–566).

25 *Siyasete muteʿallik fetvalar* f. 12b–15b (TKSMK, H. 1650).

treaties. The concept of a "truce" had another meaning than in modern international law,[26] a fact best proven by the agreements concluded by Muslim sovereigns. Classical legal thought, such as that of Abu Yusuf Yakub, did not provide much in way of details regarding temporary peace agreements.[27] An exception in this respect was al-Shaybani, who devoted separate chapters of his works to the notion of the truce (*muvada'a*).[28]

Muslim jurists tried, often unsuccessfully, to define the temporary peace comparing it with a permanent one. This confusion can be found in Hanafi legal works as well. Al-Shaybani stated that between a Muslim sovereign and a non-Muslim ruler there could be only a pact (*mu'ahada*), and al-Sarakhsi added that it could be considered a *muvada'a* because a "mutual truce (*muvada'a*) is an agreement (*mu'ahada*)." According to the scholars, a proper peace must be called *müsaleme* or *musalaha*, but it could not be concluded with non-Muslims. Hence, the term *muvada'a* was applied to the truce.[29] However, no consistency was to be found even in legal treatises, and a deeper analysis only increases the sense of confusion. For instance, according to P. Forand, the agreements concluded with the Nubians in the seventh century formally fell into the category of *sulh*. However, since they were not, strictly speaking, "treaties" or covenants in a usual sense, they should rather be regarded as "truces" (*hüdne*) or instruments of "neutralization" or "conciliation" (*muvada'a*).[30] An example from the Ottoman period was an *'ahdname* issued by Bayezid II in 1483, ratifying the peace with King Matthias Corvinus of Hungary.[31] The terms *musalaha* and *dostluk* appear to express "peace and friendship," but we cannot speak about a "permanent peace" between the rulers because the agreement was established for five years, as the text of the *'ahdname* explicitly stated.

Thus, often neither terminology nor diplomatic format served as suitable criteria for drawing a distinction between "truces" and "tributary-protection

26 Christians could only conclude truces with Muslims, in this respect quoting frequently Tubero, *Commentariorum: Turcae essimcum Christianis nulla alia Causa amititia eiguntar, nisi ut deman opprimant ineantos; unde qui illorum fidei minime credunt, maxime tuti sunt* (cf. Benda Kálmán, "Hıristiyan birliği ve XV. asırda Osmanlı Imparatorluğu-Macaristan münasebetleri." *TD*, 28–29, 1974–1975, 86–87). For definitions and features of truce in modern international law, see Rachelle Bernard, *L'armistice dans les guerres internationales*, Genève, 1947.

27 In E. Fagnan's French translation, this paragraph is entitled *Ni trêve, ni paix ne sont consenties pas des musulmans ayant la supériorite de forces*. He preferred to speak more of the treaty of Hudaibiya (Abu Yusuf, *Kitab*, 319–329).

28 Shaybani, *Kitab al-Siyar*, III, 236–335, no. 3361–3632; *Shaybani's Siyar*, 142–157.

29 Shaybani, *Kitab al-Siyar*, III, 307.

30 Forand, "Nubia," 113.

31 TKSMA, no. 5861; ANIC, mf. Turkey, r. 4, fr. 312; Maxim, *ŢRÎP*, 93–94.

compacts." It is only by addressing the contents of these documents that we can offer a clear distinction between the concepts, even though similar stipulations entered both types of *ʿahd*s. Nevertheless, a "tributary-protection compact" essentially implied the exchange between protection and tribute, while a "truce agreement" contained clauses on foreign policy, boundaries, envoys, captives and merchants. The last category thus included Ottoman agreements with European powers, such as Venice, Hungary, Poland, the Habsburgs and Russia.[32]

## 3 ʿAhdnames and Capitulations

### 3.1 *Terminology*

Imperial charter (*ʿahdname-yi hümayun*) was the term used in the Ottoman chancery until the nineteenth century for all peace agreements by which the Porte regulated its peaceful relations, alliances, international trade and the status of foreigners (called by modern historians and jurists peace treaties, treaties of alliance, treaties of friendship, treaties of commerce, treaties of vassalage etc.). The term itself is actually a compound noun, consisting of the Arabic *ʿahd* (pl. *ʿuhud*), which means oath, compact, covenant, and the Persian *name*, charter.[33] *ʿAhdname* was thus a document which confirmed in writing the grant of "protection" (*aman*), and the existence of a "contractual pact" (*ʿahd*, *ʿakd*, *ʿakd-ı ʿahd*, *sulh*) between sultans and an individual, community, or state.[34] Even though *ʿahdname*s had the form of an unilateral document, their

---

32 In the Ottoman view, peaceful relations between the Ottoman Empire and the European states were only periods of temporary peace. In this respect, one can quote the 1903 statements by Salih Munir paşa, the Ottoman ambassador in France (cf. Gemil, *Românii și otomanii*, 129, n. 321).

33 J. Schacht, "ʿAhd," *EI-2*, I, 263; M. Fayda, M. S. Kütükoğlu, "ʿAhdname," *Islam Ansiklopedisi*, Istanbul: ISAM, Türk Diayanet Vakfı, 1988, I, 535–540. Dimitrie Cantemir defined the term *ʿahdname* in the following words: "an *Arabian* Word compounded of *Ahd*, a *Covenant* or *Condition*, and *Namé*, a *Letter*. By this Name the Letters are signified which foreign Ambassadors, after a Peace obtained, procure from the Sultan, to their respective Princes, containing the Terms of the Peace (which the *Arabians* call *Mevad*) and ratified with the *Dura*, or Character of the Imperial Name" (Cantemir, *Othman History*, 88, n. 35).

34 Inalcık, Wansborough, "Imtiyazat," 1208. There were *ʿahdnames* issued for appointing dignitaries or successors (Schacht, "ʿAhd," 263). See the above-mentioned examples of *ʿahdnames* granted to religious communities, monasteries and cities.

contents implied "contract and alliance" (*ʿakd ü-ittifak*) or "pact and agreement" (*ʿahd ü-misak*).[35]

Apart from the usual term *ʿahdname*,[36] the terms *muʿahada* (*muʿahadaname*), *sulh* (*sulhname*),[37] *musalaha* (*musalahaname*)[38] were increasingly employed in the eighteenth-century Ottoman documents, either alone or in conjunction (*sulh muʿahadası*) to describe instruments of peace and treaties with European powers. Moreover, entire manuscripts were compiled to include these peace agreements.[39]

To define the Ottoman peace agreements, the Moldo–Wallachian sources focused on the practice of swearing an oath,[40] or borrowed the Ottoman term of *ʿahdname* (in Romanian transcription, *ahtiname* or *actenamede*).[41] On some occasions, attempts were made to establish an equivalency between Ottoman and European concepts. Referring to an agreement between Sultan Süleyman and John Zápolya in 1528, Moldavian chronicler Miron Costin stated that the sultan had ordered "an oath-charter be issued, which oath [the Ottomans] called *ahtiname*."[42] The Greek historian Dimitrios Ramadanis, de-

35 In the 1604 *ʿahdname* to France (Feridun, *Münşeʾat*, II, 404); in the 1612 *ʿahdname* to Holland (Groot, *OEDR*, 246).

36 The manuscript *ʿAhdname suretleri* collected the peace agreements between 1673–1733 AH/1084–1146 (TKSMK, H. 1636).

37 Since the fifteenth century, the word *sulh* designated a peace concluded with any foreign state (TKSMK. R. 1325: *risale* on the conclusion of peace (*sulh*) with the Habsburg Empire and Russia in 1739); TKSMK, E. H. 1438: *Rusya ile sulh*).

38 TKSMK, E. H. 1438, 165b–214a (on the treaties with Russia of 1791–1792).

39 The manucript *Sulhname-i ʿAmuca-zade Hüseyin paşa* related the negotiations for the peace of Karlowitz (TKSMK, R. 1311). The manuscripts *Suver-i mekatib-i musalaha Nemçe* and *Esnayi musalahada tevarüd eden mekatib* included also the treaty of Passarowitz (Pasarofça) of 1131 AH/1719 (TKSMK, R. 1946, R. 1953). The manuscript *Muʿahedat-ı hümayun <mecmuʿası>. 975–1200 Osmanlı devleti ile Nemçe ve sair devletler arasında ʿakd olunan bazı muʿahadalar* gathered the treaties with the Habsburg Empire, Russia and other states concluded between the years 975–1200 AH/1567–1796 (Belediye Kütüphanesi, Muallim Cevdet, K. 4; partially in ANIC, mf. Turcia, r. 53, fr. 894–1004). The manuscript *Risale-i muʿahedat* including the 1798 treaty with England and the secret treaty with Russia of 27 *Receb* 1213/1 January 1799 (TKSMK, fd. Bağdad 237; ANIC, mf. Turcia, r. 51, fr. 647–663).

40 In Romanian, the *ʿahdname* granted to John Zápolya in 1528 by Süleyman Kanunî was called "*carte cu giuramânt*" (Costin, *Istorie de Crăiia ungurească*, 290), while the treaty between John VI Cantacuzino and Orhan or Murad I, "*juramânt mare*" (Moxa, *Cronica*, 187).

41 For the documents granting lifelong reign to Wallachian voivode Constantin Brâncoveanu (1688–1714), Romanian words "*atişirif*," "*hatişerifuri*" (from Turkish *hatt-ı şerif*) were applied (Greceanu, *Istoria*, 126, 144–145).

42 Miron Costin, *Istorie de Crăiia ungurească*, 290 (*să iasă carte de giurământ, care ahtiname dzic ei giurământului*).

scribing the congress of Karlowitz, recounted that the Ottoman emissaries Rami-Mehmed Efendi and Alexandru Mavrocordat, returned to the capital "with peace charters in hand, *actenamedele* [...], i.e. peace treaties concluded after the war."[43]

The term *capitulations* has borne considerable controversy among scholars.[44] Medieval chanceries issued many types of internal or diplomatic documents described by this term (*capitularium, capitulatio*) whose common feature was the division of their contents into chapters. In fact, the very term originated from Latin *caput* and *capitulum* (*capitula* in plural), meaning chapter or a paragraph.[45] Therefore, this name was applied to the Ottoman instruments of peace solely due to their division into separate sections.[46]

Ottoman *ʿahdname*s contained a series of political and trade "conditions" (sing. *şart*; pl. *şartlar, şurut, şerayt*) or "issues" (*hususlar*). The beginning of articles until the end of the seventeenth century was marked by the conjunction "and" (*ve*), when the ordinal numbers were introduced under the influence of Western chanceries. Since Europeans considered the sultanic *ʿahdname*s as treaties, they applied the term *capitulations* as an equivalent to *ʿahdname*. This is well illustrated by the evidence provided by sixteenth- and seventeenth-century translations of *ʿahdname*s into European languages. For instance, comparing the Ottoman text of commercial privileges granted to English merchants in 1580 with the Italian translation of 5 April 1583, we see that the formula *ʿahdname-yi hümayun* was translated as *Imperiale Capitulazione*, while the

43 *Cronicul*, 55, n. 75. See R. A. Abou-el-Haj, "Ottoman Diplomacy at Karlowitz." *JAOS* 87, 4, (1967): 498–512.

44 On *Capitulations*, see also Maria Pia Pedani Fabris, *La Dimora della pace. Considerazioni sulle capitolazioni tra i paesi islamici e l'Europa*, Quaderni di Studi Arabi. Studi e testi, 2, Venice: Cafoscarina, 1996; Maurits van den Boogert, and Kate Fleet (eds.), *The Ottoman Capitulations: Text and Context* (in *Oriente Moderno* XXII, 3–2003), Rome: Institute per l'Oriente C.A. Nallino, 2003); Maurits van den Boogert, *The Capitulations and the Ottoman Juridical System: Qadis, Consuls, and Beratlıs in the 18th Century*, Leiden: Brill, 2005.

45 Belin, *Capitulations*, 9; Testa, *Traités*, I, 6, n. 3; Pélissié du Rausas, *Capitulations*, I, 1, n. 1; Sousa, *Capitulatory Regime*, 3; Hershlag, *Introduction*, 44. Of course, Italian words *capitolo* (pl. *capitoli*), *capitolare*, *capitolato* or the French *chapitre* and *chapitrer* have the same origin.

46 Besides *pactum* (in Italian *patto*, in French *pacte*). For details, see Belin, *Capitulations*, 7–17 (*Chapitre Ier: Sens et signification du terme capitulations; son correspondant dans les chancelleries orientales*). For example, the notion of *capitula* was applied to the Byzantine–Genoese treaty of 1304 or that concluded between Venice and Cyprus in 1328. These terms can be also found in Latin, French, Italian versions of eleventh-fourteenth-century peace and commerce treaties between Christians and Muslim North African princes. In 1186 a *capitoli della pace* was established between Pisa and Tunis. All these treaties were divided into "chapters" (Mas-Latrie, *Traités*, I, 28–30, 66–69, 283–284).

whole document was entitled *Capitoli dati alla Regina d'Inghiltera*.[47] Likewise, the Latin term *capitulationes* and its French, German and Italian derivatives were commonly used in translations of *'ahdnames* granted to France,[48] Poland,[49] the Habsburg Empire,[50] or Russia.[51]

Translating Ottoman texts, Europeans organized their contents by articles or chapters (*capitula* in Latin; *capitoli, capituli* in Italian; *chapitres, articles* in French; *articles* in English). Since any documents structured by chapters could, in the Western chancery tradition be called *capitulations*, the same label was applied to the Ottoman *'ahdnames*.[52] In fact, the Ottomans themselves adopted the notion of *Capitulation* as *Kapitülasyonlar*,[53] understood as the system of privileges granted to the foreign merchants in the Ottoman Empire,[54]

---

47 Skilliter, *Harborne*, 86–89, 232–239.

48 They were included in the seventeenth- and eighteenth-century French miscellanies, such as *Recueil des plusieurs traités entres les Puissances Chrestiennes et la Porte* (BnF, DO, Supl. Turc. 118); *Traicte et ambassades de Turquie. Recueil de pièces relatives à l'histoire des relations diplomatiques de la France avec le Levant. 1528–1640*, vols I–IV (Bibliothèque d'Arsenal, ms. 4767–4771); *les hautes et heureuses Capitulations, des anciennes Capitulations* (Hurmuzaki, *Documente*, Supl. I/1, doc. CXXIV: Henry III's letter to grand vizier Sinan paşa of 7 July 1582).

49 *Capitulatione tra sultan Selim Imperator de Turchi et Sigismondo Augusto Re di Polonia*, for the 1568 *'ahdname* (Hurmuzaki, *Documente*, vol. VIII, doc. CXCI); *Capitulations du Turc avec les Polonnois, les Capitulations de Pologne* (Hurmuzaki, *Documente*, Supl. I, vol. I, doc. CCLXVI, CCCVI (French letters of 1617 and 1623); *nostra eccelsa capitulatione*, in an Italian translation of 1564 *'ahdname* (Hurmuzaki, *Documente*, VIII, doc. CXXXIII).

50 "*Die fridens capitulation*," on the 1606 treaty, in a German letter of 16 March 1614 (Hurmuzaki, *Documente*, IV/1, doc. CCCCLXIV).

51 "*Capitulationes*," on the Ottoman–Russian treaty of 1711, in a Latin translation of an Ahmed III's ferman (Hurmuzaki, *Documente*, vol. VI, doc. LVII).

52 Other opinions: for I. de Testa, the notion of *Capitulations* had been used in European diplomacy for calling proper treaties ("bilateral documents") and could not apply to *'ahdnames* (seen as "unilateral documents"). In his opinion, the proposed synonym for *'ahdname* should be *lettres-patentes* (Testa, *Traités*, I, 6). S. Skilliter called the document of 1580 by which Murad III had granted commercial privileges to English merchants, "diploma (*berat*) incorporating the privileges" or "imperial treaty letter" (Skilliter, *Harborne*, 86–89, 232–239).

53 "Capitulation" could also be understood an agreement between two enemies which stipulated one's surrender to another. In Italian, *capitolare* means "to submit" and *capitulazione*, "surrender." From this perspective, certain scholars defined the *Capitulations* as documents which confirmed that the sultans, being forced by Western powers, gave up certain sovereign rights (D'Avril, "Protection," I, 536).

54 Sousa, *Capitulatory Regime*, 2, n. 5; Panaitescu, "Route commerciale," 53; Sertoğlu, *ROTA*, 164; Inalcık, Wansborough "Imtiyazat," 1217.

or a special treaty which regulated the position of foreigners within the empire (beginning with the eighteenth century).[55]

### 3.2 *Unilateral or Bilateral*

There are two contradictory opinions concerning the legal and diplomatic features of the *ʿahdnames*, seen either as unilateral documents[56] or as bilateral ones.[57] This divergence stemmed from interpreting Ottoman documents of the early modern period through the lens of modern international law, ignoring the peculiarities of Ottoman chancellery production and projecting individual cases of some French *ʿahdnames* and nineteenth-century commerce treaties onto the whole capitulatory regime, and even describing the notions of "unilateral" and "bilateral" in an inconsistent manner.[58]

Al-Kalkashandi, a scholar famous for the experience he acquired during his tenure in the Mamluk chancery, classified the peace agreements into two categories, depending on their structure: a) unilateral agreements granted directly by a Muslim chancery, without attendance of the second party, which received them in the form of a privilege issued by the Muslim sovereign; b) bilateral agreements elaborated in writing by both parties. In the former case, the agreement sometimes included an oath by a Muslim sovereign, which he swore after the non-Muslim ruler had done so upon receiving the text of their pact. In the latter case, the agreement appeared as a *instrumentum reciprocum*, the oaths of both rulers' included in the negotiated text.[59] In the chapters devoted to *muvadaʿa*, a term translated as a "reciprocal truce" by Muhammad Hamidullah, the famous jurists al-Shaybani and al-Sarakhsi noted that there

55 Pélissié du Rausas, *Capitulations*, I, 1, 28; Abi-Chahla, *Capitulations*, 123; Sousa, *Capitulatory Regime*, 3; Liebesny, "Privileges," 314; Ekrem, *Kapitülasyonlar*, 402.

56 *Des traités unilateraux* (Pélissié du Rausas, *Capitulations*, I, 13); "unilateral declaration" (Liebesny, "Privileges," 319–320); *lettres-patentes* (Testa, *Traités*, I, 6; Belin, *Capitulations*, 115–116); "unilateral charter of privileges" (Skilliter, *Harborne*, 89).

57 *Traités bilatéraux, conventions synallagmatiques* (Gavillot, *Capitulations*, 7–9).

58 On Ottoman diplomacy, see Palmira Brummett, *Ottoman Seapower and Levantine in the Age of Discovery*, State University of New York Press, 1994; *Ottoman Diplomacy. Conventional or Unconventional?* edited by A. Nuri Yurdusev, New York: Palgrave Macmillan, 2004 (Chapters of A. Nuri Yurdusev, "The Ottoman Attitude toward Diplomacy," 5–36; and Bülent Arı, "Early Ottoman Diplomacy: Ad Hoc Period," 36–66); *The Early Modern Ottomans. Remapping the Empire*, edited by Virginia H. Aksan and Daniel Goffman, Cambridge: Cambridge University Press, 2007 (Chapter of D. Goffman, "Negotiations with the Renaissance states: The Ottoman Empire and the new diplomacy," 61–74); Güneş Işıksel, *La diplomatie ottomane sous le règne de Selîm II: paramètres et périmètres de l'Empire ottoman dans le troisième quart du XVIe siècle*, Paris, Leuven: Peeters: Collection Turcica Vol. XX, 2016.

59 Wansborough, "Safe-Conduct," 25; Canard, "Un traité," 203–205.

were usually "two contractors" in the agreement.[60] In the case of *ʿahdname*s containing with commercial privileges, they were "unilateral" both in their form and content. According to James Porter, the documents regulating the legal status of English trade and merchants merely constituted favors granted by the Porte, without any reciprocity implied on the British side.[61] He considered the terms *Capitulation* and 'treaty' as antonyms, a concept largely confirmed in the eighteenth century, when the term *Capitulations* was applied primarily to documents of a commercial nature.

In my view, the form and contents of *ʿahdname*s were shaped largely by historical and geographical circumstances in which such documents were issued. Thus, it is instructive to consider separately instruments of peace concluded with the polities adjacent to the Ottoman domains. Taking into consideration the diplomatic form of the original texts and their translation which followed the Ottoman blueprint, the *ʿahdname*s concluded with Hungary, Poland, Venice and the Habsburgs in the fifteenth and sixteenth centuries had an unmistakeably unilateral character. In these *ʿahdname*s, the sultan was the only one to proclaim the results of the negotiations through the formula of "let it be known" (*maʾlum ola ki*)[62] and implemented the "clauses" of the agreement with the formula "the illustrious sign commands" (*nişan-ı şerif-i* [...] *hükmü oldur ki*).[63] For instance, with all the sixteenth- and seventeenth-century *ʿahdnames* which confirmed the establishment of peaceful relations with Poland, the sultan announced – prior to listing the conditions of peace – that he "gave and ordered this Imperial charter" (*işbu ʿahdname-yi hümayunu verdüm ve buyurdum ki*).[64] These formulas represent, from the point of view of diplomatics, a unilateral document issued by the sultan.

At the same time, the ways in which they were translated into Latin or Italian exhibit that the western standpoint differed from the Ottoman one. First, the Ottoman–Venetian pacts from the mid-fifteenth century, preserved in Italian or Latin, were characterized by V. L. Ménage as "bilateral agreements."[65] Sixteenth- and seventeenth-century Ottoman–Polish *ʿahdname*s were considered bilateral treaties by Polish kings, accordingly named in translations

60 Shaybani, *Kitab al-Siyar*, III, 305–334.

61 Porter, *Observations*, 362.

62 In the *ʿahdname* of 1525 granted to the Polish king (AGAD, *AKW-Tureckie*, k. 66, t. 19, no. 41).

63 In the *ʿahdname* of 1482 granted to Venice (Gallotta, "Il trattato 1482," 226). Also, in the *ʿahdnames* of 1503, 1513, 1517, 1521, 1540 (Gökbilgin, "Belgeler I," 121; Gökbilgin, "Belgeler II," 42, 47, 50).

64 In the *ʿahdnames* of 1553, 1577, 1591, 1598 (AGAD, *AKW-Tureckie*, k. 69, t. 172, no. 329; k. 71, t. 260, nr. 486; k. 71, t. 268, no. 498; k. 71, t. 280, no. 518).

65 Ménage, "Capitulation," 375–376. See G. M. Thomas, *Diplomatarium Veneto-Levantinum...*, vols. i-ii, Venice: Typis Marci Visentini, 1880–1899, passim.

*Capitulatione tra sultan Selim Imperator de Turchi et Sigismondo Augusto Re di Polonia* (of 1568) or *Capitulations du Turc avec les Polonnois*.[66] Moreover, in the Ottoman text of certain *ʿahdnames*, especially in *narratio*, the sultan affirmed that the respective peace was concluded between two contracting parties. In the 1483 Ottoman–Hungarian peace agreement, Bayezid II spoke of "peace and friendship between us and the king Matthias," (*Matyaş kıral ile bizim aramızda musalaha ve dostluk*),[67] a frequent formula of *ʿahdnames*. Some Ottoman documentary collections (*münşeʿat*) also indicate that the scribes regarded the treaties as bilateral agreements, a feature visible in the notes accompanying copied texts.[68]

In regard to their contents, some *ʿahdnames* were also seen by jurists and historians as "bilateral peace-settlements" if they included clauses formulated in a contractual manner, sometimes called "conditional privileges" or "reciprocal rights."[69] These kind of articles featured particularly in the *ʿahdnames* granted especially to neighboring states, such as Venice, Hungary or Poland.

### 3.3 *The Documentary Structure of ʿahdnames*

Information on the way Islamic peace agreements were to be drafted can be found in manuals of diplomatics, the most famous of which is by al-Kalkashandi. Another source in this respect are the treatises on "international" law, particularly al-Shaybani's *Kitab al-siyar*, annotated by al-Sarakhsi. A temporary truce (*muvadaʿa*) should begin with a standard formula naming both contracting parties, followed by the dates the truce would begin and end. Subsequently, the document would specify conditions of the agreement, which constituted the main part of the document. The oaths by both contracting parties concluded the document, warranting – according to customary practices – that the treaty would be observed.[70]

The structure most commonly applied in sixteenth- and seventeenth-century *ʿahdnames* concluding peace with foreign rulers, included the following

66 Hurmuzaki, *Documente*, VIII, doc. CXCI. A Latin copy preserved in Czartoryski Library in Cracow was entitled *Foedus inter Serenisimes Principes sultan Selimum Imperatorem Turcarum et Sigismundem Augustum Regem Poloniae* (Czartoryski Library, IV 616, 115); Hurmuzaki, *Documente*, Supl. I/1, doc. CCLXVI, CCCVI (French letters from ambassadors in Istanbul to their Kings).

67 TKSMA, no. 5861; ANIC, mf. Turkey, r. 4, fr. 312.

68 In top of the 1480–1481 *ʿahdname* copy, the scribe wrote "with the Moldavian" (*ba Kara-Boğdan*) (Decei, "Sulhname," 122; Maxim, *ȚRÎP*, 37).

69 For the Ottoman–Venetian treaties from 1419 to 1454 (Ménage, "Capitulation," 375). J. A. Gavillot used the formula *paix réciproque* for the Ottoman–Venetian treaty of 1454 (Gavillot, *Capitulations*, 16–17); Liebesny, "Privileges," 311.

70 Shaybani, *Kitab al-Siyar*, III, 306–307; M. Khadduri, "Hudna," *EI-2*, III, 566.

elements: invocatio (*daʿvet*), the invocation of the Allah's name; a *tuğra* (in Persian *nişan*), an imperial cipher or the sultan's signature written above the text;[71] intitulatio (*ʿunvan*), providing the whole list of sultan's titles; inscriptio (*elkab*), listing the addressee's position, titles and rank; salutatio (*duʿa*), a short salutation to the addressee; narratio, describing abstract of the addressee's plea for peace; dispositio (*emr/hüküm*), whereby the sultan expressed his authority in regard to peace terms, stipulated in the latter part of this section; sanctio et corroboratio (*yemin, tekid*), the sultan's solemn oath. Finally, the document concluded with datatio (*tarih*), indicating the time and place the document was issued, and the seal (*mühür*).[72]

It is important to note that not all of these elements found their way into every single *ʿahdname* or necessarily conformed to the same format. For instance, with certain *ʿahdname*s granted to Venice, Hungary or Poland in the second half of the fifteenth and at the beginning of the sixteenth century, the sultan's oath was placed before the clauses of the treaties.[73]

### 3.4 *Period of Validity*

The Prophet Muhammad concluded multiple temporary compacts with non-Muslim communities, the most famous case being the ten-year treaty of Hudaybiya in 628, that ceased hostilities with the inhabitants of Mecca.[74] This covenant subsequently provided a legal justification for Muslim jurists and sovereigns to legitimate truces with non-Muslim states.

A succession of eighth- and ninth-century peace compacts followed – most of them temporary – between the caliphs and Byzantium.[75] Similarly, diplomatic and commercial relations between North African polities and West European cities and states from the eleventh until the fourteenth centuries were settled through peace and trade agreements concluded for a limited period of

71 The *nişancı* was the official who had to write the *ʿahdnames* until the seventeenth century, including the imperial signature (F. Babinger, "Nishandji," *EI-2*, VIII (1995): 62; J. M. Landau, Ch. Pellat, "Nishan," *EI-2*, VIII (1995): 57–62. Decei, *Imp. otoman*, 212).

72 Fekete, *Diplomatik*, XXIX-LV; Guboglu, *Paleografia*, 56–67; Reychman, Zajaczkowski, *Handbook*, 140; Matuz, *Kanzleiwesen*, 93–101; Schaendlinger, *Süleyman*, vol. I, XIII-XXIX; Ménage, "Ottoman Documents," 281–304; Kütükoğlu, *Diplomatik*, 163–172.

73 But in the *ʿahdname* of 1482 granted to Venice, the oath started to be written at the end of text (Gallotta, "Il trattato 1482," 225). For the structure of fourteenth and fifteenth century treaties concluded between Venice and Anatolian emirs, see Zachariadou, *Trade and Crusade*, 180–184.

74 Al-Tabari, *Tarih*, cf. Bishai, "Negociations," 57.

75 Vasiliev, *Byzance*, passim; Hamidullah, "Nouveaux Documents," 288; Armanazi, *Islam*, 127–134.

time, up to thirty years.[76] Considering the Prophet's *sünnet* and the above-mentioned practice, al-Shaybani and al-Sarakhsi stated – along with other Hanafi jurists – that the duration of the truce had to be included in the text of the treaty.[77] Al-Kalkashandi, familiar with both the theory and practice of Mamluk diplomatics, stated that a truce with a non-Muslim ruler could be concluded for up to four months (with possible extension up to a year) if Muslims enjoyed military superiority, or up to ten years (and possibly extended for another decade) when Muslims had no advantage over the enemy.[78] The former could be concluded when Muslims intended to peacefully regulate their relations with non-Muslims.[79] I argue that a three-month truce proposed by Mehmed II to Voivode Petru Aron of Moldavia on 5 October 1455 fit the former category.[80] The latter could be concluded when Muslims had no military superiority over non-Muslims, and – as I have already emphasized – followed the model laid out by Muhammad in Hudaibiya.

The *ʿahdname*s which confirmed peace with European rulers were concluded for a limited period of time, either for a specified number of years or until both contracting parties remained on the throne. The former practice observed the rule of Islamic law which prohibited Muslims from concluding permanent peace with non-Muslims, instead requiring a limited duration of the arrangement to be included into the text of the compact.[81] In turn, the principle that the truces remained valid only for the incumbents followed a medieval custom, which lacked the concept of permanent grants and acts that would remain in place following the change on the throne.

Among the *ʿahdname*s issued for a specified period, we find those granted to Hungary, Poland (up to 1528) and the Habsburg Empire, which stated the

76 The treaty between Pisa and al-Mansur (1184–1199), an Almohad emir, of 15 November 1186, was concluded in twenty-five years: *la pace infino al termine di venticinque anni della data del presente* (Mas-Latrie, *Traités*, 28–30). The treaty of 1229 between Pisa and Tunis would be valid for thirty years: *Et termine pacis est triginte annorum* (Mas-Latrie, *Traités*, 32). For fifteen years was to be valid the commerce treaty between Tunis and France of 21 November 1270, and only for ten years the commercial privileges granted to Pisa in 1313 (Tunis) and 1358 (Morocco) (Mas-Latrie, *Traités*, 49–54).

77 Shaybani, *Kitab al-Siyar*, III, 236–252. Shafiʿi and shiʿi jurists agreed that the validity period cannot be registered in the text of treaty, but in return had to be indicated the Muslim sovereign's right to cancel unilaterally the peace (Peters, *Islam*, 29–30).

78 Cf. Wansborough, "Safe-Conduct," 26, 31; Zachariadou, *Trade and Crusade*, 179–185.

79 The legal argument was *Kur'an*, IX, 2: "Go ye, then, for four month, backwards and forwards, throughout the land, but know ye that ye cannot frustrate Allah" (Morabia, *Ǧihad*, 319–320; Peters, *Islam*, 33).

80 Mehmet, *Documente turcești*, I, doc. 1.

81 Pélissié du Rausas, *Capitulations*, I, 23–4; Liebesny, "Privileges," 327.

expected duration of truce. For instance, all Ottoman–Hungarian treaties from 1421 until 1519 were concluded for a one- to ten-year period.[82] Similarly, the agreements reached with Poland between 1489 and 1528 were to last between two and five years.[83] Although the expected duration of these truces was no more than five years,[84] the *ʿahdnames* granted to the Habsburgs from 1547 to 1591 constituted a significant change in this respect, as their duration was extended to eight years.[85] The treaty of Zsitvatörök (1606) ushered a series of even longer Ottoman–Habsburg truces, which varied between twenty and twenty-five years.[86] The treaties of Passarowitz in 1718, concluded for twenty-four years,[87] and that of Belgrade in 1739, for twenty-seven years, complete the list.[88] On the other end of the spectrum, sixteenth-century truces with Spain

82 The duration of these treaties was the following: 1421 – 5 years; 1428 – 3 years; 1444 – 10 years; 1449 – 7 years; 1451 – 3 years; 1483 – 5 years; 1488 – 3 years; 1495 – 3 years; 1498 – 3 years; 1503 – 7 years; 1510 – 3 years; 1513 – 3 years; 1519 – 1 year. For 1451, see *DRH*, D, I, doc. 305; Iorga, "Privilegiul," 20–23. For 1483, see TKSMA, E. 5861, mf. ANIC, mf. Turkey, r. 4, fr. 312; Hazai, "Urkunde. 1488," 141–145; For 1503, see TKSMA, E. 7675, mf. ANIC, mf. Turkey, r. 1, fr. 1–9; Gökbilgin, "1503," 369–390; Hammer, *Empire Ottoman*, IV, 393–400; Hurmuzaki, *Documente*, II–1, doc. XXIV. For the entire list, see Noradounghian, *Actes*, I, 396–397.

83 Two years (*ad annos duos*) were specified in the treaty of 1489; three years were concluded the treaties of 1494 (*ad decursum trium annorum fecimus*), 1519 and 1525 (*üç yıla sulhı kabul idüb*); finally, for five years were valid the treaties of 1502 (*e deba durar in fino cinque anni futuri*) and 1528 (*per anni cinque hovero*). For 1502, see *Monumenta Medii Aevi Historica, Tomus X: Acta Alexandri Regis Poloniae, Magni Ducis Lithuanie (1501–1506)*, w Krakowie, 1927, no. 117. For 1525, see Gökbilgin, "Belgeler I," 128–132. For the complete list, see Noradounghian, *Actes*, I, 398–400; Kołodziejczyk, *Ottoman-Polish Diplomatic Relations*, 197–231.

84 Only the treaty of Szegéd was an exception.

85 For 1547, see Feridun, *Münşeʾat*, II, 341–342 (*Roma imparatoru tarafına isdar buyurulan ʿahdname-yi hümayun sureti*); Petritsch, "1547," 49–80. For 1559, 1562 and 1565, see Schaendlinger, *Süleyman*, doc. 23, 25, 32. For 1568–1591, see *Nemçelü ʿAhd Defteri* 975–1210 AH/1567–1795 (BOA, *DED*, 57/1); *1567–1796 Osmanlı devleti ile Nemçe ve sair devletler arasında akd olunan bazı muʿahadalar* (ms. Belediye Kütüphanesi, Muallim Cevdet, K. 4, mf. ANIC, mf. Turkey, r. 53, fr. 894–1004). For a summary list, see Noradounghian, *Actes*, I, 385–389.

86 In 1606, twenty years (BOA, *DED* 57/1, 5–7; ANIC, mf. Turkey, r. 53, fr. 898–9; Feridun, *Münşeʾat*, II, 346–50; Fekete, *Esterhazy*, 3–14). In 1627, twenty-five years (BOA, *DED* 57/1, p. 10–4; Feridun, *Münşeʾat*, II, 330–334). In 1642, twenty years. In 1664, twenty-five years (BOA, *DED* 57/1, p. 17–9; ANIC, mf. Turkey, r. 53, fr. 905–9 (*bin yetmiş beş senesinde tecdid ʿahd olunduğda taraf-ı hümayunun Nemçe çesarına verilen ʿahdnamedir*); Silahdar, *Tarih*, in *Cronici turcești II*, 329). In 1699, twenty-five years (BOA, *DED* 57/1, p. 21–27; BOA, *Amedi Kalemi Odası, Kamil Kepeci tasnifi*, 53, 2–16 (*Amedi odası defterlerinden Nemçe çasarına virilen ʿahdname-yi hümayun kayıtı. Tarihi 1110*).

87 Sturdza, Petrescu, *Acte și documente*, I, 39–40.

88 In a Latin text: *Duret armistitium hocce et exyendatur favente Deo ad viginti septem annos et continuo sequentes a die, qua ejustem subscriptio facta fuerit* (Sturdza, Petrescu, *Acte și documente*, I, 57–58).

فرانسه پادشاهی ایله آل عثمان پادشاهی مابیننك منعقد
اولان عهدنامه درکه ذکر اولنور

ARTICLES
DV TRAICTE FAICT EN L'ANNEE
Mil ſix cens quatre, entre HENRI le Grand
Roy de France, & de Nauarre,
Et Sultan Amat Empereur des Turcs.
Par l'entremiſe de Meſſire François Sauary, Seigneur de Breues, Conſeiller du Roy en ſes Conſeil d'Eſtat & Priuè, lors Ambaſſadeur pour ſa Maieſtè à la Porte dudit Empereur.

A PARIS,
De l'Imprimerie des langues Orientales,
Arabique, Turqueſque, Perſique, &c.
Par Eſtienne Paulin, rue des Carmes, College des Lombards. MDCXV.

FIGURE 11 *Articles du traicté faict en l'année Mil six cens quatre, entre Henri le Grand Roy de France, & de Navarre, Et Sultan Amat Empereur des Turcs. Par l'entremise de Messire François Savary, seigneur de Brèves*, Paris, 1615 (title page of the bilingual edition, in Ottoman and French, of the *Capitulations* granted by Sultan Ahmed I to King Henry IV of France in 1604)

were remarkably short-term, ranging between three months and three years, reflecting a state of acute conflict between the two polities.[89]

Moreover, the Ottoman chancery issued throughout the early modern period a number of *ʿahdname*s that did not specify the duration of peace. They were usually issued to Southeastern tributaries and certain European powers, including Venice, Poland, France, England and the Dutch Republic. In case of these charters, they remained in force only throughout the sultan's reign who

89 The truce of 21 March 1580 was to last ten months (until January 1581); the truce of 7 February 1578 was negotiated for one year; the agreements of 1581, 1584 and 1587 were concluded three years (Braudel, *Mediterana*, VI, 21, 30, 34, 36).

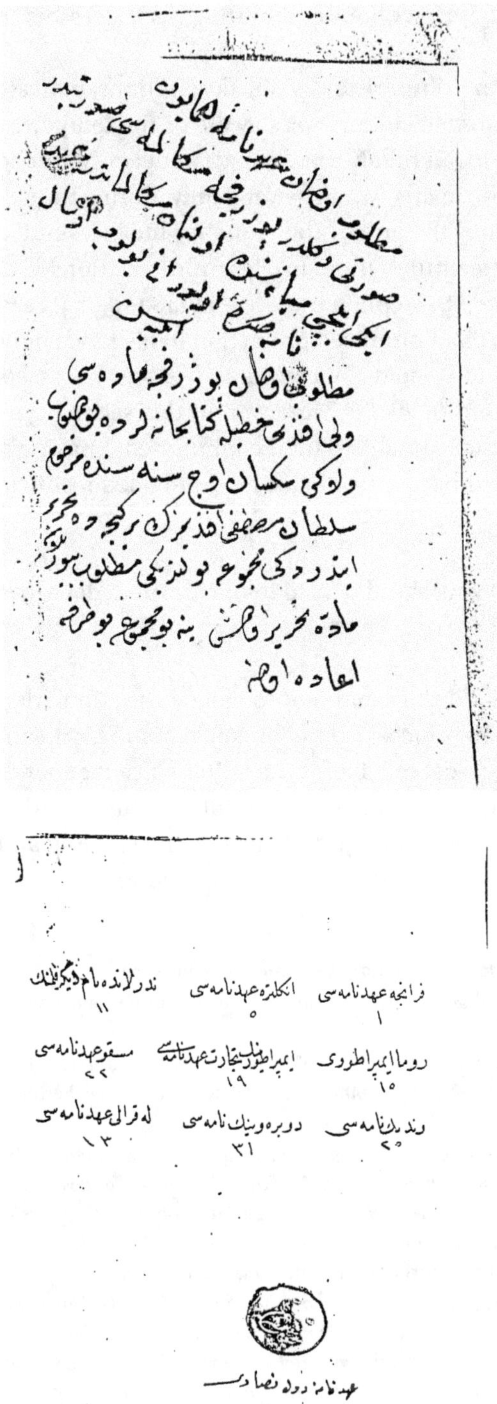

FIGURE 12
*Defter* (Register) including imperial charters (*'ahdname-yi hümayun*) granted by Mehmed IV (1648–1687) to eight European states: France (*Françe*), England (*Ingiltere*), The Nederlands (*Nederlanda*), Austria (*Roma Imparotoru*), Russia (*Mosku*), Venice (*Venedik*), Ragusa (*Dubrovnik*), Poland (*Leh kıralı*) (TKSMA, Defter 7018, f. 1; MOL, mf. Turkey, r. 10131)

applied the imperial signature (*tuğra*), without committing his successors to respect its conditions.

As for fifteenth-century Balkan tributaries, several descriptions indicate that both Christian rulers and Ottoman sultans were aware of the temporary character of the truces. According to Şükrüllah, the compact between Mehmed I Çelebi and the Wallachian voivode in 1417 was to be valid only "during the sultan's life."[90] Similar limitation, "until the end of the [sultan's] life," was noted by Ducas with regard to fifteenth-century Ottoman–Byzantine relations.[91] In the same vein, the *ʿahdname* granted to Stephen the Great in 1480–1481, if read carefully, discloses that Mehmed II had promised protection in his name only, in no way binding his successors to uphold the covenant: "neither his assets nor his country will not be attacked *by me*."[92] Moreover, in this second type of *ʿahdname*s, the Ottomans habitually qualified their commitment, making it dependent on the conduct of the other party. *Kurʾan* IX, 7 provided justification for this clause:

> As long as they stand true to you, stand true to them: for Allah does love the righteous.

Thus, the sultans promised to uphold their oath not to violate the stipulation of peace (*madam ki*), if the Christian princes had not broken it first. This meant that the stated duration of the truce lost much of its meaning, since it depended on the Ottoman authorities' will. The standard formula in this regard is ubiquitous in early modern *ʿahdname*s granted to Venice, France,[93] England and the United Provinces.[94] Similarly, in the *ʿahdname*s granted to the Polish

---

90 Şükrüllah, *Tevarih*, in *Cronici turcești I*, 32; Panaite, "Reglementări," 469–492.

91 On the peace agreements of 1416 and 1451 (Ducas, *Istoria*, 158, 288). See also Chalcocondil, *Expuneri*, 219; Sphrantzes, *Memorii*, XXX/4.

92 Mehmet, *Documente turcești*, I, doc. 5. Actually, "me, too" (*ben dahi, benden dahi*) is a standard formula of *ʿahdnames*. For the 1607 *ʿahdname* granted to Poland, see Feridun, *Münşeʾat*, II, 417.

93 *Zikr olunan ʿahd üzere mumaileyh França padişahı madam ki südde-i saʿadet penahimize sadakat ve ihlasda sabit-kadem ü rasih-dem ola ben dahi dostluğu kabul idüb ʿahd ve yemin iderim ki… bu tarafdan hilaf-ı ʿahd ü misak ve mugayir-i ʿakd ü ittifak iş olmıyub daʾima işbu ʿahdname-yi hümayun makrunumun mezmun-ı şerifiyle ʿamel oluna. Şöyle bileler,* in the 1604 *ʿahdname* granted by Ahmed I to Henri IV (Feridun, *Münşeʾat*, II, 404).

94 *Işbu zikr olunan ʿahd üzere madam ki sadakat ve ihlasda sabit-kadem ü rasih kadem olalar bu canibden dahi şerayt ʿahd ü aman kemakan merʾi ve muhterem tutılub asla bir vecihle hilafina cevaz gösterilmiye,* in the 1601 *ʿahdname* granted by Mehmed III to the Queen Elisabeth of England (Feridun, *Münşeʾat*, II, 385). For the *ʿahdname* of 1612 granted by Ahmed I to Holland, see Groot, *OEDR*, 246.

kings after 1533,[95] the period of their duration was not specified in the documents, but rather by including the formula that had already been used in instruments of peace issued for Venice.[96] To illustrate this, it is worth citing similar examples referring to tributary princes:

> As long as from his part one shall see right actions – Mehmed II stated in the 1480–1481 *ʿahdname* to the Moldavian prince –, from my part he would enjoy my same imperial benevolence (*şahanemle*) and would be protected by my same imperial magnanimity (*husrevanemle*).[97]

An identical formula can be found in the document issued by Ahmed I for Gabriel Bethlen in July 1614, confirming the latter to the Transylvanian throne.[98]

### 3.5 *Granting and Renewal of ʿahdnames*

Tributaries received imperial charters following their submission to the Porte. It is a condition emphasized by the Ottoman chancery at the very beginning of respective *ʿahdname*s:

> Formerly, because of the obedience and submission, with devotion and integrity shown by the Beys and Rector[s] of Dubrovnik in the time of my glorious forefathers [...] a charter was given unto them.[99]

According to the Islamic law, *aman* and *ʿahd* lost their validity upon the expiration of the set time period.[100] This conformed to the practice established in the Ottoman chancery, which considered *ʿahdname*s to expire with the passing of its duration or the passing away of the incumbent sultan. In effect, barring

95 For the *ʿahdname* of 1607 granted by Ahmed I, see Feridun, *Münşeʾat*, II, 416–417. For the entire series of Polish *ʿahdnames*, see Kołodziejczyk, *Ottoman-Polish Diplomatic Relations*, 234–653.

96 *Madam ki anlar ʿahdı ve dostluğu riʿayet edüb ʿahde muhalif nesne sadır olmıya benden dahi hilaf-ı ʿahd nesne vakiʾ olmıya*, in the *ʿahdnames* granted to Venice in 1513, 1517, 1521, 1540, 1595 (Gökbilgin, "Belgeler II," 46, 50, 53–54; Gökbilgin, "Belgeler I," 128; Belin, "Relations diplomatiques," 407–408).

97 Mehmet, *Documente turceşti*, I, doc. 5.

98 Gemil, *Documente turceşti*, doc. 61 (*Ben dahi bu ʿahd ve amanı mukarrer tutub hilafına zahib olmıyım*). See also T. Gökbilgin, "XVII asır başlarında Erdel hadisesi ve Bethlen Gabor'un beyliğe intihabı." *TD*, I, 1–2 (1949–1950): 1–28.

99 Biegman, *Ragusa*, 56.

100 Peters, *Islam*, 31, 35; Morabia, *Ğihad*, 321.

disagreements between the parties, the renewal of *ʿahdnames* was a legal and diplomatic necessity at the beginning of each new reign.[101]

The renewal of peace agreements when a new sovereign came to power was a medieval customary practice,[102] present in Southeastern Europe as well, and applied to the Ottomans' relations with their tributaries. Even a cursory analysis of post-1372 Ottoman–Byzantine relations clearly shows that each new sultan and emperor was anxious to renew the earlier agreements and, sooner or later, these were practically restated.[103] Similarly, referring to Ottoman–Wallachian relations in the fifteenth century, Ducas recorded several instances of earlier covenants being renewed upon ascension to the throne. He recounted that Wallachian envoys were received at the imperial court whenever a new sultan acceded the throne (Mehmed I in 1413, Murad II in 1421 and Mehmed II in 1451).[104] It has to be pointed out that Byzantine chroniclers also recorded compact-renewals each time a new voivode was confirmed in Wallachia. Ducas mentioned that Dan II sent his messengers to Murad II for peace "as soon as he came to the throne."[105] Vlad the Evil travelled to Brusa and made an acknowledgment of allegiance to Sultan Murad II immediately after "he received the throne" in 1438.[106] Kritobulos of Imbros noted the oaths between Vlad the Impaler and Mehmed II soon after the sultan "had given him the throne" in 1456.[107] An "oath of homage" by Radu the Fair accompanied his enthronement as "Hospodar and ruler of Wallachians" in 1462.[108] Although it is impossible to

101 For the renewal of Arab–Byzantine peace agreements, see Hamidullah, "Nouveaux documents," 281–298.

102 In 1421, Murad I renewed the peace agreements with Karaman and Byzantium, "according to the custom when new sultans and princes came [to throne]" (Ducas, *Istoria*, XXIII/3). Also, this practice was applied in the relations between Ragusa, Hungary, Serbia and Bosnia (Biegman, *Ragusa*, 16, n. 38), as well, in Moldavia and Wallachia's relations with Poland and Hungary (Tocilescu, *534 documente*, passim; Bogdan, *Documente. Brașov*, passim). For the relations between Ottomans and the Romanian principalities, see Maxim, "Capitulațiile," 52–60.

103 In 1389 with Bayezid I, in 1413 with Mehmed I, in 1421 with Murad II, in 1451 with Mehmed II; respectively, in 1376 with Andronicus IV, in 1379 with John V, in 1390 with John VII, in 1391 with Manuel II, in 1425 with John VIII, and in 1449 with Constantine XI Dragasses (Ducas, *Istoria*, XIII/1, XX/1, XXIII/3; Chalcocondil, *Expuneri*, 54, 137, 139).

104 Ducas, *Istoria*, XX/2, XXVIII/10, XXXIII/12.

105 In the context of his fight with another pretender, i.e. Radu II Prazanaglava, it is difficult to precise exactly what moment was about (Ducas, *Istoria*, XXIX/7).

106 Ducas, *Istoria*, XXIX/10.

107 Critobul, *Mehmed II*, IV/10, 3. See discussions on Vlad the Impaler's enthronements in 1448 and 1456 in Stoicescu, *Vlad Țepeș*, 15–25, 35–37.

108 Critobul, *Mehmed II*, IV/10, 10.

establish the conclusive form of these agreements, the examples cited above prove that the renewal of pacts was a customary practice in this period.

The Ragusan case is particularly relevant in this respect, since it provides a useful comparison for the relations between the Porte and Wallachia and Moldavia. The practice of compact-renewal was clearly affirmed in the *ʿahdname* of 1575. Murad III stated:

> In the time of my deceased father [...] sovereign Sultan Selim [...] their envoys came again and requested their charter to be renewed, and an imperial charter was given.[109]

The same practice was applied towards the Christian powers of the frontier area. Looking at the long series of Ottoman–Venetian peace agreements, one realizes that those of 1411 (Musa Çelebi), 1446–1451 (Mehmed II), 1482 (Bayezid II), 1513 (Selim I), 1521 (Süleyman Kanunî), 1567 (Selim II), 1575 (Murad III), and 1595 (Mehmed III) were concluded upon each of the sultans' enthronement. The legal and diplomatic necessity for treaty-renewal in these circumstances is further confirmed by the practice of issuing new *ʿahdnames* (like those of 1482 and 1575), despite the fact that just a few years had passed since the previous peace had been reached (in 1479, respectively, in 1573).[110] In the same vein, the series of Ottoman–Polish peace agreements proves that their renewal took place shortly after the accession of either new sultans (in 1568 Selim II, in 1577 Murad III, in 1597 Mehmed III, in 1607 Ahmed I) or Polish kings (in August 1553 Sigismund II, in 1577 Stephen Báthory, in 1591 Sigismund III Vasa).[111]

Sources indicate that the procedure of renewing an *ʿahdname* frequently began with the plea by a Christian prince, motivated either by the upcoming expiration of the treaty or the change on the throne. In 1564 Maximilian II Habsburg, upon taking over the imperial throne, pleaded to Süleyman Kanunî to issue a new charter but now "in his name."[112] Since political and military considerations encouraged the Porte to renew the peace with Ferdinand I

---

109 Biegman, *Ragusa*, 56.

110 See: Gallotta, "Il trattato 1482," 226; Gökbilgin, "Belgeler I," 121; Gökbilgin, "Belgeler II," 42, 47, 50.

111 For the debate over the renewals of Capitulations granted to Western powers, see Pélissié du Rausas, *Capitulations*, I, 23–24; Saint-Priest, *Mémoires*, 282, 290–292; Gavillot, *Capitulations*, 26; Hershlag, *Introduction*, 46–47.

112 Süleyman Kanunî informed the voivode of Transylvania, John Sigismund Zápolya, on 14 *Safer* 972/21 September 1564, and forbade him from attacking Maximilian II's territories (Mehmet, *Documente turcești*, I, doc. 58).

concluded three years prior,[113] a new *ʿahdname* was issued on 16 February 1565 in Constantinople (*Kostantiniye*).[114] At the same time, the sultans could deny request for *ʿahdname* renewal whenever the conditions of peace clashed with current Ottoman interests. For example, in 1630 Murad IV rejected the Polish king's request to renew the peace, wondering why a "new imperial charter" should be issued if the Poles had failed to uphold the stipulation of the *ʿahdname* in question.[115]

The renewal of peace agreements after military conflicts occurred when the Porte was unable to decisively prevail over the enemy and impose the conditions through *debellatio*. Ottoman relations with Moldavia and Wallachia from the end of the fourteenth until the mid-sixteenth century show that matters of war and peace were always on the agenda.[116] Both Byzantine and Ottoman historians took note of peace agreements between sultans and Wallachian princes that followed bursts of armed opposition against the Ottomans: between Mircea the Elder and Mehmed I Çelebi, Dan I and Murad II, Basarab II and Murad II, Radu the Fair and Mehmed II.[117] As concerns voivode Stephen the Great (1457–1504) of Moldavia, one can only quote the *ʿahdname* of 1480–1481 granted by Mehmed II and the peace of 1486 concluded with Bayezid II, both after periods of heated military conflicts.[118]

113 ʿAhdname of 1 *Zilhicce* 969/2 August 1562 (Schendlinger, *Süleyman*, doc. 25; Latin text in Hurmuzaki-Densușeanu, *Documente*, II/5, 507–513).

114 15 *Receb* 972 AH (Schendlinger, *Süleyman*, doc. 32; Hurmuzaki, *Documente*, VIII, doc. CXXXIII).

115 Mehmet, *Documente turcești*, I, doc. 158 (letter of *evahir-i Muharrem* 1040/ 30 August-8 September 1630). Murad IV (1623–1640) referred to the *ʿahdname* of 15 *Zilhicce* 1032/10 October 1623 (AGAD, *AKW-Tureckie*, K. 71, t. 307, no. 564; Abrahamowicz, *Documents*, 252–253). This document was the renewal of a former *ʿahdname*, issued by Mustafa I on *evasıt-ı Rebi ül-ahir* 1032/ 12–21 February 1623 (AGAD, *AKW-Tureckie*, K. 71, t. 307, no. 557; Abrahamowicz, *Documents*, 246–249).

116 Ducas, *Istoria*, XXXIV/6; Ștefănescu, *Țara Românească*, 37–100. The same image characterized the relations between the Porte and Byzantium (Hammer, *Empire Ottoman*, I, 59; Ostrogorsky, *Histoire de l'État byzantine*, 555–595).

117 Ducas, *Istoria*, XXVIII/10; Chalcocondil, *Expuneri*, in *FHDR*, IV, 477, 515, 517.

118 Mehmet, *Documente turcești*, I, doc. 5; Gorovei, "1486," 807–821.

CHAPTER 8

# Oaths as a Guarantee of Fidelity

The conclusion of covenants between the Ottoman state and the principalities of Wallachia and Moldavia from the late fourteenth until the mid-sixteenth century has sparked heated debate among Romanian historians.[1] The overriding issue has long been to find the so-called "treaties" which were supposed to have regulated the legal status of Wallachia and Moldavia over long term. Instead of looking for "treaties" that did not exist, in my view it is more important to analyse the information concerning the usual peace settlements between the Ottomans and the Balkan tribute-paying princes, most frequently called "oaths" and "pledges" (in Ottoman *ʿahd*, in Greek *horkos*, in Romanian *jurământ*) that we find in narrative sources. For a long time, these "oaths" rather than any peace agreements were the most important guarantee of fealty practiced in diplomatic relations, thus providing a fertile direction in trying to establish the evolution of the Porte's relations with its tributaries.

## 1 Oaths as Customary Practice

As was the case in Western Europe, in central and southeastern parts of the continent the oath represented a frequent diplomatic tool throughout the early modern period. It was meant to reinforce mutual trust in peace agreements and guarantee the obligations undertaken by contracting parties. It consisted usually of a solemnly worded pledge.

The special value of the oath as a diplomatic and juridical guarantee in Christendom features prominently in the agreements, alliances and commercial

1 In this respect, see: N. Beldiceanu, "Problema tratatelor Moldovei cu Poarta Otomană în lumina cronicei lui Peçevi," *Balcania* (București), V, 1, 1942, 393–407; A. Decei, "Tratatul de pace – sulhname – încheiat între sultanul Mehmed al II-lea și Ștefan cel Mare la 1479," in Decei, *RRO*, 118–129 (also in *RIR*, XV, 1945, IV, 465–494); M.M. Alexandrescu-Dersca Bulgaru, "L'origine des khatt-i șerifs de privileges des Principautés roumaines," *NEH*, VI, 1, 1980, 251–263; Ș. Papacostea, "Tratatele Țării Românești și Moldovei cu Imperiul otoman în secolele XIV–XV: ficțiune politică și realitate istorică," in *Stat, societate, națiune. Interpretări istorice*, Cluj-Napoca, 1982, 93–106; M. Maxim, "Din nou pe urmele vechilor tratate ale Moldovei și Țării Românești cu Poarta Otomană," *RdI*, 2, 1987, 157–172; Maxim, *ȚRÎP*, 25–111, 197–261; Viorel Panaite, "Câteva observații privind reglementările de pace româno-otomane în secolul XV," in *Românii în istoria universală*, III/1 eds. Ion Agrigoroaiei, Gh. Buzatu, V. Cristian, Iași: Universitatea Alex. I. Cuza, 1988, 469–492.

 | DOI:10.1163/9789004411104_009

treaties reached by Wallachian, Moldavian and Transylvanian princes with Hungarian, Polish, Habsburg or Russian sovereigns.[2] The "charter" that registered the homage paid to King Vladislav II Jagiełło (1386–1434) of Poland includes a statement from Petru I of Moldavia:

> as a token of eternal strength, I took an oath according to the rite and custom of the Eastern church, kissing with my own mouth the cross.[3]

A similar mention can be found in the document of 1496, ratifying the draft of an agreement between the Moldavian voivode Stephen the Great and Alexander, the Grand Duke of Lithuania. According to this document, the Moldavian ruler demanded a "letter of oath" to accompany the treaty:

> You shall take an oath before us [through envoys] and you shall give us that letter of oath.[4]

Even in the eighteenth century, Dimitrie Cantemir confirmed his pact with Tsar Peter I of Russia by taking an "oath of fidelity."[5]

Ottomans, as well, considered an oath a fundamental element of peace agreements with foreign princes. Fifteenth-century documents and chronicles frequently mention oath-taking as a synecdoche for peace settlements between the sultans and Southeastern European princes. In this regard, Byzantine annalists preferred the terms *horkos* (pl. *horkoi*) and *pistis*. These notions appear both in isolation and, particularly, accompany other terms suggesting the concept of peace, friendship and agreement (*eirene, agape, sponde, syntheke*). If we were to chronologically enumerate the Ottoman–Byzantine accords, all of them were dubbed "oaths" by at least one of the extant sources.[6]

According to a custom still common in the relations between Wallachian voivodes and the Ottoman sultans throughout the fifteenth century, the

2 Costăchescu, *Documente moldovenești*, II, doc. 162, 181, 183, 184; Tocilescu, *534 documente*, doc. 119, 271; Bogdan, *Documente*. Ștefan, II, 287, 293–294, 352–353, 399, 409–410 etc.; *DRH*, D, I, doc. 87, 107, 133, 306 etc.

3 Costăchescu, *Documente moldovenești*, II, doc. 162. See also doc. 162, 184; *DRH*, D, I, doc. 306.

4 Bogdan, *Documente*. Ștefan, II, doc. CLXXIII. See, also, doc. CLXXIV.

5 In a French report from L'viv from the 8 July 1711 (Hurmuzaki, *Documente*, XVI, doc. DCCCLXV).

6 Melissenos, *Cronica*, 221 (Murad I "concluded with the emperor [John V] a peace agreement strengthened by an oath" in 1372–1373), 197 ("oaths" in 1379 and 1391), 205 ("peace strengthened by an oath" in 1401), 257 ("peace strengthened by an oath" in 1424). Ducas, *Istoria*, XX/1 ("a treaty strengthened by oath" in 1413), XXII/5 ("agreements strengthened by an oath" in 1416), XXXIII/1 ("oaths" in 1449). See also Dölger, *Regesten 5*, no. 3136, 3234, 3195, 3331–4, 3364, 3414, 3524.

"oaths" were an extremely important element in settling peaceful relations. Correspondingly, peace agreements were often described as "oaths" or the phrase "pact reinforced through oath." For instance, according to Ducas, the return of Vlad the Evil to power in Wallachia in 1443 was preceded by mutual oaths taken by the voivode and Sultan Murad II. In another passage, the Byzantine chronicler states that the same sultan, fearing Hungarians, "concluded – both with the Serb *knez* and with the Wallachian voivode – pacts reinforced through oath" (*kai poiei synthekas enorkus*).[7] Laonicus Chalcocondylas, in turn, noted that Wallachians led by Vladislav II (1447–1456), feared that their presence in the Hungarian camp during the battle of Kosovo Polje (1448) would make it impossible to escape the sultan's ire "because of the oath" (*horkou*) they had taken with him.[8] Another Byzantine chronicler, Kritobulos of Imbros wrote that when Vlad the Impaler came to the throne, Mehmed the Conqueror "pledged him with pacts and oaths" (*kai synthekais* [...] *kai horkois*). Moreover, after the 1462 campaign, Mehmed II installed Radu the Fair on the Wallachian throne, "taking his oath of fealty" (*ta pista labon*).[9]

The term "oath" also appears in the few official records of Ottoman–Wallachian relations that have survived from the first half of the fifteenth century. Thus, in May–June 1432, Alexandru I Aldea was writing to an official of Temeșvar that he "pledged himself" to Murad II, and the "Turks [...] bound themselves by faith and by oath and had been guaranteed fidelity."[10] The oath thus constituted a juridical act reinforcing and guaranteeing peaceful relations between the two parties ("we brought peace to the country").[11]

Ottoman narrative sources, particularly important given the dearth of official chancery documents for this early period, in describing the conclusion of *ʿahd*s point to oath-taking as the crucial moment in the process. Şükrüllah, narrating the agreement between Mehmed I Çelebi (1413–1421) and Mircea the Older (and his co-ruler, Mihail I), simply wrote that "they took an oath" (*and etdiler*) which supported the conclusion of peace: "thus they made peace" (*barış*).[12]

Although sixteenth- and seventeenth-century practices of peace-making were more elaborate, oaths continued to play a crucial role in the conclusion and observance of peace agreements, concluded in the aftermath of military

7 Ducas, *Istoria*, XXX/5, XXXII/1 (in *FHDR*, IV, 429).

8 Chalcocondil, *Expuneri*, in *FHDR*, IV, 497.

9 Critobul, *Mehmed II*, IV, 10, 1–3 (in *FHDR*, IV, 533–535).

10 *DRH*, D, I, doc. 192.

11 *DRH*, D, I, doc. 197.

12 Şükrüllah, *Tevarih*, in *Cronici turcești I*, 32. *And* (*ant*) was one of the Ottoman terms for designating the oath (*Redhouse*, 64).

conflicts. For instance, the "guaranteeing act" (*temessük*) given to the *beylerbeyi* of Buda, Hüseyin paşa, on 2 December 1636, refers thrice to oath-making between Transylvanian Prince George Rákoczy I and Ottoman dignitaries:

> when they appointed us as ruler of Transylvania, they had taken great oaths and stipulated conditions (*andlar ve şartlar vermişlerdir*); we present ourselves again with our oath (*andımız ile*) to the happy and magnificent *padişah* [...] and the articles we laid down before, we swore to respect them! We swear to respect everything, according to our Christian law (*hıristiyan dinimiz ile and içerüz*).[13]

## 2 Oath in 'Ahdname Texts

Ottoman and Byzantine chroniclers applied the term "oath" to describe certain peace settlements, which is not surprising given the centrality of oath-taking as an essential diplomatic element in the official instruments of peace. In this regard, oath-taking remained a constant feature in *'ahdname*s throughout the early modern period. The sultans usually pledged not to break the pact for as long as (*madam ki*) Christian princes upheld their end of the bargain. A charter granted to Venice in the sixteenth century stated:

> I vow by a firm oath that [...] as long as they respect the pledge and the friendship and do nothing against me to harm the pledge, nothing shall be done on my part as well against the pledge. So be it known.[14]

This sentence features – sometimes in a more elaborate form – in the *'ahdname*s granted in the sixteenth and seventeenth centuries granted to Poland, France[15]

---

13 4 *Receb* 1046 AH (Gemil, *Documente turcești*, doc. 101). Let us note that it is about the Ottoman translation of a document written in Transylvania, in Hungarian or Latin.

14 *'Ahdname* granted to Venice by Süleyman Kanunî on 17 *Muharrem* 928 /17 December 1521 (Gökbilgin, "Belgeler II," 46). See also Gökbilgin, "Belgeler II," 50 (*'ahdname* of 1513), 53–54 (*'ahdname* of 1517); Gökbilgin, "Belgeler I," 128 (*'ahdname* of 1540); Belin, "Relations diplomatiques," 407–408 (*'ahdname* of 1595). For the Ottoman–Venetian *'ahdnames*, see H. Theunissen, *Ottoman-Venetian Diplomatics: The 'Ahdnames, The Historical Background and the Development of a Category of Political-Commercial Instruments together with an Annotated Edition of a Corpus of Relevant Documents*, PhD Dissertation, University of Utrecht, 1991 (Electronic Journal of Oriental Studies, I, 1998, no 2, 1–698).

15 *'Ahdname* granted in 1604 by Ahmed I to the king of France, Henri IV (Feridun, *Münşe'at*, II, 404).

and Holland.[16] The concluding section of the 1607 *ʿahdname* granted by Ahmed I to Sigismund III Vasa specified:

> then, on behalf of my Imperial Majesty, I vow with thorough faith [...] that this pact shall not be broken.[17]

A similar oath was taken by Ahmed I, in July 1614, in the investiture diploma (*berat*) appointing Gabriel Bethlen to the Transylvanian throne:

> then I make pledge and agreement too and swear by the thorough faith that [...] I shall see that this pledge and this favor remain unaltered and I shall not act contrary to them.[18]

However, the presence of similar statements was not universal, and we find several exceptions to the rule. For example, Mehmed II's oath is missing from the copy of the *ʿahdname* granted to Stephen the Great of Moldavia in 1480–1481,[19] although we cannot rule out if it was not just a clerical omission. Another remarkable – and difficult to explain – omission are the *ʿahdname*s granted to England, modelled on the commercial privileges granted in 1580,[20] which did not include the sultanic oath until 1641, when it was finally introduced. Yet the significance of this omission should not be exaggerated, because Ottoman documents, including *ʿahdname*s, did not have to include an oath to acquire juridical and diplomatic validity. In fact, J. Wansborough, discussing Mamluk chancery practice, noticed that oaths were not included in all pacts concluded with non-Muslim rulers; still, it was still required in two instances: when peace agreements acquired the form of *instrumentum reciprocum* and when these were negotiated in the Abode of War.[21] The place they occupied within the *ʿahdname* was by no means steady, as it was placed either at the

16 Groot, *OEDR*, 246: *ʿahdname* granted in 1612 by Ahmed I to Holland (*ben dahi ʿahd ve yemin iderim ki* [...] *bu tarafdan dahi hilaf-ı ʿahd ü-misak ve mugayir-i ʿahd ü-ittifak iş olunmıyub işbu ʿahdname-yi hümayun makrunumun mezmun-ı şerifiyle ʿamel oluna. Şöyle bileler*).

17 *Cenab-ı celalet meabim tarafından dahi iman-i galiza ile yemin ederim* (Feridun, *Münşeʾat*, II, 416–7).

18 Gemil, *Documente turcești*, doc. 61.

19 Decei, "Sulhname," 122–126; Mehmet, *Documente turcești*, I, doc. 5.

20 "There is no way to explain so grave an omission, both diplomatically and religiously, from the treaty" (Skilliter, *Harborne*, 102). Yet V. L. Ménage explained this omission by reference to the changing Ottoman diplomatics during the sixteenth century and by invoking the particular circumstances of 1580 (Ménage, "Capitulation," 378).

21 Wansborough, "Safe-Conduct," 31.

beginning or at the end of the text, under the influence of Venetian diplomacy.[22] For instance, up to the mid-sixteenth century, the sultan's oath was placed before the clauses of peace treaties with Venice or Poland. From Süleyman the Magnificent's reign onwards, the imperial oath moved to the end of the text.

## 3 Ceremony of Oath-taking

In the fifteenth century, customary practices most widespread throughout Southeastern Europe were mutual engagements concluded by the two parties. These took place either in the form of two ceremonies at respective rulers' courts or, in some instances, were taken within a single ceremony, whereby the other party committed to the terms either personally or by proxies. Basarab the Younger (1477–1482) described it to the authorities of Brașov in the following terms:

> And you shall send word right away to Bator Iştvan so he receives my envoys and pledge himself to them and then, in his turn, send a man to us, that I may pledge myself to him.[23]

According to some chronicles, the Ottomans also adopted the practice under Christian influence, given that the latter insisted on taking oaths.[24]

However, I consider this explanation rather implausible, given that the sultans, at the apex of their power, were unlikely to adapt the customs under external pressure, especially in regard to ceremonial and diplomatic protocol. Instead, this adjustment was a matter of common pragmatic considerations, shared by Islamic and Christian traditions. In any case, throughout the fifteenth and early sixteenth century, we can observe sultans making a personal pledge to uphold the clauses of an already negotiated pact, sworn in the

22 Among the treaties concluded by Anatolian emirs only those with Venice contained an oath placed before the stipulations, *capitula* (Zachariadou, *Trade and Crusade*, 184). An example from the Ottoman chancery is the Ottoman–Venetian treaty of 1454 (Hershlag, *Introduction*, 293).

23 It was about Stephen Báthory I, voivode of Transylvania between 1479–1493 (Tocilescu, *534 documente*, doc. 119).

24 From the text of Ottoman–Genoese treaty of 1387, one can infer that the oath-taking ceremony took place at the same time. V. L. Ménage insisted on this aspect (Ménage, "Capitulation," 376, 383).

presence of a delegate of a Christian prince.[25] For instance, Mehmed II swore an oath in the presence of János Hunyadi's and George Branković's envoys on 20 December 1451, a fact registered in the settlement itself: "and before the same [envoys], my Lordship has taken the oath."[26] From the second half of the sixteenth century, though the oath continued to be included in the *ʿahdname*s, it apparently disappears from the ceremony of concluding some peace agreements.[27]

### 3.1 *Invocations of Oath*

Religious identity played a decisive role in shaping the oaths, as members of each community invoked sacred authority as a guarantee to uphold their commitments. Essential elements of the Christian oath were, as following: God,[28] Jesus Christ, the Holy Cross,[29] the four Gospels,[30] as well as the Christian saints.[31] In 1636 George Rákoczy I's pledge was sworn "according to our Christian law.[32]

Muslim oath-taking, both in relations within the Islamic community and beyond, constituted a central episode in concluding peace. In effect, the oath occupied a well-defined place as early as juridical treatises of the caliphate, which codified customary practices encountered in relations with non-Muslim rulers, and Byzantine emperors in particular. Al-Sarakhsi, commenting on al-Shaybani's work, laid stress on a series of phrases that had to be included in order to reinforce such agreements. To determine the required structure of

25 Let us note the procedure of negotiation of the Ottoman–Venetian treaty of 1503, implying the Doge's oath in front of Ali, special envoy of Bayezid II, and the sultan's oath in front of the Venetian envoys (Fisher, *Foreign Relations*, 81–87; Ménage, "Capitulation," 376).

26 *DRH*, D, I, doc. 305.

27 V. L. Ménage affirmed there is no evidence that would prove that Selim II and Maximilian II took solemn oaths to strengthen the Ottoman–Habsburg treaty of 1567 (Ménage, "Capitulation," 383, n. 27).

28 "We swear by the Almighty God who created the heaven and the earth," stated the Wallachian voivode Neagoe Basarab in the "charter of fidelity" to the Hungarian king, in 1517 (Tocilescu, *534 documente*, doc. 271).

29 "We swear by touching the wood of God's cross," in the Moldavian–Polish treaty of 3 June 1433 (Costăchescu, *Documente moldovenești*, II, doc. 181).

30 "By the saint Gospels," on 17 March 1517 (Tocilescu, *534 documente*, doc. 271).

31 "*Omnes Sanctos et Sanctas Dei,*" in the oath of the Hungarian king of 1503 (Ménage, "Capitulation," 376); "we swear by the saint apostles [...] and by all saints," wrote Neagoe Basarab on 17 March 1517 (Tocilescu, *534 documente*, doc. 271).

32 Gemil, *Documente turcești*, doc. 101 (*hıristiyan dinimiz ile and içerüz*). For the Christian oaths, see Ménage, "Capitulation," 376; Tocilescu, *534 documente*, doc. 6, 121.

such an oath, al-Shaybani drew from contemporary Arab–Byzantine treaties, particularly those concluded by Caliph Harun al-Rashid:

> And each of the contracting parties invokes for the other – with respect to the accomplishment of everything that is included in this document – God's pact and engagement, God's guarantee, as well as His Envoy (the Prophet Muhammad) and that of Jesus Christ, son of Mary.

Muslims generally swore on Allah and His Envoy, Muhammad, the classic formula being *wa'llahi wa bi'llahi wa t'llahi.* Such wording posed a challenge for scholars, who would eventually forbid Muslims to swear by Allah and Muhammad, invoking the following "tradition" as an argument:

> If they ask you for the guarantee of Allah and His Envoy, you shall not give it to them, but rather offer your own and your parents' guarantee, for if you should violate your own and your parents' guarantee this will be less grievous.[33]

Subsequently, al-Sarakhsi felt the need – also citing Muhammad's example – to reassert that it was not taking an oath on the Prophet's name that was prohibited, but rather breaking it that was condemned:

> There are three [categories] of people to whom I am opposed [...] These are: a man who grants his protection and then breaks it; a man who sells a free individual (as a slave) and feeds on the money [thus obtained]; and the man who hires somebody and then does not pay him. This is a clear proof that there is no obstacle in offering [the enemy] the guarantee of the Prophet; but if there really is something to be forbidden, that is betrayal indeed.[34]

As compared to the oaths included in the treaties concluded among Muslim princes, which limited themselves to invoking Allah and Muhammad, Ottoman oaths to Christians were more elaborate. This can be seen in the following examples:

33 Shaybani, *Kitab al-siyar*, III, 307.

34 Shaybani, *Kitab al-siyar*, I, 29.

God the Creator (*per quelo che a fatto la cielo e la terra*, in 1403;[35] "for the justice of Allah, the Creator of heaven and earth"/*yeri ve göği Perverdigar hakkiçün*, swore the sultans in all *ʿahdnames* granted to the kings of Poland in the sixteenth–seventeenth centuries;[36] *We do hereby promise and swear by the one Omnipotent God the Creator of Heaven and Earth and of all creatures*, in the English translation of the 1675 *ʿahdname* granted by Mehmed IV to England);[37]

the Prophet Muhammad (*per lo mio Macometo Mustafa* in 1403;[38] Mehmed II "swears [...] by the prophet who bears the same name as his own..." in 1451;[39] "out of respect for the wonders of our grand Prophet" (*ve ulu ʿaziz Peygamberimiz Efendimiz muʿcizatı hürmetiçün*) in the Ottoman–Polish *ʿahdnames* of sixteenth–seventeenth centuries;[40] "I swear by our dearest Prophet" began Macaroğlu Ali paşa his oath taken before the Transylvanians in August 1613);[41]

the *mushaf* (*Io zuro...per lo mie VII musafi* in 1403 by Süleyman Çelebi);[42]

the 124,000 Prophets (in the 1451 agreement with Byzantium, Mehmed II "swears [...] by the angels and archangels").[43]

To these four invocations, the Ottomans also added the oath by:

the sultan's sword (in 1613, towards "all Transylvanian people" Macaroğlu Ali paşa swore, among others, "by the horse I mounted in the holy wars and by the sword we girdle"; "by the sword I girdled in the holy wars");[44]

---

35 Dennis, "Treaty 1403," 78.

36 Feridun, *Münşeʾat*, II, 417 (*ʿahdname* of 1607),

37 Hershlag, *Introduction*, 306.

38 Dennis, "Treaty 1403," 78.

39 Ducas, *Istoria*, XXXIII/12.

40 Feridun, *Münşeʾat*, II, 417 (*ʿahdname* of 1607).

41 Guboglu, "Arhive. Brașov," 252 (Letter of 12 August 1613).

42 Dennis, "Treaty 1403," 78. In 1451 Mehmed II would also "swear [...] on his... books," (Ducas, *Istoria*, XXXIII/12). *Mushaf* meant the *Kurʾan* (*Redhouse*, 800; Ménage, "Capitulation," 376).

43 Ducas, *Istoria*, XXXIII/12. The 124,000 Prophets, from Adam to Muhammad, could be the counterpart of the Christian saints from Christian oaths (Ménage, "Capitulation," 376). See, also, the unique case of the 1403 treaty, when Süleyman Çelebi swore by only one Prophet, possibly Jesus Christ: *per lo mio altissimo grande profeta che mi credemo* (Dennis, "Treaty 1403," 78; Zachariadou, "Süleyman Çelebi," 276–277 and n. 30; Ducas, *Istoria*, XIX, 7).

44 Letters of 12 and 25 August 1613 (Guboglu, "Arhive. Brașov," 252). The oath by sword should be the counterpart of the oath by cross in Christendom (Ménage, "Capitulation," 376).

the religious faith they followed ("we swear by our faith" declared Macaroğlu Ali paşa in 1613);[45]

his soul, life and head, as well as his father's and his children's ("I [...] sultan Mohamed beğ [...] I swear to you [...] by the soul of my ancestor and father, by my soul, my head and my sons' head" in the 1451 agreement with Hungary;[46] "by the head of my son" swore Macaroğlu Ali paşa in 1613).[47]

The sultan's subjects would sometimes swear by "the head of the grand *padişah*."[48]

Thus, one may conclude that the Ottoman oath represented a synthesis made up of elements originating from Turkish-Mongolian and Islamic traditions, onto which Christian influences were grafted.[49] The oath's validity did not hinge on the inclusion of all aforementioned elements, just as the peace settlement did not necessarily have to include an oath to gain validity. In the fifteenth-century *ʿahdname*s, oaths were longer and more elaborate, in some instances including all seven types of invocation discussed above. In later documents, the oath lost most of its elements, and in certain cases invoked only Allah as the guarantee, or else omitted altogether from the text of the agreement.

## 4 Oral Oaths and Written Oaths

In describing peace settlements or their renewals in Southeastern Europe, narrative sources usually employed ambiguous terms and notions, whose common thread was the establishment of peace and friendship (in Greek, *eirene* and *agape*; in Turkish, *barış* and *dostluk*). Ducas' information regarding the reception of envoys upon Mehmed I and Murad II's enthronement, which

45 Macaroğlu Ali paşa's letter to the townsmen of Brașov of 25 August 1613 (Guboglu, "Arhive. Brașov," 252). See, also, the privilege-treaty granted by the Wallachian voivode Radu Praznaglava to the merchants of Brașov on 17 May 1421 (Tocilescu, *534 documente*, doc. 6).

46 Iorga, *Acte și fragmente*, III, 23–27; DRH, D, I, doc. 305. This invocation was also included in Selim II's oath from the *ʿahdname* granted to Ragusa in 1566 (Biegman, *Ragusa*, 51). These invocations are sometimes present in Christian oaths (see Tocilescu, *534 documente*, doc. 6, 121).

47 Guboglu, "Arhive. Brașov," 252.

48 Guboglu, "Arhive. Brașov," 252.

49 The ancient Turks swore by the horse (*at*), wolf (*kurt*), dog (*köpek*) and sword (*kılıç*) (Ménage, "Capitulation," 376; Zachariadou, *Trade and Crusade*, passim).

included representatives of Wallachian voivodes, is instructive in this respect. In the case of Mehmed I, the Byzantine chronicle noted the sultan's famous answer: "peace I give and peace I take," an expression of the imperial view that increasingly gained ground at the Ottoman court. In the case of Murad II's ascension to the throne, Ducas merely states that upon receiving congratulations, Murad II "made peace (*eirene*) with them,"[50] with no additional explanation.

What realities stood behind these abstract phrases? What was the concrete diplomatic dimension to these expressions of peace and friendship? Did the fifteenth-century agreements with Wallachian and Moldavian voivodes produce Ottoman documents in this regard? I will try to address these questions below, employing a comparative approach to offset the dearth of official documents. For this purpose, I adopt two different points of reference: firstly, the theoretical model provided by Islamic legal treatises and, secondly, other tributaries in fifteenth-century Southeastern Europe.

The majority of pledges (*ʿahd*) by the Prophet Muhammad were recorded in a written form.[51] The existence of this practice and its prominence as part of the *sünnet*, provided subsequent generations of scholars with a powerful argument in this respect. Consequently, most shared the opinion that the treaties – by which they referred to temporary treaties, concluded for a fixed period of time – had to be written down. Moreover, Hanafi jurists insisted on drafting a written document, confirmed by signatures of contracting parties and witnesses, to incentivize both sides to uphold their stipulations.[52] Here is al-Shaybani's opinion, the most authoritative in this respect:

> If the Muslims and the infidels (enemies) conclude a truce for a certain precise number of years, they have to settle it in writing, for this is a limited term contract and, in this case (of such contracts) the Law orders their written formulation.[53]

The first invoked argument was extracted from *Kurʾan* II, 282, although it referred to a contract regarding debt rather than diplomatic practice per se:

> Oh, you, the believers, if you are bound by a debt for a certain time, then do it in writing. Let a righteous scribe write this between you. The scribe

50 Ducas, *Istoria*, XX/2, XXVIII/10.

51 Hamidullah, *Documents*, passim.

52 M. Khadduri, "Hudna," *EI-2*, I, 566.

53 Shaybani, *Kitab al-siyar*, III, 305.

> shall only write as God taught him. He shall write what the debtor speaks, fear God and write nothing less [...]

Al-Sarakhsi's comment on al-Shaybani's arguments even conveys a touch of intransigence:

> Hence, if the contract is for a (determined) period of time, neglecting to formulate it in writing will be a sin.[54]

The second argument invoked by the two Hanafi scholars in support of the necessity of drafting written instruments of peace was the truce concluded by Muhammad with the inhabitants of Mecca at Hudaybiya in 628. Moreover, the elaboration of two copies of this agreement, one for the Prophet and another for Mecca, was invoked by al-Shaybani's obligatory diplomatic practice for Muslims:

> This attitude (of the Prophet) has become a basic principle of this subject.

Yet, in his comment, al-Sarakhsi enumerates several new additions, whose origins can be traced to the diplomatic practice of the Abbasid caliphate:

> Another reason [to write down treaties] is that every contractor needs a copy kept in his own hand, so that in case the other party disputes one of his clauses, he can refer to the copy in his hand to counter the other party.[55]

At the same time, it is worth comparing the information provided by narrative sources and the extant official documents in regard to Ottoman peace-making practice in Southeastern Europe. An illustrative example is provided by the peace settled between Süleyman Çelebi, and the Byzantine emperor John VII and other Christian rulers in 1403. In this case, Ducas merely noted the conclusion of some "articles of peace" and their stipulations, whereas Macarie Melissenos claimed that Bayezid I's son was bound by "great friendship with the emperor."[56] Neither explicitly mentions a written compact between the two parties, and the terminology they employed suggests that the agreement took

54 Shaybani, *Kitab al-siyar*, III, 305.

55 Shaybani, *Kitab al-siyar*, III, 306.

56 Ducas, *Istoria*, XVIII/2; Melissenos, *Cronica*, I/23.

the form of verbal pledges. However, this conclusion would be a mistake, since the 1403 settlement took the form of a written document as well, and constitutes the only Ottoman–Byzantine treaty to have survived until this day, even if in an abridged Italian copy.[57]

Another example is perhaps even more instructive. In 1451, a three-year truce was reached between János Hunyadi and Mehmed II, a moment that Ducas captured in his chronicle, describing it in the following words: "concluding a three years peace (*eirenen*)" and "János, having thus taken a peace oath (*horkous* […] *agapes*) with Mehmed for three years."[58] At first sight, one is led to believe that the agreement was only verbally ratified. Yet, a document issued on 20 October 1451 by the Ottoman chancery in the name of Mehmed II survived in the form of a Latin translation. Associating the juridical procedure of an oral oath with the written pact, the sultan emphasized clearly:

> I desire to take part in the oath and abide by the agreement, that is why I have sworn and put them into writing together with them.[59]

The very same Byzantine authors inform us about the existence of written documents that complemented and accompanied verbal agreements. Several examples are here in order, originating from Ottoman–Byzantine relations. Chronologically, the first one was the settlement between Mehmed I Çelebi and Manuel II Paleologus in 1416. It is particularly important for the topic at hand, given its chronological proximity to the sultan's peace agreement with Wallachian Mircea the Elder and Mihail I. Ducas described it in the following manner:

> [Greek] envoys, having therefore received in writing the agreements reinforced by oath (*symphona engraphos kai horkous*), left.[60]

In 1455, Domenico Gattilusio was called to the sultan's court to secure his succession in Lesbos after his father, Dorino Gattilusio, passed away even though he had effectively ruled the island since 1449. Ducas took notice of the harsh conditions imposed by Mehmed II, which included the cession of Thasos and an increase in tribute to 4,000 ducats annually. Ultimately, Domenico

57 Iorga, "Privilegiul," 17–20; Dennis, "Treaty 1403," 77–80.

58 Ducas, *Istoria*, XXXIV/1, XXXVIII (in *FHDR*, 433).

59 *DRH*, D, I, doc. 305 (*volo stare in iuramento et disposicione quicquam cum eis iuravi et inscripsi*).

60 Ducas, *Istoria*, XXII/5.

Gattilusio was "dressed up in golden robe of honor" and then returned to his domains, although not before giving and receiving "written oaths" (*engraphous horkomosias*).[61] The text elucidates the diplomatic procedure of peace-making between the sultans and their tributaries in the fifteenth century. It is important to stress the conduct of negotiations before peace was concluded, which included financial and territorial concessions, but also resistance mounted against conditions Gattilusi deemed unacceptable, a refusal the Ottoman authorities had to take into account. Moreover, the outcome of negotiations materialized in the form of written pacts. These were drafted not in Istanbul or Edirne, but in a Bulgarian village of "Izlati" where the sultan's troops set up camp. These events took place about three months before the issue of a famous "summons" to the Moldavian voivode, Petru Aron, on 5 October 1455.[62] Taking into account this evidence, I argue that the notions of "peace," "peace agreement," and "oath" mentioned in Byzantine and Ottoman chronicles in regard to fifteenth-century compacts between the Porte and Wallachian voivodes were not merely verbal agreements, but written ones as well.

The existence of written instruments of peace in fifteenth-century Ottoman–Wallachian relations is further supported by a comparison between these compacts and the ones reached between the Ottomans and the Byzantine Empire, which have not survived. As I have mentioned, we are in possession of only one incomplete copy of the document from January–February 1403, concluded between Süleyman Çelebi and several Christian states (Byzantium, Venice, Genoa, and Rhodes).[63] We may even say that Romanian historiography has been more fortunate in this respect, since an Ottoman copy of the 1480–1481 *'ahdname* granted by Mehmed II to Stephen the Great exists, even though it is the only written compact of this sort that has survived to this day.

Thus, is it possible to claim that the Ottomans' relations with Byzantium, Wallachia and other polities of the region were only regulated by verbal pledges throughout the fifteenth century? I consider this hypothesis untenable, given that Byzantine chronicles clearly and unequivocally state that Ottoman–Byzantine peace settlements were put into writing. As I have demonstrated, Manuel II's envoys received the documents outlining the conditions of his agreement with the sultan in 1416. The well informed Ducas also claimed that, upon ascending to the throne in 1451, Mehmed II temporarily established peaceful relations with Byzantium by "writing new treaties and taking oaths"

61 Ducas, *Istoria*, XLIV/2. On the Gattilusi family, see W. Miller, "The Gattilusi of Lesbos," *BZ*, XXX, 1913, 407–447.

62 Mehmet, *Documente turcești*, I, doc. 1.

63 Iorga, "Privilegiul," 17–20; Dennis, "Treaty 1403," 77–80.

(*graphei neas diathekas*). It is to these treaties that the grand vizier Halil paşa (1439–1453) referred during his discussions with Byzantine envoys, who threatened – as a desperate measure – to release Ottoman pretender Orhan from custody:

> You clueless people, we have now in our hands a covenant settled by oath in writing, concluded with you just the other day and [the ink] has not yet dried on the lines of writing […][64]

This was not an isolated case. In fact, a majority of Ottoman–Byzantine peace settlements resulted in a written document. Another chronicler of the period, Kritobulos of Imbros, recounts an episode of 1452, when Constantin XII Dragasses' envoys, dispatched to oppose the construction of Rumeli Hisarı fortress, which posed a direct threat to Constantinople, reminded the sultan of the "treaties and compacts," which banned Mehmed II from erecting the fortress:

> in all peace agreements that we settled before in writing (*anagegrammenais*) during his ancestors' and his father's reigns, even during his own reign.[65]

Obviously, one can respond that the Byzantine Empire, given its prestige in Southeastern Europe, enjoyed a different status than that of peripheral Wallachia. However, the position of the empire in the fourteenth and early fifteenth-century declined considerably and was incomparably more difficult than that of Wallachia and particularly Moldavia under Stephen the Great.[66] This does not seem to have been offset by imperial prestige; hence, it seems unlikely that Ottoman–Byzantine relations were regulated by written accords, while the Porte's settlements with other tributaries merely by verbal ones. Even if we assume that the Byzantine case was distinct, a comparison of Moldavia and Wallachia with the insular lordships of Lesbos, Imbros and Lemnos leads us to similar conclusions. As I have demonstrated above, Domenico Gattilusio was confirmed as the ruler of Lesbos in 1455, receiving "written oaths" from Mehmed II. The situation repeated itself four years later (1459) in Imbros and Lemnos, whose protected status was guaranteed in exchange for 3,000 ducats of

64 Ducas, *Istoria*, XXXIII/12.

65 Critobul, *Mehmed II*, I/7, 3.

66 Dimitrios Kydones described Ottoman–Byzantine relations in 1377 in the following terms: "they order like some authoritarian potentates and we had to obey" (*Démétrius Cydonès Correspondance*, ed. G. Cammelli, Paris: Assocn. G. Budé, 1930, 59).

annual tribute, paid by Dimitrie Paleologus, the Despot of Mistra. It is worth pointing out that this took place under Mehmed II who, according to the same Kritobulos, settled with Vlad the Impaler "pacts and oaths" and concluded "peace" (*barış*) with the Moldavian prince, Petru Aron, in 1456. In regard to the framing of Imbros and Lemnos' political status and the relations between Mehmed II and Dimitrios Paleologos, Kritobulos clearly stated that "he received from the emperor the decisions in writing (*grammata*)." Moreover, his claim seems even more plausible given that he was "present [...] then at Adrianople" himself, taking part in negotiations and, implicitly, obtaining written documents in his capacity as an envoy.[67]

Even though al-Shaybani and al-Sarakhsi affirmed that written and oral peace settlements were not all the same from the Muslim perspective, we should emphasize that in the early Ottoman period verbal oaths had equal juridical value to written ones under certain political, military and diplomatic circumstances. In fact, the Hanafi jurists had already considered the testimony of witnesses more valuable than written documents. As Suraiya Faroqhi pointed out, in practice, people, including the Ottoman central administration, invoked written evidence whenever it was available.[68]

As a result of the above analysis it can be concluded that peace agreements concluded by Ottomans with Southeastern European rulers (including the princes of Wallachia and Moldavia) until the mid-sixteenth century were temporary. They were either in verbal or in written form, usually being called "oaths" and "pledges," because the oath was for a long time the most important guarantee of fidelity practiced in diplomatic relations.

67 Critobul, *Mehmed II*, I/75, 1–4.

68 Schacht, *Islamic Law*, 18; Faroqhi, "Ottoman taxpayers," 7.

CHAPTER 9

# *Pacta Sunt Servanda* and Tributary Status

Historians and jurists have devoted few pages to the Ottoman principle of *pacta sunt servanda* ("agreements must be kept"). Western scholars either deny the existence of this principle or conclude that Islamic states rarely observed it in diplomatic practice. In turn, Muslim judicial and theological works either tend to exaggerate the principle[1] (quoting especially the *Ku'ran*) or match Western accusations with accusations of their own. Quoting both violations of Christian peace agreement in Spain, and the violation of the Széged treaty of 1444 by the King of Hungary, they concluded that Christianity did not generally observe the principle *pacta sunt servanda* in relations with the Muslim world.[2]

The existence of the principle *pacta sunt servanda* in the Islamic world was one of the questions which captivated European observers of the Ottoman Empire as well. Thus, Paul Rycaut was concerned with "The regard the Turks have to their Leagues with Foreign Princes."[3] Then, Adrien Reland asked himself:

> Do the Muslims believe they are allowed to violate the agreements concluded with those called unbelievers by a principle belonging to their religion?[4]

Similarly, Dimitrie Cantemir planned to address this problem in a special chapter of his *The System of the Muhammedan Religion*, entitled "On the Muhammedan method to conclude [and break] peace with Christians."[5] Ironically,

1 Shaltut, *Koran*, 69–70; Özel, *Islam Hukuku*, 53–59: Ch. *Ahde Vefa Prensibi*.

2 "Le principe de la nullité de la parole donnée aux musulmans par les chrétiens se conserva à travers les siècles" (Rechid, "Islam," 426, 427–429). He accused the officials of the Catholic Church (in 1444, Julien Cesarini) who affirmed that the Christian princes "n'était pas obligé de tenir une parole donnée à des infideles" (Hammer, *Empire Ottoman*, II, 306–307).

3 Rycaut, *The Present State of the Ottoman Empire*, Ch. XXII, 94–96.

4 A. Reland, *La religion des Mahométans, exposée par leurs propres docteurs, avec les éclaircissements sur les opinions qu'on leur a faussement attribuées*, The Hague: Isaac Vaillant 1721, 198–204.

5 Virgil Cândea, "Studiu introductiv," in Dimitrie Cantemir, *Sistemul sau întocmirea religiei muhammedane*, ed. V. Cândea (*Opere Complete*, VIII, Tomul II) Bucharest: Ed. Academiei 1987, VII.

 | DOI:10.1163/9789004411104_010

the answers given by the scholars – which I shall quote at the appropriate moment – do not overlap, but in fact contradict each other.

From the methodological point of view, the existence of the principle *pacta sunt servanda* cannot be proven solely on the basis of the *Kur'an* or juridical texts, since they can be matched at any time confronted by quotes to the contrary. At the same time, we should avoid making sweeping generalizations based on particular solutions adopted in specific political–diplomatic circumstances. To obtain a complete outlook requires us to emphasize the relevant juridical–religious sources and to analyse political-diplomatic Ottoman practice in the long run. Thus, this task requires us to address the tangled issue of balance between two conflicting principles guiding Ottoman foreign relations – *pacta sunt servanda* and *necessitas non habet legem* ("necessity has no law").

## 1 Pacta sunt servanda in Ottoman Islam

*Pacta sunt servanda* is at the core of the law of peace and treaties.[6] Referring to the Middle Ages, it was affirmed that *pacta sunt servanda* was a "true dogma" in Christendom,[7] being considered a distinct feature of human nature.[8] The appearance of Islam also had consequences on diplomatic relations and the law of nations. Accordingly, the world of diplomatic contacts produced a split between "unbelievers" and "believers" that had to interact with one another during negotiations. In these conditions, one can ask what happened with the agreements concluded between Muslims and Christians? Setting aside the Christian standpoint,[9] my research will focus on the principle *pacta sunt servanda* from the Islamic point of view, including the Ottoman one.

In the Islamic world, the *pacta sunt servanda* principle became more a divine prescription than a customary practice. Many verses of the *Kur'an* exhorted Muslims to observe their "pacts" (*'ahd*). Two in particular were frequently invoked in juridical works and Ottoman sources:[10]

---

6 Michel du Taube, "L'inviolabilité des traités," *RdC*, 32, II, 1930, 295–389; J. B. Whitton, "La règle "pacta sunt servanda," *RdC*, 49, III, 1934, 151–275; P. I. Rusu, *Principiul respectării tratatelor. Tradiție și actualitate*, Bucharest: Ed. Științifică, 1992.

7 Redslob, *Histoire*, 122–123.

8 "What kind of man would I be, who gave my word to you and swore, and then should intend to plunder you?" the Wallachian boyar Albul, a dignitary of the hospodar Alexandru Aldea (1431–1436), asked himself in a letter written to the habitants of Brașov (Tocilescu, *534 documente*, doc. 378).

9 Redslob, *Histoire*, 122–123.

10 See also *Kur'an* V, 1 and *Kur'an* IX, 3–4.

> Fulfil the covenant of Allah (*'ahd-ı Allah*) when you have taken it, and do not violate oaths after their confirmation (*Kur'an* XVI, 91–92).
>
> Keep your agreement! Those who violate their agreement are responsible (*Kur'an* XVII, 34).[11]

Both Muslim (Ottoman) and Christian (European) scholars, such as M. Anquetil-Duperron and Dimitrie Cantemir, who affirmed the existence of the principle *pacta sunt servanda* amongst the Ottomans, have quoted these same verses, drawing on the *Kur'an* as the fundamental source of Islamic law.[12]

The *sünnet* (and the *hadis*), which followed the *Kur'an* as the second most important source of Islamic law, similarly emphasized the religious duty of Muslims to observe their commitments. Jurists and later rulers particularly referred to several pieces of advice and acts of the Prophet and the first caliphs.[13] Based on these original sources, scholars maintained that an agreement with infidels had to be respected in its entirety.[14] The *aman*, that is "protection" or "safe-conduct," had to be upheld, irrespectively whether it was granted by a Muslim ruler (*imam*) or by a simple Muslim, to an unbeliever or a non-Muslim group in times of peace and war. This way, Ibrahim al-Halebi (d. 1549) said:

> Both the stipulations of a capitulation and the protection promised [and] given to a single enemy or to a group of enemies or to a garrison of an enemy fortress will be observed;
>
> In the same time, any word violation, any breach of given allegiance are forbidden.[15]

According to European observers, the Ottomans seemed to realize that the *şeri'at* obliged them to respect treaties they concluded. Grand Vizier Çorlulu

---

11 In the Arab text, the term *'ahd* is used twice. In a recent Turkish translation *'ahd* is replaced by *söz,* which means word: *Verdiginiz sözü de yerine getirin. Çünkü verilen söz, sorunluluğu gerektirir* (*Kur'an-ı Kerim ve Türkçe Açyklamalı Meali,* Hazırlayanlar: Prof. Dr. Ali Özek, Medine-i Münevere, Istanbul, 1412 AH/1992). For A. Rechid there was no doubt that the principle *pacta sunt servanda* is present in this verse (Rechid, "Islam," 382). See also Shaltut, *Koran*, 69–70.

12 Anquetil-Duperron, *Législation*, 55; Cantemir, *Sistemul*, 323 (Virgil Cândea, who commented this work, quoted *Kur'an* II, 62–63).

13 Examples in Shaybani, *Kitab al-siyar*, I, 29, 89–90; Armanazi, *Islam*, 99–100; Özel, *Islam Hukuku*, 42.

14 Morabia, *Ğihad*, 321.

15 D'Ohsson, *Tableau*, V, 59–60 (French version of Halebi's text). More references to peace in Ibrahim Halebi, *Şerh-i Mülteka el-Ebhur* (*Mevkufat*), Tercüme ve Açıklamalar Nedim Yılmaz, vol. 2, Istanbul, 1993, 561–562.

Ali paşa (1706–1710) stated that "the Muslim law [...] would not allow them to violate their word."[16] Dimitrie Cantemir also noted, in his *System of Muhammedan Religion*, that "according to the *Kur'an*, [the Muslims] are ordered to keep their concluded treaties."[17]

Also, Ottoman sources regularly show that sultans and grand viziers were aware of the principle *pacta sunt servanda*, considered both as a custom and as a rule of *şeri'at*. In a letter sent by Süleyman Kanunî to King Sigismund II August of Poland in 1550, the sultan pointed out:

> the Empire of our Caliphate is accustomed to observe the old pacts (*'ahd*). Accordingly, as long as acts prejudicing the pact are not committed by the other part, our Caliphate shall not do anything contrary to the imperial covenant (*mu'ahede-i hümayun*).[18]

Since juridical and religious texts did not necessarily translate into practice in regard to Muslims' relations with non-Muslims, it is necessary to retrace the principle of *pacta sunt servanda* in the sources directly relating Ottoman diplomacy and politics. From this perspective, the most important sources are undoubtedly the *'ahdname*s. Thus, sixteenth- and seventeenth-century *'ahdname*s granted to Christian rulers contained sultanic oaths that provided emphatic guarantees of respecting peace.[19] The documents issued for England provide an example in this respect.

> [...] from this side also the conditions of the covenant and pact shall be held respected and observed as before [and] never in any way shall what is contrary to it be permitted.[20]

---

16 Dialogue with the French ambassador Charles de Ferriol in Istanbul, who included the conversation in the report of 1706 (Hurmuzaki, *Documente*, VI, doc. XXVI). Ambassador Guarient's letter to Emperor Joseph I, which expressed an opinion similar to Ferriol's report (Hurmuzaki, *Documente*, VI, doc. XXV).

17 Cantemir, *Sistemul*, 323. "The latter opinion was approved by all the *Ulema* with the Sultana-Mother, declaring to be unjust to wage war with an prince, who had given no cause of complaint, but had hitherto strictly observed the conditions of the truce," before the siege of Vienna in 1683 (Cantemir, *Othman History*, 296).

18 Mehmet, *Documente turcești*, I, doc. 25 (Letter of 7 *Şaban* 957/21 August 1550).

19 In early sixteenth century treaties with Venice, one can similarly read: "from my side also nothing shall be done against the pact" (*benden dahi hilaf-ı 'ahd nesne vaki' olmıya*) (Gökbilgin, "Belgeler II," 46, 50, 53–54).

20 Feridun, *Münşe'at*, II, 385; Skilliter, *Harborne*, 89, 236 (*bu canibden dahi şerayt 'ahd ü-aman kemakan mer'i ve muhterem tutılub asla bir vecihle hilafina cevaz gösterilmiye*). For the *'ahdname* of 1604 granted to France, see Feridun, *Münşe'at*, II, 404 (*ben dahi dostluğu*

The historical records concerning the Ottoman attitude towards the pacts show considerable consistency. Thus, the Ottomans can be seen emphasizing strongly the sacred nature of treaties,[21] asking the Christian princes to observe the peace agreements,[22] praising themselves for observing concluded treaties.[23] Even Christian authors praised the sultans for respecting peace agreements with Christian princes.[24]

However, there are also records which criticized the negative attitude of the Porte concerning the peace treaties with Christians.[25] The European observers

---

*kabul idüb 'ahd ve yemin iderim ki... bu tarafdan hilaf-ı 'ahd ü-misak ve mugayir-i 'akd ü-ittifak iş olmıyub daima işbu 'ahdname-yi hümayun makrunumun mezmun-ı şerifiyle 'amel oluna.* In François Savary de Brèves's French translation: *Nous promettons & iurons par la verité du grand Dieu toutpuissant...,& par l'ame de noz aieulx & bisaieulx de ne contrarier, ni contravenir à ce qui est porté par ce traité de paix & Capitulation....* (*Articles du Traicté faict en l'année mil six cens quatre...*, À Paris, MDCXV (1615). In *berat* of July 1614 granted to Gabriel Bethlen and Transylvanian nobles, Ahmed I promised: "I shall also keep always this pact and this protection and I shall not act contrary to <them>" (Gemil, *Documente turcești*, doc. 61: *ben dahi bu 'ahd ve amanı mukarrer tutub hilafina zahib olmıyım*).

21 "Our word is the [true] word and our peace is the [true] peace" (*'uhdemiz 'uhde ve sulhumuz sulhdur*), the grand vizier wrote in a 1607 letter sent to Vienna (Gemil, *Documente turcești*, doc. 24).

22 "This peace shall not be violated" (*bu sulhu bozmıyalar*), in a text of Zsitvatörök treaty of 1606 (Feridun, *Münşe'at*, II, 315. See also Guboglu, "Arhive. Brașov," 220–221). "We want strongly that all pacts concluded between us so long ago be kept and observed," Süleyman Kanunî wrote to the king of Poland in December 1532–January 1533 (Hurmuzaki, *Documente*, Supl. II/1, doc. XXVIII).

23 The same concept was present in the Christian world (Tocilescu, *534 documente*, doc. 118). During the initial stage of their contact with the Muslim world, the Turks enjoyed a good reputation regarding *pacta sunt servanda*. Thus, the poet Gaznavi (d. 1130) said that the Turks were as "angels in peace" (cf. Turan, "Ideal," 85).

24 Byzantine chroniclers considered upholding the treaties an important criterion in their positive evaluation of an Ottoman sultan (Chalcocondi, *Expuneri*, 51: about Murad I). For relations between the Ottomans, Wallachia and Hungary, see *DRH*, D, I, doc. 323; Tocilescu, *534 documente*, doc. 119.

25 Süleyman Kanunî was praised by European observers for his respect for the 1540 peace with Venice. However, in a 1541 letter to the Polish king, Moldavian voivode Petru Rareș negatively assessed Ottoman attitude towards Christians and especially towards peace treaties concluded with them: "and they do not care about the peace with you [...], but you and all Christians do not know anything about this" (Corfus, *Documente XVI*, doc. 35). For the peace settlement of 1432 between Alexandru I Aldea and Murad II, criticized by the former, see *DRH*, D, I, doc. 192 and Tocilescu, *534 documente*, doc. 28. Serb Konstantin Mihailović presents a negative portrait of Mehmed II concerning peace agreements with Christians (Mihailoviç, *Memoires*, 29, 87). For the notion of "false friendship," see Keith Hopwood, "*Müdara*: «False friendship» in Ottoman–Byzantine Relations," *CIÈPO, 9th Symposium*, Jerusalem, July 23–26, 1990 in A. Singer, A. Cohen (eds.), *Aspects of Ottoman History*, Jerusalem: The Magnes Press, 1994, 156–161.

did not forget to point out the differences between theory and practice. Thus, Dimitrie Cantemir stated:

> although according to the civil law and divine one [Muslims] obliged themselves to keep strictly and carefully established terms of peace, when the circumstances and the insignificant reasons appear they may suddenly break off peace and violate treaties.[26]

The Moldavian scholar emphasized impartially that "not only the Muslims, but also Christian princes are resourceful and experienced in this kind of thing."[27]

To prove that the principle *pacta sunt servanda* was condition by the Ottoman *raison d'état*, and that Islamic law was adjusted to the political interests of the Porte, we may compare two events in Ottoman–Habsburg relations surrounding the 1683–1699 war. Prior to the outbreak of hostilities, Dimitrie Cantemir claimed, Islamic law was cited by a war party at the court to justify breaking the Treaty of Vasvár (1664).[28] In turn, the French ambassador in Istanbul, Charles de Ferriol, baron d'Argental reported that juridical texts were brought up by Çorlulu Ali paşa (1706–1710) to emphasize the obligation of keeping the Treaty of Karlowitz (1699).[29]

## 2 Covenant Violation (nakz-ı ʿahd)

*Pacta sunt servanda* and *necessitas non habet legem* were the two basic principles for any medieval ruler,[30] each of them crucial for the conduct of diplomatic and military affairs. To justify violation of pacts without infringing on the *pacta sunt servanda* constituted a peculiarity of Islamic law, thus allowing us to say that in Ottoman Islam the state of necessity constituted "law" in itself.

To break a treaty was – even more for Muslims than for Christians – an act that required strong juridical justification in the eyes of the Muslim community (*ʿUmma*), and to a lesser extent in regard to foreign rulers. Considering so much data offered by historical and juridical sources, one can infer that the

26 Cantemir, *Sistemul*, 322–323. See also D'Ohsson, *Tableau*, V, 59; Guer, *Moeurs*, 343–366: Book IX, Ch. II: *Des deux Maximes de la Politique des Turcs*.

27 Cantemir, *Sistemul*, 322–323. Historical instances are found even in Christian sources (Sphrantzes, *Memorii*, VIII/1–3: about Ottoman–Byzantine relations in 1421).

28 Cantemir, *Othman History*, 295–298.

29 Hurmuzaki, *Documente*, VI, doc. XXVI: report to the French king of 17 September 1706. He was ambassador in Istanbul between 1700 and 1711 (Saint-Priest, *Mémoires*, 246–252).

30 Morabia, *Ğihad*, 322.

Ottomans believed the principle *pacta sunt servanda* would not be impinged if a "legitimate cause" (*legitima causa, cause légitime*)[31] could be invoked; in this case, the violation could gain legitimacy from the perspective of the Islamic law. In 1570, Sultan Selim II expressed his desire to break the treaty with Venice and invade Cyprus, although this had to take place:

> with violating neither the allegiance [due to] treaties nor the principles of law and justice.[32]

Breaking a treaty was considered such an important step that even the *şeyh ül-Islam* felt the need to cite preceding juridical sources in support of his *fetva*, although he was not obliged to clarify all matters, as lower *müftis* did. Therefore, in 1570, Ebussuud Efendi, often described as the most prominent *şeyh ül-Islam* in Ottoman history, provided a justification for attacking Venice, invoking the treaty of Hudaibiya of 628, broken by Muhammad a mere two years after its conclusion.[33] At the same time, the necessity to provide juridical argument stemmed from the fact that violation of pacts presented itself as highly irregular case; according to Colin Imber, Cyprus constituted "a unique case of a broken treaty" in the sixteenth century.[34]

Thus, what constituted a "legitimate cause" that allowed Ottomans to renege on the treaty with non-Muslims without facing accusations of trampling the principle of *pacta sunt servanda*? While an answer can be easily found in juridical texts, examining the way these theoretical constructs were applied in the practice of peace-making constitutes a far more daunting task. The sources reveal as a rule three "legitimate causes": violation of *ʿahd* by the infidels; protection of the interests of the Muslim community; and the invalidity of certain stipulations or of an entire agreement.

---

31 Hurmuzaki, *Documente*, VI, doc. XXV, XXVI; Cantemir, *Othman History*, 296.

32 In a French version from D'Ohsson, *Tableau*, V, 73–74. In Colin Imber's most recent English translation, one can read: "An explanation is sought as to whether, in accordance with the Pure *shariʿa*, this is an impediment to the Sultan's determining to break the treaty" (Imber, *Ebu's-suʿud*, 84). See also Düzdağ, *Fetvalar*, doc. 478. The differences could indicate the existence of more versions of the same *fetva*.

33 "His Excellency [Muhammad] the Apostle of God [...] made a ten-year truce with the Meccan infidels in the sixth year of the Hegira [...] Then, in the following year, it was considered more beneficial to break it and, in the eighth year of the Hegira, [the Prophet] attacked [the Meccans], and conquered Meccas the Mighty." (Imber, *Ebu's-suʿud*, 84). See also Düzdağ, *Fetvalar*, doc. 478; D'Ohsson, *Tableau*, V, 74.

34 Imber, *Ebu's-suʿud*, 85. See also Ménage, "Capitulation," 373–383.

### 2.1 *Violation of ʿahd by infidels*

In the Middle Ages, whenever one party broke agreement clauses, the other was released from its obligation contained in the oath. According to this usage, the breach of agreement by unbelievers was for the Muslims a "legitimate cause" for scrapping the *ʿahd* altogether. In fact, the *Kurʾan* considered the violation of treaties a deed unbefitting of Muslims.[35]

In Ottoman diplomatic practice,[36] the sultans observed the concluded pact as long as the Christian princes had not violated its conditions. The Kurʾanic basis of this attitude (IX, 7: "And as long as they keep their word [given] to you, you be faithful too") was constantly invoked in imperial charters, sometimes *verbatim*. Thus, the *ʿahdname* of 1521 granted to Venice by Süleyman Kanunî reads:

> Accepting the friendship with them according to this pact (*ʿahd*) which has been mentioned, I am swearing with strong oaths [...] that as long as they shall observe the pact and friendship and do nothing contrary to the pact, from my side also shall I do nothing contrary to the pact. So be it known.[37]

In a similar vein, Murad III granted the unilateral charter of privileges for English merchants in 1580, with the following statement:

> As long as you shall be steadfast and enduring in sincerity and candor, according to this agreement which has been mentioned, from this side also the conditions of the covenant and pact shall be held respected and observed as before (and) never in any way shall what is contrary to it be permitted.[38]

35 See, especially, *Kurʾan* VIII, 55–56, *Kurʾan* IX, 8–10.

36 For pre-Ottoman practices, see the response of Fatimid caliph al-Mu'izz (953–975) to a Byzantine ambassador in 955: "We shall not violate the pact and shall not betray, as you do it" (A. A. Vasiliev, *Byzance et les Arabes*, II/1, Brussels: Fondation byzantine, 1968, 421–422. See also S. M. Stern, "An Embassy of the Byzantine Emperor to the Fatimid Khaliph al-Mu'izz," *Byzantion* XX, 1950, 239–258).

37 *madam ki anlar ʿahdı ve dostluğu riʿayet idüb ʿahde muhalif nesne sadır olmıya benden dahi hilaf-ı ʿahd nesne vakiʾ olmıya. Şöyle bileler* (Gökbilgin, "Belgeler II," 46: *ʿahdname* of 17 *Muharrem* 928/17 December 1521). For the *ʿahdnames* of 1513 and 1517, see Gökbilgin, "Belgeler II," 50, 53–4.

38 *Bu canibden dahi şerayt ʿahd ü-aman kemakan merʾi ve muhterem tutılub asla bir vecihle hilafına cevaz gösterilmiye* (Skilliter, *Harborne*, 236). The same text in the *ʿahdname* of 1601: *Işbu zikr olunan ʿahd üzere madam ki sadakat ve ihlasda sabit-kadem ü rasih-kadem olalar bu canibden dahi şerayt ʿahd ü-aman kemakan merʾi ve muhterem tutılub asla bir*

In order to ensure the validity of such pacts, the sultans also demanded that Christian princes respect "the conditions of friendship" that they had concluded with the Porte.[39]

### 2.2 *Denunciation of ʿahd by Sultans*

According to Islamic law,[40] the *imam* could break off an engagement with a non-Muslim prince if he was afraid that the infidels would betray him, or considered that the respective peace no longer aligned with the interests of the Muslim community and state. Anyway, to avoid the accusations of a "treachery of the word they gave," the basic condition for such measure was to publicly declare the rejection of the pact,[41] and to warn the infidels about imminent war.[42] The former case[43] originated from the verse of *Kur'an* VIII, 58:

> If you are afraid that a person will betray you, inform him that you have decided to break [the pact concluded with him]. Because Allah does not like the traitors.

By analyzing the Ottoman sources, we can identify several actions by Christian princes that Ottoman authorities interpreted as "contrary to the old treaties" and which could destroy "the bases of peace and friendship."[44] For instance, in 1598 Mehmed III broke the *ʿahd* concluded with Michael the Brave and ordered raids against Wallachia, on the grounds that he lost all confidence in the voivode:

---

*vecihle hilafına cevaz gösterilmiye* (Feridun, *Münşe'at*, II, 385). For the *ʿahdname* of 1604, granted by Ahmed I to King Henry IV of France, see Feridun, *Münşe'at*, II, 404, and for the *ʿahdname* granted to the United Provinces in 1612, see Groot, *OEDR*, 246.

39 For the Polish case, see Mehmet, *Documente turcești*, I, doc. 23.

40 The same ideas appear in the Christian world, as well (N. Machiavelli, *Principele*, ed. N. Facon, Bucharest: Ed. Științifică, 1960, 66; Spinoza, *Tratatul teologico-politic*, ed. I. Firu, Bucharest: Ed. Științifică, 1960, 240).

41 Caurroy, "Législation," IV/17, 585; D'Ohsson, *Tableau*, V, 59–60; Shaltut, *Koran*, 69–70; Morabia, *Ğihad*, 321, 335; Rechid, "Islam," 425; Armanazi, *Islam*, 75.

42 This is why the Ottomans felt vindicated when they were attacked without a public declaration of pact violation, so "contrary to the law" (*gayr-ı hakk*). A later case of this sort occurred in 1808, when Ottoman ambassador in Paris Abdurrahim Muhib Efendi complained about sudden attack by the Russians (Veliman, *Documente turcești*, doc. 237).

43 This reason was universally accepted among Muslim jurists (Armanazi, *Islam*, 75).

44 Mehmet, *Documente turcești*, I, doc. 102: letter of *eva'il-i Zilkaʿde* 979/16–25 March 1572. For Ottoman–Polish relations in the sixteenth century, see letters sent by Süleyman Kanunî and Selim II to Sigismund I and Sigismund II Augustus (Mehmet, *Documente turcești*, I, doc. 23 (*eva'il-i Şaban* 949/10–19 November 1542); doc. 97 (*evahir-i Şaban* 979/7–16 January 1572).

> Until this moment, Michael the Damned, who is the voivode of Wallachia, shown the obeying towards my Threshold of happiness both by letters and by the envoys; because he didn't stop to lie and to practice deceptions, being naturally bad and sly, it didn't trust his word (*sözüne bir vechile* [*itimad*] *ca'iz olmamağın*).[45]

Murad II's scrapping of the covenant with Alexandru I Aldea followed the same customary practice. In 1432, the Wallachian voivode promised to pay the Ottomans back for violating their oaths on multiple occasions:

> the Turks plundered all my country although they obliged themselves by faithful oath and received faithful [...] Too many times the Turks betrayed me, so that I act in the same way, now.[46]

The latter case can be called the breaking off with a disadvantageous covenant. Muslim jurists theorized the *imam's* right to nullify a pact when it adversely affected the interest of the Muslim community and state without damaging the principle of *pacta sunt servanda*.[47] Drawing on the *Kur'an*, the majority of Hanafi jurists affirmed that the *imam* was obliged to denounce treaties once he realized that respecting their stipulations would hurt the Muslim community.[48] *Şeyh ül-Islam* Ebussuud Efendi's explanation invoked in the *fetva* of 1570 is worth citing here:

> For the Sultan of the people of Islam (may God glorify his victories) to make peace with the infidels is juridical only when there is a benefit to all Muslims. When there is no benefit, peace is never juridical. When a benefit has been seen, and it is then observed to be more beneficial to break it becomes absolutely obligatory and binding.[49]

Because the Ottomans were consistent in observing the formal rules governing the law of nations, they sought "legitimate causes" whenever they deemed *'ahd* violation necessary or beneficial. Thus, during the 1484 expedition against Kili and Akkerman, Sultan Bayezid II put the blame for scrapping the pact on the

45 *Mihai. Documente I*, doc. 75.

46 DRH, D, I, doc. 192; Tocilescu, *534 documente*, doc. 28; Maxim, *ŢRÎP*, 198.

47 Armanazi, *Islam*, 104; Morabia, *Ğihad*, 320–321, 334–335.

48 Shaybani, *Kitab al-siyar*, I, 28–29; Shaltut, *Koran*, 70. See also Caurroy, "Législation," IV/17, 585.

49 I have opted to cite the most recent English translation by Colin Imber (Imber, *Ebu's-su'ud*, 84–85). A French version in D'Ohsson, *Tableau*, V, 73–74.

Moldavian voivode Stephen the Great, claiming that "the violation of the pact and the breach of peace were provoked by him."[50]

### 2.3 *Null Clauses and Agreements*

According to the Islamic law of war and peace, some stipulations were considered illegal and invalidated the covenants that contained them. If a treaty allowed Muslim captives to remain in the hands of the enemy, ceded Muslim territories to infidels, forced Muslims to pay in exchange for peace or exempted non-Muslims from paying tribute, the *imam* was at liberty to terminate the truce unilaterally.[51]

Sources prove that these rules were not just theoretical speculations. Ottoman statesmen frequently pointed to the existence of such clauses in the pacts as the rationale for breaking them. Obtaining a favorable opinion of the *fetva* removed any existing obstacles to taking diplomatic or military action. Once again, Ebussuud Efendi's *fetva* legitimizing the 1570 invasion of Cyprus stated that the island had belonged to Muslims eight centuries prior:

> The question (*mesele*): If an infidel people in peace with the empire would own among other territories a country belonging once to Muslims (the ancient Moors) where the unbelievers would destroy the mosques, desecrate the holy places and do other irreverent acts, may the Muslims' sovereign entertained only a desire of serving religion go to conquer this country for adding it again to the Abode of Islam, without breaking neither the respect towards agreement nor the principles of law and rights? The answer (*el-cevab*): It is possible; the holy law does not object.[52]

---

50 A. Antalffy, "Două documente din Biblioteca Egipteană de la Cairo despre cucerirea Chiliei și Cetății Albe in 1484," *RI*, XX, 1934, 37–38.

51 *Shaybani's Siyar*, 154–155; Peters, *Islam*, 34. When the balance of power was tilted against Muslims, stipulations such as the killing of hostages or the sending back of the infidels converted to Islam were included in truces, but they were legally considered null.

52 D'Ohsson, *Tableau*, V, 73–74; *Journal de la bataille de Lepante*, edited and annotated by François Garnier, Paris, 1956, 52. In Colin Imber's English version: "A land was previously in the realm of Islam. After a while, the abject infidels overran it, destroyed the colleges and mosques, and left them vacant. They filled the pulpits and the galleries with the tokens of infidelity and error, intending to insult the religion of Islam with all kinds of vile deeds, and by spreading their ugly acts to all corners of the earth. His Excellency the Sultan, the Refuge of Religion, has, as zeal for Islam requires, determined to take aforementioned land from the possession of the shameful infidels and to annex it to the realm of Islam. When peace was previously concluded with the other lands in the possession of the said infidels, the aforenamed land was included. An explanation is sought as to whether, in accordance with the Pure *shari'a*, this is an impediment to the Sultan's

Moreover, according to this juridical opinion, any territorial change at the expense of the Abode of Islam, no matter when it took pace, and, by extension, the peace itself, could only be considered as temporary. The same argument (*un principe aussi monstrueux*, in d'Ohsson's view) was invoked in 1645, when Ibrahim I invaded the island of Crete.[53] Whenever territorial losses led the Muslim population to enter under infidel rule, the breaking of an *ʿahd* was not only justified, but even became an obligation.[54]

## 3 Did Tributaries Keep their Oaths?

Did the tributary voivodes of Moldavia and Wallachia keep their end of the bargain? Although this question has not been asked by Romanian historians, historical and juridical sources put it at the forefront of the present discussion.

According to the Islamic law of peace, tributary status was based on covenants (*ʿahd*) concluded between the Muslim sovereign and infidel princes. In the case of Wallachia, Moldavia and Transylvania, it is necessary to take into account three different standpoints: Ottoman official stance, local concepts and the Western position. At the same time, it is crucial to take into account the tremendous changes in the principalities' political status that took place under Süleyman Kanunî. Up until then, the voivodes of Moldavia and Wallachia retained the attributes of sovereignty, including the right to declare war, make peace and dispatch diplomatic envoys. However, from the 1530s, the control exercised by the Porte increased and the voivodes ceased to be regarded as subjects of international law. To some extent, the same applied to Transylvania.

The first standpoint to be considered is that of the Ottoman authorities. According to Islamic law, the most important breaches of *ʿahd*s committed by non-Muslims were the refusal to pay the *harac/cizye*, the conclusion of alliances with the enemies of Muslims, launching attacks against the Abode of Islam, refusing to obey a Muslim sovereign and insulting the Prophet and the

determining to break the treaty. Answer: There is no possibility that it could ever be an impediment..." (Imber, *Ebu's-suʿud*, 84).

53 D'Ohsson, *Tableau*, V, 74.

54 An example in this respect occurred between the Byzantines and the Ottomans in 1421 (Ducas, *Istoria*, XXIV/12). In 1542, Süleyman Kanunî planned to take back the territories along the Ottoman–Polish border which had once belonged to Muslims (Mehmet, *Documente turcești*, I, doc. 23).

Muslim faith.[55] Ottoman sources state that covenant violations (in Turkish, *nakzı ʿahdetmek* or *nabud etmek*)[56] by tributaries included a refusal of tribute payments, alliance with Christian rulers hostile to the Porte and attacks on adjacent *sancak*s. According to Idris Bitlisi, these actions constituted direct evidence of non-Muslims' "religious enmity" towards Muslims,[57] even though they did not imply the end of the covenant, but only the punishment of the guilty tribute-payers.

### 3.1 *Refusal to Pay Tribute as nakz-ı ʿahd*

The refusal by non-Muslim communities to pay *cizye*, a tax that provided a symbolic expression of the *imam*'s sovereignty, was regarded by Muslim jurists as a violation of *ʿahd*. Ibn Hazm (d. 1064) expressed this stance in the following passage:

> By rejecting the state of humiliation, i.e. [by] refusing to pay *cizye*, the *zimmi*s violate the protection covenant.[58]

Tribute paid in the fifteenth century by Moldavian and Wallachian rulers was considered by the Porte as a visible expression of its tributaries' commitment to the pacts. In consequence, a delay in payment of the established sum immediately put Ottoman authorities on alert. Thus, Ottoman chronicles frequently cited the failure to deliver tribute as the primary cause of punitive campaigns launched by the sultan. For instance, according to Tursun bey, "the Moldavian [Stephen the Great] became the enemy" both before the 1475–1476 campaigns and in 1484, because "he did not care to obey and pay tribute."[59] In the same way, the Hungarian historian Szamosközy recorded a similar case of violating tribute-paying arrangements by Michael the Brave in 1594:

> When the Turkish Emperor gave the reign to Michael the voivode, [the Wallachian] promised [to pay] the Emperor annually seventy thousand thalers; but he only promised, he has not paid it yet.[60]

55 For details, see Khaled Abou el Fadl, *Rebellion and Violence in Islamic Law*, Cambridge: Cambridge University Press, 2001.

56 *Redhouse*, 859, 864. The formula *nakz-ı ʿahd* was also used for defining the *ʿahd* violations by tributary princes (Veliman, *Documente turcești*, doc. 24).

57 Idris Bitlisi, *Heșt Behișt*, in *Cronici turcești I*, 165.

58 Apud Turki, "Tributaire," 42, n. 3.

59 Tursun bey, *Tarih*, in *Cronici turcești I*, 74, 76–77.

60 Szamosközy, *Însemnări ungurești*, 101.

### 3.2 *Alliance with the Porte's Enemies as nakz-ı ʿahd*

In juridical texts, the alliance with *harbis* was one of the most condemnable actions a tributary prince could undertake. According to al-Shaybani, to spy and inform the enemies of Islam about the "weak spots in the Muslim defenses" not only rendered the *ʿahd* null, but also demanded a proper punishment of the tributary prince:

> I asked: If after having entered into an agreement and having become a protected person of theirs, [the ruler] began to inform the unbelievers of the weak spots in the Muslim defenses, or provide them with guides and give refuge to their spies, would these acts constitute a violation of his pact? He replied: No, but the Muslims should punish him for so doing and throw him into prison.[61]

Ottoman statesmen similarly considered alliances between their tributaries and Christian sovereigns to be violations of the *ʿahd* the former had with the sultan. Thus, according to Koca Hüseyin, a *gaza* was launched in 1420 against the voivode Mihail I of Wallachia, "because that very dissembling infidel violated his oath and pact" (*nakz-ı ʿahd ü-misak*). How? "He concluded an alliance with the Hungarian king," the chronicler answered.[62] Accordingly, Mehmed I considered himself no longer bound by the covenant with the Wallachian voivode.

Several centuries later, in 1714, a *fetva* by *şeyh ül-Islam* Imam Mahmud Efendi (1713–1714) provided a legal sanction for the dethronement, imprisonment and beheading of the Wallachian ruler Constantin Brâncoveanu. The most important accusation against the voivode was the violation of

> the alliance and pact and agreement with the sultan (*taraf-ı sultanat ile* [...] *ittifak ve ʿahd ü-misak*) by concluding of an alliance with the infidels who are the enemies of the faith and state (*aʾda-yi din ve devlet olan kefere ile müttefik olub*).[63]

61 *Shaybani's Siyar*, 153.

62 Koca Hüseyin, *Bedaʿi ül-vekaʿi*, in *Cronici turcești I*, 446–447.

63 This *fetva* was included in the order of *evaʾil-i Rebi ül-evvel* 1126/ 17–26 March 1714 issued by Ahmed III to *mubașir* Mustafa, ordering the Wallachian voivode to be brought to Istanbul (Veliman, *Documente turcești*, doc. 11).

### 3.3 *Attack on Neighboring Sancaks as nakz-ı ʿahd*

Entering with armed forces and pillaging attack territories belonging to the Abode of Islam constituted another act strongly condemned in juridical treatises. In this respect, the traditionalist Ibn Taimiya (d. 1328), the last great theoretician of *cihad*, provides us with an important insight into the matter.[64] In such a case, the covenant immediately lost its validity upon the infidel's military campaign, freeing the Muslim leader from any obligations.[65]

Nevertheless, according to the Hanafi jurist al-Shaybani, such an attack or even the killing of Muslims did not constitute a violation of the pact per se, but rather a serious crime for which the culprits had to be severely punished:

> I asked: If he or [one of] the people of his land continued to kill Muslims by surprise attack, would this act constitute a violation of his pact? He replied: No, but [the Muslims] would investigate which one of them committed it; if evidence is established against him, they would behead him in retaliation. But if no evidence was adduced, there could be no case against him.[66]

According to the Ottoman official standpoint, the most grievous action a *haracgüzar* could undertake was launching an attack on adjacent *sancak*s. Military attacks launched by tributary voivodes from the right bank of the Danube occurred at times, and they were described in the Ottoman sources as breaches of the covenants (*nakz-ı ʿahd*). Thus, the massive destruction caused by Mircea the Elder (1386–1418) and Vlad the Evil (1436–1442; 1443–1447) on the "frontier of Islam" were regarded as serious covenant violations. According to Idris Bitlisi, the latter became one of the "villainous infidels" since by,

> violating his pact (*nakz-ı ʿahd*), he sacked and pillaged Silistre, situated in front of Wallachia, and began to show his religious and secular enmity, [even though] he had from ancient times been the tribute-payer (*haracgüzar*) of the Ottoman dynasty.[67]

---

64 Turki, "Tributaire," 55. See also A. Morabia, "Ibn Taimiya, dernier grand théoreticien du ğihad médiéval," *BEO*, 30, 2, 1978 (paru 1980), 85–100.

65 Armanazi, *Islam*, 75.

66 *Shaybani's Siyar*, 153.

67 Idris Bitlisi, *Heşt Behişt*, in *Cronici turceşti I*, 165. Employing Islamic legal terminology, Idris Bitlisi creates a false impression about Ottoman–Wallachian relations of late fourteenth and fifteenth centuries. According to him, both Mircea the Elder and Vlad the Evil were "tribute-payers" (*haracgüzar*), paid *cizye* and concluded *ʿahd-ı zimmet* with sultans.

In the same vein, in 1714, the accusations against Constantin Brâncoveanu included not only siding with enemies of the Porte, but also attacks on the lands and subjects of the sultan. The *fetva* by Imam Mahmud Efendi tackled the issue in the following manner:

> Destroying certain imperial fortresses [...] he sacked and robbed the property of the rich and poor subjects who lived and stayed [there], and killed and, indeed, he committed crimes and abuses against the people.[68]

When non-Muslims committed numerous acts contrary to their pact with Muslims, covenant violations caused more serious consequences. In fact, this was often the case. Voivodes' revolts against the Porte did not stop at their refusal to meet tributary payments, but also involved alliances with neighboring states,[69] and eventually launching attacks on Ottoman neighboring territories. For example, in the early eighteenth century, *şeyh ül-Islam* Ebu-Işak Kara Ismail Naim Efendi (1716–1718) – while still describing Wallachians as "covenant people" (*mu'ahidin*), considered their attacks on villages and towns of the right side of the Danube river as proofs of their "covenant violation" (*nakz-ı 'ahd*) and as arguments for punishing the rebels.[70] A similar *fetva* was issued as late as 1821, which categorized all "national" movements in Southeastern Europe,[71] including the Wallachian uprising led by Tudor Vladimirescu, as "rebellions" (sing. *isyan*) to be suppressed by the Porte.[72]

68 Veliman, *Documente turcești*, doc. 11.

69 Ottoman chroniclers often referred to such situations. Thus, in Transylvania George Martinuzzi (1541–1551) "came to an agreement and joined with the Habsburg king (*Nemçe kıralı*) Ferdinand, and [...] did not give his *cizye* and *harac*," although he had obeyed to the Porte and had been its tribute-payer (*haracgüzar*) (Mustafa Celalzade, *Tabakat*, in *Cronici turcești* I, 279).

70 This *fetva* was included in the hüküm of *eva'il-i Cemazi ül-evvel* 1129/ 13–22 April 1717 (Veliman, *Documente turcești*, doc. 24).

71 Charles Jelavich and Barbara Jelavich. *The Establishment of the Balkan National States, 1804–1920*. Seattle, WA: University of Washington Press, 1986.

72 Text in Zeki Arıkan, "1821 Ayvalık Isyanı," *Belleten*, LII, 206, 1988, 576 and n. 22. Frederick Anscombe argues that these uprisings had little to do with national ideology (F. Anscombe, "The Balkan Revolutionary Age," *The Journal of Modern History*, 84, 2012, 572–606). For "rebellion" in the Ottoman view see Palmira Brummett, "Classifying Ottoman Mutiny: The Act and Vision of Rebellion," *TSAB*, 22, 1, Spring 1998, 91–107.

### 3.4 *Local and Western Views*

Tributary princes realized that certain actions, such as their refusal to pay tribute or enter into alliances with polities hostile to the Porte could be interpreted as pact violations. Thus, according to Koca Hüseyin, Moldavian voivode Stephen the Great was aware of the risk concessions to the Poles would put him in, and consequently refused to allow the Polish king John Albert to march through Moldavia during the campaign of 1497. If he agreed,

> he would break off the pact [with the sultan], and consequently his country would be destroyed.[73]

A few decades later, the Moldavian boyars wrote in their letter to the Polish king that in 1538 "Prince Petru [Rareș] caused the coming of the Turks into our country."[74] Upon his revolt against the Porte in 1594, Michael the Brave was aware that he had broken his pact (*ʿahd*) with the sultan, "because the Turks had not caused any trouble or injustice to me."[75] Consequently, it is safe to say that from the tributaries' perspective power relations between them at the Porte played the role in shaping their attitudes towards existing covenants. Whenever the political and military situation worked in the tributaries' advantage, they were more likely to commit *ʿahd* violations.

In addition, several outside observers provide a different perspective that allows us to refine our traditional perception of the relationship between the Porte and its tribute-payers. Ragusan Michael Bocignoli's account of June 1524 has been intensively mined for details of the Ottoman–Wallachian relationship. However, this research has been relatively one-sided, since it ignored the accusation of violating pacts by Wallachian rulers. Referring to the new arrangements adopted by late-fifteenth- and early-sixteenth-century voivodes, Michael Bocignoli twice accused the Wallachians of breaking their covenant with the Porte:

> but Wallachians [were] continuously unsatisfied by their situation of things and looked for something else.[76]

---

73 Koca Hüseyin, *Bedaʿ ül-vekaʿi*, in *Cronici turcești* I, 465.

74 Hurmuzaki, *Documente*, Supl. II/1, doc. LXX.

75 *Mihai. Documente*, I, doc. 15. See also the statement of 17 January 1601 sent to Rudolph II (*Mihai. Documente*, I, doc. 226).

76 *Călători străini*, I, 177, 179.

## 4 The Myth of Ancient Privileges

While Ottoman sources seem to ignore the hypothesis of covenant violations by the Porte, the local tradition discussed the matter of the Porte's attitude towards pacts with its tributaries. The main grievances were against what local elites perceived as covenant violations, such as the tendency to interpret voluntary gifts as tribute payments, the increases in the *harac*, limitations imposed on voivodes' authority and forced territorial cessions.

In the short term, Wallachians and Moldavians felt the need to provide legitimacy to their acts of rebellion and accusations of the Porte's breaches in covenant made a strong case in this respect. In this regard, Moldavian boyar Petru Vartic, sent in 1542 as an envoy to the Polish court, argued that Petru Rareș's rebellion originated from Süleyman Kanunî's violation of "the pact and agreements concluded by his ancestors with Moldavians."[77] However, most complaints Moldavians and Wallachian brought against the Porte touched on long-standing grievances, and found their way into the pages of the chronicles.

In Wallachia, the claim that the Ottomans "did not keep the agreement" concluded with Mircea the Elder, was mentioned in the eighteenth century by Mihai Cantacuzino, who utilized it to justify the fact that Wallachians also failed to keep their end of the bargain.[78]

In Moldavian historiography, a similar case – albeit in a more exaggerated form – was made by Miron Costin, who claimed that

> the Turk [...] does not keep his word towards the Christian, he has no shame to deceive him, [and] he proceeds in all by opportunities.[79]

Similarly, Dimitrie Cantemir formulated multiple accusations against the Ottomans for violating ancient pacts. Thus, in his "Proclamation to the country" (1711), the voivode accused the Ottoman infringement of the "covenant with Bogdan" to justify his rebellion against the Porte and an alliance with Russia:

> the Turks, instead of performing the Treaty which was concluded for that End, did afterwards demolish our Castles, and caused the whole Country of Moldavia to be laid waste by the Tartars, upon frivolous Pretences.[80]

---

77 *Petru Rareș*, 247 (Chapter written by C. Rezachievici).

78 *Genealogia Cantacuzinilor*, 67–70. See also *Istoria politică și geografică a Țerei Romănesci*. 66.

79 Miron Costin, *Letopiseț*, 58.

80 PRUL, mf. EEN, *The British Mercury*. Numb. 209, from 23–25 July 1711, published recently in Viorel Panaite, *News in England on the Great Turkish War (1683–1699)*, Académie

A series of covenant violations was also listed by another author, Alexandru Beldiman.[81] Moreover, according to the Moldavian tradition, certain sixteenth-century rulers had rejected the Ottoman's increased financial demands, seeing them as breaches of the original covenants. Nicolae Costin, for instance, claimed that voivodes Petru Rareș and Petru the Lame gave up the throne as they were unwilling to accept an infringement on the ancient compacts with the Porte.[82]

A similar case took place in mid-seventeenth-century Transylvania and was narrated by Silahdar Fındıklılı Mehmed Ağa (d. 1723).[83] The Ottoman–Habsburg war of 1663–1664 led to a war of propaganda between Michael Apafy of Transylvania and Francisco Vesselenyi ("Palatine Bihuș"), appointed as the Habsburg governor of Middle Hungary. Both dignitaries tried to sway the inhabitants of the region, Apafy urging them "to obey to the Ottoman sultan," while Vesselenyi called for a revolt against the Porte. Trying to lure new adherents from among Transylvanian subjects, Vesselenyi emphasized the *'ahd* violations by Ottomans. He asked:

> Did the Ottomans keep their word and were they always true to their documents called imperial charters?[84]

No, the Hungarian dignitary replied, contrasting the position of the principality in the mid-seventeenth-century with that a century earlier, as well as comparing its current status with Wallachia and Moldavia's. The main arguments were similar to those invoked by the eighteenth-century Moldavian or Wallachian boyars. On the one hand, the sultan–voivode relationship became a completely obedient one:

---

Roumaine, Brăila: Institut d'Études Sud-Est Européennes, 2018, 186–189: Chapter "Dimitrie Cantemir's Manifesto – A Version from the English Press of 1711"). See also L. Boicu, *Principatele Române în raporturile politice internaționale (secolul al XVIII-lea)*, Iași: Ed. Junimea, 1986, 81.

81 Alexandru Beldiman, *Tractaturile prin care s-au închinatu țara de către Bogdan voevod, domnu al Moldovei, împărățind Bajazet al 2-lea, de Nicolae Costin/The covenants by which the voivode Bogdan, Hospodar of Moldavia, obeyed his country, during the Bayezid II's reign, by Nicolae Costin* (BAR, ms. 566, fol. 126v-136; published by M. Kogălniceanu in *Arhiva Românească*, 1845, vol. II, 347–364 and in Kogălniceanu, *Letopisețe*, III, 450–462).

82 Only Aron the Tyrant would "sign all the agreements by which the Turks wanted to charge with the people and the country" (cf. Giurescu, *Capitulațiile*, 10).

83 *Silahdar Tarihi* (*Zeyil-i Fezleke*), ms. in Bayezid Kütüphanesi, fd. Veliyüddin Efendi, no. 2369, 45r-v; ANIC, Bucharest, mf. Turkey, r. 23. On this annalist and his work, see *Cronici turcești II*, 287–290.

84 *Silahdar Tarihi*, in *Cronici turcești II*, 324.

> Think what situation was imposed in Transylvania by [the Turks]. In a short time, they have changed seven rulers in Transylvania. Let us look and realize the situation reached by Michael Apafy, prince of Transylvania! [...] He cannot do anything else than that ordered [by the Ottomans]. You, Apafy, called yourself the sovereign of Transylvania but actually you are not.

In Vesselenyi's view, the *ʿahdname*s granted to the Transylvanian princes were violated through a continuous increase of their tribute. The Palatine, clearly exaggerating, exhorted:

> How much was the tribute of Transylvania increased from the ancient times until our days![85]

As a last salvo, Vesselenyi brought up the deteriorating position of Transylvania in the seventeenth century:

> Although those of the country of Transylvania, trusting the Ottomans' word became their tribute-payers, they are not still happy. They will undoubtedly soon share the destiny of Wallachia and Moldavia.[86]

From the Ottoman standpoint, the changes that took place in the political and juridical status of Wallachia, Moldavia and Transylvania under Süleyman Kanunî (1520–1566) did not amount to a violation of pacts. This was particularly the case after 1538, when the Ottomans began to affirm the "right of the sword" (*kılıç hakkı*),[87] which provided the Porte with the authority to unilaterally decide on the status of its tributaries.[88] Their position of "annexes to the Well-Protected Domains" (*muzafat-ı Memalik-i mahrusa*),[89] part of the

85 The increase of the tribute was seen as a "treaty" violation by Moldavian scholar Dimitrie Cantemir, too (Cantemir, *Descrierea Moldovei*, 271).

86 *Silahdar Tarihi*, in *Cronici turcești II*, 324–325.

87 In 1559, Süleyman Kanunî claimed that "Wallachia and Moldavia are my countries and provinces, which were conquered and invaded with my sword – guide of victory" (*vilayet-i Eflak ve Boğdan benim şimşir-i zafer-rehberim ile feth ü-teshir olmuş memleket ü-vilayetimdir*) (Veliman, "Carte de legământ," 29).

88 According to Ibrahim Peçevi, after the campaign of 1538 "the Moldavia country entered under the rule of the Ottoman countries" (Peçevi, *Tarih*, in *Cronici turcești I*, 481).

89 In 1581, Transylvania was considered as "being one of the annexes of my Well-Protected Domains" (*Memalik-i mahrusam muzafatından olub*) (Veliman, "Carte de legământ," 36: *hüküm* of 3 July 1581 sent to the *beylerbeyi* of Buda); "Moldavia is one of the annexes of my

"Well-Protected Domains" (*Memalik-i mahrusa*)[90] or to the "properties in the sultan's inheritance" (*mülk-i mevrus*)[91] provided them with protection but also gave the sultan a right to interfere in their internal affairs and even allowed for territorial changes.

Romanian historians cited cession of Moldavian territories – in particular Bucovina and Bessarabia – as the most obvious instances of the Porte's disregard for its pacts with the principality. However, for the Ottoman authorities these decisions required no additional justification. Both in 1775, when the Porte negotiated with the Habsburgs over Bucovina, and during the 1812 talks with Russia, the matter of territorial concession was the subject of bilateral talks between Istanbul and its adversaries; Moldavian voivodes were denied a place at the negotiation table. In a document of 8 May 1775, incumbent grand vizier Izzet Mehmed paşa (1774–1775, first tenure) spoke only about "the frontiers and borders of both states' territories" and that it was the Porte that "left and conceded the specified territory" to the Habsburgs. With regard to the principalities' border with Transylvania – by then under Habsburg rule – Moldavian and Wallachian voivodes were merely instructed to "maintain the aforementioned border."[92]

## 5 Sanctions for Pact Violations

Failure to uphold the covenant and respective punishments by either Muslims or non-Muslims were stipulated by *şeri'at*. The punishments applied to non-Muslims that violated their *'ahds* can be categorized according to their

Well-Protected Domains" (*Memalik-i mahrusamız muzafatından Boğdan vilayeti*), Ahmed III affirmed in a 1692 letter sent to Khan Safa Giray (Gemil, *Documente turcești*, doc. 196).

90 "Moldavia, Wallachia and Transylvania are included in our countries and provinces like the other Well-Protected Domains which are under our own rule" – a 1572 letter by Selim II sent to King Sigismund II of Poland claimed (Mehmet, *Documente turcești*, I, doc. 103); "Wallachia is like all my other Well-Protected Domains" (*vilayet-i Eflak sayr Memalik-i mahrusam gibidir*), Osman II said in a 1618 *hüküm* (Gemil, *Documente turcești*, doc. 72).

91 In Süleyman Kanunî's letter of 1531, sent to King Sigismund I of Poland, the sultan affirmed that: "their possessions [Moldavia and Wallachia] belong to our other domains, with the same status as Bosna and Semendire, and constitute our property" (Hurmuzaki, *Documente*, Supl. II/1, doc. IX: text in Polish, with French translation). In 1808 Wallachia and Moldavia were still considered "properties of the Imperial heritage" (*mülk-i mevrus-ı şahane*) by Abdurahim Muhib Efendi, the Ottoman ambassador in Paris (Veliman, *Documente turcești*, doc. 237: document of 21 *Ramazan* 1223/10 November 1808).

92 *mahdud araziyi Devlet-i aliye Devlet-i imparatoriyeye feragat ve teslim ider* (Veliman, *Documente turcești*, doc. 173: *sened* of 7 *Rebi ül-evvel* 1189/8 May 1775).

juridical status. Juridical and historical sources carefully distinguish between sanctions for non-Muslim subjects (*zimmis*),[93] tributary princes, and rulers of sovereign states. All *fetva* collections contained a number of opinions regarding pact-breaking (*nakz-ı ʿahd*).[94] According to Hanafi legal theory, fixed penalties fell under the ruler's full discretion, which is confirmed by Colin Imber's study of Ebussuud Efendi's juridical opinions from the sixteenth century.[95]

Warnings to respect the agreements were constantly invoked to justify further sanctions in both Ottoman and Christian sources.[96] In this regard, the most frequent reference invoked in *ʿahdname*s granted to Christian princes was the verse

> Keep your agreement! Those who violate their agreement are responsible (*Kurʾan* XVII, 34).

It also appears in the imperial charter, granted in 1480–1481 to Moldavian voivode Stephen the Great.[97] The message sent by Mehmed I Çelebi to the Balkan princes in 1413 can also be considered such a warning:

> Tell your rulers that I grant peace and take peace to all of them. The God of peace will plot against those who plot against peace.[98]

93 In the *ʿahd* of 642 concluded with Isfahan, the penalties for tribute-payers were included in case they failed to fulfil their obligations: "But if you change anything, or if anyone among you changes anything and you do not hand him over, then you have no safe-conduct. If anyone insults a Muslim, he will be severely punished for it. If he strikes a Muslim, we shall kill him." (recorded by al-Tabari, in Lewis, *Islam*, I, 238). Considering the strong economic and administrative position of non-Muslim subjects (in Egypt, for instance), beginning with the rule of Harun al-Rashid (786–809), edicts were issued by caliphs to remind *zimmis* their duties assumed by the "Pact of ʿUmar" (*al-ʿahd al-ʿUmar*) (Morabia, *Ǧihad*, 435–436; Abel, "Djizya," 6; Turan, "Les souverains seldjoukides," 93; Vermeulen, "Dhimmis," 175–184).

94 See, for instance, the *fetva*s of the *şeyh ül-Islam* Zenbilli Ali Efendi (1503–1526) (*Fatava-yi ʿAli Efendi*, f. 73a-b, in SK, Fatih 2390).

95 Imber, *Ebu's-suʿud*, 89–94.

96 In Christian diplomatics, *pacta sunt servanda* was also invoked at the end of treaties, the phrase frequently complemented with oaths and penalties. This practice can be seen in the fifteenth-century commercial privileges granted to Brașov, whereby Wallachian voivodes insisted that the oaths be fulfilled (Tocilescu, *534 documente*, doc. 6: Radu Praznaglava, 17 May 1421; doc. 92: Basarab Laiotă, 11 July 1475).

97 Mehmet, *Documente turcești*, I, doc. 5.

98 Ducas, *Istoria*, XX/2.

The case of tributaries is particularly relevant for the political and juridical status of the tributary princes on the northern bank of the Danube. In the Hanafi view, the violation of a covenant by a non-Muslim tributary under the sultan's protection automatically led him to lose his status as a protected non-Muslim (*zimmi*) and become a "rebel."[99] In this respect, one can quote Abu Hanifa's opinion (in al-Mawerdi's commentary):

> Abu Hanifa says that if there is a Muslim in their territory, or there is a territory of Muslims between them and the *dar al-harb*, then it is treated as *dar al-Islam*, and those who have broken the agreement are treated as rebels. If there is no Muslim and no territory of Muslims between them and the *dar al-harb*, it is treated as *dar al-harb*. Abu Yusuf and Muhammad say that this territory is treated as *dar al-harb* in both cases.[100]

These statements provide a juridical explanation as to why Wallachia and Moldavia were sometimes considered as integral parts of the Abode of Islam, whereas Transylvania was several times described as belonging to the Abode of War.

There are some indications that until Süleyman Kanunî's reign the voivodes of Wallachia and Moldavia who did not respect their pacts with the Porte were considered "enemies" (*harbi*s). For instance, Vlad the Evil, following his attack on Silistre ceased to be an Ottoman tribute-payer (*haracgüzar*), and became "one of the villainous unbelievers."[101] Similarly, according to Tursun bey, the "Moldavian [Stephen the Great] became an enemy" on the eve of Bayezid II's campaign in 1484, because "he was careless in his obedience, and in paying the tribute."[102] Starting from the reign of Sultan Süleyman, the Wallachian, Moldavian and Transylvanian rulers became "rebels" whenever they tried to contest the sultanic authority.

In fact, the punishments for rebellion depended on the degree of the tributary's dependency on the Porte and the position of those spearheading the rebellion (the ruler, local elite, popular masses). Since the blame was usually put on the ruler, he was the first to face punishment by the Porte, usually leading to his dethronement. Until the mid-sixteenth century, the Ottomans merely

99 Referring especially to the Muslim rebels, Ibrahim al-Halebi said: "Rebels are those who revolts against the sovereign's authority, who rejects his orders or who attacks his properties by force." (D'Ohsson, *Tableau*, V, 101). For *hadis*, see Tarazi, "Statut personnel," 370.

100 Mawerdi, *Ahkam*, ed. Yate, 202.

101 Idris Bitlisi, *Heşt Behişt*, in *Cronici turceşti I*, 165.

102 Tursun bey, *Tarih*, in *Cronici turceşti I*, 76–77.

aimed at restoring the *status quo ante*, which necessitated military intervention. In the later period, given the strict control imposed by the Porte, the culprit was usually removed from the throne by a special envoy of the sultan with a military escort.

### 5.1 *Punitive Campaigns*

According to Koca Hüseyin, the violation of covenant by Mircea the Elder's successor led Mehmed I Çelebi to launch a "great holy war" against Wallachia, still described in this period as *dar al-harb*.[103] Later, in the late sixteenth century, Wallachia and Moldavia came to be considered "territories of Islam" and, accordingly, their voivodes' resistance to the Porte was labelled as a "rebellion." For instance, Ottomans regarded Michael the Brave as a "rebellious" prince (*Mihal-ı bed'fal*). The quelling of the rebellion became a hotly debated topic at the sultanic court; according to the opinion expressed by *şeyh ül-Islam* Bostanzade Mehmed Efendi, which eventually prevailed:

> removing the intrigues of the subjects who revolted in Islamic territories is more important than going up against the infidels of faraway enemy countries (*harbi küffar*).[104]

When the violation of pacts (*nakz-ı 'ahd*) was the result of a specific group rather than the whole population, only those guilty of rebellion were to be punished, and killed in case they refused to surrender; if they did, they were to be enslaved. Famous *şeyh ül-Islams' fetva* collections all included at least one juridical opinion referring to this topic.[105] Moreover, one source specifically addresses the issue in the context of protected subjects (*zimmis*) north of the Danube. The juridical opinion issued by *şeyh ül-Islam* Ebu-Işak Kara Ismail Na'im Efendi (1716–1718), and included in Ahmed III's *hüküm*, justified military reprisals against Wallachian tributaries (*haracgüzarlar*).[106] The irrevocable

103 Koca Hüseyin, *Beda'i ül-veka'i*, in *Cronici turcești* I, 447.

104 Obviously, this campaign was undertaken primarily with military concerns: "Therefore His Highness, the grand vizier, agreed [with Molla Efendi and] decided to go against Wallachia and Moldavia" (Selaniki, *Tarih*, in *Cronici turcești* I, 367). The punishment and, eventually, dethronement of "Michael the Rebel" (*Mihal-ı bed'fal*) were also demanded in 1598. Mehmed III ordered Ahmed paşa of Silistre to rally all soldiers: "to punish [the Wallachian prince] was an important matter of religion and state" (*Mihai. Documente*, I, doc. 75: *hakkından gelmesi mühimmat-i din ü-devletden olmağın*).

105 Ali Efendi Zenbilli, in office between 1503–1526: *Fetava-yi Ali Efendi*, SK, Fatih 2390, f. 73a–b. See also Ali Efendi Çatalcalı, in office in 1674–1686 and 1692: *Fetava-yi Ali Efendi*, neşreden Salih b. Ahmad Kefevi, Istanbul, 1272 AH/1855, 158.

106 Veliman, *Documente turcești*, doc. 24.

abrogation of *ʿahd* occurred if the Christian ruler colluded with rebel subjects; in this case, a military campaign was launched to punish all unbelievers, without exception.[107]

### 5.2 *Dethronement*

Dethronement (*ʿazl*) became the most ubiquitous punishment against tributary princes suspected of violating the *ʿahd*. It was implicitly included in the diploma of investiture (*berat*), particularly from the mid-sixteenth century onwards; the voivodes were considered individually and directly responsible. Under certain circumstances, dethronement could be followed by an execution (*katl*).

Even if they agreed to pay tribute, the Christian polities of Southeastern Europe were under constant threat of Ottoman *gaza* and ran the risk of being incorporated into the Abode of Islam. Thus, the tributary territories could be transformed into provinces ruled by Muslim governors, whenever such a solution was deemed more advantageous to the Ottoman interests and the sultan's troops were able to conquer the territory.[108] I will dwell more on this issue in chapter eleven, which is specifically devoted to tributary princes.

---

107 Armanazi, *Islam*, 75.

108 Following their two-decade existence as tributary polities, in 1393–1396 the tsardoms of Tarnovo and Vidin were "included in *dar al-Islam*" by Bayezid I (Idris Bitlisi, *Heșt Behișt*, in *Cronici turcești* I, 154; Sa'adeddin and Mehmed bin Mehmed, in *Cronici turcești* I, 300–301, 400–401). See also H. Inalcık, "Dar al-ʿahd," *EI-2*, 118–119; Decei, *Imp. otoman*, 133–134.

CHAPTER 10

# Customary Practices

Until this point, one can argue that both historians and jurists have dealt only with supposed long-term "covenants" and completely ignored the problem of custom in the relations between the Ottoman Empire and the principalities of Wallachia and Moldavia. This stands in stark contrast to the large number of extant sources originating from the Ottoman chancery. Thus, in the present chapter, my goal is to address this complex and ambiguous topic, investigating the role of custom in shaping the Porte's relations with Moldavia and Wallachia.

In 1656, Köprülü Mehmed paşa addressed the boyars of Wallachia in the following manner:

> You are tributary *re'aya* of the sultan; as long as you show obedience and allegiance, no viziers nor *beys* will be permitted to treat you as rebels and they are not allowed to ask you anything contrary to custom.[1]

This way, the grand vizier reminded the elite of Wallachia, including Voivode Constantin Șerban (1654–1658), of the necessity of paying homage to the sultan. What immediately draws our attention is the fact that the grand vizier cited no "pledge" (*'ahd*), "charter" (*'ahdname*) nor "diploma" (*berat*) but rather the "custom" established between Wallachian rulers and Ottoman sultans. This is not the only document to appeal to custom as the cornerstone framing tributary voivodes' rights and duties vis-à-vis the Ottoman authorities. Accordingly, the question arises as to whether custom, which constituted one of the formal sources of international law,[2] featured as the point of reference in Moldavian and Wallachian relations with the Porte. This is important given that twentieth-century criteria usually applied by scholars did not correspond to the realities on the ground in the early modern period. Thus, we should move away from looking at the topic through a modernist lens, and rather address it on its

1 Gökbilgin, "Relations turco-roumaines," 772.

2 On custom, see G. Gianni, *La coutume en droit international*, Paris: Editions A. Pedone, 1931; Ch. Rousseau, *Principes generaux du Droit international public, Tome I: Introduction, Sources*, Paris: Editions A. Pedone, 1944, 824–862; J. L. Brierly, *The Law of Nations. An Introduction to the International Law of Peace*, sixth edition, Oxford: Oxford University Press, 1963, 59–62; M. Virally, "The Sources of International Law," in *Manual of Public International Law*, edited by Max Sorensen, London, Melbourne, Toronto, New York: Macmillan, 1968, 116–175.

 DOI:10.1163/9789004411104_011

own terms. Applying such an anachronistic framework would distort the picture. We should steer away from abstract juridical concepts and instead examine the evidence regarding the role of custom in early modern Moldavian, Wallachian and Transylvanian relations with the Porte, the prominence of customary norms and their limitations in the eyes of Ottoman authorities. In other words, it is crucial to examine whether the alleged custom meant a practice accepted as a law.

## 1 Customary Practices in Historical Sources

Early modern sources are of particular interest because they provide a large number of cases – vastly outnumbering those of the previous period – that refer to custom. They can be boiled down to three distinct categories: information regarding ceremonial practice that shaped the relationship between voivodes and the Porte; recognition of the political, military and financial duties of tributary voivodes; reinforcement of specific rules pertaining to the autonomy of Wallachia, Moldavia and Transylvania.

First, Ottoman authorities and tributary voivodes resorted to custom in connection with a number of ceremonial practices and norms regarding payments between the two. For instance, when Simion Movilă (1601–1602) was confirmed on the Wallachia throne, Mehmed III (1595–1603) bestowed upon him the insignia of investiture: banner, cap and other objects, sent "according to the old habit."[3] In a similar manner, the imperial charter of July 1614, granted to the Transylvanian nobility on the occasion of Gabriel Bethlen's confirmation as the ruler of the principality, mentioned:

> and as it has been used from old times (*ve kadimden verilegelen*) to give those who became rulers of Transylvania banner and standard and sceptre and mantle on the part of my Porte of Felicity, shall henceforward give, too.[4]

Issuing a diploma of investiture[5] became a lavish ceremony in its own right. Wallachian voivode Ștefan Cantacuzino (1714–1716) was keenly aware of the custom when on 25 April 1714 he wrote to Patriarch Hrisant Nottara that an

3 Mehmet, *Documente turcești*, I, doc. 152.

4 Gemil, *Documente turcești*, doc. 61.

5 On *berat*, see: Sertoğlu, *ROTA*, 42; L. Fekete, "Berat," *EI-2*, I, 1205–1206; Matei, "Domination ottomane," 77.

Ottoman *haseki ağa* arrived from Istanbul with an imperial *berat* and mantle "in accordance with tradition" (in Romanian, *după obiceiu*).[6] Similarly, Wallachian and Moldavian agents (*kapu-kethudaları, charges d'affaires*),[7] reminded Sultan Selim III (1789–1807) "the custom (*muʿtad*) of granting the high *berat* to the voivodes of Wallachia and Moldavia."[8]

Custom was also invoked as a juridical source with regard to the payments that tributary princes – along with other Ottoman dignitaries – paid upon their appointment (*ca'ize-yi voyvodalık*); annual and triennial payments upon reconfirmation (*ca'ize-yi mukarrer* or *ıbka* in the eighteenth century); on religious *bayram* festivities (*bayramlık* or *idiye* in the eighteenth century), and upon the nomination of certain high-ranking positions (*kudumiye* in the eighteenth century).[9] In an order issued in 1716, Ahmed III referred to "the tax of reign which is given according to custom" (*muʿtad üzere verilegelen ca'ize-yi voyvodalık*) offered by Nicolae Mavrocordat upon his first appointment in Wallachia.[10] An Ottoman register of 1759 mentions "revenues" (*ava'idleri*) high-ranking officials of the Porte received upon the confirmation of Moldavian and Wallachian voivodes, "in conformity with custom" (*muʿtad üzere*). Other entries in the same document list the gifts the Moldavian ruler delivered on *bayram* "according to custom" (*muʿtad üzere*).[11] Finally, an official chronicle of Constantin Brâncoveanu's reign, penned by Radu Greceanu, informs us that the voivode "presents in accordance with custom" (*plocoane după obiceiu*) on the occasion of the grand vizier appointments in 1697 and 1702.[12]

Second, most records invoked custom as an argument to legitimize the political, military and financial duties of the tributaries. Sultans and grand viziers frequently demanded the voivodes act "according to tradition" (*muʿtad uzere, ʿadet üzere*) or "as it was used from ancient times" (*kadimden edegelduği üzere*).

6 Hurmuzaki, *Documente*, XVI/1, doc. DLXXXIV.

7 For details on these officials, see A. H. Golimas, *Despre Capuchehăile Moldovei și Poruncile Porții către Moldova până la 1829*, Iași: Tipografia Ligii Culturale, 1943; Ion Matei, *Reprezentanții diplomatici (capuchehăi) ai Țării Românești la Poarta otomană*, București: Editura Academiei Române, 2008; Panaite, *Război, pace și comerț în Islam*, 378–398.

8 Veliman, *Documente turcești*, doc. 218.

9 Veliman, *Documente turcești*, 763, 767, 773; Sertoğlu, *ROTA*, 182, 215; Mehmet, "1792. O Carte de lege," 692; Maxim, "Regimul economic," 1744–1748.

10 *Hüküm* of *evasıt-ı Şevval* 1128/28 September–7 October 1716 (Veliman, *Documente turcești*, doc. 20). See also doc. 69.

11 Document of 14 *Zilkade* – *gayet-i Zilhicce* 1172/9 July–24 August 1759 (Veliman, *Documente turcești*, doc. 139). See also doc. 13.

12 Greceanu, *Istoria*, 121, 141.

The tribute (*harac* or *cizye*)[13] paid by the voivodes was by far their most important duty. In effect, the Ottoman authorities often demanded that *harac* be sent to Istanbul "according to the old habit" (*muʿtad kadim üzere*). For instance, Mehmed III wrote to the Polish king, warning Ieremia Movilă (1595–1606) that "at the time established by custom, the usual tribute should be sent according to old practices." Similarly, the chronicler Mustafa Selaniki confirmed that the tribute establish according to *şeri'at* was paid by the Moldavian voivode "in conformity with the old tradition."[14] Later, in 1663 Mehmed IV referred to the tribute payment in the same manner, ordering the Transylvanian prince Michael Apafy to send it to the Porte of Felicity alongside the hardworking nobles "in accordance with the old habit" (*muʿtad kadim üzere*).[15] The final example comes from the beginning of the eighteenth century and is well-represented in Ottoman and Wallachian sources. A document from 1714 mentioned that Ștefan Cantacuzino would receive the investiture diploma provided that the tribute would be paid and sent in time "in accordance with the old custom" (*mut'tad kadim uzere*).[16]

Moldavian and Wallachian sources also indicate that the tribute (*birul* in Romanian) was paid "according to custom" (*după obiceiu*), that voivodes' messengers brought to Istanbul "the customary tax" (*obișnuita dajdie*) or "the usual tribute" (*haraciul obișnuit*).[17] A similar customary practice resurfaces in sixteenth- and seventeenth-century Ragusan *ʿahdname*s, which set the ceiling on the tribute that the Porte could demand from the republic at 12,500 *filori*:

> They shall send every year, in accordance with [the] old custom, the twelve thousand five hundred pieces of gold (*filori*), which they have sent since olden days to our Court, the seat of Glory, with their envoys. More *harac* than the aforementioned 12,500 *filori* shall not be demanded.[18]

Voivodes' obligation to participate in sultanic campaigns was also interpreted as a "custom" in seventeenth- and eighteenth-century sources. In 1663, Prince Michael Apafy received an order to join Köprülüzade Ahmed paşa's Hungarian campaign, which – as the document stated – "your predecessors used to do"

13 On tribute, see Cl. Cahen, A. K. S. Lambton, C. Orhonlu, "Kharadj," *EI-2*, IV, 1062–1087.

14 Hurmuzaki, *Documente*, Supl. II/1, doc. CCX; Selaniki, *Tarih*, in *Cronici turcești I*, 385.

15 Document of on *eva'il-i Zilka'de* 1073/ 7–16 June 1663 (Gemil, *Documente turcești*, doc. 136).

16 Document of *gürre-i Cemazi ül-ahir* 1126/ 14 June 1714 (Veliman, *Documente turcești*, doc. 13).

17 Gemil, *Documente turcești*, doc. 106; Veress, *Documente*, II, doc. 249; III, doc. 125; Hurmuzaki, *Documente*, Supl. I/1, doc. LVII, CCV.

18 Biegman, *Ragusa*, 57, 126–131.

(*eslafin edegeldüği üzere*).[19] Similarly, in 1707, Ahmed III reminded Antioh Cantemir that Moldavian rulers had taken part in person during Rumelian campaigns "since old times" (*zaman-i kadimden berü*).[20] In 1736, Mahmud I ordered Constantin Mavrocordat to equip soldiers "on the strength of old customs" (*mu'tad kadime*), since Wallachian rulers were obliged to participate in the European campaigns of the empire.[21]

The practice of sending hostages to the Porte to ensure their loyalty to the sultan was also considered a long-standing custom, recorded since at least the first half of the fifteenth century.[22] The earliest description of this practice as a "traditional" one, dates from Neagoe Basarab's reign in Wallachia (1512–1521): the voivode is said to have sent his son to Istanbul as a hostage "in accordance with the habit" (*cum e datina*).[23] In his 1656 order to the Wallachian boyars, Grand Vizier Köprülü Mehmed paşa also referred to the practice of paying homage to the sultan as a "custom."[24]

Gifts (*pişkeş, ava'id* or *bedaya*) delivered along with the tribute were also described as "customary" and feature frequently in diplomas and orders dispatched to the voivodes. For instance, the *berat*s granted to Wallachian voivode Mihnea II in 1577 and 1585, as well as Alexandru Iliaș in 1620,[25] clearly state that the sultans – along with tribute – expected to receive "what was usually given from old times" (*kadimden verilegelen nesneleri*). The same applied to gifts for some high-ranking Ottoman officials, including the grand vizier and the *beylerbeyi* of Rumeli, which were to receive "what had been given to them until now [...], according to old custom."[26] In a *hüküm* appointing Constantin Brâncoveanu to the Wallachian throne in 1688, Süleyman II reminded him that one of his duties was to send, besides tribute, presents "which you must give in accordance with the custom" (*mu'tad üzere hedayani*).[27] Even the agreements reached in 1687 between Grand Vizier Siyavuş paşa and the Transylvanian envoys included a stipulation that the embassy should provide each year gifts to the Porte, "according to old custom" (*mu'tad-ı kadim*

19 Gemil, *Documente turcești*, doc. 136.

20 *Hüküm* of *eva'il-i Zilhicce* 1118/ 6–15 March 1707 (Gemil, *Documente turcești*, doc. 230).

21 *Hüküm* of *evasıt-ı Rebi ül-evvel* 1149/ 20–29 July 1736 (Veliman, *Documente turcești*, doc. 79).

22 For Moldavia, see Golimas, *Capuchehăi*, 23–25.

23 Hurmuzaki, *Documente*, vol. XIV/1, doc. DCLXXX.

24 Gökbilgin, "Relations turco-roumaines," 772.

25 Gemil, "Doc. XVI-XVII," 353–356; Maxim, *CTO*, doc. 14; Feridun, *Munşe'at*, II, 398–399.

26 I am quoting from the *berat* granted to Mihnea II in 1577 (Gemil, "Doc. XVI-XVII," 353–356).

27 *Hüküm* of *evahir-i Muharrem* 1100/ 15–24 November 1688 (Gemil, *Documente turcești*, doc. 180).

*üzere*).[28] Although these documents represent the Ottoman authorities' interpretation, other sources show that the Moldavian and Wallachian stance did not differ significantly. Matei Basarab in 1649–1650, Constantin Brâncoveanu in 1711 and Ștefan Cantacuzino in 1714 also referred to gifts presented "in conformity with custom" (*'adet üzere*).[29] Apart from the members of the sultanic court and imperial administration, customary gifts were also sent to the Crimean khans and other members of the Giray dynasty. In 1720, Ahmed III instructed Moldavian voivode Mihai Racoviță to send his presents "which are given in conformity with custom" (*mu'tad üzere verilegelen*).[30]

A particular case in this respect constituted falcons delivered to the sultan as gifts. They were first mentioned as a "custom" as early as 1523, when the envoy of Moldavian voivode Ștefăniță delivered the birds of prey to Sultan Süleyman "according to tradition."[31] In 1564, the Wallachian voivode presented the same ruler with a falcon and eight horses "in conformity with an old custom."[32] Transylvanian authorities also conformed to the practice and in 1583 offered the *padişah* five falcons.[33] Two centuries later, a *hüküm* to Alexandru Moruzi is somewhat surprising in stating that twenty-five falcons should be gathered and sent to the Porte, since "there is an old custom" (*mu'tad-ı kadim olmağla*) regarding the annual supply of falcons from Wallachia.[34]

At the same time, "custom" – as juridical source – increasingly underpinned sultanic orders regarding the supply of Istanbul and Ottoman troops with foodstuffs and other goods. A *hüküm* of 11 August 1593 mentioned that "from ancient times it has been a custom" to procure mounts from the principalities for the imperial stables. Little over two decades later, Ahmed I ordered the Moldavian voivode to send, "according to the custom" (*olunageldüği üzere*), 500 horses to the Imperial fleet, along with 1000 skins, 300 *kantar* beeswax (*balmumu*), 500 *kantar* tallow (*donyağı*) to Istanbul.[35]

---

28 *Temessük* of 1 *Safer* 1099/ 7 December 1687 (Gemil, *Documente turcești*, doc. 178).

29 Gemil, *Documente turcești*, doc. 122; Mehmet, *Documente turcești*, I, doc. 201. See also *Dicționarul limbii române literare vechi (1640–1780)*, eds. M. Costinescu, M. Georgescu, F. Zgraon, Bucharest: Ed. Științifică și Enciclopedică, 1987, 222.

30 *Hüküm* of *evahir-i Receb* 1132/ 29 May – 7 June 1720 (Veliman, *Documente turcești*, doc. 40. See, also, the document from October–November 1725 (Veliman, *Documente turcești*, doc. 53). For Wallachian gifts-giving, see Gemil, *Documente turcești*, doc. 202.

31 CSISD, 402.

32 Iorga, *Istoria poporului românesc*, 418.

33 Veress, *Documente*, II, 257.

34 Veliman, *Documente turcești*, doc. 211.

35 Maxim, "Regimul economic," 1749–1758 (for 1593 *hüküm*); Gemil, *Documente turcești*, doc. 64 (for 1615 *hüküm*).

Third, "custom" provided a juridical basis that shielded voivodes and boyars from infringements and transgressions committed by Ottoman officials, troops and subjects from adjacent provinces. Among many such records, it is worth providing several examples of what was considered to be "contrary to custom" (*kadime muhalif*) or "opposite to what has been done" (*olagelmişe muhalif*): forcible seizing of lakes that had belonged to Moldavia in 1609 (*olagelmişe muhalif*); violence committed by *sipahi*s and janissaries against Wallachian merchants in 1614–1615 (*olagelmişe muhalif*); Tatar raids across the Dniester into Moldavian lands in 1608 and 1632–1633 (*hilaf-ı ʿadet*); Ottoman infringements of the Transylvanian border in Temeşvar and Lipova in 1634 (*hilaf-ı muʿtad*);[36] raids against Wallachia and forcible seizure of certain lands in 1744 (*kadime mugayir*); Tatar occupation of Moldavian lands in 1721 (*kadime mugayir*).[37] The list can be further extended and references to custom abound throughout the sources.

## 2 Terminology of Sources

In Ottoman annals and chancery sources various words and phrases were used to describe long-term practices and established customs. Among the first we come across, we find the Arabic terms *ʿadet*, *muʿtad* and *kadim*.

In its literal sense, *kadim* means "old, ancient, yore," and features frequently in expressions such as *kadimden*, *kadim ül-eyyamdan* or *zaman-i kadimden berü*, all of which carry the meaning "since the days of yore." At the same time, the notion of *kadim* appears in the adjectival sense along with other words describing custom, such as in *muʿtad-ı kadim üzere*, *ʿadet-i kadim üzere* ("according to old custom"). In some instances, the word translates directly as custom or tradition, such as in *kadime muhalif* or *kadime mugayir* ("contrary to custom").[38]

*Muʿtad* is another term meaning "customary, habitual, usual habit or custom," which was abundantly used in Ottoman records, such as in the phrases *muʿtad uzere* ("in accordance with custom"), *muʿtaddan ziyade* ("more than custom"), or *hılaf-ı muʿtad* ("contrary to custom").[39]

---

36 Gemil, *Documente turceşti*, doc. 30, 49, 62, 97, 99.

37 Veliman, *Documente turceşti*, doc. 43, 110.

38 Gemil, *Documente turceşti*, doc. 54, 68, 76, 81, 90, 104, 106, 150 (*kadimden berü*); Veliman, *Documente turceşti*, doc. 13, 16, 38, 43, 49, 53, 73, 110, 112, 129, 134 (*ez-kadim*), 145 (*mugayir-ı kadim*), 151, 195, 211, 230 etc; *Redhouse*, 577.

39 Gemil, *Documente turceşti*, doc. 99; Veliman, *Documente turceşti*, doc. 20, 40, 47, 69, 82, 86, 139; *Redhouse*, 802.

*ʿAdet* carries the meaning of custom, practice, or habit, but also a tax or duty. In my research, I have also come across it being applied to the internal practices within the principalities, such as in the phrases *ʿadet-i beled üzere* ("according to the custom of the land") and *hilaf-i ʿadet-i beled* ("contrary to the custom of the land"). In other situations, *ʿadet* was used for certain taxes and customary duties in the relations between principalities and the Porte. For instance, the former owed an *ʿadet* for the Imperial Kitchen. This Arabic term was widespread enough as to permeate into Romanian language and historical narratives of the period.[40]

Certain Ottoman documents also utilize the Persian term *ayin* to describe internal customs within the principalities, usually as *kadim ayin* ("old custom"), and traditions established in relationship with the Porte.[41]

Finally, several verbs in their continuous form were frequently employed by Ottoman scribes in the sense of "custom." This grammatical structure joined the verb *gelmek* (to come) to the root of *olmak* (to be), *etmek* (to do) or *vermek* (to give, to pay), such as in the phrases *olagelmişe muhalif* ("contrary to custom" or "contrary to what used to be"), *olageldüği üzere* ("according to custom" or "according to what used to be"), or *kadimden edegeldüği üzere* ("as was the practice since days of yore").[42]

It is also worth noting that in Wallachian and Moldavian chronicles and documents, the words *obiceiu, obicina, datina* meaning custom, habit, or tradition were used specifically to designate customary practices.[43]

## 3 A Typology of Customary Practices

First, it is necessary to see whether established practices frequently mentioned in interstate politics of this period also applied to the relationship between the Porte and its tributaries from the fourteenth until the mid-sixteenth century. In other words, my goal in this section is to examine whether the political,

40 Mehmet, *Documente turcești*, I, doc. 151; Gemil, *Documente turcești*, doc. 99; Veliman, *Documente turcești*, doc. 68, 126; *Redhouse*, 14. The Moldavian chronicler Grigore Ureche mentions "adet of country" (*adetul țării*) (Ureche, *Letopiseț*, 161). See also, Georgescu, "Coutume," 562–563.

41 Maxim, *CTO*, doc. 14; Gemil, *Documente turcești*, doc. 68; *Redhouse*, 104.

42 Gemil, *Documente turcești*, doc. 49, 62, 68, 76, 81, 86, 136 (*olagelene muhalefat*), 84 (*olubgelene muhalif*); M. Maxim, *Limba turco-osmană*, Bucharest: Editura Universității din București, 1984, 143.

43 Ureche, *Letopiseț*, 135, 161; Neculce, *Letopiseț*, 355–356; *Genealogia Cantacuzinilor*, 219, 540–541.

diplomatic and juridical framework of the latter corresponded to the wider practices of this period.[44]

Secondly, we have to take into account the influence of local traditions in each of the principalities, described as "customs of the land" (in Romanian, *obiceiurile țării*) and their role in maintaining Moldavia and Wallachia's autonomous status. Sources clearly show that the observance of the "custom of the land" was a fundamental condition required by voivodes and nobility when they negotiated with the Ottomans. Accordingly, the sultans sanctioned the principle of the inviolability of the "old customs and rules" (*kadim ayin ve 'adeti*) in the investiture diplomas granted to Moldavian and Wallachian rulers.[45] Sixteenth- and seventeenth-century Transylvanian *'ahdname*s also include safeguards protecting established customs. For instance, on Gabriel Bethlen's confirmation to the throne in July 1614, Ahmed I committed himself not to change

> the rite and regime and rules and religion, as well as the usual habits which have been practiced by them from ancient times (*aralarında cari olan 'adetlerin*).[46]

The "custom of the country," defined by Mihai Cantacuzino as the "habits which had been in practice before the country's enslavement by the Turks,"[47] subsequently became the primary juridical argument invoked against Ottoman abuses throughout the early modern period.

On the other side, it is impossible to ignore Ottoman customary practices, which – either forcibly or peacefully – were introduced and followed in the Porte's dealings with Moldavian and Wallachian rulers. This evolution began in the second half of the sixteenth century, when sultans began to regard Wallachia, Moldavia and Transylvania as Ottoman provinces, and their voivodes as governors (*bey*). Therefore, several Ottoman practices gradually made their appearance in relations with the tributary princes, ranging from ceremonies at voivodes' appointments[48] to taxes and presents given to Ottoman officials (*pișkeș, ca'ize-yi mukarrer*), *bayram* celebrations, or replacement of the Ottoman high ranking officials in their posts (*kudumiye*).

44 See François L. Ganshof, *Histoire des relations internationales,* ed. Pierre Renouvin. vol. I: *Le Moyen Age*, Paris: Hachette, 1953, 36–54, 119–156, 263–302.

45 Maxim, *CTO*, doc. 14; Feridun, *Munșe'at*, II, 398–399; Gemil, "Doc. XVI-XVII," 353–356.

46 Gemil, *Documente turcești*, doc. 61, 101.

47 *Genealogia Cantacuzinilor*, 219.

48 The case of the Moldavian voivode Ștefan Lăcustă (1538–1540) is mentioned by Ibrahim Peçevi (*Cronici turcești I*, 481).

Our interest focuses on bilateral traditions, which – according to Paul Guggenheim – apply when relations between neighboring states are not regulated by fixed rules but rather practice.[49] Without any doubt, this was the case with Moldavian–Polish relations. The conclusion of treaties between these polities in the fifteenth century on the one hand proved the existence of certain bilateral practices, while at the same time reinforcing them. A pact concluded between Stephen the Great and King Casimir IV on 4 April 1459 concluded:

> And the king is obliged to support and to protect us just like one of his subjects, according to the old custom (*iuxta consuetudinem antiquam*).[50]

Documents prove that customary practices permeated the relationship between the imperial center and the territories on the northern bank of the Danube. These included, on the one hand, rights and duties that had been in place for a long time, which began to be perceived primarily as customary practices, and were even sometimes included in charters and diplomas granted to the tributary princes. This was the case in 1589, when Transylvanian prince Sigismund Báthory stated that, to retain the throne and secure Ottoman protection, "we were accustomed to pay tribute."[51] On the other hand, a majority of practices cited in such documents regulated the voivodes' burden, the period mandated for delivering the tribute and the method of payment. For instance, the aforementioned document of 1793 not only stated that falcons should be delivered to the Porte, but also stated their number.[52] In my opinion, the records indicate the existence of certain practices accepted as laws for a longer or shorter interval.

## 4 Defining Custom

Jurists draw a clear distinction between legal customs and those remaining beyond the bounds of juridical discourse, which are seen as compulsory rules

49 Guggenheim, *Droit*, I, 109: *les situations où les rapports entre Etats voisins ne sont pas régis par des règles formulées avec precision, mais largements commandées par la pratique.*

50 *CSISD*, II, 435.

51 Veress, *Documente*, III, doc. 125.

52 Veliman, *Documente turcești*, doc. 211.

by their executors.[53] In Ottoman and Moldavian–Wallachian sources, custom was generally taken for granted as a reflection of practice established since time immemorial.

*Vetustas* ("long existence") was the determining feature of customary practices and held true for medieval Christendom,[54] as well as in the later period when European law underwent evident evolution. In the Ottoman sources, "old" or "oldness" (*eski, kadim*) were the most frequent attributes which characterized a usage, and it was referred to repetitive actions, whose origins could be traced. In her analysis of the role of "ancient" customs in petitions of sixteenth and seventeenth century, Suraiya Faroqhi pointed out that their authors traced them back to the distant past. The past played a considerable role even when the issue at hand was relatively new, such as in the case of establishing coffee-houses.[55]

## 5 Mechanism of Custom Formation

Jurists usually define custom as a "continuous practice." Therefore, for a customary rule to form, repetition is necessary, the minimal condition being a precedent.[56] As Suraiya Faroqhi noted, in the Ottoman Empire, as well as in medieval and early modern Europe

> one of the most powerful means of legitimating any kind of practice was by saying that it had a precedent.[57]

Sources inform us about one of the mechanisms that allowed for new practices to emerge and entrench themselves in relationship between the Porte and its tributaries north of the Danube, particularly the introduction of new obligations and the growing burden of older ones. This process began in the second

53 Gianni, *Coutume*, 14; Rousseau, *Droit*, 9–11. On this meaning of custom, see Valentin Al. Georgescu, "Le rôle de la théorie romano-byzantine de la coutume dans le dévelopement du droit féodal roumain," in *Mélanges Philippe Meylan*, Lausanne: Imprimerie centrale, 1963, 66, n. 23.

54 Guggenheim, *Droit*, I, 94–100; Keith Thomas, *Religion and the Decline of Magic*, Harmondsworth: Penguin, 1978, 461–517.

55 Faroqhi, "Ottoman taxpayers," 5–6.

56 Gianni, *Coutume*, 120–132 ("instant custom"); Rousseau, *Droit*, 836–837; J. Kunz, "The Nature of Customary International Law," *AJIL*, 47, 1953, 666; Geamanu, *Drept*, I, 93–95).

57 Faroqhi, "Ottoman taxpayers," 5–6. See also the papers from the collected volume *Legitimazing the Order: The Ottoman Rhetoric of State Power*, H. T. Karakete, M. Reinkowski (eds.), Leiden: Brill, 2005.

half of the sixteenth century[58] and resumed in the eighteenth century. In these instances, the precedent could originate from one of two directions: either the sultan's order[59] or the voivode's initiative.

On the one hand, the fierce competition between pretenders to the throne led to the rise of traditional obligations, the adoption of certain Ottoman practices and even the assumption of new duties, thus setting the precedent for the future. In a *hüküm* from 8 November 1592, Murad III requested – along with the tribute – the Wallachian voivode Alexandru to collect and pay his *vergi* (gift, tax), in accordance with the custom (*ʿadet üzere*). However, in this particular case, the sultan did not hesitate to refer to the precedent. A decade prior, Voivode Mihnea II the Renegade had promised to pay his dues. Thus, in just ten years, a voluntary gift (in Romanian *dar*, *plocon*) had transformed into a permanent customary tax.

A similar case can be found in a petition (*ʿarz*) by an unidentified Wallachian voivode filed at the Porte in the second half of the sixteenth century. According to its contents, the voivode's predecessor – likely Mircea the Shepherd (three-time ruler between 1545 and 1559), "had decided to give something for the imperial kitchen." Soon, the Ottoman court invoked this gift as a precedent, demanding that the voivode send "the tax for the imperial kitchen" (*mutbah-ı amire ʿadet*).[60]

On the other side, Ottoman practices or new duties could be introduced by means of imperial orders (*hüküm*). Generally, the scope of an order was limited to the matter at hand, or its validity was constrained by the lifespan of incumbent rulers. However, this could be extended and tacitly adopted as a custom. Thus, recurrent implementation transformed a single order into a customary rule.

This evolution was made possible if the voivodes adhered to the original order and upheld its validity. Although there is no doubt that their consent was not necessarily just a matter of verbal persuasion, the use of force was by no means specific to the Porte's relationship with its tributaries. Entangled in a fierce struggle for the throne, pretenders usually disregarded the potential legal consequences of their concessions. At the same time, voivodes and elites of the principalities were aware that every weakness could turn against them and

58 Maxim, "Regimul economic," 1731–1765.

59 On the relation between *örf-i ʿadet* (*lex principis*) and *kanun* in the Ottoman Law, see H. Inalcık, "Osmanlı Hukukuna Giriş. Örf-i Sultani Hukuk ve Fatihin Kanunları," *AÜSBFD*, XIII, 2, 1958, 102–126; M. A. Mehmet, "Legislaţia otomană (*Kanunname*) ca factor de organizare a societăţii balcanice. (Consideraţii generale)," *CICSEE*, V, 1988, 84–97.

60 Mehmet, *Documente turceşti*, I, doc. 151.

their descendants, as the Porte displayed a tendency to transform every concession into a custom. Thus, the Moldavian chronicler Grigore Ureche noted:

> It goes the same with the Turk, the more you give him, the more he asks, for he takes the gift for a custom, and afterwards should you not give him, he still obliges you to do so.[61]

Precisely for this reason, the Moldavian voivode Petru the Lame preferred to abandon his throne in 1591 rather than agree to new financial demands.[62] In Ureche's eyes, Moldavia would have been able to satisfy the sultan's claim only once, but this would constitute a serious threat,

> that [the duty] becomes a custom, which will not be abolished and after [the Porte] takes [the duty, new practices] will be established.[63]

We find a similar stance among Transylvanian nobility, although it managed to implement a clever policy to resist Ottoman demands. In a letter from 30 June 1583, they informed Stephen Báthory of their unwillingness to send more than five falcons (the number demanded by the sultan) "so that it does not become a custom for us."[64]

## 6 Evolution of Custom

To define custom, jurists frequently return to the notion of "evolutionary practice."[65] As Suraiya Faroqhi pointed out:

> using the past as a standard did not necessarily result in a condemnation of every new initiative, even when a religiously debatable kind of innovation.[66]

In the case of the Porte's relationship to its northern Danubian tributaries, some practices displayed considerable consistency, while others remained

61 Ureche, *Letopiseț*, 135.

62 Nicolae Costin, *Letopiseț*, 252.

63 Ureche, *Letopiseț*, 161–162.

64 Veress, *Documente*, II, 257.

65 Rousseau, *Droit*, 824–826.

66 Faroqhi, "Ottoman taxpayers," 6.

highly unstable. These divergences depended on the evolution of historical context, but also originated from the juridical differences between Muslims and non-Muslims. Issues regarding the burden of duties (in money or in kind) were subject to frequent changes, reaching their peak during the Phanariot period. Thus, eighteenth-century petitions and Ottoman documents frequently employed expressions claiming that "more than is customarily due" (*muʿtaddan ziyade*). For instance, in 1716 Nicolae Mavrocordat offered 15,000 *guruş* "over what was the custom" (*muʿtaddan ziyade*) upon his appointment to the throne of Wallachia (*mukarrer caʾizesi*), whereas the "old custom" (*muʿtad-ı kadim*) stipulated the payment of merely 30,000 *guruş*. In 1725, Voivode Mihai Racoviță of Moldavia brought a complaint to the sultan against the Crimean khan, who had demanded presents (*avaʾiet*) "more than the old custom stipulated" (*kanun-ı kadimden ziyade*).[67] The result was a permanent uncertainty over the rights and obligations specific to tributary status in relation to the Ottoman authorities. In this respect, a Wallachian boyars' opinion about the position of their polity in 1770 is significant:

> Due to the Turks' many iniquities such as infringements and the voivodes' frequent changes, the country was affected by so great a disorder, that it has not been able to keep either the old practices, or those which had been established about fifty years ago.[68]

## 6.1 *From Customs to Nizams*

A wide variety of rules concerning self-government was generally described as the "order of the land" (*nizam-ı memleket*) in the seventeenth and eighteenth centuries, and included the retention of *voyvodalık*, collection of the poll-tax, protection of Wallachian and Moldavian territories and subjects against the abuses of Ottoman administration, the conditions of commerce and the legal status of Moldavian and Wallachian subjects while in Ottoman lands.[69]

The extant *hüküm*s show that Ottoman subjects, particularly merchants and soldiers from adjacent territories of Hotin, Ibrail, Özü, Bender (Tighina) and Tarnovo were banned from entering Wallachia and Moldavia without an

67 Veliman, *Documente turcești*, doc. 47, 53, 69.

68 *Genealogia Cantacuzinilor*, 461.

69 Alexandrescu, "Khatt-ı şerif," 259–262; G.G. Florescu, "L'aspect juridiques des khatt-i chérifs. Contributions à l'étude des relations de l'Empire Ottoman avec les Principautés roumaines," *SAO*, I, 1958, 121-147.

imperial permission.[70] In a report of 1691 written by the *kadı* of Tarnovo, Ahmed Reşid, we read that:

> the interdiction of permitting to somebody from the vicinity to enter without order the countries of Moldavia and Wallachia was part of the order of the country.[71]

This regulation was announced to the Muslims of Tarnovo, by reading of the sultan's order and grand vizier's letter, which were subsequently copied in the *sicill*s.

This process of the establishment of a custom can be seen clearly in the case of three-year tenure for the voivodes in the eighteenth century, which quickly came to be considered "rule and regulation" (*ka'ide ve nizam*).[72] Finally, documents of 1776 and 1812 spoke about the regulation (*nizam*) of collecting of tribute (*cizye*) from the principalities.[73]

After 1774, local boyars put forward numerous claims in order to strengthen the distinctiveness of the Romanian principalities as political entities. As a consequence, the sultans confirmed the above-mentioned customary practices by imperial orders and laws, that is, by documents that were used to regulate the internal affairs of the empire – thus making it clear that they considered Moldavia and Wallachia to be Ottoman tributary provinces.[74] These included the *hatt-ı şerif*s of 1774, the *sened* of 1784, the *ferman*s of 1791 and 1792, the *kanunname* of 1793, and the *hattı-şerif*s of 1802, 1806 and 1826.[75] As a direct consequence of the local boyars' petitions and the Treaty of Küçük-Kaynarca

---

70 *Eflak ve Boğdan memleketlerine etrafdan kimesnenin bila-ferman duhuluna ruhsat verilmesi eğerçi nizam-ı memleketden olub* (Gemil, *Documente turcești*, doc. 190). See also Veliman, *Documente turcești*, doc. 41, 143, 148, 158 174, 184 (documents from 1720, 1760–1761, 1766, 1775, 1782).

71 Report of 6 *Receb* 1102/ 5 April 1691 (Gemil, *Documente turcești*, doc. 190). See also Veliman, *Documente turcești*, doc. 143, 148 (*memleket-i mezburenin bu def'a virilen nizamın istikrar ve istimrarı içün*), 158 (*memleket-i Boğdan'ın nizam-ı kadimi*).

72 Veliman, *Documente turcești*, doc. 120 (*hüküm* of 1749).

73 Veliman, *Documente turcești*, doc. 176, 241.

74 Panaite "The Legal and Political Status," 33.

75 Mehmet, *Documente turcești*, I, doc. 292; II, doc. 33; III, doc. 4, 10, 12, 109, 110; Veliman, *Documente turcești*, doc. 210. See also Alexandrescu, "Khatt-ı şerif," 262; Viorel Panaite "Wallachia and Moldavia according to the Ottoman Juridical and Political View, 1774–1829," in *Ottoman Rule and The Balkans, 1760–1858. Conflict, Transformation, Adaptation*, eds. Antonis Anastasopoulos and Elias Kolovos, Rethymno: University of Crete-Department of History and Archaelogy, 2007, 21– 44.

with Russia (1774), new processes of reshaping the autonomous status of Moldavia and Wallachia began, with new founding documents being issued.[76]

## 6.2 *From Established Customs to "Capitulations"*

In contrast, the Wallachian and Moldavian nobility realized that the prolonged customary practices regularly observed in the relations between the Porte and its tributary principalities could provide a basis for recuperating a real internal autonomy. Through the codification of these customary practices, "treaties" ("capitulations") were concluded between the Porte and Wallachia, as well as Moldavia: a fact that simultaneously implied the elimination of "new practices," which had been established in an abusive manner during the eighteenth century.[77] This was also the birth of the exaggerated myth of "old and long-term privileges" granted to certain Wallachian and Moldavian princes on the occasion that they acknowledged their allegiance to the Porte in the fourteenth to the sixteenth century.

According to the eighteenth-century annalists, these acknowledgments of allegiance in Wallachia would have been conditioned by "agreements of obedience" (in Romanian, *învoială* or *tocmeală*) between sultans and princes. They were traditionally assigned to Mircea the Elder and Basarab Laiotă, who would have concluded them in 1391–1393 and 1460 respectively. The stipulations (*legături*) of these two "capitulations," which defined a wide-ranging status of self-government for Wallachia, were listed by the boyars in memorials addressed to Count Orloff in 1772.[78] Concerning Moldavia, the tradition of "old privileges" became established primarily through the writings of Nicolae Costin and Dimitrie Cantemir, who registered the "instruments of the Sultans, by which they ratified the conditions" with the sons of Stephen the Great (i.e. Bogdan III the Blind and Petru Rareş) in 1511–1512 and 1529 as historical reality. According to Cantemir, these "treaties" included several stipulations:

> Among other numberless privileges granted them according to the times, the chief was that wherein it was expressly said, that *Moldavia* voluntarily and without compulsion offered her obedience to the *Turkish*

76 For Russia's implication in Southeastern Europe, see Barbara Jelavich, *History of the Balkans. Vol I: Eighteenth and Nineteenth Century*. Cambridge, London, New York: Cambridge University Press, 1983; Barbara Jelavich, *Russia's Balkan entanglements. 1806–1914*, Cambridge: Cambridge University Press, 1991.

77 They were characterized as "vile practices" (in Romanian, *obiceiuri spurcati*) by the Moldavian chronicler Ion Neculce (Neculce, *Letopiseţ*, 736).

78 *Genealogia Cantacuzinilor*, 67–70. See also *Istoria politică şi geografică a Ţerei Românesci*, 66; Fotino, *Istoria generală a Daciei*, 216–217 (616–619 in 2008 edition).

> Empire, and therefore it is the Sultan's will that all her Churches, religious Rites, and Laws be untouched, and nothing more required of the Prince, but that he send every year by faithful *Boyars* to the resplendent Port four thousand gold Crowns, forty bred Mares, twenty four Falcons, in the name of *Pishkiesh*, a present of gift.[79]

The tradition of ancient "treaties" (in Romanian, *tractaturi*) was continued and expanded upon by Alexandru Beldiman, who based his narrative on the excerpts from sources of Moldavian chronicler Nicolae Costin.[80]

In the period between 1774 and 1829, Wallachian and Moldavian nobles – enjoying the support of Russia – tried to present the "old privileges" of Wallachia and Moldavia, which had supposedly been established in writing by the so-called "capitulations," as an "integral part of European public law." Based on these apocryphal texts, the boyars tried to build a new "political identity" and to obtain the international recognition. They were indeed considered by Ottoman and Russian delegates at the negotiations leading to the Peace Treaty of Adrianople (1829), as diplomatic sources for the political status of the Romanian principalities. The "capitulations" also received European recognition, as, besides the imperial orders (*hatt-ı şerifs*) and Ottoman–Russian treaties, they were also invoked as the legal basis of the Ottoman sovereignty and the privileges enjoyed by the principalities.[81]

The tradition of "old privileges" fabricated by Wallachian and Moldavian noblemen, was also accepted by Western scholars in the eighteenth and nineteenth century.[82] William Eton, for instance, in his book *A Survey of the Turkish*

79 Dimitrie Cantemir also wrote that "The instruments of the Sultans, by which they ratified the conditions, were formerly kept among the public records of *Moldavia*, but in my time by the command or permission of *John Sobiesky* King of Poland, in his invasion of *Moldavia* in the year 1686, they were taken, and I know not whether very wisely, burnt publicly at *Jassy*, with this Declaration to the crowds of people, «Behold! his royal Majesty thus frees you from the *Turkish* yoke»" (Cantemir, *Othman History*, 188–189, n. 32).

80 Alexandru Beldiman, *Tractaturile prin care s-au închinatu țara de către Bogdan voevod, domnu al Moldovei, împărățind Bajazet al 2-lea, de Nicolae Costin/The Convents by which the country was submitted by Bogdan voivode, ruler of Moldavia, during the reign of Bayezid the Second* (BAR, ms. 566, fol. 126v-136. This text was published by Mihail Kogălniceanu in *Arhivă Românească* 2 (1845): 347–364 and then in Mihail Kogălniceanu, *Cronicele României seu Letopisețele Moldaviei și Valahiei*, III, Bucharest: Imprimeria Națională, 1874, 450–462.

81 Sturdza, Colescu, *Acte și documente*, I, 321.

82 Felix Colson, *Précis des droits des Moldaves et des Valaques, fondé sur les droit des gens et sur les traités*, Paris: Pugin, quai des Augustins, 1839; *Actes diplomatiques constant l'Autonomie Politique de la Roumanie*, ed. J. A. Vaillant, Paris, 1857; M. Mitilineu, *Les droits de la Roumanie basés sur les Traités. Par un ancien diplomate*, Bucharest, 1874.

*Empire* (printed in 1798), suggests that the legal status of Wallachia and Moldavia, as well as that of Egypt, might have been a result of peace agreements:

> They may be considered connected with the Porte rather by treaty than as integral parts of the empire.[83]

The authenticity of the texts of the "old privileges" was first questioned at the beginning of the twentieth century by the Romanian historian Constantin Giurescu, who proved that those that were supposed to have been granted by Ottomans to Moldavian *hospodars* in 1511–1513 and 1529 are actually apocryphal writings from the eighteenth century.[84] His conclusions are also valid for the so-called Wallachian "capitulations," assigned to the prince Mircea the Elder in 1391 (or 1393) and, later, to Basarab Laiotă (1473–1477, with interruptions) in 1460. Yet, Romanian historians have not given up on the idea that "special treaties" were concluded between the Porte and the Romanian principalities; treaties that would have regulated the legal and political status of Wallachia and Moldavia on a long-term basis.[85] The myth became much stronger in Romanian historiography during the Communist regime and these apocryphal writings are frequently quoted even today in nationalistic works and very recent textbooks for students as basic documents of the Ottoman–Romanian relations of the late fourteenth to the nineteenth century.

In my view, it is necessary to state clearly that the Ottomans did not grant any "special treaties" ("capitulations") during the fourteenth to the mid-sixteenth century that regulated the legal and political status of Wallachia and Moldavia on a long-term basis. The main reason being that this kind of "treaty" was contrary to Ottoman diplomatic practice. In fact, the term "capitulations" should not be used by historians and jurists at all in connection to the early relations between the Ottoman state and the principalities.[86]

83 Eton, *Turkish Empire*, 287–288, 297. In the first part of the nineteenth century, the tradition of "old privileges" was present in French writings (where I have seen the term). In his "Report on the Romanian principalities" of 10 May 1834, Bois-le-Comte emphasizes that the legal status of Wallachia and Moldavia was based on the same "terms" (*conditions*) since 1460 (?), respectively 1536 (?): *Les conditions qui furent accordées dans ce premier moment, aux Valaques et aux Moldaves, ont servis de base jusqu'à ce jour à leur constitution politique* (Hurmuzaki, *Documente*, XVII, doc. DXI, 328–334).

84 C. Giurescu, *Capitulațiile Moldovei cu Poarta Otomană*, Bucharest: Institutul de Arte Grafice Carol Göbl, 1908 (reprinted in C. Giurescu, *Studii de istorie*, Bucharest: Editura Eminescu, 1993, 473–504).

85 Ştefănescu, *Ţara Românească*, 101–140; Maxim, "Capitulaţiile," 34–68; Maxim, *ŢRÎP*, 25–111, 197–261.

86 Panaite "The Legal and Political Status," 33–37.

# PART 5

## *Tribute-Payers and Protected Peoples*

CHAPTER 11

# Sultans and Voivodes

## 1 The Reign of Süleyman the Magnificent and New Legal Sovereignty

Throughout the 1520s and 1530s, a tremendous change swept through Southeastern and Central Europe; as the Ottoman Empire reached the zenith of its power, power relations within the region were reshaped and readjusted to the new circumstances.[1]

In 1521, at the beginning of the reign of Süleyman the Magnificent, the Ottomans captured the Hungarian city of Belgrade, and five years later, in 1526, the sultan again invaded Hungary and defeated its army at the battle of Mohács. By the late 1530s, Polish claims and Habsburg attacks prompted Sultan Süleyman to consolidate Ottoman control over the territories north of the Danube. His personally-led expedition against Moldavia, undertaken in 1538, succeeded in ousting the incumbent voivode, Petru Rareș and brought the country firmly under imperial control. Three years later, Ottoman troops invaded Hungary and occupied Buda under the pretense of protecting John Sigismund Zápolya's interests against the Habsburg challenge. While all of central Hungary was incorporated into the empire, Süleyman granted Zápolya Transylvania as a tributary principality.[2]

These events, which represented but a fraction of the expanding imperial edifice in this period, had a profound impact on the Ottoman perception of legal sovereignty vis-à-vis Moldavia, Wallachia and Transylvania. As the

1 For Süleyman Kanunî's reign, see *Soliman le Magnifique et son temps*, ed. Gilles Veinstein, Paris: La Documentation français, 1992; *Süleyman the Second and his Time*, edited by Halil Inalcık and Cemal Kafadar, Istanbul: The Isis Press, 1993; *Süleyman the Magnificent and His Age. The Ottoman Empire in the Early Modern World*, edited by Metin Kunt and Christine Woodhead, London, New York: Routledge, 1995; Gilles Veinstein, "Süleyman I," *EI-2*, IX, 868–878. See also Suraiya Faroqhi, *The Ottoman Empire and the World Around It*. London, New York: I.B. Tauris, 2004; Palmira Brummett, *Mapping the Ottomans. Sovereignty, Territory and Identity in the Early Modern Mediterranean*, New York: Cambridge University Press, 2015.

2 For details, see: Berindei, Veinstein, *Documents*, 17–46; Pál Fodor, "Ottoman Policy towards Hungary, 1520–1541," *AOH*, XLV (2–3), 1991, 271–345; Cristina Feneșan, *Constituirea principatului autonom al Transilvaniei*, Bucharest: Ed. Enciclopedică, 1997; R. Constantinescu, *Moldova și Transilvania în vremea lui Petru Rareș. Relații politice și militare (1527–1546)*, Bucharest: Direcția Generală a Arhivelor Statului, 1978; Ștefana Simionescu, "Țările române și începutul politicii răsăritene antiotomane a Imperiului habsburgic (1526–1594)," *RdI*, 28, 8, 1975, 1197–1214.

 | DOI:10.1163/9789004411104_012

Ottomans' pretentions to universal sovereignty, be it secular or God-anointed,[3] reached their climax, the Porte increasingly saw tributary polities as an integral part of the "Well-Protected Domains." In line with this tendency, Süleyman Kanunî became the first sultan to claim outright ownership over the principalities and consider their inhabitants his subjects (*reʿaya*).

This emergent stance is reflected in the correspondence between the Porte and its main rivals in the region: Poland (all original letters preserved in the Central Archives of Old Documents in Warsaw) and the Habsburgs. For example, the letter of 18 April–17 May 1531 sent to King Sigismund I of Poland stated:

> The voivode of Moldavia as well as that of Wallachia are my slaves and tribute-payers, and their possessions, included among our other Well-Protected Domains like Bosna and Semendire, are my lands; even though he was informed that there are covenants between us and there is no order to attack your territories, yet the voivode dared to do contrary to our orders. Also, we are informed that the above-mentioned voivode [Petru Rareș of Moldavia] dispatched to you an envoy; who is he to dare and have audacity to send an emissary to you? He and the voivode of Wallachia are my tribute-payers and slaves; consequently, we enacted severe orders for they do not dare to dispatch envoys, no matter to whom; as well no emissary is allowed to be sent to them; if somebody has a question with them, he must appeal to our powerful Porte, which is opened all times, and acknowledge what he needs.[4]

As a result, the tradition of the "imperial conquest" of Wallachia, Moldavia and Transylvania was attributed to Süleyman Kanunî although it grew stronger in the following centuries, and was regularly invoked in Ottoman documents and chronicles.

---

3 On these legal and political changes, see Imber, *Ebu's-suʿud*, 65–79. According to Colin Imber, until around 1500 the Ottomans limited themselves "to a claim to rightful sovereignty in Anatolia and the Balkan peninsula" (Imber, *Ebu's-suʿud*, 74).

4 Hurmuzaki, *Documente*, Supl. II/1, doc. IX: *Ecrit au commencement du mois Ramazan, l'an 937 (1531)*. The same phrases are employed in a letter of *eva'il-i Cemazi ül-evvel* 938/10–19 January 1531: *Imdi sizinle sabıkda makrur olan muʿahede-yi hümayunum. Mezbur Boğdan voyvodası kulum ve haracgüzarımdır* (AGAD, AKW-Tureckie, K. 67, t. 33, no. 75; Abrahamowicz, *Katalog*, doc. 29). Likewise, in a letter from Fall 1531, Grand Vizier Ibrahim pașa pointed out the Ottoman view writing to Sigismund I in similar terms (AGAD, AKW-Tureckie, K. 67, t. 32, no. 72 and Abrahamowicz, *Katalog*, doc. 28: *evasıt-ı Rebi ül-evvel* 938/23 October–1 November 1531. A different date in Hurmuzaki, *Documente*, Supl. II/1, doc. XIV: 12 October–10 November 1531).

Increasingly, the new power relations acquired legitimizing foundations through concepts and rules adapted from classical Islamic law, whose recovery intensified in the Ottoman world after the conquest of the Arab lands. The arrival of Ibrahim al-Halebi (d. 1549) to Istanbul from Egypt in the aftermath of Selim I's conquest of the province, contributed to the proliferation and improvement of Ottoman *siyar* literature.[5] Adhering to the tradition of *şeri'at*, in his *Confluence of Seas* (*Mülteka el-Ebhür*) Ibrahim al-Halebi wrote distinct chapters on relations with non-Muslims, *Kitab al-siyar*, *Bab al-'uşr ve al-harac*, *Bab-ı ahkam al-müste'min*.[6] He was by no means the only prominent legal scholar of this period. Other famous *şeyh ül-Islam*s Zenbilli Ali Efendi (1503–1526),[7] Kemalpaşazade (1526–1534),[8] and Ebussuud Efendi (1545–1574),[9] laid the foundations for the Ottoman legal discourse. In their *fetvas*, they dealt more rigorously than before with the relationship between Ottomans and non-Muslim states and individuals, tackling the issues of sovereignty (*hükümet*), conduct of state (*siyar*), holy war (*cihad*), protected peoples (*zimmi*), tribute (*harac*), poll-tax (*cizye*) and the status of foreigners (*müste'min*).

There are certain legal texts concerning the stipulations and pacts concluded with tributary princes, which are also relevant to the alterations of the political and legal status of the principalities of Wallachia, Moldavia and Transylvania, which occurred in Süleyman Kanunî's epoch. In this respect,

5 J. Schacht, "al-Halebi," *EI-2*, III, 90; Özel, *Hanefi*, 114–115; Beldiceanu-Steinherr, "Le règne de Selim I," 35–48; al-Halebi's work was translated repeatedly from Arabic to Turkish, first by Mehmed Tahir b. Mehmed Rahimi (d. 1655) in the first half of the seventeenth century (Mehmed Tahir b. Mehmed Rahimi, *Tercüme-i Mülteka el-Ebhür* (TKSMK, E.H. 788).

6 Mehmed Mevkufati, *Şerh-i Mülteka el-Ebhür*, Istanbul, 1254 AH/1838–1839, I, 336–338; Ibrahim Halebi, *Şerh-i Mülteka el-Ebhür* (*Mevkufat*), ed. Nedim Yılmaz, vols. 1-4, Istanbul: İlmi Neşriyat, 1993 (especially, vol. 2, 559–628).

7 Zenbilli-Ali Efendi served as *şeyh ül-Islam* from 1503 until his death in 1526. I have consulted the manuscript *Fetava-yi Ali Efendi* (SK, Fatih 2390), but there are another three manuscripts in the Süleymaniye Library in Istanbul.

8 Kemalpaşazade (d. 1535), in his capacity as *kadıasker*, attended Selim I's campaign to Egypt in 1516–1517, and in 1526 accompanied Süleyman Kanunî in Hungary. Ibn Kemal studied Islamic law with Molla Lütfi (d. 1494), served as şeyh ül-Islam in 1526–1534, and authored several juridical and religious works, including some which legitimated the holy war against the Safavids of Iran (Danişmend, *OTKronolojisi*, II, 430–431; Inalcık, *Ottoman Empire*, 173–174, 178; *Cronici turcești I*, 191–192; Repp, *Müfti*, 224–240).

9 Ebussuud Efendi (d. 1574) served as *şeyh ül-Islam* for three decades between 1545 and 1574, and came to be regarded as one of the most influential Ottoman *şeyh ül-Islam*. Throughout the seventeenth and eighteenth centuries, his *fetvas* constituted a blueprint for other Islamic scholars (M. E. Duzdağ, *Şeyhüllslam Ebussuud Efendi fetvaları Işığında 16. Asır Türk Hayatı*, Istanbul: Enderun Kitabevi, 1983; Colin Imber, *Ebu's-su'ud. The Islamic Legal Tradition*, Stanford: Stanford University Press, 1997).

I find it worthwhile to cite al-Shaybani's comparison between theory and practice. Firstly, the scholar considered it illegal to conclude an agreement with a non-Muslim prince that permitted the latter to retain unlimited authority over his subjects:

> I asked: If he [the infidel ruler] did not become a Muslim nor was given the benefit of a peace agreement, nor did he become a *zimmi*, but he proposed to the Muslims [a peace agreement] on condition that he be a protected person and pay the Muslims a tribute (*harac*), on condition that he be allowed to exercise over the people of his realm such powers as he wished, such as those of beheading or crucifying, or the like, which are not proper that he should exercise in the territory of Islam, [would such an agreement be made]? He replied: It would not be right for the Muslims to make any peace agreement with him on such conditions.

In fact, this kind of agreement had been quite common, particularly along the frontier with the Christian world, including Southeastern Europe in the late fourteenth–early sixteenth centuries. However, Muslim doubts regarding this type of arrangement persisted. Was it legal to violate it entirely or to abrogate certain stipulations? Let us quote once again from al-Shaybani's *Siyar*:

> I asked, [if the Muslims] did so and entered into such an agreement with him [a non-Muslim prince] on such terms and he became a protected person of theirs, [what would the ruling be]? He replied, '[The Muslims] would look into those terms of the agreements that were illegal and improper; they would abrogate them and would observe only those terms that were proper. If the ruler accepted, [well and good]; if not, he and his followers would be allowed to return to their place of safety.'[10]

In my opinion, the modification of the legal and political status of the principalities of Wallachia and Moldavia during the reign of Süleyman Kanunî and its aggravation in the following centuries could be legally justified by the Ottomans with the aforementioned Islamic rules, even though the Wallachian or Moldavian boyars would consider them as violations of "ancient covenants."

Since the Wallachian and Moldavian voivodes of the fifteenth century, as well as Transylvanian rulers a century later, submitted to the Porte and agreed

10 *Shaybani's Siyar*, 152–153.

to pay tribute, they became "tribute-payers" (*haracgüzarlar*).[11] This concept originated from the fundamental legal duty of tribute payments and was most frequently employed in Ottoman sources to define the legal and political status of Moldavia and Wallachia well into the nineteenth century, and for Transylvania until the Habsburg conquest of the province. This term was also adopted by Western sources, such as French diplomatic reports from Istanbul. For instance, in 1554 Michel de Codignac called Moldavian and Wallachian voivodes "tributaries of the sultan" (*tributaires du Grand Seigneur*); in 1612 Achille de Harlay wrote that "all the three provinces have been, since ancient times, tributaries of the sultan" (*toutes ces troys provinces sont depuis un long temps tributaires du Grand Seigneur*). In 1702 M. de Ferriol noted that the "word tributaries is [utilized] for Wallachians and Moldavians" (*le mot de tributaires est pour les Valaques et pour les Moldaves*).[12]

At the same time, paying the tribute implied that the Porte would guarantee protection to the voivodes, who would retain control over their territories and the customs of their domains be respected. It is necessary to point out that this kind of peace, established on the exchange of tribute for protection, remained a constant feature of the relations with the Porte, in spite of different abuses and infringements throughout the early modern period. An explicit pronouncement of this principle can be found in the imperial diploma (*berat-ı hümayun*) granted by Murad III to Wallachian voivode Mihnea II the Renegade, in 1585:

> The country is under our due protection, [and] its subjects are also my tribute-payers.[13]

With Ottoman political and legal discourse, this notion of protection was expressed through several terms, which surface in relations with imperial officialdom, inhabitants of adjacent *sancak*s and Christian neighbors. Among them, by far the most frequently used were the notions of *himayet* and *siyanet*.

Even though the concepts of tribute-payer (*haracgüzar*) and protection (*himayet*) appear in fifteenth-century sources and to some extent were implemented in relation to Wallachia (from 1417) and Moldavia (from 1456), it was only under Süleyman Kanunî that the Ottoman legal–political status of the north Danubian tributaries crystallized. Thus, it would, in my opinion, be

11 Stephen the Great (1457–1504) was characterized by Tursun bey as a "tribute-payer" (Tursun bey, *Tarih*, ed. Inalcik, Murphey, 47, 61).

12 Hurmuzaki, *Documente*, Supl. I/1, doc. XVII (letter of 3 April 1554 to Henry II); doc. CCXXVII (report of 21 April 1612 from Pera); doc. DXXVII (report of 2 October 1702 to the king of France).

13 Maxim, *CTO*, doc. 14: *memleket vacib al-himayemizdir re'ayası dahi haracgüzarlarımdır*.

FIGURE 13 Sultan Süleyman The Magnificent (1520–1566) (from Demetrius Cantemir, *The History of the Growth and Decay of the Othman Empire*. Written Originally in Latin. Translated into English by N. Tindal, London, 1734)

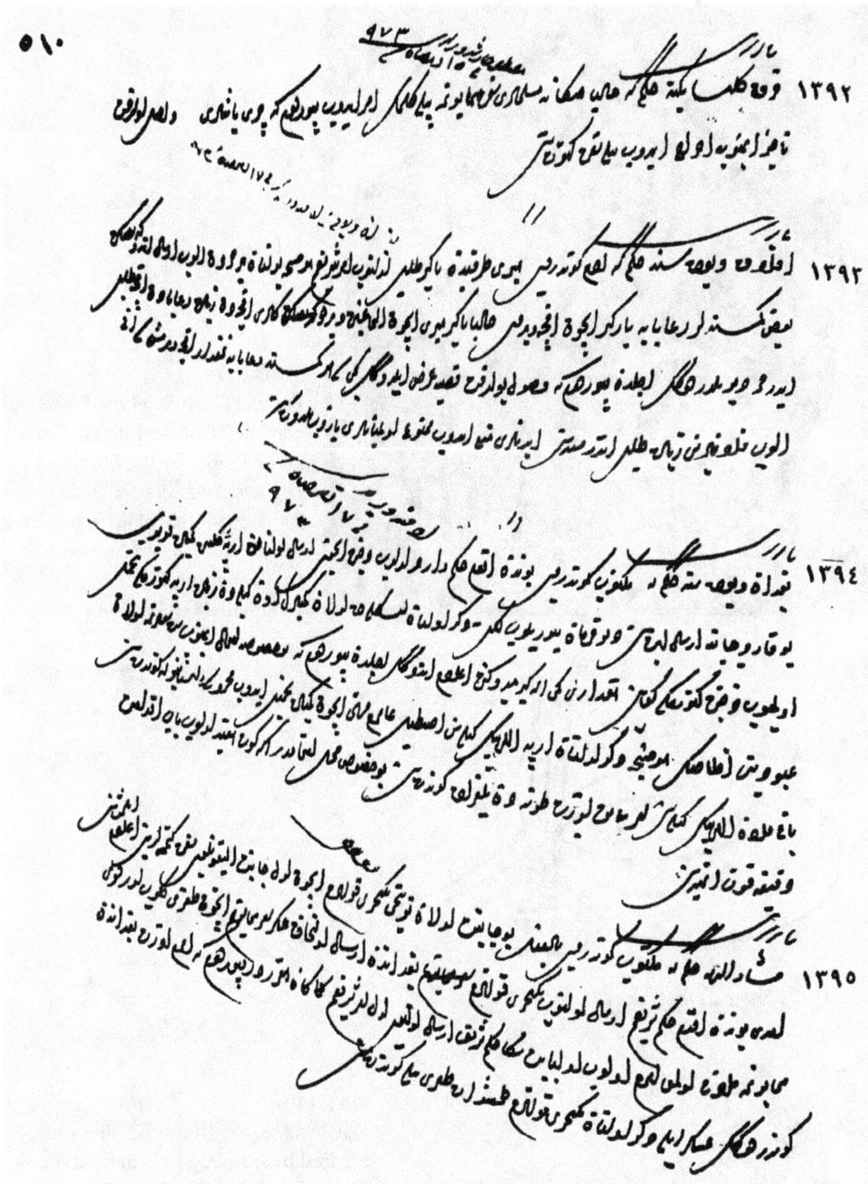

FIGURE 14 *Mühimme Defterleri* with imperial orders (*hüküm*) to the voivodes of Wallachia (*Eflak*) and Moldavia (*Boğdan*) (*5 Numaralı Mühimme Defteri, 973/1565–1566* <Tıpkıbasım>, Ankara, 1994, doc. 1393, 1394)

FIGURE 15
Portrait of Michael the Brave, voivode of Wallachia (1593–1601) made in 1601 by the Flemish engraver Aegidius Sadeler II (1570–1629) (Nicolae Iorga, *Domni români după portrete şi fresce contemporane,* Sibiu, 1930; Wikipedia. Public Domain)

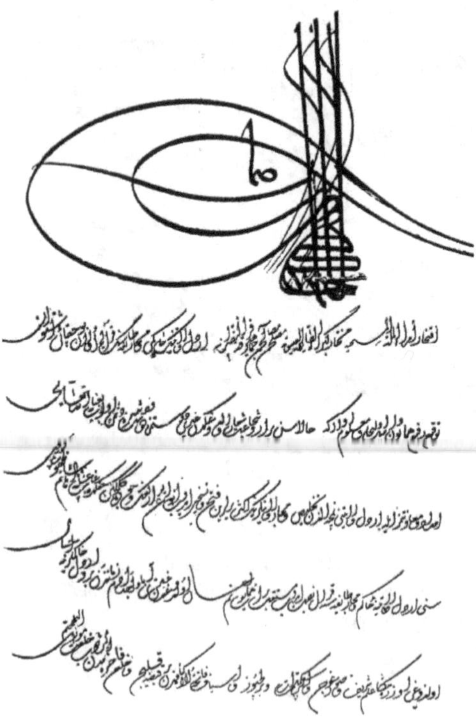

FIGURE 16
*Berat-ı hümayun* (imperial diploma) granted by Ahmed I to Prince Istvan Bocskai of Transylvania in 1604 (MOL, Budapest, Török iratok, R. 315, no. 33; Sándor Papp, *Die Verleihungs-, Bekräftigungs- und Vertragsurkunden der Osmanen für Ungarn und Siebenbürgen: Eine quellenkritische Untersuchung,* Vienna, 2003, p. 391)

FIGURE 17 Portrait of Gábor (Gabriel) Bethlen, prince of Transylvania (1613–1629) (engraving from *Theatrum Europaeum*, Band 1, Franfurt <Main>, 1662; Wikipedia. Public Domain)

FIGURE 18 Portrait of Dimitrie Cantemir (1673–1723), scholar; voivode of Moldavia between 1710–1711 (from Demetrius Cantemir, *The History of the Growth and Decay of the Othman Empire*, Written Originally in Latin. Translated into English by N. Tindal, London, 1734)

FIGURE 19 Portrait of Constantin Brâncoveanu, voivode of Wallachia (1688–1714) and his four sons, all being executed at Istanbul in 1714 (from Anton Maria del Chiaro, *Istoria delle moderne revoluzioni della Valachia*, Venezia, 1718)

FIGURE 20 *Hüküm* (Order) of Ahmed III to *mübaşir* Mustafa of *eva'il-i Rebi ül-evvel* 1714 / 17–26 March 1714, including also the legal opinion (*fetva*) which legitimated the execution of voivode Constantin Brâncoveanu of Wallachia (BOA, Ibnülemin Tasnifi, Hariciye, no. 1114; Veliman, *Documente turcești*, doc. 11 and facs. 3)

FIGURE 21 Portrait of Grigore II Ghica, four times voivode of Moldavia (1726–1733; 1735–1739; 1739–1741; 1747–1748) and two times in Wallachia (1733–1735; 1748–1752) (N. Iorga, *Domni români după portrete şi fresce contemporane,* Sibiu, 1930)

wrong to uncritically and retroactively apply sixteenth-century legal terminology to the earlier period. However, since Moldavia, Wallachia and Transylvania were completely integrated in the system *pax ottomanica* as tributary principalities in the 1530s and 1540s, this anachronistic narrative was reflected in the historiography of the period.

Explaining the ways the three principalities enjoyed tributary-protection status requires us to unpack the notions of "tribute-payer" (*haracgüzar*) and "protection" (*himayet*). Accordingly, in this part of the book my aim is to analyze the extant sources and sketch an aggregate picture of what this status entailed and how it functioned within the context of the *pax ottomanica* system.

## 2 Princes and Beys

### 2.1 *Titles*

Analyzing the power relationships embedded in the titulature, Halil Inalcık observed that for Christian rulers the Ottomans used both the original Christian titles of *kral* (*kıral*), *çar*, *çasar*, *imperator* (*imperador*), *hersek*, *voyvoda*, *hospodar*, *knez*, or *doj*, as well as Ottoman ones, such as *padişah*, or *bey*.[14] Taking note of the power relations and diplomatic interests of the Porte, the Ottoman chancery had to determine which Ottoman title corresponded to a particular Christian title: for instance, *padişah* was used for emperor, tsar, king (as the French king), and *bey* for any king, prince or voivode.[15]

Until the eighteenth century, various Christian and Ottoman titles were employed to describe the rank and status of Wallachian, Moldavian and Transylvanian rulers: *tekfür*, *hakim*, *bey*, *voyvoda*, *hospodar*, *domn*, *kıral*, *ban*, prince and duke. This lack of consistency frequently disconcerted researchers. Originally, some of these terms were specific to either Ottoman sources or non-Ottoman ones, but subsequently transcended the linguistic and cultural divide. One of the terms that appeared early in the Ottoman sources was that

14 Inalcık, "Power Relationships", 193–208.

15 Viorel Panaite, "Power Relationships in the Ottoman Empire. The Sultans and the Tribute-paying Princes of Wallachia and Moldavia from the Sixteenth to the Eighteenth Century." *IJTS*, Vol. 7, Nos. 1 & 2, Spring 2001, 26–53. For instance, the Treaty of Zsitvatörök (1606) stipulated that the Habsburg sovereign will not be called king but Caesar (*Ikinci madde budur ki: bizim sa'adetlü padişahımız hazretlerinin canib şeriflerinden yazılan name-yi hümayunda Roma-yı çasar deyü yazılub kıral nam ile yazılmıya* (Fekete, *Esterhazy*; 3–14; Köhbach, "Çasar oder imperator," 223–234; G. Bayerle, "The Compromise at Zsitvatörök." *AOtt* VI, (1980): 5–53).

of *tekfür*.[16] It originated from the Armenian *takhavor*, which meant "king," and had already been used by Arab chroniclers for designating Christian sovereigns, including Armenian princes, Greek emperors of Byzantium and Trebizond. During the Seljuk period, local Christian rulers of Asia Minor were also called *tekfür*, a usage that was subsequently adopted by Ottoman chroniclers to describe non-Muslim leaders, from military commanders to Byzantine emperors. Considering that the word *tekfür* in Arabic also referred to a Muslim accused of heresy, it is clear that it also had a derogatory meaning when referring to "infidel" Christian rulers.[17]

The term usually applied to the rulers of Moldavia and Wallachia from the sixteenth century onwards was that of *voyvoda*. This term was adopted by Ottomans from Slavic languages and was frequently used to describe a "governor" or "administrator" and in some instances was synonymous with *subaşı*, or a provincial official in charge of collecting revenue. According to Dimitrie Cantemir, *voyvoda* was a word

> signifying the General of an army, but by the *Poles* given to Governors of Provinces [...] The *Turks* are wont to call by this name the *Christian* Princes of *Moldavia*, *Walachia* and *Transylvania*, who are Tributary to them, especially in the imperial Mandates and Letters of the Prime Vizir, as *Boğdan vayvodası*, *Iflak* or *Erdel vayvodası*.[18]

The term *voyvoda* was employed in Ottoman sources to address Wallachian and Moldavian rulers and, less frequently, Transylvanian rulers. It is worth noting that the sultan's orders registered in *Mühimme Defterleri* referred to them solely by the term *voyvoda*s, included in standard formulas:

---

16 An interesting study on *tekfür* and other terms was recently published: Hasan Çolak, "*Tekfur*, *fasiliyus* and *kayser*: Disdain, Negligence and Appropriation of Byzantine Imperial Titulature in the Ottoman World," in M. Hadjianastasis (ed.) *Frontiers of the Ottoman imagination: Studies in honour of Rhoads Murphey*, Leiden–Boston: Brill, 2015, 5–28.

17 Enveri, *Destan d'Umur*, 47, n. 6; Neşri, *Tarih*, in *Cronici turcești I*, 127. Dimitrie Cantemir wrote that "formerly the Princes of *Moldavia* were, as appears in Historians, called *Tekkiur* or Kings" (Cantemir, *Othman History*, 193, n. 38).

18 Cantemir observed that sometimes the title of *voyvoda* was also given "to governors of large cities, who did not have the title of Bashas, as *Pera Vaivodesi, Galata Vaivodesi,&c*" (Cantemir, *Othman History*, 193, n. 38). See also Gustav Bayerle, *Pashas, Begs, and Effendis. A Historical Dictionary of Titles and Terms in the Ottoman Empire*, Istanbul: ISIS Press, 1997.

Order to the Wallachian voivode (*Eflak voyvodasına hüküm ki*); Order to the Moldavian voivode (*Boğdan voyvodasına hüküm ki*).[19]

Following the establishment of the Principality of Transylvania as a tributary state, the Ottoman sources usually referred to its princes as *hakim*s and *kıral*s, even though the terms *voyvoda* and *bey* can also be found. The Arabic term *hakim* (ruler, governor, judge) had already been applied to Wallachian and Moldavian voivodes in the late fourteenth and fifteenth century. Thus, Idris Bitlisi, referring to Mircea the Elder's reign, spoke about the "rulers and governors" (*hükkam ve vali*) of Wallachia. However, the use of this term shifted in the following period, and until 1699 the term was generally used for Transylvanian princes, for instance in *intitulatio* (*ʿunvan*) of Ottoman and Crimean correspondence and documents issued by the chancery (*Erdel hakimi* or *Erdel vilayetinin hakimi*).[20]

The term *kıral* (king) referred to a broader group of rulers, including monarchs of Hungary, Poland, Austria and Transylvania. Writing in the second part of the sixteenth century, Mustafa Selaniki spoke on "Yanoş's son, the King of Transylvania" (*Erdel kıralı Yanoş oğlu*) or *Erdel kıralı*.[21] The Crimean khans frequently used the term *kıral* in their letters addressed to the princes of Transylvania, e.g. *Erdel kıralının vekili* ("representative of the Transylvanian king").[22] In comparison, it was used exceedingly rarely to refer to Wallachia and Moldavia; yet, some Western sources described the voivodes as "kings" (*roys de Valachie et Moldavie*).[23] Finally, a Serbo-Croatian title *ban* was also used to describe princes of Transylvania. Thus, according to Muhieddin el-Cemalı and Mustafa Selaniki, John Zápolya was "Yanuş, the ban of the country of

19 *Mühimme Defteri* 3, 5, 6, 7, 12 passim; Mehmed, *Documente turcești*, I–III, passim; Gemil, *Documente turcești*, passim; Veliman, *Documente turcești*, passim. For comments on *hüküm*, see Heyd, *Ottoman Documents on Palestine*, 7–12.

20 Pl. *hükkam*. See: Idris Bitlisi, *Heşt Behişt*, in *Cronici turcești I*, 160–162; Gemil, *Documente turcești* doc. 171, 178; Maria Ivanics, "Formal and Lingvuistic Peculiarities of 17th Century Crimean Tatar Letters addressed to Princes of Transylvania," *AOH*, XXIX, 2 (1975), 213–224.

21 Selaniki, *Tarih*, ed. Ipşirli, 21, 564. Nineteenth century Turkish historians, as M. Nuri paşa (d. 1890) wrote as a rule on "the king of Transylvania" but used also at least for the fifteenth century the phrase "king of Moldavia" (*Boğdan kıralı*) on Stephan the Great (M. Nuri paşa, *Osmanlı Tarihi*, reviewed by M. Guboglu, in *Românii în istoria universală*, II/1, Iași: Universitatea Alex. I. Cuza, 1987, 703).

22 Ivanics, "Letters," 213–224.

23 But "tributaires du G.S. [Grand Seigneur]" (Hurmuzaki, *Documente*, Supl. I/1, doc. XVII: letter of 3 April 1554 to Henry II).

Transylvania" (*vilayet-i Erdel banı Yanuş*), and Sigismund Bathory – "the ban of Transylvania" (*Erdel banı*).[24]

Another title we frequently find in Ottoman sources was that of *bey* (*beğ*), which originated in the old Turkish word *bög*. One of the most widespread honorific titles in the Ottoman space, it was attached to high-ranking civil and military dignitaries of the Ottoman state, but also to West European sovereigns and officials.[25] Western observers adapted the term, referring to *Beigs de Valachie et de Moldavie*, a phrase that appears frequently in French ambassadors' letters.[26]

Apart from the loanwords discussed above, Western sources also employed the titles of "duke" and "prince," most frequently used for the rulers of Wallachia, Moldavia and Transylvania, like *Duke of Moldavia* for Petru Rareș and Dimitrie Cantemir in English documents and early newspapers,[27] *Principi di Moldavia e di Valacchia* in an Italian report of March 1740.[28]

Yet, nuances and variations existed. Even a brief glance at the Western sources shows that rulers of Moldavia and Wallachia were systematically called *hospodars*, a Slavonic term, which translated into Romanian as *domn*, "lord" (from Latin *dominus*), which corresponded to the tradition within the principalities.[29] In turn, the term "prince" was regularly reserved for the Transylvanian rulers. However, the sources sometimes emphasize that the titles *hospodar* and "prince" were synonyms.[30]

Without regard for the titles employed, the rulers of Wallachia, Moldavia and Transylvania were usually described, by way of compliment, as

---

24 Selaniki, *Tarih*, ed. Ipşirli, 298, 686; *Crestomaţie turcă*, 293; Cantemir, *Othman History*, 193: "the Vayvod of *Transylvania* (whom they call Ban)."

25 *Mühimme Defteri* 3, 5, 6, 7, 12 passim. Gemil, *Documente turceşti*, passim; Veliman, *Documente turceşti*, passim. The *beylik* was a country ruled by a *bey*.

26 On 15 November 1672, Nointel wrote to Pomponne on the *Beigs de Valachie et de Moldavie* (Hurmuzaki, *Documente*, Supl. I/1, doc. CCCLXXXIX).

27 Tappe, *Documents*, no. 20, 26. The Western sources borrowed the term *Kara-Boğdan*. For instance, Petru Rareș was called in this source *Caraboldan*, from the Turkish word *Kara-Boğdan*, and "Duke of Moldavia"; *The British Mercury*, Numb. 209 from 23–25 July 1711 (PRUL, mf. EEN, r. 633–684).

28 Hurmuzaki, *Documente*, IX/1, doc. DCCXCI: Report of Nicolo Erizzo to Venetian doge of 15 March 1740.

29 For the local titles of the princes used in the Wallachian and Moldavian chanceries, see Pippidi, *Tradiţia*, 18–27.

30 *The London Gazette*. 1665–1712, H. Muddiman et. al. Published by Authority. Issued twice a week (PRUL, mf. Early English Newspapers, r. 633–684). A recent analysis of English news terminology on the Romanian principalities during the Great Turkish War (1683–1699) is in Panaite, *News in England*, 33–34.

> the most excellent of the princes of the Sect of the Messia, the greatest of the Nations believing in Jesus.[31]

That said, the status of tributary princes within the diplomatic world of the period remained ambiguous, both for Ottoman and Christian authors. Some listed them along with European Christian rulers, while others emphasized that they belonged to the hierarchy of Ottoman dignitaries.

During the period of hostilities, Ottoman chroniclers frequently described the enemy by indiscriminately listing all Christian polities, often including Wallachian, Moldavian and Transylvanian princes. This can be seen in the narrative of Mustafa Ali (d. 1600), discussed by Jan Schmidt. In the preface of *History of the Ottomans until 1524* (the fourth volume of his *Essence of Histories*), Mustafa Ali provides a comprehensive list of contemporary rulers and countries, including Transylvania, Wallachia and Moldavia among them.[32] Also, on the occasion of the circumcision festivities of 1582 in Istanbul, Mustafa Ali provided a detailed list of the envoys from foreign powers and vassal polities, along with the gifts they brought. Among them, we find the representatives of Transylvania, Moldavia and Wallachia.[33]

The consolidation of the Ottoman official stance regarding tributary polities that occurred in the sixteenth century brought important changes to their perception. Wallachian, Moldavian and Transylvanian princes were included in the hierarchy of Ottoman dignitaries. They occupied the position along with Muslim *paşa*s governing imperial provinces and enjoyed a privilege of hoisting at least two horsetails (*tuğ*s), along with other banners and insignia of the viziers.[34] They were installed by means of imperial diplomas (*berat-ı hümayun*) and received orders in the form *hüküm*s, just like other officials of the Ottoman provincial administration. After 1526, Süleyman Kanunî emphasized strongly

31 Some Ottoman formulas are: *iftiharü'l-ümerai'l-izami'l-Iseviyye muhtarü'l-küberai'l-fiham fi'l-milleti'l-Mesihiyye*; or only *mefahir-i ümera'l-tayfe'l-Nasraniye* (Cantemir, *Othman History*, 50, n. 7; Gemil, *Documente turcești*, passim; Veliman, *Documente turcești*, passim; Ivanics, "Letters," 216: "to the present prince of Transylvania the pride of the leaders of the Christian people, the elect of the leaders of the Christian nation, to our old friend, to the king who shows the token of friendship and whose life may end felicitously").

32 Among the latter we find: Spaniards, French, the Pope, the Lutherans, the Andi, Georgians, Circassians, Mingrelia, Transylvania, Wallachia, Russians, Moldavia, Poles, Bohemians, the Emperor, Hungarians and Germans (Schmidt, *Mustafa Ali*, 182–183).

33 Along with *Rus*, Poland, Dubrovnik, Venice, Spain and Portugal (Schmidt, *Mustafa Ali*, 300).

34 Cantemir, *Othman History*, 11, n. 8. A *tuğ* was a horsetail attached to a helmet or flag-staff as a sign of rank: a *sancakbeyi* had one *tuğ*, a *beylerbeyi* two *tuğ*s, a vizier three *tuğ*s, the grand vizier four *tuğ*s, and the sultan six *tuğ*s.

and constantly that Wallachian and Moldavian voivodes were "my slaves and tribute-payers" (sing. *kulum ve haracgüzarımdır*), and banned direct diplomatic contacts between the voivodes and Christian powers.[35] In the same vein, Ottoman sources saw the appointment of John Sigismund Zápolya in Transylvania in the same way as an appointment of any other *sancakbeyi*.[36] Early modern *defters* concerning Moldavia and Wallachia are strikingly similar to those compiled for other Ottoman provinces. Moreover, after 1742, the outgoing orders addressed to the voivodes were included in the "Registers of orders concerning the *eyalets* of Özü și Silistra" (*Özü ve Silistre Ahkam Defterleri*).[37]

Western observers not only assimilated the titles the Porte used with regard to its tributaries, but also the political and diplomatic framework of the imperial center. Thus, Moldavian, Wallachian and Transylvanian princes were frequently regarded as "lieutenant in those parties"[38] or "servants but not sovereigns."[39]

### 2.2 *"Our Reign is Granted by Turks"*

From the reign of Süleyman Kanunî onwards, the sultans insisted on this new aspect of their power relationship with their tributaries. As Selim II stated in 1572, since "Moldavian, Wallachian, and Transylvanian countries were included in and among our countries and provinces just as the another Well-Protected Domains (*Memalik-i mahrusa*) which are under our own rule," the sultan had the right to appoint and dismiss and imprison voivodes. As they "depended on our Majesty and concern us," their position was just like that of other governors (*beys*) appointed to guard and defend imperial provinces and protect their inhabitants.[40] Whenever a new voivode was appointed, Ottoman chroniclers,

35 AGAD, AKW-Tureckie, K. 67, t. 33, no. 75; t. 32, no. 72; Abrahamowicz, *Katalog*, doc. 28, 29; Hurmuzaki, *Documente*, Supl. II/1, doc. IX, XIV.

36 "I gave [him] Transylvania as a *sancak*" (*Erdel vilayetin sancak tarikle inayet idüb*) (cf. Fodor, "Ottoman policy," 329).

37 This collection registered orders from 1155–1294 AH/1742–1877, sent to the governors of provinces attached to the two eyalets (*Silistre sancağı, Tekeyolu sancağı, Niğbolu sancağı, Kırkkilise sancağı, Özü ve Silistre eyaleti, Kefe beylerbeyiliği, Vize sancağı, Çirmen sancağı, Eflak voyvodalığı ve Boğdan voyvodalığı* (BOA. *Rehberi*, 54–56).

38 The former phrase belonged to an English source and labeled the voivode Petru Rareș of Moldavia (1527–1538, 1541–1546), called *duke* (Tappe, *Documents*, no. 20, 26).

39 Used by the French ambassador to Warsaw, Olivier de Nointel, to characterize the political and legal status of voivodes chosen from the Greeks of Phanar in the second part of the seventeenth century (Hurmuzaki, *Documente*, Supl. I/1, doc. CCCXC: Letter of 1 March 1676 to Forbin-Janson, bishop of Marseille).

40 Letter of *eva'il-i Zilhicce* 979/15–24 April 1572 to Polish king Sigismund II Augustus (ANIC, mf. Poland, r. 1, fr. 59–60; Mehmet, *Documente turcești*, I, doc. 103: *ve Boğdan ve Eflak ve*

such as Mustafa Selaniki and Şarih ül-Menaroğlu Ahmed, and non-Ottoman authors referred to long-standing customs, laws issued by sultans (*kanun*) and agreements that gave the Ottomans the right to nominate Moldavian and Wallachian rulers.[41] In 1714, Ștefan Cantacuzino remarked that "those customary [things], according to the imperial regulation," were performed upon his enthronement in Wallachia.[42] The Prime Minister's Archives in Istanbul hold numerous such documents concerning late sixteenth- and seventeenth-century nominations of tributary Moldavian and Wallachian voivodes.[43]

How did Wallachian, Moldavian and Transylvanian authors perceive the sultan's authority regarding the matters of appointing and replacing local rulers, particularly in the post-1538 period? There is no doubt that they were keenly aware of the fact that incumbency and succession to the throne depended on the sultan's will. This awareness surfaces in boyars' petitions (*'arzuhal*) sent to the Porte. A telling example in this respect is the Wallachian petition of June 1535, which states that the "*padișah* had given to us" Vlad Vintilă (1532–1535). However, following his death they elected Radu Paisie (1535–1545) and requested the sultan's consent:

> When we have seen that the country remained without voivode and His Majesty, the magnificent *padișah* is far away, and it was impossible to ask a voivode from the Gate of Felicity, and it was difficult to rule the country without voivode and, for the country to be in order, we appointed as voivode Radu, whom you know, and who, being son of voivode [Radu the Great] is fit for any imperial function and is competent and capable to rule the country. Yet, the order is of His Majesty, the *padișah*. No matter what your illustrious order will be on the issue, we will obey and observe it.[44]

---

*Erdel vilayetlerimiz... sa'ir memalik-i mahrusam gibi*)

41 "The reign of Moldavia was granted, according to the (*kanun*), to the infidel Peter," i.e. Petru Cazacul (August–24 October 1592) (Selaniki, *Tarih*, in *Cronici turcești*, I, 366). On Miron Barnovschi's execution in 1633, Şarih ül-Menaroğlu Ahmed (d. 1657) emphasized that "according to the covenants from all years and the Moldavian infidels' law inherited from ancestors [...], their hospodars were named by the High Sultanate (Şarih ül-Menaroğlu Ahmed, *Tarih*, in *Crestomație turcă*, 566). See also Mehmet, *Documente turcești*, I, doc. 152; Gemil, *Documente turcești*, doc. 61.

42 Hurmuzaki, *Documente*, XIV/1, doc. DLXXXIV.

43 For example, the document of 1075 AH/1664–1665 on Eustratie Dabija's nomination to the *Boğdan Voyvodalığı* (BOA, *Ali Emini Tasnifi*, IV Mehmed, doc. 198).

44 *'Arz* issued after 10 June 1535 (TKSMA, E. 6077; Mehmet, *Documente turcești*, I, doc. 18; M. Guboglu, "Două călătorii în Turcia pentru cercetarea arhivelor Imperiului otoman," *RA*, XII, 1, 1969, 226–227, facsimiles).

The discretion of Ottoman rulers to appoint and dismiss voivodes entered local political thought and was invoked in the principalities' dealings with Christian powers as the explanation for the rulers' continued allegiance to the Porte. The phrase "our reign is granted by Turks," cited as the title of the present chapter, was uttered by Voivode Theodosie, son of Neagoe Basarab, as he reminded the authorities of Brașov in 1521 that "in this manner the emperor appointed me to the throne of my father."[45] A few years later, Radu of Afumați brought up a similar argument in his letter to the inhabitants of Sibiu:

> the Wallachian reign was granted to me firstly by God, and then by the Turkish emperor.[46]

Although the voivode was quick to emphasize – like most rulers of the sixteenth century – that he owed his ascension to the support of local nobles, he could not deny that the maintaining of throne increasingly depended on the sultan's will. Early modern sources of the period frequently feature a standard formula that the rulers of Wallachia, Moldavia and Transylvania gained their thrones "by God's will and the sultan's decision."[47] So, what did they mean precisely when they wrote that "our reign is granted by Turks?"

### 2.3 *Authorization and Nomination by the Porte*

By the second half of the sixteenth century, direct appointment by the sultan had become a standard practice. The traditional election[48] by the local elite, followed by a confirmation by the Porte was being practiced less and less.[49]

---

45 Tocilescu, *534 documente*, doc. 274. In the conditions of extreme turmoil that beset Wallachian politics in this period, the throne alternated between numerous claimants. Among the contenders we find Vladislav III (1523; 1524; 1525) named by Süleyman Kanunî: "the emperor who gave the reign" (Popescu, *Istoriile*, 278: *au dat împăratul domniia*).

46 Tocilescu, *534 documente*, doc. 308.

47 Vlad the Younger (1530–1532) wrote to the inhabitants of Brașov on 4 June 1530 that "by the God's will and the honourable emperor's decision, I am hospodar of Wallachia, on my father's throne" (Tocilescu, *534 documente*, doc. 319). Later, on 6 June 1630, Voivode Leon wrote that "the God and the honourable emperor granted me the sceptre of Wallachia" (Hurmuzaki, *Documente*, XIV/1, doc. DCC).

48 Seen from the perspective of the year 1774, when the local boyars tried to recover their "old privileges," this would be considered as a privilege granted to Wallachia and Moldavia in the fifteenth and sixteenth centuries, and violated later, during the eighteenth century (Athanase Comnen, cf. Hurmuzaki, *Documente*, XIV/2, doc. MCCXX).

49 In 1660, the priest Gabriel Tomasić noted that "Wallachia was submitted to a hospodar named by Turks. Yet frequently the country itself chose the ruler but always with the Ottoman Porte's sanction" (*Călători străini*, VII, 127–129).

Since the appointment of Radu the Fair in 1462, the Wallachian voivodes required Ottoman consent and military support to capture and retain the throne. Each time a voivode was brought to power by way of election,[50] it was imperative for him to secure Ottoman recognition, a custom that became particularly pervasive from the 1520s onwards.[51] This can be best seen in the case of voivodes Radu Bădica (1521–1524, intermittently) and Radu of Afumați. Chosen by opposing camps among the local elite and locked in a struggle for the throne, both vied for the sultan's recognition.[52] Radu Bădica even alleged the existence of "an old custom of Wallachia," and dispatched an embassy to the Porte to obtain a "banner of rulership." But after a while the direct appointment by the Porte – applied in isolated cases before 1545 – became a rule. A statistic related to the second half of the sixteenth century shows that eleven of thirteen incumbents of this period were sultanic appointees.[53]

In Moldovia, the practice of confirming the voivodes by the Porte set in motion in the first half of the sixteenth century. Although between 1538 and 1572 the voivodes confirmed by the Porte alternated with those directly appointed from Istanbul, in the following period the latter increasingly outnumbered the former.[54] Dimitrie Cantemir and other Moldavian historians provide us with an insight into the local interpretation of this trajectory, which was subsequently adopted by Western scholarship. According to them, Süleyman Kanunî accepted the Moldavian prince's homage along with a "small sum of money," granting the local elite the right to elect their own voivodes, which would be subject to vetting by the Porte, a privilege which Moldavia would appear to have enjoyed and abused, until the beginning of the eighteenth century.[55] Cantemir continued

50 With regard to the election and Ottoman intervention, see also R. Păun, "Conquered by the (S)word: Governing the Tributary Principalities of Wallachia and Moldavia (16th–17th Centuries)," in R. Born and M. Dziewulski (eds), *Ottoman Orient in Renaissance Culture*, Krakow: The National Museum in Krakow, 2015, 19–40.

51 Giurescu, *Țara Românească*, 397 ("a regular habit"); Hurmuzaki, *Documente*, XIV/1, doc. DLXXXVII (" a stronger reinforcement of the reign").

52 Tocilescu, *534 documente*, doc. 283, 308: letter of Radu of Afumați (1521–1529) to the inhabitants of Sibiu from 1 February, without year.

53 M. Berza, in *Istoria* (Oțetea), 152–153; Murgescu, *Istorie*, 149.

54 M. Berza, in *Istoria* (Oțetea), 152–153; Murgescu, *Istorie*, 149.

55 Ion Neculce noted that this rule had been practiced before the eighteenth century: "And it was before the boyars and country's habit of electing the hospodar whom they wanted, and the Porte also nominating that [voivode]" (Neculce, *Letopiseț*, 622: *Iar mai nainte era obiceaiu de-ș alegea boiarii și țara domn, pre cine poftiia ei, și pre acela punea și Poarta*). See also Athanase Comnen, cf. Hurmuzaki, *Documente*, XIV/2, doc. MCCXX; Thornton, *Turkey*, II, 312–313.

> The *Turks* for almost a whole Century permitted according to agreement the *Moldavians* to choose their Prince but in [the] process of time, they began to appoint them Princes themselves, and usually out of the Sons of the Princes whom they detained as hostages at *Constantinople*.[56]

Certain seventeenth-century Western observers affirmed that the voivodes of Moldavia and Wallachia were at the mercy of the Porte.[57] Yet, Thomas Thornton was right to point out that local boyars continued to have a say in the process, and it was only in the eighteenth century that this practice was abandoned. For the boyars, direct appointment by the Porte was an abuse of their rights, detrimental to both the principalities and the Ottomans.[58]

In Transylvania, the practices of elected princes being confirmed by the Porte prevailed throughout the period of Ottoman rule, until the Habsburgs occupied it in the 1690s. This stood in stark contrast with Wallachia and Moldavia, where local elites increasingly lost ground on the matter. The nobility's right to elect rulers was invoked in the petitions to the Porte and acknowledged by Western authors. In 1581, the French ambassador in Istanbul, de Germigny, noted that Transylvanians were "accustomed to choosing their prince."[59] In the petition (*mahzar*) of 1 September 1652, the local noblemen informed the sultan that they had elected Francisc Rákoczy, pointing out that "from old times the nomination of the ruler [...] was granted to the country leaders' will." At the same time, they were quick to note that "it is necessary that the reign of Transylvania be reinforced by [...] His Majesty, the felicitous *padişah*."[60]

56 Cantemir, *Othman History*, 202–203, n. 67.

57 Invoking the cases of Radu Mihnea and Simion Movilă, French ambassador de Brèves wrote to Henri IV on 14 February 1602: *La grandeur de ceste porte ne luy est pas advantageuse puis ja longtemps que les Ottomans changent ceulx princes a leurs discretion; celluy cy est a cause du mauvais estat des afferes de cest Empire hors de ce danger* (Hurmuzaki, *Documente*, Supl. I/1, doc. CLXXX).

58 The reaction of the Moldavian boyars to the appointment of Nicolae Mavrocordat in 1711, without prior consultation with the local elite, was recorded by Ion Neculce (Neculce, *Letopiseț*, 622). Also, in the Crimean Khanate, the direct appointment of khans by the sultan was considered a violation of *ius electionis*. They asked this right to "remain to them hereafter" (Veress, *Documente II*, 323).

59 Letter of 22 June 1581 to Henry III (Hurmuzaki, *Documente*, Supl. I/1, doc. CX; Charrière, *Négociations*, IV, 59).

60 This procedure followed the established local practices and laws (*kadimi hayırlu ʿadet ve kanunnumuz üzere*) but also the laws issued by Ottoman sultans (*mübarek ecdad-ı izamlarından sadr olan mübarek kanunları mucibince*) (Gemil, *Documente turcești*, doc. 126). I. H. Uzunçarşılı has published numerous documents on the appointment of Akos Barçay as prince of Transylvania, carried out by Mehmed IV and Köprülü Mehmed paşa

### 2.4 *From Christian and Indigenous Princes to Christian Princes Only*

What distinguished the tributary princes of Moldavia, Wallachia and Transylvania from other Ottoman governors was their adherence to the Christian faith and their origin from among local elites.

The first feature surprised foreigners who ventured to the territories north of the Danube. De la Croix, who wondered that the position of prince "was assigned to Christian *beys*," but emphasized the financial and political benefits that the Porte drew from this state of affairs.[61] In his speech delivered to the Polish–Lithuanian *Sejm* assembled in Warsaw in 1647, the bishop of Kujawy drew a clear distinction between the lands ruled by Christian tributaries and those governed by Ottoman officials, arguing that the former offered more advantages to the Porte. According to De la Croix (1676), Wallachian–Moldavian self-government implied that the Ottomans,

> obtain much more from these Christian governors than they would obtain from Turkish [governors].[62]

During the sixteenth and seventeenth centuries, the Porte launched several attempts to replace the Christian princes with Ottoman–Muslim governors, but at each time gave up on the idea due to political, military and financial concerns.

Romanian historiography usually described these projects as attempts to transform Moldavia and Wallachia into *paşalık*s, that is territories under the authority of the *sancakbeyi*, who would have received the honorary rank of *paşa*.[63] However, since the Porte already considered tributary voivodes *paşa*s and *bey*s, their domains were in a way *paşalık*s, rendering the whole issue moot. The situation was most tenuous in the case of Wallachia, where the Ottoman influence was the strongest. Following the passing away of Neagoe Basarab in 1521, the principality faced the danger of losing its status, when "a

(I. H. Uzunçarşılı, "Akos Barçay'ın Erdel Krallığına ait tayını hakkında birkaç vesika," *Belleten*, VIII, 1943, 361–377).

61 *Călători străini*, VI, 476.

62 Hurmuzaki, *Documente*, Supl. II/3, doc. XIX; *Călători străini*, VII, 254–255.

63 For the debate in Romanian historiography, see P. P. Panaitescu, "De ce n-au cucerit turcii Țările Române," 111–119; Maxim, *ȚRÎP*, 111–141. In both cases, the notion of conquest was identified with the transformation of a tributary state into an Ottoman province, even though the Ottoman understanding of conquest was more encompassing (D'Ohsson, *Tableau*, VII, 307; Pakalın, *Sözlük*, II, 758; J. Deny, "Paşalık," *EI-2*, VIII, 282).

certain Turk, named Mehmet, took his place."[64] Since "to give the country to the Turks is not to uphold the old tradition," Wallachian boyars abandoned internal conflicts and successfully pushed back.[65] The gravity of the threat goes a long way towards explaining Radu of Afumați's joy, expressed in 1524–1524:

> The Wallachian reign was given to me [...] and I came back again alive and healthy [...], and I took the Wallachian throne and reign.[66]

According to the Moldavian tradition, Moldavia confronted similar challenges in 1538, but the sultan's plan "to establish *sancak* [*beyi*s]" failed there due to the sultan's inability to remove the local elite.[67] Three years later, Petru Rareș justified his enormous expenditure in obtaining the throne, arguing that otherwise "my place would have been taken by a Turk, like in Buda."[68] Thus, despite his triumphs in Moldavia and Hungary in 1538–1541, Süleyman Kanunî opted to retain Wallachia, Moldavia and Transylvania as autonomous principalities rather than assimilate them into the typical provincial administration. This decision was not driven by legal considerations, but rather by political, military and financial calculations, already addressed in the scholarship.[69]

A particularly dramatic moment occurred in Spring 1595. On the heels of Michael the Brave's revolt in November 1594, the Porte decided to replace the Christian voivodes of Wallachia and Moldavia with Muslim governors and transform the principalities into *saliyane* provinces, acting with more resolve than had earlier been the case.[70] Numerous steps were taken to effectuate the change, including the appointment of Muslim officials, from *beylerbeyi* to *sübaşı*, and drafting a *defter* of the Wallachian population.[71] Although the Ot-

64 This source does not tell whether this took place on the sultan's orders, instead suggesting that Mehmed bey was acting on his own initiative (*Cronica lui Macarie*, in CSR, 93). However, Radu Popescu noted that the boyars had been informed "that a Turkish ruler will be named in country" (Popescu, *Istoriile*, 272).

65 Michael Bocignoli, in *Călători străini*, I, 178.

66 Tocilescu, *534 documente*, doc. 308. Similarly, the Wallachian boyars were relieved when an attempt to impose a Muslim governor fizzled out (Tocilescu, *534 documente*, doc. 426).

67 Letter of 1540 to the Polish king (Hurmuzaki, *Documente*, Supl. II.1, doc. LXX).

68 Letter of 22 January 1542 to the Polish king, through Mikołaj Sieniawski (Hurmuzaki, *Documente*, Supl. II/1, doc. LXXX).

69 See Panaitescu, "N-au cucerit," 111–118; Maxim, *ȚRÎP*, 111–141.

70 C. Rotman, "Ocupația otomană în Țara Românească în anul 1595 (14/24 august–20/30 septembrie)." *Apulum*, XIII, 1975, 285–293.

71 Satırci Mehmed paşa, *beylerbeyi* of Anatolia, was to become the governor of Wallachia; Cafer paşa, former *beylerbeyi* of Şirvan, was to take power in Moldavia. According to

toman authorities invoked the violation of *ʿahd* as the formal cause, military and political considerations played a crucial role in radicalizing the Ottoman stance.[72] According to Akhisarı (d. 1616), who composed his *risale* during the conflict, the main reason for bringing the principalities under Muslim administration was that:

> from a political point of view, it is dangerous to keep unbeliever governors in the vicinity of big cities and in the center of the empire.[73]

It is important to note that seventeenth-century diplomatic sources provide us with a number of reports regarding alleged plans to impose Muslim governors in the principalities as punitive measures. For instance, prior to setting out on the Polish campaign of 1620, European sources claimed, Osman II planned:

> just to name Turk governors, called by them Beglierbeis, in Moldavia, Wallachia and Transylvania.[74]

---

Mustafa Selaniki's description: *vilayet-i Eflak Beglerbeğiliği virilen sabıka Anatoli Beğlerbeğisi Satırcı Mehmed Paşa dahi yaralu olduğın bildirmişler* [...] *Eflak vilayetine Beğlerbeği taʿyin olunan Satırcı Mehmed paşa'ya vezir elkabiyle hükm-i şerif yazıldığıdur. Ve vilayet-i Eflak'da kal'alar yapılup ve neferat yazılup memleket re'ayası hıfz olunup, mahsul-i mülk şerʿ-i şerif ve kanun-ı münif üzre zabd olundukdan sonra beğlerbeği ve defterdar ve ağalar ve dizdar ve piyade ve süvar olan asker yine ibtidadan dirlik alup, cümle mülk hass-ı hümayun olmak üzre tahrir olunmak re'y olunup ve müceddeden memlekete nizam u intizam virecek Satırcı Mehmed paşa'ya vezir elkabiyle hükm-i şerif-i cihan-mutaʿ yazılup, irsal olunmak ferman olundı. Fi eva'il-i muharrem, sene 1004.* (Selaniki, *Tarih*, ed. Ipşirli, II, 508; Peçevi, *Tarih*, in *Cronici turcești*, I, 502). See also Mehmet, *Documente turcești*, I, doc. 148).

72 See, generally, Ion Sârbu, *Istoria lui Mihai Vodă Viteazul, domnul Țării Românești*, Timișoara: Ed. Facla, 1976; *Mihai Viteazul. Culegere de studii*, eds. Paul Cernovodeanu and Constantin Rezachievici, Bucharest: Ed. Academiei, 1975.

73 Ak-Hisarı, *Usul el-hikam*, 286; Mehmet, "Akhisarı." 399. Other "two reasons" were learnt from spies, captives or Ottoman runaways and communicated by European envoys. On the one hand, the Ottomans wanted to retrieve "the incomes carrying before from the Moldavian and Wallachian territory." On the other hand, they wanted to establish a new outpost for further raids to the neighboring Christian territories ("when they will have garrisons here, the Tartars will be enabled to invade easier all the Christian states") (*Mihai. Documente I*, doc. 16: the report of the Polish envoy Lubienecki, of 27 July 1595, on his talks with Michael the Brave).

74 Hurmuzaki, *Documente*, Supl. I/1, doc. CCXCII. Also, in 1647, diplomatic sources related about the Polish authorities' concern of *l'intention d'abolir les Hospodarats de Moldavie et de Valachie et qu'il veut y établir des Pachas pour infester les États de Sa Majesté Royale* (Hurmuzaki, *Documente*, Supl. II/3, doc. XVI, XVII, XVIII). In 1665–1666 Venetian *baylos* narrated in their reports that the Porte planned to consolidate its control in the

Both the local elites and outside observers considered that, by way of entrenched custom, eligibility to the throne was restricted to the members of the autochthonous dynasties and boyar lineages. When in the second part of the seventeenth century the Porte tried to impose members of the Istanbul-based Phanariot community,[75] it was interpreted as a measure that would change "the custom of installing a voivode in the principalities of Transylvania, Wallachia and Moldavia."[76] In 1673, in response to the defection of Moldavian and Wallachian rulers during the Ottoman–Polish war, the Porte refrained from appointing Muslim governors, opting instead to turn to Phanariot Greeks of Istanbul.[77] In Dimitrie Cantemir's opinion, considering that even the Moldavian voivode changed sides during the battle of Hotin, thus causing the Ottoman defeat,

> the Ottoman Porte thought that in the future no Moldavian should ever be named as ruler, but rather a Greek who would have his home and relatives in Istanbul. Besides, he would be a peaceful man and ignorant of war.[78]

For the Porte, to choose the *hospodars* from the Greek subjects in Constantinople meant, as an immediate advantage, "to have their goods and family as

---

principalities by establishing of *di Bassa* (Hurmuzaki, *Documente*, IX/1, doc. CCCXI, CCCXXXIII; vol. V/2, doc. CLXXIX, CLXV).

75 On 15 April 1658, the sultan sent a *jeune Grec elevé à Constantinople pour Prince en Moldavie avec un diplome* (Hurmuzaki, *Documente*, Supl. II/3, doc. XLI). According to Matei Cantacuzino, the Köprülüs intended to impose the principle of appointing and dismissing directly by the Porte (*Genealogia Cantacuzinilor*, 308).

76 De la Haye to the French king on 15 May 1666: *la coutume d'establir aux principautés de Transilvanie, Valachie et Moldavie, un Seigneur de chaque Pays* (Hurmuzaki, *Documente*, Supl. I/1, doc. CCCLXVII).

77 Florin Constantiniu, "De la Mihai Viteazul la fanarioți: observații asupra politicii externe românești," *SMIM*, VIII, 1975, 101–136. See also R. Păun, "Some Remarks about the Historical Origins of the «Phanariot phenomenon» in Moldavia and Wallachia (16th–19th Centuries)," in G. Harlaftis and R. Paun (eds.), *Greeks in Romania in the Nineteenth Century*, Athens: Historical Archives of Alpha Bank, 2013, 47–94.

78 The Moldavian prince Ștefan Petriceicu (1672–1673; 1682–1683), and the Wallachian prince, Grigore Ghica (1660–1664; 1672–1673) (Cantemir, *Viața*, 21). In his *Othman History*, Dimitrie Cantemir mentioned some of the first Phanariot Greeks named as voivodes of Moldavia: "At length they granted this dignity to some *Constantinopolitan Greeks*, as forty years ago to *Demetrius Cantacuzenus*, thirty years since to *Antonius Rosseta*, and in my time to *Ducas Rameliota*, and *Nicolaus Maurocordatus*, first Interpreter of the *Othoman Port*, and Colleague of *Rami Mehemed, Reis Efendi* at the peace of *Carlowitz*. But of these things more largely in the Description of *Moldavia*, which I intend shortly to publish to the World." (Cantemir, *Othman History*, 203, n. 67).

hostage for their fidelity."[79] The nomination of Phanariot Greeks to the thrones of Moldavia and Wallachia became a standard practice following the reigns of Dimitrie Cantemir (1710–1711) and Constantin Brâncoveanu (1688–1714), when both rulers lent their support to the enemy during the Russo–Ottoman war of 1711. Throughout the eighteenth century, the voivodes recruited solely from this milieu and were directly appointed by the Porte. By the end of the century, this came to be widely recognized as an ancient practice:

> of old times, they were constantly chosen from *beyzade*s, and former voivodes or among the translators of the Imperial Council.[80]

### 2.5 *Ceremony of Accession*

The process of confirming a new voivode required the appointee to pay homage (in Romanian, *închinare*) to the Ottoman sultan, a ceremony which took place on each appointment.[81] This could be performed either personally[82] or by proxy (through special envoys or permanent agents, called *kapu-kethudaları*).[83] Each iteration of the ceremony was influenced by the power relations between both parties. In the 1520s, when securing Ottoman recognition became the decisive factor in the internal struggle between Radu Bădica and Radu of Afumați, each pretender approached it differently. Whereas the former merely sent several boyars to the Porte, Radu of Afumați led his delegation personally:

---

79 Hurmuzaki, *Documente*, Supl. I/1, doc. CCCLXVII: letter of French ambassador De la Haye from 15 May 1666.

80 In a 1786 *telhis* of the grand vizier to Abdul-Hamid I concerning Nicolae Mavrogheni (Veliman, *Documente turcești*, doc. 195); Aksan, "Information," 5–16.

81 In a letter of 26 June 1681 it was written on Gheorghe Duca's homage that took place "on the occasion of obtaining of a new province, according to the custom of the Porte" (Hurmuzaki, *Documente*, Supl. II/3, doc. LXX). See H. Dj. Siruni, ed. *Domnii români la Poarta Otomană*, Bucharest: Imprimeria Statului, 1941.

82 Radu Leon in 1664 and Gheorghe Duca in 1681 were confirmed to the throne of Wallachia after they came personally to Istanbul, were received in audience to the grand vizier and sultan and paid homage (*yüz sürub*) (Gemil, *Documente turcești*, doc. 148; Hurmuzaki, *Documente*, Supl. II/3, doc. LXX, LXXI). In the eighteenth century, the Phanariot hospodars' homage depreciated up to the level of that paying by foreign ambassadors. Consequently, in 1758, Ioan Teodor Callimachi complained against this mistreatment (Veliman, *Documente turcești*, doc. 134).

83 In 1605, Radu Șerban obtained the banner of reign by homage-paying embassy (Decei, *Imp. otoman*, 292).

> I went to the Turkish Porte and stood in the presence of the Turkish emperor and all dignitaries of the Turkish country.[84]

Radu of Afumați succeeded in being confirmed as the voivode of Wallachia.

Political and military circumstances influenced the ceremonial order at the Ottoman court. Whereas some appointments were carefully-crafted, solemn occasions, in other instances the whole procedure was carried out in haste.[85] Discussing the ceremonies accompanying the appointment, Dimitrie Cantemir and Thomas Thornton accurately describe the procedure at the sultan's court,[86] but provide divergent interpretations. Thornton points out that the voivodes received the investiture at the Porte with a pomp and ceremony similar to that of *paşa* and vizier appointments.[87] In turn, Cantemir emphasized some peculiarities regarding the investiture of Moldavian and Wallachian rulers. "Neither Pasha's nor Vizirs in general are created with so much pomp as the Princes of *Moldavia*," insists Cantemir, emphasizing the appointee's solemn visit to the Patriarchal Church, as was the case for virtually all Christian Ottoman officials.[88]

The first – and most significant – stage of the ceremony of accession,[89] which is at the same time the most significant, included placing a military cap (in Turkish, *kuka* or *üsküf*)[90] on the voivode's head by a Janissary officer at-

84 Tocilescu, *534 documente*, doc. 283, 308.

85 In the circumstances of a soon starting of war with the Christian alliance, in *evahir-i Receb* 999/15–24 May 1591 , Alexandru IV, the son of Bogdan Lăpuşneanu, "According to the law, appearing before the high Counsel, dressed the *bürk*, after that he was ordered to come back in his country," i.e. Moldavia (Selaniki, *Tarih*, in *Cronici turceşti I*, 363).

86 Ceremony of inauguration took place at the sultanal court, usually in Istanbul. On 23 July 1822, the ceremony took place in Silistre due to the Janissairies, although "il est d'usage l'investiture à Constantinople" (Hurmuzaki, *Documente*, XVI, doc. MMXI).

87 Thornton, *Turkey*, II, 340–341. See also Gökbilgin, "Relations turco-roumaines," 707 ("avec la pompe et les cérémonies d'usage pour la création des pachas et des vizirs").

88 "This suffices to show the manner of confirming the Princes of *Moldavia*; they who desire a larger account may consult my History of *Moldavia* which, I hope, will shortly be published" (Cantemir, *Othman History*, 192, n. 34).

89 For the eighteenth and early nineteenth centuries, see Radu Păun, "Sur l'investiture des derniers princes phanariotes. Autour d'un document ignoré," RESEE, XXXV, 1–2, 1997, 63–76.

90 *Kuka* or *üsküf* was "a crest or ornament of the head made of ostrich feathers" (Cantemir, *Othman History*, 189, n. 33). "Besides princes of Moldavia and Wallachia, with this kind of *kuka* was adorned other two Ottoman officials, the *Buluk agaları* (or Tribunes) and *Segban başı* (chief officer of the *segbans*, who is the next to the Aga of the Janissairies" (Thornton, *Turkey*, II, 340) See also Hurmuzaki, *Documente*, XVI, doc. MMXI: *La cérémonie dite de la Couca 23 iulie 1822*.

tached to the grand vizier, known as *mahzar ağa*.[91] The grand vizier himself also bestowed upon the appointee a robe of honor (*kaftan, hilʿat*). Both *kuka* and *kaftan* associated the voivode with the Janissary *ocak*. Although the donning of the *hilʿat* usually took place in the Chamber of Petitions (*ʿarz odası*), it was sometimes moved to the Chamber of Governors (*beyler odası*).[92] In the case of typical *paşa* appointment, the ceremony ended here, since

> Pasha's as soon as the Prime Vizier has put on their robe, immediately go home, and [the] next day receive the Patents of their Pashalate, with the Standard called *Sanjak*.[93]

However, in the case of Moldavian and Wallachian voivodes, the ceremonies continued. Following the bestowal of the robe of honor, the appointee proceeded to the Patriarchal Church, where the Ecumenical Patriarch consecrated him, conforming to the model established for the Byzantine emperors. He was accompanied by the whole Ottoman *divan* and awaited by the Greek clergy and notables. Dimitrie Cantemir continued:

> When the Prince comes into the Court of the Church he alights from his horse on a square stone placed there for that purpose, all the *Chaushi* repeating with a loud voice the Prayer usual on these occasions. Then the Prince's whole company honorably wait in the Court and Street his coming out. Meanwhile, the Singing men the moment the Prince treads the Threshold of the Church sing […] a Hymn composed in honor of the Virgin Mary; which ended, the Prince ascends a Throne appointed for the Princes of *Moldavia*. The Deacon […] mentions the new Prince in this manner: 'We pray also for our most pious, most serene, and most excellent Lord N. N. may be crowned with strength, victory, stability, health and security, and may the Lord our God father cooperate with him, guide him in all things, and put all his adversaries under his feet.' After this, the Patriarch in his sacred vestments, with four or more Metropolitans goes up to the Altar. The Prince also approaches the royal entrance to the Altar, where, being signed by the Patriarch with both hands in the face with the sign of the Cross, he lays his head on the Holy Table, which the

91 He is about the vizier, keeper of this court, and his deputy over the whole militia of Janissaries.

92 In March 1763, Constantin Racoviță received his *kaftan* in the "room of governors" because the grand vizier was ill (Athanase Comnen, in Hurmuzaki, *Documente*, XIV/2, doc. MCXLII).

93 Cantemir, *Othman History*, 189, n. 34.

> Patriarch covers with an *Homopher*, and reciting the Prayers that were used at the inauguration of the Orthodox Emperors, anoints his forehead with the holy oil. After these ceremonies the Prince returns to his Throne, the singers chanting this *Polychronion* [...] Then the Patriarch also goes from the Altar to his Throne and commanding silence, preaches a short Sermon to the Prince, which is followed by the foregoing *Polychronion*, pronounced by the Patriarch. At last, when all is over, the Patriarch and Prince, accompanied with all the People, go together out of the Church. In the Porch, the Prince, after kissing the Patriarch's right hand and being confirmed by him with hand and voice and the sign of the Cross, he mounts his horse, and with the same Parade as he came returns home, and dismisses his attendants with presents.[94]

After concluding these rites, the new voivode proceeded in a similar way as ordinary *paşa*s. He returned to his residence (*Boğdan Sarayı*, respectively *Eflak Sarayı*), which served also as the accommodation for his permanent agents (*kapu-kethudaları*) and awaited the arrival of the sultan's standard-bearer (*mir-i ʿalem ağa*), accompanied by a military band. The Ottoman official was received by the prince, who would take the banner (*sancak*) and kiss it.[95]

The climax of the ceremony of accession took place during a public audience when the new hospodar made his oath of allegiance and fidelity to the sultan. In August 1758, Voivode Ioan Teodor Callimachi of Wallachia requested an audience with the grand vizier, claiming that Ottoman dignitaries "since ancient times (*ez-kadim*) are given the high permission to be honored by their receiving in the imperial audience."[96] Again, here is Dimitrie Cantemir's account:

> After spending a few days in dispatching his affairs with the Court, he is conducted to the great *Divan*, where the Prime Vizir with the rest of

94 Cantemir, *Othman History*, 190, n. 34.

95 "After some days–Dimitrie Cantemir wrote–*Mir Alem Aga*, the Emperor's Standard-bearer, brings the larger Standard called *Sanjak*, with the imperial Music, *Tabulchane*, from the Palace to the Prince's house and is met in the Porch by the Prince. There he takes the Standard and kissing it, according to custom, with his mouth and forehead, delivers it into the Prince's hands. The Prince upon receiving it, kisses it in the same manner and gives it to his Standard-bearer to keep, saying: Then the Prince gives the *Mir Alem Aga*, a robe, and dismisses him with the usual present." (Cantemir, *Othman History*, 190, n. 34). See also Thornton, *Turkey*, II, 341.

96 Thornton, *Turkey*, II, 341. Radu Greceanu described how Constantin Brâncoveanu was conducted to the sultan for prostrating (Greceanu, *Istoria*, 142); Gökbilgin, "Relations turco-roumaines," 707; Veliman, *Documente turceşti*, doc. 134.

> *Kubbe Vizirleri* and the two *Cadiuleskiers* stand at the Emperor's right-hand. *Capuchilar Kiethudafi* or chief Porter, arrays the Prince with a Robe in the Porch of *Arzodasi* or Audience-room, *Muhzur Aga* bids him put the *Cucca* on his head, and cloaths all the Prince's Barons, which are usually twenty-eight, with new Robes. Thus adorned and supported on each side with two *Capujibashis*, with the chief Porter before and the Court-Interpreter behind (he is commonly a *Christian Greek*) he enters the Audience-room with four of his Barons. At the entrance he bows his head to the ground three times, and stands upright when he comes to the middle of the room, which is not extraordinary large. Then the Emperor from the Throne (*Tacht*) turning to the Vizir, bids him tell him: 'Since his faithfulness and sincerity has reached the ears of my Majesty, I graciously confer on him as a reward the Principality of *Moldavia*. It is also his duty not to fail in his fidelity and services for the future. Let him protect and defend the Provinces under his subjection, and dread to commit any thing against or beyond my Mandate.' To this the Prince replies, 'I vow on my life and head to lay out my whole endeavours in the service of my most just and gracious Emperor, son long as he does not withdraw the aspect of his clemency and Majesty from the Nothingness of his Servant' (*i. e.* from his unprofitable Servant). Upon these words the Prince goes out of the room, accompanied as when he entered, and mounting an imperial horse at the inner Gate of the Court, salutes the prime and other Vizirs as they depart, who answer with a nod; after which, the Barons and his whole Company leading the way, he returns home.[97]

Following the voivode's return to the principality, traditional rites of coronation took place, which – as Andrei Pippidi argued – was greatly influenced by Byzantine models.[98] Irrespective of whether the ruler was appointed directly by the Porte or elected by boyars, an Ottoman official was dispatched to carry out the enthronement procedure. In 1552, according to a Slavic-Moldavian chronicle, Süleyman Kanunî,

> sent one of his Turkish official to the voivode Alexandru and [in this manner] [...] he reinforced and established the reign.[99]

97 Cantemir, *Othman History*, 190–191, n. 34.

98 See, Pippidi, *Tradiția*, 17–51; Radu Păun, "Încoronarea în Țara Românească și Moldova în secolul al XVIII-lea. Principii, atitudini, simboluri," *RdI*, V, 7–8, 1994, 743–759.

99 It is about the voivode Alexandru Lăpușneanu of Moldavia (1552–1561; 1564–1568) (*Cronica lui Eftimie*, in CSR, 124). Also, in 1714, Ștefan Cantacuzino received the imperial diploma

When the voivode personally attended the sultanic court to receive the appointment, on his way to the principality he was accompanied by an Ottoman official charged with installing him on the throne. The latter are usually described in the sources through generic terms, such as "a servant" (*bir kul*), "one of the Turkish officials,"[100] or by stating his rank. In the latter category can be included *kapıcı başı* (head of the palace doorkeepers) and simple *kapıcı*s (porters),[101] *emir-i ʿalem* (the chief of banner, a *paşa* of the lowest rank),[102] *iskemle ağası* or *iskemle çavuş* (initially, that servant who kept a stool to help sultans to mount their horse). As a rule, the newly-appointed voivode expressed his gratitude by paying his respects during the ceremony and offering gifts.[103]

Dimitrie Cantemir provides a detailed description of this ceremony in Moldavia, although the procedure was similar to the Wallachian one.

> When he is about to go to his Principality, whether the Sultan be at *Constantinople* or *Adrianople*, one of the Court officers as *Sylahdar aga*, *Chocadar aga*, *Miriachoraga*, *Capujilar Kiehaiasi*, or one of the Senior *Capujibashis*, is ordered to set him on the Throne. There are also two Peiki or imperial Guards, equipped with their Gold and Silver ornaments, and two *Akkiullahlu* (so called from the white Hat they usually wear), and also as many *Capujis* and *Chaushis* as the Prince pleases. The office of these is, when the Prince mounts or alights from his horse, to make the usual acclamation *alkysh*, and in the towns and villages to take care of necessaries for the Prince's Court. The *Chaushi* go a little before him on foot, when he enters and leaves any town, and the Capujis hold his stirrups when he mounts or dismounts. In this manner he is attended till he

---

and *hilʿat* through the agency of *haseki ağa* (Hurmuzaki, *Documente*, XIV/1, doc. DLXXXIV: letter of 25 April to the Patriarch Hrisant Notara, and doc. DLXXXVII).

100 *Cronica lui Eftimie*, in CSR, 124: for Alexandru Lăpuşneanu's confirmation in 1552; Francesco Sovori, in CSISD, II, 240: for Petru Cercel's enthronement in 1583.

101 Grand Vizier Derviş Mehmed paşa wrote in his report (*telhis*) to Ahmed I about changing Constantin Movilă with Simion Movilă in 1606 that: "when the country of <Moldavia> was in good order, the *üsküf* and banner were sent to the voivodes by a head of the palace doorkeepers" (*vilayet ma'mur iken voyvodalara üsküf ve sancak bir kapucı-başı ile göderilürdi*) (Gemil, *Documente turceşti*, doc. 23). In 1592, Petru Cazacul, after his inauguration in Istanbul, was sent to Moldavia accompanied by the *kapıcı* Veli ağa (Selaniki, *Tarih*, in *Cronici turceşti I*, 366).

102 He appeared regularly in sources for investing in the princes of Moldavia and Wallachia. In *evahir-i Receb* 999/15–24 May 1591, Alexandru IV followed to be named "*bey* in his *vilayet*" by the *emir-i ʿalem* Kurt ağa (Selaniki, *Tarih*, in *Cronici turceşti*, I, 363).

103 *Cronica lui Eftimie*, in CSR, 124. In 1714, Ştefan Cantacuzino spoke about "Haseki ağa of our powerful Emperor" (Hurmuzaki, *Documente*, XIV/1, doc. DLXXXIV, DLXXXVII).

> arrives to the place of his residence, where all the great men both civil and military to the number of two thousand come to meet him. To all these the Prince gives his hand on horseback to be kissed, and having inquired of their health bids them all remount. Then the Barons attending him on each side according to their rank, and the military officers going before, he enters the City with a flow pace for the greater pomp, and first unlights in the Court of the Cathedral Church dedicated to *St. Nicolas*. The Metropolitan, accompanied with three Bishops (for Moldavia counts so many Sees, whereas Walachia has but two) and the rest of the Clergy, offers the Cross and Holy Gospels for the Prince to kiss, the imperial Music being silent during this ceremony. When the Prince comes into the Church [...] he approaches the Altar, and when Prayers are over, is anointed by the Metropolitan with the Holy Chrism, unless he has been inaugurated by the *Constantinopolitan* Patriarch, which happens when he is promoted to his dignity at Adrianople, or the Patriarch of Constantinople is absent. For he is, and is called, God's anointed. When all is over and the *Polychronion* shouted, he repairs with the sound of Trumpets and Drums and other Music to his Palace, and alighting at the *Divan*, stands before the Throne placed there, whilst the Barons who came with him take their places. Then the Officer appointed by the Emperor to attend him, gives the *Chatisherif* or imperial Mandate to *Divan Effendisi* or the scribe of the Court, who is a Turk, to be read. He rehearses the Mandate with a loud voice, sentence by sentence, which the great *Postelnik* interprets to the rest in their native Tongue. After that, the imperial officer arrays the Prince with the robe he had brought with him, and helps him with his right hand into the Throne, at which moment the guns are fired and the *Chaushis* make the usual acclamation. The Prince in his turn gives the officer a Robe lined with Ermine, but to the scribe only a plain *Caftan*. Thus established in his Throne, the Prince admits the Nobles to kiss his hand, and after saluting them, retires to his inner room. Then follows a splendid entertainment for the imperial officer, who is conducted to it by some of the Prince's Courtiers.[104]

The insignia granted to the tributary prince represented a lopsided relationship between patron and client, as they were also employed during the appointments of other Ottoman governors. These included the banner (*sancak*),

104 Cantemir, *Othman History*, 191–192, n. 34.

the robe of honor (*hilʿat, kaftan*),[105] the imperial diploma (*berat-ı hümayun*), the knitted cap with a tassel, worn usually by officers of Janissaries (*üsküf* or *kuka*), the belt (*kemer*),[106] horse (*at*), a sheath for the sword (*taklid*)[107] and the sceptre (*topuz*). However, these not were necessary to carry out the appointment, and their relative symbolic and legal value differed significantly; in practice, the banner, *kaftan* and *berat* sufficed to install the new voivode in Moldavia, Wallachia and Transylvania.[108] Ottoman symbols of investiture had been granted to Wallachian voivodes since the mid-fifteenth century. For instance, as the sultan's tribute-payer, Vlad the Impaler personally attended Mehmed II's court to deliver the tribute; on this occasion, the sultan bestowed upon him a robe of honor, a red felt hat (*bürk*) and a gold-embroidered ceremonial hat (*üsküf*).[109] With the scope of legitimizing, local princes and boyars specifically[110] requested such objects from the Porte. In 1652, Transylvanian nobles addressed Mehmed IV with a request

105 Robes of honor were granted to ambassadors, too. There were three kinds of robes of honor, i.e. *hilʿat-ı fahire* (very precious robe of honor, royal robe), *hilʿat-ı evsat* (middle robe of honor) and *hilʿat-ı edna* (usual robe of honor). From the mid sixteenth century, the Ottoman *kaftan* replaced the Byzantine *gramata*. In 1668 the agents of Wallachia and Moldavia asked to be granted two robes of honor (*iki hilʿat, iki kaftan*) for each voivode, "according to code-law" (Gemil, *Documente turcești*, doc. 149; Hurmuzaki, *Documente*, XIV/2, doc. MCXLII; *Reprezentanța*, 274; *Crestomație turcă*, 339, n. 61; Shai Har-El, *Ottoman-Mamluk*, 13–16).

106 In 1462, Radu the Fair also received a belt.

107 *Taklid*, which meant the putting on a sword, symbolized also the conferring office; *taklid-i seyf*, i.e. the girding on by the Sultan of the sword of Osman, was the equivalent of a coronation ceremony (*Redhouse*, 1089; Shai Har-El, *Ottoman-Mamluk*, 13–16).

108 The first Wallachian voivode who received signs of Ottoman investiture would be Vlad I, in 1395 (Gemil, *Românii și otomanii*, 26, n. 38). The first Moldavian voivode who received Ottoman investiture signs, e.g. the banner, robe of honor and knitted bonnet, would be Stephen the Great, after the peace of 1486 (Gorovei, "1486," 820). In Moldo-Wallachian sources, the banner of reign was considered the strongest warranty of Porte for enthroning of a new hospodar. Here are some formulas from *The Cantacuzene Annals*, concerning Radu Iliaș (July–September 1532), Matei Basarab (1632–1654) and Șerban Cantacuzino (1688–1678), in *Letopisețul cantacuzinesc*, 103, 105, 176 (*steagul Radului vodă, steag împărătesc, steag... dat la Țarigrad*). The agreement of Țuțora from 22 October 1595 also spoke about "the banner granted to Ieremia <Movilă> as symbol of reign" (Hurmuzaki, *Documente*, Supl. II/1, doc. CLXXXII).

109 It is not clear if he referred to the meteoric reign in 1448, or to the second one (Critobul, *Mehmed II*, IV/10, 3). Discussion on this topic in Stoicescu, *Vlad Țepeș*, 15–25, 35–37. Relating the campaign against the prince of Wallachia, Vlad the Impaler (*Kazıklu Voyvoda*), Tursun bey started, like other chroniclers, to define the previous legal condition of the Wallachian voivodes towards the Porte (Tursun bey, *Tarih*, ed. Inalcık, Murphey, 47, 93a–103a).

110 On this topic, a very interesting study is provided by Marian Coman, who argues that actually there were very few autochthonous insignia of power in Wallachia prior to the

> to grant [Francis Rákoczy] required [items], i.e. the imperial charter of oath and the illustrious banner and the sceptre and the horse and the sword and the needed traditional robe of honors.[111]

The insignia of investiture were recorded in treasury registers (*ruznamçe*), as necessary expenses associated with appointment and inauguration (*teşrif ü-tevcih*).[112]

It is necessary to emphasize that, *de jure*, a new voivode began his reign upon receiving the insignia of power, the date being registered in the official diploma of his appointment. Obtaining a *berat*[113] was a prerequisite, since the very authority of the official was vested in the document.[114] The same applied for Moldavian, Wallachian and Transylvanian rulers,[115] the voivodes usually receiving the document within a few months after their appointment took place. In order to secure the *berat*, the pretenders and newly-appointed voivodes made significant concessions with respect to sums they remitted to the Porte. One can invoke Martinuzzi's strategy in Transylvania in 1541:

> The relevant diploma was issued under the seal of the treasurer and was announced to the Transylvanian estates by Oruc *çavuş*. However, Martinuzzi managed to arrange for these diplomas to be preserved in Istanbul, where the witness himself saw them when he went to the sultan's capital with the first lot of tribute from Transylvania.[116]

---

Ottomans (Marian Coman, *Putere şi teritoriu. Ţara Românească medievală (secolele XIV-XVI)*, Polirom, Iaşi, 2013).

111 *Lazim gelen ʿahdname-yi hümayun ve sancak-ı alem ve topuz ve at ve kılıç ve sa'ir lazim gelen ʿadet hilʿatları ihsan edüb* (Gemil, *Documente turceşti*, doc. 126: *ʿarz* of 1 September 1652).

112 *Teşrif* means a conferring honor or rank, and *tecvih* means a conferring an office (*Redhouse*, 1162, 1165). See Maxim, *Empire ottoman*, 157–169.

113 Reychman, Zajaczkowski, *Handbook of Ottoman-Turkish Diplomatics*, 136–137.

114 "The *berat* – said Halil Inalcık – established and guaranteed the authority of the officier over a group of subjects of the Sultan, the sole and supreme authority, by whom solemn authorization and installation was therefore necessary" (Inalcık, "Appointment," 197). For the procedure of appointment at the Ottoman chancery see another study of Halil Inalcık, "Osmanlı Bürokrasisinde Aklâm ve Muâmelât," *OA/JOS* I (1980), 1–14.

115 In this respect, in 1714 Ştefan Cantacuzino wrote to the Patriarch Hrisant Notara that *haseki ağa* brought to him the *berat* and *kaftan* (Hurmuzaki, *Documente*, XIV/1, doc. DLXXXIV). In April 1795, in front of Selim III, the agents invoked "the custom of granting the high diploma to the voivodes of Wallachia and Moldavia" (*Eflak ve Boğdan voyvodalarına bu vecihle berat-ı ali iʿtası muʿtad oldığı*) (Veliman, *Documente turceşti*, doc. 218).

116 From the testimony of János Szalánczy, Isabella's envoy to the Porte, in the case of the Martinuzzi murder summarized by Gábor Barta (cf. Fodor, "Ottoman policy," 328).

Usually, the delivery of nomination documents was entrusted to the custodian of imperial warrants and his staff (*berat emini*), but in some cases the princes personally attended the Ottoman court in Istanbul or Edirne to receive their diplomas. A diploma fee (*resm-i berat*) was also demanded to issue the *berat*.[117]

Very few imperial diplomas granted to the voivodes of Wallachia[118] and Moldavia[119] have been preserved. In contrast, virtually all *berat-ı hümayun*s granted to Transylvanian princes between 1541 and 1699 survive and some were published. Considering the frequent requests and recommendations regarding the grants of *berat*s or *ʿahdname*s, one can conclude these documents were important for reinforcing the princes' loyalty towards sultans and avoiding potential abuses by Ottoman authorities.[120]

### 2.6 *Reconfirmations, Dethronements, Executions*

Once on the throne, a voivode could be reconfirmed in his function. According to seventeenth- and eighteenth-century sources, in this period reconfirmation took place every three years and required a personal acknowledgment of submission and loyalty to the Porte by the incumbent.[121] This is illustrated by the episode from Radu Leon's reign in Wallachia, as a *hüküm* of Mehmed IV states:

> Since Radu bey came to bow to the Imperial Stirrup [...] his reign was confirmed and established for three years henceforward.[122]

117 Matuz, "Transmission," 23; Maxim, *Empire ottoman*, 166–167; Veliman, "Haraci," 296, n. 73.

118 *Berat* of *evahir-i Cemazi ül-evvel* 985/6–15 August 1577 granted to Mihnea II (Bayezid Kütüphanesi, fd. Veliyüddin Efendi, no. 1970, f. 9–10; mf. ANIC, mf. Tukey, r. 74, c. 8–9; Tahsin Gemil, "Documente turceşti inedite (sfârşitul sec. XVI şi XVII)," *RA*, 3, 1981, 353–356, facsimile and translation). *Berat* granted to Mihnea II by Murad III, on 22 *Ramazan* 993/17 September 1585 (BOA, *Maliyeden Müdevver Defteri*, no. 17932, 11–12; mf. ANIC, mf. Turkey, r. 155, fr. 618–620; Maxim, *CTO*, doc. 14, facsimile and translation).

119 In Ahmed Feridun bey's anthology is included also a *berat* granted to Voivode Alexandru Iliaş (1616–1618 and 1627–1629 in Wallachia; 1620–1621 and 1631–1633 in Moldavia) (Feridun, *Münşeʿat*, II, 398–400).

120 On a sixteenth-century Wallachian hospodar (Gemil, *Documente turceşti*, doc. 1: *bize dahi ʿahdname inayet ilunmak*). On Gheorghe Martinuzzi in 1551–1552 (Mustafa Celalzade, in *Cronici turceşti*, I, 283). On Gabriel Bethlen, in 1614 (Katib Çelebi, *Fezleke-i Tarih*, in *Cronici turceşti II*, 70–71).

121 A relevant document is the "submission charter" of 28 September 1641, translated in Ottoman as *ʿubudiyetname*, by which George Rákoczy I renewed his obeisance and fidelity towards the Porte. Subsequently, he was confirmed again as prince of Transylvania (Gemil, *Documente turceşti*, doc. 106).

122 *Hüküm* of 1 *Cemazi ül-ahir* 1078/18 November 1667 (Gemil, *Documente turceşti*, doc. 148: *Radul Bey gelüb Rikab-ı hümayun şevket-makrun şehr-yari'ya yüz sürüb Eflak beyliği kemakan üç seneye değin kendüye ibka ve mukarrer kılınmağın*).

This was accompanied by the payment of a special fee, called in the eighteenth century an *ıbka*, which became a standard procedure by this time.[123]

In turn, the voivode's failure to meet his obligations was regarded by the Ottoman officials as a sign of disloyalty or incompetence, punishable by dethronement (*ʿazl*) or even execution (*katl*). In this respect, maybe the most trenchant statement was made by Selim II in 1572, when the Moldavian voivode Bogdan Lăpușneanu (1568–1572) fled and sought refuge in Poland:

> Thus, from the past until now, it is accustomed that those who do not direct – with the most faithful and greatest devotion – all their efforts towards our imperial duties, nor strive for the prosperity and development of their country and principality, nor for the happiness of their subjects and nobles, acting contrary to our illustrious benevolence, will not be forgiven at any moment, but rather, will be punished according to their crimes either by dethronement or by other methods.[124]

The usual justification of a voivode's dethronement and execution was the violation of the tributary-protection covenant (*ʿahd*), included – implicitly or explicitly – in the investiture diploma granted to the voivode.

The first instances of dethronement are recorded as early as the latter half of the sixteenth century and the Porte frequently resorted to this method throughout the early modern period. Deposed voivodes were frequently exiled to Rhodes[125] and their property and debt were seized by their successor.[126] The severity of such punishments, particularly the *katl*, led sultans to seek *fetva*s

---

123 It was about 375 *guruş* in 1759 (Veliman, *Documente turcești*, doc. 139: *Boğdan'lunun ibkalarında mu'tad üzere alınan avaidleri*).

124 Letter of *eva'il-i Zilhicce* 979/15–24 April 1572 to Sigismund II (Mehmet, *Documente turcești*, I, doc. 103). When John the Terrible was named to the Moldavian throne, Selim II insisted to remind him that "so long as you make sincere efforts and endeavors for defending and protecting the subjects there, no dethronement (*'azl*) is for you" (Mehmet, *Documente turcești*, I, doc. 122: *hüküm* of 4 *Rebi ül-ahir*/14 August 1572).

125 I am quoting here from the Ecaterina's letter of 14 January 1584 to Mărioara Adorno: "and I am in Rhodes with my son, Voivode Mihnea [...] because these people have the following custom: when a Ruler is dethroned, he is not allowed to remain in Constantinople" (Hurmuzaki, *Documente*, XIV/1, doc. VXLIII). Also, Mustafa Selaniki told about a former Wallachian prince who, in 1590–1591, "was imprisoned in Rhodes, according to an old usage" (Selaniki, *Tarih*, in *Cronici turcești I*, 363).

126 *Documente privitoare la familia Cantacuzino scoase în cea mai mare parte din arhiva D-lui G. Gr. Cantacuzino și publicate de N. Iorga*, Bucharest: Ed. Minerva, 1902, doc. LXI: letter of 1691, written by Dosoftei, Patriarch of Jerusalim.

providing the legal basis for their application.[127] For instance, *şeyh ül-Islam* stated that postponing the dismissals and executions of Miron Barnovschi (1633) and Constantin Brâncoveanu (1714), who had violated their oaths, would constitute a great sin.[128] In the case of the former, it was not only the voivode who faced an imminent threat, but also the boyars who accompanied him to the Porte. Although initially Murad IV intended to kill all members of the entourage, he was swayed by *şeyh ül-Islam*'s opinion, who had advised him to kill only "the head" of the rebellion:

> What is the people's guilt? Kill the leader, [and] the people will calm.[129]

But there are sufficient cases when the sultans assumed the right to inflict capital punishment on nobles and subjects who revolted against voivodes, based on certain legal opinions, such as the following example:

> The mufti issued the Fetwa: 'He who revolts against the ruler named by the emperor, revolts against the emperor, and the rebellion against the emperor is punished with death; therefore the rebellions against the Moldavian voivode [Constantin Cantemir (1685–1693)] are to be punished by death.' So it is written.[130]

The princes' attitudes in this matter oscillated between contrariety and resignation. Under these conditions, one can say that in September 1584, Voivode Mihnea II the Renegade of Wallachia complained in vain that:

> No evil deed was being perpetrated on my part [yet] I was dethroned from that province.[131]

Clearly, the Porte knew better who could protect and promote their interests in Wallachia.

---

127 Cantemir, *Viaţa*, 65. Also, in the fifteenth century, after the conquering of Jajce, the execution of the Bosnian king, Stephan Tomaşević (1461–1463), who was tribute-payer of Mehmed II but became a rebel after refusing to pay his *harac* in 1463, needed a *fetva* issued by the şeyh Ali Bastan (Decei, *Imp. otoman*, 110).

128 Veliman, *Documente turceşti*, doc. 11.

129 Miron Costin, *Letopiseţ*, 102. Between 1632–1634, *şeyh ül-Islam* was Ahizade Hüseyin Efendi.

130 Cantemir, *Viaţa*, 193. The most famous *şeyh ül-Islam* from this period was Çatalcalı Ali Efendi, so that is not impossible that this *fetva* belongs to him.

131 Bănescu, "Mihnea II," 181.

CHAPTER 12

# Voivodes as Tribute-Payers

From the reign of Süleyman Kanunî (1520–1566) onwards, the Ottomans understood the confirmation of tributary rulers in terms of delegating a part of sultanic power. As with the case of provincial governors, these comprised the "rule and governance of the country," "protecting and safeguarding subjects" and "defending the country."[1]

The status of tribute-paying princes tacitly perpetuated pre-conquest traditions of the country with regard to its internal authority, granting the appointee broad administrative and juridical autonomy. Sultans and grand viziers emphasized the role of Wallachian, Moldavian and Transylvanian self-governance as a crucial building block of *pax ottomanica*. Mustafa III himself stated that the status of an autonomous province implied that "all affairs of the subjects" were entrusted to the voivode's care "with full powers, according to liberty."[2] In his turn, Dimitrie Cantemir, former voivode of Moldavia, described this autonomy in the following manner:

> This remained hitherto inviolate to the Princes of *Moldavia* and *Walachia*. They fill at pleasure all the great offices, make new laws, and have full power of life and death over all. For after the Prince is authorized, no complaints of the death of any Person, Baron or other, though ever so innocent, are heard at the *Othman* Court. But if he has exacted any thing tyrannically and illegally from his Subjects, he is accountable for it.[3]

Just as the principle of taxpayer protection dominated in the Ottoman state, imperial orders regularly invoked the basic task of the voivode to protect the wealth and happiness of his subjects, defined as the sultan's *reʿaya*. This found its expression in numerous formulas employed in official documents, such as *reʿaya ve berayanın himayet ü sıyaneti* or *zabt ü sıyanet-i raʿiyet*.[4] For example, in

1 Numerous formulas were employed in official documents, such as: *hıfz ü hıraset-i memleket; memleketin zabt ü rabtı; zabt ü sıyanet-i raʿiyet* (Mehmet, *Documente turcești*, I, doc. 29, 35; Gemil, *Documente turcești*, doc. 20, 42, 204; Veliman, *Documente turcești*, doc.7)

2 *ala-vech-il-istiklal serbestiyet üzere* (Veliman, *Documente turcești*, doc. 133: *hüküm* of *evasıt-ı Ramazan* 1171/19–28 May 1758).

3 Cantemir, *Othman History*, 203, n. 68.

4 Gemil, *Documente turcești*, doc. 20 (referring to Ieremia Movilă in 1605), doc. 42 (referring to Constantin Movilă in 1609), doc. 204 (concerning Constantin Duca in 1693); Maxim, *CTO*, doc. 14.

 | DOI:10.1163/9789004411104_013

1559 Süleyman Kanunî ordered Moldavian and Wallachian hospodars to care for "subjects' wealth and happiness."[5] Over a century and a half later, upon Nicolae Mavrocordat's appointment as the Voivode of Moldavia in 1711, Ahmed III reminded him that "your subjects have to be guarded and protected."[6]

In addition, a recently-appointed voivode was assigned the task of defending his country against any enemy, which constituted an essential aspect of the notion of Well-Protected Domains. Thus, in 1559 Süleyman Kanunî charged Mircea the Shepherd in Wallachia and Alexandru Lăpușneanu in Moldavia to "defend and protect" their countries and to waste "no time to ensure the peace and safety of the *vilayet*."[7] A few years later, in a *hüküm* sent to Wallachian voivode Petru the Younger, but referring also to Prince John Sigismund Zápolya of Transylvania, the same sultan clearly defined their role in upholding the *pax ottomanica* system:

> Therefore, both are my devoted slaves, named by my person [...] as defenders of my Well-Protected Domains.[8]

As the "defense and protection of the country" (*hıfz ü hıraset-i memleket*) became another standard phrase in Ottoman documents, it was used in correspondence with the voivodes of Moldavia, Ieremia Movilă in 1605, Constantin Movilă in 1609, and Constantin Duca in 1693.[9]

Apart from the three duties discussed above, the Porte demanded that the voivodes – as Ottoman *haracgüzar*s – conform to imperial orders and perform all established political, military and financial duties (*hizmet*). For a tributary prince, these duties included paying *harac*, which was also seen as a "collection of poll-taxes" (*cizyelerinin tahsili*), and political–military obligations expressed by the formula "be a friend of our friends and an enemy of our enemies" (*dosta dostumuza ve düşman düşmanımıza olub*). In short, tribute-paying, military support and information gathering constituted the basic elements of tributary status north of the Danube.

---

5 Mehmet, *Documente turcești*, I, doc. 29, 35.

6 *Re'ayasının her vechile himayet ü sıyaneti lazim olmağla* (Veliman, *Documente turcești*, doc. 7).

7 Mehmet, *Documente turcești*, I, doc. 35. There are sufficient examples of voivodes enthroned with the order to restore public order in the name of the Porte, including Radu Mihnea, Ștefan Tomșa II, Gașpar Grațiani and Mihnea III.

8 *Imdi ikinüz dahi cenab-ı celalet-meabım kıbelinden memalik-i mahruseme hafiz ta'yin olunmuş yarar kullarımsız* (Veliman, "Carte de legământ," 31).

9 Gemil, *Documente turcești*, doc. 20, 42, 204.

## 1 Tribute-Paying

### 1.1 *Tribute of Islamic Holy Law (harac-ı şerʿiye)*

Ottoman chroniclers, like Mustafa Selaniki, labeled sums of money annually delivered by Wallachian, Moldavian and Transylvanian rulers a "tribute of Islamic holy law" (*harac-ı şerʿiye*).[10] Let us briefly analyze this concept.

In early Islamic official documents, the terms of *cizye* and *harac* were employed for the tribute paid by non-Muslims, without a clear distinction between them.[11] Although jurists tried to distinguish between the terms, equivocal definitions persisted in the legal texts and were adapted by the Ottomans. Common characteristics of these two concepts exacerbated the confusion: both were demanded from the infidels to show their abased condition in comparison with Muslims; both fed the public treasury of the Islamic empire; and both had to be paid up at the end of the year.[12]

As far as the notion of *cizye* is concerned, modern scholars have tried, unsuccessfully, to specify for what privileges non-Muslims paid this tax. Claude Cahen argued that *cizye* was paid in compensation for rejecting conversion to Islam, but M. M. Bravmann claimed that it constituted a ransom for the non-Muslim's life. Yet other specialists contended that *cizye* was imposed in lieu of non-Muslims military service against the infidels.[13] There is evidence supporting each of these hypotheses, for the *cizye* could be waived only upon its payer's conversion to Islam; enemy captives had to pay, according to an old Arab tradition, compensation to avoid being killed, and the *cizye* was imposed only on men who were able to fight.[14] In the Ottoman period, since the *cizye* was imposed only on non-Muslim subjects, it can be described as a confessional tax, intended mainly to emphasize the difference between believers

---

10 Selaniki Mustafa Efendi, *Tarih-i Selaniki*, vol. 2, ed. Ipşirli (Istanbul, 1989), p. 541 (on Ieremia Movila's case).

11 On the legal aspects of *cizye* and *harac*, see Hüsrev, *Dürer*, 192–221: including the chapter on the poll-tax (*Fasl fi al-cizye*); Halebi, *Mülteka* (ed. 1993), vol. 2, 602–614; *Fetava-yi Yahya Efendi*, SK, Hamidiye 601, f. 12a–16b (*Bab al-üşr ve al-harac*); Mawerdi, *Ahkam*, 299–331; Cl. Cahen, H. Inalcık, P. Hardy, "Djizya," *EI-2*, II , 559–566; C. Orhonlu, "Kharadj. III. Turquie ottomane," *EI-2*, IV, 1083–1086; Hossein Modarressi, *Kharaj in Islamic Law*, London: Anchor Press, 1983.

12 Caurroy, "Législation," IV/17, 573; Mawerdi, *Ahkam*, 299–331; Khadduri, *War and Peace*, 190.

13 Courbage, Fargues, *Chrétiens et Juifs*, 212; H. Inalcık, "Djizya. II. Ottoman," *EI-2*, II, 563; M. M. Bravmann, "À propos de Qur'an IX-29," *Arabica* 10:1, 1963, 94–95; M. M. Bravmann, "The Ancient Arab Background of the Qur'anic Concept al-Gizyatu' An Yadin," *Arabica*, 13:3, 1966, 307–314, and 14:1, 1967, 90–91; Maxim, "Obligațiile," 100.

14 Halebi, *Mülteka* (ed. 1993), vol. 2, 602–614; Mawerdi, *Ahkam*, 312; Cahen, "Djizya," 562–563; Bravmann, "Qur'an IX-29," 94–95.

(*mu'min*) and infidels (*kafir*).[15] In fact, *cizye* was included in the category of "religious taxes" (*tekalif-i şer'iye*), along with *zekat, harac*, and *gümrük*, as opposed to customary taxes (*tekalif-i 'örfiye*). Gradually, however, *cizye* came to be regarded as a reimbursement paid by non-Muslim subjects to not participate in the campaigns.[16]

At the same time, Muslim scholars associated payments by non-Muslims with the term *harac*, which generally meant duty. Commonly *harac* referred to two kinds of duties, the "poll-tax" (*harac-ı ru'us*), imposed on non-Muslims who accepted the supremacy of Islam, and the "land duty" (*harac-ı arazi*), on the conquered land left in the non-Muslims' possession. The *harac-ı arazi* was also defined as being a *şeri'at* tax. It was not waived upon the conversion to Islam and was also paid by Muslim landowners; it also displayed certain secular features in that it was calculated on the basis of land size or the quantity of crops.[17]

### 1.2 *Communal Tribute (harac-ı maktu')*

In the Ottoman Empire, *cizye* and *harac* were paid either as individual or as communal taxes. In the former case, *cizye* was collected in the Balkans, according to the rules of *şeri'at*, from every male non-Muslim subject who had reached puberty and was able to sustain himself (approximately between the ages of thirteen and sixty-five). The tax was imposed after a census was taken and tax-payers were divided into those who paid the highest (*evla*), the middle (*evsat*) and the lowest rate (*edna*).[18] An alternative method was a system called *maktu'* in Arabic and Ottoman Turkish, whereby a lump sum was imposed on specific

15 According to a *hadis*, "No Muslim would be obliged to pay *cizye*, as well as two *kıblas* could not exist in the same country." See also Laoust, *Ibn Taimiya*. 270; d'Ohsson, *Tableau*, V, 22–23; Khadduri, *War and Peace*, 189.

16 Hamidullah, *Documents*, 257; Lewis, *Islam*, I, 236; Akgündüz, *Osmanlı Kanunnameleri*, 1, 167–171; Gemil, *Documente turceşti*, doc. 11; Silahdar, *Zeyil-i Fezleke*, in *Cronici turcesti II*, 330.

17 D'Ohsson, *Tableau*, V, 19–20; Mawerdi, *Ahkam*, 312; Abu Yusuf Ya'kub used the term *harac* for "capitation," too (Khadduri, *War and Peace*, 190). Dimitrie Cantemir also provided a definition of *harac*: "A set tribute, which all persons that are not *Mahometans*, are obliged to pay to the *Turkish* Emperors. This imposition is grounded on the *Koran*, which enjoins, that every person of a different persuasion shall pay yearly, when come to a ripe age, thirteen drams of pure silver, if he has a mind to be a subject to the empire, and not to be obliged to embrace the *Mahometan* religion." (Cantemir, *Othman History*, 366, n. 19).

18 This method was called *'ala al-ru'us* in Arabic, meaning *per capita*. See Nedkoff, "Cizye (baş vergisi)," 599–652; Daniel S. Goffman, "The *Maktu'* System and the Jewish Community of Sixteenth-Century Safed: A Study of two Documents from the Ottoman Archives," *OA/JOS*, III, 1982, 81–90; Michael Kiel, "Remarks on the Administration of the Poll Tax (*Cizye*) in the Ottoman Balkans and Value of Poll-Tax Registers (*Cizye Defterleri*) for Demographic Research," *EB*, 26:4, 1990, 70–104.

ethnic-confessional communities and territorial entities within the empire.[19] In such instances, the *harac* was considered a communal *cizye* and, since it was established by means of a covenant (*ʿahd, sulh*), its level was in theory to remain unchanged. Hamilton Gibb and Harold Bowen described it in following terms:

> A 'Scriptural' people of the Domain of War might, according to the *şeriʿat,* contract with the conqueror in certain circumstances for the payment of a fixed sum in perpetuity, instead of submitting to the imposition of the normal *cizye per capita*; and the tributes in question were paid under this head.[20]

As for the principalities of Moldavia, Wallachia and Transylvania, *şeyh ül-Islam* Ebussuud Efendi, in a *fetva* comprised of a series of legal opinions concerning Ottoman taxes, considered the princes' annual *vergüs* to be a 1,000-*filori*-per-country poll-tax of the kind usually imposed on infidels as a result of covenants (*sulhları*) concluded with them by sultans.[21] Technically, this tribute was also a form of *cizye*.

The principalities, along with the Ragusan Republic also paid an annual tribute that fell within the category of a "communal tribute" (*harac-ı maktuʿ*) levied on non-Muslims by their representatives, such as the voivodes, in theory as a fixed sum of money.[22] This autonomous fiscal system was applied in other administrative-territorial units of the empire and was referred to by the Ottomans as *miri-i maktuʿ* and *mal-ı maktuʿ*. "You shall know that the principalities

19 Mawerdi, *Ahkam,* 312; Darling, *Revenue-Raising,* 104–105; Goffman, "Maktuʿ System," 82: "In other words, rather than attempt to impose rigorous Ottoman taxation policies upon the newly conquered peoples the Ottomans often left the tax collection to local political, religious, and social institutions in return for an agreed upon cash payment."

20 Gibb, Bowen, *Islamic Society,* 256.

21 *Bir nev'i oldur ki, Müfti Efendi Hazretlerinin fetvalarında mestur olan üzere Sultan-ı Ehl-i Islam ile keferenin rıza ve sulhları olur. Yılda bin filori gibi. Haricde misali Vilayet-i Rumda Boğdanın Eflakın ve Erdel Vilayetinin yıldan yıla verdikleri vergi gibi* (Akgündüz, *Osmanlı Kanunnameleri,* 5/1, 97).

22 Ottomans initially allowed the inhabitants of many conquered territories to pay some of their taxes in the form of a fixed sum (*maktuʿ*). In the Arab provinces, conquered in the first part of the sixteenth century, for instance, the sub-farmed districts of Lebanon paid an annual tribute to the *paşas* of Sayda and Tripoli. This was also the case in Ragusa and certain Aegean islands. Concerning "communal tribute," the Ottomans were not interested in the way the taxes were gathered, as their representatives being permitted to collect it as "poll-tax" (*cizye*) or "land-taxes" (*harac*). See Gibb and Bowen, *Islamic Society,* 256; C. Orhonlu, "Kharadj. III. Turquie ottomane," *EI-2,* IV, 1083–1086; Slot, *Archipelagus Turbatus,* 79; Biegman, *Ragusa,* 32; Inalcık, "Djizya. II. Ottoman" 562–563,

of Moldavia and Wallachia are *miri-i maktuʿ*, wrote Ahmed III in 1729 to vizier Mustafa paşa, *muhafiz* of Hotin, ordering him to refrain from "the slightest act of tyranny and abuse of the subjects of the two principalities."[23]

### 1.3 *The Voivodes from "Tenants of Tribute" to "Poll-tax Collectors"*

"Collective tribute" was usually paid through an intermediary,[24] which in the case of post-fifteenth-century principalities, meant to Moldavian and Wallachian voivodes. Even Vlad the Impaler and Stephen the Great were classified by contemporary sources as "tenants of the tribute" (*haracına mültezim*).[25] As the seventeenth- and eighteenth-century sources retrospectively applied their own legal and administrative categories to the past centuries, they regarded tribute paid by Moldavia and Wallachia as sums of individual poll-taxes paid by their inhabitants, as subjects of empire (*reʿayas*), "levied and collected and delivered continuously to my imperial treasure through its voivodes." Moreover, the voivodes came to be seen as "poll-tax collectors" (*cizyedars*),[26] Ottoman clerks of the financial domain. Consequently, other poll-tax collectors from neighboring *sancaks* were forbidden by the sultan from levying *cizye* from Wallachians Moldavians and Transylvanians.

Due to their pre-conquest status as sovereign rulers, the princes retained their traditional right to impose and collect taxes. Perceived as an "old custom" but subsequently reinforced by "high orders" issued by sultans, this right was recognized and confirmed in the very moments when it was infringed upon by Ottoman authorities.[27] In fact, even within ethnic-confessional autonomous communities, poll-tax paying was usually regulated internally and assessed by the communities themselves, whether the tax was imposed *per capita* or as a lump payment.[28]

---

23 *Boğdan ve Eflak memleketi miri-i maktuʿ olub* (Veliman, *Documente turceşti*, doc. 63: *hüküm* of *evahir-i Safer* 1142/15–23 September 1729).

24 Halebi, *Mülteka* (ed. 1993), vol. 2, 602–614; Mawerdi, *Ahkam*, 299.

25 Tursun bey, *Tarih* (ed. 1972), 110, 170.

26 Veliman, *Documente turceşti*, doc. 140: *hüküm* of *eva'il-i Muharrem* 1173/25 August-3 September 1759.

27 Veliman, *Documente turceşti*, doc. 145 (document of August 1760: "the customs and other taxes from the port of Galaţi, which is within the principality of Moldavia, had been collected since ancient times by Moldavian voivodes").

28 Similarly, in Thessaloniki, community leaders divided the burden among the congregations, with each assessing its individual members, dividing them between three categories (high, middle and low). There was no connection between this assessment and that carried out by Ottoman authorities. The internal assessment method was progressive, with the wealthy also paying the poll-tax of many of the poor (who paid no taxes at all). See Rozen, "Jewish community," 38.

### 1.4 *Tribute and Peace*

Even though the Ottomans tended to render the empire's relationship with its tributaries in a generic and unchanging vocabulary, the role and significance of tribute changed over the centuries. In D. E. Pitcher's opinion, the tribute paid by Chios, Ragusa and Naxos, and their submission to the Porte, had "commercial value"; whereas in contrast, the protection of the Holy Cities and the tribute paid by Venice carried a "prestige value." Finally, the submission of the Crimean Khanate, tributary polities north of the Danube and in other frontier areas had "military value."[29]

In regard to Moldavia, Wallachia and Transylvania, the significance of the tributes paid by the voivodes depended directly on the power relationship between them and the Porte. Under the basic rules of Islamic law of peace and war, until the 1520s and 1530s, the tribute payments registered as *cizye* and *harac* should be considered ransom for temporary peace.[30]

Of Wallachia, the Ragusan Michael Bocignoli wrote in 1524 that Basarab Laiotă "bought the peace from the Turks by paying an annual tribute of twelve thousand ducats."[31] This was also the traditional interpretation by local boyars. Thus, the money paid by late-fourteenth-century Wallachian voivodes was called "gifts" by seventeenth- and eighteenth-century chroniclers. Mircea the Elder, "coming up against the Turks' impudence, reconciled with them and presented them with gifts (*plocoane*) for his country to take rest in peace," wrote Radu Popescu, referring to a political moment following the battle "of Rovine" (1394).[32] Likewise, Alexandru I Aldea replied in 1432 to an accusation brought by the inhabitants of Sibiu:

---

29 Pitcher, *Ottoman Empire*, 130.

30 It is a general opinion in Romanian historiography that tribute did not signify their complete submission to the Ottomans. See Matei, "Regimul juridic," 462; Maxim, "Statutul politico-juridic," 109.

31 *Călători străini*, I, 177.

32 Popescu, *Istoriile*, 240. It is worth comparing the Wallachian case with the Byzantine. In 1348, Anna of Savoy accepted giving Orhan, among other things, "a great sum of money." John VI Cantacuzino compensated the Ottomans sent to help him with "plenty of gifts." After having occupied the throne in February 1347, John V Paleologus in 1379 and John VII Paleologus in 1390 made commitments to Murad I and Bayezid I, respectively, to remit annual payments – thus, a permanent tribute – of "many hundreds of gold and silver" in order to regain and obtain the Byzantine throne, see Ducas, *Istoria*, VIII/1, IX/1–2; Chalcocondil, *Expuneri*, 35, 42, 54–55; Melissenos, *Cronica*, I/13. Also see Octavian Iliescu, "Le montant du tribut payé par Byzance à l'Empire Ottoman en 1379 et 1424," *RESEE*, 9:3,1971, 427–432; Dölger, *Regesten 5*, no. 3136; Danişmend, *OTKronolojisi*, 1, 55–56.

> and if I also went to the Turks, I did it for my own needs and I bought peace to my country.[33]

From both the Ottoman–Islamic and Moldavian standpoints, irregular tribute payments by the voivodes Petru Aron and Stephen the Great of Moldavia in the second half of the fifteenth century were intended only to obtain temporary protection and the cancellation of Ottoman military expeditions.[34] Dimitrie Cantemir considered the tribute paid up until the time of Voivode Bogdan III the Blind (1504–1513), to have been a ransom for protection from oppression such as in the case of other Christian rulers.[35]

Beginning in the mid-sixteenth century, the tributes paid by Wallachian, Moldavian and Transylvanian voivodes took on new meanings from the new legal and political context created by Ottoman control over the territories north of the Danube.[36] As *harac* came to signify the Muslim community's right over conquered lands, contemporary Ottoman and Christian sources started to perceive tribute payments as a sign of the voivodes' and boyars' complete submission to the Porte and Ottoman permanent protection over these territories as parts of the Well-Protected Domains.[37] On the other hand, tribute was frequently associated with occupying the thrones and demonstrating loyalty to sultans. George Rákoczy I wrote on 28 September 1641 in his "letter of submission" (*ʿubudiyetname*):

> So that you may see that I am decided and constant in the loyalty necessary due to your Porte of happiness (*Asitane-yi saʿadetinize lazim olan sadakatımda*), I prepared the usual tribute (*harac*) of the country and my gift (*pişkeş*).[38]

Yet one constant meaning remained. The payment of tribute meant, for both Ottomans and Christians, a settlement of peaceful relations, whether temporary or permanent. According to a late-sixteenth-century observer, Michael the Brave is said to have declared,

33 *DRH, D*, I, doc. 199.

34 Guboglu, *Paleografia,* doc. 4; Decei, "Sulhname," 122; Mehmet, *Documente turcești*, I, doc. 5.

35 Cantemir invoked the case of Venice as a model (Cantemir, *Descrierea Moldovei,* 271).

36 Maxim, "Cantemir," 70–71; Gemil, *Românii și otomanii,* 211.

37 In this respect, on 8 September 1589, Sigismund Báthory admitted that "in order to rule Transylvania and obtain its protection by sultan, we have accustomed to pay tribute." (Veress, *Documente III,* doc. 125.

38 Gemil, *Documente turcești,* doc. 106.

> I could have lived at peace with the Turks and the Tartars by sending five burdens of money as a token of tribute.[39]

### 1.5 *Tribute and Pact*

Because the most important legal obligation of Southeastern European princes towards the sultans was the annual delivery of tribute deposit, it featured prominently in all oral and written engagements between the two parties.[40] In certain classical legal texts, the payment of tribute by a non-Muslim prince or community was equated by Muslims with the conclusion of a pact. Yahya b. Adam registered and accredited the answer given by an Arab scholar named al-Shaʾbi to the question of Caliph ʿUmar b. ʿAbd al-ʿAziz: "did the people of Sawad have an agreement?" The scholar responded:

> They had no pact but when the *harac* was accepted from them, that was considered their pact.[41]

Most Ottoman chroniclers tied the concept of "tribute-payer" (*haracgüzar*) to that of "pact" (*ʿahd*). Idris Bitlisi, writing about the policy of Mehmed I Çelebi (1413–1420) towards the principality of Wallachia, emphasized with some exaggeration that:

> the rulers (*hükkam*) and the governors (*valis*) of that place were tribute-payers (*haracgüzarlar*) and signatories of pact (*muʿahidin*) lasting from the reigns of the sultan's father and ancestors.

The same historian linked Vlad the Evil's status as tribute-payer to his "engagement (*ʿahd*) with the sultan,"[42] and, consequently, the traditional *ʿahd* was conditioned, first of all, by sending the tribute to the Porte.

The voivodes' status as *haracgüzar* was an integral part of imperial charters and diplomas (*ʿahdname-yi hümayun, berat-ı hümayun*) which generally regulated the sultan–voivode relationship. In a *berat* granted to Voivode Mihnea II the Renegade on 17 September 1585, we read:

---

39 *Mihai.1. Documente* doc. 55.

40 For the *ʿahdnames* granted to Dubrovnik, see Biegman, *Ragusa*, 57, 126–131.

41 Yahya bin Adam, *Kitab*, no. 126.

42 Idris Bitlisi, *Heșt Behișt*, in *Cronici turcești I*, 162–163, 165, 167.

> He shall send yearly the fixed tribute of the mentioned country, entirely and good coin [...] and with complete weight and in time.[43]

The very granting of such "investiture diplomas" to the tributary princes was contingent upon the payment of, or at least the pledge to pay, tribute to the Porte. This is clear from a document of 1714 which refers to the Wallachian voivode Ștefan Cantacuzino:

> And deeming it right that he granted my distinguished order – which all the peoples obey – on a condition that he pays off and delivers (*eda ve teslim eylemek*), in time and in season, according to the old custom, the *harac* and what he promised and the money for the *bayram*, I ordered and issued this diploma, sign of happiness and goal of joy.[44]

According to the *șeriʿat, cizye* and *harac* had to be paid annually, usually at the end of the year, and were not to be requested before this deadline.[45] In consequence, voivodes were consequently ordered to pay their tribute "on time" (*vaktiyle*), that is, "annually" (*sal-be-sal*),[46] or, in certain circumstances, "every two years."[47]

### 1.6 *The Amount of Tribute*

Until the mid-sixteenth century, Wallachian and Moldavian voivodes were not paying more than 15,000–20,000 gold pieces per year, the customary amount demanded from the tributary princes of Southeastern Europe in that period. At first, the rulers of Wallachia paid a tribute of 2,000–3,000 gold pieces; Vlad the Impaler (1456–1462) paid 10,000 gold pieces; in the third decade of the sixteenth century Radu of Afumați sent 14,000 gold pieces, and in 1540–1541 the

43 Maxim, *CTO*, doc. 14: 22 *Ramazan* 993 AH. For comparison, see the *ʿahdname* granted to Stephen the Great in 1480–1481 by Mehmed II: "and the tribute I had established in times of yore, which represented three thousand French florins every year, by doubling it, I raised it to six thousand every year" (*ve beriden üzerüme vazʿ olunan harac ki her yıl üç bin sikke-i efrenci filori idi muzaaf idüb her yıl altı bin sikke idüb*) (Decei, "Sulhname." 122, 126).

44 Veliman, *Documente turcești,* doc. 13: *nișan-ı hümayun* of *gurre-i Cemazi ül-ahir*/14 June 1714.

45 Mawerdi, *Ahkam,* 299.

46 In an *ʿahdname* granted in 1575 to the prince of Transylvania: "sending in time, yearly, their established tribute" (*taʿyın olunan haracların sal-be-sal vakti ile irsal idüb*) (Veliman, "Carte de legământ," 34).

47 This was Abdul-Hamid I's condition for granting a *berat-ı hümayun* to Grigore III Ghica, voivode of Moldavia, formulated in a *hüküm* of 21 *Receb* 1188/27 September 1774 (Mehmet, *Documente turcești,* I, doc. 291).

voivode of Wallachia paid around 20,000 gold pieces. The Moldavian voivodes were obliged to pay a *harac* of 2,000 gold pieces in 1456, 3,000 before 1473, then 5,000–6,000 gold pieces in 1480–1481, and 15,000 gold pieces in 1541.[48]

A drastic increase in Wallachian and Moldavian tribute took place after 1538–1541, especially in the second half of the sixteenth century. Upon Mircea the Shepherd's enthronement in 1545, the Wallachian tribute was increased to 50,000 gold pieces, but in 1574–1583 it reached 104,000, the maximum amount for the sixteenth century. In Moldavia, 30,000 gold pieces increased soon after 1541 to 53,000 gold pieces after 1574 and 66,000 gold pieces in 1583.[49] The tribute of the Transylvanian princes was maintained at a lower level than that of the Wallachian and Moldavian voivodes, amounting to 10,000 gold pieces until 1575 and then 15,000 until 1699. For the seventeenth and eighteenth centuries, the amount of tribute is no longer indicative as a measure of Ottoman control, as its importance receded in favor of other official or unofficial financial obligations, such as gifts (*pişkeş*) and bribes (*rüşvet*).

A rise in tribute could be initiated by voivodes,[50] or sultans.[51] It usually, but by no means uniformly, took place upon the accession of new sultans[52] or voivodes.[53] Changes could also take place when the taxable population grew

48 On the quantitative evolution of tribute paid by the princes, see: M. Berza, "Haraciul Moldovei şi Ţării Româneşti în sec. XV–XIX," *SMIM*, 2, 1957, 7–48; M. Berza, "Variaţiile exploatării Ţării Româneşti de către Poarta Otomană în secolele XVI–XVIII." *St.RdI* xi, 2, (1958): 59–71; M. A. Mehmet, "Un document turc concernant le kharatch de Moldavie et de la Valachie aux XVe-XVIe siècles," *RESEE*, 5:1–2, 1967, 265–274; M. Guboglu, "Le tribut payé par les Principautés Roumaines à la Porte jusqu'au début du XVIe siècle d'après les sources torques," *REI*, 37:1, 1969, 49–80; M. Maxim, "Circonstances de la majoration du kharadj payé par la Valachie à l'Empire ottoman durant la période 1540–1575," *AIESEE-B*, 12:2, 1974, 367–381; M. Maxim, "Haraciul Moldovei şi Ţării Româneşti în ultimul sfert al veacului XVI," *SMIM*, 12, 1994, 3–46.

49 *Istoria poporului român*, ed. Andrei Oţetea, Bucharest: Editura Ştiinţifică, 1970,152–156 (Chapter of Mihai Berza). I have taken the estimates by Bogdan Murgescu (Murgescu, *Istorie*, 150).

50 Tahsin Gemil argued that, in the fifteenth and the first half of the sixteenth century, the Wallachian and Moldavian voivodes offered to raise their tribute to defend their countries, but after 1538 the increases originated mostly from the competition for the throne (Gemil, *Românii şi otomanii*, 211).

51 Since the Moldavian, Wallachian and Transylvanian tribute was a "state tax," its amount depended solely on the sultan's will (Maxim, "Regimul economic," 1736).

52 In a report of *bailos* Marin di Cavalli and Giacomo Soranzo of 3 June 1567, they wrote on the increase of the tributes of the three principalities on the occasion of Selim II's enthronement (Hurmuzaki, *Documente*, VIII, doc. 169: *di piu per ducato dicendo che è solito ad un novo Principe accrescer li tributi alli suoi feudarij*).

53 Gaşpar Graţiani increased the tribute of Moldavia by 40,000 ducats when he was named as the voivode in 1619 (Decei, *Imp. otoman*, 318).

when new territories became attached to the tributary polity,[54] due to immigration from adjacent provinces,[55] or when poll-tax rates increased for non-Muslims across the empire. In 1567 and 1575, some of the above-mentioned motives for increases were invoked. On the other hand, the tributes of Wallachia and Moldavia were reduced after some parts of the principalities were transferred to adjacent Ottoman provinces,[56] or when military conflicts caused massive demographic and economic losses. Tribute payments could also be temporarily suspended as a reward to loyal voivodes.[57] Moreover, voivodes of Wallachia and Moldavia were obliged to annually send a certain sum to Crimean khans; Peysonnel claimed that both principalities' payments amounted to 440,000 *akçe* in the mid-eighteenth century.[58]

## 2 "Be a Friend to Our Friend and an Enemy to Our Enemy"

For Southeastern European tributary princes, including those of Wallachia, Moldavia and Transylvania, the second most important obligation to the Porte was the one expressed in the phrase "be [a] friend to friend and [an] enemy to enemy" (*dosta dost ve düşmana düşman olub*). This concise expression indicated the voivodes' duty to refrain from any actions against the sultan, to participate in the imperial campaigns, support local governors and gather information about any hostile designs by Christian neighbors.

---

54 Moldavian voivodes were ordered to pay an increased tribute after the fortress Hotin and its neighborhood had been annexed to Moldavia. In this respect, in 1740, Mahmud I ordered Grigore II Ghica to send 5,000 *guruş* (70,620 *akçe*) more as *cizye* (Veliman, *Documente turceşti*, doc. 91, 93).

55 A document of 2 November 1567 spoke of the rise in tribute (*cizye*) demanded by Selim II from the voivode of Wallachia, justified by invoking the immigration from Vidin (Alexandrescu, "Khatt-i şerifs," 256, n. 43.

56 In 1718–1719, after the Ottoman seizure of Hotin, the Moldavian voivodes petitioned the Porte for a corresponding reduction of tribute (Veliman, *Documente turceşti,* doc. 34).

57 Gemil, *Documente turceşti,* doc. 221.

58 In 1581, the khans made their participation in the Iranian campaign conditional on the payment of Moldavian tribute to them. See Hurmuzaki, *Documente,* Supl. I/1, 55–56. Each principality had to pay 500,000 *akçe*s, according to I.H. Uzunçarşılı, (Uzunçarşılı, *Osmanlı Tarihi,* 2, 434). Moreover, sending presents (*ava'idler*) to the Crimean khan and his family is mentioned in several documents, particularly from the eighteenth century. In this respect, a *hüküm* of *evahir-i Receb* 1132/29 May-7 June 1720 notes that Ahmed III asked Mihai Racoviţă to send his *ava'idleri,* according to the custom (Veliman, *Documente turceşti,* doc. 40); also, a document of October–November 1725 (Veliman, *Documente turceşti,* doc. 53). For Wallachian presents, see Gemil, *Documente turceşti,* doc. 202.

### 2.1 *Adjusting Foreign Policy*

The formulaic phrase had been widespread in the realm of diplomacy since Antiquity, and can be found in treaties concluded among Christian princes, as well as in Ottoman *ʿahdname*s ratifying peace agreements with other states.[59] Invariably, it appears in diplomatic correspondence and treaties between Wallachian–Moldavian voivodes and Hungarian and Polish kings throughout the fifteenth century. In the charter of 11 February 1450, Voivode Bogdan II of Moldavia promised Janos Hunyadi "to be friends to all His Highness' friends and enemies to all His Highness' enemies." On 28 July 1468 Stephen the Great promised to King Casimir IV of Poland that, in exchange for protection:

> we shall be friends to every friend of the king, and we shall be enemies to the king's enemies, without difference, be they Christians or Muslims.[60]

Whenever the Porte concluded peace with Christian neighbors, the formula "be [a] friend to the friends and [an] enemy to the enemies" featured prominently in political and commercial treaties. The same clause can be found in the 1480–1481 *ʿahdname* by which Mehmed II ratified the peace (*sulh*) concluded with Stephen the Great of Moldavia.[61]

Moldavian, Wallachian and Transylvanian pretenders, in their turn, made similar commitments to secure the sultan's favor. Sultan Murad III wrote on August 1580 to Christopher Báthory:

> by sending this letter [you showed that] you, always being ready [to prove] your devotion to my Imperial Threshold, are – with all noblemen and the other subjects of the Transylvanian *vilayet* – friend to our friend and enemy to our enemy (*dostumuza dost ve düşmanımıza düşman olduğun*).[62]

In 1605 Stephen Bocskái, among his other "obligations and engagements," employed the formula to declare his commitment to the commander-in-chief

59 See, for example, the treaty between Venice and Uzun Hasan from 1471, where one affirmed: *Per suo sagramento ha promesso* [...] *de preserverar perpetuamente cum noi in amicicia coniunction et union et haver li amici nostri per amici et li inimici per inimici* (Iorga, *Studii asupra evului mediu românesc*, 236, n. 54).

60 *DRH*, *D*, I, doc. 300, 316; Costăchescu, *Documente moldovenești*, II, 749–753, 762–764; Bogdan, *Ștefan. Documente*, II, doc. 135. For the phrase in the privileges granted by the Wallachian voivodes to the inhabitants of Brașov, see Tocilescu, *534 documente*, doc. 6.

61 Decei, "Sulhname," 122.

62 Veliman, "Carte de legământ," 34–35.

(*serdar*) Mehmed paşa to obtain the throne of Transylvania in the midst of Ottoman–Habsburg war. According to the letter cited by chronicler Mehmed bin Mehmed:

> We shall be friends to the Muslim *padişah*'s friends [...] Accepting submission to the Porte of Felicity and coming under the protection of the throne, we engage to serve body and soul the *padişah* and to hit by sword our old enemies, the Austrians, under whose colors and rule we are against our own will.[63]

In the sixteenth- and seventeenth-century imperial diplomas granted to voivodes on their appointment, the formula was included as an imperative demand. It can be found in the 1577 and 1585 *berats* by which Murad III enthroned Mihnea the Renegade in Wallachia, as well as in the diplomas granted to the claimant Paul Márkházy in 1581, to Sigismund Rákóczy in 1607 and to Gabriel Bethlen in 1614.[64] Likewise, Voivode Nicolae Mavrocordat acknowledged in 1710 his obligation "to conform to the will and practice of the Porte," explaining in this manner his pro-Ottoman political stance.[65]

### 2.2 *Military Support*

Throughout the Middle Ages, providing military assistance constituted an integral part of the relationship between a suzerain and his vassals. In the Muslim world, peace agreements frequently included it as a duty of the inferior party to provide support to the superior one during wartime. By a natural extension of this custom to the relations between Muslim sovereigns and Christian princes, a ban on colluding with the enemies of Islam (*harbiler*) was complemented by the tributary's obligation to participate in raids launched by his Muslim suzerain. As sources clearly show, in the Balkans, tributary princes were obliged to partake in the campaigns organized by the sultan. Prior to the battle of Kosovo Polje on 15 June 1389, Murad I dispatched messengers to several *haracgüzar* princes, ordering them to join the Ottoman army in battle. As Mehmed Neşri noted:

63 Mehmed bin Mehmed, *Tevarih*, in *Cronici turceşti* I, 433.

64 Gemil, "Doc. XVI–XVII," 353–356; Maxim, *CTO*, doc. 14; Veliman, "Carte de legământ," 40–42; Guboglu, "Arhive Braşov," doc. 1; Gemil, *Documente turceşti*, doc. 61.

65 To envoy János Pápai (*Călători străini*, VIII, 235).

> Then, the sovereign ordered the tribute paying infidels shall be prepared with their armies, too.[66]

For the same reason, in the battle of "Rovine" (1394 or 1395), we find three Christian princes from Serbia and Macedonia on Bayezid I's side, led by *Knez* Stephen Lazarević (1389–1424).[67]

This long-standing obligation of Wallachian, Moldavian and Transylvanian princes to personally lead the troops during imperial campaigns lasted well into the eighteenth century. Referring to the Ottoman raids against Hungary, Murad II's order to Vlad the Evil from 1436–1437 – recorded by Aşıkapaşazade – stated: "You shall gather your army urgently and you shall come."[68] In the early sixteenth century, Wallachians continued to join the Ottoman troops in the field. According to a Wallachian dignitary's account,

> When the Turks were plundering, their rulers sent me with an army on your estate to rob and seize you; they gave me Turkish [troops] as well; they were in my army but dressed in Wallachian clothes.[69]

After the peace of 1486, Stephen the Great was obliged as a tribute-payer to join the Ottoman forces headed by Malkoçoğlu Bali bey of Silistre, in their campaign against Poland.[70]

During the sixteenth and seventeenth centuries, the orders addressed to Wallachian and Moldavian voivodes to join military campaigns, particularly against the Habsburgs and Poland–Lithuania, became customary.[71] Voivode Petru the Younger of Wallachia (1559–1568) was solicited by Süleyman Kanunî in 1565 to join the siege of Szátmar along with the *beylerbeyi* of Temeşvar.[72] Similar military duties were imposed on Transylvanian rulers following their inclusion in the *pax ottomanica* system in 1541. For instance, in June 1663, Mehmed IV ordered Michael Apafy to participate with his troops in Köprülü-zade Fazıl

66 *andan hünkar buyurdu haracgüzar kafirlere ki anlar dahi yaraklarıyla hazır olalar* (Neşri, *Tarih*, in Veliman, "Mircea," 400–401).

67 Decei, *Imp. otoman*, 63.

68 Aşıkpaşazade, *Tevarih*, in *Cronici turceşti* I, 87.

69 In a letter of Jupân Mogoş Spătarul to Didea of Sad and Comşăi, as well as to the inhabitants of Sad and Cesnădia, from the first part of the sixteenth century (Tocilescu, *534 documente*, doc. 441).

70 Decei, *Imp. otoman*, 140.

71 Petru Rareş in 1542, Alexandru II Mircea in 1572 and Mihai Viteazul in 1594 were ordered to attend Ottoman expeditions (Pippidi, *Tradiţia*, 163, n. 98).

72 Mehmet, *Documente turceşti*, I, doc. 70.

Ahmed paşa's campaign against the Habsburgs.[73] Although the area in which they were expected to participate was generally limited to Southeastern and Central Europe,[74] some exceptions applied.[75]

Ottoman calls to arms and even the acknowledgement of military obligations towards the Porte[76] did not always translate into actual participation in the campaigns. Although local sources can be deemed as biased, Western documents also dwell on the princes' aversion to fighting against Christian neighbors, particularly when in command of Ottoman or Tatar officials. This uneasiness of the Wallachian troops, forced to attack their Christian brethren in Hungary and Transylvania until the sixteenth century, found its expression in the avoidance of plunder by the troops. A previously cited account by a Wallachian boyar ended,

> I have thus considered that you are Christians like us, and so I turned back without harming you in any way.[77]

In just one example of forced participation in Ottoman campaigns from the first part of the seventeenth century, Prince Jerzy Zbaraski informed another Polish dignitary in September 1627 that:

> The voivodes of Moldavia and Wallachia, despite their completely favorable attitude towards us, will be forced to join the Khan in his razzias against us.[78]

Ottoman orders anticipated the Christian tributary princes' aversion to fighting their brothers in faith: "should you not come, I shall not hesitate in

---

73 Gemil, *Documente turcești,* doc. 136.

74 Gemil, *Documente turcești,* doc. 230 (*hüküm* of *eva'il-i Zilhicce* 1118/6–15 March 1707, sent by Ahmed III to Antioh Cantemir); Veliman, *Documente turcești,* doc. 79 (*hüküm* of *Rebi ül-evvel* 1149/July 1736, sent by Mahmud I to Constantin Mavrocordat).

75 In 1473 Radu the Fair attended the campaign against Uzun Hasan under Mehmed II (Decei, *Imp. otoman,* 127). In 1540–1541, Alexandru Cornea was requested to join the campaign against the Hospitallers In Malta (Pippidi, *Tradiția,* 163, n. 98). In the 1565 Ottoman Malta campaign register, the Wallachian and Moldavian voivodes are not mentioned among the troops and ammunition provided for the campaign, or even among the food suppliers for the troops (Arnold Cassola, *The 1565 Ottoman Malta Campaign Register,* La Valletta: Publishers Enterprise Group, Bank of Valetta, 1998).

76 Mehmet, *Documente turcești,* I, doc. 12.

77 Tocilescu, *534 documente,* doc. 441: letter from the first part of the sixteenth century.

78 Hurmuzaki, *Documente,* Supl. II/2, doc. CCLIII.

attacking you."[79] Yet, this reluctance should not be exaggerated, for political and military interests often brought voivodes and boyars to the Ottoman side, initially on a short-term basis.

Military duty raised the difficult legal issue of the incompatibility between the payment of *cizye* and military service. In early Islam, *cizye* came to be regarded as a *zimmis*' ransom for their absence from the battlefield. Several documents show how this solution was a compromise, reconciling legal–religious rules and military necessities. "If we request help from any of you," states a letter of 639 sent to the tributary inhabitants of Dahistan and Jurjan, "this help is considered your *cizye*."[80] For the tributary princes, participating in military campaigns should have – in theory – temporarily waived tribute payments, a fact of which both Ottoman and Moldavian-Wallachian authorities were aware. In fact, Moldavian and Wallachian voivodes forced to partake in the siege of Ujvár (1664–1665), stated this issue explicitly: "Is it possible for us to pay *harac* and take part in the battle at the same time?"[81] The Porte tried to resolve this matter on a case-to-case basis, depending on the military and political circumstances. During the Ottoman–Habsburg "Long War" (1593–1606), the Grand Vizier Yemişci Hasan paşa suggested providing an alternative for the Moldavian ruler Ieremia Movilă. According to a *telhis* he presented to Mehmed III in 1603, he suggested letting the voivode choose, whether he preferred to pay his annual tribute or join a planned campaign against Wallachia and Transylvania:

> Tribute should not be required this year (*bu sene harac taleb olunmasun*); in exchange, on account of this year's tribute, recruiting many soldiers [...], he should banish [the] German and Hungarian armies from the country of Transylvania serving thus the imperial court. And if he should not commit himself to this duty [...], he shall be asked to send the *harac* in time.

In this case, the proposal to substitute military duty for tribute payments constituted a radical solution aimed at recovering the money that "for a period

79 See the case of Marko Kraljević and Konstantin Dejanović, who were obliged to fight against Mircea the Elder in 1395 (Decei, *Imp. otoman,* 63; Aşıkpaşazade, *Tevarih,* in *Cronici turcești I*, 87).

80 Hamidullah, *Documents*, doc. 257. See also Cahen, "Djizya," 559–562; Akgündüz, *Osmanlı Kanunnameleri,* 1, 167–171; Lewis, *Islam,* I, 236.

81 Silahdar, *Zeyil-i Fezleke*, in *Cronici turcești II*, 330; Maxim, "Obligațiile," 100.

of time has not even been delivered" by the cash-strapped voivode.[82] In the first half of the eighteenth century, in response to *hüküms*, demanding Moldavian–Wallachian troops to "protect and guard" the principalities, voivodes responded like Grigore III Ghica, who in September 1737 asked,

> that the amounts of money for their salaries and baksheesh and supplies and for all other expenses should be deducted from the *cizye* money of Moldavia.[83]

The official answer from Istanbul was usually affirmative. This was the case in mid-November 1716, when Ahmed III responded to Mihai Racoviță:

> the Finance Department has also issued my distinguished order that levends should be subscribed on account of the *cizye* of the Moldavian country.[84]

Documents stress a new relationship that was established in the 1520s and 1530s and remained in place until the late seventeenth century, as the three tributary polities came under permanent and firm control of the Porte. Although the Ottoman authorities often invoked "antecedents" whenever they asked the princes to follow the imperial orders, the practice did not provide any regularity in fulfilling military obligations by the tributary princes from the north of the Danube.

### 2.3 *Supporting Neighbors*

In special circumstances, a local ruler needed the neighboring governors' support to defend his "country." In this respect, the zonal security systems were organised by the Ottomans for protecting the provinces which were situated at the border with the Adobe of War. Thus any *bey* or *beylerbeyi* had an important duty to supervise, support and guard governors of adjacent provinces. Such a case was the defensive system of the northwestern border of the empire, including the areas of the Danube river and the Black Sea, which were threatened by the Habsburgs, Poles and the Cossacks of Ukraine. The following local dignitaries were parts of this security system: the tributary princes

82 *Telhis* presented to Mehmed III on 18 *Rebi ül-ahir* 1012/25 September 1603 (Gemil, *Documente turcești*, doc. 11).

83 Veliman, *Documente turcești*, doc. 82.

84 *Vilayet-i Boğdan cizyesine mahsub olmak üzere levendat tahririçün maliye tarafindan dahi emr-i şerifim sadır olmağla* (Veliman, *Documente turcești*, doc. 21). The *levends* were irregular military forces.

of Wallachia, Moldavia and Transylvania, as well as the khan of Crimea,[85] the governors-general and governors of Rumeli, Silistre, Vidin, Niğbolu, Akkerman, Bender, Özü (Ochakov), Temeşvar, Semendire, Budin and Bosnia. As proponents of Ottoman administration, they had to constantly keep an eye on the adjacent provinces, give them military support and defend them, if it was necessary.[86] The most frequent circumstances for the activation of the zonal defence system for the Danubian principalities were: a) the appointment of a new tributary prince; b) the absence of tributary princes from their country; c) fighting rebelling nobles; d) defence against external enemies.

The appointment of a new voivode always implied a rise in the level of the provinces watching over each other in order to secure his installation, protect his throne against other pretenders (such as former princes), and enforce his authority against internal and external enemies. In the following, I illustrate this point with some instances. In 1541–1542, under Süleyman Kanunî's order, Petru Rareş of Moldovia and Radu Paisie of Wallachia helped John Sigismund Zápolya to take over the throne of Transylvania.[87] In May–June 1572, following the petition of Voivode John the Terrible of Moldavia, Selim II dispatched several *hüküm*s to the *sancakbeyi*s of Silistre (Hamza bey) and Niğbolu (Mustafa bey), commanding them to camp their army at *Isakcı* (Isaccea), to watch over Moldavia. They were expected to wait for accurate news, then cross the Danube and support the new voivode in securing his throne against the former prince Bogdan Lăpuşneanu, who had run to Poland and obtained the military support of the Polish king. From the same documents we learn that in this action, the governor of Bender, the *alaybeyi* of Vidin, as well as Voivode Alexandru II Mircea of Wallachia (1568–1577, with interruption), were also implied.[88] In August 1577, Murad III ordered voivode Petru the Lame of Moldavia to support the new Wallachian hospodar, Mihnea II the Renegade:

> If in the aforementioned way, enemies would turn up from anywhere and help would be required, then, without delay, you shall support him as it is right and as he thinks it proper; you shall lose no moment in making efforts.[89]

85 See Mária Ivanics, "The Military Cooperation of the Crimean Khanate with the Ottoman Empire," in *European Tributary States*, 275–301.

86 In 1572, the *beylerbeyi* of Temeşvar was asked to defend the *sancak* of Pâncota until the new governor (who had earlier been the *bey* of Zvornik) would arrive (Mehmet, *Documente turceşti*, I, doc. 108).

87 Decei, *Imp. Otoman*, 190.

88 Mehmet, *Documente turceşti*, I, doc. 107, 110, 118, 123.

89 Mehmet, *Documente turceşti* I, doc. 135 (*hüküm* of 27 *Cemazi ül-evvel* 985/12 August 1577).

Also reading the marginal notes on the document, we learn that copies of this *hüküm* were also dispatched to the *sancakbeyi*s of Silistre and Niğbolu, who regularly meant an enforcement to the defence system of Wallachia. In 1620, Osman II ordered Stephen Bethlen, brother and deputy of Gabriel Bethlen of Transylvania, to provide "help and support" to Alexandru Iliaş, recently appointed as the voivode of Moldavia, "as you have been accustomed to do since the times of yore" (*kadimden edegeldüğün üzere*). The sultan's order was issued when the former voivode, Gaşpar Graţiani (1619–1620), defected to the Polish camp "with his perfidious supporters" once Polish troops crossed into Moldavia.[90]

A rise in the level of watching over the Romanian principalities could also be motivated by the princes' absence from their country. Tributary voivodes were sometimes asked to join imperial expeditions personally, or only to send troops. Both cases meant that the defence possibilities of the country were weakened. This is why the tributary principalities had to be protected by neighboring Ottoman governors. In March 1566, Süleyman Kanunî for the second time ordered Alexandru Lăpuşneanu to send 3,000 Moldavian soldiers and 200 *yeniçeri*s who had earlier been charged to guard him to Temeşvar for the imperial expedition. In exchange, his safety would be assured by the governors of Silistre ("will be at your disposal") and Bender ("was allowed not to come to expedition"), as well as the khan of Crimea. All these dignitaries were activated by *hüküm*s to guard Moldavia against eventual attacks from Poland.[91]

The procedure of watching over the tributary provinces was also activated when the voivodes travelled to the Porte. For instance, in March 1568, wishing to prove his fidelity, Voivode Petru the Younger of Wallachia wanted to carry his tribute to Constantinople and give it to the sultan personally. The *padişah* gave his permission, but at the same time ordered Prince John Sigismund Zápolya of Transylvania[92] to watch over Wallachia during the voivode's absence, invoking the fact that "a part of that country is close to your *vilayet*." The zonal defence system was completed with Khan Devlet Giray I of Crimea (1551–1577), who received a letter concerning the same "important question."[93]

Fighting against rebelling nobles was another circumstance for activating the zonal defending system.[94] At the beginning of 1565, Voivode Alexandru

90 In this way, he became a threat to produce "damages and evil to my Well-Protected Domains" (Gemil, *Documente turceşti*, doc. 76).

91 Mehmet, *Documente turceşti*, I, doc. 82.

92 Mehmet, *Documente turceşti*, I, doc. 89.

93 Mehmet, *Documente turceşti*, I, doc. 90.

94 See Radu Păun, "Enemies Within: Networks of Influence and the Military Revolts against the Ottoman Power (Moldavia and Wallachia, Sixteenth-Seventeenth Centuries)," in *European Tributary States*, 209–251.

Lăpuşneanu wrote a petition (*ʿarz*) to the Porte, asking for help against Moldavian rebels, who had run to Poland and planned to overcome him. From the *hüküm* of February 1565, we can learn that the governor of Akkerman, Hasan bey, was present by the side of the voivode with his troops. At the same time, at the voivode's request, new orders were sent to the governors of Silistre and Vidin, as well as to the *alaybeyi* of Niğbolu commanding them to mobilize their troops and wait for letters from Moldovia concerning the military support needed there.[95] We also have a case from 1602 concerning Wallachian rebels. In an *ʿarz* from 2 September, Voivode Simion Movilă (1600–1602, with interruption) related the rebellion of the noble family of the Buzeştis in 1601, emphasizing that he was helped by Murtaza ibn Gaybi, the chief of the timariots (*alaybeyi*s) of Bender and Akkerman.[96]

The security system of the Danubian area was based on mutual assistance and support. Defending the tributary principalities was not its only aim. It also implied that the voivodes of Wallachia and Moldavia should collaborate, in their turn, with the governors of adjacent provinces in defeating rebellions and installing the sultanic authority.[97]

The highest level of activating the zonal defence system took place when the tributary principalities needed military support against the external enemies. Almost all *hüküm*s quoted in connection with the military support of Ottoman governors to the Moldavian voivodes were related to the involvement of Poles. Despite peace agreements with the Porte, Poland preserved its traditional claim over Moldavia and used the policy of supporting pretenders to regain its influence in the country. Both Alexandru Lăpuşneanu in 1566,[98] and his son in 1568 had to be protected by the governors of Silistre and Bender, or by the khan of Crimea, against eventual attacks from Poland.[99] In 1692, in the context of the "Great Turkish War" with the Habsburgs and Poland (1683–1699), in order to defend Moldavia against an eventual Polish attack, Sultan Ahmed II (1691–1695) ordered the Tatars of Bucak to join the Crimean troops (led by Kalga Sultan Kırım Giray) and the Ottoman army (led by the *beylerbeyi* of Adana).[100]

There is abundant documentation concerning the military support against the Habsburgs as well. In 1564–1565, in a time of ongoing wars with the

95 Mehmet, *Documente turceşti*, I, doc. 65. See also doc. 76.

96 Gemil, *Documente turceşti*, doc. 6.

97 Gemil, *Documente turceşti*, doc. 103.

98 Mehmet, *Documente turceşti*, I, doc. 82.

99 *Mühimme Defteri 7*, doc. 2734; Mehmet, *Documente turceşti*, I, doc. 88.

100 Gemil, *Documente turceşti*, doc. 200.

Habsburgs, Süleyman Kanunî dispatched several *hüküms* to the governors-general and governors of Transylvania's neighboring provinces, ordering them to watch over and defend the principality's territories against enemies. The main addressees were the *beylerbeyis* of the adjacent *eyalets* of Temeşvar[101] and Budin.[102] According to other imperial commands, however, the *beyis* of Semendire and Silistre,[103] as well as the voivode of Moldavia[104] were also expected to be activated for the security system of Transylvania. Moreover, even Ahmed paşa, *beylerbeyi* of Rumeli was ordered to watch over this zonal defence system, formed by the above-mentioned local dignitaries.[105] During the war of 1683–1699, the zonal defence system from the Danube area was raised again at the highest level. Let us illustrate this with one instance concerning Wallachia. In December 1689, a *hüküm* was sent to the governor-general of Özü and to the *kadıs* and *alaybeyis* from the *sancaks* of Silistre and Niğbolu ordering them to mobilize their troops. After that, they were supposed to join the army led by Grand Vizier Mustafa paşa and the Tatar troops of the kalga sultan. They would gather and camp in the Rusçuk area, from where they had to pass the Danube, fight against the Habsburg troops and push them out from Wallachia.[106]

"Helping and supporting"[107] the adjacent provinces was an obligation of a tributary prince, as a consequence of their submission to the Porte, specific to any governor or governor-general of empire. "Helping and supporting" the neighboring governors and tributary princes from the Danubian area was also considered in *hüküms* as "an important affair" (*mühimmat*) of the empire,[108] and was based on the principle of Well-Protected Domains (*Memalik-i mahrusa*).

"Helping and supporting" the neighboring provinces, tributary princes or local governors became a rule based legally on "practice," in spite of the fact

101 Mehmet, *Documente turceşti,* I, doc. 55, 56, 58, 65, 66, 67.

102 Mehmet, *Documente turceşti,* I, doc. 55, 56, 58, 66, 67.

103 Mehmet, *Documente turceşti,* I, doc. 56.

104 Mehmet, *Documente turceşti,* I, doc. 57.

105 Mehmet, *Documente turceşti,* I, doc. 69.

106 Gemil, *Documente turceşti,* doc. 182.

107 In Ottoman documents, the terms "help and support" were used in various combinations, such as: *imdad ve muʿavenet eyleyüb; imdad ve muʿavenetde kusur ko(y)mıyub; muʿavenet ve müzaheret içün; imdad ve iʿanet eylemek; imdad ve iʿanetinde hizmetinde bulunub; imdad ve muʿavenet taleb iderler ise* (Gemil, *Documente turceşti,* passim).

108 The following are only some of the expressions which could be found in Ottoman documents: *imdad ve iʿanet eylemek mühimmatdar olmakla; husus-u mezbur mühimmatdandır; bu husus mühimmat umurdandır* (Gemil, *Documente turceşti,* doc. 19, 72).

that this "custom" was stipulated more or less explicitly in official documents. The Ottoman policy of mutual military support at the northwestern border was explicitly codified in imperial charters granted to prince of Transylvania, which are the most important pieces of evidence in this respect:

> Similarly, if there should be any necessity for a service at the borders of our empire, when it is announced by the pashas and *beys*, the *voivode* and the dignitaries of the country should – according to their enduring subservience – show their readiness personally or through sending soldiers, equipment or victuals in the necessary extent," it is stipulated in the *'ahdname* granted to István Báthory in 1575.[109]

In 1599, Mehmed III granted an imperial charter to Andrew Bathory which included a clause about the obligation for military collaboration with the Danubian principalities:

> Should Poles, Cossacks and other enemies attack Wallachia and Moldavia, the Transylvanians shall defend it if necessary.[110]

Conversely, the "custom" that the tributary voivodes of Wallachia and Moldavia should help the princes of Transylvania became a written stipulation in the *'ahdname* granted to Sigismund Báthory in 1601, when he gave an oath of fidelity to the sultan.[111] Twenty years later, in 1620, Sultan Osman II invoked "custom" as a legal source when he, as noted above, ordered Stephen Bethlen to provide "help and support" to Alexandru Iliaş of Moldavia, "as it had been a custom to do since old times" (*kadimden edegeldüğün üzere*"). The sultan ordered him to proceed "according to your custom" (*idegeldüğün üzere*).[112]

Practically, the functioning of the Ottoman zonal security system at the Danube and Black Sea areas implied three actions: watching over adjacent provinces, communicating between actors and activating military support.

109 Szabó, "Splendid Isolation," 312. See the original text of the imperial charters of 1571, 1572 and 1575 in Papp, *Die Verleihungs*, 190–194, 214–219, 221.

110 Szabó, "Splendid Isolation," 313. For the original text, see Gábor Kárman, "The 'Ahdname of Sultan Mehmed III to András Báthori, Prince of Transylvania," in *Contemporary Research in Turcology and Eurasian Studies*, eds. Stoica Lascu and Melek Fetisleam, Cluj, 2013, 435–445.

111 Szabó, "Splendid Isolation," 313. For text, see Papp, *Die Verleihungs*, 253.

112 Stephen was brother of Prince Gabriel Bethlen of Transylvania (Gemil, *Documente turceşti*, doc. 76).

Keeping watch over adjacent provinces implied a nonstop activity of supervising or spying, often expressed by the standard formula "being eyes and ears."

## 2.4 *Information Gathering*

Another crucial task of tributary princes was to gather information on any and all actions by Christian neighbors that ran against Ottoman interests.[113] The voivodes were instructed to deliver regular reports (*ʿarz, ʿarzuhal, mahzar*) on any suspicious activities and war preparations. Although the scope of this intelligence service was initially limited to Hungary and Poland, it was subsequently extended to encompass the Habsburgs and Russia. Ottoman translations of late-fifteenth- and early-sixteenth-century reports from Wallachian and Moldavian rulers prove that this obligation was established prior to the events of 1538–1541. Preserved in the Archives of the Topkapı Palace Museum, the reports show that the Porte was particularly interested in the political and military situation in Central Europe prior to its Hungarian campaign in 1526. In two letters, the voivode of Moldavia (*Boğdan voyvodası*) informed the sultan of the events in Hungary and Moldavia, focusing on the mobilization of troops in Transylvania, Cracow and Kamʾjanec.[114] This aligned well with the Moldavian voivode's awareness that the threat to Moldavia did not come from the Porte but rather from Poland. Petru Rareş's letter, sent a few months after his enthronement in 1527, informed Süleyman Kanunî about the upcoming Polish *Sejm* in Piotrków, as well as,

> the strife and affairs between the king called Ferdinand, who came from Germany to be the king of Hungary, and King János, who rose to the kingship from the Transylvanian voivodeship.[115]

It is necessary to emphasize that entrusting the voivodes with information gathering even at the early stages of their dependence on the Porte, was by no means accidental. In fact, since the end of the fifteenth century, news from Central Europe had been regularly arriving in Istanbul via Wallachia and Moldavia.[116] The standard phrase in official reports stated "that we have several

113 Morabia, *Ğihad*, 317; Biegman, *Ragusa*, 127.

114 TKSMA, E. 6512 and 6519. *ʿArzuhals* dispatched by Voivode Ştefăniţă to Süleyman Kanunî in 1521 (Mehmed, *Documente turceşti*, I, doc. 11, 13); Nigar Anafarta dated them in 1497 (Nigar Anafarta, *Osmanlı Imparatorluğu ile Lehistan (Polonya) arasındaki münasebetlerle ilgili tarihi belgeler*, Istanbul: Bilmen, 1979, doc. 1, 2).

115 Mehmed, *Documente turceşti*, I, doc. 14.

116 TKSMA, E. 1320, 5299, 5536, 6512, 6519; Nigar Anafarta, *Belgeler*, doc. 1, 2; Mehmet, *Documente turceşti*, I, doc. 8, 10, 11, 13; Fodor, "Ottoman Policy," 338–339.

times informed the felicitous court." Because the tributary voivodes could obtain information directly from their Christian neighbors, Petru Rareș would write, "The Polish King has informed me that he is in the town called Piotrków." However, the voivodes most frequently resorted to spies for procuring intelligence. Voivode Ștefăniță of Moldavia (1517–1527) assured the Porte that "we have sent people to spy for news of immediate importance."[117] In the same vein, Petru Rareș informed Süleyman Kanunî that:

> we have men who will hopefully [soon] return, and whatever news they are going to bring, we shall report to the felicitous court in accordance with the truth.[118]

Christian identity was important in this respect. Although pressure exerted by the Porte increased as the dependence grew, many princes would try to avoid fulfilling these duties whenever possible. In some instances, they reported superficial and mundane issues. "We failed, however, to learn what their intention and ideas are [...]," Petru Rareș complained in his report on the upcoming *Sejm* in Piotrków.[119] Their *ʿarzuhal*s usually contained a formula such as "we shall report to the felicitous court in accordance with the truth,"[120] which was meant to reassure the Porte, but at the same time could mask the sender's intention to feed spurious or incomplete information. However, this could also be the result of them not knowing the details. After all, information was hard to obtain and verify in this period.

The principalities of Wallachia, Moldavia and Transylvania also passed information in the opposite direction, providing Christian rulers with an important source of news on the Ottoman Empire. For instance, in the second half of the fifteenth century, "news from the Turks" regularly passed between Wallachian elites and the inhabitants of Brașov, and Wallachian princes asked for reciprocity, urging their neighbors to inform them "what you know from those parts," i.e. on Hungary.[121] Moldavia played the same role between Poland and the Ottoman Empire.[122] "As [we are] Christians," wrote Aron the Tyrant in 1594

117 Mehmet, *Documente turcești*, I, doc. 10.

118 Mehmet, *Documente turcești*, I, doc. 14.

119 Mehmet, *Documente turcești*, I, doc. 14. Uncertainty is present also in the ʿarzuhals of Voivode Ștefăniță in 1520–1521 (Mehmet, *Documente turcești*, I, doc. 10 and 11).

120 In 1559 Süleyman Kanunî ordered Voivode Mircea the Shepherd of Walllachia to send "true news" about Transylvania and other parts (Mehmet, *Documente turcești*, I, 35).

121 Tocilescu, *534 documente*, doc. 138, 408, 409; Bogdan, *Ștefan. Documente*, doc. 112.

122 Corfus, *Documente XVI*, doc. 20 (instructions for the Polish envoy in 1539, referring also to Voivode Petru Rareș).

to Jan Zamoyski, the Grand Chancellor and *Hetman* (commander-in-chief) of the Polish Crown, "we wanted to inform Your Highness of the intentions of these infidels," namely Tatar preparations for a Transylvanian campaign. This risk was assumed by the princes, who were forbidden from informing fellow infidels about the military conditions of Muslims.[123]

As the control exerted over the Danubian principalities intensified from the sixteenth through to the eighteenth centuries, sending information on Western Europe to the Ottoman court became their principal obligation. In 1740, Nicolo Erizzo wrote to the Venetian Doge that Moldavian and Wallachian voivodes received strongly-worded orders to provide news about the Habsburgs and Russia.[124] In the eighteenth century, when the voivodes hailing from the Phanariot families associated with the Dragomanate of the Imperial Divan (*divan-ı hümayun tercümanı*), they provided the Ottomans with information on Western and Central Europe. The *Hariciye* Collection from the Prime Minister's Archives in Istanbul contains numerous intelligence reports (*takrirs, tahrirs*) delivered by Wallachian and Moldavian voivodes.[125] The princes, however, frequently supplied scarce, outdated, or distorted news, denying the Sublime Porte the accurate information it needed on European politics.[126]

123 Letter of 5 March 1594 (Hurmuzaki, *Documente,* Supl. II/1, doc. 167); *Shaybani's Siyar,* 153.

124 *Dati ordini moldo pressanti a Principi di Moldavia e de Valacchia* (Hurmuzaki, *Documente,* IX/1, doc. 791: report of Nicolo Erizzo from 15 March 1740).

125 See intelligence reports (*tahrirat*) from BOA, *Cevdet Tasnifi. Eyalet-i mümtaze* (for example, doc. 76, 77, 78, 79), and BOA, *Cevdet Tasnifi. Hariciye.* Cilt I, 1025–1313 AH/1616–1896. Virginia Aksan has noted, for example, that in a 1761 report, the Moldavian voivode described the agreements reached by the Habsburgs, Great Britain and Prussia concerning the succession to the Polish throne in the event of August III's death (V. Aksan, "Ottoman Sources of Information on Europe in the Eighteenth Century," *AOtt,* 11, 1986/1988, 5–16); Neumann, "Decision Making," 34.

126 Ibrahim Emiroğlu has intentionally exaggerated the attitude of many translators and voivodes towards the Porte, considering them as traitorous dignitaries (Ibrahim Emiroğlu, *Hizmet ve Ihanetleriyle Tercümanlar: Voyvodalar ve Azınlıklar,* Izmir, 1996).

CHAPTER 13

# *Reʿaya*s and Protected Peoples

In the Ottoman Empire, non-Muslims who had taken an oath of fealty and agreed to pay tribute to the sultan were juridically called "the people of the covenant" (*ahl al-ʿahd* or *muʿahidin*). These terms derived from the Arabic word *ʿahd*, which implied engagement, agreement, convention or oath.

In Ottoman sources, whenever Wallachians, Moldavians and Transylvanians were called *muʿahidin*, the notion indicated that they were beneficiaries of "engagements" with sultans. In the fifteenth century, the term *muʿahid* was applied only to the voivodes of Wallachia and Moldavia, but during the sixteenth and seventeenth centuries, its meaning – like the notion of *haracgüzar* – expanded, encompassing all inhabitants of the principalities as well as the rulers and subjects of Transylvania.[1] This stance continued into the eighteenth century, as indicated by *şeyh ül-Islam* Ebu-Işak Kara Ismail Naʿim Efendi's *fetva* of 1717. According to the jurist, Wallachians ranked among "infidels who are beneficiaries of an engagement with Muslims" (*keferesi ehl-i Islam ile muʿahidin olan*).[2]

Islamic law recognizes two categories of "the people of covenant": *müsteʾmin*s (non-Muslim foreigners enjoying protection of the Muslim ruler) and *zimmi*s (non-Muslim Ottoman subjects).[3] In the fifteenth and early sixteenth centuries, the Wallachians and Moldavians' condition across the imperial domains was closer to that of foreigners (*müsteʿmin*). As *zimmi*s, since the mid-sixteenth century Wallachians, Moldavians and Transylvanians came to enjoy rights similar to those of other subjects of empire regarding their life, liberty, possessions and religion.[4]

---

1 Halil Inalcık, "Boğdan," *EI-2*, I, 1290–1291. *Muʿahidin* also means "contractual parts" (*Redhouse*, 784).

2 Veliman, *Documente turceşti*, doc. 24: *fetva* included in a *hüküm* of *evaʾil-i Cemazi ül-evvel* 1129/13–22 April 1717.

3 Morabia, *Ǧihad*, 290.

4 For an analysis of the Dubrovnik case, see N. H. Biegman, who wrote on the "Rights of Ragusans Resulting from Ottoman Citizenship" (Biegman, *Ragusa*, 63–69).

 | DOI:10.1163/9789004411104_014

## 1 Protected People

The legal status of *zimmi*s in the Ottoman Empire has been subject to many debates among jurists and historians, both students of the imperial history and those from other fields.[5] This notion applied to the position of Greek-Orthodox,[6] Jewish[7] and Armenian communities,[8] including monasteries such as Saint Catherine of Sinai and Saint John Prodromos of Serres.[9]

5 H. A. R. Gibb and Harold Bowen, *Islamic Society and the West. A Study of the Impact of Western Civilization on Muslim Culture in the Near East*, Volume One: *Islamic Society in the Eighteenth Century*, Part I, London: Oxford University Press, 1957, 207–262; K. Binswanger, *Untersuchungen zum Status der Nichtmuslime im Osmanischen Reich des 16 Jahrhunderts. Mit einer Neudefinition des Begriffes "Dimma,"* Munich: R Trofenik, 1977; Y. Ercan, "Türkiye'de XV-XVI yüzyılarda Gayrımuslimlerin Hukukı, Içtimai ve Iktisadi Durumu," *Belleten* 47/188, 1983, 1119–1149; R. C. Jennings, "Zimmis (Non-Muslim) in early 17th Century Ottoman Juridical Record. The Sharia Court of Anatolian Kayseri," *JESHO*, 21, 3, 1978, 225–293; Youssef Courbage and Philippe Fargues, *Chrétiens et Juifs dans l'Islam arabe et turc*, Paris: Fayard, 1992. In this respect, the work edited in 1982 by Benjamin Braude and Bernard Lewis, which gathered studies written by outstanding specialists, became a reference book *Christians and Jews in the Ottoman Empire: The Functioning of a Plural Society*, vol. 1, *The Central Lands*, London: Holmes and Meier Publishers, 1982. See in it C. E. Bosworth's "The Concept of *Dhimma* in Early Islam," 37–51; I. Metin Kunt's "Transformation of Zimmi into Askeri," 55–67; B. Braude's "Foundation Myths of the *Millet* System," 69–88.

6 Theodore H. Papadopoullos, *Studies and Documents relating to the History of the Greek Church and People under Turkish Domination*, Brussels: Librairie Scaldis, 1952; N. J. Pantazopoulos, *Church and Law in the Balkan Peninsula during the Ottoman Rule*, Thessaloniki: Institute for Balkan Studies, 1967; Josef Kabrda, "Les documents turcs relatifs aux droits fiscaux des Métropolites orthodoxes en Bulgarie au XVIIIe siècle," *AO*, 26, 1, 1958, 59–80; Steven Runciman, *The Great Church in Captivity*, Cambridge: Cambridge University Press, 1968; J. Kabrda, *Le système fiscal de l'Église Orthodoxe dans l'Empire Ottoman*, Brno: Universita J. E. Purkyne, 1969; H. Inalcık, "The Status of the Greek Orthodox Patriarch under the Ottomans," *Turcica* 21–23, 1991, 407–436.

7 Joseph R. Hacker, "Ottoman Policy toward the Jews and Jewish Attitudes Towards the Ottomans During the Fifteenth Century," in *Christians and Jews*, 117–126; Mark A. Epstein, "The Leadership of the Ottoman Jews in the Fifteenth and Sixteenth Centuries," in *Christians and Jews*, 101–115; Aryeh Shmuelevitz, *The Jews of the Ottoman Empire in the late Fifteenth and the Sixteenth Centuries: Administrative, Economic, Legal and Social Relations as reflected in the Reponsa*, Leiden: Brill, 1984.

8 Kevork B. Bargakjian, "The Rise of the Armenian Patriarchate of Constantinople," in *Christians and Jews*, 89–100.

9 Nicolas Oikonomidès, "Monastères et moines lors de la conquête ottomane," *SF*, 35, 1976, 1–10; Zdenka Veselá-Prenosilova, "À propos de la protection exercée par le gouvernement ottoman sur le Monastère de Ste. Cathérine au Sinai," *AO* 37, 1969, 326–338. Documents issued by sultans for this convent were published by Klaus Schwarz in *Osmanische Sultansurkunden des Sinai-Klosters in türkisher Sprache*, Freiburg im Breisgau: Schwarz, 1970. For a comparison with the predecessors' policy towards the Sinai Convent, see S. M.

In Islamic law, the relationship between the Muslim community and non-Muslims granted tolerance and protection by the former was regulated by a pact called *zimmet*, which in Arabic means duty, forgiveness, privilege or protection. *Harbi* people that agreed to pay tribute and obey the Muslim sovereign in exchange for protection of their lives, property and the right to practice their own religion became *ehl-i zimmet or zimmis*, i.e., "people of pact" or "protected people."[10] As a rule, Muslim jurists listed six obligations deemed absolutely "necessary" and further six considered "desirable" for securing Muslim protection.[11] Among them, the sole positive obligation was the payment of *cizye*, while others prohibited certain actions and attitudes towards Muslims. Conversely, early Islamic compacts stipulated that Muslim rulers would grant protection to the non-Muslims' life, faith and property against any aggression. "Saved are you by protection of Allah, since you have spared your blood by paying *cizye*," stipulated the *ʿahd* concluded by Khalid ibn al-Walid with an Arab chieftain in 633.[12] Just as the protection of *zimmis*' property implied their

---

Stern, "Two Ayyubid Decrees from Sinai," in *Documents from Islamic Chanceries*, ed. S. M. Stern, Cambridge: Harvard University Press, 1965, 10–25; E. Khedoori, *Charters of Privileges Granted by the Fatimids and Mamluks to St. Catherine's Monastery of Tur Sinai (ca. 500 to 900)*, Dissertation, University of Manchester, 1958. For Saint John Prodromos of Serres, see I. Beldiceanu-Steinherr, "La prise de Serres et le firman de 1372 en faveur du monastère de Saint-Jean-Prodrome," *Acta Historica. Societas Academica Dacoromana* (Munich) 4, 1965, 15–24; E. A. Zachariadou, "Early Ottoman Documents of the Prodromos Monastery (Serres)," *SF* 28, 1969, 1–12.

10 For studies concerning the status of *zimmis* in classical Islam, see: A. Fattal, *Le statut légal des non-musulmans en pays d'Islam*, Beirut: Imprimerie Catholique, 1958; A. S. Tritton, *The Caliphs and their Non-Muslims Subjects: A Critical Study of the Covenant of ʿUmar*, Routledge Library Editions: Islam, 2007 (1st ed. 1939); B. Ye'or, *Le dhimmi. Profil de l'oprimé en Orient et en Afrique du Nord depuis la conquête arabe*, Paris: Anthropos, 1980; Bernard Lewis, "L'Islam et les Non-Musulmans," *Annales* 35, 3–4 1980, 784–799; Wolfgang Kallfelz, *Nichtmuslimische Untertanen im Islam: Grundlage, Ideologie und Praxis der Politik frühislamischer Herrscher gegenüber ihren nichtmuslimischen Untertanen mit besonderem Blick auf die Dynastie der Abbasiden (749–1248)*, Wiesbaden: Otto Harrassowitz, 1995.

11 According to Majid Khadduri, *zimmis* necessarily had: to pay the *cizye*, which was the most important obligation stipulated in the tributary-protection covenant (*ʿahd-ı zimmet*); to not attack the religion of Islam nor show any disrespect to Muslim practices; to not revile or show any disrespect towards the Prophet Muhammad or to the *Kur'an*; to not injure the life or the property of a Muslim; to not marry a Muslim woman or to enter into sexual connection with her. It was desirable: not to sell wine or practice usury; not to drink wine or eat pork in public; to wear distinctive clothing; not to ride on horseback or carry weapons, but only on donkeys and mules; not to have houses higher than Muslim ones, preferably lower; not to ring church bells loudly, or not to raise voices loudly in prayer; not to bury the dead near Muslim quarters, nor to weep loudly over the dead (Khadduri, *War and Peace*, 195–197; Laoust, *Ibn Taimiya*, 270; M. Belin, "Fetoua relatif à la condition des zimmis…" *JA*, 4e série, t. xviii, (1851): 417–516; t. xix, (1852): 97–140).

12 Hamidullah, *Documents* doc. 267: document of 12 AH.

full property rights to personal estates, landed property could also be left to protected people, either as property or the right to usufruct. "Obey our authority and we shall also leave your lands to you," promised Khalid ibn al-Walid to the Persians.[13] That lenient attitude was subsequently recorded and theorized in late eighth- and early ninth-century legal treatises. At the same time, the relationship between protection and the payment of *cizye* crystallized, becoming a basic principle of Islamic law. Al-Ghazali stated:

> A *zimmi* is like a Muslim in everything which relates to the prohibition of hurting him, for Islamic law protects his honor just as it protects his life and property; he, unlike the *harbi*, must therefore not be slandered.[14]

According to R. C. Jennings, all non-Muslims who submitted themselves to Ottoman authority and paid their due taxes, were entitled to remain in the Abode of Islam with their life, property, religious practices and protection guaranteed by the sultan.[15] In other words, Christians, Jews, Armenians and other non-Muslims living within the Ottoman Empire were permitted to keep their religion and institutions, upon the condition of paying the poll-tax (*cizye*) and land-tax (*harac*).

Indeed, the Ottoman's tolerant attitude towards non-Muslim subjects stood in stark contrast to Western European polities and Safavid Iran; still, a number of religious prohibitions, the obligation to wear distinctive garments and unequal rights at *kadı* courts meant that Ottoman *zimmi*s were regarded as "second-class or inferior subjects."[16] This state of affairs continued until the nineteenth century, when during the Tanzimat reforms, Ottoman authorities

---

13 Hamidullah, *Documents*, doc. 221; Lewis, *Islam*, I, 228. In the Ottoman legal view, the "subjects and inhabitants" of the tributary principalities had the right, confirmed by seventeenth- and eighteenth-century *hüküms*, "to possess and hold their properties and lands" (Mehmet, *Documente turcești*, I doc. 260: *hüküm* of *evasıt-ı Muharrem* 1175/12–21August 1761, issued by Mustafa III for the Ottoman authorities in Vidin and Ochakov).

14 Lazarus-Yafeh, *al-Ghazzali*, 442.

15 Ronald C. Jennings, *Christians and Muslims in Ottoman Cyprus and the Mediterranean World, 1571–1640*, New York and London: New York University Press, 1993, 132.

16 Coles, *Ottoman Impact*, 54; Lazarus-Yafeh, *al-Gazzali*, 442; Fattal, *Non-musulmans*, 169. For nineteenth century modernization, see Davison, "Christian–Muslim Equality," 113; Carter D. Findley, "The Acid Test of Ottomanism: The Acceptance of Non-Muslims in the Late Ottoman Bureaucracy," in *Christians and Jews*, 339–368; Steven Rosenthal, "Minorities and Municipal Reform in Istanbul. 1850–1870," in *Christians and Jews*, 369–386; Enver Ziya Karal, "Non-Muslims Representatives in the First Constitutional Assembly. 1876–1877," in *Christians and Jews*, 387–400. There are opinions according to which non-Muslim subjects should be included among the "citizens" of the *ʿUmma* (Tarazi, "Statut personnel," 354–

developed a doctrine of equality of all Ottoman subjects, irrespective of their confession.[17] This also applied to the inhabitants of Wallachia and Moldavia. During a visit to Silistre in Spring of 1827, Mahmud II (1808–1839) stated that all his subjects had the same rights and had similar obligations, no matter their faith.[18]

In Ottoman court records and juridical works, communities of non-Muslim subjects were almost universally called *zimmis*.[19] Although from a juridical point of view the term applied to any and all non-Muslim subjects of the sultan, it usually referred to the Christian population. Other terms employed in narrative and official sources for Christians were *Isevi* ("pertaining to Jesus"), *Nasrani* and later *Hıristiyani*.[20] In popular parlance, and sometimes in official documents, *zimmis* may have also been referred to as infidels (*kefere*), although there was a distinction between non-Muslim subjects and enemy infidels (*harbi kefere*) living in the Abode of War.[21] Other words that identified Christian and non-Christian minorities, such as Greek (*Yunani*), Armenian (*Ermeni*), Maronite (*Suryani*), Jew or Hebrew (*Yahudi, Ibrani*) had significance for the practice of governance but not for the legal status of such communities.

From the fifteenth until the seventeenth century, *zimmis* constituted non-Muslim "tax-paying subjects" of the Ottoman Empire. The Arabic term *reʿaya* which can describe either a flock or a human population was translated in a variety of ways: "people subjected to a sovereign," "taxpaying subjects of the Ottoman Empire," "non-Muslim subjects of the Ottoman Empire" or "Christian

---

377: Ch. IV. *La notion de citoyenneté et de sujétion dans la théorie du droit public musulman*; Davison, "Christian-Muslim Equality," 113; Özel, *Islam Hukuku*, 210–211).

17 Maxim, *CTO*, 134–136; Davison, "Christian-Muslim Equality," 113–114.

18 Nesselrode recounted the audience of the Moldo–Wallachian voivodes, Mihail Sturza and Alexandru Ghica, who were received by Mahmud II in Silistre on 27 April 1837 (Hurmuzaki, *Documente*, Supl. I/5, doc. CCLXXX: text of 21 May 1837).

19 See Halebi, *Mülteka*, vol. 2, 559–628; Halebi, *Mülteka*, I, 328–348; *Fetava-yi Yahya Efendi*, SK, Hamidiye 601, f. 21b–25b: on *zimmis*. This is also Ronald Jennings's conclusion. After analyzing the juridical documents of the court of Lefkosa, Cyprus, Jennings affirmed that the name "Greek Orthodox" (*Rum*) was never used (Jennings, *Ottoman Cyprus*, 132).

20 *Redhouse*, 480, 548, 868. According to Cantemir "All Christians are named *Issevi*, by the Historians and in Letters, by way of compliment, as the Prince of Moldavia [...] and also *Nasrani, Nazarenes*, as *Yunani* is given to the *Greeks*, and Ibrani to the *Jews* or *Hebrews*." (Cantemir, *Othman History*, 50, n. 7).

21 Thus, in the fifteenth- to seventeenth-century *kanunnames*, the non-Muslim subjects were frequently called "tribute-payers" (*haracgüzars*), "infidels who are not from the Abode of War" (*kefere ki dar al-harb'dan olmıyan*) etc. (Anhegger, Inalcık, *Kanunname*, doc. 53, 55, 56; Biegman, *Ragusa*, 124–125: in a *ferman* of 1582).

subjects."[22] Contemporary sources also provided an alternative interpretation, according to which *reʿaya* meant tax-paying rural population in general, including both Muslim (*müsülman reʿayası*) and non-Muslim subjects (*kafir reʿayası*).[23] Indeed, according to the Ottoman notions of social hierarchy, *reʿaya* occupied the fourth place, after the "men of the sword" (*ʿasker*), the "men of the book" (*ulema*) and the "men of the pen" (bureaucrats). The payment of *cizye*, however, was incumbent only on non-Muslim subjects (*kafir reʿayası* or *zimmis*).

Since Süleyman Kanunî's reign, the Ottomans began to perceive Wallachia, Moldavia and Transylvania as part of the Well-Protected Domains (*Memalik-i mahrusa*). From the legal point of view, they were included into the Abode of Islam (*dar al-Islam*), as the Abode of Tributary Protection (*dar al-zimmet*). Consequently, the new kind of protection guaranteed to Wallachians, Moldavians and Transylvanians stemmed from the rules regarding the relationship between the Muslim sovereign and his subjects.

In Ottoman official documents, inhabitants of the tributary principalities were usually lumped together with the sultan's subjects on the Danube's southern bank. This is made clear by a phrase employed in a 1608 document, "the subjects of Moldavia are on the whole the same as the subjects of my Well-Protected Domains,"[24] which became a standard point of reference for tributary territories. Thus, it was affirmed that,

> the inhabitants of Dubrovnik are my tax-payer subjects just like other subjects.[25]

The distinct subcategory of *reʿaya* that were tribute-paying subjects (*haracgüzar olan reʿaya*) included since the early sixteenth century the inhabitants from both the territories under direct imperial administration and autonomous

---

22 On the notion of *reʿaya,* see: C.E Bosworth, Suraiya Faroqhi, "Ra'iyya,," in EI-2, VIII, 403–406; *Redhouse*, 951; Aleksandar Matkovski, "La signification historique des expressions "raia" et "beraia," in *Islam in Balkans*, 55–58; Itzkowitz, *Ottoman Empire*, 59; Mehmet, "De certains aspects," 137.

23 An opinion also adopted by Ö. L. Barkan, H. Inalcık, N. Beldiceanu and J. Kabrda (cf. Matkovski, *Raia-beraia*, 55–58). A recent study is Baki Tezcan's discussion of the *reʿaya* and *zimmi* in Christine Woodhead (ed.) *The Ottoman World*, London: Routledge, 2011, Ch. 11: Baki Tezcan, "Ethnicity, Race, Religion and Social Class: Ottoman Markers of Difference."

24 In Ahmed I's *hüküm* to Tartar prince Şehin Giray of 10 *Şaban* 1017/19 November 1608 (Gemil, *Documente turceşti*, doc. 32: *bi'l-cümle Boğdan reʿayası sa'ir gibi Memalik-i mahrusam reʿayası gibi olub*).

25 *Dubrovniklü sa'ir reʿaya gibi haracgüzar reʿayalarımdır* (Biegman, "Ragusan Spying," 238).

regions, such as Ragusa and the principalities on the northern bank of the Danube.[26]

Wallachians, Moldavians Transylvanians and Ragusans were all considered *zimmis* within the conceptual grid of Islamic law, inherited and employed by the Ottomans.[27] As their legal status was considered the same as that of imperial subjects on the right bank, it also set them apart from the inhabitants of adjacent Christian polities, *harbi* by the Hanafi tradition. This standpoint was clearly laid out in an order by Mehmed IV (1648–1687) issued in the aftermath of the Kam'janec' campaign of 1672. The sultan reminded provincial officials along the route to Istanbul and those on the shore of the Black Sea that,

> there is not my imperial permission for the [Wallachian population] be treated like the Polish one; the Wallachian population is not an enemy one; it is the same as the population of my other Well-Protected Domains.[28]

An unpublished collection of *fetvas* by Ali Efendi Akkermani (d. 1621), whose career unfolded in the region, makes an even stronger point. According to him, Moldavians clearly and unequivocally constituted *re'aya* and "protected people" (*zimmis*).[29]

Ottoman sources employed not only the juridical–religious vocabulary, but also one of politics and administration. All Ottoman documents registering the transit of Wallachians, Moldavians and Transylvanians to adjacent provinces – and particularly those crossing the Danube[30] – identified individuals. They were differentiated from other Ottoman *re'ayas* or *zimmis*; their "country"

26 In a chancery record of 1604 referring to the Wallachian subjects (Gemil, *Documente turcești*, doc. 14).

27 The 1604–1607 receipts (*tezkere*) of the tax for crossing the Danube used the term *zimmi*: *Simu nam zimmi, Fuluran nam zimmi, Yanku nam zimmi* (Gemil, *Documente turcești*, doc. 16). *Yanku nam zimmi* is mentioned in a *hüküm* of 1630–1631, too (Gemil, *Documente turcești*, doc. 16).

28 *Eflak re'ayası harbi değildir sa'ir Memalik-i mahrusamda olan re'aya gibidir* (Gemil, *Documente turcești*, doc. 155).

29 *Fetava-yi Akkermani Maa Üskubi* (SK, Hkm. 405, f. 90b). Another manuscript is *Fetava-yi 'Ali Akkermani* (TKSMK, A 842).

30 The term *zimmi* was usually accompanied by a specification of "place of residence." One merchant (*tüccar*) was identified as "a person named Iacov who is one of the inhabitants of Moldavia" (*Boğdan sakinlerinden Yakov nam kimesne*). *Sakin* meant actually "resident" (Gemil, *Documente turcești*, doc. 16).

(*vilayet*) of origin was specified,[31] and the name of their prince was often included.[32]

## 2 Protection of Tribute-Payer Subjects

### 2.1 *Protection against enslavement*

Peace agreements between Balkan princes and Ottomans were meant to halt predatory raids (*akın*) and – in conformity with medieval custom – allowed for partial ransoming of captives. Similarly, in the fifteenth and early sixteenth centuries, sultanic protection granted to Wallachian and Moldavian rulers included a temporary hiatus in Ottoman raiding activities and conquests. The immediate outcome of Alexandru I Aldea's 1432 "peace" with Murad II was the release of the voivode's subjects taken during the conflict. As he faced criticism for dealing with the "Turkish infidel" from the city council of Braşov, the voivode pointed out that he had "released 3,000 of my captives" as a proof of necessity for this decision.[33] According to a seventeenth-century Wallachian chronicle, following Vlad the Evil's reconciliation with the sultan, "the Turks released all Wallachians that they had seized before"[34] during the raids led by Firuzbeyoğlu Mehmed bey.[35]

The safety of subjects had to be ensured whenever Ottoman forces crossed Wallachian territories. This was no easy task: although the soldiers' right to take booty and slaves was restricted to the Abode of War, there was undoubtedly a temptation among the rank-and-file to seize the opportunities in the

31 E.g., "the subjects of the principality of Transylvania" (*Erdel memleketinin reʿayası*) who traveled to Lipova (then an Ottoman town), in a 1678–1679 document; "the subjects of Wallachia" (*Eflak reʿayasından olub*), in a document of 1696 (Gemil, *Documente turceşti,* doc. 161, 213); "among the subjects of Wallachia who are transiting from the principality of Wallachia to Nikopol" (*vilayet-i Eflak'dan Nikbolı tarafına mürar iden Eflak reʿayasından*), in a *hüküm* of 1717 (Veliman, *Documente turceşti,* doc. 29).

32 In 1559 Süleyman Kanunî asked the *kadı* of Rusçuk to forbid the Ottoman clerks from toubling the 'men' of the "Wallachian voivode," Petru the Younger (Mehmet, *Documente turceşti,* I, doc. 41). The denominations *Boğdanlu, Eflaklu* and *Erdellü* served to identify the Wallachian, Moldavian or Transylvanian subjects (Gemil, *Documente turceşti,* doc. 44, 119, 213). This was, as a matter of fact, the terminology used in the *ʿahdnames* by which the foreign merchants were granted the right to trade in the Ottoman territories: *Lehlü* ("the Pole"), *Venediklü* ("the Venetian"), *Ingilterelü* ("the Englishman), *Francalu* ("the Frenchman") etc.

33 *DRH*, D, I, doc. 197.

34 *Genealogia Cantacuzinilor*, 64.

35 Aşıkpaşazade, *Tevarih,* and Neşri, *Tarih*, in *Cronici turceşti I*, 86, 118.

tributary states. In 1438, the Ottoman army crossed Wallachia without plundering it because the voivode Vlad the Evil "was tributary (*haracgüzar*) and had a pledge with the sultan," and the expedition was aimed against the "land of Hungary."[36] In the early sixteenth century, the Wallachian *Spătar* (Sword-Bearer) Mogoș recounted the raids Wallachia suffered from the Turks in the late fifteenth century and the similar situation of Hungary and Transylvania during his lifetime. He emphasized that the Turks "do not still plunder" the Wallachians, but protected them once voivodes became tribute-payers.[37]

The ban on plunder and enslaving Wallachian, Moldavian and Transylvanian subjects was a recurrent topic in early modern Ottoman documents. From the end of the fifteenth century, additional juridical arguments were brought up to emphasize the necessity of protecting tax-payers. In 1574, Sultan Selim II informed Crimean Khan Devlet Giray I:

> From among *re'ayas* and *berayas* and from among those who started the fight [with Islam], a lot were made captives [such that] nobody remained to toil the land and to pay tribute.[38]

The sultan's concern originated from more mundane reasons surrounding the ideal of the relationship between the sovereign and his subjects, also alluded to in the same document:

> The people of the *Boğdan vilayeti* pay us tribute and most of provisions (*zahire*) of the well-guarded Istanbul comes from them, [this is why] our greatest desire is that [the country] be inhabited and prosperous.

Islamic law expressly stated that Muslims could not enslave tributaries and protected people, an argument brought up in Selim II's correspondence with the khan:

> Killing my subjects who pay tribute and taking them captive is against the holy law (*şeri'-i şerif*).[39]

---

36 Idris Bitlisi, *Heşt Behişt*, in *Cronici turcești I*, 167.

37 Jupân Mogoș Spătarul to Didea of Sad and Comșăi, as well as to the inhabitants of Sad and Cesnădia (Tocilescu, *534 documente*, doc. 441: letter from the first part of the sixteenth century).

38 Maxim, *CTO*, doc. 10: *name-yi hümayun of 29 Rebi ül-ahir* 982/28 July 1574.

39 Maxim, *CTO*, doc. 10.

A juridical opinion by the mufti Ali Efendi Akkermani (d. 1621) elucidates the way scholars since Süleyman's reign conceptualized Moldavians, Wallachians and Transylvanians as *zimmi*s:

> Question: A Moldavian captive belonging to Zeyd willingly became a Muslim. When all seized captives, including the above mentioned one, were set at liberty by imperial order, saying "they are subjects and protected peoples" (*reʿaya ve zimmileridir*), is it possible to set at liberty and take from the Zeyd's hand the Muslim captives, too? The answer: it is possible. The protected peoples are free [...][40]

The prohibition of plunder and enslavement (*zimmi*) can also be drawn from recurrent stipulations in sultanic charters that sanctioned any kinds of aggression, violence and abuse committed by Ottoman officials against the imperial tributaries. In regard to other sultanic *hüküm*s addressing the topic, an order by Selim II, quoted by N. H. Biegman, reinforced the immunity of Ragusans and reasserted the ban on their sale as slaves throughout the empire.[41]

The juridical aspects of plunder and enslavement are put into display by sources concerning the revolts in Wallachia and Moldavia, drawing a line between obedient and disobedient subjects. Whereas the latter were to be treated as the inhabitants of the Abode of War and thus could be captured and enslaved, the former were not to be harmed, since they continued to be "tribute-paying subjects" (*cizyegüzar reʿayalar*).

During the Ottoman–Habsburg war of 1716–1718, Sultan Ahmed III promised harsh punishments for any official who would enable or condone the enslavement and displacement of Wallachians and Moldavians as captives (*esirler*). In contrast, the Ottoman subjects were allowed to take on the southern bank of the Danube "revolting infidels" (*ʿisyan üzere olan kefereden*) or "German prisoners" (*Nemçe esirleri*) taken in Transylvania, which by that point had already come under Habsburg rule. Their captors, however, had to produce papers (*senedler*) confirming their prisoners' origin.[42] Thus, only when the *zimmi*s and tribute payers "broke the oath and throw up their revolt," irrespectively of whether they sought the assistance of the Porte's enemies; thus, it was legal

40 *Mesele: Zeydin yedinde bir Boğdan esiri rızasıyla müslüman oldukdan sonra mezkar ile sebi olunan cümle esirleri reʿaya ve zimmileridir deyü emr-i padişahi ile ıtlak etdüklerinde Zeydin müslüman olan esirlerini dahi yedinden alub ıtlaka kadır olurlar mı? El-cevab: Olurlar ruʾosa Zeydin mülki olmamışdır ehl-i zimmet ahrardır* [...] (*Fetava-yi Akkermani Maa Üskubi*, SK, Hkm. 405, f. 90b).

41 Biegman, *Ragusa*, 64–65.

42 Veliman, *Documente turcești*, doc. 30 (*hüküm* of *evaʾil-i Zilhicce* 1129/6–15 November 1717).

for them and their families to "be captured and made slaves"[43] and to plunder their "goods and effects and animals."[44] This attitude was confirmed in *fetvas* such as that issued in 1717 by *şeyh ül-Islam* Naʿim Efendi during the Ottoman–Habsburg war.[45]

The records, drafted to remind the addressees of the prohibition against killing and enslaving non-Muslim subjects, indicates that reality diverged from theoretical stipulations. While putting down the 1574 Moldavian uprising, the Tatars took scores of captives from among those "who revolted and provoked disorder and fought the people of Islam" as well the "*reʿayas* who minded their own businesses [...] and paid tribute." Selim II tried, apparently without success, to remind the Tatars of the well-known rule of *şeriʿat*, which stipulated that obedient tributaries and protected people be released, and his own *hüküm* in which he had ordered that rebels can be ransomed only by their own relatives at a set price of 1,000 *akçes* each.[46]

Historical sources register frequent abuses committed by Ottoman troops in transit through the principalities. In 1632–1633, in one of many such cases, the Moldavian voivode Alexandru Iliaş sent an *ʿarzuhal* to Murad IV complaining about the "oppression" and even "enslavement" (*esir itmişlerdir*) of Moldavian *reʿaya* by the Tatars of Bucak. Since the latter committed these abuses while en route to "the Cossack country" the hospodar asked the sultan to alter the Tatars' route: "so that they march along the other side of the Dnestr river and not enter the territory of the Moldavian country." Whenever and wherever militarily possible, the central authorities intervened to alter the direction of their (and Crimean) troops' march. In response to the voivode's plea, Murad IV noted on the document that a "firm order was issued" (*müekked-i hüküm buyurul-du*) to restrict the Tatars' passage through Moldavia in the future.[47]

### 2.2 *Principle of Tax-Payer Protection*

Since the Porte recognized that wealth was produced by subjects, its policy towards the *reʿayas* was guided by the principle of "tax-payer protection," which was not an abstract principle but a concrete necessity for Ottoman society.[48] Since this policy extended to the inhabitants of tributary principalities,

43 Veliman, *Documente turceşti*, doc. 164 (*hüküm* of *evahir-i Receb* 1183/20–29 November 1769, concerning the Russo-Ottoman war in 1769–1774).

44 Veliman, *Documente turceşti*, doc. 168 (*hüküm* of *evasıt-ı Şevval* 1183/7–16 February 1770).

45 This *fetva* was inserted in a *hüküm* of *evaʾil-i Cemazi ül-evvel* 1129/13–22 April 1717 (Veliman, *Documente turceşti*, doc. 24).

46 Maxim, *CTO*, doc. 10.

47 Gemil, *Documente turceşti*, doc. 97.

48 Decei, *Imp. otoman*, 393; Maxim, "Teritorii româneşti," I, 806–807.

sultanic orders frequently emphasized the voivodes' duty to work for the "peace and security of the subjects," the "welfare and contentment of the *reʿaya*," and the "defense and protection of the *reʿaya*."[49] On 12 July 1613, the *sancakbeyi* of Niğbolu, Macaroğlu Ali paşa wrote to the dignitaries of Braşov about the pending expedition for Gabriel Báthory's replacement but assured them that – according to the sultan's will – no subject would be harmed:

> His Majesty's will, the *padişah*, is that nobody touches what belongs to you, takes any money and troubled his *reʿayas* and *berayas*.[50]

To cause prejudices to the tribute-payer subjects (*haracgüzar olan reʿayası*) would be contrary to the *şeriʿat* and *kanun*.[51] Referring to the Wallachian subjects, a chancery note of 1604 included the following typical statement:

> An order was decided to be enacted that nobody do any harm to the tribute paying subjects, contrary to the Islamic holy law.[52]

To express the principle of tribute-payer protection and stop the abuses committed against Moldo-Wallachian subjects, seventeenth- and eighteenth-century *hüküms* used several other standard phrases. In 1608, Ahmed I stated,

> There is no imperial permission of mine that interference and violation be perpetrated [against the inhabitants of Moldavia].[53]

---

49 Maxim, *CTO*, doc. 14; Mehmet, *Documente turceşti*, I, doc. 35, 291.

50 Guboglu, "Arhive. Braşov," 242.

51 The argument most frequently invoked by sultans in this respect consisted in the similitude of their juridical condition with that of other Ottoman tax-paying subjects: "And, the Moldavian subjects is in all like the subjects of my Well-Protected Domains" (*biʾl-cümle Boğdan reʿayası gibi olub*), stated Ahmed I in a 1608 order (Gemil, *Documente turceşti*, doc. 32).

52 *Haracgüzar olan reʿayayı hilaf-ı şerʾi şerif rica olunmuştur* (Gemil, *Documente turceşti*, doc. 14).

53 *Dahl ü tecavüz olunduğuna rıza-i hümayunum yokdur* (Gemil, *Documente turceşti*, doc. 32: *hüküm* of 10 *Şaban* 1017/19 November 1608). In other documents, one can find similar formulas, such as: *reʿaya ve beraya zulm ve taʿaddiye olunduğuna rıza-yı hümayunum yokdur* (Gemil, *Documente turceşti*, doc. 68: *hüküm* of 1617); *Memalik-i mahrusamın ve sükkan ve kuttanı olan reʿaya ve berayasının himayet ü sıyanetleri aksa-yı murad-ı hümayunum oldu* (Veliman, *Documente turceşti*, doc. 127: *hüküm* of 1737). See also Veliman, *Documente turceşti*, doc. 37, 81, 130.

Similarly, in a 1719 order to the hospodar Nicolae Mavrocordat of Wallachia, Ahmed III emphasized that:

> the Wallachian subjects had to enjoy of protection and safety…; and, there being no imperial permission of mine that the above-mentioned subjects be thus ever abused and oppressed, my great noble desire is that they enjoy the tranquillity and peacefulness of mind under my shelter of my imperial justice and power.[54]

Protection was regarded by local voivodes, boyars, clergymen, and representatives (*kapu-kethüdaları*) as a legitimate right of tribute-payers' status. Thus, the abuses committed by Ottoman officials and inhabitants of adjacent provinces were promptly reported to the sultan or grand vizier.[55] These protests concerned the forcible seizure of lands belonging to Wallachian, Moldavian or Transylvanian subjects. When the Tatars raided the territory of Moldavia in 1609 and again in 1632–1633, the voivodes requested the Porte reiterate the order which prohibited them to cross the Dnestr.[56] In the same way, George Rákóczy I deemed violations committed by the Turks in the Transylvanian frontier in July 1634, as "contrary to the state of peace," and he accordingly complained to the Ottoman court.[57]

Early modern documents prove that Ottoman central authorities strove to curb any abuses committed by local officials against the Moldavian and Wallachian population.[58] For instance, in the Fall of 1714, Ahmed III, in response to transgressions perpetrated by the *nazir* of Brăila (Ibrail) "against certain places within the distinct and settled frontier of the country of Wallachia," issued a *hüküm* reminding Danubian *kadı*s that those actions were abuses contrary to custom and previous orders.[59]

---

54 Veliman, *Documente turcești,* doc. 37: *hüküm* issued by Ahmed III to Nicolae Mavrocordat in *evahir-i Cemazi ül-evvel* 1131/11–20 April 1719.

55 Veliman, *Documente turcești,* doc. 56, 57, 67, 74, 117, 118, 121, 133, 140, 145, 148 etc.

56 Gemil, *Documente turcești,* doc. 49, 97.

57 Gemil, *Documente turcești,* doc. 99.

58 Gemil, *Documente turcești,* doc. 49, 62, 99; Veliman, *Documente turcești,* doc. 16, 43, 110.

59 Veliman, *Documente turcești,* doc. 16. In a 1744 record, the principle of protection of the Wallachian territory was stated again: "[…] the distinct and settled confines of the Wallachian *vilayet* should not have suffered any interference and violation from others…" (Veliman, *Documente turcești,* doc. 110).

### 2.3 *Religious Protection*

The covenants (*ʿahd*) that survive from the time of the Prophet Muhammad and the first four caliphs uniformly stress the freedom and protection of religious cults granted to non-Muslim communities that had accepted the "political summons" and agreed to pay *cizye*. An *ʿahd* granted by Muhammad in 632 to the Christians of Nadjran provided the blueprint, which was subsequently invoked in juridical literature and diplomatic textbooks:

> God's protection and the Prophet's guarantee [...] spread over the Nadjran and its neighborhood, that is over their assets, their persons, their religious cult practices [...], over their families, their sacred temples and over everything that belongs to them, root or branch.[60]

The tolerant attitude embraced during the great Arab conquests would be codified in later Islamic law treatises. Revealing his astonishment in the question "How [does it] come [about] that the prince of Muslims leaves churches, synagogues and crosses of the non-Muslims intact?," the Hanafi jurist Abu Yusuf Ya'kub devoted a whole chapter to this issue. From the beginning, he stated, religious protection had been one of the conditions formulated by the infidels to accept the payment of *cizye*, and only in this way, could the peace be concluded.[61]

The issue of religious tolerance, prominent during the Umayyad and Abbasid caliphates, resurfaced during the period of Ottoman expansion. In the Balkans, south of the Danube, non-Muslim communities were allowed to keep their religious edifices but were in theory barred from constructing new places of worship and had to limit themselves to restoring existing ones. Obviously, as historians have already emphasized, one should not overstate the Ottoman attitude towards non-Muslims. Non-Muslim subjects could not have a church in the vicinity of a mosque and had to refrain from using bells or worshipping their God in a conspicuous manner.[62] At the same time, new Muslim communities built mosques in the area, which in the Islamic juridical view signified that these territories had entered into the Abode of Islam and thus symbolized

60 Hamidullah, *Documents*, doc. 80: document of 10 AH. It will also be included by al-Kalkashandi in his textbook. Also see Hamidullah, *Documents*, doc. 80, 262 (in the Umar's *ʿahd* granted to the inhabitants of Ludd).

61 Abu Yusuf, *Kitab*, 213–230.

62 Yet, as Géza Dávid emphasized, "These restrictions, however, were felt mainly by Christians and Jews in Istanbul and certain other urban areas; the rural populations were almost untouched by them" (Géza Dávid, "Administration," 75).

an Islamic–Ottoman conquest.[63] In the nineteenth century, the French scholar Edgar Quinet wrote,

> Wherever the Muslims lay hands on a territory, on a kingdom they began by praising their God Muhammad for their victory, and this great invoice of ownership has been marked on earth by their sacred foundations in Spain, Attica, Morea, Byzantium, Asia Minor, Serbia, Bulgaria. There is no Muslim conquest without this mark.[64]

However, the realities north of the Danube differed from this pattern, and the consequences of this divergence can be seen in the landscape of contemporary Romania. No mosques were built in Wallachia, Moldavia and Transylvania throughout the early modern period; the same was the case in other tributary territories. European travelers were eager to point out the protection that the Orthodox Church, including its architectural component, enjoyed north, though not south, of the Danube. The most evocative example in this respect is the case of Paul of Aleppo, an Orthodox priest from Syria, who expressed his astonishment at the Greek Orthodox churches in the Moldavian port Galați.[65] In a French record of 19 August 1686, describing the town of Jassy, the author did not skip over the fact that it had:

> twenty-eight very beautiful churches or convents […] that served as a refuge for the whole population and that the Turks, on purpose, never ravaged.[66]

In the middle of the nineteenth century, Edgar Quinet continued his argument for the autonomy of the Danubian principalities:

63 There is now ample literature on this topic. See Anton Minkov, *Conversion to Islam in the Balkans: Kisve Bahası and the Ottoman Social Life, 1670–1730*. Leiden and Boston: Brill, 2004; Marc David Baer, *Honoured by the Glory of Islam. Conversion and Conquest in the Ottoman Empire*. Oxford, New York: Oxford University Press, 2006; Michał Wasiucionek, "Danube-hopping, Conversion, Jurisdiction and Spatiality between the Ottoman Empire and the Danubian Principalities in the Seventeenth Century," in *Conversion and Islam in the Early Modern Mediterranean: The Lure of the Other*, ed. Claire Norton, London: Routledge, 2017, 77–99.

64 Edgar Quinet, *Românii. Reorganizarea provinciilor dunărene*, in Edgar Quinet, *Opere alese*, vol. 2, Bucharest: Editura Minerva 1983, 363.

65 Paul of Aleppo, *Jurnal de călătorie în Moldova și Valahia*, ed. Ioana Feodorov, Bucharest: Editura Academiei Române, 2014, 161, cf. Wasiucionek, "Danube-hopping," 84.

66 *auxquels les Turcs et les Tartares par politique n'ont jamais touché* (Hurmuzaki, *Documente*, XVI, doc. 282: Bethume's letter to Croissy).

> By an extraordinary exception that is striking to the eye, the Muslims, as soon as they reached this country, denied themselves the right to build a single mosque. From the beginnings till nowadays they have kept their word. What demonstration could there be more convincing for the fact that the Romanian territory is not and has never been marked by the seal of conquest, that its autonomy and sovereignty have been respected.[67]

Nevertheless, the Ottomans made no long-term commitment to grant religious protection north of the Danube, and none is included in the diplomas appointing Moldavian and Wallachian voivodes. Instead, the investiture *berat*s granted to the Transylvanian princes included stipulations concerning religious autonomy. Likewise, in the imperial diploma of July 1614, confirming Prince Gabriel Bethlen's accession to the Transylvanian throne, Ahmed I formally guaranteed the protection of:

> the rite and order and rules and faith, as well as usages practiced among them from ancient times.[68]

The practical aspects of religious protection, or religious autonomy, in Wallachia and Moldavia are revealed by numerous seventeenth- and eighteenth-century Ottoman *hüküms*. According to them, administrative and fiscal problems of the local Orthodox Church were to be resolved without interference from Ottoman authorities or the Ecumenical Patriarchate in Constantinople (*Rum patrikatı*).[69] Ahmed I, in an order of 1617 to Radu Mihnea of Moldavia, reiterated earlier orders in this respect.[70] Higher clergy had to hail from the local ecclesiastical milieu, as indicated by an ancient custom (*öteden berü*) invoked in official documents. Thus, confronting an "invasion" of Grecophone clergy, Voivode Constantin Mavrocordat demanded this tradition

67 Quinet, *Românii*, 363. Let us note that the building of mosques should be related to the existence of Muslim communities, which it was not the case in the Romanian principalities.

68 *Kadimü'l-eyyamdan suregeldikleri ayın ve kaide ve töre ve dinlerin ve aralarında cari olan ʿadetlerin tagyir ve tebdil etmeyüb* (Gemil, *Documente turceşti*, doc. 61).

69 There is an ongoing discussion regarding the extent of the power held by the patriarchate, which I think is worth citing here. The book of reference is Tom Papademetriou's *Render Unto the Sultan. Power: Authority, and the Greek Orthodox Church in the Early Ottoman Centuries*, Oxford: Oxford University Press, 2015. Most of the theses on the topic follow Paraskevos Konortas, *Les rapports juridiques et politiques entre le Patriarcat de Constantinople et l'administration ottomane de 1453 à 1600 (d'après les documents grecs et ottomans)*. PhD diss., University of Paris I, 1985.

70 Gemil, *Documente turceşti*, doc. 68.

to be re-established, and in 1755 Sultan Osman III issued a *hüküm* to that effect.[71]

Local boyars were deeply concerned about revoking the religious protections specific to the autonomous status which would cease as soon as local princes were replaced with Muslim governors. "But we fear," confessed Wallachian boyars in exile in a petition to the Transylvanian prince, dated 25 July 1604,

> that if this be on the Turks' consent, they will appoint there [in Wallachia] another ruler, a Turk among them, who shares their belief and law, and who will spoil the beautiful Christian churches and monasteries and transform them into [mosques].[72]

In the eighteenth century, apocryphal "Agreements granted and reinforced by the emperor" (in Romanian, *Legăturile celi primite și întărite de împăratul*), improperly called "capitulations" and fabricated on the basis of tradition by Moldavian and Wallachian boyars, included certain clauses regarding the protection of religious cult by the Ottomans.[73]

## 3 Wallachian, Moldavian and Transylvanian Subjects to Neighboring Sancaks

Several studies exist regarding the status of Ottomans (either Muslims or non-Muslims) from the right side of the Danube travelling and residing in the principalities;[74] few pages have been written on the regime applied to Wallachians, Moldavians and Transylvanians during their sojourns in territories

---

71 More precisely on *evahir-i Şaban* 1168/2–10 June 1755 (Veliman, *Documente turcești*, doc. 127).

72 *Dar noi ne temem că dacă va fi pe placul Turcilor lucrul, vor pune acolo alt Domn, turcesc, dintre dânșii, care e de credință și de legea lor, care vor strica frumosele biserici ceștinești și mânăstirile și le vor face să fie ale lor* (Hurmuzaki, *Documente*, VIII, doc. 403).

73 "The Christian faith that is valid in Moldavia shall never be violated or spoiled and the churches shall be free as before." Besides, "the Turks shall not be allowed to purchase estates in Moldavia, or settle, or build mosques by any reasons at all" (Giurescu, *Capitulațiile*, 475). For critical observations upon these texts, see Giurescu, *Capitulațiile*, 473–504.

74 Most studies are centered on the eighteenth century. See: M. M. Alexandrescu-Dersca, "Despre regimul supușilor otomani în Țara Românească în veacul al XVIII-lea," *St.RdI*, XIV, 1, 1961, 87–113; M. M. Alexandrescu-Dersca, "Sur le régime des ressortissants ottomans en Moldavie (1711–1829)," *SAO*, V–VI, 1967, 143–182; R. Mircea, "Sur les circonstances dans lesquelles les Turcs sont restés en Valachie jusqu'au début du XVIIe siècle," *RESEE*, V, 1–2,

directly administered by the Porte.[75] A clearer picture can be obtained, however, by examining the juridical position of merchants from Western states to the Ottoman domains (*müste'mins*) and the position of other protected peoples (*zimmis*) of the empire.[76]

Until the mid-sixteenth century, tribute-payers visited territories under direct Ottoman administration for reasons of trade, travel and diplomacy. Trade was by far the most important factor prompting Wallachians and Moldavians to cross the Danube.[77] Numerous fifteenth-century documents, some of them published by Grigore Tocilescu, show that Wallachian merchants served as intermediaries between the "Turkish" and Transylvanian merchants.[78] In the following century, the commercial exchanges between the north and the south of the Danube intensified.[79] As documents published by Nicolae Iorga show, long-standing commercial ties existed between the Moldavian centers of Kili and Akkerman, occupied by the Ottomans since 1484, and the Greek, Armenian and Jewish merchants of Constantinople.[80]

There is no doubt that the inhabitants of Wallachia and Moldavia were regarded by the Ottoman juridical sources as infidels (*küffar, kefere*) and covenant-peoples (*muʿahidin*). What status did the Wallachians and Moldavians enjoy when traveling to Ottoman territories up to the mid sixteenth century?

---

1967, 77–86; M. A. Mehmet, "Despre dreptul de proprietate al supușilor otomani în Moldova și Țara Românească în sec. XV–XVIII," *CI*, III, 1972, 65–81.

75 Ion Matei, "Românii în Imperiul Otoman. Probleme generale," *CICSEE*, III, 1986, 141–149.

76 It is worth remembering the opinion of the hospodar Vasile Lupu (1634–1653), according to which the Moldavian merchants in Poland had the status of "foreigners" and, in this situation, could ask for protection only to the voivode of Moldavia (Hurmuzaki, *Documente,* Supl. II/2, doc. 284: letter to the commander of Krakow of 22 July 1642).

77 In this respect, Idris Bitlisi, referring retroactively to the second half of the fourteenth through the first half of the fifteenth centuries in Gallipoli affirmed: "The merchants and caravans of the Arab and Persian cities, as well as of the countries of Rumeli and Hungary and Wallachia and Moldavia, and of Czech and Polish ones pass through the above-mentioned straits." (Idris Bitlisi, *Heșt Behișt*, in *Cronici turcești I*, 152).

78 Tocilescu, *534 documente,* doc. 95, 139. In the first part of the fifteenth century, in Brăila (*Ibrail*), a town on the Danube, came merchants from the lands of the infidels, i.e. Ottoman territories. See *The Bondage and Travels of Johann Schiltberger, a Native of Bavaria, in Europe, Asia, and Africa, 1396–1427*, trans. J. Buchan Telfer, London: The Hakluyt Society, 1879, 38. Also see I. Bogdan, *Documente privitoare la relațiile Țării Românești cu Brașovul în secolele XV și XVI,* vol. I, Bucharest: Carol Göbl, 1905.

79 In 1533, merchants from Pitești, Argeș and Râmnic are mentioned by sources as trading in Balkans, to the south of the Danube, from which they came back with oriental merchandise. They paid custom duties "at the Vidin passage way" (*DRH*, B, I, 147).

80 N. Iorga, *Studii și documente cu privire la Istoria Românilor.* vol. XXIII: *Acte privitoare la comerțul românesc cu Lembergul,* Bucharest, 1913, 328–399, 410–454.

A study undertaken by Halil Inalcık on the late-fifteenth- and early-sixteenth-century customs registers of Kefe and Akkerman, has shown the presence of "Franks" (*efrençiyan*) from Chios and Moldavia (at that time, tributaries to the Porte) among merchants in the commercial hubs.[81] This led the author to wonder whether these merchants were assimilated by the Ottoman authorities to the foreign merchants coming from the Abode of War, but he deemed the evidence inconclusive.[82]

The status of foreigners (*müste'min*) in Islamic law has been studied by specialists, sometimes in comparison to the status of the *zimmi*s or foreigners in Christian lands.[83] In the Ottoman context, the focus has been on the particular case of the *Capitulatory* regime, producing an impressive number of contributions.[84]

The foreigner's juridical position in Ottoman territories was that defined in the *şeri'at*. Because any Islamic law treatise includes a chapter on this topic (*bab al-müste'min*),[85] this theoretical aspect should be analysed first before proceeding to the practical ways it was implemented and protected by treaties

---

81 In fifteenth- and sixteenth-century *kanunnames*, *hüküms* and custom registers, the terms *firenk, efrenç* (pl. *efrençiyan*) and *frenk kafirleri* were used for merchants coming to the empire from European countries. See: Anhegger, Inalcık, *Kanunname,* doc. 53, 54; Cvetkova, *Villes balkaniques*, 68; Lewis, *Middle East*, 30; Cl. Cahen, "Crusade," *EI-2,* II, 65.

82 "One can justifiably wonder whether there were really any foreign traders," remarks H. Inalcık (Inalcık, "Black Sea," 100).

83 D'Ohsson, *Tableau,* V, 37–44; J. Hatschek, *Der Musta'min. Ein Beitrag zum internationalen privat und Völkerrecht das Islamischen Gesetzes*, Berlin: Walter de Gruyter, 1920; C. Cardahi, "La conception et la pratique du droit international privé dans l'islam (étude juridique et historique)," *ADIRC*, 60, II, 1937, 511–650; *Law in the Middle East. Vol. I. Origin and Development of Islamic Law*, edited by M. Khadduri and H. J. Liebesny, Washington D.C.: The Middle East Institute, 1955; A. Abel, "Le statut legal des étrangers dans l'Islam," *Recueil de la Société Jean Bodin*, IX (1958): 331–351.

84 J. C. A. Gavillot, *Essai sur les droits des Européens en Turquie et en Egypte. Les Capitulations et la reforme judicaire*, Paris: E. Dentu, 1875; Ed. Engelhardt. *La Turquie et les Principautès danubiennes sous le règime des Capitulations. Études et projet de réforme applicable à la Roumanie et à la Serbie,* Paris : Cotillon, 1879 ; G. Pélissié du Rausas, *Le régime des capitulations dans l'Empire Ottoman*, Vol. I–II, 1er édition, Paris: A. Rousseau, 1902–1905 (deuxième edition, 1910–1911); P. M. Brown, *Foreigners in Turkey. Their Juridical Status*, Princeton: Princeton University Press, 1914; A. Rechid, "La condition des étrangers dans la Republique de Turquie," *RdC*, 46, IV, 1933, 169–227; N. Sousa, *The Capitulatory Regime of Turkey. Its History, Origin and Nature*, Baltimore: Johns Hopkins Press, 1933; H. J. Liebesny, "The Development of Western Judicial Privileges," in *Law in the Middle East*, 309–333; H. Inalcık and J. Wansboroug "Imtiyazat," *EI-2*, III, 1971, 1207–1225.

85 Hüsrev, *Dürer*, I, 205–210; Halebi, *Mülteka*, I, 336–338; *Defter-i sukuk* (TKSMK K. 778); *Siyasete mute'allik fetvalar* (*Fetvas* concerning politics) (TKSMK, H. 1650). Considering the rules of *şeri'at*, one can say that the foreign merchants had a "special status." On "special status" in private international law, see I. P. Filipescu, *Drept internaţional privat*, Bucharest:

and customary rules.[86] In Islamic law, the life and property of an inhabitant of enemy territories (*harbi*) venturing into Muslim lands was without any protection, unless they were granted temporary safe-conduct (*aman*). As I have already shown, general *aman*s for Western merchants were automatically included in the *ʿahdname*s (*Capitulations*) granted to their sovereigns.[87] In a chapter of his work devoted to foreigners and entitled *Bab-ı ahkam al-müsteʾmin,* Ibrahim al-Halebi stated,

> Any enemy who enters with safe-conduct into our territories is called *müsteʾmin.*[88]

In the juridical opinions (*fetva*) issued by *şeyh ül-Islam* or lower-ranking *müfti*s, the foreigner was similarly defined:

---

Editura Academiei Române, 1991, 198–203; Grigore Geamănu, *Drept internaţional public*, I, Bucharest: Editura Didactică şi Pedagogică, 1981, 385–386.

86 In accordance with certain Ottoman documents (*name-yi hümayun, ʿahdname*), the merchants coming from Christian states (e.g., France, Venice, England, Poland, Holland) enjoyed the same commercial privileges in the Ottoman Empire. For instance, Murad III's letter to Queen Elizabeth I of England (1558–1603) of 8 *Cemazi ül-evvel* 988/21 June 1580 mentioned that: "Just as the merchants of Poland and France and Venice come and go, the merchants of your domain also shall bring wares to our Well-Protected Domains and take away wares" (*Leh ve Françe ve Venedik bazerganları gelüb gitdüği üzere sizin vilayetinizin bazerganlar dahi Memalik-i Mahrusamıza metaʾ getürüb ve metaʿ alub gidüb*). (Skilliter, *Harborne,* 247; Uzunçarşılı, "Türk-Ingiliz," 616–617). The comparison with the Polish merchants' position is found also in the ʿa*hdname* granted by Mehmed III to the same Queen in 1601 (Feridun, *Münşeʾat,* II, 382). So, one can say they had the "most favored nation clause" regime. At the same time, one must emphasize that the treaties concluded between the Porte and Venice, Hungary, Austria and Russia were different from the *ʿahdname*s given to Western states (France, England, Holland). Free access and commerce, safety of person and merchandise and individual responsibility were granted by sultans to merchants coming from the neighboring states, provided that Ottoman merchants had the same rights in the mentioned states. One can say, consequently, they had a "mutual" regime.

87 The main articles of these treaties, concerning trade and merchants can be summarized as follows: safe access by land and sea; safety of their persons and properties; the property of the deceased merchants must not be seized; freedom and security of their trade; custom dues are to be at the ordinary rates; responsibility for debts and crimes shall be individual only and not collective. For details, see Panaite, *Război, pace şi comerţ în Islam,* 230–262; Viorel Panaite, "Being a Western Merchant in the Ottoman Mediterranean. The Evidence of a Turkish Manuscript from Bibliothèque Nationale de France," in *ISAM Konuşmaları. Osmanlı Düşüncesi. Ahlak. Hukuk. Felsefe. Kelam/ISAM Papers. Ottoman Thought, Ethics-Law-Philosophy-Kalam,* edited by Seyfi Kenan, Istanbul: ISAM Yayınları, 2013, 91–135.

88 *Her harbi ki bizim darımıza aman ile dahil ola ana müsteʾmin derler* (Halebi, *Mülteka,* I, 336).

> Zeyd enemy who [comes] from the Abode of War and enters into the Abode of Islam with safe-conduct.[89]

In the fifteenth-century official documents, the concept of *müste'mins* was seldom invoked for foreign merchants, replaced by similar but ambiguous idioms. Two examples from *kanunnames* are worth citing: "infidel who was not tribute-payer" (*haracgüzar olmayan kafir*) and "infidels who come from Venice and other countries."[90] In the following centuries, foreign merchants were called by phrases specific to *şeri'at*: "infidels who come from the Abode of War"; "infidels of the Abode of War" (*dar al-harb keferesi*); "the merchants' group who comes from countries of infidels" (*kefere vilayetlerinden gelen tüccar tayfesi*); "the merchants of the house of war" (*dar al-harb tüccarı*).[91]

Although European nations, groups and individuals were almost never mentioned in Ottoman documents without the label "infidel" applied to them, one of the rare exceptions to this practice involved the *'ahdnames*. For instance, in an Ottoman–Polish charter, the terms *kafir*, *kefere* or *kufr* (unbelief) were used three or four times, usually in a clearly religious matter of Polish captives converting to Islam.[92] As Bernard Lewis argued, since Europeans coming to the Ottoman Empire saw themselves as Englishmen, Frenchmen, Venetians, Germans, or Poles, the Ottomans began to differentiate between them, albiet through the filter of political and territorial allegiance rather than that of ethnicity and national identity.[93] This necessitated a shift in official classifications, as foreign merchants were no longer called by imprecise juridical concepts (*kafir, harbi*) but by names indicating their states.[94]

---

89 *Zeyd harbi dar-i harb'dan amanla dar-ı Islam'a çıkub* (Bianchi, "Fetvas," 180–181). *Zeyd* was one of the generic names used in *fetvas* for referring to men.

90 Anhegger and Inalcık, *Kanunname*, doc. 53 ("the Frankishman who was not a tribute-payer"/*haracgüzar olmayan Firenk*), doc. 56; Berindei, Kalus-Martin, Veinstein, "Actes. Vidin," 61.

91 Barkan, *Kanunlar*, doc. 93; Veliman, *Documente turcești*, doc. 73, 122, 150.

92 From the *'ahdname* of 1577 onwards, a new article was included in the Ottoman–Polish treaties concerning: "Armenians and other infidels who live under [Polish] king's rule" (*kıralın eli altında olub ermeni ve sayr kefere*) (AGAD, AKW-Tureckie, k. 71, t. 260, no. 486).

93 "The European is different," affirmed Bernard Lewis, "but not because he belongs to another nation, is subject to another ruler, lives in another place, or speaks another language. He is different because he follows another religion" (Lewis, *Muslim Discovery*, 173).

94 *Lehlü* (Poles), *Venediklü* (Venetians), *Ingilterelü* (Englishmen), *Francalu* (Frenchmen), *Nederlandalu* (Dutchmen) and so on (Şakiroğlu, "1521," 398–399; Gökbilgin, "Belgeler I," 126; Feridun, *Münşe'at*, II, 401–402; Groot, *OEDR*, 239–245).

Unlike non-Muslim subjects (*zimmis* or *haracgüzar kafirler*), foreign merchants were still regarded as enemies (*harbi*).[95] The Hanafi jurist al-Shaybani stated that a *müste'min* "does not enjoy the *zimmi* status because he is an enemy person."[96] Also unlike a non-Muslim subject, the foreigner could only dwell in Ottoman territories for less than one year, during which time they were exempted from poll-tax; after that, they would become a *zimmi*. However, this rule of *şeriʿat* was not followed in Ottoman practice. A clause included in *ʿahdnames* regularly granted foreign merchants the privilege to remain for an unlimited time in the Ottoman Empire without paying *cizye* and becoming the sultan's subjects.[97]

The absence of any commercial stipulations in the fifteenth- and early-sixteenth-century agreements between the Porte and the voivodes of Wallachia and Moldavia seems to suggest that in this area commerce was governed by customary practices. Nevertheless, one of the first Ottoman documents intended to regulate Ottoman–Moldavian relations grants a safe conduct to Moldavian merchants. This *nişan-ı hümayun* was enacted on 9 June 1456[98] as an immediate follow-up to the peace concluded between Mehmed II and Petru Aron. As the document indicates, the sultan closely tied the establishment of peaceful relations to the guarantee of commercial activities.

The order of 1456 has been published several times but not always correctly interpreted.[99] In itself, the document is a simple order (*hüküm*) to the *sancakbeyis*, *beys*, *sübaşıs* and *kadıs* with whom the Moldavian merchants, particularly those from Akkerman, might have been in contact. Several copies of it could have been sent directly to the merchants of Akkerman, so they could

---

95 Evidence in early-seventeenth-century *ʿahdnames*, e.g., 1604 to France, 1612 to the Dutch Republic (Feridun, *Münşe'at*, II, 401–402; Groot, OEDR, 239–245).

96 *Shaybani's Siyar*, 173.

97 Gökbilgin, "Belgeler I," 126 (*ʿahdname* of 1540 for Venice); Feridun, *Münşe'at*, II, 384 (*ʿahdname* of 1601 for England), 403 (*ʿahdname* of 1604 for France). In the Ottoman–Polish treaties a similar article was absent since merchants travelling in the Ottoman territories could not in practice stay for more than one year. For details concerning trade and merchants in the Ottoman–Polish treaties, see Viorel Panaite, "Trade and merchants in the 16th Century Ottoman–Polish Treaties," *RESEE*, 32, 3–4, 1994, 259–276.

98 5 *Receb* 860 AH. Published editions: Kraelitz, *Osmanischen Urkunden*, 44–46, f. 1; Guboglu, *Paleografia*, doc. 3 and facs. 3; Mehmet, *Documente turceşti*, I, doc. 2).

99 Scholars' opinions on this are contradictory. Mihail Guboglu appreciated that the *hüküm* of 1456 was "a privilege, a Capitulation" (*imtiyaz, Kapitülasyon*) granted to the merchants of Akkerman. He rejected Mustafa A. Mehmet's statement that that document was an *ʿahdname* (Mihail Guboglu, "Osmanlılarla Romen ülkeleri arasındaki ilk devri ilişkileri (1368–1456) hakkında belirtmeler ve doğrultmalar." Off-print from *IX. Türk Tarih Kongresi*, Ankara, 1988, 841).

present them to the respective authorities. This document, which can be called a collective *aman*, granted "the merchants of his countries [of the Moldavian voivode and] of Akkerman" (*anun vilayetlerinden Akkerman'dan olan bazerganlar*) three major privileges. Commonly granted to any foreign merchant's group in that period, they were the freedom to enter, circulate and leave the Ottoman territories; the freedom to trade there; and the protection of their life, liberty and merchandise.

> In the present situation, having reconciled with Petru voivode, the *bey* of Moldavia [...] [I] put an end to our enmity and ordered that the merchants from his countries [and] from White Fortress should come by ship; [and] selling and buying to and from the inhabitants of Edirne, Brusa and Istanbul, they should trade. [And] none of my *beys* and *subaşıs* and *sipahi*s and slaves should damage and harm their soul, head and goods, when coming and when leaving.[100]

The confirmation of the commercial privileges granted to the Moldavian merchants must be viewed in the context of the resurgence, after the conquest of Constantinople, of commercial activities between the Ottoman territories in the Balkans and the northwestern coast of the Black Sea.[101] For Moldavian merchants as "covenant-people," the document of 1456 restated in new terms the trading arrangements that had prevailed between Moldavia and the Straits before 1453.[102] Unfortunately, this *hüküm* is one of the few fifteenth-century documents that speak at all of the juridical condition of Wallachians and Moldavians in territories under direct Ottoman administration.

Ottoman *'ahdname*s granted to Ragusa throughout the fifteenth and sixteenth centuries included stipulations guaranteeing the republic's merchants rights specific to *müste'min*s: freedom to enter, circulate within and leave the Ottoman territories; protection of life, liberty and goods; and in case of death,

100 *Şimdiki halde [...] Boğdan ile beyi Pitri voyvoda ile barışıklık idüb aradan duşmanlığı götürdüm ve buyurdum ki anun vilayetlerinden Akkerman'dan olan bazerganlar gemiler ile geleler; Edirne'de ve Brusa'da ve Istanbul'da halkla muamele ve mubaya'a idüb bazerganlık ideler. Gelmekde ve gitmekde benüm beylerümden ve subaşılarumdan ve sipahilerümden ve kullarudan hiç birisi bunlarun canına ve başına ve malına zarar ve ziyan getürmiye* (AGAD, Warsaw, t. 2, no. 3; ANIC, mf. Poland, r. 1, fr. 119, 243).

101 Georgieva, "Commerce," 41.

102 In 1452, the merchandise of Moldavian traders was registered in Constantinople and Pera (Iorga, *Acte și documente*, III, 31).

that their unsold goods be returned to their legal heirs.[103] In addition, the *haracgüzar* merchants were granted "privileges" from which not even the subjects of neighboring Christian states benefited, such as lower custom duties and the freedom to buy prohibited wares.[104]

Early modern sources contain frequent references to Wallachian, Moldavian and Transylvanian merchants, local dignitaries, envoys, couriers and permanent agents (*kapu-kethudaları*), who travelled and resided in territories directly administered by the Porte.[105] Since Süleyman Kanunî's reign, as *zimmi*s, the Wallachians, Moldavians and Transylvanians had been able to travel freely within the Ottoman Empire. However, following a series of abuses committed against them and reported in petitions, the Porte regularly ordered its officials to protect the *haracgüzar*s' life, liberty and goods. In 1559, Süleyman Kanunî ordered the *kadı* of Rusçuk to prevent Ottoman clerks south of the Danube from oppressing the men of Wallachian voivode Petru the Younger (1559–1568) or damaging their belongings.[106] Later, in a *hüküm* of 1609 to the *nazır* of Isaccea, Ahmed I made a general statement concerning the protection of his Moldavian *haracgüzarlar*:

> When the Moldavian crosses [the Danube] from one side to another and on other occasions you shall not allow that he be troubled [...][107]

Abuses against Wallachian, Moldavian and Transylvanian tribute-payers who ventured into neighboring districts continued despite imperial interventions. Even the voivodes, when traveling to or leaving Istanbul, had to obtain a *hüküm* to the officials along their way. Osman II's order of June 1618 sent to "Iskender paşa, as well as to the dignitaries and *kadıs* of the right side (*sağ yolda*)," regarding the former hospodar Alexandru Iliaş of Wallachia (1616–1618), stated:

> When [this order] reaches you, according to my command, you shall make sure that the above mentioned [Alexandru] and his wife and his father-in-law and his servants and his other men, together with his cattle and goods, arrive safely and completely one of you to another (*emn ü*

103 The 1430, 1442 and 1458 "privileges" (*privilegia*) (Bojović, "Dubrovnik I," doc. 2 (1430), doc. 4 (1442), doc. 6 (1458). The 1512–1513 *ʿahdname* (Bursa Şer'iye Sicilleri, A, 20, sh. 387/b; Dalsar, "Dubrovnik," 410–414; Akgündüz, *Osmanlı Kanunnameleri,* III, 385–387).

104 Biegman, *Ragusa,* 69–73.

105 Gemil, *Documente turceşti,* doc. 119 (document of 1646), doc. 213 (*boyar oğulları ve hizmetkarları,* in 1696); Veliman, *Documente turceşti,* doc. 61 (document of 1728).

106 Mehmet, *Documente turceşti,* I, doc. 41.

107 Document of *Muharrem* 1078 /April 1609 (Gemil, *Documente turceşti,* doc. 44).

> *salim bir-birinize ulaşdırub*), so that you may send them to my Porte of Felicity.[108]

According to Daniel Goffman, the *maktuʿ* system was intended to create good will among the conquered population and to grant them some sort of autonomy, but the system was often used to ensure the collection of a fixed amount of money or to avoid the abuses of the *cizye* collectors that prevailed within the Ottoman provinces, including the Danubian regions.[109] During the seventeenth and eighteenth centuries, the most frequent abuses committed on the Wallachian, Moldavian and Transylvanian travelers, as denounced by their princes to the Porte,[110] consisted of "poll-tax imposition"[111] on the crossings across the river, on the route to Istanbul, Kili, Brăila, Giurgiu, Turnu, Silistre, Rusçuk and Nikopol, and generally in neighboring *sancak*s.

In 1717, the Nikopol *cizyedar* extracted "under the pretence of poll-tax (*cizye namiyle*) 4–5 *guruş* from each of the Wallachian subjects who cross [the Danube] from Wallachia to Nikopol."[112] A Burgas tax collector in 1728 even detained a cavalryman, "chained and incarcerated him, and gave him, by force and under constraint, poll-tax paper (*cizye kağıdı verüb*)."[113] As a result of the petitions from the voivodes, sultans constantly issued orders to *kadı*s and other officials, denouncing Ottoman clerks who charged the poll-tax.[114] By the middle decades of the eighteenth century, Wallachians' exemption from *cizye* paying south of the Danube was considered a customary practice. In 1759, Mustafa III consequently invoked custom, besides previous orders:

108 Gemil, *Documente turcești*, doc. 73.

109 It was the practice of the Porte to issue orders to eradicate tax abuses by doing away with regular payments of a fixed sum (*maktuʿ*), thus substituting a household tax. Daniel S. Goffman has published documents which describe incidents of tax abuses within the Ottoman provinces of Damascus, Tripoli and Aleppo but suggests that other areas within the provinces may have suffered from similar inequities. (Gibb, Bowen, *Islamic Society*, I/2, 256; Goffman, "Maktuʿ System," 81–90).

110 Gemil, *Documente turcești*, doc. 213 (*ʿarz-u hal* of 1696 wrote by Wallachian agents, called in Ottoman *Eflak kapu-kethudaları*); Veliman, *Documente turcești*, doc. 61 (*ʿarz-u hal* of 1728 wrote by Moldavian agents, called in Ottoman *Boğdan kapukethüdaları*).

111 *Harac talebeyile* or *cizye talebiyle*, in Gemil, *Documente turcești*, doc. 119 (of 1646), 213 (of 1696); Veliman, *Documente turcești*, doc. 140 (of 1759); Mehmet, "Condica," doc. 5 (of 1792).

112 Veliman, *Documente turcești*, doc. 29.

113 Veliman, *Documente turcești*, doc. 61.

114 Gemil, *Documente turcești*, doc. 213 (*cizyedar olanlar* in 1696); Veliman, *Documente turcești*, doc. 29, 61, 140 (the Nikopol *cizyedar* in 1717, the *Bergos cizyedar* in 1728, the Silistre, Giurgiu, Rusçuk and Brăila *cizyedars* in 1759). On *cizyedar*, see Sertoğlu, *ROTA*, 60–61.

> It shall be done such that the Wallachian's subjects shall not be harmed in any way by *cizye* imposition, in opposition to the high orders and the old custom [...].[115]

In fact, the Ottoman chancery issued official orders to officials across the empire, reiterating that any and all Ottoman subjects who had paid their *cizye* were exempted from further payments. This included Wallachians, Moldavians and Transylvanians, who paid the poll-tax to their prince,[116] who then delivered it to the Porte as a "collective tribute."[117]

In a document from 1646 the Moldavians were not compared to the *zimmi*s from the right side of the Danube but were included along with *müste'min* merchants from Poland and Lithuania. Specifically, Ibrahim I ordered the *kadı* of Kili to implement a financial regulation issued in 1642–1643, referring to Moldavian and Polish merchants' exemption from poll-tax.[118] These *hüküm*s call to mind the stipulation of several *'ahdname*s granted to Christian states, which registered only the *müste'min*'s exemption from the poll-tax and set no deadlines for their return to the country of origin.[119] Certain fiscal exemptions were also granted for wares purchased in Ottoman territories on behalf of tributary princes, and an order of Ahmed I from 1608 demonstrates a custom in this respect.[120]

The right to purchase real estate or erect buildings in territories under Ottoman rule was denied to foreigners. According to the Islamic law, a *müste'min* who became the 'owner' of a piece of land within the Abode of Islam had to

115 Veliman, *Documente turcești*, doc. 140.

116 "the *harac* is paid to their voivode" (Gemil, *Documente turcești*, doc. 119: *hüküm* of 24 *Şevval* 1056/3 December 1646).

117 *Eflak cizyesi maktu' olmakla* (Gemil, *Documente turcești*, doc. 213: *hüküm* of 10 *Zilka'de* 1107 /11 June 1696).

118 "You shall not, from now on, allow anybody to trouble with poll-tax impositions those Poles and Moldavians who [...] come to Kili port for trading" (*Lehlü ve Boğdanlılardan Kili iskelesine* [...] *ticaret içün gelüb harac talebiyle rencide itdirmeyüb*) (Gemil, *Documente turcești*, doc. 119).

119 "From those who settled and are engaging in trade in our Well-Protected Domains [...] the poll-tax shall not be asked" (*Memalik-i mahrusamızda mütemekkin olanlar* [...] *rencberlik edenler anlardan harac taleb olunmıya*, in Feridun, *Münşe'at*, II, 384 (*'ahdname* of 1601 to England), 403 (*'ahdname* of 1604 to France); Groot, OEDR, 241 (*'ahdname* of 1612 to Holland). For the Venetian case, see Gökbilgin, "Belgeler I," 126; Şakiroğlu, "1521," 398.

120 "My order was issued so that steps should be taken as before" (*olageldüği üzere amel olunmak*) (Gemil, *Documente turcești*, doc. 28). This kind of fiscal exemption was a frequent practice, applied also in Southeastern Europe (Tocilescu, *534 documente*, doc. 96), and recalls the similar "privilege" guaranteed to the Western merchants.

pay both land tax (*harac*) and poll-tax (*cizye*); thus, he became a non-Muslim subject of the empire (*zimmi*).[121]

There is evidence that Wallachians and Moldavians could hold estates in adjacent *sancaks*. Voivodes owned estates in Istanbul or in towns from the right side of the Danube, such as Voivode Petru the Younger of Wallachia who owned houses in Rusçuk in 1559.[122] In any case, the voivodes could erect new buildings or repair the old ones only with administrative and legal authorization (*hüküm* and *fetva*), as was the case for the subjects from the south of the Danube. In 1644, Voivode Vasile Lupu of Moldavia needed a *fetva* to build a fountain (*çeşme*) in Varna.[123] The same year, Voivode Matei Basarab of Wallachia asked for an authorization to build a public bath in Giurgiu.[124] In 1741, however, Mahmud I ordered the *naib* and *mutessellim* of Silistre to destroy the new buildings erected around the Orthodox church Vlădica by Voivode Constantin Mavrocordat of Wallachia and he himself obtained a *fetva* from *şeyh ül-Islam*, legitimizing the demolition.[125]

To conclude briefly, in the fifteenth and early sixteenth centuries, the Wallachians and Moldavians' condition across the imperial domains was closer to that of foreigners (*müsteʿmin*). Beginning with Süleyman Kanunî's reign, the juridical position of the Wallachians, Moldavians and Transylvanians, shifted closer to that of ordinary *zimmis*. As well as the other tributaries of Southeastern Europe, the Ragusans,[126] or the inhabitants of the islands of Naxos,[127] Chios and Andros,[128] they were now allowed to circulate freely; to have their life, liberty and goods protected by Ottoman authorities; to inherit the goods of

121 D'Ohsson, *Tableau*, V, 38.

122 Mehmet, *Documente turcești*, I, doc. 41.

123 Gemil, *Documente turcești*, doc. 115.

124 Probably on the vacant space he bought from a local Muslim, Abbas Çelebi, in a sale confirmed by a juridical sentence (*ilam*) of Mustafa, *molla* of Giurgiu, and Ahmed Hüseyin, *kadı* of Rusçuk (Gemil, *Documente turcești*, doc. 114: document of *eva'il-i Zilhicce* 1053/10–20 February 1644). See also Guboglu, *Paleografia*, doc. 20.

125 Veliman, *Documente turcești*, doc. 99.

126 The *ʿahdname* of 1575 (Biegman, *Ragusa*, 48–59); BOA, *DED* 13; *Dubrovnik Ahkam Defteri*, 1013–1028 AH/1604–1618.

127 The 1564 and 1565 *ʿahdnames* which came to establish the status of Naxos island and of its dependent islands, Santorin and Paros, towards the Porte (Uzunçarşılı, *Osmanlı Tarihi*, III/2, 102–103; Safvet, "Nakşe Dukalığı, Kiklad Adaları," *TOEM*, IV, 1329, 1446–1448).

128 The *ʿahdname* granted to the Andros island in 1539, it was just one piece of a series of *ʿahdnames* (in French translation, "*lettres de privilège du sultan*") by which the status of the Cycladic islands was regulated in the first half of the sixteenth century. See R. Saulger, *Histoire nouvelle des anciens ducs et autres souverains de l'Archipel*, Paris, 1698, 349–351; Slot, *Archipaelagus Turbatus*, II, 76–77.

deceased relatives; to pay lower customs duties, and to freely buy wares prohibited to the *müste'min* merchants.[129]

129 All these rights in relation to commercial activities characterized in part the *zimmi* status of Ragusan tribute-payers (Biegman, *Ragusa,* 69–73).

CHAPTER 14

# Tributary-Protected Principalities

The juridical nature of Wallachia, Moldavia and Transylvania's relations to the Ottoman center has been at the crux of Romanian historiography's engagement with the history of the empire. Within this debate, some scholars have claimed that there existed only a *de facto* relationship, lacking any legal underpinnings and marred by abuses.[1] This assertion goes against a broad spectrum of juridical, political and administrative sources that prove the existence of a *de jure* status that the principalities had within the *pax ottomanica* system.

Romanian contributions to this topic have been characterized by a pervasive obsession with proving that the principalities enjoyed a superior status in comparison to other Balkan countries. To achieve this goal, scholars coined several concepts – sometimes ambiguous and improper for the context – to describe the principalities' status, such as "submitted states," "dependent states," "vassal states," "autonomous states," "effective dependence," "Ottoman domination," or "autonomy."

The concepts of "vassalage" and "autonomy" deserve a special treatment. A majority of historians and jurists defined the relations between tributary princes and sultans from a European juridical and political point of view, considering them as a vassal–suzerain relationship. In this respect, it is necessary to emphasize two caveats. Firstly, the notions of 'vassal' and 'suzerain' came to define the relationship between the Porte and the principalities at a late stage, particularly in eighteenth- and nineteenth-century European documents, narratives and translations of Ottoman sources.[2] In fact, it was only in the nineteenth century that Western scholars introduced the syntagma of "vassal

1 For instance L. P. Marcu, "Idei despre stat si drept în opera lui Dimitrie Cantemir," *Studii și cercetări juridice* (Bucharest), 3 (1973), 497.

2 In Western Europe this medieval notion would not be employed in nineteenth-century diplomatic vocabulary, except to define the relations between the Ottoman Empire and the Principality of Bulgaria (1878–1909) and between Great Britain and South Africa. See J. L. Brierly, *The Law of Nations: An Introduction to the International Law of Peace*, 6th edn. Oxford: Oxford University Press, 1963, 133–136. Numerous manuscripts from the Archives of the French Ministry of Foreign Affairs discuss the "vassal" provinces and countries of the Ottoman Empire: *Mémoires et documents divers sur les provinces et sur les pays vassaux de l'Empire ottoman: originaux, copies et imprimés des XVIIIe et XIXe siècles sur la période de 1700 à 1839*, AMAE, *Mémoires et documents*, vol. 13; *Mémoires et documents sur la Moldavie et la Valachie: minutes, originaux, copies et imprimés du XIXe siècles sur la période de 1825 à 1855*, AMAE, *Mémoires et documents*, vol. 48.

 | DOI:10.1163/9789004411104_015

states" to describe the political status of the Danubian principalities. This notion was complementary to the notion of suzerainty, defining the relation of dependency between a stronger state and a weaker one.[3] According to Arthur de Claparède, the secretary of the Swiss embassy in Vienna and a theoretician of diplomatic law, the "nominal vassalage status" applied to the Danubian Principalities was defined by the fact that the state was subject but *de facto* sovereign, possessing the right to conclude peace and wage war, to negotiate and be represented in foreign countries by legation.[4] This notion was subsequently deployed retroactively to describe power relations in past centuries. In their turn, Romanian historians adopted the terms of "vassalage" and "suzerainty" without regard to chronology or the uniformity of the content.[5] However, such concepts are hardly applicable to the Ottoman context. Prior to the Treaty of Adrianople in 1829, no notions equivalent to the Western concept of "suzerainty" can be found in Ottoman documents. It was only after that date that this term was abundantly used in the translation of official Ottoman documents to European languages.[6]

Within the Ottoman Empire, numerous tributary and non-tributary regions enjoyed various degrees of self-government, depending on their historical,

---

3 In this respect, Henry Wheaton spoke of "the Principalities of Moldavia, Wallachia and Serbia, under the suzerainty of the Ottoman Porte and the protectorate of Russia." (H. Wheaton, *Commentaire sur les éléments du droit international et sur l'histoire des progrès du droit des gens*, vol. 3, Leipzig: F. A. Brockhaus, 1873, 36).

4 Arthur de Claparède, *Essai sur le droit de représentation diplomatique d'après le droit international moderne*, Thèse de doctorat, Geneva: Universiţé de Genève, 1875, 113.

5 For instance, some of them came to "Westernize" the political status of the Principalities of Wallachia and Moldavia by adopting the notion of vassalage paradoxically for the period after 1538, a stage in which actually the usual Ottoman habits had begun to massively penetrate the Danubian territories. Moreover, the stages of relationship between the Porte and the two tributary Principalities being defined firstly according to the Ottoman criteria and terms (for instance, tributaries) and then according to the medieval Western ones, i.e. vassals, an ambiguous image was created. See Gh. Zagoriţ, "Stabilirea suzeranităţii turceşti în Moldova. Cu argumente că prima capitulaţie atribuită lui Bogdan III a fost facută de Ştefan cel Mare la 1497," *CL*, XLVIII/7–8 (1914), 710–728; N. A. Constantinescu, *Începuturile şi stabilirea suzeranităţii turceşti în Moldova*, Bucharest: Institutul de Arte Grafice „Flacăra," 1914.

6 For instance, in the French translation of the *ferman* of 24 October 1866 that acknowledged Prince Carol of Hohenzollern and imposed a duty to observe the Ottoman suzerainty over the United Principalities, as the part of the Ottoman Empire, the concept of "suzeraineté" is ubiquitous: *A respecter dans leur intégrité mes droits de suzeraineté sur les Principautés-Unies qui font partie intégrante de mon Empire, dans les limites fixées par les stipulations des anciennes Conventions et par le Traité de Paris de 1856* (Noradounghian, *Actes*, III, 258). This *ferman* was granted after the Grand Vizier Ali paşa's note of 19 October 1866, addressed to Prince Carol, which included the conditions of his recognition as the hereditary prince of the United Principalities, and after Prince Carol's affirmative answer of 10 October 1866.

geographical, political, diplomatic and military circumstances. The notion of "autonomy" was a creation of modern historians and jurists meant to address these realities. Of course, no specialist would deny the autonomy of Wallachia and Moldavia; yet, it is necessary to emphasize that the autonomy could exist only *within* another polity – in this case, the Ottoman Empire – rather than outside.[7]

There was no inherent contradiction between the notions of "tributary," "protection," "vassalage,' and "autonomy." Instead, they can be seen as complementary, describing various facets of the same phenomenon. The concept of a "tributary" centers on the juridical and political status from the perspective of voivodal duties, whereas "protectorate" puts Ottoman obligations at the forefront. "Vassalage" and "autonomy" encompass both aspects, the latter term indicating the protection the sultans undertook as their responsibility in return for the infidels' agreement to pay tribute.

In my opinion, the most suitable approach for identifying a proper terminology to describe the juridical and political status of Wallachia, Moldavia and Transylvania within the *pax ottomanica* is to return to the sources and refrain from introducing new notions absent from the political vocabulary of the period. Secondly, it is crucial to dissociate the topic from politically-motivated nationalist discourse and instead adopt the vantage point of Islamic law as practiced and amended by Ottoman jurists and rulers. In this chapter, my goal is to situate Wallachia and Moldavia within the wider system of the *pax ottomanica*, according to the Ottoman juridical, administrative and political terminology.

## 1 Ottoman Methods of Statecraft

The Ottoman system of governance was by no means uniform throughout the empire. Aware of this fact, contemporary European observers and modern historians made numerous attempts to decipher, classify and analyze these variations, emphasizing the pragmatism of Ottoman statesmen.[8] However, the

7 In this respect, N. H. Biegman's dilemma and conclusion are relevant. Analyzing "Dubrovnik's position within the Ottoman state," he underlined that there were many Ottoman sources which distinguished between Dubrovnik and the empire, but at the same time he realized that should be more correct to say "Dubrovnik and the rest of Turkey" than "Dubrovnik and Turkey" (Biegman, *Ragusa*, 29–45).

8 Eton, *Turkish Empire*, 287–288, 297; Thornton, *Turkey*, II, 298–307; Lybyer, *Government*, 29; Pitcher, *Ottoman Empire*, 124–134; Maxim, "Statutul politico-juridic," 112–113; Metin Kunt, "Introduction," in *Süleyman*, 33–38.

criteria they applied varied greatly, and often failed to provide a coherent picture of realities on the ground.

Some scholars, including Halil Inalcık, Suraiya Faroqhi and Metin Kunt, defined stages by which conquered territories were "Ottomanized," pointing out the evolving nature of Ottoman expansion and empire-building. Central to this efforts was Halil Inalcık's 1954 study, entitled *Ottoman Methods of Conquest*. According to the author, until the reigns of Selim I and Süleyman Kanunî, the Ottomans – like other empire-builders – practiced a policy of gradual conquest in Europe and Anatolia. Initially, Ottoman power holders sought to establish some sort of suzerainty over their neighbors and force them to pay tribute, but retaining their autonomy and refraining from the introduction of *dirlik* system and *şeri'at*. Thus, until the early sixteenth century, most princes of Southeastern Europe became tributaries as Ottoman *haracgüzar*s, with relatively uniform duties and rights. The second stage followed, which usually meant the introduction of direct control by means of ousting native dynasties, "the application of the *timar* system which was based upon a methodical recording of the population and resources of the countries on the *defter*s (official registers)."[9]

Other historians tried to provide a general description of the Ottoman system of government. Thus, according to Albert Howe Lybyer's opinion, the empire consisted of a) the majority of its territory, administered directly through an exceedingly intricate but approximately uniform system, b) regions under less direct administration, which enjoyed special status, c) numerous tributary provinces and d) protectorates or vassal states. The territories falling within these four categories constituted the empire; beyond them, there lay a belt of neutral or disputed "no man's land," vulnerable to constant raiding, which abated only somewhat during the periods of peace. Further still was *dar al-harb* (Abode of War). This classification implies that the whole Ottoman Empire was considered *dar al-Islam*:

> The order in which these several regions are mentioned, an order based on progressive diminution of control, corresponds in general to an increasing distance from Constantinople. While the Ottoman Empire was

9 Inalcık, "Methods of Conquest," 103; Metin Kunt, "Introduction," in *Süleyman*, 34–35 ("Ottoman officials and scribes arrived with their regulations and their registers to take stock of the population and resources of the area. Once revenues were estimated, taking into consideration local custom and production, they were allocated in *dirlik*s. Then *kadı* magistrates arrived, together with the newly-appointed *dirlik*-holders: thus began Ottoman administration").

growing, each sort of territory tended to absorb the next, proceeding from the centre outward.[10]

D. E. Pitcher provided a comprehensive analysis of the political geography of the imperial administration until the sixteenth century, introducing a straightforward, but somewhat confusing, distinction between two categories: "direct government" and "vassal states." The former included the *eyalet* framework of provincial administration and the "standard" *sancak* system introduced in the empire's core provinces in Rumelia and Anatolia throughout the fifteenth and sixteenth centuries. These provinces became the imperial core after the massive conquests of Selim I (1512–1520), which extended the imperial domains into the Arab lands of Syria and Egypt. Pitcher identified the newly-conquered territories as "vassal states"; in my opinion, this category comprised territories and models of governance too different to be lumped under a single label.[11] Adopting the Treaty of Zsitvatörök (1606) as a major watershed, the author further distinguished between more types of "vassal states" which retained their local institutions and political order. The first group included regions that enjoyed a greater measure of autonomy, meaning their rulers were subject to the sultan's approval, were bound to provide troops and tribute, but no Ottoman troops were garrison within the territory. According to him, Moldavia and Wallachia prior to 1606 and Transylvania from 1541 to 1699 fell into this category (however, I would argue that Süleyman's reign was more of a watershed in this respect). Regions with more limited autonomy constituted the second subset; apart from the aforementioned rights, the sultans claimed the right to appoint and dismiss officials and station Ottoman troops. The classical examples of

10 Lybyer, *Government*, 29–30. Actually, the plethora of local arrangements makes it extremely difficult to construct a comprehensive typology of the Ottoman system of governance. In Lybyer's interpretation "Crimean Tartary, Georgia, Mingrelia, and parts of Arabia were vassal territories, more or less lightly attached and paying no regular tribute. Venice's island of Cyprus, the Emperor Ferdinand's possessions in Hungary, the territories of Ragusa, Transylvania, Moldavia, and Wallachia, all paid regular tribute with occasional presents, for the privilege of maintaining their own administrations. Egypt was under a special government, adapted with slight changes from that of the Mamluks, headed by a pasha sent out from Constantinople for a term of three years, and delivering a large part of its annual revenue to the imperial treasury. The Holy Cities of Mecca and Medina, far from paying tribute, received a large annual subsidy at the cost of Egypt. North Africa, conquered by the Corsairs, was brought into the empire by Khaireddin Barbarossa principally for the sake of prestige and support; but, though in its organization it imitated the parent government, it was seldom in close obedience."

11 From those "where control was only just short of complete integration with the central administration, to those where 'tribute' might be translated by the dignity-preserving word 'gift.'" (Pitcher, *Ottoman Empire*, 124–134).

this status were the principalities of Wallachia and Moldavia in the post-Süleymanic period and the Crimean Khanate, subsidized by the Porte.[12]

Drawing on these attempts at classification, we construe an overall image of the imperial system; the majority of imperial territories consisted of the "standard" *sancak* system (also called the *eyalet* framework of government), which – as Lybyer stated – were administered directly by imperial authorities and parceled into *zeamet*s and *timar*s (*dirlik*s), such as in the case of Kefe, Silistre and Budin. Moreover, throughout Ottoman history we find various autonomous regions, communities, provinces and polities. According to their "constitutional position" or their "degree of subordination" (as D. E. Pitcher calls them), two kinds of autonomy existed within the Ottoman system. The first included parts of the empire within the *eyalet* framework of government; the second group included the areas which remained outside the system of *eyalet*s and retained their own institutions. Obviously, this classification leaves room for nuances between individual cases.

The Ottomans incorporated autonomous religious and ethnic groups by issuing special privileges to certain Muslim and non-Muslim communities, such as monastic institutions of Mount Sinai and Athos, or Albanian, Greek, Serb and Vlach communities in the Balkans. Moreover, in some regions of the empire, particularly in North Africa, locally entrenched elites wielded all the power, even though the Porte continued to appoint governors there. This was especially the case with Maghrebi *ocaklık*s, Algiers (*Cezayir*), Tunis (*Tunus*) and Tripoli of Libya (*Trablus-u Garb*).[13] The situation with North African *ocaklık*s differed greatly from that of Egypt, which was included in the category of "privileged provinces" (*eyalat-i mümtaze*), whereas the elite's ties with the

12 Fourth, there were states that recognized Ottoman suzerainty, but paid no regular tribute (the khans of Kazan, emirs of Gilan and Shirvan etc.). Finally, one could identify "secondary vassals," including tribes drawn to the Ottoman sphere of influence by their directly depended on rulers who had already been vassals to the Porte (e.g. Nogay tribes, Arab tribes from Africa) (Pitcher, *Ottoman Empire*, 124–134).

13 For details, see N. Laugier de Tassy, *Histoire des États barbaresques qui exercent la piraterie, contenant l'origine, les révolutions de l'état présent des royaumes d'Alger, de Tunis, de Tripoli et de Maroc, avec leurs forces, leurs revenus, leur politique et leurs commerce par un auteur qui a résidé plusieur années avec caractère public* (Laugier de Tassy), vol. I–II, Paris: Chaubert, 1757; Abdeljelil Temimi, "La propriété foncière et le systeme des timar et zaamat dans la régence ottomane de Tunis. 1574–1588," *AHROS*, nos. 11–13, October 1995: 179–197; H. D. de. Grammont, *Histoire d'Alger sous la domination turque. 1515–1830*, Paris: Ernest Leroux, 1887; Jean Pignon, "La milice des janissaires de Tunis au temps des Deys. 1590–1650," *Les Cahiers de Tunisie. Revue de Sciences Humaines*, Tunis, IV, 15, 1956, 301–325; Tal Shuval, "The Ottoman Algerian elite and its ideology," *IJMES*, 32, 3, August 2000, 323–344.

FIGURE 22 *Turcici Imperii Descriptio from Iodocus Hondius, Gerardi Mercatoris Atlas sive Cosmographicae*

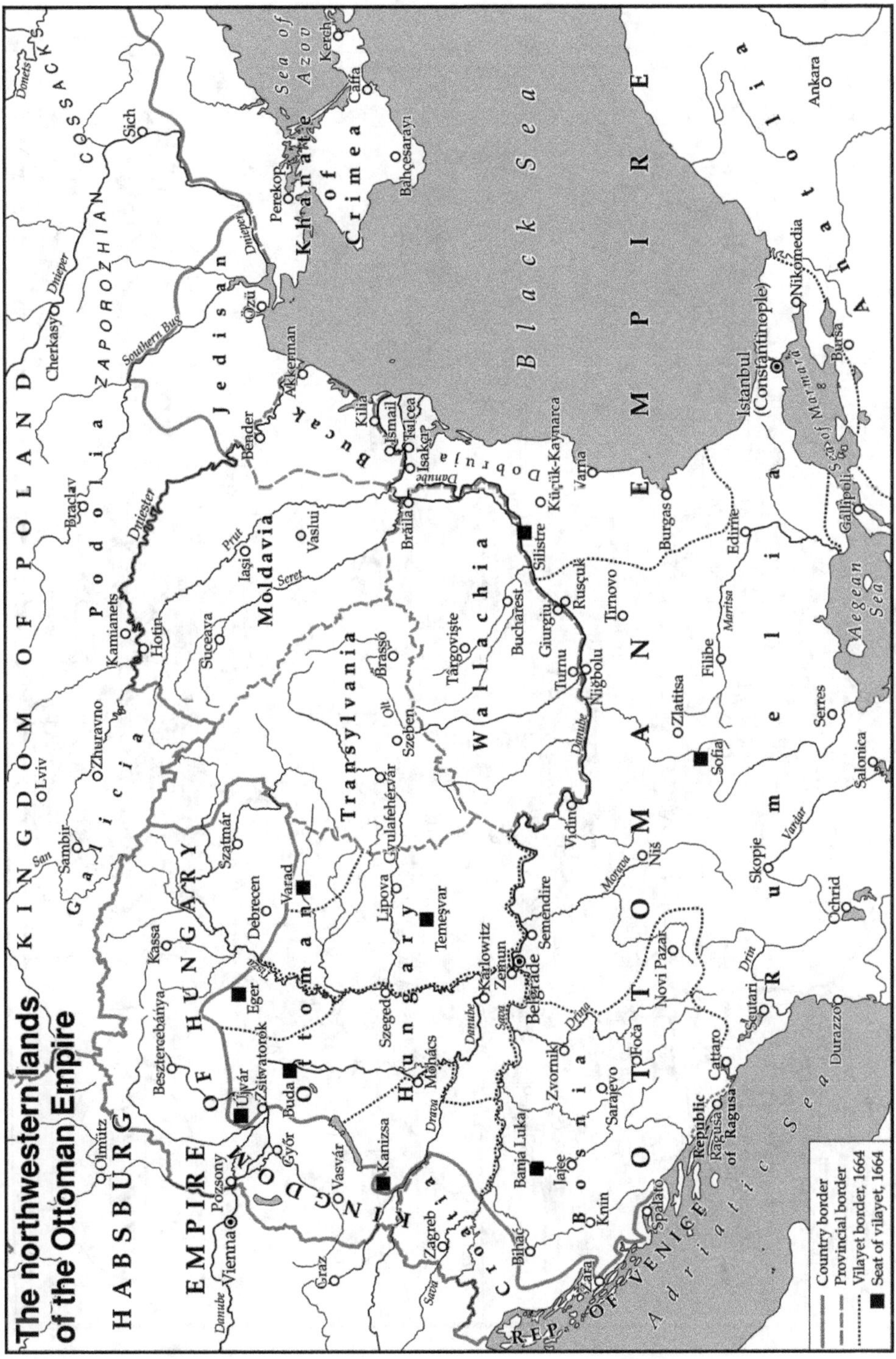


FIGURE 23 Map of Northwestern Lands of the Ottoman Empire at mid-Seventeenth Century (offered by Gábor Kárman)

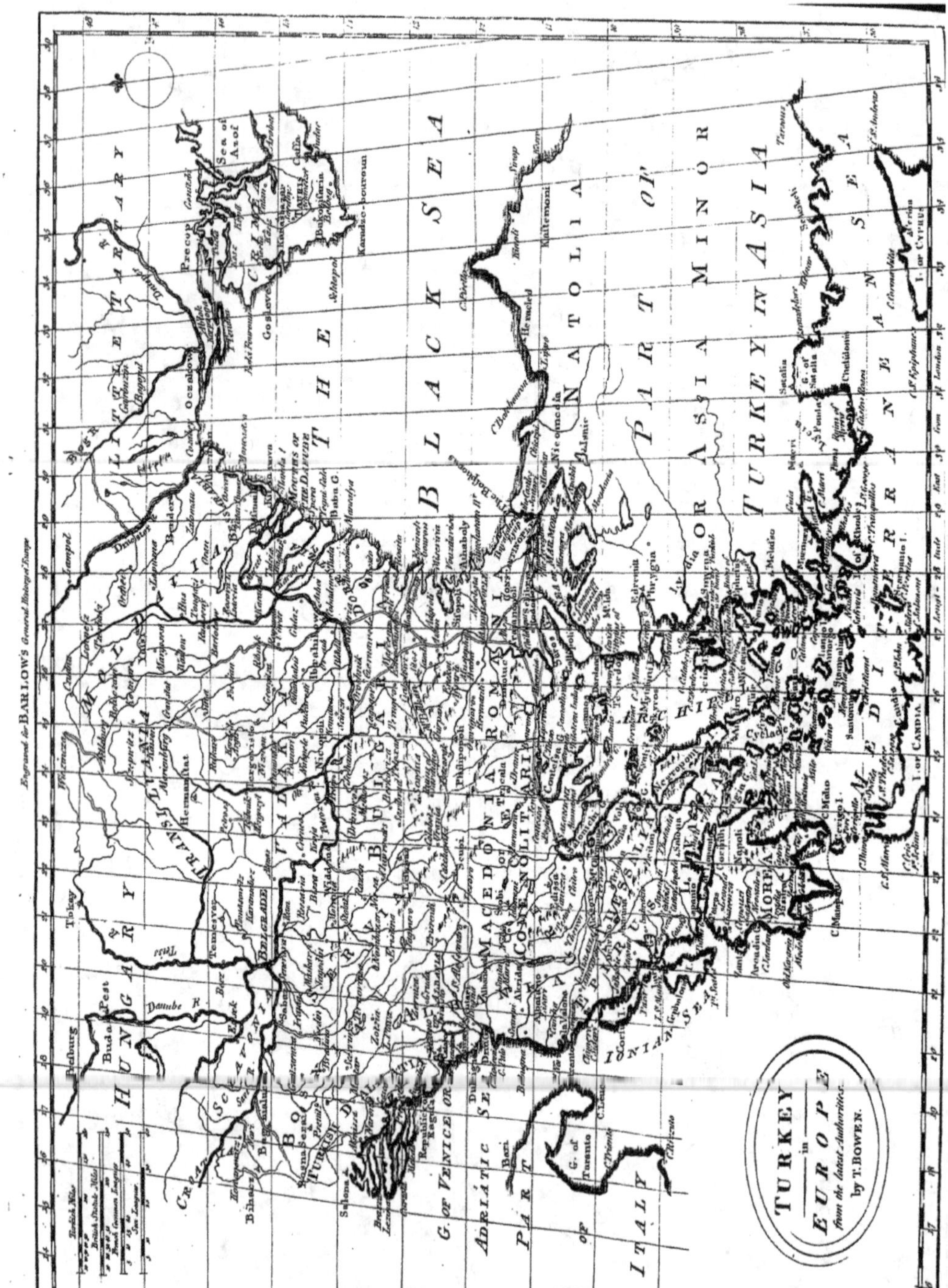


FIGURE 24 *Turkey in Europe* – Map printed in Percival Barlow, *The General History of Europe*. The

center where far more profound.[14] This kind of province is frequently called a *salyaneli* province (*saliyane* meaning "annual"). Under this model, upon covering the expenses for defense and salaries within the province, the governor remitted surplus tax revenue to the imperial treasury.[15]

In some of the regions that entered the Ottoman orbit,[16] the introduction of direct imperial administration proved impracticable due to topographical characteristics, distance from the center or resistance mounted by the local population; Pitcher, correspondingly, included them into the "vassal states" category. However, in my opinion this approach dilutes the concept itself, which should be limited to tributary-protected provinces/principalities, like Ragusa, Wallachia and Moldavia since the mid-sixteenth century, Transylvania and some Aegean islands, such as Chios and Naxos. However, there is no doubt that, differences in the degree of autonomy notwithstanding, all these areas constituted integral parts of the Ottoman Empire.

## 2 Tributary Provinces and the Pax Ottomanica System

Both Ottoman and non-Ottoman sources employed various juridical, political and administrative terminologies to describe the status of Wallachia, Moldavia and Transylvania within the Ottoman Empire. In this regard, we can discern two threads in the vocabularies employed by the early modern chancery; one

14 For Egypt, see Stanford J. Shaw, *The Financial and Administrative Organization and Development of Ottoman Egypt. 1517–1798*, Princeton: Princeton University Press, 1962; Michael Winter, *Egyptian Society Under Ottoman Rule. 1571–1798*, London and New York: Routledge, 1992. In terms of Yemen, this was a particular case, and it's not immediately clear if any system was really in place, given the precarious hold of the Ottomans on the province (Abdol Rauh Yaccob, "Yemeni Opposition to Ottoman rule: An Overview," in *Proceedings of the Seminar for Arabian Studies*, vol. 42, *Papers from the forty-fifth meeting of the Seminar for Arabian Studies held at the British Museum*, London, 28 to 30 July 2011 (2012), 411–419).

15 Salih Özbaran, "Some Notes on the *Saliyane* System in the Ottoman Empire as Organized in Arabia in the Sixteenth Century," *OA.JOS*, VI, 1986, 39–45; Metin Kunt, "Introduction," in *Süleyman*, 35; Salih Özbaran, "Ottoman Naval Policy in the South," in *Süleyman*, 68. Moreover, D. E. Pitcher included in the category of autonomous lands hereditary *sancaks* and the *sancaks* whose *beys* hailed from local communities, and therefore outside the normal system whereby a *sancakbeyi* could be transferred from one province to another (Pitcher, *Ottoman Empire*, 124–134).

16 For the case of Cossack Ukraine in the second half of the seventeenth century, see Viktor Ostapchuk, "Cossack Ukraine in and out of Ottoman Orbit, 1648–1681." In Gábor Kármán and Lovro Kuncević (eds). *The European Tributary States of the Ottoman Empire in the Sixteenth and Seventeenth Centuries*, Leiden, Boston: Brill, 2013, 123–152.

emphasized that the tributary territories had the same status as other Ottoman provinces, while the other stressed their autonomous position within the empire. In the following section, I will analyze each of them separately.

### 2.1 *Terminology of Homogeneity*

The first way in which the Ottoman chancery engaged its tributaries was through the use of homogenizing terminology, emphasizing that they had the same status as other parts of the imperial domains. By the reign of Süleyman Kanunî, Wallachia, Moldavia and Transylvania had come to be regarded – legally and politically – as the "patrimony of the sultan" (*mülk-i mevrus*), part of the Abode of Islam (*dar al-Islam*), and provinces of the Ottoman Empire (*Devlet-i Aliye*/The Exalted State, or *Memalik-i mahrusa*/The Well-Protected Domains).[17] The Porte invoked these formularies to protect its territory against the interference of both Ottoman officials and Christian neighbors.

Labeling Moldavia, Wallachia and Transylvania as parts of the Well-Protected Domains conveyed the message that the principalities were merely imperial provinces rather than distinct entities with special status. As Selim II informed King Sigismund II Augustus in 1572,

> Moldavia, Wallachia and Transylvania are among our countries and *vilayet*s just like other Well-Protected Domains under our own rule.[18]

Transylvania was also considered as an "annex of my Well-Protected Domains" (*Memalik-i mahrusam muzafatından olub*) in 1581.[19] In a similar vein, the Wallachian status was like "all the other Well-Protected Domains" as stated by Osman II in 1618.[20] Finally, in a letter sent in 1692, Ahmed II informed the Crimean Khan Safa Giray that Moldavia "is among the annexes of my Well-Protected Domains."[21] Due to obvious similarities in their legal status, Wallachia and Moldavia were frequently lumped together through such formulas as *Eflak ve Boğdan memleketleri*, *Eflak ve Boğdan voyvodalıkları*, or *Memleketeyn* ("the two

---

17 According to certain historians, all these formulas were only used to express Ottoman suzerainty: İ. H. Uzunçarşılı, *Osmanlı Tarihi*, vol. IV/1, Ankara, 1956, 6; Veliman, *Documente turcești*, 13.

18 Mehmet, *Documente turcești*, I, doc. 103: document of *eva'il-i Zilhicce* 979/15–24 April 1572.

19 *Hüküm* of 3 July 1581 to the *beylerbeyi* of Buda (Veliman, "Carte de legământ," 36). Valeriu Veliman considered that the term *muzafat* ("annex") ruled out the possibility of dependence upon the Porte. However, *Memalik-i mahrusa* was used without the attribute *muzafat* for describing the status of the Romanian principalities.

20 *Vilayet-i Eflak sa'ir Memalik-i mahrusam gibidir* (Gemil, *Documente turcești*, doc. 72: *hüküm* of 7 *Cemazi ül-ahir* 1027 /1 June 1618).

21 *Memalik-i mahrusamız muzafatından Boğdan vilayeti* (Gemil, *Documente turcești*, doc. 196: document of *evasıt-ı Rebi ül-ahir* 1103/1–10 January 1692).

countries"). I must point out that this inclusion of the principalities into the Well-Protected Domains served the Porte as a means to protect its tributaries and subjects against abuses by Ottoman officials and Christian powers alike.

The traditional notion of "sultan's patrimony" (*mülk-i mevrus*) took shape during Süleyman's reign and was frequently emphasized in the following centuries. For instance, in a *hüküm* reconfirming Grigore II Ghica on the throne in 1749, Sultan Mahmud I invoked his right to appoint voivodes on following argument:

> The country of Wallachia is my estate left as inheritance (*mülk-i mevrusum olmak*) from my glorious ancestors.[22]

Even in the early nineteenth century, Wallachia and Moldavia were considered "properties [left as] imperial inheritance" (*mülk-i mevrus-ı şahane olan*), an official position expressed by the Ottoman ambassador in Paris, Abdurrahim Muhib Efendi, in a report of 1808.[23]

The Abode of Islam was identified with the territories under Ottoman sovereignty, that is the Ottoman Empire as a whole; nonetheless, it was most often referred to as the Well-Protected Domain. One of the important attributes underlined by the Hanafi jurists (for instance, al-Shaybani) which characterized a territory of the Abode of Islam was the protection and the defense of Muslims' life and assets.[24]

It is clear that starting from the reign of Sultan Süleyman, Wallachia, Moldavia and Transylvania were no longer regarded as parts of the Abode of War. This is confirmed by a number of *hüküms*, which specifically addressed this shift. In an order issued following the Kam'janec' campaign of 1672, Mehmed IV reiterated that the "Wallachian population are not *harbis*" (*Eflak re'ayası harbi değildir*) and, consequently, Wallachia is not in the Abode of War (*dar al-harb*).[25] The same distinction was frequently conveyed through eighteenth-century orders, which prohibited exports of certain wares to countries from the Abode of War (*dar al-harb*), including Poland (*Leh*), the Habsburg Empire

22 Veliman, *Documente turcești*, doc. 120: *hüküm* of *evasıt-ı Cemazi ül-evvel* 1162/29 April-8 May 1749.

23 Veliman, *Documente turcești*, doc. 237: document of 21 *Ramazan* 1223/10 November 1808).

24 Shaybani, *Kitab al-siyar*, cf. Caurroy, "Législation," IV/17, 218; Abel, "Dar al-Islam," 430; Halebi, *Mülteka*, II, 336; Bianchi, "Fetvas," 180–181; Şükrullah, *Tevarih*, in Veliman, "Mircea," 426; Ibn Kemal, *Tevarih*, in Decei, "Mircea," 144; Parvin, Sommer, "Dar al-Islam," 4.

25 Gemil, *Documente turcești*, doc. 155. Actually, Tahsin Gemil translated "Wallachian inhabitants are not ‹in the territory› of war."

(*Nemçe*) and Venice (*Venedik*).[26] Clearly, Muslim religious practices were not carried out in public in Wallachia, Moldavia and Transylvania and the *şeriʿat* did not constitute the law of the land. Whenever the application of Islamic law was discussed, the sultans stated that "since Moldavia is not included in the Abode of Islam (*dar al-Islam olmamağin*), the [litigations] shall not be tried according to the *şeriʿat*."[27] This statement, uttered in 1585 by Murad III, was extended by modern historians to also apply to Wallachia and Transylvania, constituting a definite proof that the principalities remained outside the Abode of Islam.[28] Yet, Ottoman legal discourse differentiated between just two main categories – the Abode of War and the Abode of Islam; the latter also included tributary states and provinces under the sultan's suzerainty, even if they had no Muslim population.[29] Thus, one inevitably comes to a logical conclusion that the three principalities north of the Danube belonged to *dar al-Islam* from Süleyman Kanunî's reign onwards. This point of view was frequently embraced by Ottoman authorities. N. H. Biegman, who addressed a similar issue of litigation among Ragusan merchants in the *kadı* courts of Rumelia, arrived at a similar conclusion:

> On the evidence of this *ferman* one might contend that the Turks did not officially consider Dubrovnik as part of *dar ül-Islam*. But as it is the only known instance of such explicit differentiation between the two, it is preferable to consider it an exception to the rule, brought about by the necessity to explain to all cadis where to draw the line.[30]

### 2.2 *Terminology of Difference*

Along with vocabulary meant to emphasize homogeneity, the Ottoman chanceries also employed notions stressing the difference of status and the autonomous positions of Wallachia, Moldavia and Transylvania; this discourse, however, did not collide with the definition of the principalities as parts of the empire. In this respect, the most frequently applied terms included the Abode of Tributary Protection (*dar al-zimmet*), freedom (*serbestiyet*), and privileged provinces (*eyalat-ı mümtaze*). These formulas were as a rule invoked especially

26 Veliman, *Documente turceşti*, doc. 122: *hüküm* of 1164/1750–1751; Mehmet, *Documente turceşti*, I, doc. 265: *hüküm* of *evahir-i Zilhicce* 1177/ 21–30 June 1764.

27 Apud Maxim, "L'autonomie," 210.

28 Maxim, "Pays Roumains," 32–36; Maxim, "Statutul politico-juridic," 113–119.

29 Shaybani, *Kitab al-siyar*, cf. Caurroy, "Législation," IV/17, 218.

30 Biegman, *Ragusa*, 33–34.

whenever Moldavian–Wallachian elites petitioned the sultans for protection against local Ottoman officials and subjects from adjacent *sancak*s. In fact, Wallachia, Moldavia and Transylvania were by no means the only regions, whose status was described through these concepts, which touched upon various aspects of financial, administrative, religious and juridical autonomy within the Ottoman Empire.

One of the most controversial questions has been the Islamic juridical category in which Wallachia, Moldavia and Transylvania were included. The realities of the Umayyad and Abbasid periods have proven that a permanent state of war was unfeasible and forced the caliphal authorities to strike peace agreements with non-Muslim individuals and communities. A particularly important case in this respect was that of non-Muslim rulers who agreed to pay tribute and obeyed the caliphs but retained their internal autonomy. In these instances, Muslims scholars envisioned categories supplementary to the Abode of Islam and the Abode of War, such as *dar al-muvada'a, dar al-zimmet, dar al-ʿahd* or *dar al-sulh*.

Some Muslim jurists – particularly Yahya b. Adam, al-Shafiʾi and al-Mawerdi – advanced the concepts of *dar al-ʿahd* and *dar al-sulh*, which were variously translated by specialists as "Abode of Peace," "Abode of Pact" or "Abode of Truce."[31] It is important to note that the main criterion used by the scholars to describe these kind of territories was the existence of an "engagement" (*ʿahd*) between a Muslim sovereign and a non-Muslim leader. The famous Shafiʿi scholar al-Mawerdi (d. 1058) theorized about the concept of the *dar al-ʿahd* in the chapter on the classification of territories entering Muslim rule. Thus, al-Mawerdi understood under the *dar al-ʿahd* (*territoire du traité* in E. Fagnan's French translation), those territories that, on the basis of a contractual pact, remained in non-Muslims' possession in exchange of a tribute (*harac*) equivalent to a poll-tax (*cizye*). This point of view was comprised in a famous quotation from the twelth chapter of his *al-Ahkam al-Sultaniya:*

> Third, land which is taken through treaty, but which remains in their (its inhabitants) hands, on the understanding they pay the *harac* on it, is of two kinds: 1. the treaty is made on the understanding that the land is ours, and that it becomes *waqf* within *dar al-Islam* by way of the treaty; it is not permitted to sell it, or pledge it, and the *harac* is a rental charge which is not annulled by their becoming Muslims: thus its *harac* is also taken, if it is transferred to others who are Muslims. Such persons

31 Inalcik, "Dar al-ʿahd," 118–119; D. B. Macdonald – (A. Abel), "Dar al-sulh," *EI-2*, II, 134–135; Parvin, Sommer, "Dar al-Islam," 4; Özek, *Islam Hukuku*, 144–146; Maxim, *ŢRÎP*, 143–169.

> become people of treaty by this agreement, and, if they pay the *cizye*, they may stay there indefinitely. If they refuse to pay the *cizye*, they are not compelled to pay it, but they may only stay for the same length of time that the "people of treaty" may stay, that is four months, but (certainly) no longer than a year. There are two points of view as to whether they may stay for a period between four months and a year; II. A treaty is made such that the lands remain theirs and the *harac* tax is imposed on them, and this has the same force of law as the *cizye*, so that if they become Muslims, it is cancelled; their land does not become part of *dar al-Islam*, but remains *dar al-ʿahd* (treaty territory) such that they may sell it and pledge it, and if it is transferred to a Muslim, the *harac* is not taken; they may remain there as long as they respect the treaty, and the *cizyes* not taken from them because they are outside *dar al-Islam*...[32]

Modern historians have frequently adopted the Shafiʿi concept of *dar al-ʿahd* to define the tributary status and as a tool that could resolve apparent contradictions regarding the territories on the fence between *dar al-Islam* and *dar al-harb*.[33] However, there are two important arguments applying this term to the principalities of Wallachia and Moldavia. Firstly, the concept of *dar al-ʿahd* does not belong to the Hanafi juridical tradition adopted by the Ottomans and has been absent from the scholarly debates in the empire. In fact, al-Mawerdi himself admitted that he had not found such a concept in Hanafi works, emphasizing that Abu Hanifa had included such territories in the Abode of Islam:

> Abu Hanifa says their territory does become *dar al-Islam* by the treaty (*bi'l sulh dar al-Islamʿa*), that they themselves become *zimmis*, and that the *cizye* is taken from them.[34]

Secondly, given the historical evolution of Ottoman–Romanian relations throughout the late medieval and early modern period, it would be nigh on impossible to capture the essence of the principalities' juridical status within a single, all-encompassing term such as the Abode of Peace.

---

32 Mawerdi, *Ahkam*, ed. Fagnan, 290–291; Mawerdi, *Ahkam*, ed. Yate, 201–202.

33 For example, to define the juridical status of the tributary states in Southeastern Europe, including Wallachia, Moldavia, Transylvania, Ragusa, certain Aegean islands (Biegman, *Ragusa*, 30–32; Inalcık, "Dar al-ʿahd," *EI-2*, 118–119; Decei, "Sulhname," 139; Matei, "Domination ottomane," 95; Maxim, *ŢRÎP*, 143–168).

34 Mawerdi, *Ahkam*, ed. Fagnan, 290–291; Mawerdi, *Ahkam*, ed. Yate, 201–202. See also Decei, "Sulhname," 137.

Hanafi jurists al-Shaybani (d. 805) and al-Sarakhsi (d. 1090) distinguished between two categories of mediated territories, namely *dar al-muvada'a* (the Abode of Reconciliation, or the Abode of Truce) and *dar al-zimmet* (the Abode of Tributary Protection), depending on the criterion of sovereignty. It is crucial to keep in mind that neither of these categories existed independently of the Abode of War and the Abode of Islam, but rather they were included into these more encompassing notions.

The label of *dar al-muvada'a* (*muvada'a* meaning reconciliation or truce) applied to a territory inhabited by enemy infidels (*harbi*) who had reached an agreement with the Muslim community. Despite the existence of truce, though, such lands remained within the Abode of War, since such a peace could by definition only be temporary. According to al-Sarakhsi's comments to al-Shaybani's discussion of *harac*, *dar al-muvada'a* was "the protectorate whose inhabitants conclude peace with the stipulation that they shall pay the capitation to the Islamic ruler," but their status was not one of *zimmi*s within the Abode of Islam. Such a protectorate would pay a tribute (which in theory constituted the poll-tax from its inhabitants) but was allowed to retain its autonomy. In case the non-Muslim party broke the conditions of the treaty or was conquered by a non-Muslim with no pact with the Muslim sovereign (*harbi*), the arrangement lost its validity and would open the land to Muslim attacks. The former case invoked the principle of *pacta sunt servanda*, while in the latter, the status of a conquered country depended on that of its victor.[35]

*Dar al-zimmet* was introduced by Hanafi jurists to define the regions where non-Muslim inhabitants concluded with the Muslim sovereign pacts of tributary protection (*'ahd-ı zimmet*). Since, as I have pointed out, the term *zimmet* had more than one meaning ("obligation," "duty," "contract," "protection"), it is exceedingly difficult to provide a single translation for the term. This ambiguity only deepens once we realize that it was employed to describe two different zones which shared many common features, but also diverged in some crucial aspects. First, *dar al-zimmet* indicated an area within the Abode of War, in whose reach the non-Muslim population became tributaries of Muslim sovereigns by the consent of the local ruler; in this case, local laws and customs rather than *şeriat* applied. In its second meaning, *dar al-zimmet* was part of the Abode of Islam, whose non-Muslim population had agreed to pay tribute, obey Muslim authorities, but secured the privilege to elect their own leaders under

35 The infidels became "peoples of truce" (*ehl-i muvada'a*) (Shaybani, *Kitab al-siyar*, IV, 65–66, n. 1; Caurroy, "Législation," IV/17, 222–224; Özel, *Islam Hukuku*, 147–148). It is worth noting that the status of the Abode of Truce also applied to a territory conquered or forced into vassalage by a non-Muslim ruler whose territory had been already part of *dar al-muvada'a*.

Muslim tutelage. This ambiguity, albeit seemingly small, had important practical consequences: *dar al-zimmet* belonging to the Abode of War lost its distinct status immediately upon the breaking of the covenant by the prince.[36]

The terms of *dar al-muvadaʿa* or *dar al-zimmet* (along with the term *dar al-ʿahd*) are absent from the documents regarding Wallachia, Moldavia and Transylvania; however, their circulation can be indirectly implied from the frequent usage of related terms, such as *muvadaʿa, zimmi, cizye*, or *harac*. Thus, it is incumbent upon the historian to strike a balance between juridical vocabulary and realities on the ground, even though the former did not correspond perfectly with *de facto* political status of the principalities.

In my opinion, until the reign of Süleyman Kanunî, Moldavia and Wallachia should be regarded – due to their incomplete and discontinuous submission to the Porte – as part of the Abode of Reconciliation (*dar al-muvadaʿa*). The voivodes concluded merely temporary covenants with the Ottoman ruler, agreeing to pay *cizye/harac* in exchange for the cessation of predatory raids against their domains. As I have argued, in the Wallachian case, the major watershed was Mehmed II's campaign in 1462 and the collective homage paid by the boyars to the sultan in its aftermath.

In the first decades of the sixteenth century, the Ottoman stance on the Porte's past relations with the principalities crystallized and gained theoretical underpinning. It is in this period that the concepts and vocabulary of Islamic law were retroactively applied to the preceding period. Still, since Süleyman Kanunî, Ottoman authorities saw Wallachia and Moldavia as parts of the Abode of Tributary Protection (*dar al-zimmet*), within a wider Abode of Islam; their inhabitants agreed to pay tribute and obey the imperial authorities, but retained their right to have a Christian leader, appointed by the sultan.

The status of Transylvania merits a separate treatment, given that its juridical status seemed more equivocal. Many students of the Ottoman Empire emphasized differences between the position of the principality and the inferior status of Moldavia and Wallachia throughout the sixteenth and seventeenth century. In regard to the sixteenth century Géza Dávid and Klára Hegyi noted several areas of divergence. Ottoman troops were absent from Transylvania, whereas imperial garrisons were stationed in the capital cities of Wallachia and Moldavia; Transylvanian rulers were not expected to send hostages to the

36 Shaybani, *Kitab al-siyar*, cf. Caurroy, "Législation," IV/17, 219–223; Özel, *Islam Hukuku*, 146–147; *Redhouse*, 1286. It is likely that Selim II relied on precisely this line of argument when he claimed that Moldavia was not part of the "Abode of Islam (*dar al-Islam olmamağin*), and thus [litigation] shall not be tried according to the *şeriʿat*." (Apud Maxim, "L'autonomie," 210).

imperial court, which was demanded from the voivodes; its annual tribute was consistently lower than that imposed the other two countries, and no additional duties were demanded – such as provisioning Istanbul.[37] Despite these peculiarities of Transylvania's relationship with the Porte, I consider the principality's status to be part of the Abode of Tributary Protection (*dar al-zimmet*), within a wider Abode of Islam.

To define the administrative autonomy of Moldavia and Wallachia in the eighteenth century without diminishing the sultanic right to interfere in their internal affairs, the notions of *serbestiyet* ("freedom"), *muʿafiyet* ("immunity," "autonomy," "privilege") and *istiklaliyet* ("independence") were frequently invoked.[38] These notions frequently entered the following phrase: "separated by chancery, spared any violations and free in all respects."[39] It is worth bringing up several examples, dating mostly from the reign of Mahmud I. In 1740, a *hüküm* stated that "since the above-mentioned country has been for long free, separated by chancery and spared abuses," Mahmud I decided to intervene to adjust the amount of *cizye* following the decision to establish direct Ottoman control over the fortress of Hotin and its environs.[40] In 1742, the status of "Wallachia [...] separate through chancery and spared abuses, and free in all respects," was brought up by the sultan to confirm that litigation among Wallachian subjects and with foreigners was to be tried by the voivode.[41] Three years later, the same sultan ordered dignitaries from Brăila to Ada Kale to cease any and all actions against Wallachian inhabitants, since,

> Wallachia has been since times of yore separate in chancery and spared of abuses and [enjoys] freedom.[42]

---

37 Dávid, "Administration," 88–89 (who quoted also Klára Hegyi, "A törökök berendezkedése meghódított országaikban," *Történelmi szemle*, 3, 1981, 400–403).

38 *Serbest* means "free," "independent" (*Redhouse*, 1001–1002). *Muʿafiyet* means also "immunity," "exemption," and *muaf* "exempted." Tahsin Gemil translated *serbest* as "autonomy" in a document of 1687 (Gemil, *Documente turcesti*, doc. 178). *İstiklaliyet* also means "complete sovereignty" and *istiklal* "independent" (*Redhouse*, 556).

39 *Mefruz ül-kalem ve maktuʿ ul-kadem min-küll-il-vücuh serbest olub* (Veliman, *Documente turceşti*, doc. 93, 104, 107, 112, 140, 117, 118, 121, 127, 130, 141, 210 etc.).

40 *Memleket-i merkume öteden berü mefruz ül-kalem ve maktuʿ ul-kadem serbest oldüği ecelden* (Veliman, *Documente turceşti*, doc. 93).

41 *Eflak memleketi mefruz ül-kalem ve maktuʿ ul-kadem min-küll-il-vücuh serbest olub* (Veliman, *Documente turceşti*, doc. 104).

42 *Vilayet-i Eflak kadim ül-eyyamdan berü mefruz ül-kalem ve maktuʿ ul-kadem serbestiyet üzere* (Veliman, *Documente turceşti*, doc.112). See also doc. 107, 117, 118, 121, 127, 130, 141, 210 etc.

The frequent reference to this formulaic phrase leads us to two important conclusions. On the one hand, *serbestiyet* ("freedom"), along with *muʿafiyet* ("autonomy") and *istiklaliyet* ("independence") do not seem to have by this point had an established and specific political and juridical sense, which – as Bernard Lewis has shown – they acquired only in the nineteenth century.[43] Thus, we should refrain from applying their modern meaning to the realities of the sixteenth- and seventeenth-century Moldavia and Wallachia.

The appeal of this phrase led many Romanian scholars to invoke it as a proof that Wallachia and Moldavia remained outside the imperial space, thus separating them from the Ottoman provinces. However, once we examine the phrase "separate by chancery and spared abuses and free in all respects," it becomes clear that such an interpretation misses the point. Firstly, the formula was also invoked in regard to other regions enjoying a degree of financial and administrative autonomy, ranging from tax exemptions and lands earmarked for specific purposes (such as the imperial *hass*). For instance, in 1667 Mehmed IV claimed that Nogay Tatars in Bucak enjoyed such a privileged status.[44] In 1705, similar privileges were acknowledged for *mukataʿa*s who were earmarked as parts of sultanic domains (*havass-ı hümayun*) in the *sancak*s of Silistre and Nikopol:

> they are ruled taking into account their freedom to be in all respects, kept separate in the chancery and spared abuses.[45]

Secondly, the formula is usually only partially quoted and ignores the following section, which clearly states that the principalities enjoyed this status "since the imperial conquest" (*feth-i hakaniden berü*).[46] As I have pointed out, neither Ottoman nor local sources rendered the conquest in a negative right. Moldavian and Wallachian power holders in the seventeenth and eighteenth century frequently referred to the imperial conquest as a point of reference for preserving or reclaiming their autonomous institutions.

The massive collection of the Prime Minister's Archives in Istanbul contains numerous documents classified as "orders concerning privileged provinces," whereby the privileged provinces (*eyalat-i mümtaze*) included the lands that

---

43 In the earlier period, these concepts had a fiscal meaning (Lewis, "Sebestiyet," in *Barkan'a Armağan*, 47–52).

44 Gemil, *Documente turcești*, doc. 147.

45 *Min külli'l-vücuh mefruzü'l-kalem ve maktu'l-kadem serbestiyet üzere zabt olunagelmeğin* (Gemil, *Documente turcești*, doc. 227). *Mukata'a* designated the farming of public revenue.

46 Veliman, *Documente turcești*, docs. 93, 104, 107, 112, 140, 117, 118, 121, 127, 130, 141, 210 etc.

entered the Ottoman Empire by way of agreement and enjoyed broad internal autonomy.[47]

In the second half of the eighteenth and in the nineteenth century, the Porte increasingly emphasized that Moldavia and Wallachia were part of the empire to check the growing influence of Russia and the emancipation of the principalities following 1774. Such claims can be found as late as the Russo–Ottoman War of 1877–1878, seen by Romanians as the Independence War. In October 1874, Ottoman foreign minister Arifi paşa replied to the Romanian diplomatic agent in Istanbul that

> The Principalities are not a distinct state from Turkey, despite all rights of autonomy that they enjoy, granted by certain *fermans*, but [...] they are provinces of the Ottoman Empire.[48]

This stance was fully expressed in Midhat paşa's "Fundamental Law" (*Kanun-ı Esasi*), promulgated on 23 December 1876,[49] which stated that "the Ottoman Empire includes the actual territories and possessions and the privileged provinces"; the latter were called *eyalat-i mümtaze*, and included Romania, Serbia and Egypt.[50]

## 3 Local and Western Views

To round up and refine our understanding of Moldavia, Wallachia and Transylvania's tributary status within *pax ottomanica*, the Ottoman perspective should be complemented by the interpretations formulated by local elites and Western observers.

47 *Eyalat-i mümtaze iradeleri*: BOA, Cevdet Tasnıfı, *Eyalat-i Mümtaze*, which contains documents from 1700–1880 on *Eflak, Boğdan, Kırım Hanı, Mısır*, and *Dubrovnik* (BOA. *Rehberi*, 333–334). The category of *eyalat-i mümtaze* includes, in the long term, *Eflak ve Boğdan Voyvodalıgı, Dubrovnik, Kırım Hanlıgı, Mısır Hıdıvlığı* and in short term *Erdel Krallığı, Mekke Şerifliği, Sisam Beyliği, Cebel-i Lübnan Mutasarrıflığı, Kıbrıs Adası, Bulgaristan Prensliği, Bosna-Hersek* and *Aynoroz Emaneti*. The phrase was also employed with regard to Bulgaria between 1839–1909, Egypt between 1839–1912, Lebanon between 1842–1909, Crete between 1839–1909, and Samos between 1840–1909.

48 *Independența României. Documente. vol. IV: Documente diplomatice (1873–1881)*, Bucharest: Editura Academiei, 1978, doc. 6.

49 The first French edition was *La Constitution Ottomane du 7 Zilhidjè 1293 (23 Décembre 1876)*, with annotations by A. Ubicini, Paris: A Cotillon, 1877.

50 This formula was vehemently protested by Romanian authorities in the note of 20 January 1877 (*Independența. Documente*, III, doc. 19).

On the one hand, European powers considered and treated Wallachia, Moldavia, and Transylvania as Ottoman provinces, which found its expression in diplomatic and consular reports. In 1612, the French ambassador to the Porte, Achille de Harlay, noted that "all these three provinces have been for a long time tributaries of the Grand Seigneur."[51] On 2 September 1804, the French consul in Jassy, N. Fleury, composed a report on the "Turkish provinces of Moldavia and Wallachia."[52] In fact, this did not differ significantly from the way Western sources described the tributary status of Ragusa. In a report to Louis XV composed in 1766, Consul André Alexandre Le Maire wrote about the "total and formal subjection of the Ragusans to the Ottoman Porte" and described its inhabitants as "subject people to their sovereign" and the sultan's *reʿaya* ("this term does not imply a tributary but a subject as well").[53]

In the late eighteenth and early nineteenth centuries, Western authors made few distinctions between different provinces within the Ottoman Empire. In his work, published in 1798, William Eton spoke about "the *pashaliks* or governments most immediately connected with the seat of the empire" and "the more distant provinces"; the latter including Egypt, Wallachia and Moldavia, since,

> they may be considered connected with the Porte rather by treaty than as integral parts of the empire.[54]

A few years later, in *The Present State of Turkey*, Thomas Thornton discussed the *System of Turkish government towards the Tributary subjects*, tracing the system of governance that the Ottomans introduced in their newly conquered provinces:

> While the Turkish power was in a state of progressive aggrandizement, it was the constant policy of the government to expel the nobles and great landed proprietors from those countries which they have incorporated with their empire, and to make a new division of the lands according to the arrangements of their peculiar civil and military system.

According to Thornton's view, this constituted a general blueprint. In some cases, the Ottomans applied exceptions to the usual mode of Turkish govern-

51 *Toutes ces troys provinces sont depuis un long temps tributaires du Grand Seigneur* (Hurmuzaki, *Documente*, Supl. I/1, doc. CCXXVII: Report of 21 April 1612, from Pera).

52 *Les Provinces Turques de la Moldavie et de la Valachie* (Hurmuzaki, *Documente*, XVI, doc. MDLXIII, 146–147).

53 Zlatar, *Dubrovnik*, 1.

54 Eton, *Turkish Empire*, 287–288, 297.

ment, so that the tributary provinces of the empire, like Egypt, Wallachia, and Moldavia, were created.[55]

Since the age of Süleyman the Magnificent, Wallachian and Moldavian elites increasingly recognized the sultan as their supreme ruler and true master of the country. Two statements by sixteenth-century Moldavian and Wallachian voivodes provide what I believe to be the most comprehensive statements in this respect. In April 1537, threatened by the Polish invasion looming over Moldavia, Petru Rareș explicitly stated that:

> This country belongs to the Most Elevated and victorious Turkish emperor, my All-generous Lord, and has given us to rule over it: long live His Imperial Majesty [...] And we hope that Turkish army will come to defend the Emperor's country![56]

Several years later, the Wallachian voivode Mircea the Shepherd explicitly pointed out to the Christian inhabitants of Braşov and Sibiu that his country was the sultan's domain and that the fugitive boyars who sought refuge in Transylvania "raised their troops against my princely head and against the country of our honored emperor."[57] This opinion came to be embraced by all who experienced first-hand the sultan's right to appoint and dismiss voivodes, like a spouse of one of the voivodes:

> this country is not our inheritance; today we exist and tomorrow we no more exist, by God's will, and we are in the hands of the Turks.[58]

Following the watershed of 1774, in the context of diplomatic changes and the rise of national movements, the view of local boyars' increasingly diverged from that of Ottoman officials and Western observers, the latter of whom continued to perceive the principalities as Ottoman provinces. In 1846, Prince Gheorghe Bibescu of Wallachia shared with the French Consul Doré de Nion

55 Thornton, *Turkey*, II, 298–307.

56 Iorga, *Scrisori de domni*, doc. XXIII: *Țara aceasta e a prea-înălțatului și nebiruitului Împărat turcesc, domnul mieu cel prea-milostiv, și ni-a dat-o nouă s'o stăpânim: să trăiască Măria Sa Împărătească... Și mai nădăjduim că pentru apărarea țerii Împăratului va veni oaste turcească!*.

57 Mircea the Shepherd ruled in Wallachia three times, in 1545–1552, 1553–1554 and 1558–1559 (Tocilescu, *534 documente*, doc. 357: *s'au ridicat cu óste asupra capului domniei mele și asupra țării domnului nostru cinstitului împerat*).

58 Letter of Ecaterina, wife of Mihnea II, 20 February 1578 (Hurmuzaki, *Documente*, XIV/1, doc. CXXIX: *această țară nu e moștenirea noastră; azi suntem și mâne nu suntem, după voia lui Dumnezeu, și ne aflăm în mâna Turcilor*). See, also, letter of 2 December 1578 (Hurmuzaki, *Documente*, XIV/1, doc. CXXXII).

his astonishment that the most liberal and "worthy of respect" governments of Europe,

> did only see the Danubian Principalities as Provinces of the Ottoman Empire, their leaders, as Turkish paşas, and their inhabitants, as *reʿaya*. Then, the Wallachian prince invoked a whole series of arguments for proving that "this opinion is not grounded either *de jure* or *de facto*."

A series of questions that Doré de Nion presented to Bibescu reflects – along with European concerns regarding the ascendancy of Russia – the attitude of European powers, which sought to shore up what they perceived as the Ottoman "sick man of Europe."[59] These questions also invite us to consider the international status of the principalities in the nineteenth century:

> [...] the actual reality in particular is that it must be taken into account by the political practice, the venerable politics that is supported, on the one hand, by the immutable rules of the law of nations and, on the other side, by the reality of facts. And, in this legality, in this reality, what would be today the international existence of the Danubian provinces, if they stopped being considered as constitutive parts of the Ottoman Empire? In what other quality, different from this one, are they known by the Christian powers? What would be the basis of the commercial and neighborhood relations that Europe has with you, if [Wallachia] gave up the established and favorable position that the treaties with Turkey guarantee? [...] This relationship, which attaches you to Turkey, does not connect you to Western Europe, and is not it the one that guarantees you positive warrants and an efficient protection, in exchange for a modest tribute and a more apparent than real dependency?[60]

## 4 Wallachia, Moldavia and Transylvania as Buffer-Protectorates

In the international law, the notion of a protectorate implied a tripartite special relationship between two parties. Firstly, "protectorate" relied on bilateral agreements between "protected state" and "protecting state." Secondly, the status of a protectorate required its recognition by third parties.[61] However, these

59 It is relevant to note that the very phrase was uttered by Tsar Nicholas I.

60 Hurmuzaki, *Documente*, XVII, doc. MXLI. See also A. Iordache, A. Stan, *Apărarea autonomiei Principatelor române. 1821–1859*, Bucharest, 1987, 94. M. Chopin, A. Ubicini, *Provinces danubiennes et roumaines*.... Paris, 1856.

61 Brierly, *Law of Nations*, 133.

modern notions cannot be automatically transplanted onto the realities of the medieval world. Throughout the Middle Ages and early modern period, accepting protection of a stronger polity was a customary and commonplace practice. Similarly, protection was constantly used as a political and juridical concept in official documents which tried to define the future relations between Wallachia, Moldavia and Transylvania and the Christian sovereigns.[62] As for the Ottoman legal framework, this was a matter of simply adapting the Islamic concepts of "protected people" (*zimmi*) and "protection" (*himayet*) to European customary rules. The gist of the *ʿahd* concluded between sultans and its protégés was the exchange between protection and tribute.

The existence of the principalities of Wallachia, Moldavia and Transylvania as buffers between the Ottoman provinces and Christian powers (Hungary, Poland–Lithuania, the Habsburgs and Russia) left its mark on the treaties concluded between these polities. Thus, I believe that the notion of a "protectorate" fits well with the political status of Moldavia, Wallachia and Transylvania. From this perspective, a decisive shift took place at the end of the eighteenth century and in the early 1800s. The Treaty of Adrianople (1829) additionally stipulated that Moldavia and Wallachia would remain under Ottoman suzerainty, while at the same time becoming Russian "protectorates," a notion that was accepted and developed by nineteenth-century European jurists.[63]

### 4.1 *Temporary Protection*

For both Islamic legal theory and Moldavian–Wallachian elite, the relationship of temporary tributary protection involved the Porte as the protector of the principalities. This temporary relationship lasted until the 1520s and 1530s and was built around the exchange of the ransom for peace and the cessation of hostilities by the Ottomans. However, the sultanic campaigns against Moldavia and Wallachia as well as frontier *akın* clearly show that the principalities continued to be seen as part of the Abode of War. Thus, the 1480–1481 imperial charter (*ʿahdname*) granted to Stephen the Great contained Mehmed II's commitment that:

> your person and your property and your country will be not attacked by me, by my districts' governors or my other slaves.[64]

---

62 See the "diploma" of 10 December 1603, by which the Habsburg emperor Rudolph II granted the Wallachian throne to Radu Şerban (1602–1611, 1611) and his successors (Hurmuzaki, *Documente*, IV/1, doc. CCXCVII, CCXVIII).

63 Wheaton wrote of "the Principalities of Moldavia, Wallachia and Serbia, under the suzeraineté of the Ottoman Porte and the protectorate of Russia" (Wheaton, *Commentaire*, 36).

64 *Nefsine ve malına ve memleketine benden sancaklarım beğlerinden ve sa'ir kullarımdan*

At the same time, until the sixteenth century, Hungary acted as a protector for numerous Balkan states, including Dubrovnik, Bosnia, Serbia, and Wallachia. The Ottoman–Hungarian rivalry in the region, which continued throughout the fifteenth century, meant that smaller polities frequently found themselves under a kind of Ottoman–Hungarian polyvassalage.[65] In effect, a series of Ottoman–Hungarian peace agreements between 1428 and 1519 contained numerous clauses regarding Wallachia and Moldavia, thus establishing the latter's position as buffer states.[66]

### 4.2 *Permanent Protection*

In the following centuries, although the basis of protection was granted through the same contractual means as in the fifteenth century, legal and political underpinnings changed significantly. According to the Ottoman authorities, from the reign of Sultan Süleyman onwards, Moldavia, Wallachia and Transylvania enjoyed – along with other parts of the empire – permanent protection against official abuses by provincial governors and attacks of Christian powers.

In *berat*s granted to the voivodes, the term *himayet* was crucial for describing the Ottoman protection of sultanic tributaries. The imperial diploma issued for Mihnea II in 1585 stipulated:

> No abuse and tyranny can be explained, even if it is committed by a single person [...] And none of my grand viziers, *beylerbeyi*s, *beys* or servants of my Porte of Felicity or others shall ever do any harm to either the country of Wallachia (*Eflak vilayeti*), or to its chancellors, boyars, knezes, subjects (*re'aya*), sons and daughters [...], or to any other possessions and property belonging to them.[67]

Ahmed I inserted an almost identical clause in the *berat* appointing Gabriel Bethlen to the Transylvanian throne in 1614, declaring his commitment to protect the principality against both Christian neighbors (in this case, the Habsburgs), and Ottoman officials:

*ta'aruz olmıyub* (Decei, "Sulhname," 122; Guboglu, *Paleografia*, doc. 4; Mehmet, *Documente turcești*, I, doc. 5).

65 This term was proposed by Taras Chukhlib and discussed by Victor Ostapchuk (Victor Ostapchuk, "Cossack Ukraine in and out of Ottoman Orbit," in *European Tributary States*, 123–152).

66 DRH, D, I, doc. 305; Iorga, *Acte și fragmente*, III, 23–27; Gökbilgin, "1503," 369–390; Hammer, *Empire Ottoman*, IV, 393–400; Hurmuzaki, *Documente*, II/1, doc. XXIV.

67 Precisely, on 22 *Ramazan* 993 /17 September 1585 (Maxim, CTO, doc. 14; Maxim, "Sur la question des '*ahdnames*,'" 3–14).

> and I, in my turn, shall protect them in any way, against their enemies, whenever help and support are required [...] and absolutely none of my *beylerbeyis* and *beys*, nor my *serasker*, shall interfere in the matter.[68]

A comparison with Ragusa is in order. An *ʿahdname* granted to the Republic in 1575 stipulated, in virtually the same words that:

> By my *sancakbeyis*, *subaşıs*, fief-holders, and, in short, all those who are in the shadow of my power, no harm whatsoever shall be inflicted on their country and dominions (*vilayet ü memalik*), their castles and themselves. In the same way as their city and country were in [a state of] safety and protection (*emn ü eman*) formerly, so they shall be in a [a state of] safety and protection again.[69]

This statement of imperial protection has been preserved in other documents as well. Mahmud I's *hüküm* of 1745 contained the following clause, referring to Wallachia:

> neither his land nor his subjects and taxes should have suffered any intervention and attack of the grand viziers and generous *mirmirans* and *sancakbeyis*, and of their men and *mutesellims*, and of the *zabits* of *hass* and *vakıfs*, and of the *emins* and collectors and *nazirs* [...][70]

Islamic law regards the protection of the lands of the Abode of Islam as one of a Muslim sovereign's most important duties, and these duties extended to his tributaries. "Protection of the Islamic country is my emperor's duty" (*Memleket-i Islam hıfzı padişahumun vazifesidür*), stated *şeyh ül-Islam* Bostanzade Mehmed Efendi in 1593. In fact, this very phrase was included in the grand vizier's report to the sultan (*telhis*) regarding the imminent war with the Habsburgs, which would require defensive arrangements for Moldavia and Wallachia:

> For the protection of Wallachia and Moldavia a number of soldiers is necessary; carelessness is not a solution.[71]

---

68 *Ben dahi her vechile düşmenlerinden koruyub muʿavenet ve imdad lazim geldikde* [...] *beylerbeylerimden ve beylerimden ve seraskerimden asla kimesne dahl eylemiye* (Gemil, *Documente turceşti*, doc. 61).

69 Biegman, *Ragusa*, 57.

70 Veliman, *Documente turceşti*, doc. 112.

71 *Eflak ve Boğdan taraflarına muhafaza içün bir mikdar leşker lazimdir, ihmal deva değildir* (*Mihai. Documente*, I, doc. 2).

Ottoman authorities invoked their role as the protector of its tributaries whenever another state made its claim on the Danubian principalities or launched a military campaign. During the conflicts with Austria and Russia, the sultans and grand viziers would firmly declare – for a good reason – that Moldavia, Wallachia and Transylvania were under Ottoman protection and any attack against them was an attack against the Porte. From many examples in the sixteenth- and seventeenth-century correspondence with Polish kings and the Habsburgs, I decided to cite one. In the 1530s, both Süleyman Kanunî and Grand Vizier Ibrahim paşa addressed the Polish-Moldavian border dispute brewing at the time. In their letters to King Sigismund I, they specified the legal status of Moldavia and its incumbent ruler, Petru Rareş, insisting that "since the voivode of Moldavia is our subject and tributary, no attack is allowed against our frontier provinces."[72] Ibrahim paşa added:

> as you are bound to His Majesty the *padişah* by relations of friendship and as you know well that Moldavia is the Emperor's property [...], that voivode Petru, just like other beys, is an imperial subject appointed by His authority in this country, and that his subjects pay tribute and accomplish obligations towards the Sublime Porte, any attack on this country is equivalent to an attack against the mighty *padişah*'s dominions and represents an offence to His Majesty.[73]

In the eighteenth century, the Ottomans faced the challenge of Austria and Russia and emphasized their rights and obligations as the protectors of Wallachia and Moldavia as imperial provinces. Keeping the principalities defended would become a political principle for the Porte. For instance, in order to fulfill the duty of "protection against enemies," Mahmud I ordered in 1737 the commanders of Brăila, Rusçuk, Giurgiu, and Nikopol to send their troops to Wallachia to protect Bucharest and Voivode Constantin Mavrocordat.[74] Later, in November 1769, on the eve of war with Russia, Mustafa III made clear his duty to protect the territorial integrity of Wallachia and Moldavia, which he had "inherited from my great ancestors."[75] Although the wars with Habsburgs and

72 Hurmuzaki, *Documente*, Supl. II/1, doc. XXVIII: letter to Sigismund I of 29 December 1532–26 January 1533.

73 Hurmuzaki, *Documente*, Supl. II/1, doc. XIV: letter to Sigismund I of 12 October–10 November 1531.

74 Mehmet, *Documente turceşti*, I, doc. 224: *hüküm of eva'il-i Receb* 1150/ 25 October–3 November 1737.

75 Veliman, *Documente turceşti*, doc. 167. Also, doc. 164 ("my inherited estate").

Russia forced the Porte to cede Moldavian and Wallachian territories (1718, 1775–1776 and 1812),[76] these cessions ran against the,

> imperial burning desire [...] that no plot of their land and no individual from among their subjects shall remain in the enemy's hand.[77]

However, the balance of military and political power trumped ideological reservations.

Parallelly, the notion of "protection" recurred constantly in the political thought of the Wallachian and Moldavian elites. Given that the position of the principalities called for outside protection, local powerholders constantly sought support among neighbors.[78] Both for Ottomans and Moldavian–Wallachian elites, since the 1530s the payment of tribute constituted a proof of Ottoman protection. This is clearly shown by the correspondence of Moldavian voivodes Petru Rareş (during his second reign, 1541–1546) and Dimitrie Cantemir, who emphasized that Moldavians "voluntarily put themselves under the Protection of the *Turks*."[79] Additionally, following the second siege of Vienna, Transylvanian agents at the Porte "asked for protection in view of the imperial country's defense" against the Habsburgs in August 1687.[80] According to this standpoint, the local elites felt entitled to demand Ottoman protection, requested usually through petitions (*ʿarz, ʿarzuhal, ʿarz-ı mahzar*) to fulfill their duty to protect their subjects, property and territory against both the military invasions and official abuses.[81] As the nineteenth century set in, Wallachian and Moldavian sources began to conflate "autonomy" with "protection." Thus,

76 Banat and Oltenia were ceded to the Habsburgs in the Treaty of Passarowitz in 1718. Oltenia was reintegrated into Wallachia following the peace of Belgrade in 1739 (Veliman, *Documente turceşti*, doc. 83, 84). In 1775, the Habsburgs also annexed Bucovina, which had previously been part of Moldavia (Veliman, *Documente turceşti*, doc. 182, 206). The Russian Empire acquired Bessarabia following the Treaty of Bucharest in 1812 (Veliman, *Documente turceşti*, doc. 239, 240, 243). Romanian historians have interpreted the territorial losses of 1775 and 1812 as junctures, when the Porte reneged on its obligation to protect Moldavia and Wallachia (Adăniloaie, "Suzeranitatea otomană," 953).

77 Veliman, *Documente turceşti*, doc. 167.

78 Here, the comparison with the Ragusan case is relevant. The Ragusan patriciate had accepted Ottoman protection by mid-fifteenth century. However, following the collapse of Hungary in the aftermath of the battle of Mohács (1526) and the fall of Buda, the Republic embraced the Ottoman protection, which they utilized to conduct commercial activities despite Venetian hostility (For details, see Zlatar, *Dubrovnik*, 107–118).

79 Cantemir, *Othman History*, 74, n. 10.

80 *Memleket-i şehryarı siyaneti içün himaye rica eyleyüb* (Gemil, *Documente turceşti*, doc. 178).

81 Veliman, *Documente turceşti*, doc. 41 (1720), 49 (1723), 61 (1728), 145 (1760), 217 (1795), 244 (1813), 257 (1821).

in 1821, the Wallachian boyars wrote to the Russian authorities that paying obeisance to the sultan implied that "the Ottoman Porte shall not interfere on our land by any means at all."[82]

The notion of "protection" was also frequently used by foreign observers (travelers, envoys and merchants) and early Western contributions on the Danubian principalities and their relationship with the Porte. Jan Gniński, who in 1677–1678 was the Polish–Lithuanian ambassador to the Porte and crossed Moldavia en route to Istanbul, drew a direct connection between the relationship of "vassalage," tribute and Ottoman protection. He stated:

> The Turks call them *bogdans* because *Bogdan* was the first voivode who received Turkish protection.[83]

From the same eighth decade of the seventeenth century, let us note, despite certain confusions, the expression of Delacroix (De la Croix), secretary of the French embassy in Istanbul, twice used with regard to the early period of the Ottoman–Moldavian relations:

> [the sultan] granted him [ the Moldavian voivode] his protection in exchange for an annual tribute.[84]

In English newspapers reporting the events of the 1683–1699 war, the notion of "protection" was constantly invoked to define the political status of Wallachia, Moldavia and Transylvania towards both the Sublime Porte and the Christian powers seeking to replace it in the Danubian principalities. For instance, the letters sent from Cracow in March 1684 inform us that:

> the new Hospodars of Moldavia and Walachia, were, with the assistance of the Poles and Cossacks, established in their Governments, and it was hoped that the Transylvanians would follow their Example and put themselves under the Protection of the Crown of Poland.[85]

---

82 Petition written by Wallachian boyars who had sought refuge in Braşov (Iorga, *Studii şi documente*, XI, 192: *să nu aibă Poarta Othomanicească nici un fel de amestec în pământul nostru, câtuş de puţin*).

83 *Călători străini*, VII, 358.

84 *Luy accorda sa protection moyen d'un tribut annuel* (De la Croix, in *Călători străini*, VII, 254, 256; F. Babinger, "O relaţiune neobservată despre Moldova sub domnia lui Antonie Vodă Ruset (1676)," *AARMSI*, III, XIX, 1937, 123; Gorovei, "Însemnări," 34).

85 *The London Gazette. Numb.* 1914, 1684, March 20–24 (1683 in newspaper).

Two years later, in December 1685, a report arrived from Vienna that

> The Envoy that is here from the Prince of Transylvania has had several Conferences with the Commissioners appointed by the Emperor to Treat with him, and we are not without hopes that the Prince will be brought to quit his Engagements with the Turks, and to put himself and his Country under the Protection of his Imperial Majesty.[86]

Finally, according to an established practice, whenever two powers sought to transform a territory into a buffer zone between them, the clauses relating to their future status entered their bilateral agreements. This was also the case for Wallachia, Moldavia and Transylvania. Thus, the relations between sultans and voivodes would become one of the issues discussed between the Ottoman Empire and the Christian powers. From the mid-sixteenth until the end of the seventeenth century, the status of Moldavia was openly discussed in Polish–Ottoman treaties, starting from the one concluded in 1533;[87] similarly, clauses regarding Transylvania, Wallachia and Moldavia were included in Ottoman–Habsburg agreements.[88] During the eighteenth and early nineteenth

86 *The London Gazette. Numb.* 2096, 1685, December 17–21. Comments in Panaite, *News in England*, 35.

87 For originals of nearly all of those treaties, see AGAD, *AKW-Tureckie*, and ANIC, mf. Poland, r. 1. For copies, see BOA, *Düvel-i Ecnebiye Defterleri* (*DED*) 55/1, *Lehistan 'Ahdnamesi Defteri*, 1016–1173 AH/1607–1759. Also: for 1553–1554 (Gökbilgin, "Belgeler I," 128–132; Hurmuzaki-Bogdan, *Documente*, Supl. II/1, doc. XCIX; Mehmet, *Documente turcești*, I, doc. 45; Corfus, *Documente. XVI*, 86–87). For 1565 (Hurmuzaki- Bogdan, *Documente*, Supl. II/1, doc. CXXX). For 1577 (Mehmet, *Documente turcești*, I, 127–128). For 1591 (Hurmuzaki, *Documente*, III, doc. CXLIX; Mehmet, *Documente turcești*, I, 136–137). For 1598 (Mehmet, *Documente turcești*, I, 142–143). For 1605 (Feridun, *Münșe'at*, II, 414–7; Corfus, *Documente. XVII*, 50–51; Hammer, *Empire Ottoman*, VIII, 407–415). For the February 1623 *'ahdname* issued by Mustafa I (AGAD, *AKW-Tureckie*, k. 71, t. 304, no. 557; ANIC, mf. Poland, r. 1, f. 221–260). For the 10 October 1623 *'ahdname* issued by Murad IV (AGAD, AKW-Tureckie, k. 71, t. 307, no. 564). For the 1634 *'ahdname* issued by Murad IV to Vladislav IV (AGAD, AKW-Tureckie, k. 75, t. 362, no. 643; ANIC, mf. Poland, r. 1, f. 74–78). For the 1640 *'ahdname* issued by Ibrahim to Vladislav IV (AGAD, *AKW-Tureckie*, k. 75, t. 376, no. 663; ANIC, mf. Poland, r. 1, d. 87–91; BOA, *DED*, *LAD*, doc. 4; Feridun, *Münșe'at*, II, 435–438). For the 1667 *'ahdname* issued by Mehmed IV to Janem Kazimierzem (AGAD, *AKW-Tureckie*, k. 77, t. 453, no. 772; BOA, *DED* 55/1, *LAD*, doc. 5; Feridun, *Münșe'at*, II, 420–425). For 1678 (Czartoryski, IV, 859, 41–42). For 1699 (Czartoryski, IV, 859, 43–4). See also Dariusz Kołodziejczyk, *Ottoman-Polish Diplomatic Relations (15th -18th Century). An Annotated Edition of 'Ahdnames and Other Documents.* Leiden–Boston–Cologne: Brill, 2000.

88 Copies in: BOA, *DED* 57/1, *Nemçelü 'Ahd Defteri*, 975–1210 AH/1567–1795; Belediye Kütüphanesi, Muallim Cevdet, K. 4 and ANIC, mf. Turkey, r. 53, f. 894–1004 (*1567–1796 Osmanlı devleti ile Nemçe ve sa'ir devletler arasında 'akd olunan ba'zı mu'ahedeler*). For details, see: for

centuries, conditions regarding Wallachia and Moldavia entered the Ottoman–Habsburg peace treaties of 1718, 1739 and 1791,[89] and Ottoman–Russian peace treaties or special protocols concerning the principalities, including those of 1711, 1774, 1791–1792, 1812, 1826 and 1829.[90]

By focusing on Islamic Ottoman terminology, I have avoided describing the power relationship between sultans and princes as one of suzerainty and vassalage and therefore using the labels "vassal states" or "autonomous states" for Wallachia, Moldavia and Transylvania. To avoid terminological confusion stemming from the use of the concepts of vassalage and suzerainty in "mélange" with notions belonging to the Islamic law of peace, I have preferred to collect the abundant information and terminology of Ottoman and non-Ottoman sources under the covering of two locutions, i.e. "tributary provinces" and "buffer-protectorates," which can be expressed also in a single idiom, i.e. tributary-protected provinces and principalities.

---

1547 (Feridun, *Münşe'at*, II, 341–342: *Roma imparatoru tarafına ısdar buyurulan 'ahdname-yi hümayun sureti;* Petritsch, "1547," 49–80). For 1559 (Schaendlinger, *Süleyman*, doc. 23; Hurmuzaki, *Documente*, II/1, doc. CCCXLII; Hammer, *Empire Ottoman*, VI, 114–117. For 1562 (Schaendlinger, *Süleyman*, doc. 25; Hurmuzaki, *Documente*, II/5, doc. CCXXXI). For 1565 (Schaendlinger, *Süleyman*, doc. 32; Hurmuzaki, *Documente*, VIII, doc. CXXXIII). For 1568 (BOA, *DED* 57/1, 1–3; ANIC, mf. Turkey, r. 53, fr. 896–897: *dokuz yüz yetmiş beş senesinde merhum sultan Selim Han zamanında Nemçe çesarına virilen 'ahdname-yi hümayun*; Feridun, *Münşe'at*, II, 324–328). For 1576 (BOA, *DED*, 57/1, 2–5; ANIC, mf. Turkey, r. 53, fr. 897–8; Hurmuzaki, *Documente*, III/1, doc. 1). For 1606 (BOA, *DED* 57/1, 5–7; ANIC, mf. Turkey, r. 53, fr. 898–899; Feridun, *Münşe'at*, II, 346–350; Fekete, "Esterházy," 3–14). For 1615 (BOA, *DED* 57/1, p. 7–10; ANIC, mf. Turkey, r. 53, f. 899–904: *merhum sultan Ahmed Han zamanında bin yirğmi dört senesinde*; Feridun, *Münşe'at*, II, 321–4; Fekete, "Esterházy," doc. 2; Noradounghian, *Actes*, I, 113–8). For 1627 (BOA, *DED* 57/1, 10–14; Feridun, *Münşe'at*, II, 330–334). For 1664 (BOA, *DED* 57/1, 17–19; ANIC, mf. Turkey, r. 53, fr. 905–909: *bin yetmiş beş senesinde tecdid ahd olunduğda taraf-ı hümayunun Nemçe çasarına verilen 'ahdnamedir*). For 1699 (BOA, *DED*, 57/1, 21–27; BOA, *Amedi Kalemi Odası* (*Kamil Kepeci tasnifi*), 53, 2–16: *Amedi odası defterlerinden Nemçe çasarına verilen 'ahdname-yi hümayun kayıtı. Tarihi 1110;* IUK, ms. 3514, ANIC, mf. Turkey, r. 1, fr. 301–429: *1110 tarihindeki sulhnamesi*).

89 Copies in: BOA, *DED* 57/1, *Nemçelü 'Ahd Defteri*, 975–1210 AH/1567–1795; Belediye Kütüphanesi, Muallim Cevdet, K. 4; ANIC, mf. Turkey, r. 53, fr. 894–1004 (*1567–1796 Osmanlı devleti ile Nemçe ve sa'ir devletler arasında 'akd olunan ba'zı mu'ahedeler*). See also Sturdza, Petrescu, *Acte şi documente*, I, 32–40 (1718 Treaty of Passarowitz), 48–58 (1739 Treaty of Belgrade), 79–81 (1791 treaty of Şiştov).

90 Ottoman copies in BOA, *DED* 83/1, *Rusya 'Ahdname Defteri* 1113–1249 AH/1701–1833. For 1711 (Czartoryski Library, ms. 1685/35, 491–492; Hurmuzaki, *Documente*, VI, doc. XLV). See Sturdza, Petrescu, *Acte şi documente*, I, 131 (1774 treaty of Küçük Kaynarca); 219–225 (1791/1792 Treaty of Jassy); 298 (1812 Treaty of Bucharest); 311–314 (1826 treaty of Akkerman); 321–329 (1829 Treaty of Adrinople); 338 (1834 Treaty of St. Petersburg); 357–360 (1849 treaty of Balta Liman).

# Conclusion

The Ottoman law of war and peace comprised two main aspects: Islamic tradition and the Ottoman element. In dealing with non-Muslims, the Ottomans drew their basic rules from *siyar,* the branch of Islamic law which provided general legal guidelines for the Muslim community's relations with both the infidels from enemy territories (*harbi*) as well as the beneficiaries of a covenant (*muʿahidin*) residing temporarily (*müsteʾmin*) or permanently (*zimmi*) in the Abode of Islam. However, it would be a mistake to reduce the Ottoman law of nations to its Islamic component. On the contrary, there is enough evidence that customary practices applied in Southeastern and Central Europe, shaping the conduct of war, peace, trade and foreign relations, despite all the religious, political and legal differences between Islam and Christendom.

Studying tributary status is a matter, to a large degree, of grasping the nature of available sources and asking the right questions. In this respect, the Islamic legal and religious sources provided the Ottomans and – by extension – modern historians, with a theoretical model on how to wage war, conclude peace and define legal positions of non-Muslims. Nonetheless, to reconstruct the Ottoman standpoint on the ideology of holy war, "international" law and the status of tributary states and communities, the corpus of theoretical texts does not suffice. Apart from juridical treatises, we must take into account administrative and diplomatic documents produced within the Ottoman chancery, which remain closer to the realities on the ground. Expanding the corpus with narrative sources and non-Ottoman official documents changed and completed the perspective over the topic.

During the fifteenth and sixteenth centuries, the Ottomans justified their military expansions through the ideology of an offensive *cihad* against Christian states. The term of *kafir* (pl. *kefere, küffar*), referring to any and all non-Muslims, was ubiquitous in the Ottoman sources of this period. Since Muslim jurisprudence ignored as a rule the notion of ethnicity, the Wallachians, Moldavians and Transylvanians were also included – as Christians – into the category of "infidels" as "people of the book" (*ehl-i kitab*) and "enemies" (*harbi*). The Hanafi juridical school, adopted by the Ottomans, conceptualized the world as divided into the Abode of Islam (*dar al-Islam*), which comprised all territories under the sultan's authority, and the Abode of War (*dar al-harb*, or *dar al-kefere*). The former comprised all the territories under sultanic rule, including tributary provinces and polities, whereas the latter encompassed foreign lands and states beyond the imperial borders. Throughout the fifteenth and

 | DOI:10.1163/9789004411104_016

sixteenth centuries, much of Southeastern Europe was categorized as the latter at least temporarily.

Islamic legal theory assumed a permanent state of war between the Abode of War and the Abode of Islam; accordingly, Ottoman authorities expected the former to be brought under Islamic rule and the *pax ottomanica*. The struggle on the path of Allah provided the most adequate legal instrument to achieve this goal, carried out by means of military campaigns (*gaza*) against the Christian rulers of Southeastern and Central Europe. Extant sources refer to the military campaigns of the fifteenth and early sixteenth century against Wallachia, Moldavia and the Kingdom of Hungary as "sacred expeditions" (*gaza*, pl. *gazavat*), and associated the term of *gazi* with courage, faith, booty and martyrdom. For a century and a half, the fate of the holy war, *gazi*s and the Danube was intertwined, which led one Ottoman author to refer to the river as the "*gazi* river."

The Ottomans resorted to rules and notions specific to the classical Islamic law of peace in order to legitimize peaceful coexistence with non-Muslims, including those in Southeastern Europe; however, their actual application depended heavily on local conditions. The Moldavian scholar and voivode Dimitrie Cantemir (d. 1723) perfectly captured this reality, arguing that although the *Ku'ran* enjoined Muslims to fight Christians and spread Islam, jurists also left open the possibilities under which Muslims were allowed and had to conclude peace. Therefore, Cantemir distinguished between two scenarios. In the first one, a permanent peace with non-Muslims was established whenever they agreed to embrace Islam or pay the poll-tax, thus forcing Muslims to cease any hostilities and conclude a "firm and lasting peace," from thereon regarded as Ottoman subjects. In turn, if non-Muslims rejected the conditions of *pax ottomanica*, the Ottomans could establish merely a truce. For the sultans, the decision to halt, interrupt or cease the holy war was available only when it served the interests of the Muslim community and the Ottoman state.

Tribute payments have been of crucial importance in this legal framework and the present study. In the first two centuries of Ottoman expansion in Southeastern Europe, numerous polities entered the Ottoman orbit, with their rulers becoming imperial *haracguzars*. As I have argued throughout this study, comparing these cases with those of Wallachia and Moldavia brings to significant parallels. Although most of them entered under direct Ottoman administration, some, like certain South Aegean Cycladic islands (the Duchy of Naxos together with its dependencies, Paros and Andros) and Ragusa, retained the status of tributary-protection for centuries, much like Wallachia, Moldavia and Transylvania. The common thread of their trajectories was that while their position was that of autonomous principalities or provinces, the legal and political framework changed considerably. Finally, the Crimean Khanate – as a client state with broad autonomy and freedom of independent action – provides a crucial point of reference for Wallachia, Moldavia and Transylvania, even though the Giray rulers did not pay tribute to the sultan.

The political junctures when the voivodes accepted to pay tribute and submit themselves to the Porte were called acknowledgments of allegiance (*închinare*, in Moldavian–Wallachian chronicles). Considering the several meanings of the term *închinare*, in my opinion this should be considered as an extended process, which cannot be pinpointed to a single year or attributed to a single ruler. The tradition of homage, characterized imprecise chronology and confusion, indicated an evolutionary process, by which the Porte established and solidified its relations with the three principalities. In Wallachia, this process started during Mircea the Elder's reign (1386–1418) and concluded in 1462 with the enthronement of Radu the Fair, even though the long-term status of submission crystallized only in the 1520s. In Moldavia, the process began in 1455–1456 and came to a conclusion in 1538; however, peace agreements concluded by Stephen the Great with Mehmed II (1480–1481) and Bayezid II (1486) constituted stepping stones in the process. Finally, in the case of Transylvania, its submission to the Porte took place in the first half of the sixteenth century with the pact between Süleyman Kanunî and John Zápolya in 1528, the confirmation of Isabella and John Sigismund Zápolya as the province's rulers in 1541 and the homage paid by John Sigismund to Süleyman Kanunî in 1566. Thus, it was only during the reign of Süleyman (1520–1566) that the Ottoman stance regarding the principalities coalesced into a comprehensive doctrine that presented the tributaries as conquered territories included in the Well-Protected Domains of the sultan.

The peace agreements concluded between the Porte and Christian rulers belonged to the category of covenant (*ʿahd*), which Muslim legal texts subdivided into two kinds, *ʿahd-ı zimmet* (covenant of tributary protection) and *muvadaʿa* (truce, temporary peace agreement). In the Ottoman chancery, any agreement concluded with Muslim or non-Muslim princes was called an *ʿahdname-yi hümayun* (imperial charter).

The conclusion of covenants by the Ottoman rulers with Wallachia and Moldavia between the late fourteenth and mid-sixteenth century has sparked a heated debate in Romanian historiography. As has been definitively proven, the "old privileges" (so-called "capitulations"), allegedly granted by Ottoman rulers to Wallachian and Moldavian voivodes (1391–1393 and 1460, as well as 1511–1513 and 1529, respectively) were spurious apocryphal texts fabricated in the eighteenth century by Moldavian–Wallachian elites. The existence of such "treaties" ran against the late medieval and early modern practice of the

Ottoman chancery, which did not conclude peace agreements or charters regulating the legal and political status of its European tributaries in the long run. Instead, the Porte opted to conclude temporary truces, either written or verbal, oaths and pledges. Thus, an oath rather than any peace agreement remained the most important guarantee of loyalty in diplomatic relations. Few written Ottoman peace agreements survive from the fifteenth century and virtually none in their original form (several for Ragusa and but one for Moldavia, 1480–1481).

Concerning the principle of *pacta sunt servanda*, both Muslims and non-Muslims recognized the customary practice that covenants and oaths should be respected and observed, whether they were concluded with coreligionists or "infidels." The sources do not mention it as an explicit legal principle, adhered to by the Ottomans and Christians in their conduct of diplomatic relations; instead, its role depended upon immediate political and military interests. As I have pointed out, there is an inherent contradiction between the verses of the *Kur'an* which stipulated that the covenants should be observed, and legal texts (*kitab al-siyar* or *fetva*) that authorized the Muslim ruler to violate any peace agreement, whenever it served the interest of the Muslim state and community. Moreover, it is important not to either generalize the stipulations to uphold the treaties or the liberty to break them; neither can be extrapolated from the immediate context within which they were uttered. A careful analysis of various types of sources allows us to conclude that the Ottomans took the principle of *pacta sunt servanda* seriously and strived to legitimize any violation of an agreement, employing Islamic legal texts as a legitimizing tool.

At the same time, there was a clear contradiction between the way the Ottomans and their tributaries understood the notion of *pacta sunt servanda*. The Porte's main concern was with specific instances of violations of such agreements, particularly revolts launched and led by Moldavian and Wallachian voivodes. In turn, Wallachian and Moldavian elites took a more general perspective, shaped by the realities of the seventeenth and eighteenth centuries; thus, they accused the Porte of violating the "old privileges," allegedly granted to them in the earlier period. Thus, it is crucial to note that both the Ottomans and their tributaries scrupulously sought to justify actions that could be interpreted as a breach of a pact and by extension the very principle of *pacta sunt servanda*.

Historians and jurists dealing with Moldavia and Wallachia's relationship with the Porte have so far focused on the supposed long-term "treaties" and completely ignored the role of custom. Early modern sources generally referred to custom in three areas: ritual and ceremonial practices accompanying the relationship between the sultan, the grand vizier and the voivodes; political, military and financial duties of the tributaries; finally, reasserting specific regulations regarding the autonomy of Wallachia, Moldavia and Transylvania. Some types of sources allow us to retrace the mechanism of custom-formation, particularly with regard to the introduction of new obligations and the increase of established duties, started in the second part of the sixteenth century, and reconsidered in the eighteenth century. Fierce competition for the throne facilitated this process, as pretenders offered to expand their commitments, adopt certain Ottoman customs or even assume new duties. On the other hand, sultanic orders (*hüküms*) could also introduce innovations by imposing Ottoman models or setting up new practices in tributary principalities.

The local elites of Moldavia and Wallachia realized that long-established practices, accepted and followed by the Porte from the fifteenth century, could provide the basis for reasserting their internal autonomy. In the eighteenth century, Wallachian and Moldavian boyars claimed that these practices had been codified and turned into "capitulations" granted to Wallachian and Moldavian rulers; as such, they provided a legal basis for the attempts to eliminate "new customs." This trend gave birth to the legend of "ancient and long-term privileges" from the late fourteenth to mid-sixteenth century, upon their acknowledgement of allegiance to the Porte. This spurious tradition was subsequently accepted by modern Romanian historian, becoming a pervasive historical myth.

The Ottoman authorities did not attempt to codify the practices governing the Porte's relationship with Moldavia and Wallachia in the form of "capitulations." Pre-Ottoman Moldavian–Wallachian traditions, Ottoman customs and practices specific to the context of tributary protection operations were not laid out in a comprehensive, written document. On the contrary, the sultans reiterated and confirmed them by means of orders and law-codes, the same types of documents that regulated the empire's internal affairs.

The Porte's attitude towards Moldavia, Wallachia and Transylvania was largely conditioned through two notions, which came to the fore that emerged under Sultan Süleyman – tribute-payers (*haracgüzar*) and protected peoples (*zimmi*). After the victory of Mohács (1526) and the punitive campaign against Moldavia (1538), the Ottoman perception of its tributaries shifted considerably. This new concept was soon extended to the recently-conquered Transylvania. Therefore, Süleyman Kanunî proclaimed himself as their master, considering the three tributary principalities parts of his Well-Protected Domains (*Memalik-i mahrusa*) and their inhabitants – his subjects (*re'aya*).

At the same time and in line with this new Ottoman interpretation, Wallachian, Moldavian and Transylvanian rulers were integrated into the imperial hierarchy along with other *paşas*; they were referred to as *beys*, as governors of Ottoman provinces and enjoyed the privilege of adorning their banners with two horsetails (*tuğ*) along with other signs of rank. Just like Ottoman provincial officials, they were appointed through imperial diplomas (*berat*s) and received orders in the form of *hüküm*s.

Since the princes of Wallachia, Moldavia and Transylvania had agreed to pay tribute, they became tribute-payers (*haracgüzar*), a role which required obeying imperial orders and fulfilling all political, military and financial duties (*hizmet*) demanded by the Porte. Crucial to this status was their payment of tribute (*harac*), which was at the same time interpreted as the collection of poll-tax from their subjects; this was complemented by politico-military duties, generally expressed by the phrase "be [a] friend of our friend and [an] enemy of our enemy" (*dosta dostumuza ve düşman düşmanımıza olub*). Since Sultan Süleyman's reign, the Ottomans had seen the appointment of a new tributary ruler as a delegation of power to a provincial governor and regarded it as a sultanic prerogative. These delegated powers, according to official documents, included "rule and governance of the country," "protection and safeguarding of the subjects" and "defending of the country."

Non-Muslims who had concluded a pact with the Ottoman sultans were called "the people of covenant"; accordingly, the inhabitants of Wallachia, Moldavia and Transylvania were regularly described as *muʿahidin*. According to the Islamic legal texts two categories of "the people of covenant" exist: *müsteʾmin*s, that is foreign non-Muslims, tolerated and protected by the authorities, and *zimmi*s, non-Muslim Ottoman subjects. The latter were allowed to keep their religion and institutions as long as they paid poll-tax (*cizye*) and land-tax (*harac*). From the perspective of Ottoman law, if a *harbi* had agreed to pay tribute and obey to the sultan, he became a *zimmi*. In the Ottoman sources, such an individual is also called a tribute-payer (*haracgüzar*) or an "infidel who is not from the Abode of War" (*kafir ki dar al-harbdan olmıya*). In the fifteenth and early sixteenth century, the status of Wallachians and Moldavians straddling Ottoman territories was considered to be closer to that of *müsteʾmin*s, even though they were generally described as *haracgüzar*s. Again, it was during Süleyman's reign that the sultan began to refer to such individuals as *zimmi*s, who constituted the non-Muslim part of tax-paying subjects (*reʿaya*). Being *zimmi*s, they enjoyed basically the same rights as other subjects of the empire, with their life, freedom, property and religion protected unlike those of enemy infidels (*harbi*).

In some of the regions that entered Ottoman orbit, the introduction of direct imperial administration proved impracticable due to topographical characteristics, distance from the center or resistance mounted by local population.

However, there is no doubt that, differences in the degree of autonomy notwithstanding, all these areas constituted integral parts of the Ottoman Empire.

The Ottoman system of governance was by no means uniform throughout the empire. The majority of imperial territories consisted of the "standard" *sancak* system, which were administered directly by imperial authorities and parceled into *ze'amet*s and *timar*s (*dirlik*s). Moreover, throughout Ottoman history we find various autonomous regions, communities, provinces and polities. According to their "degree of subordination," two kinds of autonomy existed within the Ottoman system. The first included parts of the empire within the *eyalet* framework of government; the second group included the areas which remained outside the system of *eyalet*s and retained their own institutions.

The Ottomans incorporated autonomous religious and ethnic groups by issuing special privileges to certain Muslim and non-Muslim communities. Moreover, in some regions of the empire, locally entrenched elites wielded all the power, even though the Porte continued to appoint governors there. These kind of provinces were frequently called *salyaneli* provinces. Under this model, upon covering the expenses on defense and salaries within the province, the governor remitted surplus tax revenue to the imperial treasury.

Both Ottoman and non-Ottoman sources employed various juridical, political and administrative terminologies to describe the status of Wallachia, Moldavia and Transylvania within the Ottoman Empire. In this regard, we can discern two threads in the vocabularies employed by the early modern chancery; one emphasized that the tributary territories had the same status as other Ottoman provinces, while the other stressed their autonomous position within the empire.

The first way in which the Ottoman chancery engaged its tributaries was through the use of homogenizing terminology, emphasizing that they had the same status as other parts of the imperial domains. By the reign of Süleyman Kanunî, Wallachia, Moldavia and Transylvania had come to be regarded – legally and politically – as the patrimony of the sultan (*mülk-i mevrus*), part of the Abode of Islam (*dar al-Islam*), and provinces of the Ottoman Empire, or the Well-Protected Domains (*Memalik-i mahrusa*). The Porte invoked these formulas to protect its territory against the interference of both Ottoman officials and Christian neighbors.

Along with a vocabulary meant to emphasize homogeneity, the Ottoman chanceries also employed notions stressing the difference of status and the autonomous position of Wallachia, Moldavia and Transylvania; this discourse, however, did not collide with the definition of the principalities as parts of the empire. In this respect, the most frequently applied terms included the Abode of Tributary Protection (*dar al-zimmet*), freedom (*serbestiyet*), and privileged provinces (*eyalat-ı mümtaze*). These formulas were as a rule invoked especially whenever Moldavian–Wallachian elites petitioned the sultans for protection against local Ottoman officials and subjects from adjacent *sancak*s. In fact, Wallachia, Moldavia and Transylvania were by no means the only regions whose status was described through these concepts, which touched upon various aspects of the financial, administrative, religious and juridical autonomy within the Ottoman Empire.

Given that the concept of vassalage was specific to Western political language, and that the notion of autonomy originates with modern scholars, I have here striven to avoid the terms in favor of "tribute-payer" (*haracgüzar*) and "protection" (*himayet*), ubiquitous in early modern sources and constituting the central concepts within the political and juridical vocabulary of the age. Therefore, I have preferred to define the political status of Wallachia, Moldavia and Transylvania within the Ottoman Empire by two expressions: tributary principalities and buffer-protectorates. The former originated from the voivodes' duties towards sultans, while the latter took into account both the exchange of tribute for protection in imperial charters granted to the voivodes, while their position of buffer-protectorates can be found in the peace agreements between the Porte and its Christian neighbors. Thus, this entire position can be given a single label, that of tributary-protected principalities. What is more important, however, is that whatever concepts were invoked to define the legal and political status of the principalities of Wallachia, Moldavia and Transylvania, all of them should emphasize that they existed within the *pax ottomanica* system.

# Glossary of Ottoman Turkish Terms and Locutions on War, Peace and Tributaries

*ʿadet* (pl. *ʿadat*) – custom, practice, habit, usage; *ʿadet ve kanunlar üzere* – according to the usual habits and laws; *ʿadet-i beled üzere* – according to the custom of country; *ʿadetden gayri* – contrary to the custom; *aralarında carı olan ʿadetler* – the usual habits practiced among them.

*ʿahd* (pl. *ʿuhud*) – oath, promise, engagement, pact, agreement, treaty, covenant, compact; *ʿahdetmek* – to engage solemnly, to vow, to pledge, to promise with a oath; *ʿahd üzere* – according to the oath; *ʿahd ü-amana mugayir* – contrary to the oath and protection; *ʿahd-ı zimmet, ʿahd al-zimmet, ʿahd üz-zimmet* – compact of tributary-protection; *ʿahd ü-peyman* – pact and pledge, engagement and compact; *ʿahd ü-aman mukarrer olub* – renewing the pact and protection; *ʿahd ü-yeman ederim ki* – I pledge and swear that; *ʿahd ve sözünü bir kerre dahi yeniliyordu* – he renewed once again his oath and word; *ʿahde muhalif nesne sadır olmıya* – nothing will happen against the oath; *bu ʿuhud ve şurut riʿayet edüb* – observing these oaths and conditions (*berat-ı hümayun,* 1614); *zikr olunan ʿahd üzere* – according to the above-mentioned engagement.

*ʿahdname* – charter, written pact, treaty; *ʿahdname-yi hümayun* – imperial charter; *ʿahdname-yi hümayun mucebince* – according to the imperial charter; *ʿahdnamede kayd olunmağın* – because it was registered in charter; *Francaluya iʿta ve ihsan olunan ʿahdname-yi hümayunun suretidir* – it is the copy of the imperial charter, which was given and granted to the Frenchman (*ʿahdname, Defter,* 1673); *işbu ʿahdname-yi hümayun verdüm ve buyurdum ki* – I granted and decreed this imperial charter that; *Kara-Boğdan beğine varub ʿahdnamelerin gösterüb* – arriving at the prince of Moldavia, who shew his charters (*ʿarz,* 1486).

*ʿakd* – contract, treaty, agreement; *ʿakd-ı ʿahd* – contractual agreement; *ʿakd ü-ittifak* – agreement and alliance *ʿakd-ı müsalaha* – peace agreement.

*ʿalem* – standard, banner, flag; *ʿalem-i hümayun* – imperial standard; *ʿalem-i nebi* – the sacred banner of the Prophet, which is unfurled in case of a holy war.

*ʿanveten* (Ar. *ʿanwatan*) – by force

*ʿarz* – presentation, demonstration, a request addressed to one's superior; *ʿarzuhal* (*ʿarz-ı hal*) – petition, written application; *ʿarz ü-iʿlam* – presentation and communication; *ʿarz-ı ʿubudiyet* – request of obedience, presenting one's homage, homage paying; *ʿarz-ı ihlas eylemek* – to show faith; *ʿarz-ı itaʿat* – request of submission; *ʿarz-ı ʿubudiyetimiz Erdel Belgradında yazıldı* – our request of submission was written in Alba Iulia of Transylvania

 | DOI:10.1163/9789004411104_017

*ʿasker* – soldier, warrior, army; *ʿasker-i Islam* – Islamic army; *ʿasker ihracı fermanı* – order of warriors' mobilization

*ʿAtebe-yi ʿaliye, ʿAtebe-yi seni, ʿAtebe-yi ʿulya* – the Imperial Threshold, the Sultan's Court

*ʿava'id* (sing. *ʿa'ide* ) – revenues, gifts, favors

*ʿazl, ʿazil* – dismissal, discharged from office; *ʿazl olunmak* – to be discharged from office

*aʿda* ( sing. *ʿadu, ʿaduv*) – enemies; *aʿda-i din ü-devlet* – enemies of the faith and state

*ahkam* – decrees, statutes, laws; *ahkam-ı şerʿiye* – statutes of the Muslim canonical law

*Ak Deniz* – the Mediterranean Sea

*akın* – raid, *razzia*; *akıncı* (pl. *akıncılar* ) – raider, a special corps of light cavalry whose duty was to pillage the enemy.

*Akkerman* – White Fortress (Rom. Cetatea Albă)

*Al-i ʿOsman* – the Ottoman dynasty

*aman, eman* – mercy, protection, security, safe-conduct

*Anadolu* – Anatolia

*and* – oath, solemn declaration; *and bozmak* – to violate one's oath, to break an oath; *and vermek* – to take an oath

*arazi* – land, territory, estate; *harac-ı arazi, arazi-yi haraciye* – lands subject to the payment of the *harac*; *arazi-yi ʿöşriye* – tithe lands

*Asitane-yi saʿadet aşiyan* – the Threshold of the nest of the happiness, the Sultan's court, Istanbul*; Asitane-yi sultan-ı cihan-penaha gelüb* – coming to the Sultan's Threshold, shelter of the world

*ayin* – custom, law, manner; *ayin-i battalları üzere* – according to their worthless custom; *ayinleri üzere* – according to their laws

*Azak* – Azov

*bab* – gate; *Bab-ı ali* – the High Gate; *Bab-ı asafa* – the palace of the grand vizier; *Bab-ı hümayun* – the Imperial Gate (name of the outermost big gate of Topkapı Palace); *Bab-ı saʿadetim* – My Gate of Happiness (name of the innermost big gate of Topkapı Palace); the Sultan's Court; Istanbul; *Bab-ı Selam* – the Gate of Peace (name of the second big gate of Topkapı Palace)

*barış* – peace, reconciliation; *barışmak* – to make peace with one another, to be reconciled; *barışık oldukdan sonra* – after concluding the peace

*bayram* – religious festival

*beled* (pl. *bilad, biladan*) – region, country, district, territory; *bilad-ı haraciye* – tributary territories

*bende* – (P) slave, servant, subject; *bende-yi Eremia voyvoda-yı Boğdan hala* – the slave Jeremy, voivode of Moldavia at the present time (*ʿarz*, 1603); *bende-yi Nikolay voyvoda-yı Eflak hala* – the slave Nicholas, voivode of Wallachia at the present time (*ʿarz*, 1723)

*Bender* – Tighina, town in Bessarabia; *bender* – trading port, emporium *benim dostum* – my friend

*berat* – patent, diploma, warrant, title of privilege; *berat-ı hümayun, berat-ı ʿalişan, berat-ı şerif* – imperial diploma, illustrious diploma; *berat-ı hümayunumla ʿinayet olunan Simon oğlu Mihail voyvoda* – Michael voivode, Simon's son, who was granted my imperial diploma (Moldavia, 1608)

*beraya* – free subjects of the Muslim state, exempted from certain taxes

*beyʿa, beyʿat* – a shaking of hands to conclude a bargain; a touching of the hand or making other token in acknowledging of allegiance to a sovereign

*bey, beğ* – prince, ruler, chief, notable; *beylerbeyi* – bey of beys, governor-general; *beylerbeyilik* – province ruled by a governor-general; office of a governor-general

*Bosna* – Bosnia

*boyun* – neck; *boyun tutmak, boyun eğmek, boyun vermek* – to surrender, to submit

*Boğaziçi* – the Bosphorus

*Boğdan* – Moldavia; *Kara-Boğdan* – the Moldavian, Moldavia; *Boğdanlu, Boğdanlı* – the Moldavian; *Boğdan beyi Pitri voyvoda ile barışıklık edüb* – making peace with the voivode Petru, the *beyi* of Moldavia; *Boğdan haracına on bin filori ziyade edüb* – augmenting the tribute of Moldavia with 10,000 filori (*hüküm,* 1574); *Boğdan kapukethudaları* – the agents of Moldavia (*ʿarzuhal,* 1728); *Boğdan sakinlerinden Yakov nam kimesne* – somebody named Yakov, from among the inhabitants of Moldavia (*tezkere,* 1604–1607); *Boğdan ve Eflak memleketi miri-i maktuʾ olub* – the countries of Moldavia and Wallachia being separated possessions of the government (*hüküm,* 1729); *Boğdan vilayetine ve saʾir Memalik-i mahrusamıza gelüb* – coming to the country of Moldavia and to our other Well-Protected Domains (*ʿahdname,* Polonia, 1607); *Boğdan vilayetlerinin bazerganları* – merchants of the Moldavian regions (*ʿahdname,* Polonia, 1607); *Boğdan voyvodalığı* – the office of a prince of Moldavia; *Boğdan voyvodalığı hizmetde sana taʿyın olunmuşdur* – he named you in the office of voivode of Moldavia; *Boğdan voyvodalığı* [...] *Simon oğlu Mihail voyvoda üzerinde iken* – when the voivode Michael, Simon's son, was charged with the office of voivode of Moldavia (*emr,* 1608); *Boğdan voyvodası, Boğdan beği* – prince of Moldavia; *Boğdan voyvodası Eremia voyvodanın ʿarzıdır* – It is the petition of the voivode Ieremia, the voivode of Moldavia (*telhis,* 1603); *Boğdan voyvodasına ihsan olunan berat-ı şerifin suretidir* – it is the copy of the illustrious diploma granted to the voivode of Moldavia (*berat-ı hümayun, münşeʿat,* 1620); *Kara-Boğdan Hünkarın emrine imtisal etmedi* – the Moldavian did not conform to the sultan's order (Neşri, *Tarih*); *Kara-Boğdanın tekurına adam gönderüb* – sending an agent to the Christian prince of Moldavia

*Brusa* – Bursa (Gk. Prusion)

*Bükreş* – Bucharest (Rom. București)

*buyuruldu* – mandate, rescript; *buyurulmak* – to order, to decree, to command

*Cankerman* – Özü, Oczakow, Ochakov, Oceakov

*Cemaziʾlahir, Cemazi ül-ahir* – the sixth month of the Muslim year

*Cemazi'levvel, Cemazi ül-evvel* – the fifth month of the Muslim lunar year

*cevab* – answer

*cihad* (Ar. *djihad, jihad, ğihad*) – effort, holy war; *cihad fetvası* – legal opinion declaring a war sacred; *Kitab al-cihad* (Ar. *Kitab al-djihad*) – book of the holy war; *cihad fi sebil-i Allah* – effort on Allah's path

*cizye* (Ar. *djizye, jizye, ğizye*) – poll-tax, capitation; *cizye talebiyle* – with request of poll-tax; *cizye-yi gebran* – the infidels' tribute (*ruznamçe*, 1583); *cizye evrakların ve arabaların alub* – taking their poll-tax documents and their wagons (*hüküm*, 1711); *cizye kağıdı verüb* – issuing poll-tax documents (*hüküm*, 1728); *cizyedar olanlar* – those who are poll-tax collectors (*ferman*, 1696); *Bergos cizyedarı* – poll-tax collector of Burgas; *cizyegüzar re'ayalar* – poll-tax paying subjects (*nişan-ı hümayun*, 1574); *cizyeleri nefer başına olmayub haneye olmağla* – because their poll-tax is not per person but per house-hold (*'arz*, 1674)

*cülus* – accession to the throne; *cülus-u hümayun* – the accession of a sultan to the throne

*Çanakkale boğazı* – the Dardanelles

*Çirmen* – Chirmen (Gr. Kermianon, Bulg. Crnomen)

*da'vet* (Ar. *da'wa*) – summon, invitation, call, request

*dar* – abode, house, dominion, realm, region, country

*dar ül-'ahd* (Ar. *dar al-'ahd*) – Abode of covenant

*dar ül-cihad* (Ar. *dar al-djihad*) – Abode of holy war

*dar ül-harb* (Ar. *dar al-harb*) – Abode of War; *dar ül-harb'dan gelen kefere* – the infidels who come from the Abode of War (*kanunname*, 1586).

*dar ül-Islam* (Ar. *dar al-Islam*) – Abode of Islam

*dar ül-muvada'a, dar-ı muvada'a* (Ar. *dar al-muwada'a*) – Abode of truce

*dar ül-sulh* (Ar. *dar al-sulh*) – Abode of peace

*dar-ı zimmet, dar al-zimmet, dar üz-zimmet* (Ar. *dar al-dhimma*) – Abode of tributary-protection

*dergah* – court of a king; *Dergah-ı 'Ali, Dergah-ı Mu'alla* – the Sultan's court

*devlet* (pl. *düvel*) – state, government, dynasty.

*dirlik* – revenue granted as a living

*din* – faith, religion

*Divan-ı hümayun* – the Imperial Council

*diyar* – land, country, region; *diyar-ı harb* – land of war; *diyar-ı Islam* – land of Islam; *diyar-ı küffar* – land of infidels; *diyar-ı küfr* – non-Muslim country

*dost* – friend; *dostluk* – friendship; *dostluğa halel verir* – he damages the friendship; *dostluğu kabul edüb* – accepting the friendship; *dostumuza dost ve düşmanımıza düşman olduğun* – you are [a] friend to our friend and [an] enemy to our enemy (*'ahdname* Transylvania, 1580) *doyumluk* – booty, spoils of war; *doyumluk taleb eden kimesneler* – those looking for spoils (*hüküm,* 1484)

*Dubrovnik* – Ragusa; *Dubrovniklü sa'ir re'aya gibi haracgüzar re'ayalarımdır* – the Ragusans are my tribute-paying subjects like other subjects

*düşman, düşmen* – enemy

*ecnebi* – foreign; *Düvel-i ecnebiye defterleri, Ecnebi devletler defterleri* – Registers of the foreign states.

*Edirne* – Adrianople

*Eflak* – Wallachia; *Eflak voyvodası* – the voivode of Wallachia; *Eflaklu* – the Wallachian; *'an cizye-yi gebran vilayet-i Eflak* – from the tribute of the infidels of the Wallachia country; *Eflak beği elçisiyle haracın gönderüb ita'at eyledi* – the prince of Wallachia sent the tribute with his envoy <and> submitted; *Eflak canibinde olan muta' ve haracgüzar re'ayaları* – the obedient and tribute-payer subjects who are in the region of Wallachia; *Eflak cizyesi maktu' olmakla* – because the tribute of Wallachia was established (*ferman,* 1696); *Eflak kafirlerinin 'arz-ı hallarıdır* – <these> are the petitions of the Wallachian infidels (*'arz-ı hal,* 1512–1521); *Eflak kapu-kethüdaları* – the agents of Wallachia (*'arz-ı hal,* 1696); *Eflak oğlıyla bu vech üzere musalaha edüb barışıklık etdiler* – making in this way peace with the Wallachian <voivode>'s son, they reconciled (Neşri, *Tarih*); *Eflak re'ayası harbi değildir* – the subjects of Wallachia are not enemies (*hüküm,* 1672); *Eflak re'ayasından olub* – being from among the subjects of Wallachia (*hüküm,* 1696; *tezkere,* 1804); *Eflak ve Boğdan taraflarına muhafaza içün* – for defending the regions of Wallachia and Moldavia (*telhis,* 1593); *memleket-i padişahi olan Eflak memleketi* – the principality of Wallachia which is an imperial country (*'arzuhal,* 1715)

*Efrenc, Efrenğ, Firenc, Frank* (pl. *Efrenciyan Efrenciyun*) – European, Frank (*kanunname, hüküm*); *Firenc kafirleri* – European infidels

*ehl, ahl* – people, community, men; *ehl-i fesad* – intriguer, villain; *ehl-i fidye* – people of ransom; *ehl-i kitab, ehl ül-kitab* (Ar. *ahl al-kitab*) – people of the Book

*elçi* – envoy, ambassador

*elkab* – intitulatio

*emn* – safety, security; *emniyet-i kamil* – complete security; *emn ü-aman* – safety and protection; *emn ü-selamet* – peace and security

*emr* – order, command, decree; *emr-i şerif* – the imperial decree, the Sultan's order; *emr-i padişahi mucebince* – according to the imperial order

*Erdel* – Transylvania; *Erdel banı* – the ban on Transylvania; *Erdelli* – the Transylvanian; *Erdel hakimi Rakoçi Görgi* – Rákoczy George, the ruler of Transylvania (*kağıd tercemesi,* 1634); *Erdel hakimi ve Macar kıralı taraflarına isdar buyurulan 'ahdname-yi hümayunun suretidir* – It is the copy of the imperial charter which was sent to the ruler of Transylvania and the Hungarian king (*'ahdname, münşe'at,* 1614); *Erdel haracın bi't-temam tedarik ve vaktıyla irsal eyleyüb* – getting ready and delivering completely and in time the tribute of Transylvania (*inşa,* 1663); *Erdel kıralı Istefan kıral hüküm ki* – order for King Stephen, the king of Transylvania (*hüküm, mühimme defteri,* 1572); *Erdel memleketinin reʿayası* – the subjects of the country of Transylvania; *Erdel reʿayasına tecavüz ve taʿaddi üzere olub* – transgressing and attacking the subjects of Transylvania (*hüküm,* 1613); *Erdel ve Boğdan ve Eflak vilayetlerine gelüb* – coming to the countries of Transylvania and Moldavia and Wallachia (*ʿahdname,* Polonia, 1617); *Erdel vilayeti uslub-i kadim üzere kıral oğlu kulunum sancağıdır* – the country of Transylvania is the *sancak* of my servant, the king's son, according to the old manner; *Erdel vilayetin sancak tarikle inayet edüb* – I gave <him> the country of Transylvania as a *sancak*; *Erdel voyvodası* – the voivode of Transylvania

*esir* – slave, captive, prisoner of war

*eva'il* – the first ten days of a month

*evahir* – the last ten days of a month

*evasıt* – the middle ten days of a month

*eyalet* – province, principality; *eyalat-i mümtaze* – privileged provinces, the autonomous provinces of the Ottoman Empire

*farz-ı ʿayn* – duty applicable to all

*farz-ı kifaye, farz ül-kifaye* – a duty the observance of which, by some, will absolve the rest

*ferman* – imperial edict, command, order; *ferman mürüvvetlü ve izzetlü sultanım hazretlerinindir* – the order belongs to His Majesty, my generous and glorious sultan

*feth, fetih* – conquest, victory; *fetihname* – imperial letter announcing a conquest, treatise or poem describing a conquest; *feth-i hakaniden berü* – since the imperial conquest (*ʿarzuhal,* 1715); *Fetihname-yi Kara-Boğdan* – The Conquest-letter of Moldavia (1538); *ben feth-i biladan-ı Boğdanım* – I am the conqueror of the territories of Moldavia (1538)

*fetva* (Ar. *fatwa*) (pl. *fetava*) – legal opinion furnished by a mufti on application

*fey'* (Ar. *fay'*) – booty obtained from non-Muslims by a peace treaty, revenue of the Islamic state from non-Muslim subjects

*fikh, fikıh* – Muslim canonical jurisprudence

*Franca, França* – France; *Françalu* – the French; *Franca padişahı* – king of France

*Galata* – the town of Galata, part of Istanbul

*ganimet* (Ar. *ghanama*) – spoils, booty taken by Muslims during fighting

*gavur* – infidel, non-Muslim

*gaza* (Ar. *ghazwa*) (pl. *gazavat*) – holy campaign, raid; *gaza fermanı* – order for holy campaign; *Gazavatname* – Annal of holy campaigns; *gazi* – warrior in holy campaigns; frontier raider into a non-Muslim country; *Gaza-yı Kara-Boğdan* – the Holy Campaign of Moldavia (Neşri, *Tarih*); *gaza ü-cihad* – holy campaign and holy war; *gazaye hazır olalar* – they are ready for the holy campaign

*gümrük* – custom, duty, tax

*gurre* (*evvel*) – the first day of a Muslim month

*guruş* , *kuruş* – piaster, ducat.

*haber* – news, information; *haber etmek* – to send news

*Hadis* (Ar. *Hadith*) – Tradition, record of a saying or action of the Prophet Muhammad, handed down by his companions

*hakim* (pl. *hükkam* ) – ruler, governor, judge; *hakimiyet* – sovereignty, domination, rule

*Erdel hakimi olan Bator Gabor içün* – to Gabriel Báthory, who is the ruler of Transylvania (*hüküm*, 1613); *hakim-i Eflak meva'idine vefa edüb* – the ruler of Wallachia, being faithful in performing his promises

*harac* (Ar. *kharadj*) – tribute, land-tax; *harac-ı maktu'* – fixed tribute; *harac-ı arazi* – land-tax; *harac-ı şer'iye* – the tribute of holy law (Selaniki); *harac-ı ru'us* – poll-tax; *haracın zamanı* – the time <to pay> the tribute, the tribute time (*hüküm*, 1609); *haracına mültezim* – contractor of the tribute; *Kitab al-harac* (Ar. *Kitab al-kharadj*) – Book of the Land-tax; *harac talebiyle rencade etdirmeyüb* – not annoyed by the request of tribute (*hüküm*, 1646); *harac vermeğe mültezim oldı* – he contracted to give tribute; *harac-ı ma'hudı olub* – being the tribute undertaken by agreement; *haracı iltizam etdi* – he took the tribute upon himself; *haracını sen kendün getir ta kim Eflak oğlu getirir* – Bring yourself your tribute as the Wallachian bring it (Neşri, *Tarih*)

*haracgüzar* – tribute-payer; *haracgüzar olmayan Firenc* – European who is not tribute-payer (*kanunname*, 1476); *haracgüzar kafirler* – tribute-paying infidels; *haracgüzar olan re'ayayı* – tribute-paying subjects; *haracgüzar olmayan kafir* – infidel who are not tribute-payer (*kanunname*, 1476); *Eflak voyvodası gibi Hüdavendigarun haracgüzarımış* – He was Murad I's tribute-payer like the voivode of Wallachia (*Tarih*)

*harb* (pl. *hurub*) – war; *harbi* (pl. *harbiler*) – enemy; *harb i'lanı* – declaration of war; *harbi küffar, harbi kefere* – enemy infidels; *harbi vilayetleri* – enemy countries

*hat* – line, decree, imperial mandate written or signed by the Sultan's own hand; *hatt-ı şerif* , *hatt-ı hümayun* – imperial decree; mandate of the Sultan sent to the grand vizier for execution

*hediye* (pl. *hedaya* ) – gift, present

*Hersek* – Herzegovina

*Hicret* (Ar. *Hidjra*) – emigration, the Hegira, the emigration of the Prophet Muhammad from Mecca to Medina

*hizmet, hidmet* – service, duty, function; *hizmet etmek* – to serve; *bu hizmeti eda eyleyesiz* – you perform this duty (*name*, 1678); *sadakat ü-istikamet ile hizmet etmekle* – since he has served with fidelity and integrity (*hüküm*, 1609)

*hil'at* – robe of honor

*himaye, himayet* – protection, defense, patronage, support; *himayet ü-sıyanet* – protection and defense; *memleket vacib ül-himayemizdir re'ayası dahi haracgüzarlarımdır*

– the country is under our due protection, his subjects are also my tribute-payers (*berat-ı hümayun*, 1585); *memleket-i şehriyara sıyaneti içün himaye rica eyleyüb* – requesting support for protecting the imperial country (1687, Transylvania)

*Hıristiyan* – Gk. Christian

*hoca* – Muslim teacher

*hutbe* (pl. *hutab*) – sermon delivered after the Friday prayer

*hüccet* – document, title-deed

*hüdne* (Ar. *hudna*) – truce, peace, tranquility

*hudud* – frontier, boundary, border; *hududname* – boundary-charter, document demarcating a border; *hudud işareti* – border-stone

*hükm, hüküm* – decree, command, order, edict, rule, domination, authority; *hükümdar* – ruler, sovereign, monarch; *hükümet* – government, state, rule, domination authority; *hükm-ü hümayun* – imperial edict; *hükm-ü şerif verilüb* – an illustrious command was enacted

*icazet* – authorization, permission; *icazetname* – diploma, written authorization

*icmaʿ* (Ar. *idjmaʿ*) – the general concurrence in opinion of the legalists

*idiye* – bayram gift (tax)

*ihlas* – pure sincerity of heart; *sadakat ü-ihlasın mucebince* – according to your loyalty and sincerity

*ilhak* – annexation; *ilhak etmek* – to annex

*imam* – successor of the Prophet, prayer leader; *imam ül-aʿzam* – the greatest imam; title of Abu Hanifa, the founder of the Hanafi school

*iman* – faith, believing in the faith of Islam

*Ingiltere* – England; *Ingiltereli* – Englishman; *Ingiltere kıralı* – king of England

*inkıyad* – submission, obedience, *inkıyad etmek* – to submit, to be obedient, to obey

*Islam* – Islam

*Ispanya* – Spain

*Istanbul* (*Islambol*) – Gk. Istanbul

*istikamet* – uprightness, honesty, integrity

*istikametin ve sadakat üzere ʿubudiyetin izhar eyleyesin* – you manifest your submission according to your uprightness and loyalty (*inha*, 1663)

*istiklal* – independent, independence, *istiklaliyet* – absolute sovereignty

*ʿisyan* – revolt, rebellion, rioting; *ʿisyan etmek* – to rebel against; *ʿisyan üzere olan kefereden* – from among the infidels who rebelled against (*hüküm*, 1717)

*itaʿat* – obedience, submission; *itaʿat ü-inkıyad etmek* – to obey, to submit oneself

*ittifak* – accord, agreement, alliance, *ittifak ʿakdetmek* – to make an agreement

*iʿtimad* – reliance, confidence; *iʿtimad etmek* – to trust

*izin, izn* – permission

*kadı* – judge of Islamic canon, law, governor of a *kaza*

*kadim* – old, ancient

*kafir* (pl. *kafirler* , *küffar* , *kefere* ) – infidel, unbeliever, non-Muslim; *küfr, küfür* – unbelief, infidelity; *Kafiristan* – country of infidels, Europa; *kefere ile müttefik olub* – being allied with the infidels; *kefere ki dar ül-harb'dan olmıya* – infidels who are not from the Abode of War; *küffar ayrık hıyaneti zahir olmadı* – no more was the treachery of infidels evident; *küffar şevket-i Islam görecek sulh edüb* – considering the power of Islam, the infidels made peace (Kemalpaşazade)
*Kamaniçe* – Kameniça, Kam'janec, Kamjanec
*kanun* – law, rule; *kanunname* – code of laws
*kapu-kethüdası, kapı-kethüdası* – official representative of a provincial governor in Istanbul, agent
*Kara Deniz* – Black Sea
*katib* (pl. *küttab* ) – clerk, scribe, secretary
*katl, katil* – assassination, a killing
*kaza* – administrative and juridical district of a *kadı*
*Kefe* – Kaffa, town in the Crimea
*kıbla* – direction of Mecca
*kılıç hakkı* – the sword right (*name-i humayun,* 1526)
*kıral* – king; *Erdel kıralı* – the king of Transylvania
*kıyas* – comparison, analogy
*kıtal* – fight, massacre
*Kili* – Kilia (Rom. Chilia)
*Kostantiniye* – Constantinople, Istanbul
*kudumiye* – offering or present to one who arrives or by one who arrives
*kuka akçesi* – tax paid by the tribute-paying voivodes when were named in office
*kul* – slave
*Kur'an* – the Quran
*Leh vilayeti, Lehistan* – Poland; *Lehlü* – Pole, Polish; *Leh kıralı* – king of Poland; *Leh kıralına ʿinayet olunan ʿahdname-yi hümayundur* – it is the imperial charter, which was granted as a favor to the king of Poland (*ʿahdname, defter*, 1678)
*Macaristan* , *Engürüs, Ungürüs* – Hungary
*madamki, mademki* – since, as, while
*malik* – possessor, owner, king, lord; *malik ül-mülk* – Allah
*maslahat* (pl. *masalih*) – the proper cause
*Mekke* – Mecca
*Medine* – Medina
*memalik* (sing. *memleket*) – domain, dominion, country; *Memalik-i Islam* – Islamic countries; *Memalik-i mahrusa* – Well-Protected Domains; *Memleketeyn* – the two countries, i.e. Wallachia and Moldavia; *muzafat-ı Memalik-i mahrusa* – the annexes of Well-Protected Domains; *Memalik-i mahrusam muzafatından olub* – being from the annexes of my Well-Protected domains (*hüküm*, Transylvania, 1581); *muzafat-ı*

*Memalik-i mahrusamdan Eflak memleketi* – the principality of Wallachia from the annexes of my Well-Protected Domains; *sa'ir Memalik-i mahrusam gibi olub* – being like my other Well-Protected Domains
*mes'ele, mesele* – question, point under consideration
*meveddet* – friendship
*mev'id* (pl. *meva'id*) – promise, agreement
*mezheb* (Ar. *madhhab*) (pl. *mezahib*) – religious opinion, doctrine; *Mezahib-i Erba'a* – the four legal-religious Sunni schools
*Midillü* – Gk. Mytilene (Lesbos)
*Mısır, Mısr* – Egypt
*millet* – religious community, nation; *millet-başı* – head of a religious community; *millet-i Ermeni* – the Armenian community; *millet-i Rum* – the Greek-Orthodox community; *millet-i Yahudi* – the Jewish community
*miri* – public, belonging to the state, the state treasury, government tax; *miri-i maktu'* – separated possessions of the government; fixed revenues of the government
*misak* – compact, pact, treaty, solemn promise
*Moskof, Moskov, Mosku, Rusya* – Moscow, Russia
*mu'af* – exempted, free (from)
*mu'ahede, mu'ahada* (pl. *mu'ahedat* ) – treaty, pact, a mutually entering into a covenant or an alliance; *mu'ahedename* – peace treaty, agreement; *mu'ahedat-ı selam, mu'ahedat-ı sulh* – peace treaties (*name-yi hümayun,* Poland, 1550)
*mu'ahid* (pl. *mu'ahidin* ) – signatory of a treaty, beneficiary of a covenant; non-Muslim who has taken an oath of fealty and agreed to pay tribute to the Sultan; *keferesi ehl-i Islam ile mu'ahidan olan* – infidels who contracted an agreement with the people of Islam (*fetva, hüküm,* 1717)
*mu'avenet ve muzaheret eylemek* – to help and support
*Muharrem* – the first month of the Muslim lunar year
*mukarrer* – established, decided
*mukata'a* (pl. *mukata'at* ) – a farming out of public revenue
*murtad, mürted* – apostate from Islam
*musalaha* (pl. *musalahat*) – reconciliation, pacification; *musalahaname* – peace treaty (*'ahdname,* Hungary, 1483; Neșri, Tarih)
*Mushaf* – the Quran
*mu'tad* – customary practice, usual habit, custom; *mu'tad üzere verilegelen* – which is given according to the custom (*hüküm,* 1716)
*muti'* – obedient, submissive; *emrine muti' oldılar* – they obeyed his command
*muvada'a* (Ar. *muwada'a*) – forsaking enmity and becoming reconciled, reconciliation, truce
*muza'af* – doubled, multiplied
*muzaffer* – victorious, triumphant; *muzaffer daima* – always victorious

*mübarek* – holy, sacred, blessed

*mücahid* (Ar. *mudjahid*) – combatant in holy war, champion of Islam

*müctehid* (Ar. *mudjtahid*) – expounder of Islamic laws

*müfti* – official expounder of Islamic law, issuing legal opinions; *Müfti Efendi Hazretlerinin fetvalarında mestur olan üzere* – according to what is written in the legal opinions of His excellency, the Master müfti (*fetva*, Ebussuud Efendi)

*mükaleme* (pl. *mükalemat*) – diplomatic negotiation, conference

*mülhid* – heretic, irreligious

*mülk* – possession, property, state, sovereignty; *mülk-i mevrus* – inherited property

*mü'min* (pl. *mü'minan*) – believer

*münkad* – obedient, docile

*münşe'at* – writings, sets of examples of letters

*müslim* (pl. *müsliman, müslimler*) – Muslim

*müsta'kil* – independent, free, apart

*müste'min* (Ar. *musta'min*) – who applies for safety; foreigner in the Ottoman Empire

*müşrik* (pl. *müşrikin*) – polytheist, pagan

*müsaleme* (Ar. *musalama*) (pl. *müsalemat*) – peace, reconciliation, tranquility

*mütareke* (Ar. *mutaraka*) – truce

*müttefik* – allied, confederate

*nakz-ı 'ahd* – annulment of pact, covenant violation; *nabud etmek* – to destroy, to annihilate; to break an oath; *nakzı 'ahdetmek* – to break a treaty, to violate an engagement; *nakz-ı 'ahd ü-misak etdüğü içün* – because <that infidel> broke the oath and compact (*hüküm*, 1717)

*name-yi hümayun* – imperial letter, autograph letter from the Sultan; *Name-yi hümayun defterleri* – Registers of imperial letters

*nasb* – appointment, nomination; *nasb etmek* – to nominate in an office

*Nasrani* – Nazarene, Christian

*Nederlanda* – Holland, the Dutch Republic; *Nederlandalu* – the Dutchman

*Nemçe Devleti* – the Habsburg Empire, Austria; *Nemçe çasarı* – Habsburg emperor; *tecdid 'ahd olundukda taraf-ı hümayundan Nemçe çasarına verilen 'ahdnamedir* – it is the charter given to the Habsburg emperor on the imperial behalf when the pledge was renewed (*'ahdname, defter,* 1664)

*Niğbolu* – Nikopol

*nişan* – sign, mark, imperial monogram usually set over letters-patent; *nişancı* – officer whose duty it was to inscribe the Sultan's imperial monogram; *nişan-ı şerif 'alişan* – illustrious imperial sign; *nişan-ı hümayun hükmü oldur ki* – the order of the imperial monogram is that

*niyet-i gaza fi sebil-i Allah* – intention to wage holy campaigns on the Allah's path

*nizam* (pl. *nizamat*) – law, regulation, system, order; *nizam-ı memleket* – the regulation of country

*ʿOsmaniyan, ʿOsmanlılar, ʿOsman oğulları* (sing. *ʿOsman*) – Ottomans
*ʿörf, ʿurf* – common usage, sovereign right; *ʿörf ü-ʿadet* – usage and custom; *ʿörf-i sultani, ʿörf-i padişahi* – sultan's will, emperor's right.
*padişah* – emperor
*paşa* – *pasha*, the highest title of civil and military officials; *paşalık* – territory ruled by a *paşa*; the quality, rank and function of a *paşa*; *paşazade* – son of a *paşa*
*Patrik* – Gk. Patriarch; *Patrikhane* – Gk. Patriarchate
*pencik* – the fifth from the spoils; title deed delivered from the customs house to the owner of a slave on payment of the duty
*Perverdegar* – protector, God, king
*peşkeş, pişkeş* – gift, present; gift of a tributary prince brought to the sultan.
*Peygamber* – Prophet, trimis; the Prophet Muhammad
*peyman* – oath, pledge, promise, compact, treaty
*rafizi* – schismatic, heretic, Shiʿi
*Ramazan* – the ninth month of the Muslim year
*reʿaya* (sing. *raʿiyet*) – tax-paying subjects, non-Muslim subjects or Christian subjects of the Ottoman Empire; *reʿaya ve beraya* – the tax-paying and the free subjects of a country; *sa'ir Memalik-i mahrusamda olan reʿaya gibidir* – it is like the subjects of my other Well-Protected Domains (*hüküm*, 1672)
*Rebi ül-ahir, Rebi'lahir* – the fourth month of the Muslim year
*Rebi ül-evvel, Rebi'levvel* – the third month of the Muslim year
*Receb* – the seventh month of the Muslim year
*re'is ül-küttab* – head of scribes; Minister of Foreign Affairs
*Resulullah* (Ar. *Rasul al-Allah*) – the Apostle and Prophet of God, Muhammad
*riddet* (Ar. *ridda*) – apostacy from the Islamic religion
*risale* – treatise, pamphlet
*rıza-i hümayun* – imperial approval
*Rum* – Byzantium, Byzantine Empire
*Rumeli* – Rumelia, European Turkey
*Rusçuk* – Ruse
*sadakat* – faithfulness, fidelity, devotion, loyalty; *sadakat ü-istikamet* – faithfulness and uprightness; *sadakat ü-ihlasda sabit-kadem ü-rasih-i dem olalar* – they are firmly and constantly in faithfulness and honesty (sixteenth and seventeenth century *ʿahdnames*); *sadakat ü-istikametinize lazim olan* – what is inseparable from your fidelity and uprightness (*name*, 1678)
*Sefer* – the second month of the Muslim year
*saliyan, saliyane* – annual, a yearly stipend
*sancak* – flag, banner; subdivision of an Ottoman province; *sancakbeği, sancakbeyi* – governor of a *sancak*; *Sancak-ı Şerif* – the flag of the Prophet only unfurled for a holy war

*sefer-i hümayun* – imperial campaign
*selam* – peace, concord, safety
*Selanik* – Salonika, Thessalonica
*selh* – the last day of a Muslim month
*Semendire* – Semendria, Smederevo
*sened, senet* – title deed, instrument, promissory note
*serbest* – free, independent; *serbestiyet* – freedom, liberty; *serbestiyet üzere* – according to freedom; *mefruzü'l-kalem ve maktu'l-kadem min-küll-il-vücuh serbest olub* – being separated at the chancery and spared of violations and free in all respects (*hüküm*, 1742)
*serhad* – frontier; *serhadd-ı Islam* – Islamic border
*sevgend* – oath, a swearing; *sevgendname* – oath, charter
*sicil* ( pl. *sicillat* ) – register, juridical record
*sikke* – coin; *sikke ve hutbe* – the right of minting coins and of mention in a sermon, two prerogatives of the Sultan
*Silistre* – Silistra
*siyar, siyer* – conduct of government; *Kitab al-siyar* – Book of the conduct of government
*sulh* – peace, reconciliation, accord, friendly arrangement; *sulh etmek* – to make peace; *sulhname* – treaty of peace, peace charter; *sulh ü-müsalemet* – peace and reconciliation; *sulh ve emn ü aman* – peace, and safety and protection; *sulh ü-salah olması babında* – concerning the making of peace and friendship; *sulh ü-salaha mugayir* – contrary to peace and friendship (*kağıd tercemesi*, 1634)
*sulhen, sulhan* – willingly, peaceably, voluntarily
*sultan* – ruler, sovereign, sultan; *sultan-ı ʿalem* – the world's sultan; *sultan-ı ʿalim* – the wise sultan; *sultan-ı ehl-i Islam* – the sultan of the Muslims (*fetva*, Ebussuud Efendi)
*sünnet* (Ar. *Sunna*) – practices and rules not laid down in the Quran but derived from the Prophet's own habits and words
*Şaban, Şaʿban* – the eighth month of the Muslim year
*şah* – king, monarch, the Ottoman sultan; *şah-ı ʿalemin emrine imtissal edüb* – conforming to the order of the world's monarch; *şah-ı Bağdad ve ʿIrak çasar-ı Rum Mısra sultanım* – I am şah of Baghdad and Iraq, emperor of Rum, sultan of Egypt (inscription of Bender, 1538, titles of Süleyman Kanunî)
*şart* (pl. *şerayt*) – condition, stipulation, clause of agreement; *şerayt-i ʿahd ü-peyman* – stipulations of oath and agreement; *şerayt-i sulh ü-aman* – conditions of peace and protection
*şehid, şehit* – martyr, one who dies in battle for Islam; *şehadet* – testimony, martyrdom
*şerh* (pl. *şüruh*) – commentary, explanation
*şeriʿat* (*şerʿ*) (Ar. *shariʿa*) – Islamic canonical law; *şerʿ-i şerif* – holy law; *şerʿ-i şerif muhalif* – contrary to the holy law (*nişan-ı hümayun*, 1574)

*Şevval* – the tenth month of the Muslim lunar year
*şeyh ül-Islam* (Ar. *shaykh al-Islam*) – dignitary responsible for all matters connected with the canon law
*ta'arruz* (pl. *ta'arruzat*) – attack, aggression, molestation; *ta'arruz etmek* – to assault, to attack
*ta'yin* – appointment, designation; *ta'yin olunmak* – to be appointed
*taht* – throne; *tahtına geçmek* – to succeed to the throne
*tarih* (pl. *tevarih*) – history, annals; *Tevarih Al-i 'Osman* – Annals of the Ottoman dynasty
*Tatar tayfesi* – Tatar troops
*tekid* – confirmation, strengthening; *tekid etmek* – to confirm
*teklif* (pl. *tekalif* – tax, custom, obligation
*temessük* – title deed; *mühürlü temessük* – sealed document
*Temeşvar* – Timișoara
*tercüman* – interpreter, translator, dragoman
*teveccüh* (pl. *teveccühat*) – favor, kindness
*tezkere* – short note, official receipt
*ticaret* – trade
*timar, tımar* – small military fief, source of revenue; *timar almak istiyenler* – those who want to obtain a timar (*hüküm*, 1484)
*topuz* – mace
*Trabzon* – Trebizond
*tuğ* – horsetail, attached to a helmet or flag-staff as a sign of rank
*tuğra* – the Sultan's monogram; *tuğra-ı garra-ı sultanat* – illustrious imperial signature
*Tuna* – the Danube
*Turla* – the river Dniester
*'ubudiyet* – devotion, servitude, slavery; *'ubudiyet ü-rıkkiyet* – devotion and servitude; *'ubudiyet ü-ita'at* – servitude and obeisance
*uc* – frontier; *uc beyi* – frontier *bey*
*'ulema* (sing. *'alim*) – scholars in Islamic knowledge
*'Ümmet* (Ar. *'Umma*) – community (especially Muslim community)
*üsküf* – knitted bonnet, knitted cap with a tassel
*vali* – governor of a province
*vefa* – fidelity, loyalty; *vefa etmek* – to be true, faithful in performing an obligation
*Venedik* – Venice; *Venediklü* – the Venetian
*vergi, virgü* – gift, tax, tribute, duty
*vezir* – vizier, minister, rank of the great Ottoman dignitaries; *sadr-ı a'zam, vezir-i a'zam* – grand vizier; *sadr-ı a'zam tarafından Eflak boyarları tarafına yazılan emr-name-yi saminin suretidir* – it is the copy of the illustrious order-letter of the grand vizier to the nobles of Wallachia (*emr, münşe'at*, 1658)

*vilayet* (pl. *vilayetler, vilayat*) – country, province governed by a *vali; vilayet-i Boğdanın boyarlarına* [...] *hüküm ki* – order addressed to the nobles of the country of Moldavia (*hüküm*, 1711); *vilayet-i Eflak sa'ir Memalik-i mahrusam gibidir* – the country of Wallachia is like my other Well-Protected Domains (*hüküm*, 1618)

*voyvoda* – Sl. voivode, governor, administrator; *mu'tad üzere verilegelen ca'ize-yi voyvodalık* – the reigning present which is given according to the custom (*hüküm*, 1716); *sabıka Boğdan voyvodası* – the former voivode of Moldavia (*hüküm*, 1711)

*yemin* – oath; *yemin eylerim ki* – I swear that; *yeminler olub 'ahd ü-peyman etdiler* – taking oaths they concluded pact and agreement (*Tarih*)

*yeniçeri* – Janissary

*Yerköği* – Giurgiu, fortress on the left side of the Danube; *Yerköği kal'ası dizdarı* – the constable of the Giurgiu fortress (*hüküm*, 1613/1614)

*Yüce Divan* – High Court

*yüz sürmek* – to pay humble respect to a superior, to prostrate oneself humbly

*zahire* – provisions

*zekat, zakat,* – tax for helping the poor

*zarar ve ziyan olmak* – to do harm and injury (to somebody)

*Zilhicce* – the twelfth month of the Muslim year

*Zilka'de* – the eleventh month of the Muslim year

*zimmet* (Ar. *dhimma*) – duty, obligation, duty of tribute and obedience owed to the State by a non-Muslim subject; *'ahd-ı zimmet, zimmet 'ahdı, 'ahd al-dhimma, 'ahd ül-zimmet* – tributary-protection covenant.

*zimmi* (Ar. *dhimmi*), *ahl al-dhimma, ehl-i zimmet* – non-Muslim subjects; *Simu nam zimmi* – the non-Muslim subject called Simu

# Table of Correspondence

| Ottoman Sultans | Hospodars of Wallachia | Hospodars of Moldavia | Kings of Hungary. Princes of Transylvania |
|---|---|---|---|
| Osman I<br>683–726 AH<br>1284–1326 | | | |
| Orhan<br>726–761AH<br>1326–1359 | | | |
| Murad I<br>761–791 AH<br>1360–1389 | Dan I<br>1383–1386<br>Mircea cel Bătrân (the Elder)<br>1386–1418 | | Sigismund of Luxemburg<br>1387–1437 |
| Bayezid I<br>791–804 AH<br>1389–1402 | Mircea the Elder<br>1386–1418 | | Sigismund of Luxemburg<br>1387–1437 |
| Interregnum<br>804–816 AH<br>1402–1413 | Mircea the Elder<br>1386–1418 | | |
| Mehmed I Çelebi<br>816–824 AH<br>1413–1421 | Mircea the Elder<br>1386–1418<br>Mihail (Michael) I<br>1418–1420<br>Dan II<br>1420–1421 | | Sigismund of Luxemburg<br>1387–1437 |
| Murad II<br>824–855 AH<br>1421–1451 | Radu II Praznaglava<br>1421; 1423; 1424–1426; 1427; | | Sigismund of Luxemburg<br>1387–1437<br>Albert of Habsburg<br>1437–1439 |

 | DOI:10.1163/9789004411104_018

| Ottoman Sultans | Hospodars of Wallachia | Hospodars of Moldavia | Kings of Hungary. Princes of Transylvania |
|---|---|---|---|
| Murad II<br>824–855 AH<br>1421–1451 | Dan II<br>1421–1423; 1423–1424;<br>1426–1427; 1427–1431<br>Alexandru I Aldea<br>1431–1436<br>Vlad Dracul (the Evil)<br>1436–1442; 1443–1447<br>Mircea – 1442<br>Basarab II<br>1442–1443<br>Vladislav II<br>1447–1448; 1448–1456<br>Vlad Țepeș (the Impaler)<br>1448 | | Wladyslaw Jagiello<br>1440–1444<br>János Hunyadi<br>(Iancu de Hunedoara),<br>regent<br>1446–1452 |
| Mehmed II<br>Fatih<br>(The Conqueror)<br>855–886 AH<br>1451–1481 | Vladislav II<br>1448–1456<br>Vlad Țepeș (the Impaler)<br>1456–1462<br>Radu cel Frumos<br>(the Fair)<br>1462–1473; 1473–1474;<br>1474–1475<br>Basarab Laiotă<br>1473; 1474; 1475–1476;<br>1476–77<br>Vlad the Impaler<br>1476<br>Basarab cel Tânăr -Țepeluș<br>(the Younger)<br>1477–1481 | Petru Aron<br>1451–1452; 1454–<br>1455; 1455–1457<br>Alexăndrel<br>1452–1454; 1455<br>Ștefan cel Mare<br>(Stephen the Great)<br>1457–1504 | László (Ladislas) of<br>Habsburg<br>1452–1457<br>Mátyás (Matthias)<br>Corvinus<br>1458–1490 |
| Bayezid II<br>886–918 AH<br>1481–1512 | Mircea<br>1481; 1509–1510<br>Vlad Călugărul<br>(Vlad the Monk)<br>1481; 1482–1495 | Stephen the Great<br>1457–1504<br>Bogdan III cel Orb<br>(the Blind)<br>1504–1517 | Mátyás (Matthias)<br>Corvinus<br>1458–1490<br>Wladyslaw II Jagiello<br>1490–1516 |

| Ottoman Sultans | Hospodars of Wallachia | Hospodars of Moldavia | Kings of Hungary. Princes of Transylvania |
|---|---|---|---|
| Bayezid II<br>886–918 AH<br>1481–1512 | Basarab the Younger<br>1481–1482<br>Radu cel Mare<br>(the Great)<br>1495–1508<br>Mihnea cel Rău<br>(the Bad)<br>1508–1509<br>Vlad cel Tânăr–Vlăduț<br>(the Younger)<br>1510–1512 | | |
| Selim I<br>918–926 AH<br>1512 –1520 | Neagoe Basarab<br>1512–1521 | Bogdan III the Blind<br>1504–1517<br>Ștefăniță<br>1517–1527 | Wladyslaw II Jagiello<br>1490–1516<br>Lajos (Louis) II Jagiello<br>1516–1526 |
| Süleyman Kanunî<br>(The Magnificent)<br>926–974 AH<br>1520–1566 | Neagoe Basarab<br>1512–1521<br>Theodosie<br>1521<br>Radu de la Afumați<br>1522–1523; 1524;<br>1524–1525; 1525–1529<br>Vladislav III<br>1523; 1524; 1525<br>Radu Bădica<br>1523–1524<br>Moise<br>1529–1530<br>Vlad Înecatul<br>1530–1532<br>Vlad Vintilă de la Slatina<br>1532–1535<br>Radu Paisie<br>1535–1545 | Ștefăniță<br>1517–1527<br>Petru Rareș<br>1527–1538; 1541–1546<br>Ștefan Lăcustă<br>1538–1540<br>Alexandru Cornea<br>1540–1541<br>Iliaș 1546–1551<br>Ștefan 1551–1552<br>Ioan Joldea 1552<br>Alexandru<br>Lăpușneanu<br>1552–1561;1564–1568<br>Despot vodă (Ioan<br>Iacob Heraclit)<br>1561–1563 | Lajos (Louis) II Jagiello<br>1516–1526<br>János (John) Zápolya<br>1526–1540<br>Petru of Perény<br>1526–1529<br>István (Stephen) Báthory II<br>1529–1533<br>Emerik Cibak,<br>governor<br>1533–1534<br>István (Stephen) Mailat<br>1534–1539<br>István (Stephen)<br>Mailat and<br>Emeric Balassa<br>1539–1540 |

| Ottoman Sultans | Hospodars of Wallachia | Hospodars of Moldavia | Kings of Hungary. Princes of Transylvania |
|---|---|---|---|
| Süleyman Kanunî (Süleyman the Lawgiver; Süleyman the Magnificent)<br>926–974 AH<br>1520–1566 | Mircea Ciobanul (Mircea the Shepherd)<br>1545–1552; 1553–1554;1558–1559<br>Radu Ilie<br>1552–1553<br>Pătrașcu cel Bun (Pătrașcu the Good)<br>1554–1557<br>Petru cel Tânăr (Petru the Younger)<br>1559–1568 | Ștefan Tomșa<br>1563–1564 | János (John) Sigismund Zápolya<br>Isabella<br>1541–1551; 1556–1559<br>Ferdinand I of Habsburg<br>1551–1556<br>János (John) Sigismund Zápolya<br>1559–1571 |
| Selim II<br>974–982 AH<br>1566–1574 | Petru the Younger<br>1559–1568<br>Alexandru II Mircea<br>1568–1574<br>Vintilă 1574 | Alexandru Lăpușneanu<br>1564–1568<br>Bogdan Lăpușneanu<br>1568–1572<br>Ion Vodă cel Cumplit (John the Terrible)<br>1572–1574 | János (John) Sigismund Zápolya<br>1559–1571<br>István (Stephen) Báthory<br>1571–1575 |
| Murad III<br>982–1003 AH<br>1574–1595 | Alexandru II Mircea<br>1574–1577<br>Mihnea II Turcitul (Mihnea the Renegate)<br>1577–1583; 1585–1591<br>Petru Cercel (Petru the Earring)<br>1583–1585<br>Ștefan Surdul (Stephen the Deaf)<br>1591–1592<br>Alexandru cel Rău (Alexander the Bad)<br>1592–1593 | Petru Șchiopul (Petru the Lame)<br>1574–1577<br>Iancu Sasul<br>1579–1582<br>Petru the Lame<br>1582–1591<br>Aron Tiranul (Aron the Tyrant)<br>1591–1592; 1592–1595<br>Alexandru cel Rău (Alexander the Bad)<br>1592<br>Petru Cazacu 1592 | Christopher Báthory<br>1576–1581<br>Sigismund Báthory<br>1581–1597 |

| Ottoman Sultans | Hospodars of Wallachia | Hospodars of Moldavia | Kings of Hungary. Princes of Transylvania |
|---|---|---|---|
| Mehmed III<br>1003–1012 AH<br>1595–1603 | Mihai Viteazul<br>(Michael the Brave)<br>1593–1601<br>Nicolae Pătrașcu<br>1599–1600<br>Simion Movilă<br>1600–1601; 1601–1602<br>Radu Mihnea<br>1601–1602<br>Radu Șerban<br>1602–1611 | Ștefan Răzvan<br>1595<br>Ieremia Movilă<br>1595–1600; 1600–1606<br>Mihai Viteazul<br>(Michael the Brave)<br>1600 | Maria Cristierna<br>1598<br>Sigismund Báthory<br>1598–1599; 1601;<br>1601–1602<br>András (Andrew) Báthory<br>1599<br>Mihai Viteazul<br>(Michael the Brave)<br>1600–1601<br>Giorgio (George) Basta<br>1601; 1602–1603<br>Moses Székely 1603 |
| Ahmed I<br>1012–1026 AH<br>1603–1617 | Radu Șerban<br>1602–1611; 1611<br>Radu Mihnea<br>1611; 1611–1616<br>Gavril Movilă<br>1616<br>Alexandru Iliaș<br>1616–1618 | Simion Movilă<br>1606–1607<br>Mihail Movilă<br>1607<br>Constantin Movilă<br>1607; 1607–1611<br>Ștefan II Tomșa<br>1611–1615<br>Alexandru Movilă<br>1615–1616<br>Radu Mihnea<br>1616–1619 | George Basta<br>1603–1604<br>István (Stephen) Bocskai<br>1605–1606<br>Sigismund Rákóczi<br>1607–1608<br>Gábor (Gabriel) Báthory<br>1608–1613<br>Gábor (Gabriel) Bethlen<br>1613–1629 |
| Mustafa I<br>1026–1027 AH<br>1617–1618 | Alexandru Iliaș<br>1616–1618 | Radu Mihnea<br>1616–1619 | Gábor (Gabriel) Bethlen<br>1613–1629 |
| Osman II<br>1027–1031AH<br>1618–1622 | Gavril Movilă<br>1618–1620<br>Radu Mihnea<br>1620–1623 | Radu Mihnea<br>1616–1619<br>Gașpar Grațiani<br>1619–1620<br>Alexandru Iliaș<br>1620–1621<br>Ștefan II Tomșa<br>1621–1623 | Gábor (Gabriel) Bethlen<br>1613–1629 |

| Ottoman Sultans | Hospodars of Wallachia | Hospodars of Moldavia | Kings of Hungary. Princes of Transylvania |
|---|---|---|---|
| Murad IV<br>1032–1049 AH<br>1623–1640 | Alexandru Coconul<br>1623–1627<br>Alexandru Iliaș<br>1627–1629<br>Leon Tomșa<br>1629–1632<br>Radu Iliaș<br>1632<br>Matei Basarab<br>1632–1654 | Radu Mihnea<br>1623–1626<br>Miron-Barnovschi Movilă<br>1626–1629<br>Alexandru Coconul<br>1629–1630<br>Moise Movilă<br>1630–1631; 1633–1634<br>Alexandru Iliaș<br>1631–1633<br>Miron-Barnovschi Movilă<br>1633<br>Vasile Lupu<br>1634–1653 | Gábor (Gabriel) Bethlen<br>1613–1629<br>Catherine of Brandenburg<br>1629–1630<br>István (Stephen) Bethlen<br>1630<br>György (George) Rákóczi I<br>1630–1648 |
| Ibrahim<br>1049–1058 AH<br>1640–1648 | Matei Basarab<br>1632–1654 | Vasile Lupu<br>1634–1653 | György (George) Rákóczi I<br>1630–1648 |
| Mehmed IV<br>1058–1099 AH<br>1648–1687 | Matei Basarab<br>1632–1654<br>Constantin Șerban<br>1654–1658<br>Mihnea III Radu<br>1658–1659<br>Gheorghe Ghica<br>1659–1660<br>Grigore Ghica<br>1660–1664<br>Radu Leon<br>1664–1669<br>Antonie Vodă din Popești<br>1669–1672 | Vasile Lupu<br>1634–1653<br>Gheorghe Ștefan<br>1653; 1653–1658<br>Vasile Lupu<br>1653<br>Gheorghe Ghica<br>1658–1659<br>Constantin Șerban Basarab<br>1659<br>Ștefăniță Lupu<br>1659–1661; 1661 | György (George) Rákóczi II<br>1648–1660<br>Ferencz (Francis) Rhédey<br>1657–1658<br>Akos Barçay<br>1658–1660<br>János (John) Kemény<br>1661–1662<br>Mihály (Michael) Apafy I<br>1661–1690 |

| Ottoman Sultans | Hospodars of Wallachia | Hospodars of Moldavia | Kings of Hungary. Princes of Transylvania |
|---|---|---|---|
| Mehmed IV<br>1058–1099 AH<br>1648–1687 | Grigore Ghica<br>1672–1673<br>Gheorghe Duca<br>1673–1678<br>Șerban Cantacuzino<br>1678–1688 | Constantin Șerban Basarab<br>1661<br>Eustratie Dabija<br>1661–1665<br>Gheorghe Duca<br>1665–1666; 1668–1672<br>Iliaș Alexandru<br>1666–1668<br>Ștefan Petriceicu<br>1672–1673; 1683–1684<br>Dumitrașco Cantacuzino<br>1673; 1674–1675; 1684–1685<br>Ștefan Petriceicu<br>1673–1674<br>Antonie Ruset<br>1675–1678<br>Gheorghe Duca<br>1678–1683<br>Constantin Cantemir<br>1685–1693 | |
| Süleyman II<br>1099–1102 AH<br>1687–1691 | Șerban Cantacuzino<br>1678–1688<br>Constantin Brâncoveanu<br>1688–1714 | Constantin Cantemir<br>1685–1693 | Mihály (Michael) Apafy I<br>1661–1690<br>Emery (Imre) Thököly<br>1690–1691 |
| Ahmed II<br>1102–1106 AH<br>1691–1695 | Constantin Brâncoveanu<br>1688–1714 | Constantin Cantemir<br>1685–1693<br>Dimitrie Cantemir<br>1693<br>Constantin Duca<br>1693–1695 | Mihály (Michael) Apafy i<br>1690-1699<br>György (George) Bánffy<br>Habsburg governor<br>1692–1704 |

| Ottoman Sultans | Hospodars of Wallachia | Hospodars of Moldavia | Kings of Hungary. Princes of Transylvania |
|---|---|---|---|
| Mustafa II<br>1106–1115 AH<br>1695–1703 | Constantin Brâncoveanu<br>1688–1714 | Antioh Cantemir<br>1695–1700<br>Constantin Duca<br>1700–1703 | Mihály (Michael) Apafy II<br>1690-1699<br>György (George)<br>Bánffy<br>Habsburg governor<br>1692–1704 |
| Ahmed III<br>1115–1143 AH<br>1703–1730 | Constantin Brâncoveanu<br>1688–1714<br>Ștefan Cantacuzino<br>1714–1715<br>Nicolae Mavrocordat<br>1715–1716; 1719–1730<br>Ioan Mavrocordat<br>1716–1719 | Mihai Racoviță<br>1703–1705; 1707–1709; 1715–1726<br>Antioh Cantemir<br>1705–1707<br>Nicolae Mavrocordat<br>1709–1710; 1711–1715<br>Dimitrie Cantemir<br>1710–1711<br>Grigore II Ghica<br>1726–1733 | Ferencz (Francis) Rákóczi II<br>1704–1711 |
| Mahmud I<br>1143–1168 AH<br>1730–1754 | Constantin Mavrocordat<br>1730; 1731–1733; 1735–1741; 1744–1748<br>Mihai Racoviță<br>1730–1731; 1741–1744<br>Grigore II Ghica<br>1733–1735 ; 1748–1752<br>Matei Ghica<br>1752–1753<br>Constantin Racoviță<br>1753–1756 | Grigore II Ghica<br>1726–1733<br>Constantin Mavrocordat<br>1733–1735; 1741–1743; 1748–1749<br>Grigore II Ghica<br>1735–1739; 1739–1741; 1747–1748<br>Russian occupation<br>1739<br>Ioan Mavrocordat<br>1743–1747<br>Constantin Racoviță<br>1749–1753<br>Matei Ghica<br>1753–1756 | |

| Ottoman Sultans | Hospodars of Wallachia | Hospodars of Moldavia | Kings of Hungary. Princes of Transylvania |
|---|---|---|---|
| Osman III<br>1168–1171 AH<br>1754–1757 | Constantin Mavrocordat<br>1756–1758 | Matei Ghica<br>1753–1756<br>Constantin Racoviță<br>1756–1757 | |
| Mustafa III<br>1171–1187 AH<br>1757–1774 | Constantin Mavrocordat<br>1756–1758; 1761–1763<br>Scarlat Ghica<br>1758–1761; 1765–1766<br>Constantin Racoviță<br>1763–1764<br>Ștefan Racoviță<br>1764–1765<br>Alexandru Scarlat Ghica<br>1766–1768<br>Grigore III Ghica<br>1768–1769<br>Russian occupation<br>1769–1774<br>Manole Giani-Ruset<br>1770–1771 | Scarlat Ghica<br>1757–1758<br>Ioan Teodor Callimachi<br>1758–1761<br>Grigore Callimachi<br>1761–1764; 1767–1769<br>Grigore III Ghica<br>1764–1767<br>Constantin Mavrocordat<br>1769<br>Russian occupation<br>1769–1774 | |
| Andul-Hamid I<br>1187–1203 AH<br>1774–1789 | Alexandru Ipsilanti<br>1774–1782<br>Nicolae Caragea<br>1782–1783<br>Mihai Șuțu<br>1783–1786<br>Nicolae Mavrogheni<br>1786–1790<br>Austrian occupation<br>1789–1791 | Grigore III Ghica<br>1774–1777<br>Constantin Moruzi<br>1777–1782<br>Alexandru Mavrocordat<br>(Deli-bey)<br>1782–1785<br>Alexandru Mavrocordat<br>(Firaris)<br>1785–1786 | |

| Ottoman Sultans | Hospodars of Wallachia | Hospodars of Moldavia | Kings of Hungary. Princes of Transylvania |
|---|---|---|---|
| Andul-Hamid I<br>1187–1203 AH<br>1774–1789 | | Alexandru Ipsilanti<br>1786–1788<br>Austrian and Russian occupation<br>1788–1791<br>Manole Giani-Ruset<br>1788–1789 | |
| Selim III<br>1203–1222 AH<br>1789–1807 | Mihai Suțu<br>1791–1793; 1801–1802<br>Alexandru Moruzi<br>1793–1796; 1799–1801<br>Alexandru Ipsilanti<br>1796–1797<br>Constantin Hangerli<br>1797–1799<br>Alexandru Suțu<br>1802; 1806 kaymakam<br>Constantin Ipsilanti<br>1802–1806;<br>1806–1807 | Alexandru Moruzi<br>1792; 1802–1806;<br>1806–1807<br>Mihai Suțu<br>1792–1795<br>Alexandru Callimachi<br>1795–1799<br>Constantin Ipsilanti<br>1799–1801<br>Alexandru Suțu<br>1801–1802<br>Scarlat Callimachi<br>1806 | |
| Mustafa IV<br>1222–1223 AH<br>1807–1808 | Russian occupation<br>1806–1812<br>Constantin Ipsilanti<br>1807 | Russian occupation<br>1806–1812<br>Alexandru Hangerli<br>1807<br>Scarlat Callimachi<br>1807–1810 | |
| Mahmud II<br>1223–1255 AH<br>1808–1839 | Russian occupation<br>1806–1812<br>Ioan Gheorghe Caragea<br>1812–1818<br>Alexandru Șuțu<br>1818–1821<br>Scarlat Callimachi<br>1821 | Russian occupation<br>1806–1812<br>Scarlat Callimachi<br>1812–1819<br>Mihai Suțu<br>1819–1821<br>Ottoman occupation<br>1821–1822 | |

| Ottoman Sultans | Hospodars of Wallachia | Hospodars of Moldavia | Kings of Hungary. Princes of Transylvania |
|---|---|---|---|
| Mahmud II<br>1223–1255 AH<br>1808–1839 | Ottoman occupation<br>1821–1822<br>Grigore IV Ghica<br>1822–1828<br>Russian occupation<br>1828–1834<br>Alexandru Ghica<br>1834–1842 | Ion Sandu Sturdza<br>1822–1828<br>Russian occupation<br>1828–1834<br>Mihai Sturdza<br>1834–1849 | |
| Abdul-Medjid I<br>1255–1277 AH<br>1839–1861 | Alexandru Ghica<br>1834–1842<br>Gheorghe Bibescu<br>1842–1848<br>Barbu Știrbei<br>1849–1853<br>Russian, Ottoman and Austrian occupation<br>1853–1854<br>Barbu Știrbei<br>1854–1856<br>Kaymakams<br>1856–1859<br>Alexandru Ioan Cuza<br>1859–1866 | Mihai Sturdza<br>1834 1849<br>Grigore Alexandru Ghica<br>1849–1853<br>Russian occupation<br>1853–1854<br>Grigore Alexandru Ghica<br>1854–1856<br>Kaymakams<br>1856–1859<br>Alexandru Ioan Cuza<br>1859–1866 | |
| Abdul-Aziz<br>1277–1293 AH<br>1861–1876 | Alexandru Ioan Cuza<br>1859–1866<br>Carol I of Hohenzollern<br>1866–1914 | Alexandru Ioan Cuza<br>1859–1866<br>Carol I of Hohenzollern<br>1866–1914 | |
| Murad V<br>1293 AH<br>1876 | Carol I of Hohenzollern<br>1866–1914 | Carol I of Hohenzollern<br>1866–1914 | |

| Ottoman Sultans | Hospodars of Wallachia | Hospodars of Moldavia | Kings of Hungary. Princes of Transylvania |
|---|---|---|---|
| Abdul-Hamid<br>1293–1327 AH<br>1876–1909 | Carol I of Hohenzollern<br>1866–1914 | Carol I of Hohenzollern<br>1866–1914 | |
| Mehmed V<br>1327–1336 AH<br>1909–1918 | | | |
| Mehmed VI<br>1336–1341 AH<br>1918–1922 | | | |
| Abdul-Medjid II<br>1342 AH<br>1923–1924 | | | |

# Bibliography

## Unpublished Sources


Archiwum Glowne Akt Dawnych. Warsaw

AGAD, AKW-Tureckie: Karton 66, 69, 71.

Archives du Ministere des Affaires Étrangers du France. Paris

AMAE, Mémoires et documents (MD), vol. 13, *Mémoires et documents divers sur les provinces et sur les pays vassaux de l'Empire ottoman: originaux, copies et imprimés des XVIIIe et XIXe siècles sur la période de 1700 à 1839.*

AMAE, MD, vol. 48: *Mémoires et documents sur la Moldavie et la Valachie: minutes, originaux, copies et imprimés du XIXe siècles sur la période de 1825 à 1855.*

Arhivele Naţionale Istorice Centrale. Bucharest

ANIC, mf. Poland, r. 1.

ANIC, mf. Turkey, r. 53, fr. 894–1004 (Belediye Kütüphanesi, Istanbul, Muallim Cevdet, K. 4: *1567–1796 Osmanlı devleti ile Nemçe ve sa'ir devletler arasında 'akd olunan ba'zı mu'ahedeler*).

Bibliothèque Nationale de France.

BnF, Division Orientale, Supl. Turc. 118 (*Recueil des plusieurs traités entres les Puissances Chrétiennes et la Porte*).

BnF, Bibliothèque d'Arsenal, ms. 4767–4771 (*Traictés et ambassades de Turquie». Recueil de pièces relatives à l'histoire des relations diplomatiques de la France avec le Levant. 1528–1640,* Tome I-IV).

Başbakanlık Osmanlı Arşivi. Istanbul

BOA, Cevdet Tasnifi. *Eyalat-i Mümtaze* (documents from 1700–1880 on *Eflak, Boğdan, Kırım Hanı, Mısır, Dubrovnik*).

BOA, Cevdet Tasnifi. *Hariciye*. vol. I, 1616–1896 AH/1025–1313.

BOA, Amedi Kalemi Odası (Kamil Kepeci tasnifi) 53: *Amedi odası defterlerinden Nemçe çasarına virilen 'ahdname-yi hümayun kayıtı. Tarihi 1110.*

BOA, *Düvel-i Ecnebiye Defterleri*

*DED 55/1, Lehistan 'Ahdnamesi Defteri* 1016–1173 AH/1607–1759.

*DED* 57/1, *Nemçelü 'Ahd Defteri* 975–1210 AH/1567–1795.

Czartoryski Library, Krakow

Czartoryski, IV, 859.

Magyar Országos Levéltár (Hungarian National Archives), Budapest

MOL, mf. Turkey, r. 10131 (TKSMA, Defter 7018)

Princeton University Library

Department of Rare Books and Special Collections

PRUL, GYC, 1459Y: Çatalcalı 'Ali Efendi, *Fetava*, f. 57b-58b (*Kitab al-siyar*)

PRUL, GYC, 2496Y: Minkarizade Yahya, *Fetava-yı Ata'iye*, f. 27–50 (*Kitab al-siyar*)

PRUL, GYC, 3762Y: Feyzullah, *Fetava*, f. 17a-18a (*Kitab al-siyar*)

Microfilms Collection

PRUL, mf. EEN, r. 633–684: *The London Gazette*. 1665–1712, H. Muddiman et. al. Published by Authority. (Printers vary). Issued twice a week.

Süleymaniye Kütüphanesi. Istanbul

SK, Hkm. 405: *Fetava-yi Akkermani Ma'a Üskubi*, f. 87–99

SK, Süleymaniye 95: *Fetava-yi Ebussuud*, f. 85–89

SK, Hamidiye 601: *Fetava-yi Minkarizade*, f. 12–25

SK, Esad ef. 3375: *Mu'ahadat ve münşa'at ve mukarrarat.*

SK, Fatih 2390: *Fetava-yi 'Ali Efendi <Zenbilli>*, f. 73–78.

Topkapı Sarayı Müzesi Arşivi. Istanbul

TKSMA, Defter 7018

TKSMA, E. 1320, 5299, 5536, 6512, 6519

Topkapı Sarayı Müzesi Kütüphanesi. Istanbul

TKMSK, A 842: *Fetava-yi 'Ali Akkermani*

TKSMK, H. 1650: *Siyasete müte'allik fetvalar*, 16 f.

TKSMK, B. 107: *Fetava fi hakk-i müsadere*, 9 f.

## Published Sources

*16. Asırda Yazılmış Grekçe Anonim Osmanlı Tarihi. Giriş ve Metin (1373–1512)*, Ankara: Hazırlayan: Şerif Baştav, 1973.

Abrahamowicz, Z. *Katalog Dokumentow Tureckich...Catalogue des documents turcs. Documents concernant la Pologne et les Pays Voisins de 1455 à 1672*, Warsaw : Państwowe Wydawnictwo Naukowe 1959.

Abu Yusuf Ya'koub. *Le livre de l'impôt foncier* (*Kitâb al-kharâdj*), translated and edited by E. Fagnan, Paris : Paul Geuthner,1921.

Akgündüz, Ahmed. *Osmanlı Kanunnameleri ve Hukukî Tahlilleri*. 1–11. Kitap, Istanbul: Fey Vakfı, 1990–2016.

Akhisarı, Hasan al-Kâfi el-Bosnevi. *Usûl el-hikam fi nizam el-alem*, BAR, Filiala Cluj-Napoca, ms. Oriental no. 258; "Principes de Sagesse, touchant l'art de gouverner, par Ac-hissari (Petit Traité traduit du turc par M. Garcin de Tassy)." *JA* IV, (1824): 213 226, 283–290.

Anafarta, Nigar. *Osmanlı Imparatorlugu ile Lehistan (Polonya) arasındaki münasebetlerle ilgili tarihi belgeler (Historical Documents concerning Relations between the Ottoman Empire and Lehistan (Poland)*, Istanbul: Bilmen, 1979.

Anhegger, R. and H. Inalcık., *Kanunname-i Sultanı ber muceb-i örf-i Osmani. II.Mehmed ve II. Bayezid devirlerine ait yasakname ve kanunnameler*, Ankara: Türk Tarih Kurumu Basımevi, 1956.

Anquetil-Duperron, A. H. *Législation orientale. Ouvrage dans lequel, en montrant quels sont en Turquie, en Perse et dans l'Indoustan, les principes fondamentaux du gouvernement*, Amsterdam: Marc Michel Rey, 1778.

Antalffy, A. "Două documente din Biblioteca Egipteană de la Cairo despre cucerirea Chiliei şi a Cetăţii Albe în 1484." *RI* XX, (1934): 37–38.

Argenti, Philip P. (ed.). *Diplomatic Archive of Chios. 1577–1841*, vols. I–II, Cambridge: Cambridge University Press, 1954.

Aristarchi Bey, Grégoire, *Législation ottomane ou recueil des lois, règlements, ordonnances, traités, capitulations et autre documents officiels de l'Empire Ottoman*, vols. I–VII, Constantinople: Demétrius Nicolaides, 1873–1888.

Aşıkpaşazade, *Tevarih* – Fr. Giese. *Die altosmanische Chronik des Aşıkpaşazade*, Leipzig, 1929 (excerpts in *Cronici turceşti I*, 81–105; *Crestomaţie turcă*, 77–101). Also in Çiftcioğlu N. Atsız, *Osmanlı Tarihleri*, I, Istanbul, 1949, 77–319.

Atsız, Çiftcioğlu N. (ed.). *Osmanlı Tarihleri*, vol. I, Istanbul, 1949.

Averroes, *Jihad in Mediaeval and Modern Islam. The Chapter on Jihad from Averroes' legal handbook "Bidâyat al-Mudjtahid."* Translated and annotated by Rudolph Peters, Leiden: Brill, 1977, 9–25.

Bănescu, Nicolae. "Opt scrisori turceşti ale lui Mihnea II «Turcitul»." *AARMSI*, s. III, VI, 8, (1926): 177–191.

Bannâ'. *Five Tracts of Hasan al-Bannâ' (1906–1949). A Selection from the Majmû'at Rasâ'il al-Imâm al-Shahîd Hasan al-Bannâ'*, Translated from the Arabic and annotated by Charles Wendell, Berkeley, Los Angeles, London: University of California Press, 1978.

Barkan, Ö. L. *XV ve XVI-inci asırlarda Osmanlı Imparatorluğunda ziraî ekonominin hukukî ve malî esasları. Birinci Cilt: Kanunlar*, Istanbul, Bürhaneddin matbaasi, 1943.

*Başbakanlık Osmanlı Arşivi Rehberi*, Ankara : T.C. Başbakanlık Devlet Arşivleri Genel Müdürlüğü, 1992.

Behrnauer, F. A. "Sultân Ahmad's I. Bestallungs-und Vertrags- Urkunde für Gabriel Báthory von Somlyó, Fürsten von Siebenbürgen, vom Jahre 1608 der Christlichen Zeitrechnung." *AKOG* XVIII, (1857): 299–300.

Beldiman, Alexandru. *Tractaturile prin care s-au închinatu ţara de către Bogdan voevod, domnu al Moldovei, împărăţind Bajazet al 2-lea, de Nicolae Costin* (BAR, ms. 566, fol. 126v-136; published in Mihail Kogălniceanu, *Cronicele României seu Letopiseţele Moldaviei şi Valahiei*, III, Bucharest, (1874): 450–462).

Belin, M. "Fetoua relatif à la condition des zimmis et particulièrement des chrétiens en pays musulmans, depuis l'établissement de l'islamisme, jusqu'au milieu du VIIIe siècle de l'Hégire. Traduit de l'arabe." *JA*, 4e série, t. XVIII, (1851): 417–516; t. XIX, (1852): 97–140.

Belin, M. *Étude sur la propriété foncière en pays musulmane et spécialement en Turquie (rite hanéfite)*, Paris, 1862 (offprint from *JA*, XVIII, (1861) : 477–517; XIX, 74, (1862) : 156–212; XIX, 75, (1862) : 257–358).

Bennigsen, Alexandre, Pertev Naili Boratov, Dilek Desaive, Chantal Lemercier-Quelquejay (eds). *Le Khanat de Crimée dans les Archives du Musée du Palais de Topkapy*, Paris: La Haye, 1978.

Berindei, M., and G. Veinstein. "Règlements fiscaux et fiscalité de la province de Bender-Aqkerman. 1570." *CMRS* XXII, 2–3, (1981): 251–328.

Berindei, M., M. Kalus-Martin and G. Veinstein, "Actes de Murad III sur la région de Vidin et remarques sur les qânun ottomans." *SF*, XXXV, (1976): 11–68.

Berindei, Mihnea and Gilles Veinstein, *L'Empire Ottoman et les Pays Roumains. 1544–1545. Étude et documents*, Paris: Éditions de l'ÉHÉSS, Cambridge : Harvard Ukrainian Research Institute, 1987.

Bianchi, M. "Recueil des Fetvas, écrit en turc et en arabe, par Hafiz Mohammed ben Ahmad ben Elcheich Moustafa Elkedousy." *JA* IV, (1824): 171–185.

Blochet, E. *Catalogue des Manuscrits Turcs de la Bibliothèque Nationale,* vol. I: Ancien Fonds, nos. 1–396, Supplément nos. 1–572. vol II: Supplément nos. 573–1419, Paris: Bibliothèque Nationale, 1932.

Bogdan, I. *Documente privitoare la relaţiile Ţării Romaneşti cu Braşovul în secolele XV şi XVI,* vol. I, Bucharest: Carol Göbl, 1905.

Bogdan, I. *Documentele lui Ştefan cel Mare,* vol. I–II, Bucharest, Atelierele Grafice Socec, 1913.

Bojović, Bosko I. "Dubrovnik (Raguse) et les Ottomans. II: Onze actes de Mehmed II en vieux-serbe. 1473–1476." *Turcica*, XXIV, (1992) : 155–181.

Bojović, Bosko I. "Dubrovnik et les Ottomans (1430–1472). 20 actes de Murad II et de Mehmed II en médio-serbe." *Turcica* XIX, (1987): 119–173.

Bojović. Boško I. *Raguse (Dubrovnik) et l'Empire Ottoman (1430–1520). Les actes imperiaux ottomans en vieux-serbe de Murad II à Selim Ier,* Paris: Association Perre Belon, 1998.

Brancovici, Gheorghe. *Cronica Românească,* critical edition by Damaschin Mioc and Marieta Adam-Chiper, Bucharest : Editura Academiei, 1987.

*Byzantium, Europe, and the Early Ottoman Sultans, 1373–1513: An Anonymous Greek Chronicle of the Seventeenth Century (Codex Barberinus Graecus 111)*. Translated and Annotated by Marios Philippides, New Rochelle, New York: A.D. Caratzas, 1990.

Cammelli, G. (ed.). *Démétrius Cydonès Correspondance*, Paris : Assocn G. Budé, 1930.

Cantemir, Demetrius, *The History of the Growth and Decay of the Othman Empire*. Part I. *Containing the Growth of the Ottoman Empire from the Reign of Othman the Founder, to the Reign of Mahomet IV. That is from the Year 1300, to the Siege of Vienna, in 1683.* Translated into English, from the Author's own Manuscript, by N. Tindal, M.A., Vicar of Great Waltham in Essex, London, 1734, 1–272. Part II. *The History of the Decay of the Othman Empire from the Reign of Mahomet IV. to the Reign of Ahmed III. Being the History of the Author's own Times.* Written Originally in Latin, by... late Prince of Moldavia. Translated into English, from the Author's own Manuscript, by

N. Tindal, M.A., Vicar of Great Waltham in Essex, London, 1735, 273–454. + *Preface* (I–XVI) + *The Life of Demetrius Cantemir, Prince of Moldavia*, 455–460.

Cantemir, Dimitrie. *Descrierea Moldovei* (*Descriptio antiqvi et hodierni statvs Moldaviae*), translated by Gh. Guțu, introduced by M. Holban, commentary by N. Stoicescu, Bucharest, Editura Academiei, 1973.

Cantemir, Dimitrie. *Viața lui Constantin Cantemir* (ed.). Radu Albala, Bucharest: Editura de Stat pentru Literatură și Artă, 1973.

Cantemir, Dimitrie. *Sistemul sau întocmirea religiei muhammedane* (*The System of Muhammedan Religion*) (ed.). Virgil Cândea, Bucharest, Editura Minerva, 1977 (re-edited together with the Russian original text in *Opere Complete*, VIII, II, Bucharest: Editura Academiei, 1987).

Cantimir, Demetrius. *Istoria creșterilor și a descreșterilor Curții Othman[n]ice sau Aliothman[n]ice de la primul început al neamului, adusă pînă în vremurile noastre, în trei cărți*, Translated by Dan Slușanschi, Ediția a II-a revizuită, Bucharest: Editura Paideia, 2012.

Çatalcalı Ali Efendi. *Fatava-yi Ali Efendi*, neșreden Sâlih b. Ahmad Kefevi, Istanbul, 1272 AH/1855.

Caurroy, M. Du. "Législation musulmane sunnite: rite hanéfi." *JA* IV série, vol. 12, (1848): 5–44; IV/13 (1849), 120–63; IV/16 (1850), 476–519; IV/17 (1851), 211–55, 568–91; IV/18 (1851), 290–321; IV/19 (1852), 519–50; V/1 (1853), 39–91; V/2 (1853), 471–528.

Celalzade, Mustafa. *Tabakat ül-memalik ve derecat ül-mesalik* (ed.). Sa'adeddin Tokdemir, Istanbul, 1937 (excerpts in *Cronici turcești I*, 257–77).

Chalcocondil, Laonic. *Expuneri istorice*, trans. V. Grecu, Bucharest: Editura Academiei, 1958 (in *FHDR*, IV, 450–517).

Charrière, E. *Négociations de la France dans le Levant ou correspondances, mémoires et actes diplomatiques des ambassadeurs de France à Constantinople*, vols. I–IV, Paris: Imprimerie Nationale, 1848–1860.

Corfus, Ilie (ed.). *Documente privitoare la istoria României culese din arhivele polone. Secolul al XVI-lea*, Bucharest: Editura Academiei, 1979.

Corfus, Ilie (ed.). *Documente privitoare la istoria României culese din arhivele polone. Secolul al XVII-lea*, Bucharest: Editura Academiei, 1983.

Costăchescu, M. (ed.). *Documente moldovenești înainte de Ștefan cel Mare*, vols. 1–2, Iași: Viața Românească, 1932.

*Crestomație pentru studiul istoriei statului si dreptului RPR, II, Feudalismul I*, Șt. Pascu and V. Hanga (eds). Bucharest: Editura Științifică, 1958.

*Crestomație turcă* – Mihail Guboglu (ed.). *Crestomație turcă. Izvoare narative privind istoria Europei centrale și orientale (1263–1683)*, University of Bucharest, 1977.

Critobul din Imbros, *Din domnia lui Mehmed al II-lea. Anii 1451–1467*, edited by V. Grecu, Bucharest: Editura Academiei 1963 (also in *FHDR*, IV, 518–537). Other edition:

Critovoulos, *History of Mehmed the Conqueror by Critovoulos*, translated from the Greek by Charles T. Riggs, Westport, Connecticut: Greenwood Press, 1954.

*Cronici turcești privind Țările române. Extrase. Vol. I. Sec. XV – mijlocul sec. XVII* (ed.). Mihail Guboglu and Mustafa Mehmet, Bucharest: Editura Academiei, 1966.

*Cronici turcești privind Țările române. Extrase. Vol. II. Sec. XVII – începutul sec. XVIII* (ed.). Mihail Guboglu, Bucharest: Editura Academiei, 1974.

*Cronici turcești privind Țările române. Extrase. Vol. III. Sfârșitul sec. XV – începutul sec. XIX* (ed.). Mustafa Mehmet, Bucharest: Editura Academiei, 1980.

*Cronicul lui Chesarie Daponte de la 1648–1704*, in C. Erbiceanu, *Cronicarii greci carii au scris despre români în epoca fanariotă*, textul grecesc și traducerea românească, Bucharest: Tipografia cărților bisericesci, 1888, 5–63.

D'Ohsson, Ignace Mouradgea. *Tableau général de l'Empire Othoman,* vol. I–VII, Paris : l'Imprimerie de Monsieur, 1787–1824.

Dalsar, F., "Selim I'in Dubrovnik Cumhuriyeti ile yaptiği muahede." *TV*, vol. II, 12, (1943): 410–414.

Hurmuzaki, *Documente* – Eudoxiu de Hurmuzaki, I. Bogdan, N. Densușeanu, et al. (eds). *Documente privitoare la istoria românilor culese de Eudoxiu de Hurmuzaki,*, Bucharest: I/2 (1346–1450), 1890; II/1 (1451–1575), 1891; II/5 (1552–1575), 1897; III/1 (1576–1599), 1880; IV/1 (1600–1649), 1880; VI (1700–1750), 1878; VIII (1376–1650), 1894; XI (1517–1612), 1900; XIV/3 (1560–1820), 1936; XVII (1825–1846), 1913; Supl. I/1 (1518–1700), 1886; Supl. I/5 (1822–1838), 1894; Supl. I/1 (1510–1600), 1893; Supl. II/2 (1601–1640), 1895; Supl. II/3 (1641–1703), 1900.

*Documenta Romaniae Historica. A. Moldova,* vol. II (1449–1486), Bucharest: Editura Academiei, 1976.

*Documenta Romaniae Historica. D. Relațiile între Țările Române,* vol. I, Bucharest: Editura Academiei, 1977.

Ducas. *Istoria turco-bizantină* (*1341–1462*), critical edition by V. Grecu, Bucharest: Editura Academiei, 1958 (in *FHDR*, IV, 416–37); Doukas, *Decline and Fall of Byzantium to the Ottoman Turks, An Annotated Translation of "Historia Turco-Byzantina"* by Harry J. Magoulias, Detroit: Wayne State University Press, 1975.

Düzdağ, M. E. *Şeyhülslam Ebussuud Efendi fetvalar ışığında 16. asır türk hayat,* Istanbul: Enderun, 1983.

Enveri, *Düsturname* – Irène Mélikoff-Sayar, *Le Destan d'Umur Pacha*, Paris: Presses Universitaires de France, 1954; Mükrimin Halil, *Düsturname-yi Enveri,* Istanbul, 1928 (excerpts in *Cronici turcești I,* 33–45).

Erbiceanu, C. *Cronicarii greci carii au scris despre Români în epoca fanariotă*, Greek text and Romanian translation, Bucharest: Tipografia cărților bisericesci, 1888.

Eton, W. *A Survey of the Turkish Empire. In which are considered, I. Its Government, Finances, Military and Naval Force, Religion, History, Arts, Sciences, Manners, Commerce, and Population. II. The State of the Provinces III. The Causes of the Decline of*

*Turkey.* IV. *The British Commerce with Turkey*, London: T. Cadell and W. Davies, 1798 (reprinted in 1973).

*Eyyubî Efendi Kânûnnâmesi.* Tahlil ve Metin. Yayına Hazırlayan: Prof. dr. Abdülkadir Özcan, Istanbul: EREN Yayıncılık, 1994.

Fekete, L. *Einführung in die osmanisch – türkische Diplomatik der türkischen Botmässigkeit in Ungarn. Faksimiles*, Budapest: Könighliche Ungarische Universitätsdruckerei, 1926.

Fekete, L. *Turkische Schriften aus des Palatins Nikolaus Esterhazy*, Budapest: Archives princières Esterhazy, 1932.

Feridun, Ahmed Bey. *Mecmuʿa-ı Münşeʾat es-Selâtin*, I–II, Istanbul: Takvimhane-yi Âmire, 1264–1265 AH / 1848–1849.

Filstich, Johann. *Încercare de Istorie Românească*, edited by Adolf Ambruster, Bucharest: Editura Ştiinţifică şi Enciclopedică, 1979.

Fotino, Dionisie. *Istoria generală a Daciei sau a Transilvaniei, Ţării Munteneşti şi a Moldovei*, trans. George Sion, Bucharest: Imprimeria Naţională a lui Iosef Romanov et Companie, 1859 (reedited in 2008).

Gemil, Tahsin. *Relaţiile Ţărilor române cu Poarta otomană în documente turceşti. 1601–1712*, Bucharest: Direcţia Generală a Arhivelor Statului, 1984.

*Genealogia Cantacuzinilor de Banul Mihai Cantacuzino* (ed.). Nicolae Iorga, Bucharest: Institutul de Arte Grafice și Editura Minerva, 1902.

Gökbilgin, M. T. "Korvin Matthias (Máttyás)'ın Bayezid II.e mektupları tercümeleri ve 1503 Macar-Osman muahedesinin Türkçe metni / La traduction des lettres de Korvin Matthias à Bayezid II et le texte turc du traité hungaro-turc de 1503 (909)." *Belleten*, XXII, 87, (1958): 369–390.

Göllner, Carl. *Turcica.* Vols. I–II. *Die europäischen Türkendrucke des XVI. Jahrhunderts*, Bucharest, Editura Academiei, Berlin: Akademie-Verlag, 1961; Bucharest: Editura Academiei, Baden-Baden: Verlag Librarie Hertz, 1968; III. Vol. *Die Türkenfrage in der öffentlichen Meinung Europas im 16. Jahrhundert*, Bucharest: Editura Academiei, Baden-Baden: Verlag Librarie Hertz, 1978.

Greceanu, Radu logofătul. *Istoria domniei lui Constantin Basarab Brâncoveanu Voievod (1688–1714)*, critical edition by Aurora Ilieș, Bucharest: Editura Academiei, 1970.

Grotius, Hugo. *Despre dreptul războiului și al păcii*, edited, annotated, and commentary by George Dumitriu, Bucharest: Editura Științifică, 1968 (Romanian translation of Hugonis Grotii, *De iure belli ac pacis. Libri tres. In quibus ius nature & Gentium: item iuris publici praecipua explicantur*, Paris : Nicolaum Buon, 1625).

Guboglu, Mihail. "Șapte documente turcești din arhivele Brașovului privind relațiile Transilvaniei cu Poarta otomană la începutul secolului al XVII-lea." *RA*, VIII, 1, (1965): 213–256.

Guboglu, Mihail. *Catalogul documentelor turcești*, Bucharest: Direcția Generală a Arhivelor Statului, vol. I, 1960; vol. II (1455–1829), 1965.

Guer, M. *Moeurs et usages des Turcs, leur religion, leur gouvernament civil, militaire et polititque, avec un abrégé de l'histoire ottomane*, I–II, Paris: Merigot & Piget, 1746–1747.

Halebi, Ibrahim. *Şerh-i Mülteka el-Ebhür* (*Mevkufat*), Tercüme ve Açıklamalar Nedim Yılmaz, vols. 1–4, Istanbul : İlmi Neşriyat, 1993 (especially, vol. 2, 559–628); Mehmed Mevkufati, *Şerh-i Mülteka el-Ebhür*, vols. I–II, Istanbul, 1254 AH/1838–1839.

Hamidullah, Muhammad. *Documents sur la diplomatie musulmane à l'époque du Prophète et des Khalifes Orthodoxes*, Paris: G. P. Maisonneuve, 1935.

Hamidullah, Muhammad. "Nouveaux documents sur les rapports de l'Europe avec l'Orient musulman au Moyen Âge." *Arabica*, VII, (1960): 281–298.

Hasan Vecihi, *Tarih*, TKSMK, Revan 1153 (excerpts in *Cronici turcești II*, 166–188).

Holban, M., M. M. Alexandrescu-Dersca Bulgaru, and P. Cernovodeanu (eds). *Călători străini despre Țările Române*, Bucharest: Editura Științifică și Enciclopedică; Editura Academiei Române, I, 1968; II, 1970; III, 1971; IV, 1972; V, 1973; VI, 1976; VII, 1980; VIII, 1983.

Hüsrev, Molla. *Dürer ül-hukkam fî șerh gürer ül-ahkam*, I, Istanbul : Matbaa-i Amire, 1258 AH/1842–1843, 205–210.

Idris Bitlisi, *Heşt Behişt*, translated by Abdulbaki Sa'di, 1146 AH/1733 (excerpts in *Cronici turcești I*, 149–174).

Inalcık, H., M. Oguz (eds). *Gazavat-i Sultan Murad bin Mehmed Han. Izlâdi ve Varna savaşları (1443–1444) üzerine Anonim Gazavatnâme*, Ankara: T.T.K. Basımevi, 1978.

*Independența României. Documente. vol. IV: Documente diplomatice (1873–1881)*, Bucharest: Editura Academiei, 1978.

Ionașcu, I., P. Bărbulescu, Gh. Gheorghe (eds). *Relațiile internaționale ale României în documente (1368–1900). Culegere selectivă de tratate, acorduri, convenții și alte acte cu caracter internațional*, Bucharest: Editura Politică, 1971.

Iorga, Nicolae. "Privilegiul lui Mohammed al II-lea pentru Pera (1-iu iunie 1453)." *AARMSI*, seria II, vol. XXXVI, Bucharest, 1913 (offprint).

Iorga, Nicolae. *Acte și fragmente cu privire la Istoria Românilor*, III, Bucharest: Imprimeria statului, 1897.

Iorga, Nicolae, *Scrisori de boieri. Scrisori de domni*, ediția a II-a, Vălenii-de-Munte : Așezământul Tipografic „Datina Românească", 1925.

Iorga, Nicolae. *Studii și documente cu privire la Istoria Românilor*. vol. XI: *Cercetări și regeste documentare*, Bucharest: Editura Ministerului de Instrucție, 1906; vol. XXIII: *Acte privitoare la comerțul românesc cu Lembergul*, Bucharest: Editura Ministerului de Instrucție, 1913, 328–399; 410–454.

*Istoria politică și geografică a Țerei Românesci de la cea mai veche a sa întemeere până la anul 1774, dată mai ântâiu în limba grecească la anul 1806 de Frații Tunusli*, translated by G. Sion, Bucharest : Tipographia Națională a lui Stephan Rassidescu, 1863.

Kara-Çelebi-Zade, *Ravdat ül-ebrar*, Bulak, 1248 AH/1832–1833 (excerpts in *Cronici turcești* I, 541–559); *Süleymannâme*, Bulak, 1248 AH/ 1832–1833 (excerpts in *Cronici turcești* I, 527–540).

Karatay, Fehmi Edhem. *Topkapı Sarayı Müzesi Kütüphanesi Türkçe Yazmalar Kataloğu, vol. I. Din, Tarih, Bilimler. No. 1–1985; vol. II. Filoloji, Edebiyat, Mecmualar. No. 1986–3088*, Istanbul: Topkapı Sarayı Müzesi, 1961.

Kárman, Gábor. "The 'Ahdname of Sultan Mehmed III to András Báthori, Prince of Transylvania." in *Contemporary Research in Turcology and Eurasian Studies: A Festschrift in Honor of Professor Tasin Gemil on the Occasion of Hi Cluj University Press s 70th Birthday* (eds). Stoica Lascu and Melek Fetisleam, Cluj: Cluj University Press, 2013, 435–345.

Kâtib Çelebi (Hacı Halifa), *Fezleke-i Tarih*, Istanbul, I–II, 1286–1287 AH/ 1869–1870 (excerpts in *Cronici turcești* II, 29–104).

Kemalpaşazade (Ibn Kemal) *Tevarih-i Al-i Osman. VII. Defter*, Ankara: hazırlayan: Şeraffetin Turan, 1954, Ankara, 1957 (excerpts in *Cronici turcești*, I, 191–218); Ibn Kemal, *Tevarih-i Al-i Osman. I. Defter*, Ankara: TTK Basımevi, 1970, *II. Defter*, Ankara: TTK Basımevi, 1983.

Kemalpaşazade, *Fetihname-i sefer-i Mohaç li-mevlana Kemalpaşazade* (excerpts in *Crestomație turcă*, 299–362).

Khadduri, M. (ed.). *Shaybani's Siyar – The Islamic Law of Nations. Shaybani's Siyar*, Baltimore, Maryland: The Johns Hopkins Press, 1966.

Kıvami, *Fetihnâme* – F. Babinger, *Fetihnâme-i Sultan Mehmed*, müellifi: *Kıvami*, Istanbul: Maarif Basımevi, 1955.

Knolles, Richard. *The Generall Historie of the Turkes, from The first beginning of that Nation to the rising of the Othoman Familie: with all the notable expeditions of the Christian Princes against them. Together with the Lives and Conquests of the Othoman Kings and Emperors. Faithfullie collected out of the best Histories, both auntient and moderne, and digested into one continuat Historie until this present yeare 1603*, London: Printed by Adam Islip, 1603 (my quotations are made from the 6th Edition, 1687: *The Turkish History, from the Original of that Nation, to the Growth of the Ottoman Empire: with the Lives and Conquests of their Princes and Emperors.* By Richard Knolles sometime Fellow of Lincoln College in Oxford. *With a Continuation to this Present Year MDCLXXXVII. Whereunto is added The Present State of the Ottoman Empire.* By Sir Paul Rycaut, late Consul of Smyrna. The Sixth Edition, with the Effigies of all the Kings and Emperors. The first Volume. London, 1687).

Koca Hüseyin, *Beda'i ül-veka'i* (ed.). A. S. Tveretinova, I–II, Moscow, 1961 (excerpts in *Cronici turcești* I, 437–468).

Kogălniceanu, Mihail. *Cronicele României seu Letopisețele Moldaviei și Valahiei*, I–III, Bucharest: Imprimeria Națională, 1872–1874 (vol. I–II 1872; vol. III 1874).

Kołodziejczyk, Dariusz. *Ottoman-Polish Diplomatic Relations (15th -18th Century). An Annotated Edition of 'Ahdnames and Other Documents.* Leiden–Boston–Cologne: Brill, 2000.

Kraelitz, Fr.. "Kanunnamé des Sultans Mehmeds des Eroberers." *MOG*, Vienna, I, (1921): 13–48.

*Kur'an – The Glorious Kur'an*, Translation and Commentary by Abdallah Yousuf Ali, Lahore, 1973; *Le Saint Coran,* translation and commentary by Muhmmad Hamidullah, New Edition, Publiée par Amana Corporation, 1989; *Kur'an-ı Kerim ve Türkçe Açıklamalı Meali,* Hazırlayanlar: Ali Özek, Medine-i Münevere, 1412 AH/1992; *Coranul*, translated from the Arabic by Dr. Silvestru Octavian Isopescul, Chernivtsi: Editura Autorului, 1912 (reedited Cluj-Napoca: Editura ETA, 1992).

Laoust, H. *Contribution à l'étude de la méthodologie canonique de Takî-d-dîn Ahmad b. Taimîya*, Le Caire : Institut français d'archéologie orientale, 1939.

Laoust, H. *La profession de foi d'Ibn Batta*, text and traduction, Damascus: Institut français, 1958.

*Letopisețul cantacuzinesc. Istoria Țării Românești. 1290–1690*, critical edition C. Grecescu and D. Simonescu, Bucharest: Editura Academiei Române, 1960.

Lewis, Bernard. *Islam from the Prophet Muhammad to the Capture of Constantinople,* I–II, London: Macmillan, 1976.

Lütfi pașa, *Tevarih-i Al-i Osman*, Istanbul: Matbaa-i Amire, 1341 AH/1923 (excerpts in *Cronici turcești I*, 233–250, and in *Crestomație turcă*, 363–376).

Majda, T. "A Letter by Sultan Mehmed III to King Sigismund III in Polish Transcription." *RO,* XXXVIII, 1976, 199–203.

Mas Latrie, M. L. de. *Traités de paix et de commerce et documents divers concernant les relations des Chrétiens avec les Arabes de l'Afrique septentrionale au Moyen Âge,* Paris: Henri Plon, 1866.

Mawerdi, Aboul-Hasan Ali. *Al-Ahkâm al-Sultâniyah* (*Les Statuts Gouvernementaux ou règles de droit public et administratif*). Traduction et notes de E. Fagnan, Alger, Paris : Typographie Adolphe Jourdan, 1915; *Al-Ahkam as-Sultaniyyah. The Laws of Islamic Governance,* by Abu'l-Hasan 'Ali ibn Muhammad ibn Habib al-Basri al-Baghdadi al-Mawardi (d. 450 H.), translated by Dr. Asadullah Yate, London, 1996.

Mawerdi. *Le droit du Califat*, introduction, translation and notes by Comte Léon Ostrorog, Paris: Ernest Leroux, 1925.

Maxim, *CTO* – Maxim, Mihai, *Culegere de texte otomane. Fasc.I. Izvoare documentare și juridice* (*sec. XV-XX*), University of Bucharest, 1974.

Mehmed bin Mehmed, *Nuhbet üt-Tevarih ve'l-ahbar,* Istanbul, 1276 AH/1860 (excerpts in *Cronici turcești I,* 399–436).

Mehmed Halife. *Tarih-i Gılmanı* (ed.). A. Refik, in *TOEM*, (1924–1925), no. 78–83; Mehmed Halife, *Tarih-i Gılmanı,* Hazırlayan: Kâmil SU, Ankara, 1986 (excerpts in *Cronici turcești II*, 189–202).

Mehmed paşa, *Tarih-i Nişancı Mehmed Paşa* (ed.). Ahmed Vefik Paşa, Istanbul, 1279 AH/1862; Karamanlı Nişancı Mehmed paşa, *Tevarih al-Selatin al-Osmaniye,* in *Osmanlı Tarihleri,* I, 321–62 (excerpts in *Cronici turceşti I,* 289–98).

Mehmed Raşid, *Tarih,* I–V, Istanbul, 1282 AH/1856–1866 (excerpts in *Cronici turceşti III,* 129–252).

Mehmet, M. A. *Documente turceşti privind istoria României. vol. I (1455–1774)*, Bucharest : Editura Academiei, 1976; M. A. Mehmet, *Documente turceşti privind istoria României. Vol. II (1774–1791)*, Bucharest : Editura Academiei, 1983; M. A. Mehmet, *Documente turceşti privind istoria României. Vol. III (1791–1812)*, Bucharest : Editura Academiei, 1986.

Melissenos, Macarie. *Cronica 1258–1481*. In Georgios Sphrantzes, *Memorii. 1401–1477*. Annex: Pseudo-Phrantzes: Macarie Melissenos, *Cronica. 1258–1481*, critical edition by V. Grecu, Bucharest: Editura Academiei, 1966.

*Menakib-i Sultan Bayezid Han ibn Mehmed Han* (excerpts in *Cronici turceşti I,* 135–140).

Mihăescu, H., R. Lazarescu, N. Ş. Tanaşoca, et al. (eds). *Fontes Historiae Daco-Romanae,* vol. IV: *Scriitori şi acte bizantine. Secolele IV-XV*, Bucharest: Editura Academiei, 1982.

*Mihai Viteazul în conştiinţa europeană. 1. Documente externe,* Bucharest: Editura Academiei, 1982.

Mihailović, Konstantin. *Memoirs of a Janissary,* translated by B. Stolz, Ann Arbor, MI: The University of Michigan Press, 1975.

Miron Costin. *Letopiseţul Ţărîi Moldovei de la Aron vodă încoace,* in Miron Costin, *Opere,* critical edition by P. P. Panaitescu, Bucharest: Editura de Stat pentru Literatură şi Artă, 1958, 41–201.

Miron Costin. *Opere,* critical edition by P.P. Panaitescu, Bucharest: Editura de Stat pentru Literatură şi Artă, 1958, 277–314.

Moxa, Mihail, *Cronica universală,* critical edition by G. Mihăilă, Bucharest : Editura Minerva, 1989.

Mühieddin el-Cemâlı, *Tevarih* – Fr. Giese, *Die altosmanischen anonymen Chroniken* (*Tevarih-i Âl-i Osman*), Teil I, Breslau, 1922 (excerpts in *Cronici turceşti,* I, 188–190, and in *Crestomaţie turcă,* 271–298).

*Mühimme Defteri 3 – 3 Numaralı Mühimme Defteri (966–968/1558–1560) <Özet ve Transkripsiyon>*, Ankara: T.C. Başbakanlık Devlet Arşivleri Genel Müdürlüğü,, 1993.

*Mühimme Defteri 5 – 5 Numaralı Mühimme Defteri (973/1565–1566). <Özet ve Indeks>* and *<Tıpkıbasım>*, Ankara: T.C. Başbakanlık Devlet Arşivleri Genel Müdürlüğü, 1994.

*Mühimme Defteri 6 – 6 Numaralı Mühimme Defteri (972/1564–1565). <Özet – Transkripsyon ve Indeks>*, I–II, Ankara: T.C. Başbakanlık Devlet Arşivleri Genel Müdürlüğü, 1995.

*Mühimme Defteri 7 – 7 Numaralı Mühimme Defteri (975–976/1567–1569). <Özet – Transkripsyon – Indeks>*, I–II, Ankara: T.C. Başbakanlık Devlet Arşivleri Genel Müdürlüğü, 1998.

*Mühimme Defteri 12 – 12 Numaralı Mühimme Defteri (978–979/1570–1572). <Özet – Transkripsyon ve Indeks>*, I–II, Ankara: T.C. Başbakanlık Devlet Arşivleri Genel Müdürlüğü, 1996.

Müneccimbaşı, *Saha'if ül-ahbar*, III, Istanbul: Matbaa-yı Amire, 1285 AH/1868–1869 (excerpts in *Cronici turceşti III*, 231–75).

Mustafa Ali. *Künh ül-Ahbar* (ed.). Ahmed Cevdet, Istanbul, 1277 AH/1862 (excerpts in *Cronici turceşti I*, 333–56).

*Naima Tarihi*, Istanbul, 1280 AH/1863–1864 (excerpts in *Cronici turceşti*, III, 1–128, and *Crestomaţie turcă*, 660–768). Other edition: Mustafa Naima, *Annals of the Turkish Empire, from 1591 to 1659 of the Christian Era*. Translated by Ch. Fraser, vol. I, London: The Oriental Translation Fund, 1832.

Nasuh Matrakçi, *Fetihnâme-yi Kara-Boğdân*, TKSMK, R. 1284 (excerpts in *Cronici turceşti I*, 219–32).

Neculce, Ion. *Opere. Letopiseţul Ţării Moldovei şi O samă de cuvinte*, edited by Gabriel Ştrempel, Bucharest: Editura Minverva, 1982.

Neşri, *Tarih* – Franz Taeschner, *Gihannüma. Die altosmanische Chronik des Mevlâna Mehemmed Neschrî*, vol. I, Leipzig, 1951, vol. II, Leipzig, 1955 (excerpts in *Cronici turceşti I*, 110–134, and in *Crestomaţie turcă*, 243–270). Other edition used: Mehmed Neşri, *Kitâb-ı Cihan-nüma. Neşri Tarihi* (ed.). Faik Reşit Unat, Mehmed A. Köymen, vols. I–II, Ankara: TTK Basımevi, 1987 (1st edition 1947).

Nicolae, Costin. *Letopiseţul Ţării Moldovei de la zidirea lumii până la 1601*, edited by C. Stoide and I. Lăzărescu, Iaşi : Editura Junimea, 1971.

Noradounghian, Gabriel. *Recueil d'actes internationaux de l'Empire Ottoman*, vols. I–IV, Paris: F. Pichon, 1897–1903 (especially, vol. I: 1300–1789), Paris, 1897.

Orhonlu, Cengiz. *Osmanlı tarihine aid belgeler. Telhisler (1597–1607)*, Istanbul: İstanbul Üniversitesi Edebiyat Fakültesi yayınları, 1970.

Oruc bin Adil, *Tevarih* – Fr. Babinger, *Jahrbücher des Urudsc. Nach den Handschriften*, Hanovra, 1925; *Oruç Beğ Tarihi* (ed.). A. Nihal Atsız, Istanbul, 1972; excerpts in *Cronici turceşti I*, 47–64, and *Crestomaţie turcă*, 208–242.

Panaite, Viorel. *News in England on the Great Turkish War (1683–1699)*, Académie Roumaine, Institut d'Études Sud-Est Européennes, Brăila: Editura Istros a Muzeului Brăilei "Carol I", 2018.

Panaitescu, P. P. (ed.). *Cronicile slavo-române din sec. XV-XVI, publicate de Ioan Bogdan*. Revised and completed edition, Bucharest: Editura Academiei, 1959.

Papp, Sándor. *Die Verleihungs-, Bekräftigungs- und Vertragsurkunden der Osmanen für Ungarn und Siebenbürgen: Eine quellenkritische Untersuchung*, Vienna: VÖAW, 2003.

Paul of Aleppo. *Jurnal de călătorie în Moldova şi Valahia* (ed.). Ioana Feodorov, Bucharest: Editura Academiei Române, 2014.

Peçevi, *Tarih – Tarih-i Peçevi* (ed.). Kemal Efendi, I–II, Istanbul, 1281–1283 AH/1864–1867 (excerpts in *Cronici turceşti* I, 469–525). Other editions used: *Peçevi Tarihi* (ed.). B. Ş. Baykal, vols. I–II, Ankara, 1981–1982.

Petritsch, E. D., "Der Habsburgisch-Osmanische Friedensvertrag des Jahres 1547." *MOS* 38, (1985): 49–80.

Popescu, Radu, *Istoriile domnilor Țărîi Româneşti de Radu Popescu*, in *Cronicari munteni* (ed.). Mihail Gregorian, vol. I, Bucharest: Editura pentru literatură, 1961, 225–578.

Porter, James, *Observations. The State of the Turkey Trade from its Origin to the Present Time*, London: J. Nourse, 1771.

*Războieni. 500 de ani de la Campania din 1476* (ed.). Manole Neagoe, Bucharest : Direcția Generală a Arhivelor Statului, 1977.

Reland, A. *La religion des Mahométans, exposée par leurs propres docteurs, avec les éclaircisments sur les opinions qu'on leur a faussement attribuées*, The Hague: Isaac Vaillant, 1721.

*Reprezentanța diplomatică a Moldovei la Constantinopol (30 august 1741-decembrie 1742). Rapoartele inedite ale agenților lui Constantin Mavrocordat* (ed.). Ariadna Camariano-Cioran, Bucharest: Editura Academiei, 1985.

Rustem paşa, *Tarih* – L. Forrer, *Die Osmanische Chronik des Rustem Pascha* (*Tarih-i Al-i Osman*), Leipzig: Mayer & Műller, 1923, and excerpts in *Cronici turceşti*, I, 251–256.

Rusu, P. I. *Principiul respectării tratatelor. Tradiție și actualitate*, Bucharest: Editura Științifică, 1992.

Rycaut, Paul. *The History of the Turkish Empire From the year 1623. to the year 1677. Containing the Reigns of the Three Last Emperours, Viz. Sultan Morat, or Amurat IV. Sultan Ibrahim, and sultan Mahomet IV. his Son, The XIII. Emperour now Reigning.* By Sir Paul Rycaut Efq; late Consul of Smyrna. London: Printed by J. M. for John Starkey, 1680 (2nd edition in 1687).

Rycaut, Paul. *The History of the Turks. Beginning with the year 1679. Being a full Relation of the Last Troubles in Hungary, with the Sieges of Vienna, and Buda, and all the several Battles both by Sea and Land, between the Christians, and the Turks, until the End of the Year 1698, and 1699. In which The Peace between the Turks, and the Confederate Christian Princes and States, was happily Concluded at Carlowitz in Hungary, By the Mediation of His Majesty of Great Britain, and the States General of the United Provinces.* London: Printed for Robert Clabell, in St. Paul's Church-Yard, and Abel Roper against St. Dunstan's Church in Fleetstreet, 1700.

Rycaut, Paul. *The Present State of the Ottoman Empire. Containing the Maxims of the Turkish Politie, the most material Points of the Mahometan Religion, their Sects and Heresies, their Convents and Religious Votaries. Their Military Discipline with an exact*

*Computation of their Forces both by Land and Sea*, London: Printed John Starkey and Henry Brome, 1668. (French translation: Paul Ricaut, *Tableau de l'Empire Ottoman, ou l'on trouve les moeurs et coutumes des turcs, leurs lois, leur religions, leur differentes sectes, l'état de leurs forces par mer et par terre; et généralment tout ce qui concerne leur gouvernament civil, militaire et ecclesiastique*, The Hague, 1709).

Sa'adeddin, Mehmed Hoca, *Tac üt-Tevarih*, Istanbul, I–II, 1279–1280 AH/1862–1863; Hoca Sa'adeddin, *Tacü't-Tevarih* (ed.). Ismet Parmaksızoğlu, Istanbul, 1979 (excerpts in *Cronici turcești I*, 297–332).

Saint-Priest, Le Comte de. *Mémoires sur l'ambassade de France en Turquie et sur le commerce des Français dans le Levant*, Paris: Ernest Leroux, 1877.

Şakiroğlu, M .H. "1521 tarihli Osmanlı-Venedik andlaşmasının aslı metni." TED, 12, (1981–1982): 387–403.

Şakiroğlu, M. H. "1503 tarihli Türk-Venedik Andlaşması." In *VIII. Türk Tarih Kongresi*, vol. III, cilt'ten aırıbasım, Ankara: TTK Basımevi, 1983, 1559–1569.

Sarakhsi, *Şerh* – al-Sarakhsi, *Şerh al-Siyar al-Kabir*, türkçeye tercüme: Mehmed Münib 'Ayntabi, vols. I–II, Istanbul, 1241 AH/1825.

Savary. *Les lois morales, religieuses et civiles de Mahomet, extraites du Koran*, trans. de Savary, I–II, Paris : V. Lecou, 1850.

Schaendlinger, Anton C. *Die Schreiben Süleymans des Prächtingen au Karl V., Ferdinand I, und Maximilian II*, vol. I: *Transkriptionnen und Übersetzungen*; vol. II: *Faksimle*, Vienna : VÖAW, 1983.

Schiltberger, Johann. *The Bondage and Travels of Johann Schiltberger, a Native of Bavaria, in Europe, Asia, and Africa, 1396–1427*. Translated by J. Buchan Telfer, with notes by P. Bruun, London: The Hakluyt Society, 1879 (reprinted Frankfurt am Main: Institute for the History of Arabic-Islamic Science at the Wolfgang Goethe Universty, 1995).

Schwarz, Klaus. *Osmanische Sultansurkunden des Sinai-Klosters in türkisher Sprache*, Freiburg im Breisgau: Klaus Schwarz Verlag, 1970.

Selaniki, Mustafa Efendi. *Tarih-i Selaniki, I (971–1003 AH/1563–1595); II (1003–1008 AH/1595–1600*, Hazırlayan: Prof. dr. Mehmed Ipşirli, Istanbul: TTK Yayınları, 1989; *Tarih-i Selaniki Mustafa Efendi*, Istanbul: Matbaa-i amire 1281 AH/1864 (excerpts in *Cronici turcești I*, 357–98).

Selle, Friedrich. *Prozessrecht des 16. Jahrhunderts im Osmanischen Reich. Auf Grund von Fetwas des Scheichulislams Ebussuud und anderer unter des Regierung des Sultans Süleiman des Prächtingen*, Wiesbaden: Otto Harrassowitz, 1962.

Shaybani, *Kitab al-siyar* – Muhammad ibn al-Hasan ach-Chaibânî, *Le Grand Livre de la Conduite de l'Etat* (*Kitâb as-Siyar al-Kabîr*). *Commenté par… as-Sarakhsî*. Translated by M. Hamidullah, vols I–IV, Ankara: Editions Türkiye Diyanet Vakfi, 1989–1991.

Silahdar, Fındıklılı Mehmed Ağa. *Nusretname* (ed.). Ismet Parmaksızoğlu, I–II, Istanbul, 1962–1969 (excerpts in *Cronici turcești II*, 421–539); *Silahdar Tarihi*, I–II (ed.). A. Refik, Istanbul, 1928 (excerpts in *Cronici turcești II*, 287–420).

Siruni, H. Dj. "Acte turcești privitoare la hotarele dunărene ale Țării Românești." *RA*, v, 1, (1942): 129–165.

Siruni, H. Dj. ed. *Domnii români la Poarta Otomană. După un manuscris turcesc conținând note și însemnări despre ceremoniile și recepțiunile din palatul împărătesc din Stambul între anii 1698–1782*, Bucharest: Imprimeria Statului, 1941.

Siruni, H.Dj. "O corespondență turcească a lui Scarlat Callimachi, domnul Moldovei." *RI*, XVII, 7–9, (1931): 177–185.

Solakzade, Mehmed Hemdemi, *Tarih-i Solakade*, Istanbul, 1297 AH/1880 (excerpts in *Cronici turcești II*, 125–165).

Sphrantzes, Georgios. *Memorii. 1401–1477*, critical edition by V. Grecu, Bucharest: Editura Academiei, 1966 (in *FHDR*, IV, 438–449).

Stern, S.M. ed. *Documents from Islamic Chanceries*, Columbia: University of South Carolina Press, 1965.

Sturdza, D.A., and C. Colescu-Vartic (eds). *Acte şi documente relative la istoria renascerei României. Actes et Documents relatifs à l'histoire de la régénération de la Roumanie*, vol. 1, *1391–1841*, Bucharest : Institutul de Arte C. Göbl, 1900.

Sturdza, D. A., D. C. Sturdza, and G. Petrescu (eds). *Acte și documente relative la Istoria Renascerei României*, vol. I, Bucharest: Tipografia Carol Göbl, 1888.

Şükrullah, *Tevarih – XVinci asır tarihçisi Şükrullah: Dokuz boy Türkler ve Osmanlı sultanları tarihi* (ed.). Hüseyin Nihal Atsız, Istanbul, 1939 (excerpts in *Cronici turcești I*, 29–32).

Sulami, "Kitab al-djihad" – E. Sivan, "La genèse de la contre-croisade: un traité damasquin du début du XII-e siècle." *JA*, CCLIV, 2, (1966): 197–225 (Sulami's text was recently published in a critical edition: Niall Christies (ed.). *The Book of the Jihad of 'Ali ibn Tahir al-Sulamî (d. 1106)*, Aldershot: Ashgate, 2015).

Szamosközy, *Însemnări* – Ioachim Crăciun ed., *Cronicarul Szamosközy și însemnările lui privitoare la români. 1566–1608*, Cluj: Ardealul, 1928.

Tassy, Laugier de. *Histoire des États barbaresques qui exercent la piraterie, contenant l'origine, les révolutions de l'état preesent des royaumes d'Alger, de Tunis, de Tripoli et de Maroc, avec leurs forces, leurs revenus, leur politique et leurs commerce par un auteur qui a résidé plusieur années avec caractère public* (Laugier de Tassy), translated from English, 2 vols. Paris: Chaubert, 1757.

Tappe, E. D. *Documents concerning Romanian History (1427–1601) collected from British Archives*, The Hague: Mouton, 1964.

Testa, I. de. *Recueil des traités de la Porte Ottomane avec les puissances étrangères*, vols. I–VIII, Paris : Amyot, 1864–1896; vol. IX–X, edited by A. de Testa and L. de Testa, Paris, 1898–1901.

*Tevarih* – Fr. Giese, *Die altosmanischen anonymen Chroniken (Tevarih-i Al-i Osman)*, Teil I, *Text und Varianten*, Breslau: im Selbstverlag, 1922, vol. II, Leipzig, 1925;

A. Antalffy, "Veche cronică otomană ca izvor pentru istoria românilor." *RI*, XXIII, 7–9, (1937): 217–235 (excerpts in *Cronici turceşti*, I, 180–187, and *Crestomaţie turcă*, 271–298).

Thibault-Lefebvre. *Situation diplomatique de la Valachie à l'égard des puissances européennes*, Paris, 1857, 689–705 (offprint from *Correspondant de Paris*, 1857).

Theunissen, H. *Ottoman-Venetian Diplomatics: The 'Ahdnames, The Historical Background and the Development of a Category of Political-Commercial Instruments together with an Annotated Edition of a Corpus of Relevant Documents*, Dissertation, University of Utrecht, 1991 (EJOS: Electronic Journal of Oriental Studies, I, no 2, 1998, 1–698).

Thomas, George Martin. *Diplomatarium Veneto-Levantinum sive Acta et Diplomata res Venetas Graecas atque Levantis illustratia a.1300–1454*, vols. I-II, Venice: Typis Marci Visentini, 1880–1899.

Thornton, Thomas, *The Present State of Turkey or A Description of the Political, Civil and Religious, Constitution, Government and the Laws of the Ottoman Empire.... Together with the Geographical, Political, and Civil, State of the Principalities of Moldavia and Wallachia. From observations made during a residence of fifteenth years in Constantinople and the Turkish provinces*, vols. I–II, The second edition, with corrections and additions, London: Joseph Mawman, 1809.

Tietze, Andreas (ed.). *Mustafa Ali's Counsel for Sultans of 1581*, Vienna: Verl. d. Österr. Akad. d. Wiss, 1979.

Tijani, *Voyage – Voyage du Scheikh et-Tidjani dans la régence de Tunis, pendant les années 706, 707 et 708 de l'Hégira* (*1306–1309* de J.C.) translated from Arabic by M. Alphonse Rousseau, Paris: Imprimerie Impériale, 1853.

Tocilescu, Gr. G. *534 documente istorice slavo-române din Ţara Românească şi Moldova privitoare la legăturile cu Ardealul. 1346–1603*, Bucharest : Librăria „Cartea Românească", 1931.

Tornauw, Nicolas de. *Droit musulman exposé d'après les sources*, trans. M. Eschbach, Paris : Cotillon, 1860.

Turpin, Fr. H. *Histoire de l'Alcoran, où l'on découvre le systéme politique et religiuex de Faux-Prophète et les sources où il a puisé sa législation*, I–II, London, Paris : De Hansy, 1775.

Tursun Bey, *Tarih-i Ebü'l Feth Sultan Mehmed Han*, Hazırlayan. A. Mertol Tulum, Istanbul, 1972; *The History of Mehmed the Conqueror by Tursun Beg*, Text Published in Facsimile with English Translation by Halil Inalcık and Rhoads Murphey, Minneapolis & Chicago: Bibliotheca Islamica, 1978 (excerpts in *Cronici turceşti I*, 65–80).

Ubicini, A. ed. *La Constitution Ottomane du 7 Zilhidjè 1293* (*23 Décembre 1876*), with annotations by A. Ubicini, Paris: A Cotillon, 1877.

Ureche, Grigore. *Letopiseţul Ţării Moldovei*, edited by P. P. Panaitescu, Bucharest : Editura Minerva, 1987.

Uzunçarşılı, I. H. "On dokuzuncu asir başlarına kadar Türk-Ingiliz münasebetlerine dair vesikalar." *Belleten*, XIII, 51, (1949): 615–622.

Văcărescu, Ianache. *Istorie a prea puternicilor înpărați othomani*, in Poeții Văcărești, *Opere* (ed.). Cornel Cîrstoiu, Bucharest : Editura Minerva, 1982, 181–312.

Veliman, Valeriu. *Relațiile româno-otomane. (1711–1821). Documente turcești*, Bucharest : Direcția Generală a Arhivelor Statului, 1984.

Veress, Andrei. *Documente privitoare la istoria Ardealului, Moldovei și Țării Românești. Vol. II. Acte și scrisori (1573–1584)*, Bucharest : Cartea Românească, 1930; *Vol. III. Acte și scrisori (1585–1592)*, Bucharest: Cartea Românească, 1931.

Williams, J. A. *Themes of Islamic Civilisation*, Los Angeles, London: University of California Press Berkeley, 1971.

Yahya bin Adam, *Kitâb – Taxation in Islam. Volume I: Yahya bin Adâm's Kitâb al-kharâj*, edited, translated, annotated, and introduced by A. Ben Shemesh, Revised Second Edition, Leiden: Brill, 1967, 23–109.

## Studies

Abel, A. "La convention de Nedjrân et le developement du "droit des gens" dans l' Islam Classique." *RIDA* 2, (1949): 1–17.

Abel, A. "Le statut legal des étrangers dans l'Islam," *Recueil de la Société Jean Bodin*, IX (1958): 331–51.

Abel, A. "La djizya: tribut ou rançon?" *SI*, XXXII, (1970): 3–21.

Abi-Chahla, H. *L'Extinction des capitulations en Turquie et dans les régions arabes*, Paris, 1924.

Abou el Fadl, Khaled. *Rebellion and Violence in Islamic Law*, Cambridge: Cambridge University Press, 2001.

Abou-el-Haj, Rifa'at Ali. "Ottoman Diplomacy at Karlowitz." *JAOS* 87, 4, (1967): 498–512.

Abou el-Haj, Rifa'at Ali. "The Formal Closure of the Ottoman Frontier in Europe: 1699–1703." *JAOS* 89, 3, (1969): 467–475.

Abou-el-Haj, Rifa'at Ali. "Ottoman Attitudes toward Peace Making: The Karlowitz Case." *Der Islam* 51, 1, (1974): 130–137.

Adăniloaie, Nichita. "Despre suzeranitatea otomană și nerespectarea de către Poartă la 1775 și 1812 a obligațiilor de apărare a teritoriilor Țărilor Române." *RdI* 35, 8, (1982): 950–955.

Ágoston, Gábor, "Defending and Administering the Hungarian frontier," in Christine Woodhead (ed.). *The Ottoman World*, (London, New York: Routledge, 2012), 220–236.

Aksan, Virginia. "Ottoman Sources of Information on Europe in the Eighteenth Century." *AOtt*, XI, (1986) [1988]: 5–16.

Aksan, Virginia H. and Daniel Goffman. *The Early Modern Ottomans. Remapping the Empire,* Cambridge: Cambridge University Press, 2007 (especially Daniel Goffman, "Negotiations with the Renaissance states : the Ottoman Empire and the new diplomacy")

Alexandrescu-Dersca Bulgaru, M.M. "Rolul hatișerifurilor de privilegii în limitarea obligațiilor către Poartă." *St.RdI* 11, 6, (1958): 101–121.

Alexandrescu-Dersca Bulgaru, M.M., "Sur le régime des ressortissants ottomans en Moldavie (1711–1829)." *SAO* V–VI, (1967): 143–182.

Alexandrescu-Dersca Bulgaru, M.M. "Les relations du prince de Valachie Mircea l'Ancien avec les émirs seldjoukides d'Anatolie et leur candidat Musa au tróne Ottoman." *TAD* VI, (1968): 10–11; (1972): 113–225.

Alexandrescu-Dersca Bulgaru, M.M. "L'origine des khatt-i șerifs de privilèges des Principautés roumaines." *NEH* VI, 1, (1980): 251–263.

Allen, W. Ed. *Problems of Turkish Power in the Sixteenth Century*, London: Central Asian Research Centre, 1963.

Andreescu, Șt. "Limitele cronologice ale dominației otomane în Țările Române." *RdI* 27, 3, (1974): 399–412.

Andreescu, Șt. *Vlad Țepeș (Dracula). Între legendă și adevăr*, Bucharest: Editura Minerva, 1976.

Angelov, D. "Certains aspects de la conquête des peuples balkaniques par les Turcs." *BS* XVII, 2, (1956): 220–275.

Anooshahr, Ali. *The Ghazi Sultans and the Frontiers of Islam,* London and New York: Routledge, 2009.

Anscombe, Frederick. "The Balkan Revolutionary Age." *JMH* 84 (September 2012): 572–606.

Armanazi, Najib. *L'Islam et le droit international,* Paris : Picart, 1929.

Arntz, E. R. N. "De la situation de la Roumanie au point de vue du droit international." *Revue de droit international et de legislation comparée* (Gand), X, 1877 (reprinted in *Independența României. Documente. vol. III. Presa Străină,* Bucharest : Editura Academiei, 1977, 41–61).

Babinger, Franz. "Cel dintîi bir al Moldovei către sultan," Bucharest, 1936 (off-print from *Omagiu fraţilor Alexandru şi Ion I. Lepedatu,* București 1936).

Babinger, Franz. *Mahomet II le Conquérant et son temps (1432–1481). La grande peur du monde au tournant de l'histoire,* Paris: Payot, 1954.

Bacqué-Grammont, J. L. *Les Ottomans, les Safavides et leurs voisins. Contribution à l'histoire des relations internationales dans l'Orient islamique de 1514 à 1524,* Nederlands Historisch-Achaelogisch Instituut te Istanbul, 1987.

Baer, Marc David. *Honoured by the Glory of Islam. Conversion and Conquest in the Ottoman Empire.* Oxford, New York: Oxford University Press, 2006.

Bailly, M. A. *Dictionnaire grec-français*, Paris: Hachette, 1894.

Barkan, Ö. L. "Caractère religiuex et caractère séculier des institutions ottomanes." In *Contributions à l'histoire économique et sociale de l' Empire ottoman*, Louvain: Editions Peeters, 1983, 11–58.

Barta, Gábor. *La route qui mene à Istanbul 1526–1528*, Budapest: Akadémiai Kiadó, 1994.

Basri Erk, Hasan. *Meşhur Türk Hukukçuları (Célébres juristes turcs)*, Istanbul, n. d.

Baxter, R. R. "Treaties and custom." *RdC* vol. 129, I, (1970): 27–105.

Bayerle, Gustav "The Compromise at Zsitvatorok." *AOtt* VI, (1980): 5–53.

Bayerle, Gustav. *Pashas, Begs, and Effendis. A Historical Dictionary of Titles and Terms in the Ottoman Empire*, Istanbul: The ISIS Press, 1997.

Beldiceanu-Steinherr, Irène. "La conquête d'Adrinople par les Turcs: la pénétration turque en Thrace et la valeur dea chroniques ottomanes." In *Travaux et Mémoires* I, Paris, (1965): 439–61.

Beldiceanu-Steinherr, Irène. "La prise de Serres et le firman de 1372 en faveur du monastère de Saint-Jean-Prodrome." *Acta Historica. Societas Academica Dacoromana* (Munich) 4, 1965, 15–24.

Beldiceanu-Steinherr, Irène. "En marge d'un acte concernant le pengyek et les aqıngı." *REI*, XXXVII, I, 1969, 21–47.

Beldiceanu-Steinherr, Irène. "Le règne de Selim I: tournant dans la vie politique et religieuse de l'Empire Ottoman." *Turcica* 6, (1975): 35–48.

Beldiceanu, Nicoară. "Problema tratatelor Moldovei cu Poarta Otomană în lumina cronicei lui Peçevi." *Balcania* (Bucharest), V, 1, (1942): 393–407.

Beldiceanu, Nicoară. "La campagne ottomane de 1484: ses préparatifs militaires et sa chronologie." *RER* 5–6, (1957–1958) (Paris, 1960) : 66–77.

Beldiceanu, Nicoară. "La conquête des cités marchandes de Kilia et Cetatea Albă par Bayezid II." *SF* XXIII, (1964): 36–90.

Beldiceanu, Nicoară. *Le monde ottoman des Balkans (1402–1566). Institutions, société, économie*, London: Variorum Reprints, 1966.

Beldiceanu, Nicoară. *Recherche sur la ville ottomane au XVe siécle. Étude et actes*, Paris: A Maisonneuve, 1973.

Beldiceanu, Nicoară. *Le timar dans l'État ottoman: début XIVe-début XVIe siècle*, Wiesbaden: Harrasowitz, 1980.

Belin, F. A. *Des Capitulations et des traités de la France en Orient*, Paris : Challamel, 1870.

Berchem, Max von. *La propriété territoriale el l'impôt foncier sous les premiers califes*, Geneva: H. Georg, 1886.

Berindei, Mihnea. "Le problème des «Cosaques» dans la seconde moitié du XVIe siècle. À propos de la révolte de Ion vodă, voiévode de Moldavie." *CMRS* XIII, 3, (1972): 338–367.

Berindei, Mihnea. "Porte Ottomane, voiévode et boyards de Moldavie en 1552." In *Quand le Crible était dans la paille... Homage à Pertev Naili Boratov*, Paris: G.-P. Maisonneuve et Larose, 1978, 105–118.

Bernard, Rachelle. *L'armistice dans les guerres internationales*, Geneva: Impremerie Genevoise, 1947.

Berza, Mihai. "Haraciul Moldovei și Țării Românești în sec. XV-XIX." *SMIM* II, (1957): 7–47.

Berza, Mihai. "Variațiile exploatării Țării Românești de către Poarta Otomană în secolele XVI-XVIII." *St.RdI* XI, 2, (1958): 59–71.

Berza, Mihai. "Turcs, Empire Ottoman et relations roumano-turques dans l'historiographie moldave des XVe-XVIIe siècles." *RESEE* X, 3, (1972): 595–627 (reprinted in M. Berza, *Pentru o istorie a vechii culturi românești* (ed.). Andrei Pippidi, Bucharest, 1985).

Biegman, N. H. "Ragusan Spying for the Ottoman Empire. Some 16th Century Documents from the State Archive at Dubrovnik." *Belleten* XXVII, 106, (1963): 237–255.

Biegman, N. H. *The Turco-Ragusan Relationship. According to the Firmans of Murad III (1575–1595) extant in the State Archives of Dubrovnik*, The Hague–Paris: Mouton, 1967.

Binswanger, Karl. *Untersuchungen zum Status der Nichtmuslime im Osmanischen Reich des 16 Jahrhunderts. Mit einer Neudefinition des Begriffes "Dimma,"* Munich: R. Trofenik, 1977.

Bishai, W. B. "Negotiations and Peace Agreements between Muslims and Non-Muslims." In Sami A. Hanna (ed.). *Medieval and Middle Eastern Studies. In Honor of Aziz Suryal Atiya*, Leiden: Brill, 1972, 50–61.

Bogdan, I. *Vlad Țepeș și narațiunile germane și rusești asupra lui*, Bucharest: Editura Librăriei Socecu & Comp., 1896.

Boisard, M. *L'Islam et la morale internationale*, Paris: A. Michel, 1979.

Bonner, Michael. *Aristocratic Violence and Holy War. Studies in thre Jihad and the Arab-Byzantine Frontier*, New Haven: American Oriental Society, 1996.

Boogert, Maurits van den, and Kate Fleet (eds). *The Ottoman Capitulations: Text and Context* (in *Oriente Moderno* XXII, 3–2003), Rome: Istituto per l'Oriente C.A. Nallino. 2003.

Boogert, Maurits van den. *The Capitulations and the Ottoman Juridical System: Qadis, Consuls, and Beratlıs in the 18th Century*, Leiden: Brill, 2005.

Brătianu, Gh. I. "Formules d'organisation de la paix dans l'histoire universelle. Première partie." *RHSEE* XXII, (1945) 67–104 and "Deuxième partie," *RHSEE* XXIII, (1946): 31–56.

Brătianu, Gh. I. *Marea Neagră de la origini până la cucerirea otomană*, I–II (ed.). Victor Spinei, Bucureşti, 1988.

Braude, Benjamin and Bernard Lewis (ed.). *Christians and Jews in the Ottoman Empire. The Functioning of a Plural Society. vol. I: The Central Lands*, New York–London: Holmes and Meier Publishers, 1982.

Braudel, Fernand. *Mediterana şi lumea mediteraneană în epoca lui Filip al II-lea*, I–VI, Bucharest, 1986 (in English, *The Mediterranean and the Mediterranean Wold in the Age of Philip II*. Translated by Siân Reynolds. New York: Harper & Row, Publishers, 1972).

Bravmann, M. M. "À propos de Qur'ân IX-2." *Arabica* X, 1, (1963): 94–5.

Bravmann, M. M. "The Ancient Arab Background of the Qur'anic Concept al-Gizyatu 'an Yadin." *Arabica* 3, (1966): 307–14; 1, (1967): 90–1; 3, (1967): 326–7.

Bravmann, M. M. *The Spiritual Background of Early Islam. Studies in Ancient Arab Concepts*, Leiden: Brill, 1972.

Brezeanu, Stelian. *O istorie a Imperiului bizantin*, Bucharest: Editura Albastros, 1981.

Brierly, J. L. *The Law of Nations. An Introduction to the International Law of Peace*, 6th edn., Oxford: Oxford University Press, 1963 (first edition 1928).

Brown, P. M. *Foreigners in Turkey. Their Juridical Status*, Princeton: Princeton University Press, 1914.

Brummett, Palmira. *Ottoman Seapower and Levantine Diplomacy in the Age of Discovery*, State University of New York Press, 1994.

Brummett, Palmira. *Mapping the Ottomans. Sovereignty, Territory and Identity in the Early Modern Mediterranean*, New York: Cambridge University Press, 2015.

Bulliet, R. W. "The Shaykh al-Islam and the Evolution of Islamic Society." *SI* XXXV, 1, (1972): 53–69.

Burak, Guy. *The Second Formation of Islamic Law. The Hanafî School in the Early Modern Ottoman Empire*, New York: Cambridge University Press, 2015.

Çagatay, N. "Laiklik nedir. Şeriat nedir? (Qu'est-ce que le laicisme, qu'est-ce que le Şeriat?)." *Belleten* XLII, 167 (1978): 427–36.

Cahen, Cl. "Documents et notules: C IX-29 – Hattâ yu'tûl -gizyata 'an yadin wa-hum sâgirûna." *Arabica* IX, 1, (1962): 76–9.

Canard, Marius. "La guerre sainte dans le monde islamique et dans le monde chrètien." *Revue Africaine* (Algeria), (1936): 605–23.

Canard, Marius. "Une lettre de Muhammad ibn Tugj al-Ishid émir d'Egypte à l'empereur Roman Lacapène." *Byzantion*, XI, fasc. 2, 1936, 717–28.

Canard, Marius. "Un traité entre Byzance et l'Egypte au XIIIe siècle et les relations de Michel Paléologue avec les sultans mamluks Baibers et Qalâ'un." In *Mélanges Gaudefroy-Demombynes,* Le Caire : Imprimerie de l'Institut fran¸ais d'archéologie orientale, 1937, 197–224.

Canard, Marius. "La prise d'Héraclée et les relations entre Hârûn ar-Rashîd et l'empereur Nicéphore I." *Byzantion* XXXII, (1962): 345–79.

Carra de Vaux. *Les penseurs de l'Islam,* IV–V, Paris: Paul Geuthner, 1923.

Cassola, Arnold. *The 1565 Ottoman Malta Campaign Register*, La Valletta : Publishers Enterprise Group, Bank of Valetta, 1998.

Castellan, A. L. *Moeurs, usages, costumes des Othomans et abrégé de leur histoire*, I–II, Paris: Nepveu, 1812.

Cazacu, M. and K. Kevonian. "La chute de Caffa en 1475 à la lumière de nouveaux documents." *CMRS* XVII, 4, (1976): 499–538.

Cernovodeanu, Paul (ed.). *Mihai Viteazul. Culegere de studii*, Bucharest: Editura Academiei, 1975.

Ceterchi, Ioan. *Istoria dreptului românesc*, Bucharest: Editura Academiei,, vol. I, 1980; vol. II/1, 1984.

Chaygan, M. *Essai sur l'histoire de droit public musulman aux premiers siècles de sa formation*. Thèse pour le doctorat, Paris, 1934.

Chopin, M. and A. Ubicini. *Provinces danubiennes et roumaines. Bosnie, Servie, Herzegovine, Bulgarie, Slavonie, Illyrie, Croatie, Dalmatie, Montenegro, Albanie,* par M. Chopin. *Valachie, Moldavie, Bukovine, Transylvanie, Bessarabie, par A. Ubicini*, Paris: Firmin Didot Frères Editeure, 1856 (reprinted, Iași, 1993).

Ciocîltan, Virgil. "Între sultan și împărat: Vlad Dracul în 1438." *RdI* 29, 11, (1976): 1767–90.

Ciocîltan, Virgil. "Competiția pentru controlul Dunării inferioare. 1412–1420." *RdI* 10, (1982): 1090–1100 and 11, (1982): 1191–1203.

Ciocîltan, Virgil. "Poarta Osmană și Gurile Dunării în secolul al XV-lea." *RdI* 11, (1985): 1058–74.

Ciurea, D. "Relațiile externe ale Moldovei în secolul al XVI-lea." *AIIAI* X, (1973): 1–47.

Claparède, Arthur de. *Essai sur le droit de représentation diplomatique d'après le droit international moderne*, Thèse de doctorat, Geneva: Universiţé de Genève, 1875,

Cohen, Mark R. *Under Crescent and Cross. The Jews in the Middle Ages*, 4th ed. Princeton: Princeton University Press, 1996.

Coles, P. *The Ottoman Impact on Europe*, London: Thames and Hudson, 1968.

Colson, Felix. *Précis des droits des Moldaves et des Valaques, fondé sur les droit des gens et sur les traités*, Paris : Pugin, quai des Augustins, 1839.

Coman, Marian. *Putere și teritoriu. Țara Românească medievală (secolele XIV-XVI)*, Iași: Polirom, 2013.

Constantin, Gh. I. "Le traité entre le sultan Baiazet I et la Valachie." *Der Islam* 59, 2, (1982): 254–84.

Constantinescu, N. A. *Începuturile și stabilirea suzeranității turcești în Moldova*, Bucharest: Institutul de Editură și Arte Grafice „Flacăra", 1914.

Constantinescu, R. *Moldova și Transilvania în vremea lui Petru Rareș. Relații politice și militare (1527–1546)*, Bucharest: Direcția Generală a Arhivelor Statului, 1978.

Constantiniu, Florin. "De la Mihai Viteazul la fanarioți: observații asupra politicii externe românești." *SMIM* VIII, (1975):101–36.

Cooke, W. S. *The Ottoman Empire and its Tributary States (excepted Egypt). With a Sketch of Greece*, Amsterdam: B.R. Grüner, 1968.

Courbage, Youssef and Philippe Fargues. *Chrétiens et Juifs dans l'Islam arabe et turc*, Paris: Fayard, 1992.

Cvetkova, B. A. "Vie économique de villes et ports balkaniques aux XVe et XVIe siècles." *REI* XXXVIII, (1970): 267–356.

Danişmend, I. H. *Izahlı Osmanlı Tarihi Kronolojisi*, Cilt 1–5, Istanbul: Türkiye Yayınevi, 1947–1948 (reprinted, 1971).

Darling, Linda T. *Revenue-Raising and Legitimacy. Tax Collection and Finance Administration in the Ottoman Empire. 1560–1660*. Leiden. New York. Cologne: Brill, 1969.

Dávid, Géza and Pál Fodor (eds). *Hungarian-Ottoman Military and Diplomatic Relations in the Age of Süleyman the Magnificent*, Budapest: Loránd Eötvös University, Hungarian Academy of Sciences, 1994.

Dávid, Géza. "Administration in Ottoman Empire." In Kunt, Metin and Christine Woodhead (eds). *Süleyman the Magnificent and His Age. The Ottoman Empire in the Early Modern World*, London and New York, 1995, 71–90.

David, René. *Les grands systèmes de droit contemporains*, Septième édition, Paris: Dalloz, 1978.

Davison, Roderic H. "Turkish Attitudes Concerning Christian-Muslim Equality in the Nineteenth Century." *American Historical Review* 59, 4, 1954, 844–64 (reprinted in Roderic H. Davison, *Essays in Ottoman and Turkish History. The Impact of the West*, London: Saqi Books, 1990, 112–32).

Davison, Roderic H. *Reform in the Ottoman Empire. 1856–1876*, New York: Gordian Press, 1973.

Decei, Aurel. "A participat Mircea cel Bătrân la lupta de la Ankara?" *RIR* VII, fasc. III–IV, (1937): 339–357 (also in Decei, *RRO*, 5–14).

Decei, Aurel. "Tratatul de pace – sulhname – încheiat între sultanul Mehmed al II-lea și Ștefan cel Mare la 1479." In Aurel Decei, *Relații româno-orientale. Culegere de studii*, Bucharest: Editura Științifică și Enciclopedică, 1978, 118–129 (also in *RIR*, XV, 1945, fasc. IV, 465–494).

Decei, Aurel. "Expediția lui Mircea cel Bătrân împotriva acîngiilor de la Karinovasi (1393)." In Decei, *RRO*, 140–55 (in French in *RER*, I (1953): 130–151).

Decei, Aurel. "Două documente turcești privitoare la expedițiile sultanilor Baiazid I și Murad al II-lea în Țările Române." In Decei, *RRO*, 209–222 (in French in *RRH* xiii, 3, (1974): 395–413).

Decei, Aurel and V. Veliman. "Izvoare turcești despre Mihai Viteazul." *RA*, XXXVII, anul LII, 2, (1975): 157–168.

Decei, Aurel. "Relațiile lui Mihai Viteazul cu Imperiul Otoman." *RRH* XIV, 3, (1975): 457–82 (in Decei, *RRO*, 223–245).

Decei, Aurel. *Istoria Imperiului otoman până la 1656*, Bucharest: Editura Științifică și Enciclopedică, 1978.

Decei, Aurel. *Relații româno-orientale. Culegere de studii*, Bucharest: Editura Științifică și Enciclopedică, 1978.

Delilbaşı, Melik. "Ortaçağ'da Türk hükümdarları tarafından batılılara ahidnamelerle verilen imtiyazlara genel bakış." *Belleten*, XLVII 185, (1983): 95–104.

*Dicționarul limbii române literare vechi (1640–1780)* (eds). M. Costinescu, M. Georgescu, F. Zgraon, Bucharest: Editura Științifică și Enciclopedică, 1987.

*Dictionnaire Arabe – Française – Anglais. Langue classique et moderne. Arabic – French – English Dictionary*, par Régis Blachère, Moustafa Chouémi et Claude Denizeau, vol. I–III, Paris, 1972.

Dölger, Franz. *Regesten der Kaiserrurkunden des Ostromischen Reiches von 565–1453. 5 Teil (Schluss) Regesten von 1341–1453*, Munich und Berlin : Verlag R. Oldenburg, 1965.

Duțu, Alexandru. *Călătorii, imagini, constante*, Bucharest: Editura Eminsecu, 1985.

El-Shakankiri. "Loi divine, loi humaine et droit dans l'histoire juridique de l'Islam." *RIDC* 3, (1981): 767–789.

Emiroğlu, Ibrahim. *Hizmet ve Ihanetleriyle Tercümanlar, Voyvodalar ve Azınlıklar*, Izmir, 1996.

Engelhardt Ed. *La Turquie et les Principautès danubiennes sous le règime des Capitulations. Études et projet de réforme applicable à la Roumanie et à la Serbie*, Paris : Cotillon, 1879.

Ercan, Yavuz. "Türkiye'de XV-XVI yüzyıllarda Gayrımüslimlerin Hukuku, Içtimai ve Iktisadi Durumu." *Belleten* XLVII, 188, (1983) : 1119–1149.

Eskenasy, Victor. "Omagiul lui Ștefan cel Mare de la Colomeea (1485). Note pe marginea unui ceremonial medieval." *AIIAI* XX, (1983) : 257–267.

Farah, Caesar E. (ed.). *Decision Making and Change in the Ottoman Empire*, Missouri: The Jefferson University Press, 1993.

Faroqhi, Suraiya. "Political Activity among Ottoman Taxpayers and the Problem of Sultanic Legitimation (1570–1650)." *JESHO* XXXV, 1, (1992): 1–39.

Faroqhi, Suraiya. *The Ottoman Empire and the World Around It.* London, New York: I.B. Tauris, 2004.

Fattal, Antoine. *Le statut légal des non-musulmans en pays d'Islam*, Beirut : Imprimerie Catholique, 1958.

Feneșan, Cristina. *Constituirea principatului autonom al Transilvaniei*, Bucharest: Editura Enciclopedică, 1997.

Filipescu, I. P. *Drept internațional privat*, Bucharest : Editura Academiei Române, 1991.

Filitti, Ioan C. "România față de Capitulațiile Turciei." *AARMSI*, s. II, vol. XXXVIII, 7, 1915 (reprinted in I. C. Filitti, *Opere alese* (ed.). Georgeta Penelea, Bucharest, 1985, 1–59).

Firestone, Reuven. *Jihad. The Orgin of Holy War in Islam*, Oxford University Press, 1999.

Fischer, Alan W. "Les rapports entre l'Empire ottoman et la Crimée. L'aspect financier," CMRS, XIII 3, (1972), 368–381.

Floresçu, G. G. "L'aspect juridiques des khatt-i chérifs. Contributions à l'étude des relations de l'Empire Ottoman avec les Principautés roumaines." *SAO* I, (1958): 121–147.

Florescu, G. G. "La procedure de l'investiture et le ceremonial de la reception du prince regnant Cuza à Constantinople. Contribution à l'étude des relations entre les Principautés Unies et l'Empire Ottoman." *SAO* II, (1960): 71–87.

Florescu, Radu and Raymond T. McNally, *Dracula: A Biography of Vlad the Impaler. 1431–1476*, New York: Hawthorn, 1973.

Fodor, Pál. "Ahmedî's Dâsitân as a Source of Early Ottoman History." *AOH* XXXVIII, (1–2), (1984): 41–54.

Fodor, Pál. "Ottoman Policy towards Hungary, 1520–1541." *AOH* 55, 2–3, (1991): 271–345.

Fodor, Pál. "Ungarn und Wien in der osmanischen Eroberungsideologie (im Spiegel der Târîh-i Beç krâlı – 17. Jahrhundert)." *JTS* 13, (1989): 81–98.

Forand, P. "Early Muslim Relations with Nubia." *Der Islam* 48, 1, (1971): 111–121.

"Forme ale păcii" – Andrei Pippidi, Tudor Teoteoi, Alex. Duțu, V. A. Georgescu, M. A. Mehmet, Sergiu Iosipescu, E. Stănescu, "Forme ale păcii în sud-estul european în secolele XIV-XVII. Dezbatere la Institutul de Studii Sud-Est Europene. 10 iunie 1981." *RdI*, 35, 1, 1982, 139–160.

Gallotta, Aldo. "Il trattato turco-veneto del 12 gennaio 1482." In *Studia turcologica memoriae Alexii Bombaci dicata*, Naples: Istituto universitario orientale, 1982, 219–235.

Ganshof, François L. *Histoire des relations internationales* (ed.). Pierre Renouvin. vol. I: *Le Moyen Age*, Paris: Hachette, 1953.

Gardet, Louis. *Dieu et la destinée de l'homme*, Paris: Vrin, 1967.

Garnier, François (ed.). *Journal de la bataille de Lepante*, Paris : Éditions de Paris, 1956.

Gauggenheim, Paul. *Traité de droit international public. Avec mention de la pratique internationale et suisse*, vol. I, Geneva, 1967.

Gavillot, J. C. *Essai sur les droits des Européens en Turquie et en Egypte. Les Capitulations et la reforme judiciaire*, Paris : E. Dentu, 1875.

Geamănu, Grigore. *Drept international public*, I–II, Bucharest : Editura Didactică și Pedagocică, 1981, 1984.

Gemil, Tahsin. "Două documente tătărăști referitoare la campania din 1476 a sultanului Mehmed al II-lea în Moldova." *AIIAI* V, (1968): 183–194.

Gemil, Tahsin. "Din relațiile moldo-otomane în primul sfert al secolului al XVI-lea. Pe marginea a două documente din arhivele de la Istanbul." *AIIAI*, IX, (1972): 132–144.

Gemil, Tahsin. "Date noi privind haraciul Țărilor române în secolul al XVII-lea." *RdI* 8, (1977): 1433–1446.

Gemil, Tahsin. *Țările Române în contextul politic internațional (1672–1621)*, Bucharest: Editura Academiei, 1979.

Gemil, Tahsin. "Documente turcești inedite. Sfârșitul sec. XVI și sec. XVII." *RA* 3, (1981): 351–361.

Gemil, Tahsin. "Fetih-nâme a sultanului Mehmed al II-lea privind campania din 1476 împotriva Moldovei." *RA* XLIV, 3, (1982): 252–258.

Gemil, Tahsin. "Observații referitoare la încheierea păcii și stabilirea hotarului dintre Moldova și Imperiul otoman (1486)." *RA* IX, 2, (1983): 117–128.

Gemil, Tahsin. "'Capitulațiile' Transilvaniei de la jumătatea secolului al XVII-lea." *AIIAI* XXXIII, 2, (1986): 717–721.

Gemil, Tahsin. "Raporturile româno-otomane în vremea lui Mircea cel Mare." In *Marele Mircea Voievod.* ed. I. Pătroiu, Bucharest: Editura Academiei, 1987, 330–364.

Gemil, Tahsin. *Românii și otomanii în secolele XIV-XVI*, Bucharest: Editura Academiei Române, 1991.

Georgescu, Valentin Al. "La place de la coutume dans le droit des états feodaux roumains de Valachie et de Moldavie jusqu'au milieu de XVIIe siècle. " *RRH* VI, 4, (1967): 553–586.

Georgieva, Cvetana. "Les rapports de commerce entre l'Empire Ottoman et la Pologne et les terres bulgares au XVIe siècle." *BHR* 3, (1978): 38–49.

Gerber, Haim. *State, Society, and Law in Islam. Ottoman Law in Comparative Perspective,* Albany, New York: State University of New York Press, 1994.

Ghiață, Anca. "Condițiile instaurării dominației otomane în Dobrogea." In *Studii istorice sud-est europene,* I, Bucharest, (1974): 43–126.

Ghunaimi, M. Talaat al-. *The Muslim Conception of International Law and the Western Approach,* The Hague: M. Nijhoff, 1968.

Gianni, Grégoire. *La coutume en droit international,* Paris: Editions A. Pedone, 1931.

Gibb, H. A. R. and Harold Bowen (eds). *Islamic Society and the West. A Study of the Impact of Western Civilization on Muslim Culture in the Near East, Volume One: Islamic Society in the Eighteenth Century,* Parts I–II, London: Oxford University Press, 1957.

Gibbons, H. A. *The Foundation of the Ottoman Empire. A History of the Osmanlis up to the Death of Bayezid I (1300–1403)*, New York: The Century Co., 1916.

Giurescu, C. C. and Dinu C. Giurescu, *Istoria românilor. vol. 2: De la mijlocul secolului al XIV-lea până la începutul secolului al XVII-lea*, Bucharest: Editura Științifică, 1976.

Giurescu, C. C. "Despre caracterul relațiilor dintre români și turci." In *Probleme controversate în istoriografia română*, Bucharest, 1977, 87–122.

Giurescu, Constantin. *Capitulațiile Moldovei cu Poarta Otomană,* Bucharest: Institutul de Arte Grafice Carol Göbl, 1908 (reprinted in C. Giurescu, *Studii de istorie*, Bucharest: Editura Eminescu, 1993, 473–504).

Giurescu, Dinu C. *Țara Românească în secolele XIV și XV*, Bucharest : Editura științifică, 1973.

Giurescu, C. C. (ed.). *Istoria României în date,* Bucharest: Editura Enciclopedică Română, 1971.

Goffman, Daniel S. "The Maktu' System and the Jewish Community of Sixteenth-Century Safed: A Study of two Documents from the Ottoman Archives." *OA.JOS* III, (1982): 81–90.

Gökbilgin, Tayyib. "XVII asır başlarında Erdel hadisesi ve Bethlen Gabor'un beyliğe intihabı." *TD*, I, 1–2, (1949 –1950): 1–28.

Gökbilgin, Tayyib. "La structure des relations turco-roumaines et des raison de certains hüküms, ferman et berat et des ordres de sultans adressés aux princes de la Moldavie et de la Valachie aux XVI-e siècles." *Belleten*, XLII, 165–168, (1978): 761–773.

Goldziher, I. *Le dogme et la loi de l'Islam*, Paris: Librairie orientaliste Paul Geuthner, 1920.

Golimas, A. H. *Despre Capuchehăile Moldovei și Poruncile Porții către Moldova până la 1829. Contribuții la cunoașterea raporturilor de drept dintre Moldova și Turci*. Teză de doctorat, Iași : Tipografia Ligii Culturale, 1943.

Golimas, A. H. "Sensul închinării de la Vaslui a lui Petru Vodă Aron. Din legăturile de drept ale Moldovei cu Poarta Otomană," Iași, 1941 (off-print from *Cuget moldovenesc,* Iași, 9–12, 1940).

Gorovei, Șt. S. "Pacea moldo-otomană din 1486." *RdI*, 7, 1982, 807–821 (also in *RRH*, 3–4, (1982): 405–421).

Gorovei, Ștefan S. "Câteva însemnări pentru istoria relațiilor româno-otomane în veacurile XV-XVI." In *Românii în istoria universală* (eds). Ion Agrigoroaiei, Gh. Buzatu, V. Cristian, Iași: Universitatea Alex. I. Cuza, vol. I, 1986, 31–41.

Gorovei, Ștefan S. "Moldova în 'Casa Păcii'. Pe marginea izvoarelor privind primul secol de relații moldo-otomane." *AIIAI*, XVII, (1980): 629–667.

Grammont, H. D. de. *Histoire d'Alger sous la domination turque. 1515–1830*, Paris: Ernest Leroux, 1887.

Granara, William. "*Jihâd* and Cross-Cultural Encounter in Muslim Sicily." *Harvard Middle Eastern and Islamic Review* (Cambridge) 3, 1/2, 1996: 42–61.

Green, Maryan N. A. *International Law. Law of Peace*, London: Macdonald and Evans Ltd., 1973.

Grignaschi, Mario. "Una raccolta inedita di «Münşeât»: Il Ms. Veliyüddin Ef. 1970 della Biblioteca Beyazit Umumi e gli Ahdnâme concesii dalla Sublima Porta à Chio (muharrem 927 h), à Firenze (muharrem 934) e ad Antivari (ramadan 983)." In *Studi preottomani e ottomani. Atti del Convegno di Napoli. 24–26 settembre 1974*, par Aldo Gallotta (ed.). Napoli: Istituto Universitario Orientale, 1976, 105–127.

Grignaschi, Mario. "Le problème du droit coutumier dans l'Empire Ottoman." In *La coutume. Custom, Troisième partie. Third Part. Europe Orientale, Asie et Islam. Eastern Europe, Asia and Islam*, Transactions of the Jean Bodin Society for Comparative Institutional History, Brussels: De Boeck University, 1992, 281–298.

Grigoraș, N. *A existat un tratat de pace între Mehmed II și Ștefan cel Mare?* Iași: Institutul de Istorie Națională „A.D. Xenopol", 1948.

Grigoraş, N. "Relaţiile Moldovei cu Imperiul Otoman până la domnia lui Ştefan cel Mare." *RdI* 28, 1, (1975): 33–49.

Groot, OEDR – Groot, A. H. de. *The Ottoman Empire and the Dutch Republic. A History of the Earliest Diplomatic Relations. 1610–1630*, Leiden–Istanbul, 1978.

Guboglu, Mihail, "L'inscription turque de Bender relative à l'expedition de Soliman le Magnifique en Moldavie (1538)." *SAO*, I, (1957): 175–187.

Guboglu, Mihail. *Paleografia şi diplomatica turco-osmană. Studiu şi album*, Bucharest: Editura Academiei, 1958.

Guboglu, Mihail. "Le tribut payé par les Principautés Roumaines à la Porte jusqu'au début du XVIe siècle d'après les sources turques." *REI*, 37, 1, (1969): 49–80.

Guboglu, Mihail. "Izvoare turco-persane privind relaţiile lui Ştefan cel Mare cu Imperiul Otoman." *RA*, LIX, vol. XLIV, 2, (1982): 134–145.

Guboglu, Mihail. "Kanunî Sultan Süleyman'in Boğdan seferi ve zaferi (1538/945 H.)." *Belleten*, vol. L, (1987): 727–806.

Guboglu, Mihail. "Osmanlılarla Romen ülkeleri arasındaki ilk devri ilişkileri (1368–1456) hakkında belirtmeler ve doğrultmalar." Off-print from *IX. Türk Tarih Kongresi*, Ankara: Türk Tarih Kurumu, 1988, 829–843.

Guilmartin, John F. "Ideology and Conflict: The Wars of the Ottoman Empire, 1453–1606." *Journal of Interdisciplinary History* (MIT Press), XVIII, 4, (1988): 721–747.

Hadrovics, L. *Le peuple Serbe et son Église sous la domination turque,* Paris : Presses universitaires de France, 1947.

Hamidullah, Muhammad. *Muslim Conduct of State. Being a Treatise on Siyar, that is the Islamic Notion of Public International Law, consisting of the Laws of Peace, War and Neutrality, together with Precedents from Orthodox Practice and Preceded by a Historical and General Introduction*, 4th Edition, Revised and Enlarged, Lahore, 1953 (1st edition in 1941–1942).

Hammer, J. de. "Memoir on the Diplomatic Relations between the Courts of Dehli and Constantinople in the Sixteenth and Seventeenth Centuries." *Transactions of the Royal Asiatic Society of Great Britain and Ireland* (Cambridge) II, (1830): 462–487.

Hammer, J. de. *Histoire de l'Empire Ottoman depuis son origine jusqu'à nos jours,* traduit de 'Allemand par J. J. Hellert, vols. I–XVIII, Paris : Bellizard, Barthés, Dufour et Lowell 1837–1841 (Joseph von Hammer-Purgstall, *Geschichte des Osmanischen Reiches*, I–X, Pest, 1827–1835, reprint Graz, 1963).

Hatschek, J. *Der Musta'min. Ein Beitrag zum internationalen privat und Völkerrecht das Islamischen Gesetzes*, Berlin: Walter de Gruyter, 1920.

Hazai, G. "Urkunde des Friedensvertrages zwishen König Matthias, und dem türkischen Sultan 1488." In *Beiträge zur Sprachwissenschaft Volkskunde und Literaturforschung* (*Steinitz-Festschrift*), Berlin: Akademie-Verlag, 1965, 141–145.

Hershlag, Z. Y. *Introduction to the Modern Economic History of the Middle East*, second revisted edition, Leiden: Brill, 1980.

Heyd, Uriel. *Ottoman Documents on Palestine. 1552–1615. A Study of the Firman according to the Muhimme Defteri,* Oxford: Clarendon Press, 1960.

Heyd, Uriel. "Some Aspects of the Ottoman *Fetva*." BSOAS, XXXII, 1, (1969): 35–56.

Heyd, Uriel. *Studies in Old Ottoman Criminal Law*, Oxford: Clarendon Press, 1973.

Hill, D. R. *The Termination of Hostilities in the Early Arab Conquests.* AD *634 – 656,* London: Luzac and Co. Ltd., 1971.

Hitti, Phillip K. *Précis d'histoire des Arabes*, Paris: Payot, 1950.

Holt, P. M., A. K. S. Lambton and B. Lewis. *The Cambridge History of Islam. vol. 1: The Central Lands. vol. 2: Further Lands. Islamic Society and Civilisation*, Cambridge: Cambridge University Press, 1970.

Hopwood, Keith. "Müdara: False friendship. in Ottoman–Byzantine Relations," in CI.PO, 9th Symposium, Jerusalem, July 23–26, 1990 (published in A. Singer, A. Cohen (ed.). *Aspects of Ottoman History*, Jerusalem: The Magnes Press, 1994, 156–161.

Houdas, O. "La Guerre Sainte islamique." *Revue des Sciences Politiques*, XXXIII, (1915): 87–95.

Huart, Cl. "Le droit de la guerre," *RMM*, II, (1907): 331–347.

Huart, Cl. "Le Khalifat et la Guerre Sainte." *RHR*, LXXII, (1915): 288–302.

Hupchick, Denis P. *Culture and History in Eastern Europe,* New York: St. Martin's Press, 1994.

Iliescu, Octavian. "Le montant du tribut payé par Byzance à l'Empire Ottoman en 1379 et 1424." *RESEE* IX, 3, (1971): 427–432.

Imber, Colin. "The Persecution of the Ottoman Shî'ites according to the Mühimme Defterleri. 1565–1585." *Der Islam* 56, no. 2, (1979): 245–273.

Imber, Colin. "Paul Wittek's "De la défaite d'Ankara à la prise de Constantinople." *OAJOS* V, (1986): 65–79.

Imber, Colin. "The Ottoman Dynastic Myth." *Turcica* XIX, (1987): 7–28.

Imber, Colin. *The Ottoman Empire. 1300–1481*, Istanbul: The Isis Press, 1990.

Imber, Colin. "Ideals and legitimation in early Ottoman history." In Kunt, Metin and Christine Woodhead (eds). *Süleyman the Magnificent and His Age. The Ottoman Empire in the Early Modern World*, London, New York: Routledge, 1995, 138–153.

Imber, Colin. *Ebu's-su'ud. The Islamic Legal Tradition,* Stanford: Stanford University Press,1997.

Imber, Colin. *The Ottoman Empire, 1300–1650. The Structure of Power.* New York: Palgrave Macmillan, 2002.

Inalcık, Halil. *Fatih Devri üzerinde tetkikler ve vesikalar*, I, Ankara: TTK Basımevi, 1954 (2. Baskı, 1987).

Inalcık, Halil. "Ottoman Methods of Conquest." SI, II, 1954, 104–129 (reprinted in Halil Inalcık, *The Ottoman Empire. Conquest, Organization and Economy. Collected Studies*, London: Variorum Reprints, 1978).

Inalcık, Halil. "An Ottoman Document on Bayezid I expedition into Hungary and Wallachia." In *Actes du X Congrès International d'Etudes Byzantines*, Istanbul: Comité d'Organisation du X. Congrés Internationale d'Etudes byzantines, 1957, 220–222.

Inalcık, Halil. "Osmanlı Hukukuna Giriş. Örf-i Sultanî Hukuk ve Fatih'in Kanunları." *AÜSBFD*, XIII, 2, (1958): 102–126.

Inalcık, Halil. "Osmanlılar'da raiyyet rüsûmu." *Belleten* 92, (1959): 575–610.

Inalcık, Halil. "The Emergence of the Ottomans." In P. M. Holt, A. K. S. Lambton and B. Lewis (eds). *The Cambridge History of Islam*, vol. I, Cambridge: Cambridge University Press, 1970, 263–291.

Inalcık, Halil and J. Wansborough, "Imtiyâzât." *EI*-2, III, (1971): 1207–1225.

Inalcık, Halil. *The Ottoman Empire. Conquest, Organization and Economy. Collected Studies*, London: Variorum Reprints, 1978.

Inalcık, Halil. "The Question of the Closing of the Black Sea under the Ottomans." *Arheion Pontou* (Athens), 35 (1979): 74–110.

Inalcık, Halil. "Osmanlı Bürokrasisinde Aklâm ve Muâmelât." *OA.JOS* I, (1980): 1–14.

Inalcık, Halil. "Dâr al-'ahd." *EI*-2, II, (1991): 118–119.

Inalcık, Halil. "Power Relationships Between Russia, the Crimea and the Ottoman Empire as Reflected in Titulature." In *Passé turco-tatar, présent soviétique: Études offertes à Alexandre Bennigsen* (eds). Ch. Lemercier-Quelquejay, G. Veinstein, E. S. Wimbush, Louvain–Paris: Éditions Peeters, 1986, 193–208.

Inalcık, Halil. *The Middle East and the Balkans under the Ottoman Empire. Essays on Economy and Society*, Bloomington: Indiana University Turkish Studies, 1993.

Inalcık, Halil and Cemal Kafadar (eds). *Süleyman the Second and his Time*, Istanbul: The Isis Press, 1993.

Inalcık, Halil. "The Appointment Procedure of a Guild Warden (Kethüda)." In H. Inalcık, *The Middle East and the Balkans under the Ottoman Empire. Essays on Economy and Society*, Bloomington: Indiana University Turkish Studies, 1993, 194–204.

Inalcık, Halil. *The Ottoman Empire. The Classical Age. 1300–1600*, Translated by Norman Itzkowitz and Colin Imber, New York, Washington: Prager Publishers, 1973.

Iorga, Nicolae. "Latins et Grecs d'Orient et l'etablissement des Turcs en Europe (1342–1362)." *BZ*, XV, vol. 1–2, (1906), 179–222.

Iorga, Nicolae. *Istoria poporului românesc* (ed.). Georgeta Penelea, Bucharest, 1985 (1st Romanian ed. [illegible]).

Iorga, Nicolae, *Ce este sud-estul european?* Bucharest: Datina Românească, 1940.

Iorga, Nicolae, *Domni români după portrete şi fresce contemporane*, Sibiu, 1930.

Iorga, Nicolae. *Istoria Românilor*, I–X, Bucharest: Tipografia Datina Românească, 1936–1939 (2nd ed., Bucharest: Editura Enciclopedică, 1988–2017; French edition: N. Iorga, *Histoire des Roumains et de la romanité orientale*, Bucharest: 1937–1945).

Iorga, Nicolae. *Istoria vieţii bizantine. Imperiul şi civilizaţia. După izvoare* (ed.). M. Holban, Bucharest : Editura Enclopedică Română, 1974.

Iorga, Nicolae. *Studii asupra evului mediu românesc* (ed.). Şerban Papacostea, Bucharest: Editura Ştiinţifică şi Enciclopedică, 1984.

Iorga, Nicolae. *Locul românilor în istoria universală* (ed.). Radu Constantinescu, Bucharest : Editura Ştiinţifică şi Enciclopedică, 1985.

Itzkowitz, Norman. *Ottoman Empire and Islamic Tradition*, Chicago and London: The University of Chicago Press, 1972 (2nd ed, 1980).

Ivanics, Mary. "Formal and Lingvuistic Peculiarities of 17th Century Crimean Tatar Letters adressed to Princes of Transylvania." *AOH* (Budapest), XXIX, 2 (1975): 213–224.

Işıksel, Güneş. *La diplomatie ottomane sous le règne de Selîm II: paramètres et périmètres de l'Empire ottoman dans le troisième quart du XVIe siècle*, Paris, Leuven: Peeters: Collection Turcica Vol. XX, 2016.

Jaroslav, César (ed.). *Ottoman Rule in the Middle Europe and Balkan in the 16th and 17th Centuries: Papers presented at the 9th joint Conference of the Czechoslovak-Yugoslav Historical Commitee*, Prague: Oriental Institute in Academia, 1978.

Jelavich, Barbara. *History of the Balkans. Vol I: Eighteenth and nineteenth Century.* Cambridge, London, New York: Cambridge University Press, 1983.

Jelavich, Barbara. *Russia's Balkan Entanglements. 1806–1914*, Cambridge: Cambridge University Press, 1991.

Jelavich, Charles and Jelavich, Barbara. *The Establishment of the Balkan National States, 1804–1920*. Seattle, Washington: University of Washington Press, 1986.

Jennings, Ronald. C. "Zimmîs (Non-Muslim) in early 17th Century Ottoman Juridical Record. The *Shari'a* Court of Anatolian Kayseri." *JESHO*, 21, 3, (1978): 225–293.

Jennings, Ronald. C. "Some Thoughts on the Gazi-Thesis." In *WZKM* (*Festschrift Andreas Tietze zum 70. Geburtstag*), 76, 1986, 151–161.

Jennings, Ronald C. *Christians and Muslims in Ottoman Cyprus and the Mediterranean World, 1571–1640*, New York and London, New York University Press, 1993.

Jurji, J. E. "The Islamic Theory of War." *The Moslem World* (London), 30, (1940): 332–442.

Kabrda, J. *Le système fiscal de l'Église Orthodoxe dans l'Empire Ottoman*, Brno: Universita J. E. Purkyne, 1969.

Kader, Ali Abd al-. "Land Property and Land Tenure in Islam." *IQ*, V, 2 (1959): 4–11.

Kafadar, Cemal. *Between Two Worlds: The Construction of the Ottoman State*, Berkley, Los Angeles, London: University of California Press, 1995.

Káldy-Nagy, Gy. "The Holy War (jihâd) in the First Centuries of the Ottoman History." *HUS*, III–IV, no. 1, (1979–1980): 467–473.

Kallfelz, Wolfgang. *Nichtmuslimische Untertanen im Islam: Grundlage, Ideologie und Praxis der Politik frühislamischer Herrscher gegenüber ihren nichtmuslimischen Untertanen mit besonderem Blick auf die Dynastie der Abbasiden (749–1248)*, Wiesbaden: Otto Harrassowitz, 1995.

Karadja, C. I. "Poema lui Michel Beheim despre cruciadele împotriva turcilor din anii 1443 și 1444." *Bul.Com.Ist.*, XV, (1936): 3–59.

Karakete, H. T. and M. Reinkowski (eds). *Legitimazing the Order. The Ottoman Rhetoric of State Power*, Leiden: Brill, 2005.

Kármán, Gábor and Lovro Kuncević (eds). *The European Tributary States of the Ottoman Empire in the Sixteenth and Seventeenth Centuries*, Leiden, Boston: Brill, 2013.

Karpat, Kemal. *An Inquiry into the Social Foundations of Nationalism in the Ottoman State: From Social Estates to Classes, from Millets to Nations*, Princeton, NJ: Princeton University Press, 1973.

Kastritsis, Dimitris J. *The Sons of Bayezid. Empire Building and Representation in the Ottoman Civil War of 1402–1413*, Leiden, Boston: Brill, 2007.

Kélékian, Diran. *Dictionnaire Turc-Français*, 1st edition, Constantinople: Mihran, 1911.

Khadduri, Majid and Herbert J. Liebesny (eds). *Law in the Middle East.* vol. I. *Origin and Development of Islamic Law*, Washington D.C.: The Middle East Institute, 1955.

Khadduri, Majid. "The Impact of International Law upon the Islamic World Order." *AJIL* 66, 4, (1972): 46–50.

Khadduri, Majid. "The Islamic System: Its Competion and Coexistence with Western Systems." In R. H. Nolte (ed.). *The Modern Middle East*, New York, 1963, 150–155.

Khadduri, Majid. "The Islamic Theory of International relations and its Contemporary Relevance." In J. H. Proctor (ed.). *Islam and International Relations*, London, 1965, 24–34.

Khadduri, Majid. Art. "Hudna." *EI*-2, III, 184–185.

Khadduri, Majid. *War and Peace in the Law of Islam*, Baltimore: The Johns Hopkins Press, 1955 (2nd ed. 1969).

Kiel, Machiel. "Remarks on the Administration of the Poll Tax (*Cizye*) in the Ottoman Balkans and Value of Poll Tax Registers (*Cizye Defterleri*) for Demographic Research." *EB* 26, 4, (1990): 70–104.

Kister, M. J. "«'An Yadin» (Qur'ân IX/29) an Attempt at Interpretation." *Arabica*, XI, Sept. 1964, 272–279.

Koç, Yunus. "Early Ottoman customary law: the genesis and development of Ottoman codification," in *Shattering tradition: Custom, Law and the Individual in the Muslim Mediterranean*. Ed. Walter Dostal and Wolfgang Kraus (The Islamic Mediterranean, 8). London: I. B. Tauris, [illegible]

Köhbach, M. "*Çasar* oder *imperator?* Zur titulatur de römischen Kaiser durch die Osmanen nach dem Vertrag von Zsitvatorok (1606)." *WZKM* (*In memoriam Anton C. Schendlinger*), 82, (1992): 223–34.

Kohlberg, E. "The Development of the Imâmi Shii Doctrine of Jihâd." *ZDMG*, 126, 1, (1976): 64–88.

Köprülü, M. F. *Les origines de l'Empire Ottoman*, Paris: E. de Boocard, 1935 (in Turkish, *Osmanlı Devleti'nin Kuruluşu*, Ankara: TTK Basımevi, 1959).

Kortepeter, Carl M. "Ottoman Imperial Policy and the Economy of the Black Sea Region on the Sixteenth Century." *JAOS*, 86, 2, (1966): 86–113.

Kortepeter, Carl M. "Gazi Giray II, Khan of the Crimea, and Ottoman Policy in Eastern Europe and the Caucasus, 1588–1594." *SEER*, XLIV 102 (1966): 139–166.

Kortepeter, Carl Max. "How the Ottomans governed the Arabs: The Observations recorded by Evliya Çelebi in 1672." In *Studia Turcologica Memoriae Alexii Bombaci Dicata*, Naples: Istituto universitario orientale, 1982, 318–333.

Kramers, J. K. "Droit de l'Islam et droit islamique." *AHDO*, I, (1937): 401–414.

Krekić, B. *Dubrovnik (Raguse) et le Levant au Moyen-Age*, Paris : Mouton, 1961.

Królikowska, Natalia. "Sovereignty and Subordination in Crimean–Ottoman Relations (Sixteenth–Eighteenth Centuries)." In Gábor Kármán, and Lovro Kuncević (eds). *The European Tributary States of the Ottoman Empire in the Sixteenth and Seventeenth Centuries*, Leiden, Boston: Brill, 2013, 43–66.

Krstić, Tijana. *Contested Conversions to Islam: Narratives of Religious Change in the Early Modern Ottoman Empire*. Stanford: Stanford University Press, 2011.

Kruger, Hilmar. *Fetwa und Siyar*, Wiesbaden: Otto Harrassowitz, 1978.

Kruse, Hans. "Al-Shaybani on International Instruments." *JPHS*, 1, (1953): 90–100.

Kruse, Hans. "The Foundation of International Islamic Jurisprudence (Muhammad al-Shaybani – Hugo Grotius of the Muslims)." *JPHS*, III, IV (1955): 231–67 (See, also, the German original text: H. Kruse, "Die Begrundung der islamischen Volkerrechtslehre – Muhammad al-Shaybani – Hugo Grotius der Moslimen." *Saeculum* (Munich), 5, (1954): 221–41; and the Turkish translation: H. Kruse, "Islam Devletler Hukukunun ortaya Cıkışı (Muslumanların Hugo Grotius'u Muhammad eş-Şeybânî." *ITED*, IV, 3–4, (1971): 54–82).

Kruse, Hans. "The Islamic Doctrine of International Treaties." *IQ*, I 3 (1954): 152–158.

Kunt, Metin. "State and sultan up to the age of Süleyman: frontier principality to world empire." In Kunt, Metin and Christine Woodhead (eds). *Süleyman the Magnificent and His Age. The Ottoman Empire in the Early Modern World*, London, New York: Routledge, 1995, 3–29.

Kunt, Metin and Christine Woodhead (eds). *Süleyman the Magnificent and His Age. The Ottoman Empire in the Early Modern World*, London, New York: Routledge, 1995.

Kütükoğlu, Mübahat S. *Osmanlı Belgelerinin Dili (Diplomatik)*, Istanbul: Kubbealtı Akademisi Kültür ve San'at Vakfı, 1994.

Lambton, A.K.S. "A Nineteenth Century View of Jihâd." *SI*, XXXII, (1970): 181–193.

Lazarus-Yafeh, H. *Studies in al-Ghazzali*, Jerusalem: The Magnes Press, 1975.

Lemercier-Quelquejay, Ch., G. Veinstein and E.S. Wimbush (eds.), *Passé turco-tatar, présent soviétique. Études offertes à Alexandre Bennigsen*, Louvain–Paris : Éditions Peeters, 1986.

Lemerle, Paul. *L'emirat d'Aydin, Byzance et l'Occident. Recherches sur «La geste d'Umur Pacha»*, Paris : Presses universitaires de France, 1957.

Lévi-Provençal, E. *Histoire de l'Espagne musulmane,* vols. I–III, Paris : Maisonneuve et Larose, 1952–1953.

Lewis, Bernard. *The Middle East and the West,* Bloomington: Indiana University Press, 1964.

Lewis, Bernard. "Politics and War." In J. Schacht and C. E. Bosworth (eds). *The Legacy of Islam,* Oxford: Clarendon Press, 1974, 156–210.

Lewis, Bernard. "The Ottoman Proclamation of Jihâd in 1914." *IQ,* 19, 3–4, (1975): 157–163.

Lewis, Bernard. "L'Islam et les Non-Musulmans." *Annales,* 35, 3–4, (1980): 784–799.

Lewis, Bernard. *The Muslim Discovery of Europe,* New York, London: W.W. Norton, 1982.

Lewis, Bernard. "Serbestiyet." In *Ord. Prof. Ömer Lütfi Barkan'a Armağan,* Istanbul, 1985, 47–52.

Liebesny, H. J. "The Development of Western Judicial Privileges." In M. Khadduri and H. J. Liebesny (eds). *Law in the Middle East,* Washington: Middle East Institute, 1955, 309–333.

Linder, Rudi Paul. "Stimulus and Justification in Early Ottoman History." *GOTR,* 27, 2, (1987): 207–224.

Little, Donald P (ed.). *Essays on Islamic Civilization. Presented to Niyazi Berkeş,* Leiden: Brill, 1976.

Lowry, Heath. *The Nature of the Early Ottoman State,* Albany, NY: Suny Press, 2003.

Lybyer, Albert Howe. *The Government of the Ottoman Empire in the Time of Suleiman the Magnificent,* Cambridge: Harvard University Press; London: Henry Frowde, Oxford University Press, 1913.

Mahmassani, Sobhi. "The Principles of International Law in the Light of Islamic Doctrine." *RdC,* I, (1966): 205–328.

Makdisi, G. "The Significance of the Sunni Schools of Law in Islamic Religious History." *IJMES,* 10, 1, (1979): 1–8.

Manselli, Raoul and R. I. Burns, Philippe Contamine, Y. Amino, "Formes et problèmes de la paix dans l'histoire. 1. Moyen Age." In *Actes XVe Congrès international des sciences historiques, Bucarest, 10–17 août 1980. Grandes thèmes et méthodologie,* Bucharest : Editura Academiei, 1980, vol I. 149–190; IV/1, 123–196.

Mantran, Robert (ed.). *Histoire de l'Empire Ottoman,* Paris: Fayard, 1989.

Marcu, L. P. "Idei despre stat și drept în opera lui Dimitrie Cantemir," *Studii și cercetări juridice* (Bucharest), 3 (1973).

Massignon, Louis. "La guerre sainte supreme de l'Islam arabe." In Louis Massignon, *Opera Minora,* II, Paris : Dar al-Maaref, 1969, 305–320.

Matei, Ion. "Quelques problemes concernant le régime de la domination ottomane dans les Pays roumains (concernant particulièrement la Valachie)." *RESEE* X, 1, (1972): 66–81; XI, no. 1, (1973): 81–95.

Matei, Ion. "Regimul juridic al relaţiilor internaţionale." In Ioan Ceterchi (ed.). *Istoria dreptului românesc*, vol. I, Bucharest : Editura Academiei, 1980, 458–470.

Matei, Ion. "Românii în Imperiul Otoman. Probleme generale." *CICSEE*, III, (1986): 141–149.

Matei, Ion. *Reprezentanţii diplomatici (capuchehăi) ai Ţării Româneşti la Poarta otomană*, Editura Academiei Române, Bucureşti, 2008.

Matkovski, A. "La Signification historique des expressions «raia» et «beraia»." In J.M. Scarce (ed.). *Islam in the Balkans: Persian Art and Culture of the 18th and 19th Centuries*, Edinburgh: Royal Scottish Museum, 1979, 55–58.

Matuz, Josef. *Das Kanzleiwesen Sultan Süleymâns des Prachtigen*, Wiesbaden: Franz Steiner Verlag, 1974.

Matuz, J. E. "Transmission of Directives from the Center to the Periphery in the Ottoman State from the Beginning until the Seventeenth Century." In Caesar E. Farah (ed.) *Decision Making and Change in the Ottoman Empire*, At Northeast Missouri State University: The Thomas Jefferson University Press, 1993, 19–29.

Maxim, Mihai. "Circonstances de la majoration du kharâdj payé par la Valachie à l'Empire ottoman durant la période 1540–1575." *AIESEE-B*, XII, 2, (1974): 367–381 (also, in Maxim, *Empire ottoman*, 215–226).

Maxim, Mihai. "Haraciul moldovenesc în opera lui Dimitrie Cantemir." *AUBI*, XXIII, (1974): 69–78.

Maxim, Mihai. "L'autonomie de la Moldovie et de la Valachic dans les actes officiels de la Porte au cours de la seconde moitié du XVI-e siècle." *RESEE*, XV, 2 (1977): 207–230 (also, in Maxim, Empire ottoman, 11–40).

Maxim, Mihai. "Obligaţiile militare, în muncă şi transport ale Moldovei şi Ţării Româneşti faţă de Poartă în a doua jumătate a secolului al XVI-lea." *AUBI*, XXVIII, (1979): 99–109.

Maxim, Mihai. "Regimul economic al dominaţiei otomane în Moldova şi Ţara Românească în a doua jumătate a secolului al XVI-lea." *RdI* 32, 9, (1979): 1731–1765.

Maxim, Mihai. "Le statut de la Moldavie et de la Valachie à l'égard de la Porte ottomane dans la seconde moitié du XVIe siècle." *NÉH*, VI-1 1980, 237–250.

Maxim, Mihai. "Teritorii româneşti sub administraţie otomană în secolul al XVI-lea (I)." *RdI*, 8, (1983): 802–817 şi (II), in RdI, 9, 1983, 879–890.

Maxim, Mihai. "Din istoria relaţiilor româno-otomane – «Capitulaţiile»." *AI*, XXVIII, 6, (1982): 34–68 (reprinted in *Din cronica relaţiilor poporului român cu popoarele vecine*, Bucharest, 1984, 68–118).

Maxim, Mihai. "Le statut des Pays Roumains envers la Porte Ottomane aux XVI-XVIIIe siècles." *RRH*, XXIV, 1–2, (1985): 29–50.

Maxim, Mihai. "Cu privire la statutul de 'ahd al Ţărilor Române faţă de Poartă. Consideraţii pe marginea unor izvoare otomane." *RdI* 6, (1986): 523–534.

Maxim, Mihai. "Din nou pe urmele vechilor tratate ale Moldovei și Țării Românești cu Poarta Otomană." *RdI* 2, (1987): 157–172.

Maxim, Mihai. "Statutul politico-juridic al Țărilor Române în evul mediu" (off-print), University of Bucharest, 1983, 105–126.

Maxim, Mihai. "Sur la question des *'ahdnames* octroyés par les sultans ottomans aux princes de la Moldavie et de la Valachie." *Transylvanian Review*, III, 1, 1994, 3–14.

Maxim, Mihai. *L'Empire Ottoman au Nord du Danube et l'autonomie des Principautés Roumaines au XVIe siècle. Études et documents,* Istanbul : Isis Press, 1999.

Maxim, *ȚRÎP* – Maxim, Mihai. *Țările Române și Înalta Poartă. Cadrul juridic al relațiilor româno-otomane în evul mediu,* Bucharest : Editura Enciclopedică, 1993.

Mehmet, M. A. "Din raporturile Moldovei cu Imperiul Otoman în a doua jumătate a veacului al XV-lea." *St.RdI,* XIII, 5, (1960): 165–178.

Mehmet, M. A. "La politique ottomane à l'égard de la Moldavie et du Khanat de Crimée vers la fin du règne du sultan Mehmed II "Le Conquérant." *RRH* 3, (1974): 509–533.

Mehmet, M. A. *Istoria turcilor,* Bucharest : Editura Științifică și Enciclopedică, 1976.

Mehmet, M. A., "La crise ottomane dans la vision du Hasan Kiafi Akhisari (1544–1616)." RESEE 13, 3, (1975): 385–402.

Mehmet, M. A., "O condică domnească din a doua jumătate a veacului al XVIII-lea, scrisă în limba turcă, privind țara Românească." *RA* 2, (1958): 248–260.

Mehmet, M. A., "De certains aspects de la société ottomane à la lumière de la Legislation (Kanunnâme) du sultan Mahomed II (1451–1481)." *SAO*, II, (1960): 127–160.

Mehmet, M. A., "Un document turc concernant le kharatch de Moldavie et de la Valachie aux XVe-XVIe siècles." *RESEE,* V, 1–2, (1967): 265–274.

Mehmet, M. A. "Despre dreptul de proprietate al supușilor otomani în Moldova și Țara Românească în sec. XV–XVIII," *CI*, III, 1972, 65–81.

Mehmet, M. A., "O nouă reglementare a raporturilor Moldovei și Tării Românești față de Poartă la 1792 (O carte de lege – Kanunname – în limba turcă)." *St.RdI* XX, 6, (1976): 691–707.

Ménage, V. L. "The English Capitulation of 1580. A Review Article." *IJMES*, (1980): 373–383.

Ménage, V. L. "On the Constituent Elements of Certain Sixteenth Century Ottoman Documents." *BSOAS*, XLVII, 2, (1985): 283–304.

Meron, Ya'kov. "The Development of Legal Thought in Hanefi Texts." *SI*, xxx, (1969): 73–119.

Miller, W. "The Gattilusi of Lesbos." *BZ,* XXX, (1913): 407–447.

Milliot, Louis. "La réception du droit occidental dans les systèmes juridiques orientaux." *Mémoires de l'Académie Internationale de Droit Comparé* (Paris), III, 4, (1955): 111–126.

Milliot, Louis. *Introduction à l'étude du droit musulman,* Paris : Sirey, 1953.

Mills, Ch. *Histoire du mahométisme, contenant la vie et les traits du caractère du prophète arabe. Avec un aperçu des divers empires fondés par les armes mahométanes,* Paris : Boulland, 1825.

Minea, I. *Principatele române și politica orientală a împăratului Sigismund. Note istorice,* Bucharest : Convorbiri literare, 1919.

Minea, I. *Vlad Dracul și vremea sa,* Iași, 1928 (offprint from *Cercetări istorice,* IV).

Minkov, Anton. *Conversion to Islam in the Balkans: Kisve Bahası and the Ottoman Social Life, 1670–1730.* Leiden and Boston: Brill, 2004.

Miović, Vesna. "Diplomatic Relations between the Ottoman Empire and The Republic of Dubrovnik." In Gábor Kármán, and Lovro Kuncević (eds). *The European Tributary States of the Ottoman Empire in the Sixteenth and Seventeenth Centuries,* Leiden, Boston: Brill, 2013, 187–208.

Miquel, André. *L'Islam et sa civilisation* (*VIIe – XXe siècles*), Paris : Armand Colin, 1977 (in Romanian, vol. I–II, Bucharest : Editura Meridiane, 1995).

Miquel, André. *La géographie humaine du monde musulman jusqu'au milieu de 11e siècle. Géographie et géographie humaine dans la littérature arabe des origines à 1050,* Paris: La Haye, Mouton, 1967.

*Mircea – Marele Mircea Voievod.* ed. I. Pătroiu, Bucharest: Editura Academiei, 1987.

Mircea, I. R. "Sur les circonstances dans lesquelles les Turcs sont restés en Valachie jusqu'au début du XVIIe siècle." *RESEE*, V, 1–2, (1967): 77–86.

Mitilineu, Mihail. *Les droits de la Roumanie basés sur les Traités,* Bucharest, 1874.

Mitler, Louis. "The Genoese in Galata: 1453–1682." *IJMES,* 10, 1, (1979): 71–91.

Modarressi, Hossein. *Kharâj in Islamic Law,* London : Anchor Press, 1983.

Mokri, Mohammad. "Un farmân de Sultân Husayn Bâyqarâ recommandant la protection d'une ambassade ottomane en Khorâsân en 879/1479." *Turcica,* v, (1975): 68–80.

Morabia, Alfred. *La notion de ğihad dans l'Islam médiéval* (*des origines à al-Gazali*), thèse presenté devant l'Université de Paris IV, 1er Juillet 1974, Université de Lille III, 1975.

Morabia, Alfred. "Ibn Taimiyya, dernier grand théoreticien du *ğihad* médiéval." *BEO* 30, 2, 1978 (paru 1980), 85–100.

Mureșan, C. *Iancu de Hunedoara,* Bucharest : Editura Științifică, 1968.

Murgescu, B. *Istorie românească-istorie universală* (*600–1800*), Bucharest : Teora, 1999.

Murgescu, Bogdan. "O nouă reglementare de pace moldo-otomană în 1481?" *SAI* LI–LII, (1985): 268–274.

Murgescu, Bogdan. "Avatarurile unui concept: monopolul comercial otoman asupra Țărilor Române." *RI* I, 9–10, (1990): 819–845.

Murgescu, Bogdan. *Țările Române între Imperiul Otoman și Europa creștină,* Iași: Polirom, 2012.

Naff, Thomas. "Ottoman Diplomatic Relations with Europe in the Eighteenth Century: Patterns and Trends." In Thomas Naff and Roger Owe (eds). *Studies in Eighteenth Century Islamic History*, London and Amsterdam: Southern Illinois University Press, 1977, 88–107.

Naff, Thomas. "Reform and the Conduct of Ottoman Diplomacy." *JAOS* 83, (1963): 295–315.

Nedkoff, B. C. "Osmanlı Imparatorluğunda cizye (baş vergisi). Bulgaristan hususî bir surette nazarı itibara alınmıştır." *Belleten* 8, 32, (1944): 599–652.

Neumann, F. "Decision Making without Decision Makers: Ottoman Foreign Policy circa 1780." In Farah, Caesar E. ed. *Decision Making and Change in the Ottoman Empire*, Missouri: The Jefferson University Press, 1993, 29–35.

Oikonomidès, Nicolas. "Monastèes et moines lors de la conquëte ottomane," *SF*, 35, 1976, 1–10.

Orhonlu, C., Cl. Cahen, and A. K. S. Lambton. "Kharâdj. I. Islam classique, II. Iran, III. Turquie ottomane." In *EI-2*, IV, 1062–1087.

Ostapchuk, Viktor, "Cossack Ukraine in and out of Ottoman Orbit, 1648–1681." In Kármán, Gábor and Lovro Kuncević (eds). *The European Tributary States of the Ottoman Empire in the Sixteenth and Seventeenth Centuries*, Leiden, Boston: Brill, 2013, 123–152.

Ostrogorsky, Georges. "Byzance. État tributaire de l'Empire turc." *Zbornik Radova* (Novi Sad), vol. V, (1958): 49–58.

Ostrogorsky, Georges. "La prise de Serres par les Turcs." *Byzantion*, 35, (1965): 302–319.

Ostrogorsky, Georges. *Histoire de l'État byzantine*, trans. French J. Gouillard, Paris: Payot, 1977.

Oțetea, Andrei (ed.). *Istoria poporului român*, Bucharest: Editura Ştiinţifică, 1970.

Özel, Ahmed. *Islam Hukukunda Ülke Kavramı. Dar ül-Islam. Dar ül-harb*, Istanbul: Iklim Yayınları, 1988.

Özel, Ahmed. *Hanefi Fıkıh Âlimleri*, Ankara: Türkiye Diyanet Vakfı, 1990.

Pakalın, Mehmet Zeki. *Osmanlı Tarih Deyimleri ve Terimleri Sözlüğü*, vols. I–III, Istanbul: ikinci basılış, 1971.

Pall, F. "Notes du pélerin William Wey à propos des opérations militaires des Turcs en 1462." *RHSEE* XXII, (1945): 246–266.

Pall, F. "La condizioni e gli achi internationali della lotta antiottoman del 1442–1443 condotta da Giovanni di Hunedoara." *RESEE* III, (1965): 433–463.

Panaite, Viorel. "Din istoria dreptului islamic al popoarelor: doctrina djihâd-ului." *AIIAI* XXII/2, (1985): 707–18 and XXIII/1, (1986): 409–418.

Panaite, Viorel. "Câteva observații privind reglementările de pace româno-otomane în secolul XV." In *Românii în istoria universală*, vol. III/1 (eds). Ion Agrigoroaiei, Gh. Buzatu, V. Cristian, Iași: Universitatea Alex. I. Cuza, 1988, 469–492.

Panaite, Viorel. "Reprezentanța diplomatică a Țării Românești la Poarta Otomană în epoca lui Constantin Brâncoveanu." *RdI*, 41, 9, (1988): 877–894.

Panaite, Viorel. "Considerații privind legea păcii în Islamul medieval." *AIIAI* XXIV/2, (1987): 567–586; XXV/2, (1988): 397–413 and XXVI/1, (1989): 481–497.

Panaite, Viorel. "Custom in the 16th – 18th Centuries Ottoman-Romanian Relationships. Starting Points for a Historiographical Debate." *RESEE* vol. XXXI, 1–2, (1993): 171–185.

Panaite, Viorel. "Străinii în viziune juridică otomană. Veacurile XVI-XVII." *AIIC*, XXXII, (1993): 29–38.

Panaite, Viorel. "Trade and Merchants in the 16th Century Ottoman-Polish Treaties." *RESEE* XXXII, 3–4, (1994): 259–276.

Panaite, Viorel. "Regimul negustorilor straini în '*ahdnâme*-lele otomane din secolele XV-XVII. O radiografie." In *Sud-Estul si Contextul European. Buletin*, Bucharest, II, (1994): 100–14; III, (1995): 95–112; IV, (1995): 115–130.

Panaite, Viorel. "Ethnicity and Religion in the Ottoman *'Ahdnâmes* (16th – 17th c). Terminological Considerations." In *Chrétiens et Musulmans à l'époque de la Renaissance*, Tunis: Zaghouan, 1997, 201–212.

Panaite, Viorel. *Pace, război și comerț în Islam. Țările române și dreptul otoman al popoarelor. Secolele XV-XVII*, Bucharest: Ed. All, 1997.

Panaite, Viorel. *The Ottoman Law of War and Peace. The Ottoman Empire and Tribute Payers*, Boulder, New York: Columbia University Press, East European Monographs, 2000.

Panaite, Viorel. "The Status of *Kharâj-güzârlar.* A Case Study: Wallachians, Moldavians and Transylvanians in the 15th – 17th Centuries." In *The Great Ottoman-Turkish Civilisation, vol. I. Politics and Institutions* (ed.). Kemal Çicek, Ankara: Yeni Turkiye Yayınları, 2000, 227–238.

Panaite, Viorel. "Peace Agreements in Ottoman Legal and Diplomatic View. 15th – 17th Centuries." In *Pax Otomana. Studies in Memoriam Prof. Dr. Nejat Göyünç*, edited by Kemal Çiçek, Ankara & Haarlem: Yeni Türkiye & Sota, 2001, 277–308.

Panaite, Viorel. "Pacta sunt servanda and Tribute-Payers in the Ottoman Empire. A Case Study: Wallachia, Moldavia, Transylvania (15th – 17th Centuries)." *Archív orientální. Perspectives on Ottoman Rule and Its Heritage. Dedicated to the Living Memory of Zdenka Veselá-Prenosilová (30.9.1930–4.3.1998)*. Praha, vol. 69, no. 2, (May 2001): 235–264.

Panaite, Viorel. "Power Relationships in the Ottoman Empire. The Sultans and the Tribute-paying Princes of Wallachia and Moldavia from the Sixteenth to the Eighteenth Century." *IJTS* vol. 7, nos. 1 & 2, (Spring 2001): 26–53.

Panaite, Viorel. "Islamic Tradition and Ottoman Law of Nations." In *The Turks. vol. 3: The Ottomans*, Ankara: Yeni Türkiye Yayınları, 2002, 597–604.

Panaite, Viorel. "Ottoman Expansion to the North of the Danube: Wallachia and Moldavia. 14th-16th century." In *The Turks. vol. 3: The Ottomans,* Ankara: Yeni Türkiye Yayınları, 2002, 111–122.

Panaite, Viorel. "Notes on Islamic-Ottoman Law of Peace." *RESEE* XLI, 1–4, (2003): 191–206.

Panaite, Viorel. "The *Re'ayas* of the Tributary-Protected Principalities. The Sixteenth through Eighteenth Centuries." *IJTS,* vol. 9, (2003): 79–104.

Panaite, Viorel. "The Voivodes of the Danubian Principalities – as *Harâcgüzarlar* of the Ottoman Sultans." *IJTS,* vol. 9, (2003): 59–78.

Panaite, Viorel. "Wallachia and Moldavia according to the Ottoman Juridical and Political View, 1774–1829." In Antonis Anastasopoulos and Elias Kolovos (eds). *Ottoman Rule and The Balkans, 1760–1858. Conflict, Transformation, Adaptation,* Rethymno: University of Crete-Department of History and Archaelogy, 2007, 21– 44.

Panaite, Viorel. "From Allegiance to Conquest. Ottomans and Moldo-Wallachians from the Late Fourteenth to Mid Sixteenth Centuries (I)." *RESEE* XLVIII, 1–4, (2010): 211–31; and (II), in *RESEE* XLIX, 1–4, (2011): 197–212.

Panaite, Viorel. "«Our Reign is granted by Turks...» Ottoman Sultans and Tributary Voyvodas of Wallachia and Moldavia (Sixteenth–Seventeenth Centuries)." In Maria Baramova, Plamen Mitev, Ivan Parvev and Vania Racheva (eds). *Power and Influence in South-Eastern Europe 16th – 19th century,* Zürich–Berlin: LIT Verlag, 2013, 177–189.

Panaite, Viorel. "The Legal and Political Status of Wallachia and Moldavia in Relation to the Ottoman Porte." In Gábor Kárman and Lovro Kuncević (eds). *The European Tributary States of the Ottoman Empire in the Sixteenth and Seventeenth Centuries,* Leiden, Boston: Brill, 2013, 9–43.

Panaite, Viorel. "Being a Western Merchant in the Ottoman Mediterranean. The Evidence of a Turkish Manuscript from Bibliothèque Nationale de France," in *ISAM Konuşmaları. Osmanlı Düşüncesi.Ahlâk. Hukuk. Felsefe-Kelâm / ISAM Papers. Ottoman Thought, Ethics-Law-Philosophy-Kalam* (ed.). by Seyfi Kenan, Istanbul: ISAM Yayınları, 2013, 91–135.

Panaite, Viorel. *Război, pace şi comerţ în Islam. Ţările române şi dreptul otoman al popoarelor,* 2nd revised and enlarged edition, Iași: Polirom, 2013.

Panaite, Viorel. "The Danubian Principalities." In Kate Fleet, Gudrun Krämer, Denis Matringe, John Nawas, Everett Rowson (eds). *The Encyclopaedia of Islam. Three,* Leiden: Brill, 2014, 85–89.

Panaitescu, P. P. "De ce n-au cucerit turcii Țările Române." In *Interpretări românești. Studii de istorie economică și socială* (eds). Șt. S. Gorovei and M. M. Székely, Bucharest: Editura Enciclopedică, 1994, 111–119 (1st ed. in *RFR* XI, 5, 1944).

Panaitescu, P.P. "La route commerciale de Pologne à la Mer Noire au Moyen Age." *RIR* III, fasc. II–III, (1933): 172–193.

Panaitescu, P. P. *Mircea cel Bătrân*, Bucharest, 1944.

Panaitescu, P.P. and N. Stoicescu, "La participation des Roumains à la bataille de Varna (1444)." *RRH* IV, 2, (1965): 221–231.

Pantazopoulos, N. J. *Church and Law in the Balkan Peninsula during the Ottoman Rule*, Thessaloniki: Institute for Balkan Studies, 1967.

Papacostea, Şerban. "De la Colomeea la Codrul Cozminului (Poziţia internaţională a Moldovei la sfârşitul secolului al XV-lea)." *Romanoslavica* (Bucharest) XVII, (1970): 525–553.

Papacostea, Şerban. "La Moldavie tributaire de l'empire ottoman au XVe siècle: le cadre international des rapports établis en 1455–1456." *RRH* XIII, 3, (1974): 445–461.

Papacostea, Şerban. "Relaţiile internaţionale în răsăritul şi sud-estul Europei în secolele XIV-XV." *RdI*, vol. 34, 5, (1981): 899–918.

Papacostea, Şerban. "Tratatele Ţării Româneşti şi Moldovei cu Imperiul otoman în secolele XIV-XV: ficţiune politică şi realitate istorică." In N. Edroiu, A. Răduţiu, P. Teodor (eds). *Stat, societate, naţiune. Interpretări istorice*, Cluj-Napoca: Editura Dacia, 1982, 93–106.

Papacostea, Şerban. "Relaţiile internaţionale ale Moldovei în vremea lui Ştefan cel Mare." *RdI*, 5–6, (1982): 607–638.

Papacostea, Şerban. "La Valachie et la crise de structure de l'Empire Ottoman (1402–1413)." *RRH* XXV, 1–2, (1986): 23–33.

Papademetriou, Tom. *Render unto the Sultan. Power, Authority, and the Greek Orthodox Church in the Early Ottoman Centuries*, Oxford: Oxford University Press, 2015.

Papadopoulos, Theodore H. *Studies and Documents relating to the History of the Greek Church and People under Turkish Domination*, Brussels: Librairie Scaldis, 1952.

Paraskevos, Konortas, *Les rapports juridiques et politiques entre le Patriarcat de Constantinople et l'administration ottomane de 1453 à 1600 (d'après les documents grecs et ottomans)*. PhD diss., University of Paris I, 1985.

Parry, V. J. "The Reigns of Bâyezîd I and Selim I, 1481–1520." In Parry, V. J., H. Inalcık, et al. (eds). *A History of the Ottoman Empire to 1730. Chapters from The Cambridge History of Islam and The New Cambridge Modern History*, Cambridge, London, New York, Melbourne: Cambridge University Press, 1976, 54–78.

Parvev, Ivan. *Habsburgs and Ottomans between Vienna and Belgrade (1683–1739)*, Boulder, New York: East European Monographs, 1995.

Parvin, M. and M. Sommer, "Dar al-Islam: the Evolution of Muslim Territoriality and its Implication for Conflict Resolution in the Middle East." *IJMES* 11, 1, (1980): 1–21.

Păun, Radu. "Încoronarea în Ţara Românească şi Moldova în secolul al XVIII-lea. Principii, atitudini, simboluri," *RdI*, V, 7–8, 1994, 743–759.

Păun, Radu. "Sur l'investiture des derniers princes phanariotes. Autour d'un document ignoré." *RESEE* XXXXV, (1997): 1–2, 63–76.

Păun, Radu. "Some Remarks about the Historical Origins of the «Phanariot phenomenon» in Moldavia and Wallachia (16th – 19th Centuries)." In G. Harlaftis and R. Păun (eds). *Greeks in Romania in the Nineteenth Century*, Athens, 2013, 47–94.

Păun, Radu. "Conquered by the (S)word: Governing the Tributary Principalities of Wallachia and Moldavia (16th -17th Centuries)." In R. Born and M. Dziewulski (eds). *Ottoman Orient in Renaissance Culture*, Kraków, 2015, 19–40.

Peacock, Andrew (ed.). *The Frontiers of the Ottoman World*, Oxford, New York: Oxford University Press, 2009.

Pedani Fabris, Maria Pia. *La Dimora della pace. Consideranzioni sulle capitolazioni tra i paesi islamici e l'Europa,* Quaderni di Studi Arabi. Studi e testi, 2, Venice: Cafoscarina, 1996.

Pedani, M. P. *The Ottoman-Venetian Border (15th-18th Centuries),* translated by Mariateresa Sala, Venice: Edizioni Ca' Foscari – Digital Publishing, 2017.

Pélissié du Rausas, G. *Le régime des capitulations dans l'Empire Ottoman*, I-II, 1er édition, Paris : A. Rousseau, 1902–1905 (deuxième edition, 1910–1911).

Perjés, Géza. *The Fall of the Medieval Kingdom of Hungary: Mohács 1526 – Buda 1541,* Boulder, New York, East European Monographs, 1989.

Peters, Rudolph. "Djihad: War of Aggression or Defense?" *AAWG* 98, (1976): 282–289.

Peters, Rudolph. *Islam and Colonialism. The Doctrine of Jihad in Modern History*, The Hague: Uitgeverij Mouton's Gravenhage, 1979.

Pienaru, Nagy. "Relațiile lui Mircea cel Mare (1386–1418) cu Mehmed I Çelebi (1413–1421)." *RdI* 8, (1986): 774–794.

Pignon, Jean. "La milice des janissaires de Tunis au temps des Deys (1590–1650)," *Les Cahiers de Tunisie. Revue de Sciences Humaines (Tunis),* IV, 15, (1956): 301–325.

Pilat, Liviu and Ovidiu Cristea, *The Ottoman Threat and Crusading on the Eastern Border of Christendom during the 15th Century,* Leiden: Brill, 2017.

Pippidi, Andrei. *Contribuții la studiul legilor războiului în evul mediu,* Bucharest: Editura militară, 1974.

Pippidi, Andrei. "Formules d'organisation de la paix dans l'histoire universelle par G. I. Brătianu," AIIAI, XXIV, 1987/2, 45–61.

Pippidi, Andrei. *Tradiția politică bizantină în Țările române în secolele XVI-XVIII*, Bucharest: Editura Academiei, 1983.

Pippidi, Andrei. *Visions of the Ottoman World in Renaissance Europe,* London: Hurst &Company, 2012.

Pitcher, D. E. *An Historical Geography of the Ottoman Empire from Earliest Times to the End of the Sixteenth Century*, Leiden: Brill, 1972.

Poliak, A. N. "Classification of Lands in the Islamic Law and its Technical Terms." *AJSMLL* 1, (1940): 50–63.

Proctor, J.H. (ed.). *Islam and International Relations,* New York: Frederick A. Praeger, 1965.

Quinet, Edgar. *Românii. Reorganizarea provinciilor dunărene*, in Edgar Quinet, *Opere alese*, vol. 2, Bucharest: Editura Minerva, 1983, 288–364.

Rechid, Ahmed. "La condition des étrangers dans la Republique de Turquie." *RdC*, 46, IV, (1933): 169–227.

Rechid, Ahmed. "L'Islam et le droit des gens." *RdC* 60, II, (1937): 375–504.

*Redhouse yeni Türkçe-Ingilizce Sözlük. New Redhouse Turkish-English Dictionary*, 12th edition., Istanbul: Redhouse Yayınevi, 1991.

Redhouse, James W. *A Turkish and English Lexicon Shewing in English the Significations of the Turkish Terms*, 2nd edition, Istanbul: Cagri Yayinlari, 1992.

Redslob, Robert. *Histoire des grandes principes du droit des gens, depuis l'antiquité jusqu'à la veille de la grande guerre*, Paris: Librairie Arthur Rousseau, 1923.

Repp, R. C. *The Müfti of Istanbul. A Study in the Development of the Ottoman Learned Hierarchy*, Oxford: Oxford University Press, 1986.

Reychman, Jan and Ananiasz Zajaczkowski, *Handbook of Ottoman-Turkish Diplomatics*, The Hague, Paris: Mouton, 1968.

Rouillard, Clarence Dana. *The Turk in French History, Thought and Literature (1520–1660)*, Paris: Boivin, 1938.

Rousseau, Charles. *Principes generaux du Droit international public. vol. 1: Introduction. Sources*, Paris: Editions A. Pedone, 1944.

Rozen, Minna. "The Corvée of operating the mines in Siderokapisi and its effects on the Jewish community of Thessaloniki in the 16th century." *BS* 34, 1, (1993): 29–46.

Runciman. Steven. *The Great Church in Captivity*, Cambridge: Cambridge University Press, 1968.

Samy-Bey, Ch. Fraschery. *Dictionnaire Français-Turc*, Éditeur-Imprimeur: Mihran, Constantinople, 1882.

Savvas-Paşa. *Étude sur la théorie du droit musulman*, vols. I-II, Paris: Marchal et Billard, 1892, 1898.

Savvides, A. "Nakshe." *EI-2*, VII, 939–941 (with bibliography in Greek).

Savvides, A. "Para." *EI-2*, VIII, 265–266.

Savvides, A. and N.A. Bées, "Mora." *EI-2*, VII, 236–241.

Scelle, Georges. "Règles générales du droit de la paix." *RdC* vol. 46, IV, (1933): 5–163.

Schacht, Joseph. *An Introduction to Islamic Law*, Oxford: Clarendon Press, 1964.

Schmidt, Jan. *Pure Water for Thirsty Muslims. A Study of Mustafâ 'Âlî of Gallipoli's Künhü l-Ahbâr*, Leiden: Het Oosters Instituut, 1991.

Schmitt, Oliver Jens, *Skanderbeg (Der neue Alexander auf dem Balkan)*, Regensburg: Pustet, 2009.

Schmitt, Oliver Jens (ed.) *The Ottoman Conquest of the Balkans. Interpretations and Research Debates*, Wien: Verlag der Österreichische Akademie der Wissenschaften, 2016.

Schwarz, Klaus. *Osmanische Sultansurkunden des Sinai-Klosters in türkisher Sprache*, Freiburg im Breisgau: Schwarz, 1970.

Seфériades, S. "Principes généraux du droit internationale de la paix." *RdC* vol. 34, IV, (1930): 181–439.

Sertoğlu, Midhat. *Resimli Osmanlı Tarihi Ansiklopedisi*, Istanbul: Inkılap ve Aka Kitabevleri, 1958.

Seton-Watson, R. W. *A History of the Roumanians. From Roman Times to the Completion of Unity,* Archon Books, 1963 (1st ed. Cambridge University Press, 1934).

Setton, Kenneth M. *Venice, Austria and the Turks in the Seventeenth Century,* Philadelphia: The American Philosophical Society, 1991.

Shai Har-El. *Struggle for Domination in the Middle East. The Ottoman-Mamluk War. 1485–1491,* Leiden, New York, Cologne: Brill, 1995.

Shaw, Standford. *History of the Ottoman Empire and Modern Turkey. Vol I: Empire of the Gazis: The Rise and Decline of the Ottoman Empire. 1280–1808,* London, New York, Melbourne: Cambridge University Press, 1976.

Shaw, Stanford J. *The Financial and Administrative Organization and Development of Ottoman Egypt. 1517–1798,* Princeton, NJ: Princeton University Press, 1962

Shuval, Tal. "The Ottoman Algerian elite and its ideology." *IJMES* 32, 3, (August 2000): 323–44

Şimanschi, Leon. "«Închinarea» de la Vaslui (5 <iunie>) 1456." *AIIAI* XVIII, (1981): 613–38.

Simionescu, Ştefana. "Ţările române şi începutul politicii răsăritene antiotomane a Imperiului habsburgic (1526–1594)." *RdI* 28, 8, (1975): 1197–1214.

Simionescu, Ştefana. "Les relations de la Moldavie avec les Habsbourg pendant le règne de Petru Rareş (1527–1538; 1541–1546)." *RRH* XVI, 3, (1977): 463–65.

Siruni, H. Dj. *Haşmetlu. Pe marginea titulaturii domnilor români în Cancelaria Otomană,* Bucharest, 1942 (off-print *Hrisovul*, 2, Bucharest, 1942, 139–202).

Sivan, Emmanuel. *L'Islam et la Croisade: Ideologie et propagande dans les reactions musulmans aux Croisades*, Paris: Librairie d'Amérique et d'Orient Adrien Maisonneuve, 1968.

Skilliter, Susan. *William Harborne and the Trade with Turkey. 1578–1582. A Documentary Study of the First Anglo-Ottoman Relations*, London: Oxford University Press, 1977.

Slot, B. J. *Archipelagus Turbatus. Les Cyclades entre colonisation latine et occupation ottomane. c.1500–1718,* vol. I-II, Istanbul: Nederlands Historish – Archaeologisch Institut Te Istanbul, 1982.

Soucek, S. "Midilli." *EI-2,* VI, 1035–1037.

Soucek, S. "Tashoz." *EI-2,* X, 352–353.

Sourdel, D. and J. Sourdel-Thomine, *La Civilisation de l'Islam CLassique,* Paris: B. Arthoud, 1968 (In Romanian *Civilizaţia Islamului clasic,* transl. E. Filotti, vol.I-III, Bucharest: Editura Meridiane, 1975).

Sousa, N. *The Capitulatory Regime of Turkey. Its History, Origin and Nature*, Baltimore : Johns Hopkins Press, 1933.

Stănescu, Eugen. "Le coup d'état nobiliaire de 1538 et son rôle dans l'asservissement de la Moldavie par l'Empire Ottoman." *NEH*, Bucharest, (1955): 241–264.

Ștefănescu, Ștefan. *Țara Românească de la Basarab I "Intemeietorul" până la Mihai Viteazul*, Bucharest: Editura Academiei, 1970.

Stein, Mark L. *Guarding the Frontier. Ottoman Border Forts and Garrisons in Europe*, London, New York: I.B. Tauris, 2007.

Stern, S.M. "An Embassy of the Byzantine Emperor to the Fatimid Khaliph al-Mu'izz." *Byzantion* XX, (1950): 239–258.

Stoian, E. *Vlad Țepeș. Mit și realitate istorica*, Bucharest: Albatros, 1989.

Stoicescu, Nicolae. *Dicționar al marilor dregători din Țara Românească și Moldova. Sec. XIV-XVII*, Bucharest: Editura enciclopedică română, 1971.

Stoicescu, Nicolae. *Vlad Țepeș*, Bucharest: Editura Academiei, 1976.

Stoicescu, Nicolae. *Radu de la Afumați*, Bucharest: Editura Militară, 1983.

Sugar, Peter F. *Southeastern Europe under Ottoman Rule. 1354–1804*, Seattle and London: University of Washington Press, 1977.

Süreyya, Mehmed. *Sicill-i 'Osmânî. Osmanlî Ünlüleri.* Istanbul: Tarih Vakfı Yurt Yayınları, cild 1–6, Istanbul, 1996. The edition in Ottoman: Mehmed Süreyya, *Sicill-i 'Osmânî (The Ottoman National Biography)*, I–III, Istanbul, 1308 AH/1890–1315 AH/1897.

Tarazi, Salah el-Dine. "La solution des problèmes de statut personnel dans le droit des pays arabes et africains." *RdC* 159, I, (1978): 348–463.

Tekin, Șinasi. "XIV. yüzyılda yazılmış Gazilik Tarikası "Gâziligin Yolları" adlı bir eski Anadolu Türkçesi metni ve *gazâ / cihâd* kavramları hakkında." *JTS.TBA* 13, (1989): 139–204.

Temimi, Abdeljelil. "La propriété foncière et le systeme des timar et zaamat dans la régence ottomane de Tunis. 1574–1588," *AHROS*, nos. 11–13, (October 1995): 179–197.

*The Encyclopaedia of Islam*, I-IV. First Edition, edited by H.Th. Houtsma, R. Basset, T.W. Arnold, R. Hartmann, Leyden: Brill, 1913–1936.

*The Encyclopaedia of Islam.* I–XIII. Second Edition., edited by P. Bearman, Th. Bianquis, C.E. Bosworth, E. van Donzel and W.P. Heinrichs, Paris, Leyden: Brill, 1986–2004 (some quotations are from the French edition *L'Encyclopédie de l'Islam. Nouvelle édition*, I–XII, edited by P. Bearman, Th. Bianquis, C.E. Bosworth, E. van Donzel and W.P. Heinrichs, Paris: Maisonneuve et Larose, Leiden: Brill, 1955–2005, where the pagination slightly differs).

Todorov, N. *La ville balkanique aux XVe-XIXe siècles. Développement socio-économique et démographique*, Bucharest : AIESEE, 1980.

Todorova, Maria. *Imagining the Balkans*, Oxford: Oxford University Press, 1997.

Topolski, J. *Metodologia istoriei*, translated by Aura Țapu, Bucharest: Editura Științifică și Enciclopedică, 1987.

Tritton, A. C. *The Caliphs and their Non-Muslims Subjects: A Critical Study of the Covenant of 'Umar*, Routledge Library Editions: Islam, 2007 (1st ed. 1939).

Turan, Osman. "Les souverains seldjoukides et leur sujets nonmusulmans." *SI* I, (1953): 65–101.

Turan, Osman. "The Ideal of the World Domination among the Medieval Turks." *SI* IV, (1955): 77–90.

Turan, S. "Sakız'ın türk hakimiyeti altına alınması," *TAD*, IV (1966), 173–184.

Turki, Abdelmagid. "Situation du «Tributaire» qui insulte l'Islam." *SI* XXX, (1969): 39–73.

Tyan, E. "Méthodologie et sources de droit en Islam." *SI* X, (1959): 79–111.

Tyan, E. and J. R. Walsh, "Fatwâ." *EI-2*, II, 866–867.

Umur, Suha. *Osmanlı Padişah Tuğraları*, Istanbul: Cem Yayınevi, 1980.

Uzunçarşılı, Ismail Hakki. "On sekizinci asırda Bogdan'a voyvoda tayini." *Tarih Semineri Dergisi* (Istanbul), vol. 1, (1937): 32–38.

Uzunçarşılı, Ismail Hakki. "On altıncı yüzyıl ortalarında Islâmiyeti kabul etmiş olan bir Boğdan voyvodası." *Belleten* XVIII, 69, (1954): 83–87.

Uzunçarşılı, Ismail Hakki. *Osmanlı Tarihi*, I-IV vol., Ankara: TTK Basımevi, 1947–1959.

Uzunçarşılı, Ismail Hakki. *Osmanlı Devletimim ilmiye teşkilâtı*, Ankara: TTK Basımevi, 1965.

Vacalopoulos (Bakalopoulos), A. E. *History of Macedonia. 1354–1833*, translated by Peter Megann, Thessaloniki: Institute for Balkan Studies, 1973.

Vacalopoulos (Bakalopoulos), A. E. *The Greek Nation, 1453–1669*, New Brunswick: Rutgers University Press, 1976.

Vasiliev, A. A. *Byzance et les Arabes, vol. II/1: La dynastie Macédonienne (867–959)*, French edition by M. Canard, Brussels: Fondation byzantine, 1968.

Vaughan, M. Dorothy. *Europe and the Turk. A Pattern of Alliances (1350–1700)*, Liverpool : Liverpool University Press, 1954.

Veinstein, Gilles. "Les préparatifs de la campagne navale franco-turque de 1552 à travers les ordres du duvan ottoman." *ROMM*, 39, (1985): 35–67.

Veinstein, Gilles. "L'occupation ottomane d'Oceakov et le problème de la frontière lituano-tatars. 1538–1544." In *Passé turco-tatar. Présent soviétique…*, Louvain–Paris, Éditions Peeters, 1986, 123–155.

Veinstein, Gilles (ed.). *Soliman le Magnifique et son temps.* Paris: La Documentation français, 1992.

Veliman, Valeriu, "O carte de legământ (ahid-nâme) din 1581 privitoare la Transilvania." *AIIAI* XXV, (1988)/1: 27–44.

Veliman, V. "Câteva considerații privind haraciul Moldovei la mijlocul secolului al XVI-lea." *AIIAI* XIX, (1982): 285–301.

Veliman, V. "Date noi cu privire la circumstanțele alegerii mitropolitului Moldovei (1792) și statutul juridico-politic al Principatelor Române." *AIIAI* XXIII, 2, (1986): 599–617.

Veliman, V. "Domnia lui Mircea cel Mare în viziunea istoriografiei otomane (sec. XV-XVII)." In *Marele Mircea Voievod*. ed. I. Pătroiu, Bucharest: Editura Academiei, 1987, 397–429.

Vermeulen, U. "The Rescript of Al-Malik As-Sâlih Sâlih against the Dhimmis (755 AH/1354 AD)." *OLP* 9, (1978): 175–184.

Veselá-Prenosilova, Zdenka. "Contributions aux rapports de la Sublime Porte avec le Transylvanie pendant la deuxième moitié du XVIIe s." (off-print, III, Athens, 1970), 753–760.

Veselá-Prenosilova, Zdenka. "À propos de la protection exercée par le gouvernement ottoman sur le Monastère de Ste. Cathérine au Sinai." *AO* 37, (1969): 326–338.

Virally, M. "The Sources of International Law." In *Manual of Public International Law*, edited by Max Sorensen, London, Melbourne, Toronto, New York: Macmillan, 1968, 116–175.

Visscher, Charles de. "Coutume et traité en droit international public." *RGDIP* 3, (1955): 353–369.

Wansborough, J. "The Safe-Conduct in the Muslim Chancery Practice." *BSOAS* XXXIV, 1, (1971): 20–35.

Wasiucionek, Michał. "Danube-hopping. Conversion, jurisdiction and spatiality between the Ottoman Empire and the Danubian principalities in the seventeenth century." In *Conversion and Islam in the Early Modern Mediterranean: The Lure of the Other* (ed.). Claire Norton, London: Routledge, 2017, 77–99.

Watt, W. Montgomery. *Mahomet à la Mecque,* trad. F. Dourveil, Paris: Payot, 1958.

Watt, W. Montgomery. *Mahomet à la Medine*, Paris: Payot, 1959.

Watt, W. Montgomery. "Conditions of Membership of the Islamic Community." *SI,* XXI, (1964): 5–13.

Watt, W. Montgomery. *A History of the Islamic Spain*, Edinburgh: Edinburgh University Press, 1965.

Watt, W. Montgomery. "The Christianity criticized in the Qur'ân." In *Atti del Terzo Congresso di Studi arabi e islamici*, Naples: Istituto universitario orientale, 1967, 651–656.

Watt, W. Montgomery. "The Significance of the Theory of Jihâd." *AAWG* (*Akten des VII. Kongresses für Arabistik und Islamwissenschaft Göttingen, 15 bis 22 august 1974*), 98, (1976): 390–394.

Wenner, Manfred W. "The Arab/Muslim Presence in the Medieval Central Europe." *IJMES* 12, 1, (1980): 59–79.

Wheaton, H. *Commentaire sur les éléments du droit international et sur l'histoire des progrès du droit des gens*, vol. 3, Leipzig: F. A. Brockhaus, 1873.

Winter, Michael. *Egyptian Society Under Ottoman Rule 1571–1798.* London and New York: Routledge, 1992.

Wittek, Paul. "Deux chapitres de l'histoire des Turcs de Roum." *Byzantion*, XI, fasc. 1, (1936): 285–319.

Wittek, Paul. "Le Sultan de Rûm." *AIPHOS*, VI, (1938): 361–390.

Wittek, Paul. *The Rise of the Ottoman Empire*, London: B. Franklin, 1938.

Xenopol, A. D. *Istoria românilor din Dacia Traiană*, vol. II–IV, ediția a IV-a, Bucharest: Editura Științifică și Enclopedică, 1986–1993 (1st edition ended in 1893).

Xenopol, A. D. "Lupta dintre Dănești și Drăculești." *AARMSI* 2, XXX, (1907): 183–272.

Yaccob, Abdol Rauh. "Yemeni opposition to Ottoman rule: an overview." In *Proceedings of the Seminar for Arabian Studies*, vol. 42, Papers from the forty-fifth meeting of the Seminar for Arabian Studies held at the British Museum, London, 28 to 30 July 2011 (2012): 411–419.

Ye'or, B. *Le dhimmi. Profil de l'opprimé en Orient et en Afrique du Nord depuis la conquête arabe*, Paris: Anthropos, 1980.

Yurdusev, A. Nuri (ed.). *Ottoman Diplomacy. Conventional or Unconventional?* New York: Palgrave Macmillan, 2004.

Yusuf, S. M. "The Supremacy of Shari'at Law in Islamic Society." *IQ*, 1–2, 1978: 15–22.

Zachariadou, E. A. "Early Ottoman Documents of the Prodromos Monastery (Serres)." *SF* XXVIII, (1969): 1–12.

Zachariadou, E. A. *Trade and Crusade. Venetian Crete and the Emirates of Menteshe and Aydyn (1300–1415)*, Venice: Hellenic institute of Byzantine and post-Byzantine studies, 1983.

Zachariadou, E. A. "Süleyman Çelebi in Rumili and the Ottoman Chronicles." *Der Islam*, vol. 60, no. 2, (1983): 268–296.

Zachariadou, E. A. *Romania and the Turks (c.1300-c.1500)*, London: Variorum Reprints, 1985.

Zachariadou, E. A. "Holy War in the Aegean during the Fourteenth Century." *MHR* 4, (1989): 212–225.

Zagoriț, Gh. "Stabilirea suzeranității turcești în Moldova. Cu argumente că prima capitulație atribuită lui Bogdan III a fost făcută de Ștefan cel Mare la 1497." *CL*, XLVIII, 7–8, (1914): 710–728.

Zakythinos, Denis A. *Le despotat grec de Morée. Vie et institutions*, vol. II (ed.). Chryssa Maltézou, London : Variorum, 1975.

Zlatar, Zdenko. *Between the Double Eagle and the Crescent. The Republic of Dubrovnik and the Origins of the Eastern Question,* Boulder, New York: East Euroepan Monographs, 1992.

# Index

This index includes historical and geographical proper names. The words Ottoman Empire (the Porte), Wallachia, Moldavia, Transylvania, Southeastern Europe, as well as their derivatives, are not included as they appear throughout the text.

www.ingramcontent.com/pod-product-compliance
Lightning Source LLC
LaVergne TN
LVHW010638300926
049161LV00005B/971
* 9 7 8 9 0 0 4 4 0 6 3 7 7 *